THE ROUGH GUIDE TO

London

This eleventh edition updated by

Samantha Cook, Neil McQuillian, Andrew Mickel,
Matt Norman and Alice Park

roughguides.com

Contents

OPPOSITE ROYAL ALBERT HALL AND HYDE PARK **PREVIOUS PAGE** FRANK'S CAFÉ, PECKHAM

Introduction to
London

Historic, sprawling, sleepless: London is a wonderful place to visit. Monuments from the capital's glorious past are everywhere, from medieval banqueting halls to the great churches of Christopher Wren, while the modern-day skyline is dominated by a new generation of eye-grabbing buildings – from Ferris wheels to giant walkie talkies. Whether you spend your time relaxing in Bloomsbury's quiet Georgian squares, drinking real ale in a Docklands riverside pub or checking out Peckham's galleries, you will find that London is still identifiably a collection of villages, each with a distinct personality. It is also incredibly diverse, offering cultural and culinary delights from right across the globe. And, of course, London is also rather big. In fact, it's the largest capital in the European Union, stretching for more than thirty miles from east to west, and with a population fast approaching nine million. In other words, it really is the archetypal buzzing metropolis.

The capital's traditional landmarks – Big Ben, Westminster Abbey, Buckingham Palace, St Paul's Cathedral, the Tower of London and so on – continue to draw in millions of tourists every year. Things change fast, though, and the regular emergence of new attractions ensures that there's plenty to do even for those who've visited before. London's world-class **museums**, **galleries** and institutions are constantly reinventing themselves, from the V&A to the British Museum. With Tate Modern and the Shard, the city boasts the world's largest modern art museum and Europe's highest building. And thanks to the 2012 Olympics, the East End has had a boost, an entirely new park has been created, and the tourist and transport infrastructure has had a major overhaul.

The biggest problem for newcomers is that the city is bewilderingly amorphous. Londoners cope with this by compartmentalizing their city, identifying strongly with the neighbourhoods in which they work or live, just making occasional forays into the West End, London's busy shopping and entertainment heartland. As a visitor, the key to

ABOVE COLUMBIA ROAD FLOWER MARKET

enjoying London, then, is not to try and do everything in a single trip – concentrate on one or two areas and you'll get a lot more out of the place. And remember to take some time out in the city's surprisingly large expanses of greenery: Hyde Park, Green Park and St James's Park are all within a few minutes' walk of the West End, while, further afield, you can enjoy the rolling landscapes of Hampstead Heath and Richmond Park.

You could spend days just **shopping** in London, too, mixing with the upper classes in the "tiara triangle" around Harrods, or sampling the offbeat weekend markets of Portobello Road, Brick Lane and Camden. The **music**, **clubbing** and **LGBT** scenes are second to none, with an ever-growing selection of clubs and bars around Shoreditch and Dalston and new music festivals cropping up every summer. Mainstream **arts** are no less exciting, with regular opportunities to catch outstanding theatre companies, dance troupes, exhibitions and opera. The city's pubs have always had heaps of atmosphere, and beer-lovers are spoilt for choice, but food is a major attraction too, with over sixty Michelin-starred **restaurants** and the widest choice of cuisines on the planet.

What to see

Although most of the city's sights are north of the **River Thames**, which loops through the centre from west to east, there is no single focus of interest. That's because London hasn't grown through centralized planning but by a process of random agglomeration. Villages and urban developments that once surrounded the core are now lost within the vast mass of Greater London, leaving London's highlights widely spread, and meaning that visitors should make mastering the public transport system, particularly the Underground (tube), a top priority.

If London has a centre, it's **Trafalgar Square**, home to Nelson's Column and the National Gallery. It's also as good a place as any to start exploring the city, especially as the area to the south of here, **Whitehall and Westminster**, is one of the easiest bits to discover on foot. This was the city's royal, political and ecclesiastical power-base for centuries, and

MULTIETHNIC LONDON

With around three hundred languages spoken and all the major religions represented, London is Europe's most ethnically **diverse** city. First-, second- and third-generation immigrants make up over thirty percent of the population, with many more descended from French Huguenot refugees. The first immigrants were invaders like the Romans, Anglo-Saxons, Vikings and Normans, while over the last four centuries the city has absorbed wave after wave of foreigners fleeing persecution or simply looking for a better life. In the postwar period thousands came here from the Caribbean and the Indian subcontinent; today's arrivals are more likely to come from the world's trouble spots (Somalia, Afghanistan, Iraq) or from new EU member states like Poland or Romania.

London doesn't have the sort of ghettoization that's widespread in the US, but certain areas have become **home from home** for the more established communities. Brixton and Hackney are the most prominent African-Caribbean and African districts; Dalston, along with Haringey, is home to the largest Turkish and Kurdish communities; Southall is predominantly Punjabi; Wembley is a Gujarati stronghold; Acton has a sizeable Polish community; Hoxton is a Vietnamese neighbourhood. The East End, London's top immigrant ghetto, has absorbed several communities over the centuries, and is currently the heart of Bengali London, while the Jewish community has more or less abandoned the East End, and now has its largest Orthodox communities in Stamford Hill and Golders Green.

you'll find some of London's most famous landmarks here: Downing Street, Big Ben, the Houses of Parliament and **Westminster Abbey**. The grand streets and squares of **St James's**, **Mayfair** and **Marylebone**, to the north of Westminster, have been the playground of the rich since the Restoration, and now contain some of the city's busiest shopping zones: Piccadilly, **Bond Street**, **Regent Street** and, most frenetic of the lot, **Oxford Street**.

East of Piccadilly Circus, **Soho**, **Chinatown** and **Covent Garden** are also easy to walk around and form the heart of the West End entertainment district, where you'll find the largest concentration of theatres, cinemas, shops, cafés and restaurants. Adjoining Covent Garden to the north, the university quarter of **Bloomsbury** is the location of the ever-popular **British Museum**, a stupendous treasure house that boasts a wonderful central, covered courtyard. To the north of Bloomsbury lies **King's Cross**, home to the **British Library** and the city's Eurostar terminal at St Pancras, and now at the centre of a massive redevelopment project with galleries, restaurants and a swimming pond.

Welding the West End to the financial district, **Holborn** is a little-visited area, but offers some of central London's most surprising treats, among them the eccentric Sir John Soane's Museum and the secluded quadrangles of the Inns of Court, where the country's lawyers learn and ply their trade. Fashionable **Clerkenwell**, to the east of Holborn on the northern edge of the City, is visited mostly on weeknights for its many popular bars and restaurants, but also has vestiges of London's monastic past and a radical history to be proud of.

A couple of miles downstream from Westminster, **The City** – or the City of London, to give it its full title – is the original heart of London, simultaneously the most ancient and the most modern part of the metropolis. Settled since Roman times, the area became the commercial and residential heart of medieval London, with its own Lord Mayor and its own peculiar form of local government, both of which survive (with considerable pageantry) to this day. The Great Fire of 1666 obliterated most of the City, and although it was rebuilt, the resident population has dwindled to insignificance. Yet this remains

OPPOSITE HOUSES OF PARLIAMENT AND LONDON EYE

one of the great financial centres of the world, with the most prominent landmarks these days being the hi-tech **skyscrapers** of banks and insurance companies. However, the Square Mile, as it's known, boasts its fair share of historic sights too, notably the **Tower of London** and a fine cache of Wren churches that includes the mighty **St Paul's Cathedral**.

East of the City, the **East End** and **Docklands** are equally notorious, but in entirely different ways. Traditionally working-class, the East End is not conventional tourist territory, but its long history of immigration is as fascinating as is its more recent emergence as a bolthole for artists. With its converted warehouse apartments and hubristic tower blocks, Docklands is the converse of the edgy East End, with the **Canary Wharf** tower – for three decades the country's tallest building – epitomizing the pretensions of the 1980s' Thatcherite dream.

The **South Bank**, **Bankside** and **Southwark** together make up the small slice of central London that lies south of the Thames. The Southbank Centre itself, London's concrete culture bunker, is now ingrained on the tourist map – thanks, in part, to the nearby London Eye, which spins gracefully over the Thames. Bankside is also going from strength to strength, with the Millennium Bridge linking St Paul's Cathedral with the former power station that's home to **Tate Modern**, London's beloved museum of modern art.

In **Hyde Park** and **Kensington Gardens** you'll find a large segment of greenery that separates wealthy west London from the city centre. The museums of **South Kensington** – the Victoria and Albert Museum, the Science Museum and the Natural History Museum – are a must, and if you have shopping on your agenda you may well want to investigate the hive of plush stores in the vicinity of Harrods, superstore to the upper echelons.

Some of the most appealing parts of north London are clustered around the Regent's Canal, which skirts the northern edge of **Regent's Park** and serves as the focus for the capital's busiest weekend market, held around **Camden Lock**. Further out, in the chic literary suburbs of Hampstead and Highgate, there are unbeatable views across the city from half-wild **Hampstead Heath**, the sprawling stomping ground of dog walkers and kite flyers.

The glory of south London is **Greenwich**, with its nautical associations, royal park and observatory (not to mention its Dome). Finally, there are plenty of rewarding day-trips up the Thames, southwest of the city centre from **Chiswick** to **Hampton Court**, an area that is liberally peppered with the stately homes and grounds of the country's royalty and former aristocracy, from Syon and **Kew**, to **Richmond** and Ham.

When to go

Considering how temperate the London **climate** is (see p.28), it's amazing how much mileage the locals get out of the subject. The truth is that summers rarely get really hot and the winters aren't very cold. In fact, it's impossible to say with any certainty what the weather will be like in any given month. May might be wet and grey one year and gloriously sunny the next; November stands an equal chance of being crisp and clear or foggy and grim. So, whatever time of year you come, be prepared for all eventualities, and bring a pair of comfortable shoes, as, inevitably, you'll be doing a lot of walking.

FROM TOP LITTLE VENICE; GUARDS OUTSIDE BUCKINGHAM PALACE; COVENT GARDEN PIAZZA

17

things not to miss

It's not possible to see everything that London has to offer in one visit – and we don't suggest you try. What follows, in no particular order, is a selective taste of the city's highlights, from outstanding art collections and historic architecture to vibrant markets and picturesque parks. Each highlight has a page reference to take you straight into the Guide, where you can find out more.

1

1 BRITISH MUSEUM
Page 119

The spectacular Great Court and the renovated Round Reading Room have brought new life to the world's oldest and greatest public museum.

2 TOWER OF LONDON
Page 176

Bloody royal history, Beefeaters, lots of armour, the Crown Jewels and ravens – and a great medieval castle.

3 HIGHGATE CEMETERY
Page 302

The city's most atmospheric Victorian necropolis, thick with trees and crowded with famous corpses, with Karl Marx topping the bill.

4 KING'S CROSS REDEVELOPMENT
Page 136

Take a stroll around the brilliant King's Cross redevelopment, where galleries, restaurants and public squares have transformed the industrial landscape.

5 HAMPSTEAD HEATH
Page 299

Fly kites, look across London and walk over to Kenwood, for fine art, tea and cakes.

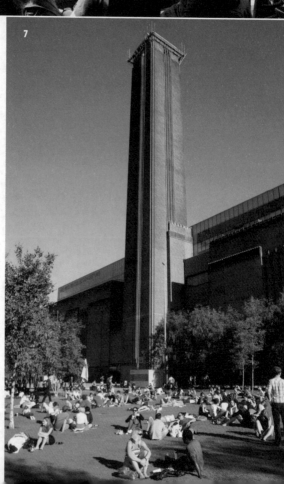

Itineraries

London is a city of neighbourhoods, and each of these day-long itineraries covers one of the city's most distinctive areas. They can all be covered on foot, or with just a few short hops by bus or tube.

FREE WEST END

London can be an expensive place, but there are lots of things to enjoy that are free. We've picked a few lesser-known sights, in some of the city's poshest parts, none of which will break the bank.

Wallace Collection Escape from nearby Oxford Street and pop into this miniature eighteenth-century French chateau and wallow in the luxury and excess of the Ancien Régime. **See p.92**

Mayfair auction houses Of the area's three major auction houses, Sotheby's is the most approachable. Sift through the lots, imagine what you'd buy if you had the money and then have a coffee at the café. **See p.82**

Royal Institution Not only is the RI one of the country's most venerable scientific institutions, it also has a great building to explore, from the museum to the famous lecture hall. **See p.82**

Lunch Have a picnic in the manicured gardens of the Inns of Court. **See p.139**

Covent Garden buskers Performers in the Piazza have to audition, so a certain quality is guaranteed – expect everything from opera to slapstick. **See p.107**

Horse Guards Don't fret that you missed Changing the Guard at 11am. The 4pm daily inspection by an Officer of the Guard involves lots of cavalry and is just as much fun. **See p.48**

Evensong at Westminster Abbey You can save yourself the hefty entrance fee by turning up for choral evensong at 5pm. **See p.53**

A SOUTH BANK STROLL

You can stroll the wonderful traffic-free footpath for three miles along the South Bank from the London Eye to Rotherhithe.

Southbank Centre London's concrete culture bunker is a vibrant venue for pop-up festivals and outdoor stalls. A tour of the National Theatre is well worth it, or just take a peek backstage from the Sherling High Level Walkway. **See p.217**

View from the Oxo Tower No need to buy a drink in the pricey bar, just ask the way to the public viewing gallery for one of the best free views this side of the river. **See p.220**

Tate Modern Already the largest modern art museum in the world, this awesome edifice is expanding below and behind the original power station. **See p.227**

Shakespeare's Globe Groundling tickets are only just over a fiver, so there's no excuse not to catch a play or visit the museum. **See p.230**

Borough Market Whatever your favourite food indulgence is, you'll find it at Borough – taste the finest English cheeses, slurp down an oyster, feast on roasted hog or devour a divine brownie. **See p.233**

Tower Bridge Climb to the top of one of the city's most famous sights, or phone ahead to check the bridge opening times. **See p.184**

Butler's Wharf A lesson in how to preserve and enhance an old warehouse, marking the start of the South Bank's Docklands. **See p.237**

ABOVE ST PAUL'S CATHEDRAL **OPPOSITE** SUMMER FOUNTAIN OUTSIDE THE SOUTHBANK CENTRE

Mayflower pub, Rotherhithe Continue for one mile beyond Tower Bridge and you leave behind the tourist crowds. Sink a pint of real ale at this historic pub riverside from which the Pilgrim Fathers set out in 1620. **See p.238 & p.394**

OFFBEAT CITY

The City of London is one of the world's major financial centres, but dig deeper and you'll find centuries of history just below the surface.

Barbican Conservatory Discover the Barbican's stunning greenhouse gardens – an unlikely tropical oasis in the brutalist cultural centre. **See p.164**

St Bartholomew-the-Great Hidden between the Barbican and Smithfield, the church's *Cloister Café* is an atmospheric spot for a brew. **See p.163**

Postman's Park Tiny park with a curious, slightly mawkish memorial to have-a-go heroes of the Victorian era (and today). **See p.165**

The Black Friar Settle into an alcove, nurse a pint and soak in this pub's fantastically over-the-top 1905 Art Nouveau interior. **See p.390**

Bow Lane This lovely, narrow street takes you back to pre-Fire City – popular during the week for its sandwich bars and pubs. **See p.160**

Old Bailey Watch the proceedings from the visitors' gallery of the court that heard the trials of the Kray Twins and the Angry Brigade. **See p.161**

Leadenhall Market Visit this ornate, covered arcade during the week to shop for exotic seafood, fine wines and caviar. **See p.172**

HEADING EAST

London's East End is one of the capital's most historic and distinctive quarters, perfect for a Sunday of browsing and grazing.

Columbia Road flower market Pick up a pastry at cute artisanal bakery Lily Vanilli (see p.430) before checking out the fragrant blooms and browsing the lively indie shops. **See p.194**

Geffrye Museum This endearing museum re-creates period living spaces in a set of eighteenth-century almshouses. **See p.194**

Vintage shops You could spend days exploring the markets and artist's spaces near Brick Lane, but vintage is where the area excels. Start with the department store-style Blitz before moving on to Absolute Vintage and a final rummage in Beyond Retro. **See p.428**

Whitechapel Gallery Check out the cutting-edge art at this fine old establishment, which gave first UK exhibitions to such luminaries as Pollock, Rothko, Kahlo and Gilbert and George. **See p.197**

Tayyabs While the East End has some seriously cool and experimental restaurants, our bet's on old favourite *Tayyabs* for fresh, flavour-filled Pakistani food at low prices. **See p.379**

Dalston nightlife Head out of the East End proper for a night on the tiles in hipster-hub Dalston, where gritty basement clubs and pop-up bars jostle for space with Turkish takeaways and charity shops. **See p.392 & p.403**

BUS OUTSIDE ST PAUL'S

Basics

Getting there

London has five airports (see p.20) and is a major destination for most international airlines, so airfares tend to be keenly competitive. How much you pay to fly to London depends on how far in advance you book, how flexible you need your ticket to be and to some extent which airport you arrive at. From Paris, Brussels and further afield, Eurostar trains arrive at St Pancras station.

Flights from the US and Canada

All major US and Canadian airlines run direct services from North America to London, Europe's busiest gateway. Two of London's airports – **Heathrow** and **Gatwick** – handle transatlantic flights. Figure on around six hours' flying time from New York; it's an hour extra going the other way, because of headwinds. Add three or four hours more for travel from the West Coast. Most eastbound flights cross the Atlantic overnight, arriving the next morning; flying back, departure times tend to be morning or afternoon, arriving in the afternoon or evening of the same day.

The cheapest return **fares** (including taxes) from New York or Chicago (and even LA) start from around US$700 (though US$1000 and up is average); or from around Can$800 from Toronto; and from around Can$1100 from Vancouver.

Flights from Australia and New Zealand

Flight time from Australia and New Zealand to London is at least 22 hours, and can be more depending on routes and transfer times. There are a wide variety of routes, with those touching down in Southeast Asia the quickest and cheapest on average. Given the length of the journey involved, you might be better off including a night's stopover

in your itinerary; some airlines include one in the price of the flight.

The cheapest direct scheduled flights to London are usually to be found on one of the Asian airlines. Average return **fares** (including taxes) are Aus$1700–2500 depending on the season. Return fares from Auckland to London range between NZ$2500 and NZ$3500 depending on the season, route and carrier.

By plane or train from Ireland

Travel from Ireland is quickest by **plane**, with the likes of Aer Lingus (W aerlingus.com) and Ryanair (W ryanair.com) offering return tickets from Dublin, Derry, Cork or Shannon to London Stansted or Gatwick for as little as €55. From Belfast International, easyJet (W easyjet.com) has return fares to London Luton, Gatwick or Stansted from around £60, if you book far enough in advance; flybe (W flybe.com) has similar fares from Belfast City to London City. A fully flexible fare can cost three or four times that amount, but will allow you to change your plans after purchasing the ticket.

Flying may be quick, but the **ferry** and **train** fares are pretty competitive and much more flexible, with Irish Ferries (W irishferries.com) offering SailRail return fares of around €100 to London (via Holyhead) from anywhere in the Republic; journey time is around eight hours from Dublin. From Belfast, you need to travel via Dublin or Cairnryan and Glasgow, which takes around eleven hours (from £106; book through W virgintrains.co.uk).

Arrival

The majority of visitors arrive in London at one of its five main airports, all but one of which can involve an expensive trip to the centre. Those arriving by train or bus are dropped right in the middle of the city, with easy access to public transport.

A BETTER KIND OF TRAVEL

At Rough Guides we are passionately committed to travel. We feel that travelling is the best way to understand the world we live in and the people we share it with – plus tourism has brought a great deal of benefit to developing economies around the world over the last few decades. But the growth in tourism has also damaged some places irreparably, and climate change is exacerbated by most forms of transport, especially flying. All Rough Guides' trips are carbon-offset, and every year we donate money to a variety of charities devoted to combating the effects of climate change.

By plane

Heathrow, Gatwick, Stansted, Luton and City airports are all less than an hour from the city centre.

Heathrow

Heathrow (W heathrowairport.com) lies around fifteen miles west of central London, and is the city's busiest airport, with five terminals and three train/tube stations: one for terminals 1, 2 and 3, and separate ones for terminals 4 and 5 (last train and tube departure times vary slightly by terminal). The fastest (and most expensive) trains into London are the nonstop **Heathrow Express** services to Paddington station (Mon–Sat 5am–11.40pm, Sun 6am–11.40pm; every 15min; journey 15min; £21.50 one way, £35 return, more if you purchase your ticket on board the train, online group deals available; W heathrowexpress.com). **Heathrow Connect** trains stop at some intermediate stations (Mon–Sat 5am–11.30pm, Sun 7am–10.45pm; every 30min; journey 30–40min; £10.10 one way, £20.20 return; W heathrowconnect.com). Cheapest of all is to take the **Piccadilly Underground line** (W tfl.gov .uk), which connects the airport to numerous tube stations across central London (daily 5am–11.40pm; Fri & Sat 24hr to terminals 1, 2, 3 & 5; every 5min; journey 50min–1hr; tickets cost just £3.10 off-peak, £5.10 peak (Mon–Fri 6.30–9.30am) with a pay-as-you-go Oyster card (see p.22).

National Express bus services run from Heathrow to Victoria Coach Station (daily 4.20am–10.10pm every 20min–1hr; 40min–1hr; £9.50 one way; W nationalexpress.com). If arriving after 11.30pm, check W tfl.gov.uk for nightbus routes. **Taxis** are plentiful, but will set you back between £50 and £85 to central London, and take around an hour (much longer in the rush hour); an UberX car (see p.23) will cost £30–47.

Gatwick

Gatwick (W gatwickairport.com) is around thirty miles south of London, and has a train station at the South Terminal. Nonstop **Gatwick Express** trains run between the airport and London Victoria (daily 4.30am–1.30am; every 15min; journey 30–35min; W gatwickexpress.com); tickets cost around £20 single, £35 return (less online). A cheaper option is to take a **Southern** train service to Victoria (every 15min; journey 35min; W southernrailway.com), which stops at a couple of intermediate stations, or a **Thameslink** train to various stations within London (every 15–30min; journey 30–45min; from £19 return; W thameslinkrailway.com), including

Blackfriars and St Pancras; advance online tickets for either cost from £15 single.

From the North and South terminals **easyBus** runs buses to West Brompton tube near Earl's Court (daily 4.30am–midnight every 20min; 1hr 5min; W easybus.co.uk), with online tickets from only £2 single (£10 if you buy on board); buses to Waterloo only go from South terminal (1hr). **National Express** buses run from Gatwick direct to central London (daily 24hr, except 1–2am; 1–2 hourly; 1hr 30min); tickets cost £6–£11 single. A **taxi** will set you back £100 or more, and take over an hour.

Stansted

Designed by Norman Foster, Stansted (W stanstedairport.com) lies roughly 35 miles northeast of the capital. The fastest trains are run by **Stansted Express** to Liverpool Street (daily 5.30am–12.30am; every 15–30min; journey 45min; W stanstedexpress.com), and cost £19 single, £32 return; online advance and group offers available. Ever-reliable **easyBus** runs buses to Baker Street tube (daily 4am–1am; every 15min; 1hr 15min) and Old Street (daily 4am–1am; every 15min; 60min), with online tickets for both going for as little as £2 single (£10 if you buy on board). **National Express** runs buses 24 hours to Victoria Coach Station or Liverpool Street (every 30min; journey 1hr 30min–1hr 45min), with tickets £11 single. **Terravision** (W terravision.eu) also runs coaches to Liverpool Street and Victoria (daily 6am–1am; every 30min; 1hr 15min to Victoria, 55min to Liverpool St), with tickets £8–9 single. A **taxi** will set you back £100, and take at least an hour.

City Airport

City Airport (W londoncityairport.com), London's smallest, used primarily by business folk, is situated in the Royal Albert Docks, ten miles east of central London, and handles European flights only. The **Docklands Light Railway** (DLR) takes you straight to Bank in the City (Mon–Sat 5.30am–12.15am, Sun 7am–11.15pm; every 8–15min; journey 20min), where you can change to the tube. A **taxi** from the airport to the City's financial sector will cost around £20, and take half an hour or so.

Luton

Luton Airport (W www.london-luton.co.uk) is roughly thirty miles north of London and mainly handles charter flights. A free shuttle bus (every 10min) takes five minutes to transport passengers to **Luton Airport Parkway station**, which is connected by train to St Pancras (every 15–30min; journey 25–35min) and other stations in central London;

single tickets cost around £14. **Green Line** (ⓦgreen line.co.uk) runs the #757 coach from Luton Airport to Victoria Coach Station (24hr; every 20–30min; journey 1hr 20min; £10), stopping at several locations en route, including Baker Street. **National Express** runs buses to Victoria Coach Station (24hr every 30min–1hr; journey time 1hr 5min–1hr 20min); for £6–12 one way. A **taxi** will cost in the region of £70–80 and take at least an hour to central London.

Arriving by train or bus

Eurostar (ⓦeurostar.com) trains arrive at St Pancras International next door to King's Cross. Trains from the **Channel ports** arrive at Charing Cross or Victoria, while **boat trains** from Harwich arrive at Liverpool Street. Arriving by train from elsewhere in Britain, you'll come into one of London's numerous mainline stations, all of which have adjacent Underground stations linking into the city centre's tube network. Coming into London by coach, you're most likely to arrive at Victoria Coach Station, a couple of hundred yards south down Buckingham Palace Road from Victoria train station and tube.

City transport

London's transport system is highly complex and can be subject to disruption in places thanks to a never-ending programme of renovation and expansion, but generally will get you across this sprawling city fairly efficiently. It is, however, one of the most expensive transport systems in the world – get an Oyster card (see box, p.22).

Transport for London (TfL) provides excellent free maps and details of bus and tube services from its six **Travel Information Centres**: the most central one is at Piccadilly Circus tube station (Mon–Fri 8am–7pm, Sat & bank hols 9.15am–7pm, Sun 9.15am–6pm); there are other desks at the arrivals at Heathrow (terminals 1, 2 & 3), Victoria, Euston, King's Cross and Liverpool Street train stations; plus Visitor Information Centres at Gatwick, Paddington and Euston. There's also a 24-hour helpline and website for information on all bus and tube services (ⓣ0343 222 1234, ⓦtfl.gov.uk).

For transport purposes, London is divided into six concentric zones (plus a few extra in the northwest), with fares calculated depending on which zones you travel through: the majority of the city's sights lie in zones 1 and 2. If you cannot produce a valid ticket for your journey, or travel further than your ticket allows, you will be liable to a Penalty Fare of £80, reduced to £40 if you pay within 21 days. Try to avoid travelling during the rush hour (Mon–Fri 8–9.30am & 5–7pm) if possible, when tubes become unbearably crowded and hot, and some buses get so full they won't let you on.

Within the centre, **walking** can be a practical option – it's always worth checking the distance on foot between central tube stations, as the schematic tube map can be misleading. Setting out on two feet can also be the best way to discover some of London's most interesting corners, in particular along its waterways: the Regent's Canal (see p.282) and Thames Path (see p.238).

The tube

Except for very short journeys, the **Underground** – or **tube**, as it's known to Londoners – is by far the quickest way to get about for all but the shortest journeys. Eleven different lines cross much of the metropolis, although south of the river is not very well covered. Each line has its own colour and name – all you need to know is which direction you're travelling in: northbound, eastbound, southbound or westbound (this gets tricky when taking the Circle Line). As a precaution, it's also worth checking the final destination displayed on the front of the train, as some lines, such as the District and Northern lines, have several different branches.

Services are frequent (whole network: Mon–Sat 5.30am–12.30am, Sun 7.30am–11.30pm), and you rarely have to wait more than five minutes for a train between central stations. In addition there is a 24hr **Night Tube** service planned, which will run every ten minutes on Friday and Saturday nights on all of the main Underground lines (expected to start at some point in 2016). Tickets must be bought in advance from automatic machines or from a ticket booth in the station entrance hall. An **Oyster card** is by far your best option (see p.22); single **fares** with paper tickets are never the best choice – a journey in the central zone costs £4.80 with a paper ticket, £2.30 with an Oyster.

Overground and DLR

Somewhere between a tube line and suburban rail, the orange **Overground** is a large network that connects with the tube system and stretches out to Richmond in the west, Stratford in the east and Crystal Palace in the south, forming an orbital railway, a sort of outer Circle Line. It's particularly useful for reaching parts of Hackney and Hoxton.

The **Docklands Light Railway**, or **DLR**, runs driverless trains from Bank in the City, and from Tower Gateway (close to Tower Hill tube and the Tower of London) above ground to the financial centre of Docklands, plus other areas in the East End and also below ground to Greenwich and Woolwich. Oyster cards and travelcards (see below) are valid on both these networks.

Buses

London's famous red double-decker buses are fun to ride on, with most running a frequency of five to ten minutes during the day. Some stops have live departure information, or if you've got a smartphone,

there are several apps (and the TfL website) that will do the same for you. A single journey bus **fare** is £1.50, anytime and for any distance travelled. Cash is not accepted on buses: you need an Oyster card, contactless debit card or travelcard; you only need to touch in on buses (if you touch out, you will be charged again).

A lot of bus stops are request stops (easily recognizable by their red sign), so if you don't stick your arm out to hail the bus you want, it will pass you by, and if you don't ring the bell for the bus to stop, it will just keep on going.

Some buses run a **24-hour service**, but most run between 5am and midnight, with a network of night buses (prefixed with the letter "N") operating outside this period. Night-bus routes depart every twenty to thirty minutes, more frequently on Friday

---

OYSTER CARDS, CONTACTLESS PAYMENT AND TICKETS

By far the cheapest, easiest way to get about London is to use an **Oyster card**, London's transport smartcard, available from all tube stations and Travel Information Centres, and valid on the bus, tube, Docklands Light Railway (DLR), Tramlink, Overground, all suburban rail services and Thames Clipper boats. You can use an Oyster card either to store a weekly/monthly/yearly **season ticket**, or as a **pay-as-you-go** card – you can top up your card at all tube stations and at some newsagents. As you enter the tube or bus, simply touch in your card at the card reader – if you're using pay-as-you-go, the fare will be taken off your card. If you're using the tube or train, you need to touch out again even if the gate is open or a maximum fare of up to £8.80 may be deducted. A pay-as-you-go Oyster operates daily price-capping, so there's a maximum you will be charged in a 24-hour period, depending on the zones you travel through. For zones 1–2 this is £6.40; for zones 1–6 this is £11.70. Single tube fares on Oyster are £2.30 for zone 1 and zone 1–2 off peak; (zone 1–2 peak is £2.90), £5.10 for a journey between zones 1 and 6; some outer journeys will cost more. If you're making a journey with a change that doesn't require going through zone 1, tap a pink Oyster reader, which you'll see in some stations (mainly DLR and Overground stations), to avoid paying a zone 1 fare. Oyster cards are free for those purchasing monthly or yearly tickets; everyone else needs to pay a £5 refundable deposit; visitors can buy a pay-as-you-go Visitor Oyster card for just £3, plus the amount of credit you want.

If you have a debit or credit card with a **contactless payment** function, you can use this in the same way as a pay-as-you-go Oyster card, with the same fares and price-capping (make sure you use the same card all day). British Visa, MasterCard and American Express cards work; for cards issued outside the UK, American Express and most but not all MasterCard and Visa with contactless payment should work. However, any overseas bank charges will apply to each use.

Alternatively, you can buy a paper **Travelcard** at tube and train stations, but the cheapest is £12 for zones 1–6. Pay-as-you-go Oyster cards also have a Monday–Sunday price cap of £32.10 for zones 1 & 2, which is the same price as a seven-day paper travelcard.

Children under 11 travel free; children aged 11–15 travel free on all buses and trams and at child-rate on the tube; children aged 16 or 17 can travel at half the adult rate on all forms of transport. Children over 10 need a Zip Oyster photocard to be eligible for the discounts – these should be applied for in advance online and will cost £10; visitors from outside the UK will need to pick this up from a Travel Information Centre (see p.21). Alternatively, you can register a normal Oyster card for a Young Visitor discount at Travel Information Centres, but you must go along with the child. Railcard holders can buy a Day Off-Peak Travelcard (zones 1–9) for children aged 11–15 for just £2.30, providing they're travelling with an adult. Other **concession rates** are available, such as for those over 65 and people with other railcards; check Ⓦtfl.gov.uk for details.

and Saturday nights. All stops are treated as request stops, so you must signal to get the bus to stop, and press the bell in order to get off.

Suburban trains

Large areas of London's suburbs are only served by the suburban train network. Wherever a sight can only be reached by train, we've indicated the nearest train station (and, if relevant, the central terminus from which trains depart). Oyster cards and Travelcards are valid on all suburban train services within Greater London.

The most useful train line to cross the capital is the **Thameslink** service (W thameslinkrailway.com), which runs north–south via St Pancras and Black-friars (Mon–Sat every 15min, Sun every 30min).

For information on train services and ticket prices, contact National Rail Enquiries (T 0845 748 4950, W nationalrail.co.uk).

Boats

Boat trips on the Thames are a fun way of sight-seeing, either on a tour (see p.24) or using the **Thames Clipper** service. You can buy tickets at a pier, but there is a discount if you buy online in advance or use an Oyster card. With a travelcard (either paper or on an Oyster) the discount is a third; with pay-as-you-go Oyster it is around 10–15 percent. Timetables and services are complex, and there are numerous companies and small charter operators. The largest is Thames Clippers (W thamesclippers.com), which runs a regular commuter service (Mon–Fri 6am–8pm, Sat & Sun 8 or 9am–9.30pm, then infrequent service until around 10.30pm which may not cover all stops; every 20–30min) between the London Eye and Greenwich (including the Dome), with some boats going as far as Woolwich. There are piers on both sides of the river, including Embankment, Bankside, Blackfriars, London Bridge and Tower. There are three zones: Central, East and West. Typical fares are £7.50 Central zone single (£6.30 with pay-as-you-go Oyster), with an unlimited hop-on, hop-off River Roamer costing £14.70 if bought online, £17.35 from the pier.

Other companies run boats upstream from Westminster to Kew, Richmond and Hampton Court from April to October (see p.328).

Taxis

Compared to most capital cities, London's metered **black cabs** are an expensive option unless there are three or more of you. The minimum fare is £2.40, and a ride from Euston to Victoria, for example, costs around £12–15 (Mon–Fri 6am–8pm). After 8pm on weekdays and all day during the weekend, a higher tariff applies, and after 10pm, it's higher still. Tipping is customary. An illuminated yellow light over the windscreen tells you if the cab is available – just stick your arm out to hail it. London's cabbies are the best-trained in Europe; every one of them knows the shortest route between any two points in the capital, and they won't rip you off by taking another route. The cabs are also wheelchair accessible. To order a black cab in advance, phone T 0871 871 8710, and be prepared to pay an extra £2. You can also hail a black cab (and book minicabs) via the **Hailo** app (W hailoapp.com).

Minicabs and apps

Minicabs look just like regular cars and are consider-ably cheaper than black cabs, but they cannot be hailed from the street. All minicabs should be **licensed** and able to produce a TfL ID on demand. There are hundreds of minicab firms, but the best way to pick is to take the advice of the place you're at. TfL's **Cabwise** app can provide the numbers of minicab firms near where you are. Avoid illegal taxi touts, who hang around outside venues alongside licensed cabs, and always establish the fare before-hand, as minicabs are not metered.

The **Uber** app (W uber.com) is handy if you have a smart phone (and internet access). The app connects you to the nearest Uber driver, and it normally takes around ten to fifteen minutes to reach you (you can't book ahead). You pay through the app rather than paying the driver, so there's no need for cash. Prices for the standard UberX service can be up to fifty percent cheaper than black cabs. Be aware, though, that "surge" pricing operates at peak times (typically pub closing time), when they can be three times as much, but the app will let you know when this is operating. There are fixed rates from Heathrow (£30–47) and Gatwick (£50–63) into London.

Driving

Given the traffic jams, parking hassle and pollution caused, driving in London – especially central London – is by far the worst transport option available. However, if you must drive, bear in mind the rules of the road. Seatbelts are compulsory front and back and the speed limit is 30mph, unless it says otherwise.

Your biggest nightmare as a driver is undoubtedly **parking**. The basic rules are that double **red and double yellow lines** mean no waiting or stopping, as do the zigzag lines that you'll see near a pedestrian crossing. **Single yellow** and single red lines mean that you can park on them after 6pm or 7pm, and at the weekends, but times vary from borough to borough, so read the signs before leaving your vehicle. Parking at a meter or pay-and-display will cost you up to around £4 an hour, though again meters are often free in the evenings and at weekends. In some boroughs, you'll need a mobile phone and credit card with you to pay for your parking. Finally, you can go to a car park – NCP are the largest operators ⓦ ncp.co.uk – which costs between £7 and £24 for two hours during the day (West End parking spaces are particularly expensive). If you park your car illegally, you will get a Penalty Charge Notice, issued by the local borough (up to £130, reduced by up to 50 percent if you pay within fourteen days), possibly get clamped or get towed away (£200 and upwards). If you suspect your vehicle has been towed away, phone ⓣ 0845 206 8602.

Cycling

Cycling is more popular than ever in London, not least because it's the cheapest and – for short journeys in the centre, at least – fastest way to get around. The easiest way to get cycling is to use the city's cycle hire scheme, officially Santander Cycles but universally known as **Boris Bikes** after Boris Johnson, Mayor of London at the time they were introduced. There are over seven hundred docking stations across central London, though south London has largely been ignored by the scheme. With a credit or debit card, you can buy 24 hours' access to the bikes for just £2. You then get the first half-hour on a bike free, so if you hop from docking station to docking station you don't pay another penny. Otherwise, it's £2 for each additional thirty minutes. For more details see ⓦ tfl.gov.uk.

If you want to rent a better bike for longer than an hour or so, try **London Bicycle Tour Company,** on the South Bank at 1 Gabriel's Wharf, SE1 (ⓣ 020 7928 6838, ⓦ londonbicycle.com), which has hybrid and mountain bikes for rent at £3–4 an hour or £20

SIGHTSEEING TOURS AND WALKS

BUS TOURS

Standard sightseeing tours are run by several rival bus companies, their open-top double-deckers setting off every thirty minutes from Victoria station, Trafalgar Square, Piccadilly and other conspicuous tourist spots. You can hop on and off several different routes as often as you like with **The Original Tour** for around £26 if booked online (daily 8.30am–6pm; every 15–20min; ⓣ 020 8877 1722, ⓦ theoriginaltour.com).

The cheapest option is to hop on a real **London double-decker**. For example, the #11 bus (with its fleet of "Boris Buses" with open rear platforms and roving conductors) from Victoria station, will take you past Westminster Abbey, the Houses of Parliament, up Whitehall, round Trafalgar Square, along the Strand and on to St Paul's Cathedral. You can also take an old double-decker Routemaster, on "heritage" route #15 (daily every 15min 9.30am–7pm) from Trafalgar Square to Tower Hill.

BOAT TOURS

For unbeatable views of some of the major city sights, you need to get on the water. You can either just take a Thames Clipper service (see p.23), perhaps from the London Eye as far as Greenwich, or one of the numerous **boat tours**, including City Cruises, from Westminster to Greenwich (every 30min; tickets from £8.91; ⓣ 020 7740 0400, ⓦ citycruises.com). Feel the need for speed? London Rib Voyages (£37.97 for 50min trip from the London Eye; ⓣ 020 7928 8933, ⓦ londonribvoyages.com) and Thames Rib Experience (from £24.50 for 20min trip from Tower Bridge pier; ⓣ 020 3245 1177; ⓦ thamesribexperience.com) both offer speedboat tours.

WALKING TOURS

Appealing and informative, a good **walking tour** can really get under the skin of a neighbourhood, mixing solid historical facts with juicy anecdotes in the company of a local specialist. Walks on offer range from a literary pub crawl round Bloomsbury to a roam around the East End. Tours cost around £10 and take around two hours; normally you can simply show up at the starting point and join. **Original London Walks** (ⓣ 020 7624 3978, ⓦ walks.com) are a well-established and reliably good company. If you want to plan – or book – walks in advance, contact ⓦ guidelondon.org.uk or ⓦ britainsbestguides.org.

CONGESTION CHARGE

All vehicles entering central London on weekdays between 7am and 6pm are liable to a **congestion charge** of £11.50 per vehicle (£10.50 if you sign up online to pay automatically each time you travel in the zone). Drivers can pay the charge in advance or on the day online or over the phone (lines open Mon–Fri 8am–10pm, Sat 9am–3pm; ☎ 0343 222 2222, ⓦ tfl.gov.uk) and must do so before midnight; paying the following day costs £14; 24 hours later, you'll be liable for a £130 Penalty Charge Notice (reduced to £65 if you pay within fourteen days). Disabled travellers, motorcycles, minibuses and some alternative-fuel vehicles are exempt from the charge, and local residents get a ninety percent discount, but you must register in order to qualify.

for the first day, £10 per day thereafter, £50 for the week; or On Your Bike, The Vaults, Montague Close, SE1 (☎ 020 7378 6669, ⓦ onyourbike.com), which has a whole range of bikes to rent for £18 for the day, £10 per day thereafter.

There are restrictions on taking **bikes on public transport**: no bikes other than folding bikes are allowed on any part of the system (with a few minor exceptions) from Monday to Friday between 7.30am and 9.30am, and from 4pm to 7pm. Bikes are also restricted on the tube, but allowed on the District, Circle, east London, Hammersmith & City and Metropolitan lines, plus certain sections of other tube lines and the Overground. Restrictions on the suburban trains vary from company to company, so check before you set out.

Festivals

London hosts an enormous number of festivals throughout the year, several of which are worth planning a trip around. The biggest street festival is still the Notting Hill Carnival, which takes place at the end of August, and the longest-running event is still the Proms, whose series of classical music concerts takes place for around eight weeks over the summer. There are also regular free events held throughout the year on Trafalgar Square. The list of events below really just skims the surface – there is also an excellent range of sporting events (see p.435) and music festivals (see p.404).

JANUARY

London New Year's Day Parade Jan 1 ⓦ lnydp.com; admission charge for grandstand seats in Piccadilly, otherwise free. A procession of floats, marching bands, cheerleaders and clowns wends its way from Parliament Square to Green Park.

London International Mime Festival Late Jan ⓦ mimelondon .com. Annual mime festival that takes place over much of January at the

Southbank Centre, and other venues across London. It pulls in some very big names in mime, animation and puppetry.

Chinese New Year Late Jan/early Feb ⓦ chinatownlondon.org; ⊖ Leicester Square; free. Celebrations in Soho's Chinatown, Leicester Square and even Trafalgar Square erupt in a riot of dancing dragons and firecrackers – expect serious human congestion.

FEBRUARY

Clowns Service First Sun of month 3pm. Usually Holy Trinity Church, Beechwood Rd, E8 ⓦ clowns-international.com; ⊖ Dalston Kingsland or Dalston Junction; free. The Joseph Grimaldi Memorial Service for clowns, commemorating the great clown, with a clown show afterwards in the church hall (see box, p.290).

Pancake Day Shrove Tuesday. Free. There are several places to enjoy a public pancake race: go to Brick Lane for frivolity, and the Guildhall Yard for seriously silly costumes courtesy of the Poulters' Guild.

MARCH

Women of the World Festival Early March ⓦ southbankcentre .co.uk. ⊖ Waterloo. A weekend of talks, events and performances celebrating – you guessed it – women of the world. It takes over the Southbank Centre for a weekend close to International Women's Day (March 8).

St Patrick's Day March 15 ⓦ london.gov.uk; free. Events all over London and a parade that sets off at noon and ends up at Trafalgar Square, where there's a festival of Irish culture; also plenty of events in the week building up to the day.

Head of the River Race Sat in late March or early April ⓦ www .horr.co.uk; free. Less well known than the Oxford and Cambridge race, but much more fun, since there are over four hundred crews setting off on the ebb tide at ten-second intervals and chasing each other from Mortlake to Putney.

The Boat Race Last Sat in March or first Sat in April ⓦ theboatrace.org; free. Since 1829 rowers from Oxford and Cambridge universities have battled it out over four miles from Putney to Mortlake, setting off on the flood tide. Since 2015, a women's race has taken place on the same stretch and on the same day. The pubs at prime vantage points pack out early.

APRIL

London Marathon Third or fourth Sun in month ⓦ london-marathon.co.uk; free. The world's most popular marathon, with around forty thousand masochists sweating the 26.2 miles from Greenwich to

The Mall. A handful of world-class athletes enter each year, but most of the competitors are running for charity, often in ludicrous costumes.

MAY

IWA Canalway Cavalcade May Bank Holiday weekend. Little Venice ⓦ waterways.org.uk; ⊖ Warwick Avenue; free. Lively three-day celebration of the city's inland waterways, with scores of decorated narrow boats, and lots of stalls and children's activities.

May Fayre and Puppet Festival Sun nearest May 9. St Paul's Churchyard; ⊖ Covent Garden; free. The gardens of Covent Garden's St Paul's Church play host to puppet booths to commemorate the first recorded Punch and Judy show in England, seen by diarist Samuel Pepys in 1662.

State Opening of Parliament May or June ⓦ parliament.uk; ⊖ Westminster. The Queen arrives by coach at the Houses of Parliament at 11am accompanied by the Household Cavalry and gun salutes. The ceremony itself takes place inside the House of Lords and is televised; it also takes place whenever a new government is sworn in.

Chestnut Sunday Sun nearest May 11. Bushy Park ⓦ royalparks .gov.uk; ⇌ Hampton Court; free. Parade of antique bicycles, classic cars, motorcycles and carriages along Chestnut Ave, with the trees in full blossom.

Chelsea Flower Show Late May. Royal Hospital, Chelsea ⓦ rhs .org.uk/Chelsea; ⊖ Sloane Square; tickets from £37 for half-day. The world's finest horticultural event, with over 150,000 visitors over two days, is a solidly bourgeois affair. RHS members only on the first two days.

JUNE

Beating Retreat Two consecutive eves in early June 9pm. Horse Guards Parade ⓦ army.mod.uk; ⊖ Charing Cross, Embankment or Westminster. Annual military display on Horse Guards Parade over two evenings, marking the old custom of drumming and piping the troops back to base at dusk. Soldiers on foot and horseback provide a colourful ceremony which precedes a floodlit performance by the Massed Bands of the Foot Guards and the Mounted Bands of the Household Cavalry.

Stoke Newington Literary Festival Weekend in early June ⓦ stokenewingtonliteraryfestival.com. Literary festival in venues across this north London neighbourhood, which celebrates the area's radical history, and often attracts an impressive selection of speakers.

Spitalfields Summer Music Festival June ⓦ spitalfieldsmusic .org.uk; ⊖ Liverpool Street and Shoreditch High St. The festival is held over two weeks in various venues across the East End, focusing on early classical music, with the odd nod to world music. There's also a smaller, winter festival held in December.

Trooping the Colour Second Sat in month ⓦ army.mod.uk; ⊖ Charing Cross, Embankment or Westminster. Celebration of the Queen's official birthday (her real one is on April 21) featuring massed bands, gun salutes, fly-pasts and crowds of tourists and patriotic Britons. The royal procession along the Mall allows you a glimpse for free, and there are rehearsals (minus Her Majesty) on the two preceding Saturdays.

Meltdown Mid-June. Southbank Centre ⓦ southbankcentre.co.uk; ⊖ Waterloo. Week of groovy gigs, films and other events on the South Bank, chosen and presided over by a different seminal musician each year.

City of London Festival Late June to late July ⓦ colf.org. For one month, churches (including St Paul's Cathedral), livery halls, corporate buildings and even the streets around the City play host to classical and jazz concerts, performers and a host of talks and interesting events, some ticketed and some free.

Open Garden Squares Weekend in mid-June ⓦ opensquares.org. Around two hundred gardens — private squares, community gardens, roof gardens — open to visitors for one weekend.

Gay Pride Late June ⓦ prideinlondon.org. Traditional Gay Pride march through the West End, finishing up in Trafalgar Square for speeches, music and dancing. Other celebrations and events throughout the city for the week.

JULY

Hampton Court Palace Flower Show Early July. Hampton Court Palace ⓦ rhs.org.uk; ⇌ Hampton Court; half-day tickets from £20. Six-day international flower extravaganza that rivals its sister show in Chelsea. RHS members only on the first two days.

Doggett's Coat & Badge Race July or early Aug ⓦ www .doggettsrace.org.uk; free. World's oldest rowing race, which runs from London Bridge to Chelsea, established by Thomas Doggett, an eighteenth-century Irish comedian, to commemorate George I's accession to the throne. Six young watermen battle it out in modern sculling boats.

Lambeth Country Show Weekend in mid-July. Brockwell Park ⓦ lambeth.gov.uk; ⇌ Herne Hill; free. A traditional country show comes to Brixton's Brockwell Park for a splendidly idiosyncratic two-day festival featuring sheep shearing, animals from Vauxhall City Farm, local produce stalls, a vegetable sculpture competition that has to be seen to be believed, Somerset cider, jerk chicken, falconry displays and a couple of stages of live music, normally featuring a few legends of reggae, roots and world music.

The Proms or Henry Wood Promenade Concerts Mid-July to early Sept ⓦ bbc.co.uk/proms; ⊖ South Kensington or High Street Kensington. This series of nightly classical concerts, over the course of two months at the Royal Albert Hall (and elsewhere), is a well-loved British institution (see p.413).

Italian Procession Sun nearest July 16. St Peter's Italian Church ⓦ italianchurch.org.uk; ⊖ Farringdon; free. Big, boisterous Italian Catholic parade, party and stalls; starts on Clerkenwell Road and roams the streets of what used to be London's very own Little Italy (see p.146).

Cart Marking Wed 11am in mid-July. Guildhall ⓦ thecarmen .co.uk; ⊖ Bank; free. Recalling a 1681 Act which restricted to 421 the number of horse-drawn carts allowed in the City, this arcane ceremony involves vintage vehicles congregating in Guildhall Yard in a branding ceremony organized by the Worshipful Company of Carmen.

AUGUST

Ride London Early Aug ⓦ prudentialridelondon.co.uk; free. Weekend festival of cycling, including an eight-mile traffic-free loop around the capital — more than eighty thousand people take part every year.

Brixton Splash Sun in Aug (noon–7pm) ⓦ brixtonsplash.org; ⊖ Brixton. A one-day street party to celebrate Brixton's diversity. Stages and soundsystems on Windrush Square, Atlantic Road, Coldharbour Lane and Pope's Road make the neighbourhood throb with music, while food and other stalls spread out across the neighbourhood.

Great British Beer Festival Mid-Aug. London Olympia ⓦ gbbf
.org.uk; ⊖ Kensington Olympia. A five-day binge organized by the
Campaign for Real Ale (CAMRA). With up to eight hundred brews to
sample, the entrance fee – about £20, which includes £5 in beer tokens
– is a small price to pay to drink yourself silly.

London Mela Sun in Aug or early Sept. Gunnersbury Park
ⓦ londonmela.org; ⊖ Gunnersbury; free. Around eight thousand
revellers come to this big open-air Asian festival of live music, dance and
the arts, washed down with the best festival food in the capital.

Notting Hill Carnival Sun & Mon of Aug Bank Holiday weekend
ⓦ thenottinghillcarnival.com; check transport options online,
nearby stations often close; free. World-famous two-day street
festival, a tumult of imaginatively decorated floats, eye-catching
costumes, thumping soundsystems, live bands, irresistible food and huge
crowds (see p.279).

SEPTEMBER

Great River Race Sat in mid-Sept ⓦ greatriverrace.co.uk; free.
Hundreds of boats are rowed or paddled for 21 miles from Island Gardens
on the Isle of Dogs to Ham House, Richmond. Starts are staggered and
any number of weird and wonderful vessels take part.

Totally Thames Sept ⓦ totallythames.org; ⊖ Southwark; free.
The Mayor of London's family-orientated festival takes place over a month
on both banks of the river, with river races, a Thames beach, dancing,
music, fireworks and a night-time parade.

Open House Third weekend in month ⓦ londonopenhouse.org; free.
A once-a-year opportunity to peek inside over seven hundred buildings
around London, many of which don't normally open their doors to the public.
You'll need to book in advance for some of the more popular places.

Great Gorilla Run Last Sat in month ⓦ greatgorillarun.org; free
(to watch). Don a gorilla suit and join (or simply watch) 750 gorillas
running 8km through the City for mountain gorilla conservation.

Costermongers Harvest Festival Parade Service Last Sun in
month 1pm. Guildhall to St Mary-le-Bow ⓦ pearlysociety.
co.uk; ⊖ Bank or St Paul's; free. Cockney festival in the City, with
donkeys and carts, marching bands and Pearly Kings and Queens in their
traditional pearl-button-studded outfits.

OCTOBER

Judges' Service Early Oct ⓦ westminster-abbey.org.
⊖ Westminster; free. To mark the opening of the legal year the judiciary,
in full regalia, attends a service at 11.30am in Westminster Abbey.
Afterwards they process to the House of Lords for their "Annual Breakfast".

London Film Festival Mid- to late Oct ⓦ bfi.org.uk/lff. A
two-week cinematic season with scores of new international films
screened at the BFI Southbank and some West End venues.

Frieze London Art Fair Mid-Oct ⓦ friezelondon.com;
⊖ Regent's Park or Great Portland Street; tickets around £30. The
international art set descend on Regent's Park for five days as it plays host
to the huge Frieze Art Fair, plus the parallel Frieze Masters. It's shopping
on a grand sale for the world's uber-wealthy, but the general public can
enjoy the spectacle of works by some of the biggest names in
contemporary art, and there are events, such as a free sculpture garden,
that run alongside.

London Literature Festival Two weeks in Oct ⓦ southbankcentre
.co.uk ⊖ Waterloo. The capital's chief wordfest is held over a fortnight at
the Southbank Centre, with music, poetry and debate.

Return to Camden Town Late Oct & early Nov. London Irish
Centre, 50–52 Camden Square, and nearby pubs and venues
ⓦ returntocamden.org; ⊖ Camden Road. Two long weekends of
traditional Irish music, song and dance featuring a great line-up of
performers as well as talks and workshops.

NOVEMBER

London to Brighton Veteran Car Run First Sun in month. Hyde
Park ⓦ veterancarrun.com; free. In 1896 Parliament abolished the Act
that required all cars to crawl along at 2mph behind someone waving a
red flag. A rally was set up to mark the occasion, and more than a century
later five hundred or so pre-1905 vehicles still set off from Hyde Park at
sunrise and travel the 58 miles to Brighton along the A23 at the heady
average speed of 20mph.

Bonfire Night Nov 5 or nearest weekend; free. In memory of Guy
Fawkes – executed for his role in the 1605 Gunpowder Plot to blow up
King James I and the Houses of Parliament – effigies of the hapless
Fawkes are traditionally burned on bonfires all over the capital, though
now the celebrations are dominated by fireworks. See local listings or
head for Alexandra Palace, which provides a good vantage point from
which to take in several displays at once.

London Jazz Festival Mid-Nov ⓦ londonjazzfestival.org.uk. Big
ten-day international jazz fest held in all London's jazz venues, large
and small.

Lord Mayor's Show Second Sat in month ⓦ lordmayorsshow.org;
free. The investiture of a new Lord Mayor is marked with a day of pomp
and ceremony, including a river pageant, and a vast ceremonial
procession of seven thousand participants, headed by a gilded coach,
from Mansion House to the Law Courts in the Strand, where the oath of
office is taken. From there the coach and its train make their way back.
After dark, there's a fireworks display on the Thames.

Remembrance Sunday Sun nearest Nov 11; free. A day of
commemorative ceremonies for the dead and wounded of the two world
wars and other conflicts. The principal ceremony, attended by the Queen
and the prime minister, takes place at the Cenotaph in Whitehall,
beginning with a march-past of veterans and building to a one-minute
silence at the stroke of 11am.

Christmas Lights Late Nov to Jan 5; free. Assorted celebrities flick
the switches, and Bond, Oxford and Regent streets are bathed in festive
illumination from dusk to midnight until January 6. Also, each year since
the end of World War II, Norway has acknowledged its gratitude to the
country that helped liberate it from the Nazis with the gift of a mighty
spruce tree that appears in Trafalgar Square in early December. Decorated
with lights, it becomes the focus for carol singing versus traffic noise each
evening until Christmas Eve.

DECEMBER

Christmas markets and ice rinks Dec–Jan. Numerous locations
across London set up "German-style" Christmas markets and/or ice rinks.
The biggest by far is the popular (and sometimes overcrowded) Winter
Wonderland in Hyde Park, with an ice rink, Bavarian-style beer hall and

funfair, while the South Bank has stalls and pop-up Christmassy bars. You can skate outside the Natural History Museum, at Somerset House, Kew Gardens and elsewhere.

Christmas Day Race Christmas Day. Serpentine Lido Ⓦ serpentineswimmingclub.com; ⊖Knightsbridge; free. Brave (or foolhardy) members of the Serpentine Swimming Club have taken an icy 100yd plunge and competed for the Peter Pan Cup in the Lido every year since 1864.

New Year's Eve Ⓦ london.gov.uk; free. New Year is welcomed by thousands of revellers who get to enjoy a spectacular firework display centred on the London Eye. For a Thames-side view you need to get a ticket in advance, released a few months ahead. Transport for London runs free public transport all night.

Travel essentials

Addresses

London addresses come with postcodes at the end. Each street name is followed by a letter or letters giving the geographical location of the street in relation to the City (E for "east", WC for "west central" and so on) and a number that specifies its location more precisely. Unfortunately, this number doesn't correspond to the district's distance from the centre (as in most cities). So W11 (Notting Hill) for example, is closer to the centre of town than W4 (Chiswick), and SE3 (Blackheath) lies beyond the remote-sounding SE10 (Greenwich). Full postal addresses end with a digit and two letters, which specify the individual block, and will locate a building on Google Maps or a sat nav.

Climate

Despite the temperateness of the English climate, it's impossible to say with any degree of certainty that the weather will be pleasant in any given month. English summers rarely get unbearably hot, while the winters don't get very cold – though they're often wet. However, whenever you come, be prepared for all eventualities: it has been known to snow at Easter and rain all day on August Bank Holiday weekend.

TIPPING

There are no fixed rules for **tipping** in London. However, there's a certain expectation in restaurants or cafés that you should leave a tip of about ten percent of the total bill – check first, though, that "optional" service has not already been included. Taxi drivers also expect tips – add about ten percent to the fare – as do traditional barbers. The other occasion when you'll be expected to tip is in upmarket hotels where porters, bellboys and table waiters rely on being tipped to bump up their often dismal wages.

Costs

The high cost of accommodation (see p.354), and food (see p.366) and drink, makes London a **very expensive** place to visit. The minimum expenditure for a couple staying in a budget hotel and eating takeaway meals, pizzas or other such basic fare would be in the region of at least £50 per person per day. You only have to add in the odd better-quality meal, plus some major tourist attractions, a few films or other shows, and you're looking at around £75–100 as a daily budget, even in decidedly average accommodation.

Most attractions and many cinemas and theatres offer **concessions** for senior citizens, the unemployed, full-time students and under-16s, with under-5s being admitted free almost every-where – although proof of eligibility will be required in most cases.

If you're not a student, but you're 25 or younger, you can get an International Youth Travel Card or **IYTC**, which costs the same as the ISIC and carries the same benefits. Visit Ⓦ isic.org for more details.

Crime and personal safety

The traditional image of the friendly British "bobby" is a bit of a tired old cliché, but in the normal run of events the police continue to be approachable,

---

ENGLISH HERITAGE AND NATIONAL TRUST

A few of London's historic properties come under the control of the private **National Trust** (☎0844 800 1895, Ⓦnationaltrust.org.uk), or the state-run **English Heritage** (☎0370 333 1181, Ⓦenglish-heritage.org.uk). These properties are denoted in the guide by "NT" or "EH" after the opening times. Annual membership, which allows free entry to their properties, is £60 for the National Trust and £50 for English Heritage. A few small London sights offer discounted entry for National Trust members.

AVERAGE MONTHLY TEMPERATURES AND RAINFALL

	Jan	Feb	Mar	Apr	May	Jun	Jul	Aug	Sep	Oct	Nov	Dec
LONDON												
Max/min (°C)	6/2	7/2	10/3	13/6	17/8	20/12	22/14	21/13	19/11	14/8	10/5	7/4
Max/min (°F)	43/36	44/36	50/37	56/43	62/46	69/53	71/57	71/56	65/52	57/45	50/41	44/39
Rainfall (mm)	54	40	37	37	46	45	57	59	49	57	64	48

helpful and, for the most part, unarmed. Police officers on street duty wear a distinctive domed hat with a silver tip. In general, London is a very safe city, but like any other capital, it has its dangerous spots, but these tend to be obscure parts of the city where no tourist has any reason to be. The chief risk on London's streets is pickpocketing, and there are some virtuosos at work on the big shopping streets and the Underground (tube).

Should you have anything stolen or be involved in an incident that requires reporting, go to the local police station or phone ☎101 – the ☎999 number should only be used in emergencies. Central 24hr Metropolitan police stations include Charing Cross, Agar St, WC2 (⊖Charing Cross) and West End Central, 27 Savile Row, W1 (⊖Oxford Circus); see ⓦmet.police.uk. The City of London Police are separate from the Metropolitan Police and have a 24hr police station at 182 Bishopsgate, EC2 (☎020 7601 2222, ⓦcityoflondon.police.uk; ⊖Liverpool Street). If there's an incident on public transport, you should call the British Transport Police (☎0800 405 040, ⓦbtp.police.uk). If you have a complaint against the police, take the officer's badge number and report it to the relevant police force, which you can do via the Independent Police Complaints Commission (☎0300 020 0096, ⓦwww.ipcc.gov.uk).

Electricity

Electricity supply in London conforms to the EU standard of approximately 230V. Sockets are designed for British three-pin plugs, which are totally different from those in the rest of the EU and North America.

Entry requirements and working in London

Citizens of all European countries – except Albania, Bosnia, Macedonia, Montenegro, Serbia and the former Soviet republics (other than the Baltic states) – can enter Britain with just a passport, for up to three months (indefinitely if you're from the EU). All Swiss nationals and EEA citizens can work in London without a permit (other nationals need a work permit in order to work legally in the UK). US, Canadian, Australian and New Zealand citizens can stay for up to six months, providing they have a return ticket and adequate funds to cover their stay. Citizens of most other countries require a **visa**, obtainable from the British consular or mission office in the country of application. To check if you need a visa and find UK Visa and Immigration services outside the UK, visit ⓦgov.uk/check-uk-visa.

Note that visa regulations are subject to frequent changes, so it's always wise to contact the nearest British embassy or High Commission before you travel.

THE LONDON PASS

If you're thinking of visiting a lot of fee-paying attractions in a short space of time, it's worth considering buying a **London Pass** (ⓦlondonpass.com), which gives you free entry to some of London's top attractions including Hampton Court Palace, Kensington Palace, Kew Gardens, London Zoo, St Paul's Cathedral, the Tower of London, Westminster Abbey and Windsor Castle. You can choose to buy the card with an **All-Zone Oyster Travelcard** thrown in; the extra outlay is relatively small, but does not include travel out to Windsor. The pass costs £52 for one day (£35 for kids), rising to £116 for six days (£80 for kids), or £65 with a Travelcard (£41 for kids) rising to £159 (£110 for kids). The London Pass can be bought online or in person from tourist offices and London's mainline train or chief underground stations.

EMERGENCIES
Police, fire and ambulance ☎999

EMBASSIES AND HIGH COMMISSIONS

Australian High Commission Australia House, Strand, WC2 ☎ 020 7379 4334, ⓦ uk.embassy.gov.au; ⊖Charing Cross
Canadian High Commission Trafalgar Square (entrance on Cockspur Street), SW1 ☎ 020 7004 6000, ⓦ unitedkingdom.gc.ca; ⊖Charing Cross
Irish Embassy 17 Grosvenor Place, SW1 ☎ 020 7235 2171, ⓦ embassyofireland.co.uk; ⊖Hyde Park Corner
New Zealand High Commission New Zealand House, 80 Haymarket, SW1 ☎ 020 7930 8422, ⓦ nzembassy.com; ⊖Piccadilly Circus
South African High Commission South Africa House, Trafalgar Square, WC2 ☎ 020 7451 7299, ⓦ southafricahouseuk.com; ⊖Charing Cross
US Embassy 24 Grosvenor Square, W1 ☎ 020 7499 9000, ⓦ london.usembassy.gov; ⊖Bond Street

Health

For minor complaints, pharmacists (known as chemists in England) can dispense a limited range of drugs without a doctor's prescription. Most pharmacies are open standard shop hours, though some stay open later: Zafash, 233–235 Old Brompton Rd, SW5 (☎020 7373 2798, ⓦzafashpharmacy.co.uk; ⊖Earl's Court), is open 24 hours, while Bliss, at 5–6 Marble Arch, W1 (☎020 7723 6116, ⓦblisslife.co.uk;⊖Marble Arch), is open daily 9am till midnight.

EU and EEA citizens are entitled to free medical treatment within the National Health Service (ⓦnhs.uk), on production of an EHIC (European Health Insurance Card). Australia, New Zealand, Russia and several other non-EU countries also have reciprocal health-care arrangements with the UK. If it's an emergency, go to the Accident and Emergency (A&E) department of your local hospital, or phone for an ambulance (☎999). Centrally located A&E departments include: St Thomas's Hospital, Westminster Bridge Rd, SE1 (⊖Westminster); University College London Hospital, 235 Euston Rd, NW1 (⊖Euston Square or Warren Street); Royal London Hospital, Whitechapel

Rd, E1 (⊖Whitechapel); and St Mary's Hospital, Praed St, W2 (⊖Paddington).

For non-emergencies get medical advice from the NHS's 24-hour helpline ☎111.

Insurance

Even though EU healthcare privileges apply in the UK, it's as well to take out an insurance policy before travelling to cover against theft, loss and illness or injury. Non-EU citizens should check whether they are already covered before buying a new policy.

Internet access

Most hotels and hostels in London have internet access. Otherwise, your best bet is to find a café or venue with wi-fi. The Southbank Centre has free wi-fi and the British Library and St Pancras Station both have free wi-fi, too. Some public libraries also offer free access.

Laundry

Most hotels offer a laundry service and most hostels have washing machines. Self-service laundrettes exist all over London, although they are harder to find in the centre – there's Red & White laundrette at 78 Marchmont St, WC1 (daily 6.30am–10.30pm; ☎020 7387 3667; ⊖King's Cross).

Left luggage

All left luggage facilities cost around £10/24hr.
Airports Gatwick: South Terminal (24hr; ☎01293 734887). Heathrow: Terminal 2 (daily 5am–11pm; ☎020 3642 9178); Terminal 3 (daily 5am–11pm; ☎020 3468 4589); Terminal 4 (daily 5.30am–11pm; ☎020 3468 4565); Terminal 5 (daily 5am–11pm; ☎020 3468 4558). London City (Mon–Fri 5am–10pm, Sat 5am–1pm, Sun 11am–10.20pm;

ROUGH GUIDES TRAVEL INSURANCE

Rough Guides has teamed up with **WorldNomads.com** to offer great travel insurance deals. Policies are available to residents of over 150 countries, with cover for a wide range of adventure sports, 24hr emergency assistance, high levels of medical and evacuation cover and a stream of travel safety information. Roughguides.com users can take advantage of their policies online 24/7, from anywhere in the world – even if you're already travelling. And since plans often change when you're on the road, you can extend your policy and even claim online. Roughguides.com users who buy travel insurance with WorldNomads.com can also leave a positive footprint and donate to a community development project. For more information go to ⓦroughguides.com/travel-insurance.

☎020 7646 0000). Luton (24hr; ☎01582 809582). Stansted (24hr; ☎0844 824 3109).

Train stations Excess Baggage Company (Ⓦleft-baggage.co.uk): Charing Cross (daily 7am–11pm; ☎020 3468 4662); Euston (daily 7am–11pm; ☎020 3468 4670); King's Cross (daily 7am–11pm; ☎020 3468 4690); Liverpool Street (daily 7am–11pm; ☎020 3468 4552); Paddington (daily 7am–11pm; ☎020 3468 4709); St Pancras (Mon–Sat 6am–10pm, Sun 7am–10pm; ☎020 3468 4685); Victoria (daily 7am–midnight; ☎020 3468 4551); Waterloo (daily 7am–11pm; ☎020 3468 4553).

Lost property

Airports Gatwick, South Terminal (daily 10am–4pm; ☎01293 503162); Heathrow, Terminals 3 & 5 (daily 9.30am–4.30pm; ☎0844 824 3115); London City ☎020 7646 0000; Luton ☎01582 809174; Stansted (daily 1–5pm; ☎0844 824 3109).

Eurostar (Mon–Fri 10am–5pm; ☎0344 822 44 11).

Train stations Euston (Mon–Fri 9am–5pm; ☎020 7387 8699); King's Cross (Mon–Fri 9am–5pm; ☎020 7278 3310); Liverpool Street (Mon–Fri 9am–5pm; ☎020 7247 4297); Paddington (Mon–Fri 9am–5pm; ☎020 7262 0344); St Pancras (Mon–Fri 9am–5pm; ☎020 7837 4334); Victoria (Mon–Fri 9am–5pm; ☎020 7963 0957); Waterloo (Mon–Fri 7.30am–7pm; ☎020 7401 7861).

Transport for London Lost Property Office, 200 Baker St, NW1 (Mon–Fri 8.30am–4pm; ☎0343 222 1234, Ⓦtfl.gov.uk; ⊖Baker Street; map p.89). Contact TfL about property lost on buses, tubes or in black cabs.

Mail

The postal service is pretty efficient. First-class **stamps** to anywhere in the UK currently cost 63p and mail should arrive the next day; if the item is anything approaching A4 size, it will be classed as a "Large Letter" and will cost 95p; if you want to guarantee next-day delivery, ask for Special Delivery (from around £6.45). Second-class stamps cost 54p, taking up to three days; airmail to the rest of Europe and the world costs £1 and should take three days within Europe, five days further afield. Stamps can be bought at post offices, and from newsagents and supermarkets, although they usually only sell books of four or ten first-class UK stamps.

Almost all London's **post offices** are open Monday to Friday 9am–5.30pm, Saturday 9am–noon. The exception is the Trafalgar Square Post Office (24–28 William IV St, WC2N 4DL; Mon & Wed–Fri 8.30am–6.30pm, Tues 9.15am–6.30pm, Sat 9am–5.30pm). To find out your nearest post office, see Ⓦpostoffice.co.uk.

Maps

The maps in this book should be adequate for sightseeing purposes. Alternatively, the Geographers' A–Z map series produces a whole range of street-by-street maps of London, from pocket-sized foldouts to giant atlases. The best map shop in London is Stanfords on Long Acre (see p.430). Free maps of the Underground and bus networks can be picked up at tourist offices and TfL information offices (see p.21).

Media

The free **listings magazine**, *Time Out*, comes out every Tuesday and carries critical appraisals of a selection of the week's theatre, film, music, exhibitions, restaurant openings and children's events, though for comprehensive coverage, you need to visit their website Ⓦtimeout.com/london. London's only daily **newspapers** are both tabloids: the *Metro* is available on the public transport system in the morning, and the *Evening Standard* all over town from mid-afternoon onwards – both are free. Each of the London boroughs has a local paper, usually printed twice weekly and filled mostly with news of local crimes and cheap adverts.

Useful websites

There's a vast quantity of useful London-related information online. These are a handful of good general sites:

Ⓦ **culture24.org.uk** Useful national website, with up-to-date information on virtually every single museum, large or small, in London (and elsewhere in the UK).

Ⓦ **derelictlondon.co.uk** Pictorial catalogue of the city's abandoned cinemas, pubs, theatres and even toilets, plus other forgotten derelict gems.

Ⓦ **hot-dinners.com** All the latest London foodie news on new openings, pop-up restaurants and so on, plus some reader offers.

Ⓦ **londonist.com** London listings, reviews, news and interesting articles on the many faces of London.

Ⓦ **londonnet.co.uk** Web guide to London with useful up-to-date listings on eating, drinking and nightlife.

Ⓦ **thisislocallondon.co.uk** Forty of the capital's local newspapers on one local news website.

Money

The currency in the UK is the pound sterling (£), divided into 100 pence (p). Coins come in denominations of 1p, 2p, 5p, 10p, 20p, 50p, £1 and £2. Notes come in denominations of £5, £10, £20 and £50. Many shopkeepers may not accept £50 notes – the best advice is to avoid having to use them. At the time of writing, £1 was worth $1.55, €1.35, Can$1.85, Aus$1.95 and NZ$2.10. For the most up-to-date exchange rates, visit ⓦxe.com.

The easiest way to get hold of your cash is to use your **credit/debit card** in a "cash machine" (ATM); check in advance whether you will be subject to a daily withdrawal limit. There are ATMs all over the city, outside banks, supermarkets and post offices – beware of stand-alone ATMs in small shops, which charge up to £2 for each withdrawal. The opening hours for most **banks** are Monday to Friday 9.30am–4.30pm, with some branches opening on Saturday mornings. Post offices charge no commission, and are therefore a good place to change money and cheques. Lost or stolen credit/debit cards should be reported to the police and the following numbers: MasterCard ☎0800 964767, Visa ☎0800 891725.

Opening hours and public holidays

Generally speaking, **shop opening hours** are Monday to Saturday 9am or 10am to 5.30pm or 6pm – with some places in central London staying open till 8pm, and later on Thursdays and Fridays (around 9pm) – and Sundays and Bank Holidays noon to 6pm. There are still plenty of stores that close completely on Sundays and Bank Holidays. That said, numerous family-run corner shops stay open late every day of the year. The big supermarket chains tend to open Monday to Saturday from 8am to 10pm, Sunday 10am or 11am to 4pm or 5pm. Note that many petrol (gas) service stations in London are open 24 hours and have small shops.

UK OPERATOR SERVICES
Domestic operator ☎100
International operator ☎155

Tourist attractions and **museums** are typically open daily 10am to 6pm, occasionally with shorter hours on Sundays and public holidays (see box below). Most places are closed on December 25 and 26. Several museums now have late-night openings until 9pm or 10pm, either once or twice a week or as monthly special events.

Phones

Public **payphones** on the streets of London are iconic, ubiquitous and little-used, other than for photo opportunities. Most take coins from 10p upwards – the minimum charge of 60p will get you thirty minutes calling a UK landline. Paying using a credit card is expensive (20p per minute).

If you're taking your **mobile/cellphone** with you, check with your provider that roaming is activated. If you're staying for a while, it's easier to buy a handset and SIM card when you arrive – a basic pay-as-you-go phone can cost as little as £20.

London phone numbers are prefixed by the area code ☎020. Mobile numbers are prefixed with ☎07; numbers with ☎0800, 0808 and 0500 prefixes are free of charge (unless calling from a mobile); ☎03 numbers are charged at local rates; ☎0845 and ☎0870 numbers are charged at special higher rates. Beware of premium-rate numbers which usually have the prefix ☎09, as these are charged at anything up to £1.50 a minute.

For directory enquiries, there are numerous companies offering the service, all with six-figure numbers beginning with ☎118. Whichever one you choose, the minimum charge you'll get away with is 40p. The best known is ☎118 118; for an online UK phone directory, visit ⓦukphonebook.com.

PUBLIC HOLIDAYS
You'll find all banks and offices closed on the following Bank Holidays, while everything else pretty much runs to a Sunday schedule (except on Christmas Day, when most places shut down): **New Year's Day** (January 1); **Good Friday** (late March/early April); **Easter Monday** (late March/early April); **Spring Bank Holiday** (first Monday in May); **May Bank Holiday** (last Monday in May); **August Bank Holiday** (last Monday in August); **Christmas Day** (December 25); **Boxing Day** (December 26). Note that if January 1, December 25 or December 26 falls on a Saturday or Sunday, the holiday falls on the following weekday.

PHONING HOME

To Australia ☎0061 + area code without the zero + number
To Ireland ☎00353 + area code without the zero + number
To New Zealand ☎0064 + area code without the zero + number
To South Africa ☎0027 + area code without the zero + number
To US and Canada ☎001 + area code + number

Smoking

Smoking is banned in all indoor public spaces including all cafés, pubs, restaurants, clubs and public transport. E-cigarettes are not allowed on public transport and generally prohibited in museums and many other public buildings; for restaurants and bars it depends on the individual proprietor.

Tax

Most goods in Britain are subject to **Value Added Tax** (VAT), which increases the cost of an item by 20 percent, although the prices displayed nearly always include VAT. Visitors from non-EU countries can save money through the **Retail Export Scheme** (tax-free shopping), which allows a VAT refund on goods taken out of the country. Note that not all shops participate in this scheme (those doing so will display a sign to this effect) and that you cannot reclaim VAT charged on hotel bills or other services.

Time

Greenwich Mean Time (GMT) is used from the end of October to the end of March; for the rest of the year the country switches to British Summer Time (BST), one hour ahead of GMT. GMT is five hours ahead of the US East Coast; eight ahead of the US West Coast; and nine behind Australia's East Coast.

Toilets

There are surprisingly few public toilets in London. All mainline train and major tube stations have toilets (with a charge for usage). Department stores and free museums and galleries are another good option.

Tourist information

The official tourist information body is Ⓦvisitlondon .com, though they don't run any tourist offices just a kiosk outside Holborn tube station (Mon–Fri 8am–6pm). More useful is **The City Information Centre** on the south side of St Paul's Cathedral (Mon–Sat 9.30am–5.30pm, Sun 10am–4pm; Ⓦcityoflondon. gov.uk; ⊖St Paul's), run by the City of London. They have information about sights across London (and England), free wi-fi and a currency exchange, and you can buy tickets and the London Pass here and find out about walking tours of the City (several daily; £7). Another useful borough tourist office is Greenwich in the old Royal Naval College (daily 10am–5pm; ☎0870 608 2000; ⊖Cutty Sark DLR).

Travellers with disabilities

London is an old city, not well equipped for disabled travellers. That said, all public venues are obliged to make some effort towards accessibility and even public transport is slowly improving, with most buses now wheelchair-accessible. The ancient tube and rail systems, designed, for the most part, in the nineteenth century, are still a trial for those with mobility problems. Around 25 percent of all tube stations are step-free – the majority on the Docklands Light Railway – and are indicated by a blue symbol on the tube map. For a more detailed rundown, get hold of the free *Tube Access Guide* or use the TfL website to plan a step-free journey (Ⓦtfl.gov.uk).

Tourism For All has lots of useful information on accessibility for visitors to London (☎0845 124 9971, Ⓦtourismforall.org.uk). Another valuable service is provided by Artsline (Ⓦartsline.org.uk), which can give up-to-date information and advice on access to arts venues and events in London.

Whitehall and Westminster

The monuments and buildings in Westminster include some of London's most famous landmarks – Nelson's Column, Big Ben, the Houses of Parliament and Westminster Abbey, plus two of the city's top permanent art collections, the National Gallery and Tate Britain and its finest architectural set piece, Trafalgar Square. This is one of the easiest parts of London to walk round, with all the major sights within a mere half-mile of each other, and linked by one of London's most triumphant – and atypical – avenues, Whitehall. However, despite the fact the area is a well-trodden tourist circuit, for the most part there are only a few shops or cafés and little commercial life (nearby Soho and Covent Garden are far better for this).

Political, religious and regal power has emanated from **Whitehall** and **Westminster** for almost a millennium. It was King Edward the Confessor (1042–66) who first established Westminster as a royal and ecclesiastical power base, some three miles west of the City of London. The embryonic English parliament used to meet in the abbey and eventually took over the old royal palace of Westminster when Henry VIII moved out to Whitehall. Henry's sprawling Whitehall Palace burnt down in 1698 and was slowly replaced by government offices, so that by the nineteenth century Whitehall had become the "heart of the Empire", its ministries ruling over a quarter of the world's population. Even now, though the UK's world status has diminished and its royalty and clergy no longer wield much real power or receive the same respect, the institutions that run the country inhabit roughly the same geographical area: Westminster for the politicians, Whitehall for the ministers and civil servants.

While Westminster is as much an institution as a place, The City of Westminster is the full title for one of the two most central London boroughs (the other being The City) and actually covers most of the West End, which is why you will see street signs from Marylebone to Covent Garden carrying the name.

Trafalgar Square

⊖ Charing Cross

As one of the few large public squares in London, **Trafalgar Square** has been both a tourist attraction and the main focus for political demonstrations for over a century and a half (see box below). Nowadays, most folk come here to see **Nelson's Column**, or to visit the **National Gallery**, though a huge range of events, commemorations and celebrations are staged here throughout the year, from St Patrick's Day shenanigans to Diwali. Each December, the square is graced with a giant Christmas tree covered in fairy lights, donated by Norway in thanks for Britain's support during World War II, and carol singers battle nightly with the traffic.

For centuries, Trafalgar Square was the site of the **King's Mews**, established in the thirteenth century by Edward I, who kept the royal hawks and the falconers here (the term "mews" comes from falconry: the birds were caged or "mewed up" there while changing their plumage). In the 1760s, George III began to move the mews to Buckingham Palace, and by the late 1820s, **John Nash** had designed the new square (though he didn't live to see his plan executed). The Neoclassical National Gallery filled up the northern side in 1838, followed shortly afterwards by the central focal point, Nelson's Column, though the famous bronze lions didn't arrive until 1868. The development of the rest of the square was equally haphazard, though the overall effect is unified by the safe Neoclassical style of the buildings, and the square remains one of London's grandest architectural highlights.

A HISTORY OF PROTEST

Installed in 1845 in an attempt to deter the gathering of urban mobs, the Trafalgar Square fountains have failed supremely to prevent the square from becoming a focus of **political protest**. The first major demo was held in 1848 when the Chartists assembled to demand universal suffrage before marching to Kennington Common. Protests were banned until the 1880s, when the emerging Labour movement began to gather here, culminating in **Bloody Sunday**, 1887, when hundreds of demonstrators were injured, and three killed, by the police. To allow the police to call quickly for reinforcements, a police phone box was built into one of the stone bollards in the southeast corner of the square, with a direct link to Scotland Yard.

Throughout the 1980s, there was a continuous **anti-apartheid demonstration** outside South Africa House, and in 1990, the square was the scene of the **Poll Tax Riot**, which precipitated the downfall of Margaret Thatcher. Smaller demos still take place here, but London's largest demonstrations – like the ones against military intervention in Iraq and Afghanistan – simply pass through, en route to the more spacious environs of Hyde Park.

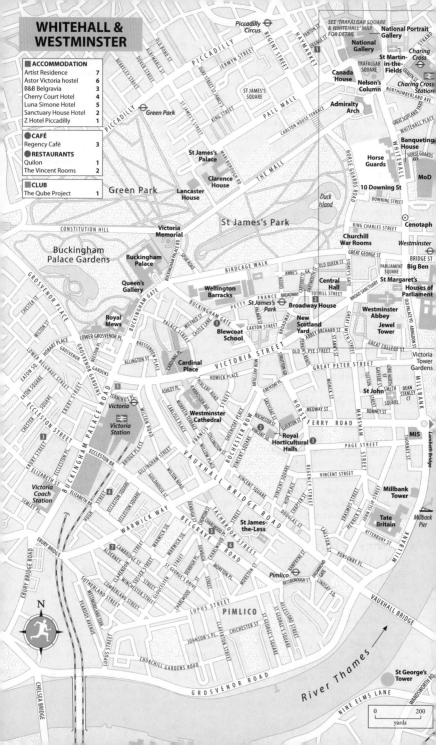

WHITEHALL & WESTMINSTER

ACCOMMODATION
Artist Residence	7
Astor Victoria hostel	6
B&B Belgravia	3
Cherry Court Hotel	4
Luna Simone Hotel	5
Sanctuary House Hotel	2
Z Hotel Piccadilly	1

CAFÉ
Regency Café	3

RESTAURANTS
Quilon	1
The Vincent Rooms	2

CLUB
The Qube Project	1

N

0   200
yards

Nelson's Column

Raised in 1843, and now one of London's best-loved monuments, **Nelson's Column** commemorates the one-armed, one-eyed admiral who defeated the French at the Battle of Trafalgar in 1805, but paid for it with his life. The sandstone statue which surmounts a 151-foot granite column is more than triple life-size but still manages to appear minuscule. The acanthus leaves of the capital are cast from British cannons, while bas-reliefs around the base – depicting three of Nelson's earlier victories as well as his death aboard HMS *Victory* – are from captured French armaments. Edwin Landseer's four gargantuan **bronze lions** guard the column and provide a climbing frame for kids (and demonstrators).

Keeping Nelson company at ground level, on either side of the column, are bronze **statues** of Napier and Havelock, Victorian major-generals who helped keep India British; against the north wall are busts of Beatty, Jellicoe and Cunningham, admirals from the last century. To the right of them are the imperial standards of length – inch, foot and yard – "accurate at 62 degrees Fahrenheit", as the plaque says, and still used by millions of Brits despite the best efforts of the European Union. Above this is an equestrian statue of George IV (bareback, stirrup-less and in Roman garb), which he himself commissioned for the top of Marble Arch, but which was later erected here "temporarily".

South Africa House and Canada House

There's an unmistakable whiff of empire about Trafalgar Square, with **South Africa House** erected in 1935 on the east side, complete with keystones featuring African animals, and a gilded springbok. **Canada House**, constructed in warm Bath stone on the opposite side of the square, was built by Robert Smirke in the 1820s as a gentlemen's club and home for the Royal College of Physicians. It retains much of its original Neoclassical interior, and is now in the hands of the Canadian High Commission.

St Martin-in-the-Fields

Trafalgar Square • Mon, Tues & Fri 8.30am–1pm & 2–6pm, Wed 8.30am–1.15pm & 2–5pm, Thurs 8.30am–1.15pm & 2–6pm, Sat 9.30am–6pm, Sun 3.30–5pm • Free • ☎ 020 7766 1100, 🌐 stmartin-in-the-fields.org • ⊖ Charing Cross

At the northeastern corner of Trafalgar Square stands the church of St Martin-in-the-Fields, fronted by a magnificent Corinthian portico and topped by an elaborate tower and steeple, designed in 1721 by James Gibbs – it was subsequently copied widely in the American colonies. The barrel-vaulted interior features ornate, sparkling white Italian plasterwork and is best appreciated while listening to one of the church's long-running series of free lunchtime concerts (Mon, Tues & Fri at 1pm) or ticketed, candle-lit evening performances (box office in the crypt).

As the official parish church for Buckingham Palace, St Martin's maintains strong royal and naval connections – there's a royal box on the left of the high altar, and one

---

THE FOURTH PLINTH

The **fourth plinth**, in the northwest corner of Trafalgar Square, was originally earmarked for an equestrian statue of William IV. In the end, it remained empty until 1999, since when it has been used to display works of modern sculpture, which are changed every year or two. Highlights have included: Marc Quinn's *Alison Lapper Pregnant*, a statue of a nude woman without arms – a larger, inflatable version of which appeared in the 2012 Paralympics opening ceremony; Antony Gormley's *One & Other*, where several thousand individuals each had an hour to occupy the plinth; and Yinka Shonibare's *Ship in a Bottle*. In March 2015, German artist Hans Haacke's *Gift Horse* was unveiled, a four-and-a-half-metre tall skeleton of a horse with a London Stock Exchange ticker fixed to its leg; replaced in 2016 by David Shrigley's *Really Good* sculpture, a giant hand with an elongated thumb aloft – it's the artist's hope that this public and prominent thumbs-up will instill some optimism into life here.

1

for the admiralty on the right. Far from being a church for the "establishment", however, this distinctly liberal institution has a strong tradition of working with the homeless and continues to provide grants helping people out of poverty. Down in the newly expanded crypt – accessible via either of the two smaller entrances flanking the main door at the front or a winding staircase inside a completely detached entrance north of the church – there's a licensed café (see p.367), shop, gallery and brass-rubbing centre.

National Gallery

Trafalgar Square • Daily 10am–6pm, Fri till 9pm • Free • ☎ 020 7747 2885, ⓦ nationalgallery.org.uk • ⊖ Charing Cross

Taking up the entire north side of Trafalgar Square, the sprawling Neoclassical hulk of the **National Gallery** houses one of the world's greatest art collections. Unlike the Louvre or the Hermitage, the National Gallery is not based on a former royal collection, but was begun as late as 1824 when the government reluctantly agreed to purchase 38 paintings belonging to a Russian émigré banker, John Julius Angerstein. The collection was originally put on public display at Angerstein's old residence, on Pall Mall, until today's purpose-built edifice was completed in 1838. A hostile press dubbed the gallery's diminutive dome and cupolas "pepperpots", and poured abuse on the Greek Revival architect, William Wilkins, who retreated into early retirement and died a year later.

The gallery now boasts a collection of more than 2300 paintings, whose virtue is not so much its size as its range, depth and quality. Among the thousand paintings on permanent display are **Italian masterpieces** by the likes of Botticelli, Leonardo and Michelangelo, dazzling pieces by Velázquez and Goya and an array of **Rembrandt** paintings that features some of his most searching portraits. In addition, the gallery has a particularly strong showing of **Impressionists**, with paintings by Monet, Degas, Van Gogh and Cézanne, plus several early Picassos. There are also showpieces by Turner, Reynolds and Gainsborough, but for a wider range of British art, head for Tate Britain (see p.62). **Special exhibitions** are held in the basement of the Sainsbury Wing and usually charge admission.

INFORMATION AND TOURS

Arrival There are four entrances to the National Gallery: Wilkins' original Portico Entrance up the steps from Trafalgar Square, the Getty Entrance on the ground floor to the east, the Sainsbury Wing to the west and the back entrance on Orange St. The Getty Entrance and the Sainsbury Wing both have an information desk, where you can buy a floorplan, and disabled access, with lifts to all floors.

Tours Audioguides (£4, concessions £3.50, free for under-12s accompanied by an adult) are available – much better, though, are the gallery's free guided tours, which set off from the Sainsbury Wing foyer (daily 11.30am & 2.30pm, plus Fri 7pm; 1hr). Alternatively, download one of the gallery's free 'Printed trails' from the website.

Eating By the Getty Entrance is the *National Café* (Mon–Fri 8am–11pm, Sat 9am–11pm, Sun 9am–6pm), which has a self-service area, and a large brasserie, with an entrance on St Martin's Place. More formal dining is available at the *National Dining Rooms* (daily 10am–5.30pm, Fri till 8.30pm; ☎ 020 7747 2525), serving excellent British cuisine, in the Sainsbury Wing, with views over Trafalgar Square.

The Sainsbury Wing

The original design for the gallery's modern **Sainsbury Wing** was dubbed by Prince Charles "a monstrous carbuncle on the face of a much-loved and elegant friend". So instead, the American husband-and-wife team of Venturi and Scott-Brown were commissioned to produce a softly-softly, postmodern adjunct, which playfully imitates elements of William Wilkins' Neoclassicism and even Nelson's Column and, most importantly, got the approval of Prince Charles, who laid the foundation stone in 1988.

Chronologically the gallery's collection begins in this wing, which houses the National's oldest paintings from the thirteenth to the fifteenth centuries, mostly early

Italian Renaissance masterpieces, with a smattering of early Dutch, Flemish and German works.

Giotto to Van Eyck

The gallery's earliest works by **Giotto**, "the father of modern painting", and **Duccio**, a Sienese contemporary, are displayed in room 52. So too, in a "side chapel" is the "Leonardo Cartoon" – a preparatory drawing for a painting which, like so many of Leonardo's projects, was never completed. The cartoon was known only to scholars until the gallery bought it for £800,000 in the mid-1960s. In 1987, it gained further notoriety when an ex-soldier blasted the work with a sawn-off shotgun in protest at the political status quo.

Next door, you can admire the extraordinarily vivid **Wilton Diptych**, one of the few medieval altarpieces to survive the Puritan iconoclasm of the Commonwealth. It was painted by an unknown fourteenth-century artist for King Richard II, who is depicted kneeling, presented by his three patron saints to the Virgin, Child and assorted angels.

Whatever you do, don't miss **Paolo Uccello**'s brilliant, blood-free *Battle of San Romano*, which dominates room 54. The painting commemorates a recent Florentine victory over her bitter Sienese rivals and was commissioned as part of a three-panel frieze for a Florentine palazzo.

Room 56 explores the beginnings of oil painting, and one of its early masters, **Jan van Eyck**, whose intriguing *Arnolfini Portrait* is celebrated for its complex symbolism. No longer thought to depict a marriage ceremony, the "bride" is not pregnant but simply wearing a fashionable dress that showed off just how much excess cloth a rich Italian cloth merchant like Arnolfini could afford.

Botticelli to Piero della Francesca

You return to the Italians in room 57, which boasts **Leonardo da Vinci**'s melancholic *Virgin of the Rocks* (the more famous *Da Vinci Code* version hangs in the Louvre) and two contrasting Nativity paintings by **Botticelli**: the *Mystic Nativity* is unusual in that it features seven devils fleeing back into the Underworld, while in his *Adoration of the Kings*, Botticelli himself takes centre stage, as the best-dressed man at the gathering, resplendent in bright-red stockings and giving the audience a knowing look. In room 58 is his *Venus and Mars*, depicting a naked and replete Mars in deep postcoital sleep, watched over by a beautifully calm Venus, fully clothed and somewhat less overcome.

Further on, in room 62, hangs one of **Mantegna**'s best early works, *The Agony in the Garden*, which demonstrates a convincing use of perspective. Close by, the dazzling dawn sky in the painting on the same theme by his brother-in-law, **Giovanni Bellini**, shows the artist's celebrated mastery of natural light. Elsewhere, there are paintings from Netherlands and Germany, among them **Dürer**'s sympathetic portrait of his father (a goldsmith in Nuremberg), in room 65, which was presented to Charles I in 1636 by the artist's home town.

Finally, at the far end of the wing, in room 66, your eye will probably be drawn to **Piero della Francesca**'s monumental *Baptism of Christ*, one of his earliest surviving pictures, dating from the 1450s and a brilliant example of his immaculate compositional

---

TEN PAINTINGS NOT TO MISS

Battle of San Romano Uccello. Room 54

Arnolfini Portrait Van Eyck. Room 56

Virgin of the Rocks Da Vinci. Room 57

Venus and Mars Botticelli. Room 58

The Ambassadors Holbein. Room 4

Self-Portrait at the Age of 63 Rembrandt van Rijn. Room 23

The Cornfield Constable. Room 34

Rain, Steam & Speed Turner. Room 34

Gare St Lazare Monet. Room 43

Van Gogh's Chair Van Gogh. Room 45

1

technique. Blindness forced Piero to stop painting some twenty years before his death, and to concentrate instead on his equally innovative work as a mathematician.

The main building

The collection continues in the gallery's **main building** with paintings from the sixteenth century to the early twentieth century. This account follows the collection more or less chronologically.

Veronese, Giorgione and Titian

The first room you come to from the Sainsbury Wing is the vast Wohl Room (room 9), containing mainly large-scale sixteenth-century Venetian works. The largest of the lot is **Paolo Veronese**'s lustrous *Family of Darius before Alexander*, its array of colourfully clad figures revealing the painter's remarkable skill in juxtaposing virtually the entire colour spectrum in a single canvas. Less prominent in this room are two perplexing paintings attributed to the elusive **Giorgione**, a highly original Venetian painter, only twenty of whose paintings survive. Here, too, at opposite ends of the room, are all four of Veronese's erotic *Allegories of Love* canvases, designed as ceiling paintings, perhaps for a bedchamber.

More Venetian works hang in room 10, including **Titian**'s consummate *La Schiavona*, a precisely executed portrait within a portrait. His colourful early masterpiece *Bacchus and Ariadne*, and his much gloomier *Death of Actaeon*, painted some fifty years later, amply demonstrate the painter's artistic development and longevity. *The Virgin and Child* is another typical late Titian, with the paint jabbed on and rubbed in.

Bronzino, Michelangelo and Raphael

In room 8, **Bronzino**'s strangely disturbing *Venus, Cupid, Folly and Time* is a classic piece of Mannerist eroticism, once owned by François I, the decadent, womanizing, sixteenth-century French king (incidentally, Cupid's foot features in the opening animated titles of *Monty Python's Flying Circus*). Here too are **Michelangelo**'s early, unfinished *Entombment*, which depicts Christ's body being carried to the tomb, and the National's major paintings by **Raphael**. These range from early works such as *St Catherine of Alexandria*, whose sensuous serpentine pose is accentuated by the folds of her clothes, and the richly coloured *Mond Crucifixion*, both painted when the artist was in his 20s, to later works like *Pope Julius II* – his (and Michelangelo's) patron – a masterfully percipient portrait of old age.

Holbein, Cranach, Bosch and Bruegel

Room 4 contains several masterpieces by **Hans Holbein**, most notably his extraordinarily detailed double portrait from the Tudor court, *The Ambassadors* – note

---

BORIS ANREP'S FLOOR MOSAICS

One of the most overlooked features of the National Gallery is the mind-boggling **floor mosaics** executed by Russian-born Boris Anrep between 1927 and 1952 on the landings of the main staircase leading to the Central Hall. The *Awakening of the Muses*, on the halfway landing, features a bizarre collection of famous figures from the 1930s – Virginia Woolf appears as Clio (Muse of History) and Greta Garbo plays Melpomene (Muse of Tragedy). The mosaic on the landing closest to the Central Hall is made up of fifteen small scenes illustrating the *Modern Virtues*: Anna Akhmatova is saved by an angel from the Leningrad Blockade in *Compassion*; T.S. Eliot contemplates the Loch Ness Monster and Einstein's Theory of Relativity in *Leisure;* Bertrand Russell gazes on a naked woman in *Lucidity*; Edith Sitwell, book in hand, glides across a monster-infested chasm on a twig in *Sixth Sense*; and in the largest composition, *Defiance*, Churchill appears in combat gear on the white cliffs of Dover, raising two fingers to a monster in the shape of a swastika.

the anamorphic skull in the foreground. Among the other works by Holbein is his intriguing *A Lady with a Squirrel and a Starling*, and his striking portrait of the 16-year-old Christina of Denmark, part of a series commissioned by Henry VIII when he was looking for a potential fourth wife. Look out, too, for Holbein's contemporary, **Lucas Cranach the Elder**, whose *Cupid Complaining to Venus* is a none-too-subtle message about dangerous romantic liaisons – Venus's wonderfully fashionable headgear only emphasizes her nakedness.

Next door, in room 5, hangs the National's one and only work by **Hieronymus Bosch**, *Christ Mocked*, in which four manic tormentors (one wearing an Islamic crescent moon and a Jewish star) bear down on Jesus. The painting that grabs most folks' attention, however, is **Massys**'s caricatured portrait of an old woman looking like a pantomime dame. Nearby, in room 14, you'll find the gallery's only work by **Jan Bruegel the Elder**, the tiny *Adoration of the Kings*, with some very motley-looking folk crowding in on the infant; only Balthasar looks at all regal.

Claude, Poussin and Dutch landscapes

The English painter **J.M.W. Turner** left specific instructions in his will for two of his Claude-influenced paintings to be hung alongside a couple of the French painter's landscapes. All four now hang in the octagonal room 15, and were slashed by a homeless teenager in 1982 in an attempt to draw attention to his plight. **Claude**'s dreamy classical landscapes and seascapes, and the mythological (often erotic) scenes of **Poussin**, were favourites of aristocrats on the Grand Tour, and made both artists very famous in their time. Claude's *Enchanted Castle*, in particular, caught the imagination of the Romantics, allegedly inspiring Keats' *Ode to a Nightingale*. Nowadays, rooms 19 and 20, which are given over entirely to these two French artists, are among the quietest in the gallery.

Of the Dutch landscapes in rooms 21 and 22, those by **Aelbert Cuyp** stand out due to the warm Italianate light which suffuses his works, but the finest of all is, without a doubt, **Hobbema**'s tree-lined *Avenue at Middelharnis*. The market for such landscapes at the time was limited, however, and Hobbema quit painting at the age of just 30. **Jacob van Ruisdael**, Hobbema's teacher, whose works are on display nearby, also went hungry for most of his life.

Rembrandt and Vermeer

Rooms 23 and 24 feature mostly works by **Rembrandt**, including the highly theatrical *Belshazzar's Feast*, painted for a rich Jewish patron. Look out also for two of Rembrandt's searching self-portraits, painted thirty years apart, with the melancholic *Self Portrait Aged 63*, from the last year of his life, making a strong contrast to the sprightly early work. Similarly, the joyful portrait of Saskia, Rembrandt's wife, from the most successful period of his life, contrasts with his more contemplative depiction of his mistress, Hendrickje, who was hauled up in front of the city authorities for living "like a whore" with Rembrandt. The portraits of Jacob Trip and his wife, Margaretha de Geer, are among the most honestly realistic depictions of old age in the entire gallery.

Room 25 harbours **de Hooch**'s classic *Courtyard of a House in Delft*, and a (probable) self-portrait by Carel Fabritius, one of Rembrandt's pupils. Fabritius died in the explosion of the Delft gunpowder store, the subject of another painting in the room. Also here is the seventeenth-century **van Hoogstraten Peepshow**, a box of tricks that reflects the Dutch obsession of the time with perspectival and optical devices. Two typically serene works by **Vermeer** hang here (or in a nearby room) and provide a counterpoint to one another: each features a "young woman at a virginal", but where she stands in one, she sits in the other; she's viewed from the right and then the left, in shadow and then in light and so on.

1

HIDDEN GEMS OF THE NATIONAL GALLERY

Wilton Diptych Room 53
An Allegory with Venus and Cupid
Bronzino. Room 8
Supper at Emmaus Caravaggio. Room 32
A Young Woman standing at a
Virginal Vermeer. Room 25
The Avenue at Middleharnis Hobbema
Room 21

Self-Portrait in a Straw Hat Elisabeth
Louise Vigée le Brun. Room 33
Marriage à la Mode Hogarth. Room 35
Portrait of Hermine Gallia Klimt.
Room 44
After the Bath Degas. Room 46
Boris Anrep's mosaics See box, p.40

Rubens

Three adjoining rooms, known collectively as room 29, are dominated by the expansive, fleshy canvases of **Peter Paul Rubens**, the Flemish painter whom Charles I summoned to the English court. The one woman with her clothes on is the artist's future sister-in-law, Susanna Fourment, whose delightful portrait became known as *Le Chapeau de Paille* (*The Straw Hat*) – though the hat is actually made of black felt and decorated with white feathers. At the age of 54, Rubens married Susanna's younger sister, Helena (she was just 16), the model for all three goddesses posing in the later 1630s version of *The Judgement of Paris*. Also displayed here are Rubens' rather more subdued landscapes, one of which, the *View of Het Steen*, shows off the very fine prospect from the Flemish country mansion Rubens bought in 1635.

Velázquez, El Greco, Van Dyck and Caravaggio

The cream of the National Gallery's Spanish works are displayed in room 30, among them **Velázquez**'s *Rokeby Venus*, one of the gallery's most famous pictures. Velázquez is thought to have painted just four nudes in his lifetime, of which only the *Rokeby Venus* survives, an ambiguously narcissistic image that was slashed in 1914 by suffragette Mary Richardson, in protest at the arrest of Emmeline Pankhurst.

Another Flemish painter summoned by Charles I was **Anthony van Dyck**, whose *Equestrian Portrait of Charles I*, in room 31, is a fine example of the work that made him a favourite of the Stuart court, romanticizing the monarch as a dashing horseman. Nearby is the artist's double portrait of *Lord John and Lord Bernard Stuart*, two dapper young cavaliers about to set out on their Grand Tour in 1639, and destined to die fighting for the royalist cause shortly afterwards in the Civil War.

Caravaggio's art is represented in the vast room 32 by the typically salacious *Boy Bitten by Lizard*, and the melodramatic *Supper at Emmaus*. The latter was a highly influential painting: never before had biblical scenes been depicted with such naturalism – a beardless and haloless Christ surrounded by scruffy disciples. At the time it was deemed to be blasphemous, and, like many of Caravaggio's religious commissions, was eventually rejected by the customers. One of the most striking paintings in this room is Giordano's *Perseus turning Phineas and his Followers to Stone*, in which the hero is dramatically depicted in sapphire blue, with half the throng already petrified.

British art 1750–1850

When the Tate Gallery opened in 1897, the vast bulk of the National's British art was transferred there, leaving just a few highly prized works behind. Among these are several superb late masterpieces by **Turner**, two of which herald the new age of steam: *Rain, Steam and Speed* and *The Fighting Temeraire*, in which a ghostly apparition of the veteran battleship from Trafalgar is pulled into harbour by a youthful, fire-snorting tug, a scene witnessed first-hand by the artist in Rotherhithe. Here, too, is **Constable**'s *Hay Wain*, painted in and around his father's mill in Suffolk, as is the irrepressibly popular *Cornfield*. There are landscapes, as well as the portraits, by **Thomas Gainsborough** – his

FROM TOP HOUSES OF PARLIAMENT (P.50); TRAFALGAR SQUARE (P.34); THE NATIONAL GALLERY (P.38) >

1

feathery, light technique is seen to superb effect in *Morning Walk*, a double portrait of a pair of newlyweds. **Joshua Reynolds**' contribution is a portrait, *Lady Cockburn and her Three Sons*, in which the three boys clamber endearingly over their mother. And finally, the most striking portrait in the whole room is George Stubbs' pin-sharp depiction of the racehorse Whistlejacket rearing up on its hindlegs.

More works by Gainsborough and Reynolds hang in room 35, including the only known self-portrait of the former with his family, painted in 1747 when he was just 20 years old. On the opposite wall are the six paintings from **Hogarth**'s *Marriage à la Mode*, a witty, moral tale that allowed the artist to give vent to his pet hates: bourgeois hypocrisy, snobbery and bad (ie Continental) taste.

French art 1700–1860

The large room of British art (room 34) is bookended with two small rooms of French art. In room 33, among works by the likes of Fragonard, Boucher and Watteau, there's a portrait of Louis XV's mistress Madame de Pompadour in the year of her death and a spirited self-portrait by the equally well-turned-out **Elisabeth Louise Vigée-Lebrun**, one of only three women artists in the National Gallery.

In room 41, the most popular painting is **Paul Delaroche**'s slick and pretentious *Execution of Lady Jane Grey*, in which the blindfolded, white-robed, 17-year-old queen stoically awaits her fate. Look out, too, for **Gustave Courbet**'s languorous *Young Ladies on the Bank of the Seine*, innocent enough to the modern eye, scandalous when it was first shown in 1857 due to the ladies' "state of undress".

Impressionism and beyond

Among the gallery's busiest section are the four magnificent rooms (43–46) of Impressionist and post-Impressionist paintings, where rehangings are frequent. The National boasts several key works by **Manet**, including his famous *Music in the Tuileries Gardens*, and the unfinished *Execution of Maximilian*, one of three versions he painted. There are also canvases from every period of **Monet**'s long life: from early works like *The Thames below Westminster* and *Gare St Lazare* to the late, almost abstract paintings executed in his beloved garden at Giverny.

Other major Impressionist works include **Renoir**'s *Umbrellas*, **Seurat**'s classic pointillist canvas, *Bathers at Asnières* – one of the National's most reproduced paintings – and **Pissarro**'s *Boulevard Montmartre at Night*. There are also several townscapes from Pissarro's period of exile, when he lived in south London, during the Franco-Prussian War. There's a comprehensive showing of **Cézanne** with works spanning the great artist's long life. *The Painter's Father*, one of his earliest extant works, was originally painted onto the walls of his father's house outside Aix. *The Bathers*, by contrast, is a late work, whose angular geometry exercised an enormous influence on the Cubism of Picasso and Braque.

Van Gogh's famous, dazzling *Sunflowers* hangs here, as does the beguiling *Van Gogh's Chair*, dating from his stay in Arles with Gauguin, and *Wheatfield with Cypresses*, which typifies the intense work he produced shortly before his suicide. Finally, look out for **Picasso**'s sentimental Blue Period *Child with a Dove*; **Rousseau**'s imagined junglescape, *Surprised!*; Klimt's *Hermine Gallia*, in which the sitter wears a dress designed by the artist; and a trio of superb **Degas** canvases: *Miss La-La at the Cirque Fernando*, the languorous pastel drawing *After the Bath* and the luxuriant *La Coiffure*.

National Portrait Gallery

St Martin's Place • Daily 10am–6pm, Thurs & Fri till 9pm • Free • ☎ 020 7306 0055, ⊛ npg.org.uk • ⊖ Charing Cross

Around the east side of the National Gallery lurks the **National Portrait Gallery**, founded in 1856 to house uplifting depictions of the good and the great. Though it undoubtedly has some fine works among its collection of over ten thousand portraits, many of the studies are of less interest than their subjects. Nevertheless, it's interesting to trace who has been deemed worthy of admiration at any one time: aristocrats and artists in previous centuries, warmongers and imperialists in the early decades of the twentieth century, writers and poets in the 1930s and 1940s. The most popular part of the museum by far is the contemporary section, where the whole thing degenerates into a sort of high-brow Madame Tussauds, with photos and portraits of today's celebrities. However, the special exhibitions (for which there is often a charge) are well worth seeing – the photography shows, in particular, are often excellent.

INFORMATION

Arrival There are two entrances to the NPG: there is step-free access from Orange St, while the main entrance is on St Martin's Place. Once inside, head straight for the Ondaatje Wing, where there's an information desk – you can pick up an audioguide (£3), which gives useful biographical background on many of the pictures.

Eating and drinking There's a little café in the basement, and the excellent but pricey rooftop *Portrait* Restaurant on Floor 3, with incredible views over Trafalgar Square (Sun–Wed 10am–5pm, Thurs–Sat 10am–8.30pm, ☎ 020 7312 2490). If you want a beer with your Bailey try the Late Shift bar (Thurs & Fri 6–9pm) in the Main Hall, where you can sometimes catch a talk or some live music.

The Tudors and Stuarts

To follow the collection chronologically, take the escalator to the trio of **Tudor Galleries**, on Floor 2. Here, you'll find Tudor portraits of pre-Tudor kings as well as Tudor personalities: a stout **Cardinal Wolsey** looking like the butcher's son he was and the future **Bloody Mary** looking positively benign in a portrait celebrating her reinstatement to the line of succession in 1544. Pride of place goes to Holbein's larger-than-life cartoon of **Henry VIII**, showing the king as a macho buck against a modish Renaissance background, with his sickly son and heir, **Edward VI**, striking a deliberately similar pose close by. The most eye-catching canvas is the anamorphic portrait of Edward, an illusionist painting that must be viewed from the side.

Also displayed here are several classic propaganda portraits of the formidable Elizabeth I and her dandyish favourites. Further on hangs the only known painting of **Shakespeare** from life, a subdued image in which the Bard sports a gold-hoop earring; appropriately enough, it was the first picture acquired by the gallery. To keep to the chronology, you must turn left here into room 5, where the quality of portraiture goes up a notch thanks to the appointment of Van Dyck as court painter. Among all the dressed-to-kill Royalists in room 5, **Oliver Cromwell** looks dishevelled but masterful.

The eighteenth century

The **eighteenth century** begins in room 9, with members of the **Kit-Kat Club**, a group of Whig patriots, painted by one of its members, Godfrey Kneller, a naturalized German artist, whose self-portrait can be found in room 10. Next door, room 11 contains a hotchpotch of visionaries including a tartan-free **Bonnie Prince Charlie** and his saviour, the petite Flora MacDonald. In room 12 there are several fine self-portraits, including a dashing one of the Scot Allan Ramsay. Room 14 is dominated by *The Death of Pitt the Elder*, who collapsed in the House of Lords having risen from his sickbed to try and save the rebellious American colonies for Britain – despite the painting's title, he didn't die for another month.

In room 17, you'll find a portrait of **George IV** and the twice-widowed Catholic woman, Maria Fitzherbert, whom he married without his father's consent. His official wife, **Queen Caroline**, is depicted at the adultery trial at which she was acquitted, and again, with sleeves rolled up, ready for her sculpture lessons, in an audacious portrait by Thomas Lawrence, who was called to testify on his conduct with the queen during the painting of the portrait.

1

The Romantics dominate room 18, with the ailing **John Keats** painted posthumously by Joseph Severn, in whose arms he died in Rome. Elsewhere, there's **Lord Byron** in Albanian garb, an open-collared **Percy Bysshe Shelley**, with his wife, Mary, nearby, and her mother, **Mary Wollstonecraft**, opposite.

The Victorians

Down on the first floor, the **Victorians** feature rather too many stuffy royals, dour men of science and engineering and stern statesmen such as those lining the corridor of room 22. Centre stage, in room 21, is a comical statue of **Victoria and Albert** in Anglo-Saxon garb. The best place to head for is room 24, which contains a deteriorated portrait of the **Brontë sisters** as seen by their disturbed brother Branwell; you can still see where he painted himself out, leaving a ghostly blur between Charlotte and Emily. Nearby are the poetic duo, **Robert** and **Elizabeth Barrett Browning**, looking totally Gothic in their grim Victorian dress.

In room 28, it's impossible to miss the striking Edwardian portrait of **Lady Colin Campbell**, posing in a luxurious black silk dress. Finally, in room 29, there are some excellent **John Singer Sargent** portraits, and several works by students of the Slade: **Augustus John**, looking very confident and dapper at the age of just 22, his sister, Gwen John, **Walter Sickert** (by Philip Wilson Steer) and Steer (by Sickert). Steer founded the New English Arts Club, at which the last two portraits were originally exhibited.

The twentieth century and beyond

The **twentieth-century** collection begins in room 30, with Sargent's group portrait of the upper-crust generals responsible for the slaughter of World War I. The interwar years are then generously covered in room 31. The faces on display here are frequently rotated, but look out for Sickert's excellent small, smouldering portrait of **Churchill**, Augustus John's portrayal of a ruby-lipped Dylan Thomas, Ben Nicolson's double portrait of himself and Barbara Hepworth and a whole host of works by, or depicting, the **Bloomsbury Group**.

Out on the Balcony Gallery, there's a who's who (or was who) of **Britain 1960–90**. Even here, amid the photos of the Swinging Sixties, there are quite a few genuine works of art by the likes of Leon Kossoff, R.B. Kitaj, Lucien Freud and Francis Bacon. The **Contemporary Galleries** occupy the ground floor, and are a constantly changing, unashamedly populist trot through the media personalities of the last decade or so. As well as a host of photo portraits, you can sample such delights as Michael Craig

TRAFALGAR SQUARE & WHITEHALL

■ ACCOMMODATION
Northumberland House 1

● CAFÉ
Café in the Crypt 1

■ PUBS & BARS
The Chandos 1
St Stephen's Tavern 2

Martin's LCD portrait of architect Zaha Hadid, or the cartoon-like quadruple portrait of pop band Blur by Julian Opie.

Whitehall

Whitehall, the unusually broad avenue connecting Trafalgar Square to Parliament Square, is synonymous with the faceless, pinstriped bureaucracy charged with the day-to-day running of the country. Yet during the sixteenth and seventeenth centuries, it was, in fact, the site of the chief royal residence in London. **Whitehall Palace** started out as the London seat of the Archbishop of York, but was confiscated and enlarged by Henry VIII after a fire at Westminster Palace forced the king to find alternative accommodation; it was here that he celebrated his marriage to Anne Boleyn in 1533, and here that he died fourteen years later. Described by one contemporary chronicler as nothing but "a heap of houses erected at diverse times and of different models, made continuous", it boasted some two thousand rooms and stretched for half a mile along the Thames. Very little survived the fire of 1698 and, subsequently, the royal residence shifted to St James's and Kensington.

Since then, all the key governmental ministries and offices have migrated here, rehousing themselves on an ever-increasing scale. The **Foreign & Commonwealth Office**, for example, occupies a palatial Italianate building, built by George Gilbert Scott in 1868, and well worth a visit on Open House weekend (see p.27). The process reached its apogee with the grimly bland **Ministry of Defence (MoD)** building, completed in 1957, underneath which is Britain's most expensive military bunker, the £125 million Pindar.

Banqueting House

Whitehall • Daily 10am–5pm but frequent early closures so ring before visiting; last entry 45 mins before closure time • £6, concessions £5, under-16s free • ☎ 020 3166 6154, ⓦ hrp.org.uk • ⊖ Charing Cross

The only sections of Whitehall Palace to survive the 1698 fire were Cardinal Wolsey's wine cellars (now beneath the Ministry of Defence) and Inigo Jones's **Banqueting House**, the first Palladian (or Neoclassical) building to be built in central London. Opened in 1622 with a performance of Ben Jonson's *Masque of Augurs*, the Banqueting House is still used for state occasions (hence the closures at short notice). The one room open to the public – the main hall upstairs – is well worth seeing for the superlative ceiling paintings, commissioned by Charles I from **Rubens** and installed in 1635. A glorification of the divine right of kings, the panels depict the union of England and Scotland, the peaceful reign of Charles's father, James I and, finally, his apotheosis.

CHARLES I

Stranded on a traffic island to the south of Nelson's Column, on the site of the medieval **Charing Cross** (see p.112), an equestrian statue of **Charles I** gazes down Whitehall to the place of his execution in 1649, outside the Banqueting House. The king wore two shirts in case he shivered in the cold, which the crowd would take to be fear, and once his head was chopped off, it was then sewn back on again for burial in Windsor – a very British touch. The statue itself was sculpted in 1633 and was originally intended for a site in Roehampton, but was sold off during the Commonwealth to a local brazier, John Rivett, with strict instructions to melt it down. Rivett made a small fortune selling bronze mementoes, allegedly from the metal, while all the time concealing the statue in the vaults of St Paul's, Covent Garden. After the Restoration, in 1675, the statue was erected on the very spot where eight of those implicated in the king's death were disembowelled in 1660. Until 1859, "King Charles the Martyr" Holy Day (Jan 30) was a day of fasting, and his execution is still commemorated here on the last Sunday in January with a parade by the royalist wing of the Civil War Society.

1

Given the subject of the paintings, it's ironic that it was through the Banqueting House that **Charles I** walked in 1649 before stepping onto the executioner's scaffold from one of its windows. **Oliver Cromwell** moved into Whitehall Palace in 1654, having declared himself Lord Protector, and kept open table in the Banqueting House for the officers of his New Model Army; he died here in 1658. Two years later **Charles II** celebrated the Restoration here, and kept open house for his adoring public – Samuel Pepys recalls seeing the underwear of one of his mistresses, Lady Castlemaine, hanging out to dry in the palace's Privy Garden. (Charles housed two mistresses and his wife here, with a back entrance onto the river for courtesans.) To appreciate the place fully, it's worth getting hold of one of the free audioguides. Currently undergoing lengthy renovations, the whole building, both outside and in, is being slowly restored to its former glory.

Horse Guards and the Household Cavalry Museum

Whitehall • Daily: April–Oct 10am–6pm; Nov–March 10am–5pm, last entry 45 mins before closing • £7, concessions £5 • ☏ 020 7930 3070, ⓦ householdcavalrymuseum.co.uk • ⊖ Charing Cross or Westminster

During the day, two mounted sentries and two horseless colleagues are posted at **Horse Guards**, a modest building compared to much of the surrounding architecture, designed by William Kent in 1758, and originally the formal gateway to St James's and Buckingham Palace. The best times to visit are when one of the Changing the Guard ceremonies takes place (see box below). The black dot over the number two on the building's clock face denotes the hour at which Charles I was executed close by in 1649. The sentries are part of the Queen's Life Guard, provided by the Household Cavalry Regiments and round the back of the building, you'll find the **Household Cavalry Museum.** Here you can try on a trooper's elaborate uniform, complete a horse quiz and learn about the regiments' history with help from the free audioguides. With the stables immediately adjacent, it's a sweet-smelling place, and – horse-lovers will be pleased to know – you can see the beasts in their stalls through a glass screen. Don't miss the pocket riot act on display, which ends with the wise warning: "must read correctly: variance fatal".

Downing Street

Whitehall • ⊖ Westminster

London's most famous address, **10 Downing Street**, is the terraced house that was presented to the First Lord of the Treasury, Robert Walpole, Britain's first prime minister or PM, by George II in the 1730s. It has been the PM's official residence ever

---

CHANGING THE GUARD

Changing the Guard takes place at two London locations: the Foot Guards hold theirs outside Buckingham Palace (May–July daily 11.30am; Aug–April alternate days; no ceremony if it rains; ⓦ royal.gov.uk), but the more impressive one is held on Horse Guards Parade, behind Horse Guards, where a squad of mounted Household Cavalry arrives from Hyde Park to relieve the guards at the Horse Guards building on Whitehall (Mon–Sat 11am, Sun 10am) – alternatively, if you miss the whole thing, turn up at 4pm for the daily inspection by the Officer of the Guard, who checks the soldiers haven't knocked off early. If you want to see something grander, check out **Trooping the Colour**, and the **Beating Retreat**, which both take place in June (see p.26).

The Queen is colonel-in-chief of the seven **Household Regiments**: the Life Guards (who dress in red and white) and the Blues and Royals (who dress in blue and red) – princes William and Harry were both in the Blues and Royals – are the two Household Cavalry Regiments; while the Grenadier, Coldstream, Scots, Irish and Welsh guards make up the Foot Guards.

The Foot Guards can only be told apart by the plumes (or lack of them) in their busbies (fur helmets), and by the arrangement of their tunic buttons. The three senior regiments (Grenadier, Coldstream and Scots) date back to the seventeenth century, as do the Life Guards and the Blues and Royals. All seven regiments still form part of the modern army as well as performing ceremonial functions such as Changing the Guard.

1

WHITEHALL STATUES AND THE CENOTAPH

The **statues** dotted along Whitehall recall the days of the empire. Kings and military leaders predominate, starting outside Horse Guards with the **2nd Duke of Cambridge** (1819–1904), whose horse was shot from under him in the Crimean War. As commander-in-chief of the British Army, he was so resistant to military reform that he had to be forcibly retired. Next stands the **8th Duke of Devonshire** (1833–1908), who failed to rescue General Gordon from the Siege of Khartoum in 1884–85. Appropriately enough, **Lord Haig** (1861–1928), who was responsible for sending thousands to their deaths in World War I, faces the Cenotaph, his horse famously poised ready for urination. Before you get to the Cenotaph, there's a striking memorial to the **Women of World War II**, featuring seventeen uniforms hanging on a large bronze plinth.

At the end of Whitehall, in the middle of the road, stands Edwin Lutyens' **Cenotaph**, built in 1919 in wood and plaster to commemorate the Armistice, and rebuilt in Portland stone the following year. The stark monument, which eschews Christian imagery, is inscribed simply with the words "The Glorious Dead" – the lost of World War I, who, it was once calculated, would take three and a half days to pass by the Cenotaph marching four abreast. The memorial remains the focus of the **Remembrance Sunday** ceremony held on the Sunday nearest November 11. Between the wars, however, a much more powerful, two-minute silence was observed throughout the entire British Empire every year on November 11 at 11am, the exact time of the armistice at the end of World War I.

since, with no. 11 the official home of the Chancellor of the Exchequer (in charge of the country's finances) since 1806, and no. 12 official headquarters of the government's Chief Whip (in charge of party discipline). These three are the only remaining bit of the original seventeenth-century cul-de-sac, though all are now interconnected and house much larger complexes than might appear from the outside. The public have been kept at bay since 1990, when Margaret Thatcher ordered a pair of iron gates to be installed at the junction with Whitehall, an act more symbolic than effective – a year later the IRA lobbed a mortar into the street from Horse Guards Parade, coming within a whisker of wiping out the entire Tory cabinet.

Churchill War Rooms

King Charles St • Daily 9.30am–6pm; last admission 5pm • £18, concessions £14.40, under-15s £9, under-5s free • ☎ 020 7930 6961, Ⓦ iwm.org.uk • ❸ Westminster

In 1938, in anticipation of Nazi air raids, the basement of the Treasury building on King Charles Street was converted into the **Churchill War Rooms**, protected by a three-foot-thick concrete slab, reinforced with steel rails and tramlines. It was here that Winston Churchill directed operations and held cabinet meetings for the duration of World War II. By the end of the war, the six-acre site included a hospital, canteen and shooting range, as well as sleeping quarters; tunnels fan out from the complex to outlying government ministries, and also, it is rumoured, to Buckingham Palace itself, allowing the Royal Family a quick getaway to exile in Canada (via Charing Cross station) in the event of a Nazi invasion.

The rooms remain much as they were when they were abandoned on VJ Day, August 15, 1945, and make for an atmospheric underground trot through wartime London. To bring the place to life, pick up one of the free audioguides, which includes various eyewitness accounts by folks who worked here. The best rooms are Winnie's very modest emergency bedroom (though he himself rarely stayed here, preferring to watch the air raids from the roof of the building, or rest his head at the *Savoy Hotel*), and the Map Room, left exactly as it was on VJ Day, with its rank of multicoloured telephones, copious ashtrays and floor-to-ceiling maps covering every theatre of war.

Churchill Museum

When you get to Churchill's secret telephone hotline direct to the American president, signs direct you to the self-contained Churchill Museum, which begins with his finest

1

moment, when he took over as PM and Britain stood alone against the Nazis. You can hear snippets of Churchill's speeches and check out his trademark bowler, spotted bow tie and half-chewed Havana, not to mention his wonderful burgundy zip-up "romper suit". Fortunately for the curators, Churchill had an extremely eventful life and was great for a soundbite, so there are plenty of interesting anecdotes to keep you engaged.

Houses of Parliament

Parliament Square • ☎ 020 7219 4114, ⓦ parliament.uk • ⊖ Westminster

The Palace of Westminster, better known as the **Houses of Parliament**, is among London's best-known icons. The city's finest Victorian edifice and a symbol of a nation once confident of its place at the centre of the world, it's best viewed from the south side of the river, where the likes of Monet and Turner once set up their easels. The building's most famous feature is its ornate, gilded clock tower popularly known as **Big Ben**, at its most impressive when lit up at night. Strictly speaking, it's the Elizabeth Tower – "Big Ben" is just the nickname for the thirteen-ton bell that strikes the hour (and is broadcast across the world by the BBC), after either the former Commissioner of Works, Benjamin Hall, or a popular heavyweight boxer of the mid-nineteenth century, Benjamin Caunt.

The original Palace of Westminster was built by **Edward the Confessor** in the eleventh century to allow him to watch over the building of his abbey. Westminster then served as the seat of all the English monarchs until a fire forced Henry VIII out, and he eventually decamped to Whitehall. The Lords have always convened at the palace, but it was only following Henry's death that the House of Commons moved from the abbey's Chapter House into the palace's St Stephen's Chapel.

In 1834, a fire reduced the old palace to rubble. Save for Westminster Hall, a few pieces of the old structure buried deep within the interior and the House of Commons chamber, redesigned by Sir Giles Gilbert Scott after it was destroyed in 1941 during the Blitz, most of what you see today is the work of **Charles Barry**, who wanted to create something that expressed national greatness through the use of Gothic and Elizabethan styles. The resulting orgy of honey-coloured pinnacles, turrets and tracery is the greatest achievement of the Gothic Revival. Inside, the Victorian love of mock-Gothic detail is evident in the maze of over one thousand committee rooms and offices, the fittings of which were largely the responsibility of Barry's assistant, **Augustus Pugin**.

INFORMATION AND TOURS

Sitting times To find out exact "sitting times" and dates of "recesses" (holiday closures), phone ☎ 020 7219 4272, or visit ⓦ parliament.uk. If the House of Commons is in session after dark there's a light above the clock face on Big Ben, known as the Ayrton Light.

Public galleries To watch proceedings in either the House of Commons – the livelier of the two – or the House of Lords, simply join the queue for the public galleries at the Cromwell Green visitor entrance. For the House of Commons, the public are let in from about 2.30pm on Mondays, 11.30am on Tuesdays and Wednesdays, and 9.30am on Thursdays and Sitting Fridays. Security is tight and the whole procedure can take a while, so to avoid the queues, turn up an hour or so later or on a Sitting Friday.

Question Time From Mondays to Thursdays both the House of Commons and the House of Lords start the day's debating with questions to Government ministers, lasting

around an hour and half-an-hour respectively. UK residents can book in advance through their MP and though anyone can turn up on the day without booking they will only be let in if there is space. UK residents are given the exclusive right to attend Prime Minister's Question Time – when the House of Commons is at its liveliest – on Wednesdays from 12 noon to 12.30pm, but they must book in advance with their local MP.

Guided tours On Saturdays throughout the year and on most weekdays during Parliamentary recesses (including summer, Christmas and Easter) there are guided tours (9am–4.15pm; £25, concessions £20, under-15s £10, under-5s free) and self-guided audio tours (9.20am–4.30pm; £18, concessions £15.50, 1 under-15 accompanied by an adult is free, subsequent under-15s £7.20, under-5s free). There are also occasional specialist tours (from £18). Tours take between 60 and 90 minutes and it's a good idea to book in advance (☎020 7219 4114; ⓦparliament.uk). You can buy tickets on the day from the ticket office at the front of Portcullis House, the modern building on Victoria Embankment. UK residents are entitled to a free guided tour of the palace (Mon–Fri, times vary), as well as a guided tour up the Elizabeth Tower to see Big Ben (Mon–Fri 9am, 11am & 2pm; no under-11s); both need to be organized well in advance through your local MP or a member of the House of Lords. Visitors for Big Ben must enter via Portcullis House.

Westminster Hall

One of only five surviving sections of the medieval Palace of Westminster is the bare expanse of **Westminster Hall**, which you enter after passing through security. Built by William II in 1099, it was saved from the 1834 fire by the timely intervention of the PM, Lord Melbourne, who took charge of the firefighting himself. The sheer scale of the hall – 240ft by 60ft – and its huge oak hammer-beam roof, added by Richard II in the late fourteenth century, make it one of the most magnificent secular medieval halls in Europe. It has also witnessed some nine hundred years of English history and been used for the lying-in-state of members of the royal family and a select few non-royals. Until 1821 every royal coronation banquet was held here and during the ceremony, the Royal Champion would ride into the hall in full armour to challenge any who dared dispute the sovereign's right to the throne.

Until the nineteenth century the hall was also used as the country's highest court of law: **William Wallace** had to wear a laurel crown during his treason trial here; **Thomas More** was sentenced to be hanged, drawn and quartered (though in the end was simply beheaded); **Guy Fawkes**, the Catholic caught trying to blow up Parliament on November 5, 1605, was also tried here and actually hanged, drawn and quartered in Old Palace Yard. The trial of **Charles I** took place here, but the king refused to take his hat off, since he did not accept the court's legitimacy. **Oliver Cromwell**, whose statue now stands outside the hall, was sworn in here as Lord Protector in 1653, only to be disinterred after the Restoration and tried here (while dead). His head was displayed on a spike above the hall for several decades until a storm dislodged it. It's now buried in a secret location at Cromwell's old college in Cambridge University.

St Stephen's Hall

From Westminster Hall, visitors pass through the tiny **St Stephen's Hall**, designed by Barry as a replica of the palace's Gothic chapel (built by Edward I), where the

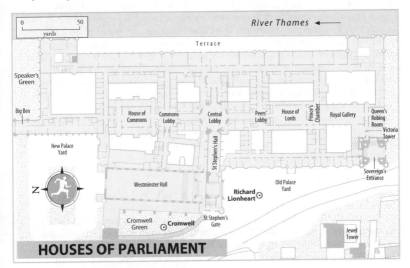

HOUSES OF PARLIAMENT

1

Commons met from 1550 until the 1834 fire. It was into that chapel that Charles I entered with an armed guard in 1642 in a vain attempt to arrest five MPs who had made a speedy escape down the river – "I see my birds have flown", he is supposed to have said. Shortly afterwards, the Civil War began, and no monarch has entered the Commons since. It was on the steps of the hall, in 1812, that Spencer Perceval – the only British prime minister to be assassinated – was shot by a merchant whose business had been ruined by the Napoleonic Wars.

Central Lobby

Next you come to the bustling, octagonal **Central Lobby**, where constituents can "lobby" their MPs. In the tiling of the lobby Pugin inscribed the Biblical quote in Latin: "Except the Lord keep the house, they labour in vain that build it." In view of what happened to the architects, the sentiment seems like an indictment of parliamentary morality – Pugin ended up in Bedlam mental hospital and Barry died from overwork within months of completing the job.

The House of Commons

If you're going to listen to proceedings in the **House of Commons**, you'll be asked to sign a form vowing not to cause a disturbance and then led up to the Public Gallery. Protests from the gallery used to be a fairly regular occurrence: suffragettes have poured flour, farmers have dumped dung, Irish Nationalists have lobbed tear gas and, over in the House of Lords, gay-rights protesters have abseiled down into the chamber, but a screen now protects the MPs. An incendiary bomb in May 1941 destroyed Barry's original chamber, so what you see now is a rather lifeless postwar reconstruction. Barry's design was modelled on the palace's original St Stephen's Hall, hence the choir-stall arrangement of the MPs' benches. Members of the cabinet (and the opposition's shadow cabinet) occupy the two "front benches"; the rest are "backbenchers". The chamber is at its busiest during Question Time, though if more than 427 of the 650 MPs turn up, a large number have to remain standing. For much of the time, however, the chamber is almost empty, with just a handful of MPs present from each party.

The House of Lords

On the other side of the Central Lobby, a corridor leads to the **House of Lords** (or Upper House), the appointed, as opposed to elected, chamber peopled by Lords and Ladies, plus a smattering of bishops. Their home boasts much grander decor than the Commons, full of regal gold and scarlet, and dominated by Pugin's great canopied gilded throne where the Queen sits for the state opening of Parliament in May. Directly in front of the throne, the Lord Speaker runs the proceedings from the scarlet Woolsack, an enormous cushion stuffed with wool, which harks back to the time when it was England's principal export. Until 1999, there were one thousand plus hereditary Lords (over a quarter of whom had been to Eton) in the House. Today, just 92 hereditary peers sit in the House, along with 26 senior bishops, while the rest are made up of life peers, appointed by the Queen on the advice of the Prime Minister. However, for the most part, the Lords have very little real power, as they can only advise, amend and review parliamentary bills.

The royal apartments

To see any more of parliament's pomp and glitter you'll need to go on a **tour** (see p.50). Beyond the House of Lords is the **Princes' Chamber**, where the portraits lining the walls include Henry VIII and all six of his wives. Beyond here you enter the **Royal Gallery**, a cavernous writing room for the House of Lords, hung with portraits of royals past and present, and two 45-foot-long frescoes of Trafalgar and Waterloo. Next door is the **Queen's Robing Chamber**, which boasts a superb coffered ceiling and lacklustre

1

Arthurian frescoes. As the name suggests, this is the room where the monarch dons the crown jewels before entering the Lords. Lastly, you get to see the Norman Porch, every nook of which is stuffed with busts of eminent statesmen, and the **Royal Staircase**, which is lined with guards from the Household Cavalry when the Queen arrives for the annual state opening of Parliament in May.

Jewel Tower

Apr–Sept daily 10am–6pm, Oct daily 10am–5pm, Nov–Mar Sat & Sun 10am–4pm, last admission 30mins before close • £4.20, concessions £3.80, under-15s £2.50 • ☎ 020 7222 2219, Ⓦ english-heritage.org.uk • ⊖ Westminster

The **Jewel Tower** across the road from the Sovereign's Entrance, is the only other accessible remnant of the medieval palace apart from Westminster Hall. Constructed in 1365 by Edward III as a giant strongbox for his most valuable possessions, the tower formed the southwestern corner of the original exterior fortifications (there's a bit of moat left, too), and was called the King's Privy Wardrobe. Later, it was used to store the records of the House of Lords, and then as a testing centre by the Board of Trade's Standards Department. Nowadays, there's a small exhibition here on the history and changing role of the Jewel Tower itself, as well as a model of the 'lost' medieval Palace of Westminster.

Victoria Tower Gardens

To the south of Parliament's Victoria Tower are the leafy **Victoria Tower Gardens**, which look out onto the Thames. Visitors are greeted by a statue of Emmeline Pankhurst, leader of the suffragette movement, who died in 1928, the same year women finally got the vote on equal terms with men; medallions commemorating her daughter Christabel, and a WPSU Prisoners' Badge, flank the statue. Round the corner, a replica of Rodin's famous sculpture, *The Burghers of Calais*, makes a surprising appearance here, while at the far end of the gardens stands the **Buxton Memorial**, a neo-Gothic fountain, made from a real potpourri of exotic materials, erected in 1865 to commemorate the 1834 abolition of slavery in the British Empire.

Westminster Abbey

Parliament Square • Hours can vary: Mon–Sat 9.30am–4.30pm, Wed until 7pm, last admission on any day 1hr before close • £20, concessions £17, under-16s £9, under-5s free • ☎ 020 7654 4900, Ⓦ westminster-abbey.org • ⊖ Westminster

The Houses of Parliament overshadow their much older neighbour, **Westminster Abbey**, a still mighty and magnificent structure but one which appears to have been squeezed awkwardly onto the western edge of Parliament Square. Yet this single building has stood here longer than any other and embodies much of the history of England: it has been the venue for every coronation since the time of William the Conqueror, and the site of just about every royal burial for some five hundred years between the reigns of Henry III and George II. Scores of the nation's most famous citizens are honoured here, too – though many of the stones commemorate people buried elsewhere – and the interior is cluttered with literally hundreds of monuments, reliefs and statues.

With over 3300 people buried beneath its flagstones and countless others commemorated here, the abbey is, in essence, a giant mausoleum and is now more mass tourist attraction than house of God.

INFORMATION AND TOURS

Information If you have any questions, ask the vergers in the black gowns, the marshals in red or the abbey volunteers in green. Note that on Sundays, when the rest of the abbey is closed to visitors, you can visit the Chapter House, the Cloisters and the College Garden for free by entering via Dean's Yard. a large quadrangle used by Westminster School to the west of the Abbey.

Tours There are guided tours by the vergers, which allow access to the Confessor's Tomb (Mon–Fri 4 to 5 times a day, Sat 2 to 3 times a day, start times vary; ring or see website for details; 1hr 30min; £5 in addition to entrance fee). A free audioguide is available to all entrance ticket holders and the same narrated guide can be downloaded to your smartphone from the website.

1

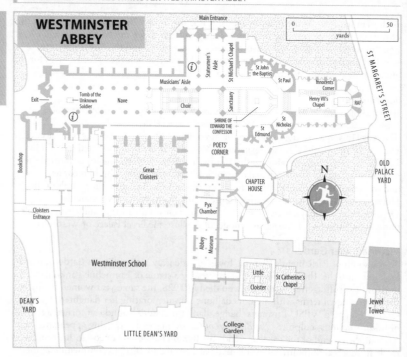

Services Admission to the daily services at the abbey (check website for details) is, of course, free. Evensong is at 5pm on weekdays.

Eating The thoughtfully designed *Cellarium Café*, in the abbey's fourteenth-century storehouse, adjacent to the Cloisters (☎ 020 7222 0516, ⊛ cellariumcafe.com).

Brief history

By the tenth century there was a small Benedictine monastery on this site, for which **Edward the Confessor** built an enormous church. Nothing much remains of Edward's church, which was consecrated on December 28, 1065, just eight days before his death. The following January his successor, Harold, was crowned, and, on Christmas Day, William the Conqueror rode up the aisle on horseback, thus firmly establishing the tradition of royal coronation within the Confessor's church.

It was in honour of Edward (who had by now been canonized) that **Henry III** began to rebuild the abbey in 1245, in the French Gothic style of the recently completed Rheims Cathedral. The monks were kicked out during the Reformation, but the church's status as the nation's royal mausoleum saved it from any physical damage. In the early eighteenth century, Nicholas Hawksmoor designed the quasi-Gothic west front, while the most recent additions can be seen above the west door: a series of statues representing twentieth-century martyrs, from Dietrich Bonhöffer to Martin Luther King.

Statesmen's Aisle and the Sanctuary

The north transept, where you enter, is littered with overblown monuments to long-forgotten empire-builders and nineteenth-century politicians, and traditionally known as **Statesmen's Aisle**. From here, you can go straight to the central **Sanctuary**, site of the royal coronations. The most precious work of art here is the thirteenth-century Italian floor mosaic known as the **Cosmati pavement**. It depicts the universe with interwoven circles and squares of Purbeck marble, glass, and red and green porphyry, though it's sometimes covered by a carpet to protect it. The richly gilded high altar, like the ornately carved **choir stalls**, is, in fact, a neo-Gothic construction from the nineteenth century.

The side chapels

Some of the best funereal art is tucked away in **St Michael's Chapel**, east of the Statesmen's Aisle, where you can admire the remarkable monument to **Francis Vere** (1560–1609), one of the greatest soldiers of the Elizabethan period, made out of two slabs of black marble, between which lies Sir Francis; on the upper slab, supported by four knights, his armour is laid out, to show that he died away from the field of battle. The most striking grave, by Roubiliac, is that in which **Elizabeth Nightingale**, who died from a miscarriage, collapses in her husband's arms while he tries to fight off the skeletal figure of Death, who is climbing out of the tomb.

In the **north ambulatory**, two more chapels contain ostentatious Tudor and Stuart tombs that replaced the altarpieces that had graced them before the Reformation. One of the most extravagant tombs is that of Lord Hunsdon, Lord Chancellor to Elizabeth I, which dominates the **Chapel of St John the Baptist**, and, at 36ft in height, is the tallest in the entire abbey.

Henry VII's Chapel

From the Chapel of St Paul you can climb the stairs and enter the Lady Chapel, better known as **Henry VII's Chapel**, the most dazzling architectural set piece in the abbey. Begun by Henry VII in 1503 and dedicated to the Virgin Mary, it represents the final gasp of the English Perpendicular style, with its beautiful, light, intricately carved vaulting, fan-shaped gilded pendants and statues of nearly one hundred saints, high above the choir stalls. The stalls themselves are decorated with the banners and emblems of the Knights of the Order of the Bath, established by George I. **George II**, the last king to be buried in the abbey, lies in the burial vault under your feet, along with Queen Caroline – their coffins were fitted with removable sides so that their remains could mingle.

Beneath the altar is the grave of Edward VI, the single, sickly son of Henry VIII, while behind lies the chapel's centrepiece, the black marble **sarcophagus of Henry VII** and his spouse – their lifelike gilded effigies, modelled from death masks, are obscured by an ornate Renaissance grille by Pietro Torrigiano, who fled from Italy after breaking Michelangelo's nose in a fight. James I is also interred within Henry's tomb, while the first of the apse chapels, to the north, hosts a grand monument by Hubert le Sueur to James's lover, George Villiers, Duke of Buckingham, the first non-royal to be buried in this part of the abbey, who was killed by one of his own disgruntled soldiers.

The side chapels

The easternmost **RAF Chapel** sports a stained-glass window depicting airmen and angels in the Battle of Britain and a small piece of bomb damage from World War II. In the floor, a plaque marks the spot where Oliver Cromwell rested, briefly, until the Restoration, whereupon his mummified body was disinterred, dragged through the streets, hanged at Tyburn and beheaded. The last of the apse chapels contains another overblown Le Sueur monument, in which four caryatids, holding up a vast bronze canopy, weep for Ludovic Stuart, another of James I's "favourites".

North aisle: Elizabeth I and the Innocents

Before descending the steps back into the ambulatory, pop into the chapel's north aisle, which is virtually cut off from the chancel. Here James I erected a huge ten-poster tomb to his predecessor, **Elizabeth I**. Unless you read the plaque on the floor, you'd never know that Elizabeth's Catholic half-sister, "Bloody Mary", is also buried here, in an unusual act of posthumous reconciliation. The far end of the north aisle, where James I's two infant daughters lie, is known as **Innocents' Corner**: Princess Sophia, who

1

died aged three days, lies in an alabaster cradle, her face peeping over the covers, just about visible in the mirror on the wall; Princess Mary, who died the following year aged 2, is clearly visible, casually leaning on a cushion. Set into the wall between the two is the Wren-designed urn containing (what are thought to be) the bones of the **Princes in the Tower**, Edward V and his younger brother, Richard (see p.179).

South aisle: Mary Queen of Scots

The south aisle of Henry VII's Chapel contains a trio of stellar tombs, including James I's mother, **Mary, Queen of Scots**, whom Elizabeth I had beheaded. James had Mary's remains brought from Peterborough Cathedral in 1612, and paid significantly more for her extravagant eight-postered tomb, bristling with Scottish thistles and complete with a terrifyingly aggressive Scottish lion, than he had done for Elizabeth's; the 27 hangers-on (including the Cavalier Prince Rupert and the "Winter Queen", Elizabeth of Bohemia) who are buried with her are listed on the nearby wooden screen.

The Coronation Chair

As you leave Henry VII's Chapel, look out for Edward I's **Coronation Chair**, a decrepit oak throne dating from around 1300. The graffiti-covered chair, used in every coronation since 1308, was custom-built to incorporate the **Stone of Scone**, a great slab of red sandstone which acted as the Scottish coronation stone for centuries before Edward pilfered it in 1296. The stone remained in the abbey for the next seven hundred years, apart from a brief interlude in 1950, when some Scottish nationalists managed to steal it back and hide it in Arbroath. In 1997 the then Conservative government returned the stone to Edinburgh Castle, where it now resides until the next coronation.

The Shrine of Edward the Confessor

Behind the chair lies the tomb of **Henry V**, who died of dysentery in France in 1422 at the age of just 35, and was regarded as a saint in his day. Above him rises the highly decorative, H-shaped Chantry Chapel, where the body of Henry's wife, Catherine of Valois, was openly displayed for several centuries – Pepys records kissing her corpse on his 36th-birthday visit to the abbey. The chapel acts as a sort of gatehouse for the **Shrine of Edward the Confessor**, the sacred heart of the building, and site of some of the abbey's finest tombs, now only accessible on a guided tour (see p.53). With some difficulty, you can just about make out the battered marble casket of the Confessor's tomb and the niches in which pilgrims would kneel.

Poets' Corner

In the south transept, you'll find the ever popular **Poets' Corner**. The first occupant, **Geoffrey Chaucer**, was buried here in 1400, not because he was a poet, but because he had been Clerk of the King's Works, and his battered tomb, on the east wall, wasn't built for another 150-odd years. When **Edmund Spenser** chose to be buried close to Chaucer in 1599, his fellow poets – Shakespeare among them (possibly) – threw their own works and quills into the grave. Nevertheless, it wasn't until the eighteenth century that this zone became an artistic pantheon, since when the transept has been filled with tributes to all shades of talent.

Among those who are actually buried here, you'll find – after much searching – grave slabs or memorials for everyone from John Dryden and Samuel Johnson to **Charles Dickens** and Thomas Hardy (though his heart was buried in Dorset). Among the merely commemorated is **William Shakespeare**, whose dandyish statue is on the east wall. Even mavericks like Oscar Wilde, commemorated in the Hubbard window, are acknowledged here, though William Blake was honoured by a Jacob Epstein sculpture only in 1957, and Byron was refused burial for his "open profligacy", and had to wait until 1969.

1

South choir aisle

Before you enter the cloisters, it's worth seeking out several wonderful memorials to undeserving types in the **south choir aisle**, though you may have to ask a verger to allow you to see them properly. The first is to **Thomas Thynne**, a Restoration rake, whose tomb incorporates a relief showing his assassination in his coach on Pall Mall by three thugs, hired to kill him by his Swedish rival in love. Further along lies **Admiral Clowdisley Shovell**, lounging in toga and wig. One of only two survivors of a shipwreck in 1707, he was washed up alive on a beach in the Scilly Isles, off southwest England, only to be killed by a fisherwoman for his emerald ring. Above Shovell is a memorial to the court portrait painter **Godfrey Kneller**, who declared, "By God, I will not be buried in Westminster – they do bury fools there". In the event, he has the honour of being the only artist commemorated in the abbey (most are in St Paul's); the tomb is to his own design, but the epitaph is by Pope, who admitted it was the worst thing he ever wrote – which is just as well, as it's so high up you can't read it.

The cloisters

Cloisters daily 10am–6pm; Chapter House daily 10.30am–4pm • Entry included in cost of ticket to abbey but free on Sundays when entry is via Dean's Yard entrance

Doors in the south choir aisle lead to the **Great Cloister**, rebuilt after a fire in 1298 and paved with yet more funerary slabs, including, at the bottom of the ramp, that of the proto-feminist writer **Aphra Behn**, upon whose tomb "all women together ought to let flowers fall", according to Virginia Woolf, "for it was she who earned them the right to speak their minds".

At the eastern end lies the octagonal **Chapter House**, built in the 1250s and used by Henry III's Great Council, England's putative parliament. The House of Commons continued to meet here until 1395, though the monks were none too happy about it, complaining that the shuffling and stamping wore out the expensive tiled floor. Despite their whingeing, the paving tiles have survived well, as have sections of the remarkable apocalyptic wall-paintings, which were executed in celebration of the eviction of the Commons. Be sure to check out the southern wall, where the Whore of Babylon rides the scarlet seven-headed beast from the Book of Revelation.

Pyx Chamber and Museum

Daily: Pyx Chamber 10.30am–3.30pm; museum 10.30am–4pm • Entry included in cost of ticket to abbey but free on Sundays when entry is via Dean's Yard entrance

The nearby **Pyx Chamber** was a medieval high-security safe-deposit box and is one of the few surviving Norman sections of the abbey, along with the neighbouring **Museum**. The latter contains a real mixed bag of exhibits, from replica coronation regalia used during rehearsals to the ring given by Elizabeth I to her lover, the Earl of Essex. The most bizarre items, though, are the lifelike wood and wax royal funereal effigies (several of which are wigless), used in royal burials (1307–1660) instead of an open coffin, including that of Lady Frances Stuart, the Duchess of Richmond and Lennox and model for Britannia on the old penny coin, complete with her pet parrot, which died a few days after she did.

College Garden and the Little Cloister

Tues–Thurs: April–Sept 10am–6pm; Oct–March 10am–4.30pm • Entry included in cost of ticket to abbey but free on Sundays when entry is via Dean's Yard entrance

From the Great Cloister, beyond the museum, you can make your way to the **Little Cloister**, where sick or elderly monks would spend time recuperating and resting, and where, on the east side, you can look into **St Catherine's Chapel Garden**, a tiny plot dotted with medieval ruins. From here a passage leads to the little-known **College Garden**, with a nine hundred-year-old stretch of green, originally used as a herb garden by the monastery's doctor. The garden now provides a quiet retreat and a croquet lawn for pupils of Westminster School; brass-band concerts take place in the summer (July & Aug Wed 12.30–2pm).

The nave
It's only when you finally leave the cloisters that you get to enter the **nave** itself. Narrow, light and, at over a hundred feet in height, by far the tallest in the country, the nave is an impressive space. The first monument to head for is the **Tomb of the Unknown Warrior**, by the west door, with its garland of red poppies commemorating the million British soldiers who died in World War I. Close by is a large floor slab dedicated to **Winston Churchill**, though he chose to be buried in his family plot in Bladon, Oxfordshire.

A tablet in the floor near the Unknown Warrior marks the spot where **George Peabody**, the nineteenth-century philanthropist whose housing estates in London still provide homes for those in need, was buried for a month before being exhumed and removed to Massachusetts; he remains the only American to have been buried in the abbey. On the pillar by St George's Chapel, right by the west door, is a doleful fourteenth-century portrait of **Richard II**, painted at his coronation at the age of 10, and the oldest known image of an English monarch painted from life. Above the west door, **William Pitt the Younger**, Prime Minister at just 23, teaches Anarchy a thing or two, while History takes notes.

The choir screen and the side aisles
The dried and salted body of the explorer and missionary **David Livingstone** is buried in the centre of the nave – except for his internal organs, which, following the tradition of the African people in whose village he died, were buried in a box under a tree. To the left of the gilded neo-Gothic choir screen is a statue of **Isaac Newton**, who, although a Unitarian by faith, would no doubt have been happy enough to be buried in such a prominent position. Other scientists' graves cluster nearby, including non-believer **Charles Darwin**, who, despite being at loggerheads with the Church for most of his life over *On the Origin of Species*, was given a religious burial in the abbey.

In the far corner of the south aisle, the eighteenth-century marble memorial to **General Hargrave** by Roubiliac, has the deceased rising from the grave in response to the Last Trumpet; at the time there was a public outcry that such an undistinguished man – he was Governor of Gibraltar – should receive such a vast memorial. Another controversial grave is that of poet and playwright **Ben Jonson**, who, despite being a double murderer, was granted permission to be buried here, upright so as not to exceed the eighteen square inches he'd been allowed.

Parliament Square
Parliament Square was laid out in the mid-nineteenth century to give the new Houses of Parliament and the adjacent Westminster Abbey a grander setting, though nowadays it functions primarily as a traffic roundabout and as a favoured protest spot. Statues of notables – Abraham Lincoln, Benjamin Disraeli and Nelson Mandela, to name but a few – are scattered amid the swirling cars and buses, with Winston Churchill stooping determinedly in the northeast corner of the central green. At the beginning of **Westminster Bridge**, you can also spot **Boudicca**, depicted keeping her horses and daughters under control without the use of reins – the imperialist boast "regions Caesar never knew, thy posterity shall sway" adorns the plinth.

St Margaret's Church
St Margaret St • Mon–Fri 9.30am–3.30pm, Sat 9.30am–1.30pm, Sun 2–4.30pm • Free • ⓦ westminster-abbey.org/st-margarets-church • ⊖ Westminster

Sitting in the shadow of Westminster Abbey, **St Margaret's Church** has been the unofficial parliamentary church since 1614, when Puritan MPs decided to shun the elaborate liturgy of the neighbouring abbey. St Margaret's has also long been a

1

fashionable church to get married in – Pepys and Milton were followed in the twentieth century by Churchill and Mountbatten – and it gets a steady stream of visitors simply by dint of being so close to the abbey (and because it's free, unlike the abbey). The present building dates back to 1523, and features some colourful Flemish stained glass above the altar, commemorating the marriage of Henry VIII and Catherine of Aragon (depicted in the bottom left- and right-hand corners).

Supreme Court

Parliament Square • Mon–Fri 9.30am–4.30pm • Free; guided tours cost £5 and must be booked in advance, payment on arrival • ☎ 020 7960 1500, ⓦ supremecourt.uk • ⊖ Westminster

The House of Lords was the country's final court of appeal from medieval times until 2009, when the **Supreme Court** took over, separating the most senior judges from Parliament. It's housed in the former Middlesex Guildhall, a quasi-medieval town hall, replete with lugubrious gargoyles and sculptures, actually built in 1913, on the west side of Parliament Square, and previously a crown court. The public are welcome to explore the building, including an engaging exhibition area in the basement, where the crown court cells were located, detailing the history and role of the Supreme Court, and sit in on any sessions going on (Mon–Thurs only) – plus there's a very nice **café** with free wi-fi in the tiled and roofed inner light well. A self-guided tour booklet is available for £1 from the reception desk or, on most Fridays, there are guided tours led by court staff, at 11am, 2pm and 3pm.

Methodist Central Hall Westminster

Storey's Gate • Mon–Sat 9am–5pm • Free guided tours 9.30am–5pm • ☎ 020 7222 8010, ⓦ c-h-w.com • ⊖ Westminster

Set back from Parliament Square, on Storey's Gate, stands **Methodist Central Hall**, the Methodist Church's national headquarters, established here in 1912. In order to avoid the Gothic of the abbey, and the Byzantine of the nearby Catholic cathedral (see opposite), the Methodists opted for Edwardian Beaux-Arts and created a regal-looking building, featuring Europe's largest self-supporting concrete dome ceiling. Central Hall has been used over the years as much for political meetings as religious gatherings, and was the unlikely venue for the inaugural meeting of the **United Nations** in 1946. If there's no event on, you're free to wander round the building and – after donning black gloves – to look at the Historic Roll, a fifty-volume list of the folk who donated a guinea towards the cost of the building. The free **guided tours** take you up to the stone balustrade atop the reinforced concrete dome.

North of Victoria Street

The one tower block north of Victoria Street that deserves special mention is the soon-to-be ex- headquarters of the Metropolitan Police, **New Scotland Yard**, on Broadway. The famous revolving sign, familiar from countless TV news reports, is moving, along with the Met itself, to a new HQ on Victoria Embankment. The tower block was bought in 2014 for £370 million by an investor from Abu Dhabi who plans to tear the building down and replace it with luxury apartments.

Further up the street is 55 Broadway, the tallest building in London when it was built in 1929 by Charles Holden and home to St James's Park tube station. The building's exterior nude statues by, among others, Eric Gill, Henry Moore and Jacob Epstein, gained a certain notoriety at the time, in particular the boy figure in *Day*, whose penis had to be shortened to appease public opinion.

There's some delightful Queen Anne architecture just to the north in **Queen Anne's Gate** and **Old Queen Street**, two exquisite streets, originally separated by a wall, whose position is indicated by a weathered statue of Queen Anne herself.

South of Victoria Street

The area between **Millbank** – the busy riverside road that runs past Tate Britain – and **Victoria Street** – the link forged in the 1860s between Parliament and the newly built Victoria train station – is home to various governmental ministries that can't quite fit into Whitehall. It's also a favourite place for MPs to have their London bases, and many of the restaurants and pubs in the area have "division bells", which ring eight minutes before any vote in the House of Commons. As for sights, the area boasts one of the city's most exotic and unusual churches, the Catholic Westminster Cathedral.

Westminster Cathedral

Victoria St • **Bell tower viewing gallery** Mon–Fri 9.30am–5pm, Sat & Sun 9.30am–6pm • £6, concessions £3 **Cathedral** Mon–Fri 7am–7pm, Sat 8am–7pm, Sun 8am–8pm • Free • ☎ 020 7798 9055, ⓦ westminstercathedral.org.uk • ⊖ Victoria

Set back from the stark 1960s and sleek contemporary architecture of Victoria Street, you'll find one of London's most surprising churches, the stripy neo-Byzantine concoction of the Roman Catholic **Westminster Cathedral**. Begun in 1895, it's one of the last and wildest monuments to the Victorian era: constructed from more than twelve million terracotta-coloured bricks, decorated with hoops of Portland stone, it culminates in a magnificent tapered bell tower which rises to 273ft. From the small piazza to the northwest, you can admire the cathedral and the neighbouring mansions on Ambrosden Avenue, with their matching brickwork.

The **interior** is still only half-finished, and the domed ceiling of the nave – the widest in the country – remains an indistinct blackened mass, free of all decoration. To get an idea of what the place will look like when it's eventually completed, explore the series of **side chapels** – in particular the Holy Souls Chapel, the first one in the north aisle – whose rich, multicoloured decor makes use of over one hundred different marbles from around the world. Further down the north aisle is the Chapel of St George and the English Martyrs, where lies the enshrined body of St John Southworth, who was hanged, drawn and quartered as a traitor at Tyburn in 1654. Be sure, too, to check out the striking baldachin, held up by mustard-yellow pillars, and the low-relief Stations of the Cross sculpted by the controversial Eric Gill during World War I. The view from the **bell tower** is definitely worth taking in as well, especially as you don't even have to slog up flights of steps, but can simply take a lift; the entrance is in the north aisle.

St John's, Smith Square

Smith Square • ☎ 020 7222 1061, ⓦ sjss.org.uk • ⊖ Westminster

Hidden away in the backstreets west of Millbank is the beautiful early Georgian architectural ensemble of **Smith Square**, home to the church of **St John**, a rare and totally surprising slice of full-blown Baroque, completed in 1728. With its four distinctive towers topped by pineapples, it was dubbed the "footstool church" – the story being that Queen Anne, when asked how she would like the church to look, kicked over her footstool. Bombed in 1941, the interior was totally gutted and has since been restored as a classical music venue, so to visit you'll have to go to a concert. The church's atmospheric café-restaurant (Mon–Fri 8.30am–5pm and on concert evenings) is in the brick-vaulted crypt beyond the box office (access from Dean Stanley St).

St James-the-Less

Vauxhall Bridge Rd • Mon–Fri 9am–1pm • Free • ☎ 020 7630 6282, ⓦ sjtl.org • ⊖ Pimlico

Another sight worth seeking out is the remarkable High Victorian church of **St James-the-Less**, designed by George Edmund Street in the 1860s, which lies on the south side of Vauxhall Bridge Road, amid an unprepossessing 1960s Lillington Gardens housing estate. The red-and-black brickwork patterning on the exterior is exceptional, but pales in comparison to the red, black, cream and magenta tiling inside. The capitals of the church's rounded pillars hide biblical scenes amidst their

1

acanthus-leaf foliage, and the font boasts similarly rich adornments, while above the chancel arch there's a wonderfully colourful fresco by G.F. Watts.

Tate Britain

Millbank • Daily 10am–6pm, last admission 5.15pm; usually first Fri of month until 10pm • Free • ☎ 020 7887 8888, ⦿ tate.org.uk • ⊖ Pimlico or Vauxhall

Founded in 1897 with money from Henry Tate, who brought the sugar cube to Britain, **Tate Britain** showcases British art from 1500 to the present day. In addition, the gallery has a whole wing devoted to Turner, as well as putting on large-scale temporary exhibitions (for which there is a charge) and sponsoring the **Turner Prize**, the country's most infamous modern-art award. Works by a shortlist of four British artists under 50 are displayed in the gallery a month or two prior to the December prize-giving.

What you see is only a fraction of the collection, and rooms are periodically re-hung. What follows, therefore, is a rundown of the artists usually featured, plus some of the best works Tate owns, many of which are on show more or less permanently.

INFORMATION AND TOURS

Arrival The traditional entrance on Millbank leads up the steps to a small information desk. A larger entrance with disabled access is on Atterbury St, and leads down to information desks and the cloakroom. The Clore Gallery, which houses the Turner Bequest, can be reached via the modern-art galleries, but it also has its own entrance and information desk to the right of the original gallery entrance.

Tate boat If you're coming from, or going to, Tate Modern, there's a Tate Boat that plies between the two galleries (every 40min; 15min; £7.15 single, £12.60 return, under-16s £3.60); ⦿ thamesclippers.com.

Tours There are free guided tours (daily 11am, noon, 2 & 3pm; 45min) and you can rent multimedia guides for £3.50 or download the gallery's free audioguide app to your smartphone from the website.

British art from 1540 to 1810

The collection's earliest works are richly bejewelled portraits of the Elizabethan and Jacobean nobility, the most striking being the richly symbolic portrait of *Captain Thomas Lee*, a bare-legged swashbuckling English soldier. Another eye-catching work is the *Cholmondeley Ladies*, who were born on the same day, married on the same day and "brought to bed" on the same day, but are not now thought to be twins. Despite a smattering of English talent – **William Dobson**'s portrait of courtier *Endymion Porter* is a perennial favourite – the Stuarts relied heavily on imported Dutch talent such as Van Dyck and Peter Lely (several of whose "lovelies" are usually on display) and the German Godfrey Kneller, who used to sign himself "Pictor Regis" such was the longevity of his royal patronage.

Hogarth and Constable

You can be guaranteed a good selection of works by the first great British artist, **William Hogarth**, including *O the Roast Beef of Old England*, a particularly vicious visual dig at

---

THE SECRET SERVICE

The green-and-beige postmodernist ziggurat across the water is Vauxhall Cross, the indiscreet Secret Intelligence Service or **MI6 headquarters** (⦿ sis.gov.uk), designed in the 1990s by Terry Farrell. It has featured in several Bond films and is connected by tunnel to Whitehall. Such conspicuousness comes at a price, however, and in 2000, the building, known as "Legoland" to those who work there, was hit by a rocket attack courtesy of some dissident Irish-republican terrorists. **MI5** (⦿ mi5.gov.uk), the UK's domestic Security Service, occupies the much more anonymous Thames House on the corner of MIllbank and Horseferry Road.

the French, whom Hogarth loathed. **John Constable**'s most famous work, *Hay Wain*, hangs in the National Gallery, but the same location – Flatford Mill in his native Stour valley in Suffolk – features in many of the paintings owned by the Tate. Another painter to look out for is **George Stubbs**, for whom "nature was and always is superior to art", and who portrayed animals – horses in particular – with a hitherto unknown anatomical precision.

Gainsborough and Reynolds

Works by **Thomas Gainsborough** and **Joshua Reynolds** are sprinkled across several rooms. Of the two, Reynolds, first president of the Royal Academy, was by far the more successful, elevating portraiture to pole position among the genres and flattering his sitters by surrounding them with classical trappings as in *Three Ladies adorning a Term of Hymen*. Gainsborough was equally adept at flattery, but preferred instead more informal settings, concentrating on colour and light, as in *Giovanna Baccelli*. At the outset of his career, Gainsborough was also a landscape artist, often painting the Stour valley in Suffolk, where he – like Constable – was born.

The Pre-Raphaelites

Tate is justifiably renowned for its vast collection of paintings by the **Pre-Raphaelites**, seven of whom formed their Brotherhood, the PRB, in 1848 in an attempt to re-create the humble, pre-humanist, pre-Renaissance world. One of the first PRB paintings to be exhibited was **Rossetti**'s *Girlhood of Mary Virgin*, which was well received by the critics, but his *Annunciation*, with its emaciated heroin-chic Virgin, the model for which was his sister, caused outrage. So too did **Millais**' *Christ in the House of His Parents*; Dickens described the figure of Jesus as "a hideous, wry-necked, blubbering, red-headed boy in a bed-gown". Millais also got into trouble for *Ophelia*, after his model, Elizabeth Siddal, caught a chill from lying in the bath to pose for the picture, prompting threats of a lawsuit from her father. Siddal later married Rossetti, and is also the model in his *Beata Beatrix*, painted posthumously, after she died of an opium overdose in 1862.

The Academy and the Impressionists

Throughout Tate Britain, the term "British" is very loosely applied, so you'll find several works by the French artist, **James Tissot**, whose Impressionist take on English life (and, in particular, English ladies in frilly frocks) was very popular. **Lord Leighton**'s *Bath of Psyche* is a typical piece of Victorian soft porn, the likes of which made him by far the most successful Royal Academician of his generation. Moralizing paintings such as A. L. Egg's *Past and Present* abound, as do heavily symbolist efforts like G.F. Watts' *Hope* (once one of the most popular paintings in the Tate). Look out for **John Singer Sargent**'s well-known and much-loved *Carnation, Lily, Lily-Rose* and the American-born **Whistler**'s portrait of the precocious *Miss Cecily*, who looks as pissed off as she clearly felt after interminable sittings.

Twentieth-century British art

You'll find works by the same twentieth-century and contemporary British artists displayed in both Tate Modern and Tate Britain, so it's very hard to predict what will be on show here. Works by sculptors **Barbara Hepworth**, Jacob Epstein, Eric Gill, Giacometti and **Henry Moore** usually feature prominently, while paintings by Walter Sickert, Paul Nash, Ben Nicholson and Francis Bacon crop up regularly. Vanessa Bell and Duncan Grant, from the Bloomsbury Group, are represented more often than not, and there are nearly always several paintings by **Stanley Spencer**, who saw his home village of Cookham, on the Thames, as paradise and used it as a background for all his Biblical paintings.

1

Some less well-known artists to look out for include the Vorticist **David Bomberg**, who forged his own brand of Cubo-Futurism before World War I; **Ivon Hitchens**, whose distinctive use of blocks of colour harks back to the late works of Cézanne; and the self-taught St Ives painter **Alfred Wallis**. There's usually a fairly good selection of work, too, by modern painters such as **Lucian Freud** and R.B. Kitaj, as well as established living artists such as **David Hockney**, Frank Auerbach and op-art specialist Bridget Riley, and contemporary artists such as Rachel Whiteread, Damien Hirst, Chris Ofili and the ever-popular Antony Gormley.

The Turner Collection

J.M.W. Turner, possibly the greatest artist Britain has ever produced, bequeathed over one hundred oil paintings to the nation, and the gallery now has three hundred, plus a staggering 19,000 watercolours and drawings. Turner's one condition was that the paintings should be housed and exhibited together – the original idea behind the Clore Gallery, the strangely childish building by James Stirling from 1987. The Turner Galleries still exhibit probably the world's largest collection of works by Turner, but you'll also find other artists' works here, and several of Turner's major works hang in the National Gallery. Turner was superb at depicting awe-inspiring scenes – what the Romantics liked to call "the sublime" – particularly marine scenes, and one of the finest examples is *The Shipwreck*. Other natural cataclysms include the *Deluge*, and, in this case as part of a grand historical painting, *Snow Storm: Hannibal and His Army Crossing the Alps*. His financial independence allowed him to develop his own style freely and it's worth seeking out Turner's late works, great smudges of colour that seem to anticipate Monet in their almost total abandonment of linear representation. *Snow Storm – Steam Boat off a Harbour's Mouth* is a classic late Turner, a symbolic battle between the steam age and nature's primeval force. It was criticized at the time as "soapsuds and whitewash", though Turner himself claimed he merely painted what he saw, having been "lashed to a mast" for four hours.

William Blake

Two rooms on the upper floor of the Turner Wing are devoted to the visionary works of the poet **William Blake**, who was considered something of a freak by his contemporaries. He rejected oil painting in favour of watercolours, and often chose unusual subject matter which matched his highly personal form of Christianity. He earned a pittance producing illuminated books written and printed entirely by himself, and painted purely from his own visions: "Imagination is My World; this world of Dross is beneath my notice", he wrote. He also executed a series of twelve large colour prints on the myth of the Creation, now considered among his finest works, several examples of which are normally on display here. Blake's works were originally intended for a room back in the southern corner of the main building, which is decorated by Boris Anrep's floor mosaics, accompanied by quotes from Blake's poem *The Marriage of Heaven and Hell*.

J.M.W. TURNER (1775–1851)

Born in **Covent Garden**, Turner's childhood was blighted by the death of his younger sister and the mental illness of his mother, who died in Bedlam in 1804. Nevertheless, he became an extremely successful artist, exhibiting his first watercolours in the window of his father's barbershop in Maiden Lane while still a boy, and at the **Royal Academy** when he was just 14. He travelled widely in Europe, but when returning to England, lived increasingly as a recluse. He never married, but had two children with an older widow, and lived for thirty years with his father who worked as his studio assistant. Turner's only known **self-portrait** (he had no pretensions as a portraitist and was rather ashamed of his ruddy complexion) is usually on display.

EARLY EVENING IN ST JAMES'S PARK

St James's

An exclusive little enclave sandwiched between St James's Park and Piccadilly, St James's was laid out in the 1670s close to the royal seat of St James's Palace. Even today, regal and aristocratic residences overlook nearby Green Park and the stately avenue of The Mall; gentlemen's clubs cluster along Pall Mall and St James's Street; and jacket-and-tie restaurants and expense-account shops line St James's and Jermyn Street. Hardly surprising, then, that most Londoners rarely stray into this area, though plenty of folk frequent St James's Park, with large numbers heading for the Queen's chief residence, Buckingham Palace. If you're not in St James's for the shops, the best time to visit is on a Sunday, when it's quieter, the nearby Mall is closed to traffic, and the royal chapels – plus Spencer House, the one accessible Palladian mansion – are open to the public.

St James's Park

St James's Park is the oldest of London's royal parks, having been drained and turned into a deer park by Henry VIII. It was redesigned and opened to the public by Charles II, who used to stroll through the grounds with his mistresses and courtiers, feed the ducks and even take a dip in the canal. By the eighteenth century, when some 6500 people had access to night keys for the gates, the park had become something of a byword for robbery and prostitution: diarist James Boswell was among those who went there specifically to be accosted "by several ladies of the town". The park's current landscaping was devised by Nash in the 1820s in an elegant style that established a blueprint for later Victorian city parks.

Today, the banks of the tree-lined lake are a favourite picnic spot for the civil servants of Whitehall and an inner-city reserve for wildfowl. James I's two crocodiles have left no descendants, alas, but the pelicans (which have resided here ever since a pair was presented to Charles II by the Russian ambassador) can still be seen at the eastern end of the lake, and there are exotic ducks, swans and geese aplenty. From the bridge across the lake there's a fine view over to Westminster and the jumble of domes and pinnacles along Whitehall.

The Mall

⊖ St James's Park, Charing Cross or Westminster

The tree-lined sweep of **The Mall** – London's nearest equivalent to a Parisian boulevard (minus the cafés) – is at its best on Sundays, when it's closed to traffic. It was laid out in the first decade of the twentieth century as a memorial to Queen Victoria, and runs along the northern edge of St James's Park. The bombastic **Admiralty Arch** (until recently a Cabinet building, but set to become a luxury hotel) was erected to mark the entrance at the Trafalgar Square end of The Mall, while at the other end stands the ludicrous **Victoria Memorial**, Edward VII's overblown 2300-ton marble tribute to his mother: *Motherhood* and *Justice* keep Victoria company around the plinth, which is topped by a gilded statue of *Victory*, while the six outlying allegorical groups in bronze confidently proclaim the great achievements of her reign.

The Mall's most distinctive building is John Nash's **Carlton House Terrace**, whose graceful, cream-coloured Regency facade lines the north side of The Mall from Admiralty Arch. Among other things, it serves as the unlikely home of the **Institute of Contemporary Arts** or **ICA** (Tues–Sun 11am–11pm; £1 for day membership; ☎020 7930 3647, ⓦica.org.uk), an avant-garde institution which moved here in 1968 and has put on a programme of regularly provocative exhibitions, films, talks and performances ever since. A little further down the terrace, there are statues of George VI, erected in 1955, and his wife, the Queen Mum, erected in 2009 but depicted at the age she would have been when her husband died – on either side bronze reliefs depict the couple visiting the East End during the Blitz and having a day out at the races.

Wellington Barracks Guards' Chapel and Museum

Birdcage Walk • Museum daily 10am–4pm, last admission 3.30pm • £6, concessions £3, under-16s free • ☎ 020 7414 3271, ⓦ theguardsmuseum.com • ⊖ St James's Park

Named after James I's aviary, which once stood here, Birdcage Walk runs along the south side of St James's Park, with the Neoclassical facade of the **Wellington Barracks**, built in 1833 and fronted by a parade ground, occupying more than half its length. Several of the barracks' buildings are open to the public, all of them gathered around **Chapel Square** – more an open space than a square, really – about halfway along Birdcage Walk. Of the various buildings here it's the modernist lines of the **Guards' Chapel** (Mon–Thurs 10am–4pm, Fri 10am–3pm) that come as the biggest surprise. Hit by a V1 rocket bomb on the morning of Sunday, June 18, 1944 – killing 121 worshippers – the chapel was rebuilt in the 1960s. Inside it retains the ornate Victorian apse, with Byzantine-style gilded mosaics, from the old chapel.

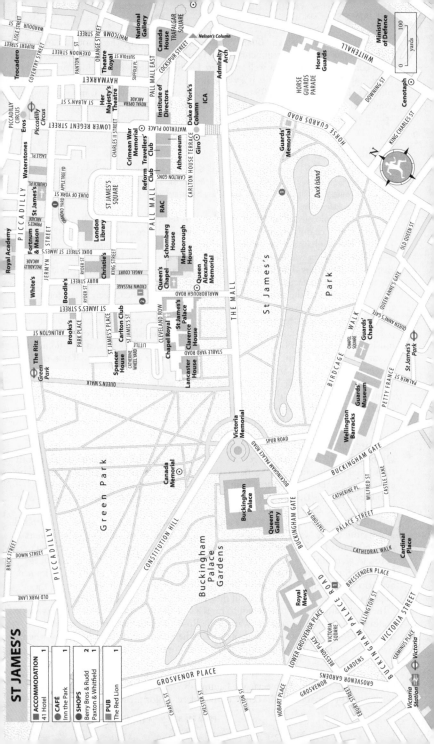

In a bunker opposite is the **Guards' Museum**, which displays the glorious scarlet-and-blue uniforms of the five regiments of the Queen's Foot Guards (see p.48) and explains their complicated history, as well as a potted military history of the country since the Civil War. Among the exhibits is a whole load of war booty, from Dervish prayer mats plundered from Sudan in 1898 to items taken from an Iraqi POW during the first Gulf War. Also on the square is **The Guards' Toy Soldier Centre** (Sat–Thurs 10am–4pm), selling an impressive array of toy soldiers.

Buckingham Palace

The Mall • Late July to Aug daily 9.30am–7.30pm, last admission 5.15pm; Sept 9.30am–6.30pm, last admission 4.15pm • State Rooms £20.50, concessions £18.80, under-17s £11.80, under-5s free; State Rooms & Garden Highlights £29.50, concessions £26.70, under-17s £17.70, under-5s free; State Rooms, Queen's Gallery & Royal Mews £35.60, concessions £32.50, under-17s £20, under-5s free • ☎ 020 7766 7300, ⓦ royalcollection.org.uk • ⊖ Green Park

The graceless colossus of **Buckingham Palace** has served as the monarch's permanent London residence only since Queen Victoria's reign. It began its days in 1702 as the Duke of Buckingham's city residence and was sold by the duke's son to George III in 1762. The building was overhauled by John Nash in the late 1820s for the Prince Regent, and again by Aston Webb in 1913 for George V, producing the blandest of all the existing royal palaces.

For ten months of the year there's little to do here, with the Queen in residence and the palace closed to visitors – not that this deters the crowds who mill around the railings all day, and gather in some force to watch the **Changing of the Guard** (see box, p.48), in which a detachment of the Queen's Guards marches to appropriate martial music from Wellington Barracks (unless it rains, that is). If the Queen is at home, the Royal Standard flies from the roof of the palace and four guards patrol; if not, the Union flag flutters aloft and just two guards stand out front.

Since 1993, the hallowed portals of the palace have been grudgingly opened for two months of the year when the royals stay in Scotland's Balmoral Castle instead. **Timed tickets** can be purchased online or from the box office on the south side of the palace; queues vary enormously, but you may have some time to wait before your allocated slot.

The interior

Of the palace's 775 rooms you get to see around twenty of the grandest ones, but with the Queen and her family in Scotland, there's usually very little sign of life. The visitors' entrance is via the **Ambassadors' Court** on Buckingham Palace Road, which lets you into the enormous **Quadrangle**, from where you can see the Nash facade, built in warm Bath stone, that used to overlook St James's Park.

Through the courtyard, you hit the **Grand Entrance**, decorated like some gloomy hotel lobby, from where Nash's rather splendid winding, curlicued **Grand Staircase**, with its floral gilt-bronze balustrade and white plaster friezes, leads past a range of very fine royal portraits, all beautifully lit by Nash's glass dome. Beyond, the small Guard Chamber leads into the **Green Drawing Room**, a blaze of unusually bright green silk walls, framed by lattice-patterned pilasters, and a heavily gilded coved ceiling. It was here that the Raphael Cartoons used to hang, until they were permanently loaned to the V&A.

The scarlet and gold **Throne Room** features a Neoclassical plaster frieze in the style of the Elgin Marbles, depicting the Wars of the Roses. The thrones themselves are disappointingly un-regal – just two pink his 'n' hers chairs initialled ER and P – whereas George IV's outrageous sphinx-style chariot seats, nearby, look more the part.

From the Picture Gallery to the Ballroom

Nash originally designed a spectacular hammer-beam ceiling for the **Picture Gallery**, which stretches right down the centre of the palace. Unfortunately, it leaked and was

eventually replaced in 1914 by a rather dull glazed ceiling. Still, the paintings on show here are excellent and include several Van Dycks, two Rembrandts, two Canalettos, a Poussin, a de Hooch and a wonderful Vermeer. Further on, in the East Gallery, check the cherub-fest in the grisaille frieze, before heading into the palace's rather overwrought **Ballroom**. It's here that the Queen holds her State Banquets, where the annual Diplomatic Reception takes place, and where folk receive their honours and knighthoods.

The west facade rooms

Having passed through several smaller rooms, you eventually reach the **State Dining Room**, whose heavily gilded ceiling, with its three saucer domes, is typical of the suite of rooms that overlooks the palace garden. Next door lies Nash's not very blue, but incredibly gold, **Blue Drawing Room**, lined with flock wallpaper interspersed with thirty fake onyx columns. The room contains one of George IV's most prized possessions, the "Table of the Grand Commanders", originally made for Napoleon, whose trompe-l'oeil Sèvres porcelain top features cameo-like portraits of military commanders of antiquity.

Beyond the domed **Music Room** with its enormous semicircular bow window and impressive parquet floor, the **White Drawing Room** features yet another frothy gold and white Nash ceiling and a superb portrait of Queen Alexandra, wife of Edward VII. Before you leave the palace, be sure to check out the Canova sculptures: *Mars and Venus* at the bottom of the Ministers' Staircase, and the pornographic *Fountain Nymph with Putto* in the Marble Hall.

If you've booked for the Garden Highlights Tour, you'll now get shown round the Queen's splendiferous herbaceous border, rose garden and veg patch, plus the wisteria-strewn summer house and the tennis court where George VI and Fred Perry used to knock up in the 1930s. There's a **café** overlooking the gardens if you want to linger longer before exiting onto busy Grosvenor Place.

Queen's Gallery
Daily: Oct–July 10am–5.30pm; Aug & Sept 9.30am–5.30pm; last admission 4.15pm • £10, concessions £9.20, under-17s £5.20, under-5s free • ☎ 020 7766 7301 • ➔ Victoria

A modern Doric portico on the south side of the palace forms the entrance to the **Queen's Gallery**, which puts on temporary exhibitions drawn from the **Royal Collection**, a superlative array of art that includes works by Michelangelo, Raphael, Holbein, Reynolds, Gainsborough, Vermeer, Van Dyck, Rubens, Rembrandt and Canaletto, as well as the world's largest collection of Leonardo drawings, the odd Fabergé egg and heaps of Sèvres china. The Queen holds the Royal Collection, which is three times larger than the National Gallery, "in trust for her successors and the nation" – note the word order. However, with over seven thousand works spread over the numerous royal palaces, the Queen's Gallery and other museums and galleries around the country, you'd have to pay a king's ransom to see the lot.

Royal Mews
Feb, March & Nov Mon–Sat 10am–4pm; April–Oct daily 10am–5pm; last admission 45min before closing • £9, concessions £8.30, under-17s £5.40, under-5s free • ☎ 020 7766 7302 • ➔ Victoria

On the south side of the palace, along Buckingham Palace Road, you'll find the **Royal Mews**, built by Nash in the 1820s. The horses are on view in sheds, but it's the royal carriages, lined up in coach houses, that are the main attraction. The most ornate is the **Gold State Coach**, made for George III in 1762, smothered in 22-carat gilding and panel paintings by Cipriani, and weighing four tons, its axles supporting four life-size Tritons blowing conches. Eight horses are needed to pull it and the whole experience apparently made Queen Victoria feel quite sick; since then it has only been used for coronations and jubilees. The mews also house the royal family's fleet of three Rolls Royce Phantoms and three Daimlers, none of which is obliged to carry number plates.

THE ROYAL FAMILY

The popularity of the **royal family** with foreign tourists never seems to flag, but at home it has always waxed and waned. The Queen herself, in one of her few memorable Christmas Day speeches, accurately described 1992 as her **annus horibilis** (or "One's Bum Year" as the *Sun* put it). That was the year that saw the marriage break-ups of Prince Charles and Prince Andrew and the divorce of Princess Anne, and ended with the fire at Windsor Castle. The royals decided to raise some of the money needed to pay for restorations to the castle by opening Buckingham Palace to the public for the first time (and by cranking up the admission charges on all the royal residences).

To try and deflect some of the bad publicity from that year, the Queen agreed to reduce the number of royals paid out of the state coffers, and, for the first time in her life, pay **taxes** on her personal fortune. The death of Princess Diana in 1997 was a low point for the royals, but their ratings have improved steadily since the new millennium, partly because the family have got much better at PR. Efficiencies and cost-cutting have also taken place, though public subsidy is still considerable, with around £40 million handed over each year in the Sovereign Grant and millions more spent on **luxuries** such as the Royal Squadron (for air travel) and the Royal Train.

Boosted by the hysteria around the **wedding** of Prince William and Kate Middleton (not to mention the births of their two children), and the Queen's **Diamond Jubilee** (which coincided with the 2012 Olympics), the Windsors are currently riding high on a wave of good publicity at home. Modernizing continues apace, with female heirs to the throne no longer passed over in preference of younger males, and marriage to a Roman Catholic no longer an issue, although the sovereign still has to be a full-blooded Protestant. However, with none of the mainstream political parties advocating scrapping the monarchy, the royal soap opera looks safe to run for many years to come.

Pall Mall

Running west from Trafalgar Square to St James's Palace, the wide thoroughfare of **Pall Mall** is renowned for its gentlemen's clubs, whose discreet Italianate and Neoclassical facades, fronted by cast-iron torches, still punctuate the street. It gets its bizarre name from the game of *pallo a maglio* (ball to mallet) – something like modern croquet – popularized by Charles II and played here and on The Mall. Crowds gathered here in 1807 when it became London's first gas-lit street – the original lampposts (erected to reduce the opportunities for crime and prostitution) are still standing.

Lower Regent Street

Lower Regent Street, a quarter of the way down Pall Mall, was the first stage in John Nash's ambitious plan to link the Prince Regent's magnificent Carlton House with Regent's Park. Like so many of Nash's grandiose schemes, it never quite came to fruition, as George IV, soon after ascending the throne, decided that Carlton House – the most expensive palace ever to have been built in London – wasn't quite luxurious enough, and had it pulled down. Its Corinthian columns now support the main portico of the National Gallery.

Waterloo Place

Lower Regent Street opens into **Waterloo Place**, which Nash extended beyond Pall Mall once Carlton House had been demolished. At the centre of the square stands the **Crimean War Memorial**, fashioned from captured Russian cannons in 1861, and commemorating the 2152 Foot Guards who died during the Crimean War. The horrors of that conflict were witnessed by Florence Nightingale (see p.222), whose statue – along with that of Sidney Herbert (Secretary at War at the time) – was added in 1914.

South of Pall Mall, Waterloo Place is flanked by St James's two grandest gentlemen's clubs: the former **United Services Club** (now the Institute of Directors), to the east, and the **Athenaeum**, to the west. Their almost identical Neoclassical designs are by Nash's protégé Decimus Burton: the better-looking is the Athenaeum, its portico sporting a garish gilded statue of the goddess Athena and, above, a Wedgwood-type frieze inspired

2

by the Elgin Marbles, which had just arrived in London. The Duke of Wellington was a regular at the United Services Club, and the horse blocks – confusingly positioned outside the Athenaeum – were designed so the duke could mount his steed more easily.

Appropriately enough, an equestrian statue of that eminently clubbable man **Edward VII** stands between the two clubs. More statues line the railings of nearby Waterloo Gardens: **Captain Scott** was sculpted by the widow he left behind after failing to complete the return journey from the South Pole; New Zealander **Keith Park**, the World War I flying ace and RAF commander who organized the fighter defence of London and southeast England during the Battle of Britain, was erected in 2010.

Duke of York's Column

To the south of Waterloo Place, overlooking St James's Park, is the **Duke of York's Column**, erected in 1833, ten years before Nelson's more famous one. The "Grand Old Duke of York", second son of George III, is indeed the one who marched ten thousand men "up to the top of the hill and… marched them down again" in the famous nursery rhyme. The 123ft column was paid for by stopping one day's wages of every soldier in the British Army, and it was said at the time that the column was so high because the duke was trying to escape his creditors, since he died £2 million in debt.

Carlton House Terrace

Having pulled his old palace down, George IV had Nash build **Carlton House Terrace**, whose monumental facade now looks out onto St James's Park. No. 4, by the exquisitely tranquil Carlton Gardens, was handed to de Gaulle for the headquarters of the Free French during World War II; nos. 7–9, by the Duke of York steps, served as the German embassy until World War II. Albert Speer designed the interior under the Nazis, while outside a tiny grave for *ein treuer Begleiter* (a true friend) lurks behind the railings near the column – it holds the remains of **Giro**, the Nazi ambassador's pet Alsatian, accidentally electrocuted in February 1934.

St James's Square

Around the time of George III's birth at no. 31 in 1738, **St James's Square** boasted no fewer than six dukes and seven earls, and over the decades it has maintained its exclusive air: no. 10 was occupied in turn by prime ministers Pitt the Elder, Lord Derby and Gladstone; at no. 16 you'll find the East India Club, a 160-year-old gentlemen's club; no. 4 was home to Nancy Astor, the first woman MP to take her seat in parliament, in 1919; while no. 31 was where Eisenhower formed the first Allied HQ during World War II. The narrowest house on the square (no. 14) is the **London Library**, a private library founded in 1841 by Thomas Carlyle, who got sick of waiting up to two hours for books to be retrieved from the British Library shelves only to find he couldn't borrow them (he used to steal them instead).

The square is no longer residential and, architecturally, it's not quite the period piece it once was, but its proportions remain intact, as do the graceful central **gardens** (Mon–Fri 10am–4.30pm), which feature an equestrian statue of **William III**, depicted tripping over on the molehill that killed him at Hampton Court. In the northeastern corner, there's a memorial marking the spot where police officer **Yvonne Fletcher** was shot dead in 1984, during a demonstration by Libyan dissidents outside what was then the Libyan embassy, at no. 5. Following the shooting, the embassy was besieged by armed police for eleven days, but in the end the diplomats were simply expelled and no one has ever been charged.

Schomberg House

80–82 Pall Mall

The unusual seventeenth-century mansion of **Schomberg House** is one of the few to stand out on Pall Mall, thanks to its Dutch-style red brickwork and elongated caryatids. In 1769, the house was divided into three, and the artist Thomas Gainsborough, who was at the height of his fame, lived in no. 80, the western portion, until his death in 1788. Next door, at no. 81, a Scottish quack doctor, James Graham, ran his Temple of Health and Hymen, where couples having trouble conceiving could try their luck in the "grand celestial bed" for £50 a night (a fortune in those days).

79 Pall Mall

Charles II housed **Nell Gwynne** at 79 Pall Mall, and even gave her the freehold, so that the two of them could chat over the garden wall, which once backed onto the grounds of St James's Palace. It was from one of the windows overlooking the garden that Nell is alleged to have dangled her 6-year-old, threatening to drop him if Charles didn't acknowledge paternity and give the boy a title, at which Charles yelled out "Save the Earl of Burford!"; another, more tabloid-style version of the story alleges that Charles was persuaded only after overhearing Nell saying "Come here, you little bastard", then excusing herself on the grounds that she had no other name by which to call him.

Marlborough House

Pall Mall • Mon–Fri 10am–4.45pm • Visits by guided tour only, of groups of 15 or more • ☎ 020 7747 6164, ⓦ thecommonwealth.org/marlborough-house • ⊖ Green Park

Marlborough House itself is hidden from Marlborough Road by a high brick wall, and only partly visible from The Mall. Queen Anne sacrificed half her garden in granting this land to her lover, Sarah Jennings, Duchess of Marlborough, in 1709. The duchess, in turn, told Wren to design her a "strong, plain and convenient" palace, only to sack him later and finish the plans off herself. The highlight of the interior is the **Blenheim Saloon**, with its frescoes depicting the first duke's eponymous victory, along with ceiling paintings by Gentileschi transferred from the Queen's House in Greenwich. The royals took over the building in 1817, though the last one to live here was Queen Mary, wife of George V. Since 1965, the palace has been the headquarters of the Commonwealth Secretariat, and can only be visited on a guided tour.

THE GENTLEMEN'S CLUBS

The **gentlemen's clubs** of Pall Mall and St James's Street remain the final bastions of the male chauvinism and public-school snobbery for which England is famous. Their origins lie in the coffee- and chocolate-houses of the eighteenth century, though the majority were founded in the post-Napoleonic peace of the early nineteenth century by those who yearned for the life of the officers' mess; drinking, whoring and gambling were the major features of early club life. **White's** – the oldest of the lot, and with a list of members that still includes numerous royals (Prince Charles held his [first] stag party here), prime ministers and admirals – used to be the unofficial Tory party headquarters, renowned for its high gambling stakes, while opposite, was the Whigs' favourite club, **Brooks's**. Bets were wagered over the most trivial of things to relieve the boredom – "a thousand meadows and cornfields were staked at every throw" – and in 1755 one MP, Sir John Bland, shot himself after losing £32,000 in one night.

In their day, the clubs were also the battleground of sartorial elegance, particularly **Boodle's**, in whose bay window the dandy-in-chief Beau Brummell set the fashion trends for the London upper class and provided endless fuel for gossip. It was said that Brummell's greatest achievement in life was his starched neckcloth, and that the Prince Regent himself wept openly when Brummell criticized the line of his cravat. More serious political disputes were played out in clubland, too. The **Reform Club** on Pall Mall, from which Phileas Fogg set off in Jules Verne's *Around the World in Eighty Days*, was the gathering place of the liberals behind the 1832 Reform Act, and remains one of the more "progressive" – it was one of the first to admit women as members in 1981. The **Carlton Club** was created in 1832 to represent the Tories' opposition to the Reform Act – bombed by the IRA in 1990, it's still the leading Conservative club, and only admitted women as full members in 2008 (Mrs Thatcher was made an honorary member).

St James's Palace

St James's Palace was built on the site of a lepers' hospital which Henry VIII bought in 1532. Bloody Mary died here in 1558 (her heart and bowels were buried in the Chapel Royal), and it was here that Charles I chose to sleep the night before his execution, so as not to have to listen to his scaffold being erected. When Whitehall Palace burnt down in 1698, St James's became the principal royal residence and even today it remains the official residence, with every ambassador to the UK accredited to the "Court of St James's", even though the monarchy moved over to Buckingham Palace in 1837. The main red-brick gate-tower, which looks out on to St James's Street, is a survivor from Tudor times; the rest of the modest, rambling, crenellated complex, largely hidden from view behind high walls, was restored and remodelled by Nash, and is now the London residence of Princess Anne, Princess Alexandra, Princess Beatrice and Princess Eugenie.

Chapel Royal

Open for services only: Oct to Easter Sun 8.30am & 11.15am · ⊖ Green Park

St James's Palace is off-limits to the public, with the exception of the **Chapel Royal**, which is accessed from Cleveland Row. Charles I took Holy Communion in the chapel on the morning of his execution, and here, too, the marriages of William and Mary, George III and Queen Charlotte, Victoria and Albert and George V and Queen Mary took place. One of the few remaining sections of Henry VIII's palace, it was redecorated in the 1830s, though the gilded strap-work ceiling matches the Tudor original erected to commemorate the brief marriage of Henry and Anne of Cleves (and thought to have been the work of Hans Holbein).

Queen's Chapel

Open for services only: Easter to July Sun 8.30am & 11.15am · ⊖ Green Park

Despite being on the other side of Marlborough Road, the **Queen's Chapel** is officially part of St James's Palace. A perfectly proportioned classical church, it was designed by Inigo Jones (with Gibbons and Wren helping with the decoration) for the Infanta of Spain, intended child bride of Charles I, and later completed for his French wife, Henrietta Maria, who was also a practising Catholic. A little further down Marlborough Road is the glorious Art Nouveau memorial to **Queen Alexandra** (wife of Edward VII), the last work of Alfred Gilbert (of Eros fame), comprising a bronze fountain crammed with allegorical figures and flanked by robust lampposts.

Clarence House

Aug Mon–Fri 10am–4.30pm, Sat & Sun 10am–5.30pm, last admission 1hr before closing · £9.80, under-17s £5.80, under-5s free · ☎ 020 7766 7303, ⓦ royalcollection.org.uk · ⊖ Green Park

John Nash was also responsible for **Clarence House**, which is attached to the southwest wing of St James's Palace. Built in the 1820s for William IV and used as his principal residence, it was occupied by various royals until the death of George VI, after which it became the home of the Queen Mother, George's widow for nearly fifty years. It's currently the official London home of Charles and Camilla (ⓦ princeofwales.gov.uk), but a handful of rooms can be visited over the summer when the royals are in Scotland. Visits (by guided tour) must be booked in advance, as they are extremely popular. The rooms are pretty unremarkable, so apart from a peek behind the scenes in a working royal palace, or a few mementoes of the Queen Mum, the main draw is the twentieth-century British paintings on display by the likes of Walter Sickert and Augustus John.

St James's Street and Jermyn Street

St James's Street and **Jermyn Street** (pronounced "German Street"), have been, along with Savile Row in Mayfair, the spiritual home of English gentlemen's fashion since the

---

HIDDEN GEMS: SHOPS AND SIGNAGE

As you stroll along St James's and Jermyn streets keep an eye out for some of the unique shops and signs – antiquated epithets are part of Jermyn Street's quaint appeal – including:

Berry Brothers 3 St James's St. The oldest wine merchants in the world, with acres of cellars, and a sloping wooden floor of great antiquity.

James Lock & Co 6 St James's St. The first company to sell a bowler, they have the Duke of Wellington's hat on display, alongside a replica of the cocked hat they made for Nelson.

James J. Fox 19 St James's St. Fox supplied Winston Churchill with his cigars and Oscar Wilde with Sobranie cigarettes – there's a small museum inside and a smoking room for sampling the wares.

Turnbull & Asser 71–72 Jermyn St. Describe themselves as "Hosiers & Glovers".

Bates the hatters, housed within the shirtmakers **Hadditch & Key**, 73 Jermyn St. Bates still displays Binks, the stray cat which entered the shop in 1921 and never left, now stuffed and sporting a cigar and top hat in a glass cabinet.

Taylor of Old Bond Street 74 Jermyn St. Established in 1854 on Bond Street, this family business has been providing 'herbal remedies for hair and skin' ever since – there's a barber's here too, dubbed "Gentlemen's Court Hairdresser".

Foster & So 85 Jermyn St. A shoe shop styled as "Bootmakers since 1840".

Floris 89 Jermyn St. Renowned for covering up the royal family's body odour with its ever-so-English fragrances.

Paxton & Whitfield 93 Jermyn St. Boasts an unrivalled selection of cheeses.

2

advent of the clubs (see box above). The window displays and wooden-panelled interiors (see box, above) still evoke an age when mass consumerism was unthinkable, and when it was considered that gentlemen "should either be a work of art or wear a work of art", as Oscar Wilde put it.

Green Park

Green Park was established by Henry VIII on the burial ground of the old lepers' hospital that became St James's Palace. It was left more or less flowerless – hence its name (officially "The Green Park") – and, apart from the springtime swathes of daffodils and crocuses, it is mostly meadow, shaded by graceful London plane trees. In its time, however, it was a popular place for duels (banned from neighbouring St James's Park), ballooning and fireworks displays. One such display was immortalized by Handel's *Music for the Royal Fireworks*, performed here on April 27, 1749, to celebrate the Peace of Aix-la-Chapelle, which ended the War of the Austrian Succession – over ten thousand fireworks were let off, setting fire to the custom-built Temple of Peace and causing three fatalities. The music was a great success, however.

Along the east side of the park runs the wide, pedestrian-only **Queen's Walk**, laid out for Queen Caroline, wife of George II, who had a little pavilion built nearby. At its southern end, there's a good view of **Lancaster House** (closed to the public), a grand Neoclassical palace built in rich Bath stone in the 1820s by Benjamin Wyatt, and used for government receptions and conferences since 1913.

Spencer House

27 St James's Place • Feb–July & Sept–Dec Sun only 10am–4.45pm • £12, concessions £10, no under-10s • ☎ 020 7499 8620, Ⓦ spencerhouse.co.uk • ⊖ Green Park

Princess Diana's ancestral home, **Spencer House**, is one of London's finest Palladian mansions. Erected in the 1750s, its most hansdome facade looks out over Queen's Walk to Green Park, though access is from St James's Place. Inside, tour guides take you through nine of the state rooms, returned to something like their original condition by current owners, the Rothschilds. The Great Room features a stunning coved and coffered ceiling in green, white and gold. The most outrageous decor, though, is in Lord Spencer's Room, with its astonishing gilded palm-tree columns.

THE ROYAL ARCADE, OFF ALBEMARLE STREET

Mayfair and Piccadilly

Although shops, offices, embassies and hotels outnumber aristocratic
pieds-à-terre nowadays, the social cachet of the luxury apartments and
mews houses of Mayfair has remained much the same. This is, after all, where
the fictional Bertie Wooster – the perfect upper-class Englishman – and his
faithful valet Jeeves, of P.G. Wodehouse's interwar novels, lived. Piccadilly
may not be the fashionable promenade it once was, but a whiff of exclusivity
still pervades Bond Street and its tributaries, where designer clothes emporia
jostle for space with jewellers, bespoke tailors and fine art dealers. Most
shoppers, however, stick to Regent and Oxford streets, home to the flagship
branches of the country's most popular chain stores and two of the busiest
streets in the West End.

Along with neighbouring St James's and Marylebone, **Mayfair** emerged in the eighteenth century as one of London's first real residential suburbs. Sheep and cattle were driven off the land by the area's big landowners (the largest of whom were the Grosvenor family, whose head is the Duke of Westminster, one of the ten richest men in Britain) to make way for London's first major planned development: a web of brick-and-stucco terraces and grid-plan streets feeding into a trio of grand, formal squares, with mews and stables round the back. The name comes from the infamous fifteen-day fair, which bit the dust in 1764 after the newly ensconced wealthy residents complained of the "drunkenness, fornication, gaming and lewdness". Mayfair quickly began to attract aristocratic London away from hitherto fashionable Covent Garden and Soho, and set the westward trend for upper-middle-class migration.

Piccadilly Circus

Tacky and congested it may be, but for many visitors, Piccadilly Circus is up there with Trafalgar Square as a candidate for London's city centre. A much-altered product of Nash's grand 1812 **Regent Street** plan, and now a major bottleneck, with traffic from Piccadilly, Shaftesbury Avenue and Regent Street all converging, it's by no means a picturesque place, and is probably best seen at night, when the spread of illuminated signs (a feature since the Edwardian era) gives it a touch of Times Square dazzle, and when the human traffic flow is at its most frenetic.

3

As well as being the gateway to the West End, this is also prime tourist territory, thanks mostly to the celebrated Shaftesbury Memorial, popularly known as **Eros**. The fountain's aluminium archer is one of London's top tourist attractions, a status that baffles all who live here – when it was first unveiled in 1893, it was so unpopular that the sculptor, Alfred Gilbert, lived in self-imposed exile for the next thirty years. The figure depicted is not Eros, but his lesser-known brother Anteros, who was the god of requited love, although in this case he commemorates the selfless philanthropic love of the Earl of Shaftesbury, a Bible-thumping social reformer who campaigned against child labour.

Behind Eros, it's worth popping into **The Criterion** restaurant, at no. 224 Piccadilly, just for a drink, so you can soak in probably the most spectacular Victorian interior in London, with its Byzantine-style gilded mosaic ceiling.

Trocadero

Piccadilly Circus • ⓦ londontrocadero.com • ⊖ Piccadilly Circus

Just east of the Circus, **Trocadero** was originally an opulent restaurant, from 1896 until its closure in 1965. Since then, millions have been poured into this glorified amusement arcade, casino and multiplex cinema, in an unsuccessful attempt to find a winning formula. Save for a few tacky shops just inside the main entrance, most of the building is currently inaccessible. The whole place is being gutted, redeveloped and, according to the latest reports, converted into a 585-bedroom hotel.

Ripley's Believe It or Not!

Piccadilly Circus • Daily 10am–midnight, last admission 10.30pm • £26.95, concessions £24.95, under-16s £19.95, under-4s free • ⓣ 020 3238 0022, ⓦ ripleyslondon.com • ⊖ Piccadilly Circus

Next door to Trocadero, in what was once the London Pavilion music hall, is the world's largest branch of **Ripley's Believe It or Not!**, which bills itself as an odditorium. Delights on display include a chewing gum sculpture of The Beatles and Tower Bridge rendered in 264,345 matchsticks whilst interactive attractions include a mirror maze and "rotating vortex tunnel". Book online to save a few pounds off the stratospheric admission charge.

Regent Street

Regent Street was drawn up by John Nash in 1812 as both a luxury shopping street and a triumphal way between George IV's (now demolished) Carlton House and Regent's Park to the north. It was the city's first stab at slum clearance, creating a tangible borderline to shore up fashionable Mayfair against the chaotic maze of neighbouring Soho. Today, it's still possible to admire the stately intentions of Nash's plan, even though the original arcading of the **Quadrant**, which curves westwards from Piccadilly Circus, is no longer there.

Regent Street enjoyed eighty years as Bond Street's nearest rival, before the rise of the city's middle classes ushered in heavyweight stores catering for the masses. Two of the oldest established stores can be found close to one another on the east side of the street: **Hamleys**, which claims to be the world's largest toy shop, and **Liberty**, the department store that popularized Arts and Crafts designs. Liberty's famous mock-Tudor entrance, added in the 1920s, is round the corner on Great Marlborough Street – inside there's a

● SHOPS							
Alexander McQueen	**10**	Hamleys	**6**	Liberty	**5**	Vivienne Westwood	**7**
Browns	**3**	Hatchards	**12**	Marks & Spencer	**1**	Waterstones	**13**
Dover Street Market	**9**	John Lewis	**4**	Selfridges	**2**	Wolf and Badger	**8**
Fortnum & Mason	**11**						

● CAFÉS	
Claridge's	**2**
Fortnum & Mason	**9**
The Ritz	**7**
Tibits	**5**
The Wolseley	**8**

● RESTAURANTS	
Kiku	**6**
Little Social	**3**
Rasa W1	**1**
Wild Honey	**4**

■ PUBS & BARS	
The Windmill	**1**
Ye Grapes	**2**

MONOPOLY

Although **Monopoly** was patented during the Depression by an American, Charles Darrow, it was the British who really took to the game, and the UK version was the one used in the rest of the world outside of the US. In 1935, to choose appropriate streets and stations for the game, the company director of Waddington's in Leeds sent his son, Norman Watson, and his secretary, Marjorie Phillips, on a day-trip to London. They came up with an odd assortment, ranging from the bottom-ranking Old Kent Road (still as tatty as ever) to an obscure dead-end street in the West End (Vine Street), and chose only northern train stations. All the properties have gone up in value since the board's inception (six zeros need to be added to most), but Mayfair and Park Lane (its western border), the most expensive properties, are still aspirational addresses.

central roof-lit well, surrounded by wooden galleries carved from the timbers of two old naval battleships.

Piccadilly

3

Piccadilly apparently got its name from a local resident who manufactured the ruffs or "pickadills" worn by the dandies of the late seventeenth century. Despite its fashionable pedigree, it's no place for promenading in its current state, with traffic careering down it nose to tail most of the day and night. Infinitely more pleasant places to window-shop are the **nineteenth-century arcades**, built to protect shoppers from the mud and horse dung on the streets, but now equally useful for escaping exhaust fumes.

Waterstones and Hatchard's

One of the most striking shops on Piccadilly, at nos. 203–206, is the sleek modernist 1930s facade of Simpsons department store, now the multistorey flagship bookstore of **Waterstones**. While Piccadilly may not be the shopping heaven it once was, it still harbours several old firms that proudly display their royal warrants. London's oldest bookshop, **Hatchard's**, at no. 187, was founded in 1797, as a cross between a gentlemen's club and a library, with benches outside for servants and daily papers inside for the gentlemen to peruse. Today, it's owned by Waterstones, elegant still, but with its old traditions marked most overtly by an unrivalled section on international royalty.

St James's Church

197 Piccadilly • Daily 8am–7pm • ☎ 020 7734 4511, ⓦ sjp.org.uk • ⊖ Piccadilly Circus

At the eastern end of Piccadilly, two blocks from Piccadilly Circus, stands **St James's Church**, Wren's favourite parish church (he built it himself). The church has rich furnishings, with the limewood reredos, organ-casing and marble font all by the master sculptor **Grinling Gibbons**. St James's is a radical campaigning church, which runs a daily craft market (Tues–Sat 10am–6.30pm), a food market (Mon 11am–3pm) and a café at the west end of the church; it also puts on top-class, free lunchtime concerts and regularly displays contemporary outdoor sculptures in the churchyard.

Fortnum & Mason

181 Piccadilly • Mon–Sat 10am–8pm, Sun 11.30am–6pm • ☎ 020 7734 8040, ⓦ fortnumandmason.com • ⊖ Green Park or Piccadilly Circus

One of Piccadilly's oldest institutions is **Fortnum & Mason**, the food emporium established in 1707 by Hugh Mason (who used to run a stall at St James's market) and William Fortnum (one of Queen Anne's footmen). Over the main entrance, the figures of its founders bow to each other on the hour as the clock clanks out the Eton school anthem – a kitsch addition from 1964. The store is most famous for its opulent food hall and its picnic hampers, first introduced as "concentrated lunches" for hunting and shooting parties, and now *de rigueur* for Ascot, Glyndebourne, Henley and other society events. Fortnum's is credited with the invention of the Scotch egg in 1851, and was also the first store in the world to sell Heinz baked beans in 1886.

Royal Academy of the Arts

Burlington House, Piccadilly • Daily 10am–6pm, Fri until 10pm • £10–15 • John Madejski Fine Rooms guided tours Tues 1pm, Wed–Fri 1 & 3pm, Sat 11.30am; free • ☎ 020 7300 8000, ⓦ royalacademy.org.uk • ⊖ Green Park

The **Royal Academy of Arts** occupies Burlington House, one of the few survivors from the ranks of aristocratic mansions that once lined the north side of Piccadilly. Rebuilding in the nineteenth century destroyed the original curved colonnades beyond the main gateway, but the complex has kept the feel of a Palladian *palazzo*. The academy itself was the country's first formal art school, founded in 1768 by a group of painters including Thomas Gainsborough and Joshua Reynolds. Reynolds went on to become the academy's first president, and his statue now stands in the courtyard, palette in hand ready to paint the cars hurtling down Piccadilly.

The academy's alumni range from Turner and Constable to Hockney and Tracey Emin, though the college has always had a conservative reputation for both its teaching and its shows. As well as hosting exhibitions, the RA has a small selection of works from its permanent collection in the white and gold **John Madejski Fine Rooms**. Highlights include a Rembrandtesque self-portrait by Reynolds, plus works by the likes of Constable, Hockney and Stanley Spencer. To see the gallery's most valuable asset, Michelangelo's marble relief, the *Taddei Tondo*, head for the narrow glass atrium of Norman Foster's Sackler Galleries, at the back of the building.

The Wolseley and the Ritz

On the south side of Piccadilly, on the corner of Arlington Street, **The Wolseley** is a superb Art Deco building, originally built as a Wolseley car showroom in the 1920s, now a café (see p.368). The most striking original features are the zigzag inlaid marble flooring, the chinoiserie woodwork and the giant red Japanese lacquer columns. Across St James's Street, with its best rooms overlooking Green Park, stands the **Ritz Hotel**, famous for its afternoon teas (see p.378) and a byword for decadence since it first wowed Edwardian society in 1906. The hotel's design, with its two-storey French-style mansard roof and long arcade, was based on the rue de Rivoli in Paris.

Burlington Arcade

Mon–Fri 8am–8pm, Sat 9am–8pm, Sun 11am–6pm • Free • ⓦ burlington-arcade.co.uk • ⊖ Green Park

Along the side of the Royal Academy runs the **Burlington Arcade**, London's first shopping arcade, built in 1819 for Lord Cavendish, then owner of Burlington House, to prevent commoners throwing rubbish into his garden. Today, it's London's longest and most expensive nineteenth-century arcade, lined with mahogany-fronted luxury shops, including Linley, run by the Queen's nephew. Upholding Regency decorum, it's still illegal to whistle, sing, hum, hurry or carry large packages or open umbrellas on this small stretch, and the arcade's beadles (known as Burlington Berties), in their Edwardian frock coats and gold-braided top hats, take the prevention of such criminality very seriously.

THE SUMMER EXHIBITION

The most famous event in the Royal Academy's calendar is the **Summer Exhibition**, which has been held annually since 1769, and runs from June to mid-August. It's an odd event: anyone can enter paintings in any style. Around ten thousand entries are surveyed at considerable speed) by the RA's Hanging Committee (great name) and around one thousand lucky winners get hung, in extremely close proximity, and sold. In addition, the eighty "Academicians" are allowed to display up to six of their own works – no matter how awful. The result is a bewildering display, which gets annually panned by the critics. However, with thirty percent of the purchase price going to the RA, it generates at least £2 million in income.

Piccadilly and Princes arcades

Ⓦ piccadillyarcade.com, Ⓦ princesarcade.com • ⊖ Green Park or Piccadilly Circus

Neither of Piccadilly's other two arcades can hold a torch to the Burlington, though they are still worth exploring if only to marvel at the strange mixture of shops. The finer of the two is the **Piccadilly Arcade**, an Edwardian extension to the Burlington on the south side of Piccadilly, whose squeaky-clean bow windows display, among other items, Russian icons, model soldiers and buttons and cufflinks supplied to Prince Charles. The **Princes Arcade**, to the east, exudes a more discreet Neoclassical elegance and contains Prestat, purveyors of handmade, hand-packed chocolates and truffles to the Queen.

Bond Street

Bond Street runs more or less parallel to Regent Street, extending north from Piccadilly all the way to Oxford Street. It is, in fact, two streets rolled into one: the southern half, laid out in the 1680s, is known as **Old Bond Street**; its northern extension, which followed less than fifty years later, is known as **New Bond Street** (the split is at the junction with Burlington Gardens). In contrast to their international rivals, rue de Rivoli and Fifth Avenue, both Bond streets are pretty unassuming architecturally – a mixture of modest Georgian and Victorian townhouses – but the shops that line them are among the flashiest in London.

3

Bond Street shops

Unlike its overtly masculine counterpart, Jermyn Street (see p.74), **Bond Street** caters for both sexes, and although it has its fair share of long-established names, it's also home to flagship branches of multinational **designer clothes** outlets like Prada, D&G, Louis Vuitton, Chanel and so on. This designer madness also spills over into **Conduit Street**, connecting Bond Street to Regent Street and home to Donna Karan, Vivienne Westwood and Rigby & Peller, corsetieres to the Queen. On parallel Dover Street, two blocks away at the Piccadilly end, nos. 17–18 house the original Comme des Garçons market store, **Dover Street Market**, a huge six-floor fashion bazaar that could easily be mistaken for a modern art gallery, stocking the Japanese label's own clobber alongside a host of other cutting-edge brand names.

Bond Street also has its fair share of perfumeries and **jewellers**, many of them long-established. One of the most famous is **Asprey**, founded in 1781 by a family of Huguenot craftsmen, and now jewellers to the royals. The facade of the store, at no. 167, features a wonderful parade of arched windows, flanked by slender Corinthian wrought-iron columns. Close by is *Allies*, a popular double statue of **Winston Churchill and President Roosevelt**, enjoying a chat on a bench – you can squeeze between the two of them, in the space where Stalin should be, for a photo opportunity.

Auction houses and art galleries

In addition to fashion, Bond Street is renowned for its **auction houses** (see box, p.82) and **art galleries**, although the latter are actually outnumbered by those on neighbouring **Cork Street**. The main difference between the two is that the Bond Street dealers are basically heirloom offloaders, where you might catch an Old Master or an Impressionist masterpiece, whereas Cork Street galleries and others dotted throughout Mayfair – such as the Mason's Yard outpost of White Cube (see p.237) – show largely contemporary art.

Smythson

40 New Bond St • Mon–Wed & Fri 9.30am–7pm, Thurs 10am–8pm, Sat 10am–7pm, Sun noon–6pm • Ⓦ smythson.com • ⊖ Bond Street

One Bond Street institution you can feel free to walk into is **Smythson**, the bespoke stationers, founded in 1887, who made their name printing Big Game books for

3

AUCTION HOUSES

A very Mayfair-style entertainment lies in visiting the area's trio of auction houses. **Sotheby's**, 34–35 New Bond St (☎020 7293 5000, ⌨sothebys.com), was founded in 1744 and is the oldest of the three (and the fourth oldest in the world), though its pre-eminence only really dates from the last war. Above the doorway of Sotheby's is London's oldest outdoor sculpture, an Egyptian statue dating from 1600 BC. **Bonhams**, founded in 1793 (and now merged with Phillips), is at 101 New Bond St (☎020 7447 7447, ⌨bonhams.com); and **Christie's**, founded in 1766, and now the world's largest auction house, is actually over in St James's at 8 King St (☎020 7839 9060, ⌨christies.com).

Viewing takes place from Monday to Friday, and also occasionally at the weekend, and entry to the galleries is free of charge, though if you don't buy a catalogue, the only information you'll glean is the lot number. Thousands of the works that pass through the rooms are of museum quality, and, if you're lucky, you might catch a glimpse of a masterpiece in transit between private collections. Anyone can attend the auctions themselves, though remember to keep your hands firmly out of view unless you're bidding.

Sotheby's is probably the least intimidating: there's an excellent **café**, and staff offer free valuations, if you have an heirloom of your own to check out. There's always a line of people unwrapping items under the polite gaze of valuation staff, who call in the experts if they see something that sniffs of real money. Only Bonhams remains British-owned; Christie's and Sotheby's, once quintessentially English institutions, are now under French and US control.

colonialists to record what they'd bagged out in Africa and India. At the back of the shop is a small octagonal museum encrusted with shells and mirrors, and a few artefacts: photos and replicas of the book of condolence Smythson created for JFK's funeral, and the cherry calf-and-vellum diary given to Princess Grace of Monaco as a wedding gift.

Albemarle Street

Running parallel to Old Bond Street to the west is **Albemarle Street**, connected by the **Royal Arcade**, a short High Victorian shopping mall with tall arched bays and an elegant glass roof. It was designed so that the wealthy guests of nearby **Brown's** hotel could have a sheltered and suitably elegant approach to the shops on Bond Street. Apart from being a posh hotel opened in the 1830s by James Brown, Byron's former valet, *Brown's* is famous as the place where the country's first telephone call was placed by **Alexander Graham Bell** in 1876, though initially he got a crossed line with a private telegraph wire. Also in Albemarle Street, at no. 50, are the offices of **John Murray**, the publishers of Byron and of the oldest British travel guides. It was here in 1824 that Byron's memoirs were burnt to cinders, after Murray persuaded Tom Moore, to whom they had been bequeathed, that they were too scurrilous to publish.

Royal Institution

21 Albemarle St • Museum Mon–Fri 9am–6pm • Free • ☎020 7409 2992, ⌨rigb.org • ⊖ Green Park

The weighty Neoclassical facade at 21 Albemarle Street heralds the **Royal Institution**, a scientific body founded in 1799 "for teaching by courses of philosophical lectures and experiments the application of science to the common purposes of life". The RI is best known for its six Christmas Lectures, begun by Michael Faraday and designed to popularize science among schoolchildren. The building houses an archive and reading rooms but the easiest way to visit is to walk round the enjoyably interactive **Faraday Museum** aimed at both kids and adults. In the basement, you can learn about the ten chemical elements that have been discovered at the RI, and about the famous experiments that have taken place here: Tyndall's blue-sky tube, Humphry Davy's early lamps and Faraday's explorations into electromagnetism – there's even a reconstruction of Faraday's lab from the 1850s. The ground floor has displays on the fourteen Nobel

Prize winners who have worked at the RI, while on the first floor, you can visit the semicircular hall where the Christmas Lectures take place and see some of the apparatus used in lectures over the decades. There's also a great café-bar-restaurant on the ground floor.

Savile Row

Running parallel with New Bond Street, to the east, **Savile Row** has been *the* place to go for bespoke tailors since the early nineteenth century. Gieves & Hawkes, at no. 1, were the first to establish themselves here back in 1785, with Nelson and Wellington among their first customers; more recently, they made the military uniform worn by Prince William at his wedding. More modern in outlook, Kilgour, at no. 5, famously made Fred Astaire's morning coat for *Top Hat*, helping to popularize Savile Row tailoring in the US. Henry Poole & Co, who moved to no. 15 in 1846 and have cut suits for the likes of Napoleon III, Dickens, Churchill and de Gaulle, invented the short smoking jacket (originally designed for the future Edward VII), later popularized as the "tuxedo".

Savile Row also has connections with the pop world. **The Beatles** used to buy their suits from Tommy Nutter's House of Nutter established in 1968 at no. 35, now occupied by Gary Anderson, and in the same year set up the offices and recording studio of their record label **Apple** at no. 3, until the building's near physical collapse in 1972. On January 30, 1969, The Beatles gave an impromptu gig (their last live performance) on the roof here, stopping traffic and eventually attracting the attentions of the local police – as captured on film in *Let It Be*.

Mayfair's squares

Mayfair has three showpiece Georgian squares: **Hanover**, the most modest of the three, **Berkeley** and **Grosvenor**, the most grandiose, named after two of the district's big private landowners, Sir Richard Grosvenor and the Lords Berkeley of Stratton. Planned as purely residential locations, all have suffered over the years, and have nothing like the homogeneity of the Bloomsbury squares. Nevertheless, they are still impressive urban spaces, and their social lustre remains more or less untarnished, though the west side of Hanover Square is now a huge Crossrail building site (see box, p.105) and by 2018 will be one of two new ticket halls for the massively expanded Bond Street station. Each square is worth visiting, and travelling between them gives you a chance to experience Mayfair's backstreets and, en route, visit one or two hidden sights.

St George's Church, Hanover Square

1–2 Hanover Square • Mon–Fri 8am–4pm, Wed till 6pm, Sun 8am–noon • Free • ⓦ stgeorgeshanoversquare.org • ⊖ Bond Street

At the very southern tip of **Hanover Square** stands the Corinthian portico of **St George's Church**, the first of its kind in London when it was built in the 1720s. Nicknamed "London's Temple of Hymen", it has long been Mayfair's most fashionable church for weddings. Among those who tied the knot here are the Shelleys, Benjamin Disraeli, Teddy Roosevelt and George Eliot. The composer, Handel, a confirmed bachelor, was a warden here for many years and even had his own pew. North of the church, the funnel-shaped St George Street splays into the square itself, which used to boast the old Hanover Square Rooms venue, where Bach, Liszt, Haydn and Paganini all performed before the building's demolition in 1900.

Handel House Museum

25 Brook St • Tues–Sat 10am–6pm, Thurs till 8pm, Sun noon–6pm • £6.50, concessions £5.50, under-17s £2 and free at weekends, under-5s free • ☎ 020 7495 1685, ⓦ handelhouse.org • ⊖ Bond Street

The **Handel House Museum**, one block west of Hanover Square, is where the composer Handel lived for 36 years from 1723 until his death. He used the ground floor as a shop where subscribers could buy scores, while on the first floor, there was a rehearsal and performance room, plus a composition room at the back. The museum has few original artefacts, but the house has been redecorated to how it would have looked in Handel's day. Further atmosphere is provided by the harpsichord students who often practise in the rehearsal room; to find out about the regular recitals, visit the website. Access is via the chic, cobbled yard at the back of the house.

Berkeley Square

Berkeley Square is where, according to the music-hall song, nightingales sing (though it's probable they were, in fact, blackcaps). Laid out in the 1730s, only the west side of the square has any surviving Georgian houses to boast of, including Maggs Bros, at no. 50, the oldest antiquarian booksellers in the world – they also sell signatures and famously bought Napoleon's penis in 1916. A few doors up, in the basement of the Georgian mansion at no. 44, is *Annabel's*, the private members' nightclub where Princess Diana and Sarah Ferguson turned up dressed as a police officer and a traffic warden, and were refused entry on the grounds that no uniforms were allowed inside. What saves the square aesthetically, however, is its wonderful parade of two hundred-year-old **London plane trees**. With their dappled, exfoliating trunks, giant lobed leaves and globular spiky fruits, these pollution-resistant trees are a ubiquitous feature of the city, and Berkeley Square's specimens are among the finest. The square has further royal connections, as the Queen was born just off it, at 17 Bruton St, and then lived at 145 Piccadilly until 1936.

Bourdon House: Alfred Dunhill

2 Davies St • Mon–Sat 10am–7pm, Tues till 8pm • ☎ 020 7853 4440, ⓦ dunhill.com • ⊖ Bond Street

Just north of Berkeley Square, it's possible to see inside **Bourdon House**, a lovely Georgian mansion on the corner of Davies and Bourdon streets. Former private

---

HANDEL AND HENDRIX

Born **Georg Friedrich Händel** (1685–1759) in Halle, Saxony, Handel first visited London in 1710, composing *Rinaldo* in fifteen days flat. The furore it produced – not least when Handel released a flock of sparrows for one aria – made him a household name. The following year he was commissioned to write several works for Queen Anne, eventually becoming court composer to George I, his one-time patron in Hanover.

London quickly became Handel's permanent home: he anglicized his name and nationality and lived out the rest of his life here, producing all the work for which he is now best known, including the *Water Music*, the *Fireworks Music* and his *Messiah*, which failed to enthral its first audiences, but which is now one of the great set pieces of Protestant musical culture. George II was so moved by the *Hallelujah Chorus* that he leapt to his feet and remained standing for the entire performance. Handel himself fainted during a performance in 1759, and died shortly afterwards in his home, now a museum (see p.83); he is buried in Westminster Abbey. Today, Handel's birthday is celebrated with a concert at the Foundling Museum (see p.130), and an annual Handel Festival (ⓦ london-handel-festival.com) takes place at St George's Church, Hanover Square (see p.83).

Two centuries later, **Jimi Hendrix** (1942–70) moved into the top-floor flat of 23 Brook St, next door to Handel's old address, and lived there for eighteen months or so. Born in Seattle in 1942, Hendrix was persuaded to fly over to London in 1966 by The Animals. Shortly after arriving, he teamed up with two British musicians, Noel Redding and Mitch Mitchell, and formed The Jimi Hendrix Experience. It was at the beginning of 1969 that Hendrix moved into Brook Street with his girlfriend, Kathy Etchingham; apparently he was much taken with the fact that it was once Handel's residence, ordering Kathy to go and buy some Handel albums for him. It was also in London that Hendrix met his untimely death, on September 18, 1970. At the *Samarkand Hotel* in Notting Hill, after a gig at *Ronnie Scott's* in Soho, Hendrix, with alcohol still in his system, swallowed a handful of sleeping pills, later vomiting in his sleep and slipping into unconsciousness. He was pronounced dead on arrival at St Mary's Hospital, Paddington, and is buried in Seattle.

residence of the Duke of Westminster, the house is now the flagship store of **Alfred Dunhill**. the luxury men's clothing and accessories retailer. As well as a shop, Dunhill's has a bar, a barber's and a screening room where they show classy masculine documentaries. On the first floor, they display a few items from the days of Dunhill Motorities, gadget suppliers to Rolls Royce, whose slogan was "everything but the motor". This wonderful range made hip flasks disguised as books, "Bobby Finders" for detecting police cars, in-car hookahs and even a motorist's pipe with a windshield for open-top toking.

Grosvenor Square

Grosvenor Square is the largest of Mayfair's squares. Its American connections go back to 1785, when John Adams (future US President) established the first American embassy in a house in the northeast corner. During World War II, it was known as "Little America" – General Eisenhower, whose statue stands in the square, ran the D-Day campaign from no. 20. As well as Eisenhower, there are statues of Roosevelt and Reagan, and a memorial garden dedicated to the 67 British victims of 9/11. The entire west side of the square is occupied by the monstrous, heavily guarded **US Embassy**, built in 1960. The embassy is watched over by a giant gilded aluminium eagle and has been the victim of numerous attacks over the decades. The first major incident occurred in 1967 when Spanish anarchists machine-gunned the embassy in protest against US collaboration with Franco. The most famous (and violent) protest took place in 1968, when a demonstration against US involvement in Vietnam turned into a riot. Mick Jagger, so the story goes, was innocently signing autographs in his Bentley at the time, and later wrote *Street Fighting Man*, inspired by what he witnessed. Most weeks, there's some group or other camped out objecting to US foreign policy – in fact, American security concerns are such that in 2017, the embassy will move to a purpose-built $1 billion complex near Vauxhall.

Claridge's

49 Brook St • ☎ 020 7629 8860, ⓦ claridges.co.uk • ⊖ Bond Street

Claridge's, one of the most renowned luxury hotels in London, started out in 1812 as *Mivart's Hotel* in a small terraced house, but has grown considerably larger since those days. The current building dates from 1898, has over two hundred rooms and a Gordon Ramsay restaurant, and still attracts Hollywood and pop glitterati. Its royal connections are also second to none. Most famously, King Peter II of Yugoslavia spent most of World War II in exile at the hotel – suite 212 was ceded to Yugoslavia for a day on June 17, 1945 so that his son and heir, Crown Prince Alexander, could be born on Yugoslav soil. A room in the hotel, painted "whorehouse pink", served as General Eisenhower's initial wartime pied-à-terre, and it was also the wartime hangout of the OSS, forerunner of the CIA. It was here in 1943 that Szmul Zygielbojm, from the Polish government-in-exile, was told that Roosevelt had refused his request to bomb the rail lines leading to Auschwitz; the following day he committed suicide.

Grosvenor Chapel

24 South Audley St • Mon–Fri 9.30am–4.30pm • Free • ☎ 020 7499 1684, ⓦ grosvenorchapel.org.uk • ⊖ Bond Street or Green Park

American troops stationed in Britain used to worship at the **Grosvenor Chapel**, two blocks south of *Claridge's* on South Audley Street, a simple classical building that formed the model for early settlers' churches in New England and is still popular with the American community. The church's most illustrious corpse is radical MP John Wilkes ("Wilkes and Liberty" was the battle cry of many a mid-eighteenth-century riot). The interior comes as something of a surprise, however, as it was redesigned in Anglo-Catholic style by Ninian Comper in 1912, and features an elaborate tableau of gilded statuary: Christ crucified is flanked by Mary and one of the disciples, with two angels kneeling below with chalices ready to catch the sacred blood.

3

THE CATO STREET CONSPIRACY

Modern British history is notably short on political assassinations: one prime minister, no kings or queens and only a handful of MPs. One of the most dismal failures was the 1820 **Cato Street Conspiracy**, drawn up by sixteen revolutionaries in an attic off the Edgware Road in Marylebone. Their plan was to decapitate the entire Cabinet as they dined with Lord Harrowby at 44 Grosvenor Square. Having beheaded the Home Secretary and another of the ministers, they then planned to sack Coutts Bank, capture the cannon on the Artillery Ground, take Gray's Inn, Mansion House, the Bank of England and the Tower, torching the barracks in the process, and proclaiming a provisional government.

As it turned out, one of the conspirators was an *agent provocateur*, and the entire mob was arrested in the Cato Street attic on the night of the planned coup, February 23, 1820. In the melee, one Bow Street Runner was killed but eventually eleven of the conspirators were arrested and charged with high treason. Five of the ringleaders were hanged at Newgate, and another five were transported to Australia. Public sympathy for the uprising was widespread, so the condemned were spared being drawn and quartered, though they did have their heads cut off afterwards. (The hangman was later attacked in the streets and almost castrated.)

Farm Street: Church of the Immaculate Conception

114 Mount St • Daily 8am–7pm • Free • ☎ 020 7493 7811, ⓦ farmstreet.org.uk • ⊖ Bond Street or Green Park

Built in ostentatious neo-Gothic style in the 1840s, the **Church of the Immaculate Conception Farm Street** is the London stronghold of the Jesuits, and as such is a fascinating and unusual church. Every surface is covered in decoration, but the reredos of gilded stone by Pugin (of Houses of Parliament fame) is particularly impressive. Behind the chapel are the beautifully secluded **Mount Street Gardens**, dotted with two hundred-year-old plane trees and enclosed by nineteenth-century red-brick mansions.

Oxford Street

As wealthy Londoners began to move out of the City during the eighteenth century, in favour of the newly developed West End, so **Oxford Street** – the old Roman road to Oxford – gradually replaced Cheapside as London's main shopping street. Today, despite successive recessions and sky-high rents, this hotchpotch of shops, over a mile long, is still one of the world's busiest streets, its Christmas lights switched on by the briefly famous, and its traffic controllers equipped with loud-hailers to prevent the hordes of Christmas shoppers from losing their lives at the busy road junctions. The stretch west of Oxford Circus is slightly more upmarket and home to a string of department stores; east of Oxford Circus, the street forms a scruffy border between Soho and Fitzrovia.

Selfridges

400 Oxford St • Mon–Sat 9.30am–9pm, Sun 11.30am–6pm • ⓦ selfridges.com • ⊖ Bond Street

The one long-standing landmark on Oxford Street is **Selfridges**, a huge Edwardian department store fronted by giant Ionic columns, with the Queen of Time riding the ship of commerce and supporting an Art Deco clock above the main entrance. Opened in 1909 by Chicago millionaire Harry Gordon Selfridge, Selfridges is the second largest shop in London (after Harrods), and is credited with selling the world's first television set, as well as introducing the concept of the "bargain basement", "the customer is always right", the irritating "only ten more shopping days to Christmas" countdown and the nauseous bouquet of perfumes from the cosmetics counters, strategically placed at the entrance to all department stores. Selfridge himself was a big spender and eventually died in Putney in poverty in 1947 at the age of 90. Today, while Harrods may have the snob value and the longer pedigree, it's a conservative institution compared to Selfridges, which keeps reinventing itself and successfully remains ahead of the field, particularly in fashion – the window displays alone are worth the journey here.

Marylebone

Marylebone may not have quite the social pedigree of neighbouring Mayfair, but it's still a wealthy and aspirational area. Compared to the brashness of Oxford Street, which forms its southern border, Marylebone's backstreets are a pleasure to wander, especially the chi-chi village-like quarter around Marylebone High Street. This is where the city's leading private specialists in medicine and surgery have had their practices since they gravitated here in the nineteenth century. And it was here that The Beatles (and many others since) took up residence when they hit the big time in the 1960s. The area's more conventional sights include the free art gallery and aristocratic mansion of the Wallace Collection, Sherlock Holmes' old stamping ground around Baker Street and the massively touristy Madame Tussauds.

Marylebone was once the outlying village of St Mary-by-the-Bourne (the bourne in question being the Tyburn stream) or St Marylebone (pronounced "marra-le-bun"), and when Samuel Pepys walked through open countryside to reach its pleasure gardens in 1668, he declared it "a pretty place". During the course of the next century, the gardens were closed and the village was swallowed up as its chief landowners – among them the Portlands and the Portmans – laid out a mesh of uniform Georgian streets and squares, much of which survives today.

Langham Place

North of Oxford Circus, Regent Street forms the eastern border of Marylebone, but stops abruptly at **Langham Place**, which formed an awkward twist in John Nash's triumphal route to Regent's Park in order to link up with the pre-existing Portland Place. Nash's solution was to build his unusual All Souls Church, now the only Nash building left in this star-studded chicane that's home to the BBC's Broadcasting House and the historic *Langham Hotel*.

All Souls Church

Langham Place • Mon–Sat 9.30am–5.30pm, Sun 8am–2pm & 5.30–8.30pm • Free • ☎ 020 7580 3522, ⓦ allsouls.org • ⊖ Oxford Circus

John Nash's simple and ingenious little **All Souls Church** was built in warm Bath stone in the 1820s, and is the architect's only surviving church. The unusual circular Ionic portico and conical stone spire, which caused outrage in its day, are cleverly designed to provide a visual full stop to Regent Street and lead the eye round into Portland Place and ultimately to Regent's Park.

Broadcasting House

Portland Place • Guided tours Mon–Sat 10am–4.30pm, Sun 10.45am–4.30pm; £15, students £11.25, children aged 9–15 £10, no under-9s • ☎ 0370 901 1227, ⓦ bbc.co.uk/broadcastinghouse • ⊖ Oxford Circus

Behind All Souls lies the totalitarian-looking Art Deco **Broadcasting House**, BBC radio headquarters since 1932 and now the London home of the BBC itself. The figures of Prospero and Ariel (pun intended) above the entrance are by Eric Gill, who caused a furore by sculpting Ariel with overlarge testicles and, like Epstein a few years earlier at Broadway House, was forced in the end to cut the organs down to size. You can book a guided tour (1hr 30min; online bookings only; ⓦ bbc.co.uk/showsandtours/ tours) to see the results of the decade-long, £1 billion refurbishment which finished in 2012, including the state-of-the-art open-plan newsroom, the Radio Theatre and some of the studios.

Langham Hotel

Opposite Broadcasting House stands the **Langham Hotel**, built in grandiose Italianate style and opened by the Prince of Wales in 1865 as the city's most modern hotel, with over one hundred water closets. It features in several Sherlock Holmes mysteries, and its former guests have included Antonín Dvořák (who courted controversy by ordering a double room for himself and his daughter to save money), exiled emperors Napoleon III and Haile Selassie, and Oscar Wilde. Following

---

MARYLEBONE HIGHLIGHTS

Alfie's Antique Market Rummage for treasures in this vast indoor market. See p.433
Daunt Books This gorgeous store sells everything from guidebooks to classics. See p.429
Royal Academy of Music Pop in on a Friday for a lunchtime concert. See p.414
The Providores and Tapa Room Enjoy small plates in a cool contemporary setting. See p.369
Tours of Broadcasting House Take a tour of the BBC's state-of-the-art studios. See above

World War II, it was taken over by the BBC and used to record legendary shows such as *The Goons*, only returning to use as a luxury hotel in 1991.

Portland Place

After the chicane around All Souls, you enter **Portland Place**, laid out by the Adam brothers in the 1770s and incorporated by Nash in his grand Regent Street plan. Once the widest street in London, it's still a majestic avenue, still lined here and there with Adam-style houses, boasting wonderful fanlights and iron railings. At the northern end of Portland Place, Nash originally planned a giant "circus" as a formal entrance to Regent's Park (see p.286). Only the southern half – two graceful arcs of creamy terraces known collectively as **Park Crescent** – was completed, now cut off from the park by busy Marylebone Road.

Chinese Embassy

Several embassies occupy properties on Portland Place, but the most prominent is the **Chinese Embassy** at no. 49, opposite which there's usually a small group of protesters positioned objecting either to Chinese policies in Tibet or the suppression of Falun Gong. It was here in 1896 that the exiled republican leader Sun Yat-sen was kidnapped

DOCTORS AND DENTISTS

Harley Street was an ordinary residential Marylebone street until the nineteenth century when doctors, dentists and medical specialists began to colonize the area in order to serve London's wealthier citizens. Private medicine survived the threat of the postwar National Health Service, and the most expensive specialists and hospitals are still to be found in the streets around here.

The national dental body, the **British Dental Association (BDA)** has its headquarters at nearby 64 Wimpole St, along with a **museum** (Tues & Thurs 1–4pm; free; ☎ 020 7563 4549, ⓦ bda.org; ⊖ Bond Street) displaying the gruesome contraptions of early dentistry and old prints of agonizing extractions. Although dentistry is traditionally associated with pain, it was, in fact, a dentist who discovered the first anaesthetic.

and held incognito, on the orders of the Chinese emperor. Eventually Sun managed to send a note to a friend, saying "I am certain to be beheaded. Oh woe is me!". When the press got hold of the story, Sun was finally released; he went on to found the Chinese Nationalist Party and became the first president of China in 1911.

Royal Institute of British Architects (RIBA)

66 Portland Place • Mon–Fri 8am–5.30pm, Tues till 8pm, Sat 8am–5pm • Free • ☎ 020 7580 5533, ⓦ architecture.com • ⊖ Regent's Park or Great Portland Street

The **Royal Institute of British Architects** or RIBA at no. 66 is arguably the finest building on Portland Place, with its sleek Portland-stone facade built in the 1930s amid the remaining Adam houses. Its Art Deco stylings are more profuse inside, the main staircase a wonderful example of the genre, with its etched glass balustrades and walnut veneer, and with two large black marble columns rising up on either side. You can view the interior en route to the institute's excellent ground-floor bookshop (Mon–Fri 9.30am–5.30pm, Sat 10am–5pm), first-floor exhibition galleries and bistro (Mon–Fri 10am–3.30pm). The *RIBA Café Bar* (Mon–Sat 8am–5pm, Sun 10am–5pm) is next to the main entrance.

Marylebone High Street

Marylebone High Street is all that's left of the village street that once ran along the banks of the Tyburn stream. It's become considerably more upmarket since those bucolic days, though the pace of the street is leisurely by central London standards. A couple of shops, in particular, deserve mention: the branch of *Patisserie Valerie*, at no. 105, was previously *Maison Sagne*, another patisserie, founded in 1921 by a Swiss pastry-cook, and the original mock-Pompeian frescoes that adorned it when it was founded remain; Daunt, a purpose-built bookshop from 1910, at no. 83, specializes in travel books, and has a lovely, long, galleried hall at the back, with a pitched roof of stained glass.

St James's Church, Spanish Place

22 George St • Mon–Fri 7am–7pm, Sat 10am–7pm, Sun 8am–8pm • ☎ 020 7935 0943, ⓦ sjrcc.org.uk • ⊖ Bond Street or Baker Street

Despite its name, **St James's Church, Spanish Place,** is actually tucked away on neighbouring George Street, just off Marylebone High Street. A Catholic chapel was built here in 1791 thanks to the efforts of the chaplain at the Spanish embassy, though the present neo-Gothic building dates from 1890. Designed in a mixture of English and French Gothic, the interior is surprisingly large and richly furnished, from the white marble and alabaster pulpit to the richly gilded heptagonal apse. The Spanish connection continues to this day: Spanish royal heraldry features in the rose window, and there are even two seats reserved for the royals, denoted by built-in gilt crowns high above the choir stalls.

WALLACE COLLECTION (P.92) >

Wallace Collection

Manchester Square • Daily 10am–5pm • Free • ☎ 020 7563 9500, ⊕ wallacecollection.org • ⊖ Bond Street

It comes as a great surprise to find the miniature eighteenth-century French chateau of Hertford House in the quiet Georgian streets just to the north of busy Oxford Street. Even more remarkable is the house's splendid **Wallace Collection** within, a public museum and art gallery combined, which boasts paintings by Titian, Rembrandt and Velázquez, the finest museum collection of Sèvres porcelain in the world and one of the finest displays of Boulle marquetry furniture, too. The collection was originally bequeathed to the nation in 1897 by the widow of Richard Wallace, an art collector and the illegitimate son of the fourth Marquess of Hertford. The museum has preserved the feel of a grand stately home, an old-fashioned institution with exhibits piled high in glass cabinets and paintings covering every inch of wall space. However, it's the combined effect of the exhibits set amid superbly restored eighteenth-century period fittings – and a massive **armoury** – that makes the place so remarkable. Labelling is deliberately terse, so as not to detract from the aristocratic ambience, but there are information cards in each room, free highlights tours most days (11.30am & 2.30pm) and themed audioguides available (for a fee).

Ground floor

The ground-floor rooms begin with the **Front State Room**, to the right as you enter, where the walls are hung with several fetching portraits by Reynolds, and Lawrence's typically sensuous portrayal of the author and society beauty, the Countess of Blessington, which went down a storm at the Royal Academy in 1822. The decor of the **Back State Room** is a riot of Rococo, and houses the cream of the house's gaudily spectacular Sèvres porcelain. Centre stage is a period copy of Louis XV's desk, which was the most expensive piece of eighteenth-century French furniture ever made. On the other side of the adjacent Dining Room, in the **Billiard Room**, you'll find an impressive display of outrageous, gilded oak and ebony Boulle marquetry furniture. From the Dining Room, with its Canalettos, you can enter the covered courtyard, home to *The Wallace Restaurant* (Sun–Thurs 10am–5pm, Fri & Sat 10am–11pm), and head down the stairs to the temporary exhibition galleries and the **Conservation Gallery** where folk of all ages can try on some medieval armour.

Back on the ground floor, the **Sixteenth-Century Gallery** displays a wide variety of works ranging from *pietre dure*, bronze and majolica to Limoges porcelain and Venetian glass. In the **Smoking Room**, a small alcove at the far end survives to give an idea of the effect of the original Minton-tiled decor Wallace chose for this room. The next three rooms house the extensive **European Armoury** bought *en bloc* by Wallace around the time of the Franco-Prussian War (it was in recognition of the humanitarian assistance Wallace provided in Paris during that war that he received his baronetcy). A fourth room houses the **Oriental Armoury**, collected by the fourth Marquess of Hertford, including one of the most important Sikh treasures in Britain, the sword of Ranjit Singh (1780–1839).

First floor

The main staircase, with its incredible Parisian wrought-iron balustrade and its gilded, fluted columns, is overlooked by **Boucher**'s sumptuous mythological scenes. In the gloriously camp pink **Boudoir**, off the landing and conservatory, you'll find Reynolds' doe-eyed moppets, while the adjacent passageway boasts an unbelievably rich display of gold snuff boxes and miniatures. The **Study** features more Sèvres porcelain, Greuze's soft-focus studies of kids and a lovely portrait by Elisabeth Vigée-Lebrun, one of the most successful portraitists of pre-Revolutionary France. Next door, in the sky-blue **Oval Drawing Room**, one of Fragonard's coquettes flaunts herself to a smitten beau in *The Swing*, alongside more Boucher nudes – the soft porn of the *ancien régime*.

In addition to all the French finery, a good collection of Dutch paintings hangs in the **East Galleries**, including de Hooch's *Women Peeling Apples*, oil sketches by Rubens and landscapes by Ruisdael, Hobbema and Cuyp. On the opposite side of the house, the **West Galleries** feature works by the British landscape artist Richard Parkes Bonington and Delacroix, his great friend and admirer.

Great Gallery

Finally, you reach the largest room in the house, the **Great Gallery**, reopened in 2014 after an eighteen-month refurbishment and wonderfully lit thanks to its new glass ceiling. Specifically built by Wallace to display his finest paintings, the gallery includes works by Murillo and Poussin, several vast Van Dyck portraits, Rubens' *Rainbow Landscape* and **Frans Hals**' *Laughing Cavalier*. Here, too, are *Perseus and Andromeda*, a late work by **Titian**, and **Velázquez**'s *Lady with a Fan*. At one end of the room are three portraits of the actress Mary Robinson as Perdita: one by Romney, one by Reynolds and, best of the lot, **Gainsborough**'s deceptively innocent portrayal, in which she insouciantly holds a miniature of her lover, the 19-year-old Prince of Wales (later George IV), who is portrayed in a flattering full-length portrait by Lawrence.

Baker Street and Marylebone Road

Running north–south through Marylebone, **Baker Street** is a fairly nondescript one-way highway. Despite its unprepossessing nature, its associations with the fictional detective Sherlock Holmes are, naturally, fully exploited. At the northern edge of Marylebone, Baker Street is bisected by the six-lane highway of **Marylebone Road**. Built as the New Road in the 1750s, to provide London with its first bypass, it remains one of London's major traffic arteries, and is no place for a casual stroll. There are, however, a couple of minor sights, such as **St Marylebone Church** and the **Royal Academy of Music**, and one major tourist trap, **Madame Tussauds**, that are all an easy stroll from Baker Street tube.

4

Madame Tussauds

Marylebone Rd • Sept–June Mon–Fri 9.30am–5.30pm, Sat & Sun 9am–6pm; July, August, Christmas & Easter daily 8.30am–7pm • £33, under-16s £28.80 • ☎ 0871 894 3000, ⓦ madametussauds.com • ⊖ Baker Street

The wax models at **Madame Tussauds** have been pulling in the crowds ever since the good lady arrived from France in 1802 bearing the sculpted heads of guillotined aristocrats (she was lucky to escape the same fate – her uncle, who started the family business, was less fortunate). The entrance fee might be extortionate and the likenesses dubious, but some of London's biggest queues form here – to avoid joining them (and to save up to 40 percent on the door price), book online, or whizz round after 5pm for half-price.

There are **photo opportunities** galore in the first few sections, which are peppered with contemporary celebrities from the BBC to Bollywood. Look out for the diminutive Madame Tussaud herself, and the oldest wax model, Madame du Barry, Louis XV's mistress.

The interactive **Star Wars** experience was launched in 2015, featuring sixteen of the characters and eleven iconic scenes from the movies, allowing you to take a seat next to Chewbacca in the Millenium Falcon, visit Jabba the Hutt and the captive Princess Leia in Jabba's throne room or remind yourself just how bad the prequel movies were by stepping into scenes from Episodes I and III.

Tussauds also features the **Spirit of London**, an irreverent five-minute romp through the history of London in a miniaturized taxicab.

Sherlock Holmes Museum

239 Baker St • Daily 9.30am–6pm • £10, under-16s £8 • ☎ 020 7224 3688, ⓦ sherlock-holmes.co.uk • ⊖ Baker Street

Baker Street, which cuts across Marylebone Road, is synonymous with London's languid super-sleuth, Sherlock Holmes, who lived at no. 221b. The detective's address was always fictional, although the most likely inspiration was, in fact, no. 21, at the south end of the street. However, the statue of Holmes's creator, Arthur Conan Doyle, is at the north end of the street, outside Baker Street tube, round the corner from the

MARYLEBONE STATION

Probably London's most discreet train terminal, **Marylebone Station** is hidden in the backstreets north of Marylebone Road on Melcombe Place, where a delicate and extremely elegant wrought-iron canopy links the station to the former *Great Central Hotel* (now *The Landmark*). Opened in 1899, Marylebone was the last and most modest of the Victorian terminals, originally intended to be the terminal for the Channel tunnel of the 1880s, a scheme abandoned after only a mile or so of digging, when Queen Victoria got nervous about foreign invasions. The station enjoyed a brief moment of fame after appearing in the opening sequence of The Beatles film *A Hard Day's Night* and now serves the Birmingham and Buckinghamshire commuter belt.

Sherlock Holmes Museum, at no. 239 (the sign on the door says 221b). Unashamedly touristy – you can have your photo taken in a deerstalker – the museum is nevertheless a competent exercise in period reconstruction, stuffed full of Victoriana and life-size models of characters from the books.

St Marylebone Church

Marylebone Rd • Daily 9am–5pm • ☎ 020 7935 7315, ⓦ stmarylebone.org • ⊖ Baker Street or Regent's Park

St Marylebone Church, its beehive cupola-topped tower visible from Marylebone High Street, was consecrated in 1817, and is a bold construction for a parish church, complete with eight Corinthian columns lining the grand portico. It was at this church that prominent Victorian poet **Elizabeth Barrett** and one of her admirers, writer and fellow poet **Robert Browning,** were secretly married in 1846. After the ceremony Elizabeth – six years older than Robert, an invalid, morphine addict and virtual prisoner in her father's house on nearby Wimpole Street – returned home and acted as if nothing had happened. A week later the couple eloped to Italy, where they spent most of their married life (the whole affair is portrayed in a play and two subsequent films, *The Barretts of Wimpole Street*, the 1957 production of which features the church itself). There's a small chapel in the church crypt, which was a burial ground until 1853, and not opened for public use until 1987, after an extensive renovation and the reburial of its cadaverous occupants. There's a craft, clothing and textile market in the church gardens every Saturday (11am–5pm).

Royal Academy of Music

Marylebone Rd • Mon–Fri 11.30am–5.30pm, Sat noon–4pm, closed Dec • Free • ☎ 020 7873 7443, ⓦ ram.ac.uk • ⊖ Baker Street or Regent's Park

On the other side of Marylebone Road from St Marylebone Church stands the **Royal Academy of Music**, which was founded in 1823 and has taught the likes of Arthur Sullivan, Harrison Birtwistle, Dennis Brain, Evelyn Glennie, Elton John, Michael Nyman and Simon Rattle. As well as putting on free lunchtime and evening concerts, the academy houses a small **museum** at the corner of Marylebone Road and York Gate. Temporary exhibitions, a short history of the academy and a shop are on the ground floor, while the Strings Gallery on the first floor, includes a world-class collection of Cremonese violins, several by Stradivari. The exhibition on the second floor in the Piano Gallery follows the development of the grand piano in England and gives you a peek into the resident luthier's workshop. Listening-posts on each floor allow you to experience the instruments in live performance.

Soho and Fitzrovia

Bounded by Regent Street to the west, Oxford Street to the north and Charing Cross Road to the east, Soho is very much the heart of the West End. It was the city's premier red-light district for centuries and retains an unorthodox and slightly raffish air that's unique for central London. It has an immigrant history as rich as that of the East End and a louche nightlife that has attracted writers and revellers of every sexual persuasion since the eighteenth century. Conventional sights in Soho are few and far between, yet there's probably more street life here than anywhere else in the city centre. Most folk head to Soho to go to the cinema or theatre, and to have a drink or a bite to eat in the innumerable bars, cafés and restaurants that pepper the tiny area and Fitzrovia, the quieter Soho spillover, north of Oxford Street.

5

Soho

Soho's historic reputation for tolerance made it an obvious place of refuge from dour, postwar Britain. **Jazz** and skiffle proliferated in the 1950s, folk and **rock** in the 1960s, and punk at the end of the 1970s. London's artistic cliques still gather here and the **media**, film and advertising industries have a strong presence. The area's most recent transformation has seen it become London's most high-profile gay quarter, especially around **Old Compton Street**. The attraction, though, remains in the unique mix of people who drift through Soho. There's nowhere else in the city where such diverse slices of London come face to face: businessmen, drunks, theatregoers, fashion victims, market-stallholders, pimps, prostitutes and politicians. Take it all in, and enjoy – for better or worse, most of London is not like this.

Leicester Square

Most adult Londoners tend to avoid **Leicester Square**, a short hop east of Piccadilly Circus, unless they're heading for one of the cinemas. In the eighteenth century, this once pleasant leafy square was home to the fashionable "Leicester House set", headed by successive Hanoverian princes of Wales who didn't get on with their fathers at St James's. Nowadays it attracts a hectic mix of tourists, day-trippers, cinemagoers, buskers and, especially at weekends, drunken groups of teenagers and stag- and hen-do parties. With its uninspired selection of chain restaurants and bars, Leicester Square resembles a scaled-up version of city centres across the country and remains an unfulfilling place. On sunny days the central, scrappy lawn, surrounding a statue of Shakespeare, makes a convenient place for eating lunch outside if you're touring the area but, like the rest of the square, it would be so much more inviting if some imagination were used in its make-up.

The square has been an **entertainment zone** since the mid-nineteenth century, when it boasted Turkish baths and music halls such as the grandiose Empire, now a huge cinema and, close by, the Hippodrome – designed by Frank Matcham in 1900 – the UK's biggest casino and one of three now on the square. Purpose-built movie houses moved in during the 1930s, a golden age evoked by the sleek black lines of the Odeon on the east side, a favourite for red-carpet premieres, and maintain their grip on the area, though newer arrivals, like M&Ms World, help to lower the tone.

Notre-Dame de France

5 Leicester Place • Daily 9am–9pm • Free • ☎ 020 7437 9363, ⓦ ndfchurch.org • ⊖ Leicester Square

One little-known sight, north of Leicester Square, is the modern Catholic church of **Notre-Dame de France**, heralded by an entrance flanked by two pillars decorated with biblical reliefs. The main point of interest within the unusual circular interior is the Chapelle de la Vierge Marie, which contains a series of simple frescoes of the Annunciation, Crucifixion and Assumption by Jean Cocteau from 1960 and an altar mosaic of the Nativity by Boris Anrep.

Chinatown

Hemmed in between Leicester Square and Shaftesbury Avenue, **Chinatown**'s self-contained jumble of **shops**, **cafés** and **restaurants** makes up one of London's most distinct ethnic enclaves. Only a minority of the capital's Chinese live in the three small blocks of Chinatown, with its ersatz touches – telephone kiosks rigged out as pagodas

---

SOHO HIGHLIGHTS

Bar Italia This tiny Soho institution is the perfect place for a 2am espresso. See p.369
Cecil Court bookshops Discover specialist bookshops in this Victorian alleyway. See p.424
The French House Rub shoulders with literary greats in this bijou French bar. See p.387
Ronnie Scott's Tap your foot to the world's best saxophonists and scatters. See p.402
Society Club This bohemian bookshop/gallery will transport you to another era. See p.430

SOHO & FITZROVIA

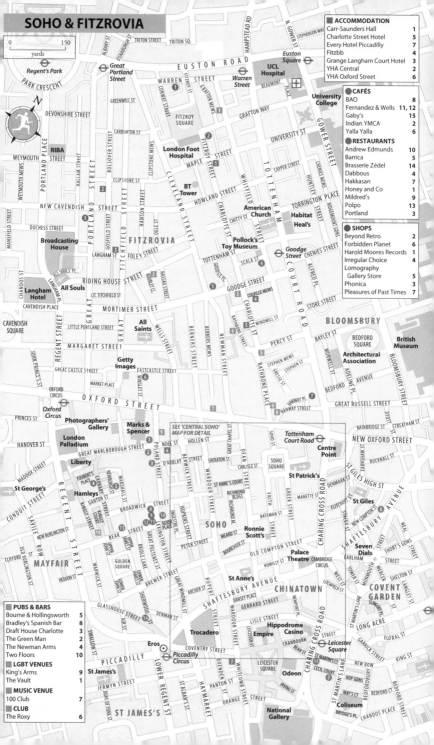

0   150
yards

SEE 'CENTRAL SOHO'
MAP FOR DETAIL

5

SOHO'S WHO'S WHO

When **Soho** – named after the cry that resounded through the district when it was a popular place for hunting hares – was built over in the seventeenth century, its streets were among the most sought-after addresses in the capital. Princes, dukes and earls built their mansions around Soho and Leicester squares, which became the centre of high-society nightlife, epitomized by the wild masquerades organized by Viennese prima donna Theresa Cornelys (who had a daughter by Casanova), which drew "a riotous assembly of fashionable people of both sexes", a traffic jam of hackney carriages and a huge crowd of onlookers. By the end of the eighteenth century, however, the party was over, the rich moved west, and Soho began its inexorable descent into poverty and overcrowding. Even before the last aristocrats left, Soho had become one of the city's main cultural melting pots: French Huguenots moved in followed by Italians, Irish, Jews and eventually the Chinese.

For several centuries, Soho has also been a favourite haunt of the capital's creative bohos, **literati** and rebels. It was at Soho's *Turk's Head* coffee shop, in 1764, that Joshua Reynolds founded "The Club", to give Dr Johnson unlimited opportunities for talking. Thomas de Quincey turned up in 1802, and was saved from starvation by a local prostitute, an incident later recalled in his *Confessions of an English Opium Eater*. Wagner arrived destitute in 1839, Marx lived in poverty here after the failure of the 1848 revolution, and Rimbaud and Verlaine pitched up after the fall of the Paris Commune in 1871. "Such noise and chaos. Such magnificent and terrible abandon. It's like stepping into the future", wrote Verlaine.

and formal entrances or *paifang* – yet the area remains a focus for the community, a place to do business or the weekly shopping, celebrate a wedding or just meet up on Sundays for dim sum. Most Londoners come to Chinatown simply to eat, but if the mood takes you, you can easily while away several hours sorting through the Chinese trinkets, ceramics and ornaments in the various arts and crafts shops, or amassing the perfect ingredients for a demon stir-fry. It's a pleasant spot for a wander, with increased pedestrianization in recent years helping to enhance the appeal beyond the completely traffic-free main drag, Gerrard Street.

The first Chinese immigrants were sailors who arrived here from the late eighteenth century onwards on the ships of the East India Company. London's first Chinatown grew up around the docks at Limehouse and eventually boasted over thirty Chinese shops and restaurants. Predominantly male, this closed community achieved a quasi-mythical status in Edwardian minds as a hotbed of criminal dives and opium dens, a reputation exploited in Sax Rohmer's novels (later made into films) featuring the evil Doctor Fu Manchu. Wartime bomb damage, postwar demolition and protectionist union laws all but destroyed Limehouse Chinatown. However, following the Communist takeover in China, a new wave of Chinese refugees began to buy up cheap property around **Gerrard Street**, eventually establishing the nucleus of today's Chinatown. For a calendar of events taking place in Chinatown and comprehensive eating and drinking listings for the area see ⓦchinatownlondon.org.

Charing Cross Road

Created in the 1880s as part of the Victorians' slum clearance drive, **Charing Cross Road** has always been liberally peppered with **bookshops**. One of the first to open here, in 1906, was **Foyles**, a vast book emporium, now at no. 107 following a successful refit in 2014, where George Bernard Shaw, Walt Disney and Arthur Conan Doyle were all once regular customers. Once famous for its antiquated system for selling books that required customers to queue three times, it's now a much more vibrant, if less idiosyncratic place, with a busy café and regular live jazz and classical music gigs.

One of the nicest places for secondhand-book browsing is **Cecil Court**, connecting the southern end of Charing Cross Road and St Martin's Lane. This short, civilized, late-Victorian paved alley boasts specialist bookshops such as Goldsboro Books and

5

Watkins Books, home of the occult, plus various antiquarian dealers selling modern first editions, old theatre posters, coins and notes, cigarette cards, maps and children's books.

The northern end of Charing Cross Road, and the corner of Soho that it runs along, is currently the site of one of the West End's most dramatic redevelopments in decades, to include a new theatre and public square, all propelled by the Crossrail project (see box, p.105).

Shaftesbury Avenue

Sweeping through the southern part of Soho, the gentle curve of **Shaftesbury Avenue** is the heart of the West End's **Theatreland**, with theatres and cinemas along its entire length. Built in the 1870s, ostensibly to relieve traffic congestion but with the dual purpose of destroying the slums that lay in its path, the street was ironically named after Lord Shaftesbury, whose life had been spent trying to help the likes of those dispossessed by the road. The most impressive theatre architecturally is the grandiose terracotta **Palace Theatre**, overlooking Cambridge Circus, which opened in 1891 as the Royal English Opera House; it folded after just one year, and, since the 1920s, has mostly hosted musicals. Just off Cambridge Circus, hidden away down West Street, is St Martin's Theatre, where Agatha Christie's record-breaking murder-mystery *The Mousetrap* has been on nonstop since 1952, notching up over 25,000 performances.

Old Compton Street

If Soho had an official main drag, it would be **Old Compton Street**, which runs parallel with Shaftesbury Avenue, and forms the heart of Central Soho. The shops, boutiques and cafés in the narrow surrounding streets are typical of the area and a good barometer of the latest Soho fads. Several places have survived the vicissitudes of fashion, including the original *Patisserie Valerie*, opened by the Belgian-born Madame Valerie in 1926, the Algerian Coffee Store, The Vintage House and Gerry's, both off-licences, and I Camisa & Son, an Italian deli where they've been slicing Soho's salami since 1961.

The liberal atmosphere of Soho has made it a permanent fixture on the **gay scene** since the last century: gay servicemen frequented the *Golden Lion*, on Dean Street, from World War II until the end of National Service, while a succession of gay artists found refuge here during the 1950s and 1960s. Nowadays the scene is much more upfront, with every type of gay business jostling for position on and off Old Compton Street.

Greek Street

The streets off Old Compton Street are lined with Soho institutions past and present, starting in the east with **Greek Street**, named after the Greek church that once stood nearby. South of Old Compton Street, at no. 28, stands *Maison Bertaux*, London's oldest French patisserie, founded in 1871. The *Coach and Horses*, one door down at

---

THE SWISS CORNER

For no particularly good reason, the area in the northwest corner of Leicester Square has a Swiss theme to it. The impetus was the building of the Swiss Centre – a sort of trade centre-cum-tourist office – in 1968 and the renaming of the area as Swiss Court. After forty years of alpine theming, the much unloved Swiss Centre was finally demolished in 2008, the space now occupied by M&M's World, leaving behind a slightly surreal **Swiss glockenspiel**. This tall steel structure is topped by a Swiss railway clock and features a glass drum decorated with the 26 cantonal flags which lower on the hour (Mon–Fri noon & 5–8pm, Sat & Sun 2–4pm), to sound a 27-bell carillon, thus revealing a procession of Helvetic cows and peasants making their way up the mountain.

5

no. 29, was lorded over for years by the boozy gang of writer Jeffrey Bernard, painter Francis Bacon and jazz man George Melly, as well as the staff of the satirical magazine, *Private Eye*.

Frith Street

Frith Street is home to **Ronnie Scott's**, London's longest-running jazz club, founded in 1958 and still pulling in the big names. Opposite is *Bar Italia*, a tiny, quintessentially Italian café established in 1949, whose late-night hours make it a clubbers' favourite. It was in this building, appropriately enough for such a media-saturated area, that **John Logie Baird** made the world's first public television transmission in 1926. Next door, a plaque recalls that the 7-year-old Mozart stayed here in 1763, having wowed George III and London society.

Soho Square

Soho Square is one of the few patches of green amid the neighbourhood's labyrinth of streets and alleys. It began life as a smart address, surrounded by the houses of the nobility and centred on an elaborate fountain topped by a statue of Charles II. Charles survives, if a little worse for wear, on one of the pathways, but the fountain is now an octagonal, mock-Tudor garden shed. As for the buildings around the square, they are a typical Soho mix: 20th Century-Fox; the Victorian Hospital for Sick Women (now the Soho Centre, a walk-in health clinic); the British Board of Film Classification (the national guardians of film censorship) and two red-brick churches, **St Patrick's**, the first Catholic church built in England after the Reformation and the **Église Protestante**, the sole survivor of London's once numerous Huguenot churches.

Dean Street

One block west of Frith Street runs **Dean Street**, once home to *The Colony Room*, a private drinking club that was at the heart of Soho's postwar bohemian scene, and still home to the members-only *Groucho Club* at no. 45, where today's literati and media types preen themselves. Nearby, at no. 49, *The French House* is an open-to-all bohemian landmark, where the most popular drink is Ricard, and they only serve beer in halves.

SOHO ON RECORD

Soho has been a popular meeting point for the capital's up-and-coming pop stars since the late 1950s, when the likes of Cliff Richard, Tommy Steele and Adam Faith used to hang out at the **2 i's coffee bar**, 59 Old Compton St, and perform at the rock'n'roll club in the basement. Marc Bolan, whose parents ran a market stall on Berwick Street, also worked at the café in the early 1960s. The Rolling Stones first met in a pub on Broadwick Street in early 1962 and, by the mid-1960s, were playing Soho's premier rock venue, the **Marquee**, originally at 90 Wardour St. David Bowie performed there (as David Jones) in 1965, Pink Floyd played their "Spontaneous Underground" sessions the following year, Led Zeppelin had their first London gig there in 1968 and Phil Collins worked for some time as a cloakroom attendant.

In November 1975, The Sex Pistols played their first gig at **St Martin's School of Art** (now Foyles) on Charing Cross Road, during which Sid Vicious (in the audience rather than the band, at the time) made his contribution to dance history when he began to "pogo". The classic punk venue, however, was the **100 Club** on Oxford Street, where the Pistols, The Clash, Siouxsie, The Damned and The Vibrators all played. The Pistols used to rehearse in the studios on **Denmark Street**, London's own version of New York's Tin Pan Alley, off Charing Cross Road (still lined with music shops). The Rolling Stones, The Kinks and Genesis all recorded songs there, and Elton John got his first job at one of the street's music publishers in 1963. There's a whiff of Soho's pop music past still in **Berwick Street**, pictured on the cover of the Oasis album *(What's The Story) Morning Glory* and where a cluster of independent and secondhand record shops survive.

CENTRAL SOHO & CHINATOWN

● CAFÉS
Bar Italia	5
Maison Bertaux	8
Patisserie Valerie	7

● RESTAURANTS
Bar Shu	9
Bocca di Lupo	11
Ceviche	8
Four Seasons	13
Mr Kong	15
New World	10
The Palomar	14
Pizza Pilgrims	1
Rasa Sayang	12
Stockpot	4
Tonkotsu	6
Yauatcha	2

● SHOPS
Absolute Vintage	2
Algerian Coffee Stores	11
Any Amount of Books	16
Berwick Street Market	8
Foyles	7
Gerry's	12
Gosh!	9
I. Camisa & Son	13
Kokon to Zai	4
Loon Fung Supermarket	15
Paul A Young	3
Quinto	14
Reign Wear	5
Sister Ray	1
Society Club	6
The Vintage House	10

■ PUBS & BARS
The Blue Posts	28
The Dog & Duck	8
The French House	22
The Lyric	27
Phoenix Artist Club	9

■ MUSIC VENUES
Borderline	5
Jazz@Pizza Express	3
Ronnie Scott's	10

■ CLUB
Café de Paris	30

■ LGBT VENUES
The Admiral Duncan	16
Balans	13, 18
Circa	6
Comptons of Soho	21
Duke of Wellington	23
The Edge	2
Freedom	14
G-A-Y Bar	12
G-A-Y Late	4
Ku Bar	17, 29
Miabella	7
Muse Soho	11
Rupert Street	25
Shadow Lounge	29
She Soho	15
Star at Night	1
Titania	26
Village Soho	20
The Yard	24

■ ACCOMMODATION
Dean Street Townhouse	3
Hazlitt's	2
Nadler Soho	1
Z Hotel Soho	4

OXFORD STREET
NEW OXFORD ST
NOEL STREET
HOLLEN STREET
FAREHAM ST
GREAT CHAPEL ST
RATHBONE PL.
Tottenham Court Road
Centre Point
Église Protestante
SOHO ST.
DIADEM CT.
SHERATON ST.
DEAN STREET
CARLISLE STREET
Charles II
SOHO SQUARE
St Patrick's
SUTTON ROW
FALCONBERG MEWS
DENMARK PLACE
GOSLETT YARD
DENMARK ST
D'ARBLAY STREET
WARDOUR MEWS
PORTLAND MEWS
LIVONIA ST.
ST ANNE'S COURT
BROADWICK ST.
WARDOUR STREET
FLAXMAN
RICHMOND BLDGS
RICHMOND MEWS
Soho Theatre
FRITH STREET
BATEMAN'S BUILDINGS
GREEK STREET
MANETTE ST.
CHARING CROSS ROAD
Foyles
FLITCROFT ST.
PHOENIX ST.
BROADWICK ST.
BERWICK STREET
DUCK LANE
KEMP'S CT.
INGESTRE PLACE
SILVER PL.
HOPKINS STREET
TYLER'S COURT
Berwick Street Market
SOHO
MEARD STREET
BATEMAN ST.
PETER STREET
GREEN COURT
WALKER'S COURT
BOURCHIER STREET
Ronnie Scott's
OLD COMPTON STREET
MOOR STREET
BREWER STREET
TISBURY COURT
WINNETT ST.
ROMILLY STREET
Palace Theatre
CAMBRIDGE CIRCUS
WEST ST.
St Anne's
Curzon Cinema
SMITH'S CT.
GREAT WINDMILL STREET
HAM YARD
ARCHER ST.
RUPERT STREET
SHAFTESBURY AVENUE
MACCLESFIELD ST.
DANSEY PLACE
HORSE & DOLPHIN YD
GERRARD PL.
NEWPORT PLACE
LITCHFIELD ST.
CHARING CROSS ROAD
GERRARD STREET
CHINATOWN
NEWPORT COURT
GREAT NEWPORT ST
DENMAN ST.
WARDOUR STREET
RUPERT COURT
LISLE STREET
Prince Charles Cinema
LITTLE NEWPORT ST.
LEICESTER COURT
GREAT WINDMILL ST.
HAYMARKET
Trocadero
LEICESTER STREET
Empire
LEICESTER PLACE
Notre-Dame de France
Hippodrome Casino
STREET
Leicester Square
Piccadilly Circus
COVENTRY STREET
Comedy Store
OXENDON ST.
SWISS CT.
Glockenspiel
LEICESTER SQUARE
BEAR STREET
CRANBOURN
Odeon
ST MARTIN'S CT.

0   100
yards

N

5

Opened by a German as the *York Minster* pub, it was bought by a Belgian, Victor Berlemont, when the German owner was deported in 1914, and transformed into a French émigré haunt. Dylan Thomas and Brendan Behan were both regulars, and during World War II it was frequented by de Gaulle and the Free French forces.

Soho's most famous Jewish immigrant was **Karl Marx**, who in 1850 moved into two "evil, frightful rooms" on the top floor of no. 28, with his wife and maid (both of whom were pregnant by him) and four children, having been evicted from his first two addresses for failing to pay the rent.

Wardour Street

A kind of dividing line between the busier eastern half of Soho and the marginally quieter western zone, much of **Wardour Street** is given over to the media industry, though it's sprinkled with a few pubs and is stacked with restaurants at the southern end. It's also one of the few streets in Soho consistently plagued by traffic. Just north of Shaftesbury Avenue are **St Anne's Churchyard Gardens** (April–Oct 10am–6pm, Nov–March 10am–4pm), a small park laid out in front of **St Anne's Church**, a largely modern structure. The first church to stand on this spot was consecrated in 1686 but nothing of the original structure remains, its nineteenth-century tower, which replaced the original tower in 1803, the only section that survived a Second World War bombing raid.

Brewer Street

West of Wardour Street, along **Brewer Street**, the sex industry has a long history and retains a foothold. It was at the **Windmill Theatre**, on nearby Great Windmill Street, that the famous "Revuedeville" shows, featuring static nude performers (movement was strictly forbidden by the censor), were first staged in the 1930s. The shows continued pretty much uninterrupted right through World War II – the subject of the 2005 film *Mrs Henderson Presents* – eventually closing in 1964. Meanwhile, back on Brewer Street, the **Raymond Revuebar** opened in 1952 as a "World Centre of Erotic Entertainment", finally succumbing, in 2004, to competition from the slick **lap-dancing clubs** that now prevail.

SOHO VICE

Prostitution is nothing new to Soho. Way back in the seventeenth and eighteenth centuries, prince and prole alike used to come here (and to Covent Garden) for paid sex. Several prominent courtesans were residents of Soho, their profession recorded as "player and mistress to several persons", or, lower down on the social scale, "generally slut and drunkard; occasionally whore and thief". *Hooper's Hotel*, a high-class Soho brothel frequented by the Prince of Wales, even got a mention in the popular, late eighteenth-century book *The Mysteries of Flagellation*. By Victorian times, the area was described as "a reeking home of filthy vice", where "the grosser immorality flourishes unabashed from every age downwards to mere children". And it was in Soho that Prime Minister Gladstone used to conduct his crusade to save prostitutes – managing "to combine his missionary meddling with a keen appreciation of a pretty face", as one perceptive critic observed.

By World War II, **organized gangs**, like the notorious Messina Brothers from Malta, controlled a huge vice empire in Soho, later taken over by one of their erstwhile henchmen, Bernie Silver, Soho's self-styled "Godfather". In the 1960s and 1970s, the sex trade threatened to take over the whole of Soho, aided and abetted by the police themselves, who were involved in a massive protection racket. The complicity between the gangs and the police was finally exposed in 1976, when ten top-ranking Scotland Yard officers were charged with bribery and corruption on a massive scale and sentenced to prison for up to twelve years (Silver himself had been put inside in 1974). The combined efforts of the Soho Society and Westminster Council have enormously reduced the number of sex establishments, but, with the rise of the lap-dancing club, the area's vice days are not quite over yet.

ART AND HERESY IN SOHO

The streets around Poland Street have more than their fair share of artistic and heretical associations. A blue plaque at 74 Broadwick St records that **William Blake** was born there in 1757, above his father's hosiery shop; it's also where, from the age of 9, he had visions of "messengers from heaven, daily and nightly". He opened a print shop of his own next door to the family home, and later moved nearby to 28 Poland St, where he lived six years with his "beloved Kate" and wrote perhaps his most profound work, *The Marriage of Heaven and Hell*, among other poems. Poland Street was also **Shelley**'s first halt after having been kicked out of Oxford in 1811 for distributing *The Necessity of Atheism*, and **Canaletto** ran a studio just south on Beak Street for a couple of years while he sat out the Seven Years War in exile in London. And it was in the *Old King's Arms* pub on Poland Street in 1781 that the **Ancient Order of Druids** was revived.

Berwick Street

Ⓦ berwickstreetlondon.co.uk • ⊖ Piccadilly Circus

Pop down Walker's Court, a tiny alley off Brewer Street, past the triple-X-rated film shops, and you come out into **Berwick Street** where the unlikely sight of one of the capital's traditional fruit and veg markets greets you (see p.433). The street itself is no beauty spot but the barrow displays are works of art in themselves. Here and nearby you'll find some of London's best specialist record shops like Sister Ray (see p.432) and Reckless Records, both further up Berwick Street, and Sounds of the Universe, round the corner on Broadwick Street.

Broadwick Street

It was a water pump on **Broadwick Street** that caused the deaths of some five hundred Soho residents in the **cholera epidemic** of 1854. Dr John Snow, Queen Victoria's obstetrician, traced the outbreak to the pump, thereby proving that the disease was waterborne rather than airborne, as previously thought. No one believed him, however, until he removed the pump handle and effectively stopped the epidemic. The original pump stood outside the pub now called the *John Snow*, on which there's a commemorative plaque and an easily missed red-granite kerbstone.

Carnaby Street

Until the 1950s, **Carnaby Street** was a backstreet on Soho's western fringe, occupied, for the most part, by sweatshop tailors who made up the suits for nearby Savile Row in Mayfair. Then, in 1954, Bill Green opened a shop in neighbouring Newburgh Street, selling outrageous clothes to the gay men who were hanging out at the local baths. He was followed by **John Stephen**, a Glaswegian grocer's son, who opened His Clothes in Beak Street. In 1960, Stephen moved his operation to Carnaby Street and within a couple of years owned a string of trendy boutiques catering for the new market in flamboyant men's clothing, including the wonderfully named I Was Lord Kitchener's Valet. By 1964 – the year of the official birth of the Carnaby Street myth – Mods, West Indian Rude Boys and other "switched-on people", as the *Daily Telegraph* noted, had begun to hang out in Carnaby Street. By the time Mary Quant sold her first miniskirt here, the area had become the heart of London's **Swinging Sixties**, its street sign the capital's most popular postcard. A victim of its own hype, Carnaby Street quickly declined into an avenue of overpriced tack. Nowadays, it's pedestrianized and smart again, but dominated by chains – for any sign of contemporary London fashion, you need to go round the corner to **Fouberts Place**, **Newburgh Street** and **Kingly Court** or head over to east London. The relatively recent pedestrianization of parallel **Kingly Street** has injected some night-time energy into this corner of Soho, the punters spilling out onto the street from the restaurants and bars now filling its eastern side, including one of London's longest running blues bars at no. 20.

5

Photographers' Gallery

16–18 Ramillies St • Mon–Sat 10am–6pm, Thurs till 8pm, Sun 11.30am–6pm • Free • ☎ 020 7087 9300, ⓦ thephotographersgallery
.org.uk • ⊖ Oxford Circus

Established in 1971, the **Photographers' Gallery** was the first independent gallery
devoted to photography in London, and is now the city's largest public photographic
gallery. This former warehouse hosts three floors of exhibitions that change regularly
and are invariably worth a visit, as are the bookshop and café. There's also a **camera
obscura** on the third floor (Fri–Sun 11am–1pm).

Fitzrovia

Fitzrovia is the very much quieter northern extension of Soho, beyond Oxford Street.
Like its neighbour, it has a raffish, cosmopolitan history, attracting its fair share of
writers and bohemians over the last hundred years or so, including the
Pre-Raphaelites and members of the Bloomsbury Group. That said, it's a lot less edgy
than Soho, with just two real sights to visit – an ornate Victorian church on
Margaret Street and Pollock's Toy Museum – and one unavoidable landmark, the
former Post Office Tower.

All Saints, Margaret Street

Margaret St • Daily 7am–7pm • ⓦ allsaintsmargaretstreet.org.uk • ⊖ Oxford Circus

Few London churches are as atmospheric as **All Saints, Margaret Street**, built by
William Butterfield in the 1850s. Patterned brickwork characterizes the entire
ensemble of clergy house, choir school (Laurence Olivier sang here as a boy) and
church, set around a small courtyard entered from the street through a pointed
arch. The church interior – one of London's gloomiest – is best visited on a sunny
afternoon when the light pours in through the west window, illuminating the
fantastic polychrome marble and stone which decorates the place from floor to
ceiling. Several of the walls are also adorned with Pre-Raphaelite Minton-tile
paintings, the east window is a neo-Byzantine quasi-iconostasis with saintly images
nestling in gilded niches, and the elaborate pulpit is like the entire church in
miniature.

Charlotte Street and around

Fitzrovia's main street, **Charlotte Street** is lined with lively cafés and restaurants, as are
its neighbours **Percy Street**, **Goodge Street** and **Rathbone Street**. The real heyday of this
part of Fitzrovia was in the 1930s, when Percy Street, at the foot of Charlotte Street,
was home to the *Tour Eiffel*, where Wyndham Lewis and Ezra Pound launched the
Vorticist magazine *Blast* (the site is now occupied by *Bam-Bou*, a southeast Asian
restaurant). *L'Étoile*, further up Charlotte Street at no. 30, was patronized by the likes
of Dylan Thomas and T.S. Eliot, while it was above what is now *Wahaca* that Eliot,
John Berger and Christopher Isherwood used to meet at the Wednesday Club in the
1950s, by which time Fitzrovia was beginning to lose its rebellious edge. The same
crowd would get plastered in the nearby and still-standing *Fitzroy Tavern* – from which
the area got its sobriquet – along with rather more outrageous bohemians, like the
hard-drinking Nina Hamnett, the self-styled "Queen of Bohemia", who used to boast
that Modigliani once told her she had the best tits in Europe.

Pollock's Toy Museum

1 Scala St (entrance on Whitfield St) • Mon–Sat 10am–5pm • £6, concessions £5, children £3 • ☎ 020 7636 3452, ⓦ pollockstoys.com •
⊖ Goodge Street

Housed above a wonderful toy shop in the backstreets of Fitzrovia is the highly
atmospheric, doll's-house-like **Pollock's Toy Museum**. Its collections include a fine
example of the Victorian paper theatres popularized by Benjamin Pollock, who sold

CROSSRAIL

Near where Tottenham Court Road tube station used to be, there's now a very large hole in the ground – just one of several prominent sites across London marking the £15 billion **Crossrail** project. Aimed at relieving congestion on the tube, Crossrail will provide a super-fast method of travelling between the east and west of the city by digging a thirteen-mile long, deep-bore tunnel, reducing travel time between Heathrow Airport and Liverpool Street train station to just forty minutes. As well as the expansion at Tottenham Court Road, major new Crossrail stations are now emerging at Paddington, Bond Street, Farringdon, Liverpool Street, Whitechapel and Canary Wharf. The development around the new station at Tottenham Court Road alone is going to cost around £1 billion, and the first trains are due to run in 2018, with the whole line, stretching from Reading to the west of London and stations in Kent and Essex to the east, set to be operational in 2019. If you want to learn more about the project, visit ⓦ crossrail.co.uk

them under the slogan "a penny plain, two pence coloured". The other exhibits range from vintage teddy bears to Sooty and Sweep, and from Red Army soldiers to wax dolls, filling every nook and cranny of the museum's six tiny, rickety rooms and the stairs – be sure to look out for the dalmatian, Dismal Desmond.

Post Office Tower

Exploring Fitzrovia, it's impossible to ignore the looming presence of the former **Post Office Tower** (now officially known as the BT Tower), a glass-clad pylon on Cleveland Street, designed in the early 1960s by a team of bureaucrats in the Ministry of Works. The city's tallest building until the NatWest Tower (now Tower 42) topped it in 1981, it's still a prominent landmark north of the river. Sadly, after a bomb attack in 1971, the tower closed to the public, and the revolving restaurant followed in 1980.

Tottenham Court Road

It's been centuries since there was a stately mansion – the original Tottenham Court – at the northern end of **Tottenham Court Road**, which has consistently made a strong challenge for London's least prepossessing central shopping street. Considered the boundary between Fitzrovia and Bloomsbury, the northern end is today peppered with furniture-makers – the street's original vendors – from the upmarket Habitat and Heal's to cheap sofa outlets, while for decades the southern end has been dominated by a rash of stores flogging discounted electrical equipment. Several huge building projects are, however, set to completely transform this southern end of the street, along with the northern end of Charing Cross Road: the landmark Centre Point office tower, built in 1966 at the Oxford Street crossroads, is to be converted into luxury apartments (average price: £3.2 million) with a new public square and retail development built around its base; another new shopping complex is taking shape along the wide stretch of pavement at this end, dubbed Tottenham Court Walk by some marketing geniuses; while Tottenham Court Road tube station is undergoing one of the most ambitious expansions of the giant Crossrail project (see box above).

STREET PERFORMER IN COVENT GARDEN

Covent Garden and the Strand

Covent Garden's transformation from a workaday fruit and vegetable market into a fashionable *quartier* is one of the most miraculous and successful developments of the 1980s. More mainstream and commercial than neighbouring Soho, it's also a lot more popular thanks to the buskers, street entertainers and human statues that make the traffic-free Covent Garden Piazza an undeniably lively place to be. As its name suggests, the Strand, on the southern border of Covent Garden, once lay along the riverbank until the Victorians created the Embankment to shore up the banks of the Thames. One showpiece river palace, Somerset House, remains, its courtyard graced by a lovely fountain in summer, and its chambers home to the Courtauld Gallery's superb collection of Impressionist and Post-Impressionist paintings.

Covent Garden

Covent Garden has come full circle: what started out in the seventeenth century as London's first luxury neighbourhood is once more an aspirational place to live, work and shop. Boosted by buskers and street entertainers, the piazza is now one of London's major tourist attractions, and the streets to the north – in particular, Long Acre, Neal Street and Floral Street – are home to fashionable clothes and shoe shops.

Most visitors are happy enough simply to wander around watching the street life, having a coffee and doing a bit of shopping, but there are a couple of specific sights worth picking out. One of the old market buildings houses the enjoyable **London Transport Museum**, while another serves as the public foyer for the **Royal Opera House** and boasts a great roof terrace overlooking the piazza.

6

The piazza

Covent Garden's **piazza** – London's oldest planned square – was laid out in the 1630s, when the Earl of Bedford commissioned Inigo Jones to design a series of graceful Palladian-style arcades based on his design for the portico of the cathedral in the main square of Livorno, Tuscany. Initially it was a great success, its novelty value alone attracting a plutocratic clientele, but over time the tone of the place fell as the **market** (set up in the earl's back garden) expanded and theatres, coffee houses and brothels began to proliferate.

By the beginning of the nineteenth century, the market dominated the area, and so in the 1830s a proper market hall was built in the middle of the piazza in the Greek Revival style. A glass roof was added in the late Victorian era, but otherwise the building stayed unaltered until the market's closure in 1974, and only public protests averted yet another office development. Instead, the elegant market hall and its environs were restored to house shops, restaurants and arts-and-crafts stalls. In its early days, the area had an alternative hippy vibe, a legacy of the area's numerous squats. Nowadays, upmarket chain stores occupy much of the market hall and the arcades, with a huge Apple Store on the north side of the piazza, a sign of how far the area has come from its origins.

St Paul's Church

Covent Garden Piazza • Mon–Fri 8.30am–5pm, Sat times vary depending on events, Sun 9am–1pm • ☎ 020 7836 5222, ⓦ actorschurch.org • ⊖ Covent Garden or Leicester Square

Covent Garden piazza is overlooked from the west by the Tuscan portico of **St Paul's Church**. The Earl of Bedford allegedly told Inigo Jones to make St Paul's no fancier than a barn, to which the architect replied, "Sire, you shall have the handsomest barn in England." It's better known nowadays as the **Actors' Church**, and is filled with memorials to thespians from Noel Coward to Gracie Fields. The cobbles in front of the building (though the entrance is round the back) – where Eliza Doolittle was discovered selling violets by Henry Higgins in George Bernard Shaw's *Pygmalion* – are now a legalized venue for buskers and street performers, who must audition for a slot.

The neatly tended, bench-filled, fronded **churchyard gardens** squeezed up against the surrounding buildings on the Bedford Street side of the church provide a tranquil respite from the activity outside. In keeping with Covent Garden's street entertainment traditions, a **Punch and Judy Festival,** called May Fayre, is held in the gardens on the second Sunday in May.

London Transport Museum

Covent Garden Piazza • Daily 10am–6pm, Fri from 11am, last entry 5.15pm • Adults £16, concessions £13.50, under-18s free • ☎ 020 7379 6344 or for booking depot tours ☎ 020 7565 7298, ⓦ ltmuseum.co.uk • ⊖ Covent Garden

A former flower-market shed on the piazza's east side houses the ever-popular **London Transport Museum**. A sure-fire hit for families with kids, it's a must-see for any transport enthusiast, though restrictions of space mean that there are only a handful of large exhibits.

Still, the story of London's transport is a fascinating one – to follow it chronologically, start upstairs on Level 2, where you'll find a replica 1829 Shillibeer's Horse Omnibus, which provided the city's first regular **horse-bus** service, and a double-decker horse-drawn tram, introduced in the 1870s. Level 1 tells the story of the world's first underground system and contains a lovely 1920s Metropolitan Line carriage, fitted out in burgundy and green with pretty, drooping lamps.

Back on the ground floor, the museum's one double-decker electric **tram** is all that's left to pay tribute to the world's largest tram system, which was dismantled in 1952. Look out, too, for the first **tube** train, from the 1890s, whose lack of windows earned it the nickname "the padded cell". Most of the interactive stuff is aimed at kids, but visitors of all ages should check out the tube driver simulator.

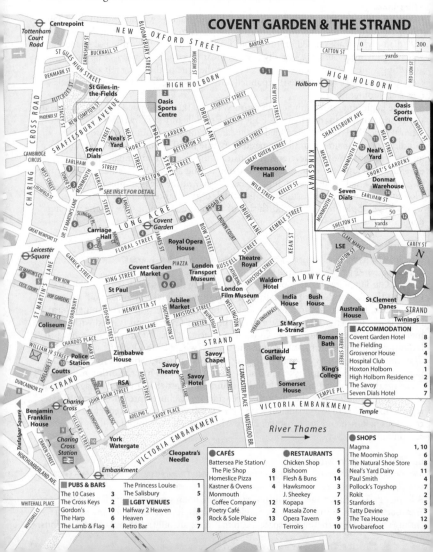

COVENT GARDEN & THE STRAND

■ ACCOMMODATION
Covent Garden Hotel	8
The Fielding	5
Grosvenor House	4
Hospital Club	3
Hoxton Holborn	2
High Holborn Residence	2
The Savoy	6
Seven Dials Hotel	7

■ SHOPS
Magma	1, 10
The Moomin Shop	6
The Natural Shoe Store	8
Neal's Yard Dairy	11
Paul Smith	4
Pollock's Toyshop	7
Rokit	2
Stanfords	3
Tatty Devine	3
The Tea House	9
Vivobarefoot	5

● CAFÉS
Battersea Pie Station/	
The Pie Shop	8
Homeslice Pizza	11
Kastner & Ovens	4
Monmouth	
Coffee Company	12
Poetry Café	2
Rock & Sole Plaice	13

● RESTAURANTS
Chicken Shop	1
Dishoom	6
Flesh & Buns	14
Hawksmoor	3
J. Sheekey	9
Kopapa	15
Masala Zone	5
Opera Tavern	12
Terroirs	10

■ PUBS & BARS
The 10 Cases	3
The Cross Keys	2
Gordon's	10
The Harp	6
The Lamb & Flag	4
The Princess Louise	1
The Salisbury	5

■ LGBT VENUES
Halfway 2 Heaven	8
Heaven	9
Retro Bar	7

COFFEE HOUSES AND BROTHELS

By the eighteenth century the piazza was known as "the great square of Venus", home to dozens of gambling dens, bawdy houses and so-called "bagnios". Some bagnios were plain Turkish baths, but most doubled as **brothels**, where courtesans stood in the window and, according to one contemporary, "in the most impudent manner invited passengers from the theatres into the houses".

London's most famous **coffee houses** were concentrated here, too, attracting writers such as Sheridan, Dryden and Aphra Behn. The rich and famous frequented places like the piazza's *Shakespeare's Head*, whose cook made the best turtle soup in town, and whose head waiter, John Harrison, was believed to be the author of the anonymously published "Who's Who of Whores", *Harris's List of Covent Garden Ladies*, which sold over a quarter of a million copies in its day.

The *Rose Tavern*, on Russell Street (immortalized in Hogarth's *Rake's Progress*), was one of the oldest brothels in Covent Garden – Pepys mentions "frigging with Doll Lane" at the *Rose* in his diary of 1667 – and specialized in "Posture Molls", who engaged in flagellation and striptease, and were deemed a cut above the average whore. Food was apparently excellent, too, and despite the frequent brawls, men of all classes, from royalty to ruffians, made their way there.

6

A good selection of London Transport's stylish **maps and posters** are usually on display, many commissioned from well-known artists, and you can buy copies at the shop on the way out. You can visit the reserve collection at the **Museum Depot** in Acton on one of the two annual open weekends, usually in March and September, or on one of the pre-booked guided tours which take place at least twice a month (more details on the website).

London Film Museum

45 Wellington St • Daily 10am–6pm, Sat till 7pm, last entry 1hr before close • Adults £14.50, concessions & under-16s £9.50, under-5s free • ☎ 020 7836 4913, Ⓦ londonfilmmuseum.com • ⊖ Covent Garden

Since early 2014 the **London Film Museum** has been dominated by the Bond in Motion exhibition, a collection of many of the original vehicles featured in the **James Bond** films, including the amphibious Lotus Esprit S1 from *The Spy Who Loved Me* and the most famous Bond car of them all, the classic Aston Martin DB5. Also on display are boats, motorbikes, sleds and aircraft while clips from the films accompany the hardware and there's plenty of other memorabilia, original props and background information, making this a must for Bond fans and a decent bit of fun for anyone who has even just a small soft spot for the movies.

Bow Street

Covent Garden's dubious reputation was no doubt behind the opening of **Bow Street** magistrates' office in 1748. The first two magistrates were Henry Fielding, author of *Tom Jones*, and his blind half-brother John – nicknamed the "Blind Beak" – who, unusually for the period, refused to accept bribes. Finding "lewd women enough to fill a mighty colony", Fielding set about creating London's first police force, the **Bow Street Runners**. Never numbering more than a dozen, they were employed primarily to combat prostitution, and they continued to exist a good ten years after the establishment of the uniformed Metropolitan Police in 1829. Bow Street police station and magistrates court (both now closed) had the honour of incarcerating Oscar Wilde after he was arrested for "committing indecent acts" in 1895 – he was eventually sentenced to two years' hard labour. In 1908 Emmeline Pankhurst appeared here, charged with leafleting supporters to "rush" the House of Commons, and, in 1928, Radclyffe Hall's lesbian novel *The Well of Loneliness* was deemed obscene by Bow Street magistrates and remained banned in this country until 1949.

6

Royal Opera House

Bow St • Foyer: daily 10am–3.30pm • Several tours including backstage tours (1hr 15min) take place regularly and can be booked in advance: usually Mon–Fri 10.30am, 12.30pm & 2.30pm, Sat 10.30am, 11.30am, 12.30pm & 1.30pm • £12, concessions £11, under-16s £8.50 (not suitable for under-8s) • ☎ 020 7304 4000, ⓦ roh.org.uk • ⊖ Covent Garden

The main entrance to the **Royal Opera House** – a splendid Corinthian portico – stands opposite the former Bow Street magistrates' court. The original theatre witnessed the premieres of Goldsmith's *She Stoops to Conquer* and Sheridan's *The Rivals* before being destroyed by fire in 1808. To offset the cost of rebuilding, ticket prices were increased; riots ensued for 61 performances until the manager finally backed down. The current building dates from 1858, and is the city's main opera house, home to both the Royal Ballet and Royal Opera. A covered passageway connects the piazza with Bow Street, and allows access to the ROH box office, and upstairs to the beautiful Victorian wrought-iron-and-glass **Floral Hall**. Continuing up the escalators, you reach the *Amphitheatre* bar-restaurant, with a fine terrace overlooking the piazza.

Drury Lane

One block east of Bow Street runs **Drury Lane**, nothing to write home about in its present condition, but in Tudor and Stuart times a very fashionable address. During the Restoration, it became a permanent fixture in London's theatrical and social life, but by the eighteenth century, it had become a notorious slum rife with prostitution. Nevertheless, it was at no. 179 that J. Sainsbury (founder of the supermarket chain) opened his first food store in 1869 – "Quality perfect, prices lower" – and it is here, of course, that the Muffin Man lives in the children's nursery rhyme.

Theatre Royal, Drury Lane

Drury Lane • ⓦ reallyusefultheatres.co.uk • ⊖ Covent Garden

The most famous building in the street is the **Theatre Royal, Drury Lane** first established

---

COVENT GARDEN'S SHOPPING STREETS

Apple may have arrived on the piazza, but the shopping streets to the north hold plenty of less ubiquitous brand names and some independent stores, restaurants, cafés and pubs too. **Floral Street**, a quiet cobbled backstreet, running east–west one block north of the piazza, is a good place to start. At the eastern end is a strange helix-shaped walkway connecting the Royal Ballet School with the Royal Opera House. In the western half you can inspect the tongue-in-cheek window displays of three adjoining shops run by top-selling British designer Paul Smith (nos. 40–44). Another quirky outlet is the shop entirely dedicated to Tintin, the Belgian boy-detective (no. 34). Meanwhile, squeezed beside a very narrow alleyway off Floral Street is the **Lamb and Flag**, the pub where the Poet Laureate, John Dryden, was beaten up in December 1679 by a group of thugs, hired most probably by his rival poet, the Earl of Rochester, who mistakenly thought Dryden was the author of an essay satirizing him.

One block north, **Long Acre** has long been Covent Garden's main shopping street, though it originally specialized in coach manufacture. The most famous shop on the street is **Stanfords**, the world's oldest and largest map shop (see p.430), packed to the rafters with Rough Guides and other travel guidebooks. Look out, too, for **Carriage Hall**, an old stabling yard originally used by coachmakers (currently undergoing redevelopment to increase the size of its shopping space), surrounded by cast-iron pillars and situated between Long Acre, Floral Street and two of the tiny alleys linking them together, Banbury Court and Conduit Court. Running north from Long Acre, **Neal Street** features some fine Victorian warehouses, complete with stair towers for loading and shifting goods between floors, from the days of the fruit, vegetable and flower market. The street is currently dominated by shoe stores. **Neal's Yard** is a tiny little courtyard off Shorts Gardens, stuffed with cafés and prettily festooned with flower boxes and ivy. The three streets branching off the western side of Neal Street combine with Mercer Street to form the tentacles of the **Seven Dials**, a worthwhile visit for style-seekers with its vintage-style clothes and accessories shops, streetwear specialists and cosmetics stores.

here in 1663 – the current theatre (the fourth on the site) dates from 1812, faces onto Catherine Street and, under the ownership of Andrew Lloyd Webber, churns out big-budget musicals. It was at the original theatre that women were first permitted to appear on stage in England (their parts having previously been played by boys), but critics were sceptical about their competence at portraying the fairer sex and thought their profession little better than prostitution – most had to work at both to make ends meet. The scantily clad women who sold oranges to the audience were considered even less virtuous, the most famous being **Nell Gwynne** who from the age of 14 was playing comic roles on stage. At the age of 18, she became Charles II's mistress, the first in a long line of Drury Lane actresses who made it into royal beds.

It was also at the Theatre Royal that **David Garrick**, as actor, manager and part-owner from 1747, revolutionized the English theatre, treating the text with more reverence than had been customary, insisting on rehearsals and cutting down on improvisations. The rich, who had previously occupied seats on the stage itself, were confined to the auditorium, and the practice of refunding those who wished to leave at the first interval was stopped. However, an attempt to prevent half-price tickets being sold at the beginning of the third act provoked a riot and had to be abandoned. Despite Garrick's reforms, the Theatre Royal remained a boisterous and often dangerous place of entertainment: George III narrowly escaped an assassination attempt, and ordered the play to continue after the assassin had been apprehended, and the orchestra often had cause to be grateful for the cage under which they were forced to play. The theatre has one other unique feature: two royal boxes, instigated in order to keep George III and his son, the future George IV, apart, after they had a set-to in the foyer.

Freemasons' Hall

60 Great Queen St • Museum and library Mon–Fri 10am–5pm; free • Guided tours Mon–Fri usually 11am, noon, 2, 3 & 4pm; free • ☎ 020 7395 9257, Ⓦ freemasonry.london.museum • ⊖ Covent Garden

Looking east off Drury Lane, down Great Queen Street, it's difficult to miss the austere, Pharaonic mass of the **Freemasons' Hall**, built as a memorial to all the Masons who died in World War I. Whatever you may think of this reactionary, secretive, male-dominated organization, the interior is worth a peek for the **Grand Temple** alone, whose pompous, bombastic decor is laden with heavy symbolism. To see the Grand Temple, sign up for one of the **guided tours** and bring some ID with you. The cultishness of the Freemasons is in evidence in the museum, with its assortment of objects inscribed or engraved with Masonic heraldry and there are also items that belonged to famous Freemasons, including Winston Churchill. There's a shop for all your Masonic merchandise needs – such as aprons, wands, rings and books about alchemy – with several alternative outlets on Great Queen Street.

The Strand

As its name suggests, the **Strand** – the main road from Westminster to the City and built specifically to link the two – once ran along the banks of the River Thames. From the twelfth century onwards, it was famed for its riverside residences, owned by bishops, noblemen and courtiers, which lined the south side of the street, each with their own river gates opening onto the Thames. In the late 1860s, the Victorians built the **Embankment**, simultaneously relieving congestion along the Strand, cutting the aristocratic mansions off from the river and providing an extension for the tube and a new sewerage system. By the 1890s, the mansions on the Strand were outnumbered by **theatres**, giving rise to the music-hall song *Let's All Go Down the Strand* (have a banana!), and prompting Disraeli to declare it "perhaps the finest street in Europe". A hundred years later, several theatres survive, from the sleek Art Deco Adelphi to the Rococo Lyceum, but the only surviving Thames palace is **Somerset House**, which houses gallery and exhibition space, a selection of restaurants and cafés and boasts a wonderful fountain-filled courtyard.

Charing Cross Station

The Strand begins at **Charing Cross Station**, fronted by the French Renaissance-style Amba Hotel *Charing Cross*, built in the 1860s. Standing rather forlorn, in the station's cobbled forecourt, is a Victorian version of the medieval **Charing Cross**, removed from nearby Trafalgar Square by the Puritans. The original thirteenth-century cross was the last of twelve erected by Edward I, to mark the overnight stops on the funeral procession of his wife, Eleanor of Castile, from Lincoln to Westminster in 1290.

6

The Savoy

Strand • ☎ 020 7836 4343, ⓦ fairmont.com/savoy-london • ⊖ Charing Cross or Embankment

On the south side of the Strand, the blind side street of Savoy Court – the only street in the country where the traffic drives on the right – leads to **The Savoy**, one of London's grandest hotels, built in 1889 by Richard D'Oyly Carte. César Ritz was the original manager, Auguste Escoffier the chef, who went on to invent the *pêche Melba* at the hotel. The hotel's *American Bar* introduced cocktails into Europe in the 1930s, Guccio Gucci started out as a dishwasher here and the list of illustrious guests is endless: Monet and Whistler both painted the Thames from one of the south-facing rooms, Sarah Bernhardt nearly died here, and Strauss the Younger arrived with his own orchestra. It's worthwhile strolling up Savoy Court to check out the hotel's Art Deco foyer, the polygonal glass fish fountain and the silver and gold statue of John of Gaunt, whose medieval palace stood on the site (see below). If you fancy a drink at the *American Bar* you'll need to be suitably attired (smart casual, no sportswear) and prepared to hand over £15 for a cocktail. The adjacent **Savoy Theatre**, with its outrageous 1930s silver and gold fittings, was originally built in 1881 to showcase Gilbert and Sullivan's comic operas, witnessing eight premieres, including *The Mikado* – the theatre's profits helped fund the building of the hotel.

Savoy Chapel

Savoy Hill • Mon–Thurs 9am–4pm, Sun 10.30am–1pm • Free • ☎ 020 7836 7221, ⓦ royalchapelsavoy.org • ⊖ Charing Cross or Embankment

Nothing remains of John of Gaunt's medieval Savoy Palace, which stood here until it was burnt down in the 1381 Peasants' Revolt, though the **Savoy Chapel** (or The Queen's Chapel of the Savoy to give its full title), hidden round the back of the hotel down Savoy Street, dates from the time when the complex was rebuilt as a hospital for the poor in 1512. The chapel is much altered, but it became a fashionable venue for weddings when the hotel and theatre were built next door – all three were the first public buildings in the world to be lit by electricity. Talking of lighting, don't miss London's last remaining **Patent Sewer Ventilating Lamp**, halfway down Carting Lane and powered by methane collected in a U-bend in the sewers below. The original lamp, erected in the 1880s, was replaced by this replica after being damaged in a traffic accident.

Victoria Embankment

To get to the **Victoria Embankment**, from the Strand, head down Villiers Street, beside Charing Cross Station. Completed in 1870, the embankment was the inspiration of engineer **Joseph Bazalgette**, who used the reclaimed land for a new tube line, new sewers, and a new stretch of riverside parkland – now filled with an eclectic mixture of statues and memorials from Robbie Burns to the Imperial Camel Corps. The 1626 **York Watergate**, in the Victoria Embankment Gardens to the east of Villiers Street, gives you an idea of where the banks of the Thames used to be: the steps through the gateway once led down to the river.

CLOCKWISE FROM TOP COVENT GARDEN MARKET HALL (P.107); ROYAL OPERA HOUSE (P.110); THE TEA HOUSE, NEAL ST (P.431) >

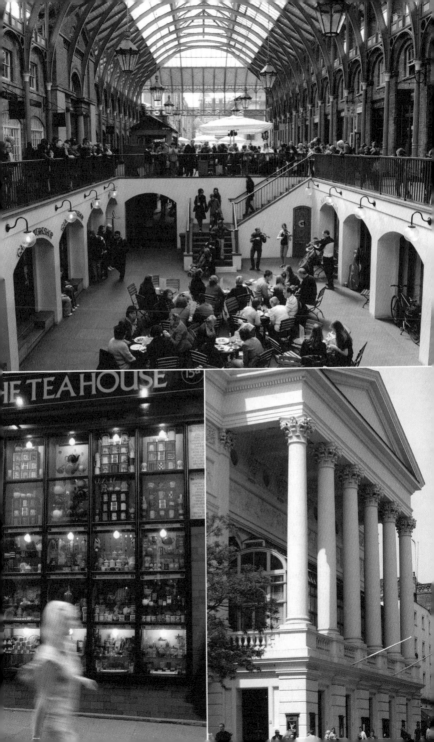

6

Cleopatra's Needle

A 60ft-high, 180-ton stick of granite languishing little noticed on the Thames side of the busy Victoria Embankment, guarded by two Victorian sphinxes (facing the wrong way), **Cleopatra's Needle** is London's oldest monument. It did not actually arrive in the city until the late nineteenth century and has spent most of its 3500 years in Egypt. It's one of a pair originally erected in Heliopolis (near Cairo) in 1475 BC (the other one wound up in New York's Central Park) and taken to Alexandria by Emperor Augustus fifteen years after Cleopatra's suicide. This obelisk was presented to Britain in 1819 by the Turkish viceroy of Egypt, but nearly sixty years passed before it made the treacherous voyage, in its own purpose-built boat, all the way to London. It was erected in 1878 above a time capsule containing, among other things, the day's newspapers, a box of hairpins, a railway timetable and pictures of the country's twelve prettiest women.

RSA House

8 John Adam St · Tours by appointment only · ☎ 020 7930 5115, ⓦ thersa.org · ⊖ Charing Cross or Embankment

Founded in 1754, the "Royal Society for the encouragement of Arts, Manufactures and Commerce", better known now as the Royal Society of Arts or **RSA**, moved into a purpose-built, elaborately decorated house designed by the Adam brothers in 1774. The building contains a small display on the Adelphi and retains several original Adam ceilings and chimneypieces. The highlight, however, is The Great Room, with six paintings on *The Progress of Human Knowledge and Culture* by James Barry, forming a busy, continuous pictorial frieze around the room, punctuated by portraits of two early presidents by Reynolds and Gainsborough. The RSA is one of a number of Adam houses that survive from the magnificent riverside development built between 1768 and 1772 by the Adam brothers and known as the **Adelphi**, which was, for the most part, demolished in 1936.

Benjamin Franklin House

36 Craven St · **Architectural tours** Mon noon, 1, 2, 3.15 & 4.15pm · £3.50, under-16s free **Historical Experience shows** Wed–Sun noon, 1, 2, 3.15 & 4.15pm · £7, under-16s free · ☎ 020 7925 1405, ⓦ benjaminfranklinhouse.org · ⊖ Charing Cross or Embankment

From 1757 to 1775, **Benjamin Franklin** (1706–90) had "genteel lodgings" here. While Franklin was espousing the cause of the British colonies (as the US then was), the house served as the first de facto American embassy; eventually, he returned to America to help draft the Declaration of Independence and frame the US Constitution. On Mondays, the emphasis is on the **Benjamin Franklin House**'s architecture and restoration, as well as Franklin's own story. For the Historical Experience, a costumed guide and a series of impressionistic audiovisuals transport visitors back to the time of Franklin, who lived here with his "housekeeper" in cosy domesticity, while his wife and daughter languished in Philadelphia.

Aldwych

The wide crescent of **Aldwych**, forming a neat "D" on its side with the eastern part of the Strand, was driven through the slums of this zone in the early twentieth century. A confident ensemble occupies the centre, with the enormous Australia House and India House sandwiching **Bush House**, home of the BBC's World Service from 1940 to 2012. Despite its thoroughly British associations, Bush House was actually built by the American speculator Irving T. Bush, whose planned trade centre flopped in the 1930s. The giant figures on the north facade and the inscription, "To the Eternal Friendship of English-Speaking Nations", thus refer to the friendship between the US and Britain, and are not, as many people assume, the World Service's declaratory manifesto.

Not far from these former bastions of Empire, up Houghton Street, lurks that erstwhile hotbed of left-wing agitation, the **London School of Economics**. Founded in 1895, the LSE gained a radical reputation in 1968, when a student sit-in protesting against the Vietnam War ended in violent confrontations that were the closest London came to the heady events in Paris that year. Famous alumni include John F. Kennedy, Mick Jagger and, among its sixteen Nobel Prize winners, philosopher Bertrand Russell.

Somerset House

Strand • **Fountain Court** Daily 7.30am–11pm • Free **Riverside terrace** Daily 8am–11pm • Free **Guided tours** Tues 12.45 & 2.15pm, Thurs 1.15 & 2.45pm, Sat 12.15, 1.15, 2.15 & 3.15pm • Free **Embankment galleries** Daily 10am–6pm • £6 **East and West Wing Galleries** Daily 10am–6pm during exhibitions • Usually free • ☎ 020 7845 4600, ⓦ somersethouse.org.uk • ⊖ Temple or Covent Garden

With four wings enclosing a large courtyard rather like a Parisian *hotel*, **Somerset House** is the sole survivor of the grandiose river palaces that once lined the Strand. Although it looks like an old aristocratic mansion, the present building was, in fact, purpose-built in 1776 by William Chambers, to house governmental offices (including the Navy Office). Nowadays, Somerset House's granite-paved courtyard is a great place to relax thanks to its 55-jet **fountain** that spouts straight from the cobbles, and does a little syncopated dance every half-hour (daily 10am–11pm). The courtyard is also used for open-air performances, concerts, installations and, in winter, an ice rink.

The interior is a network of corridors, staircases and exhibition spaces, also housing half a dozen cafés and restaurants. In the north wing is the **Courtauld Gallery**, best known for its outstanding Impressionist and Post-Impressionist paintings. The south wing has a lovely riverside terrace with a café-restaurant and, down at riverbank level, the **Embankment Galleries**, which host innovative special exhibitions on contemporary art and design. There are galleries in the east and west wings too where temporary exhibitions of visual arts, from sculpture to photography, are staged through most of the year and are usually free. Before you head off to one of the collections, however, make sure you go and admire the Royal Naval Commissioners' superb gilded eighteenth-century barge in the **King's Barge House**, below ground level in the south wing.

Courtauld Gallery

Somerset House, Strand • Daily 10am–6pm, last entry 5.30pm, occasional Thurs until 9pm • £7, concessions £6, students and under-18s free • ☎ 020 7848 2526, ⓦ courtauld.ac.uk • ⊖ Temple or Covent Garden

Founded in 1931 as part of the University of London, the Courtauld Institute was the first body in Britain to award degrees in art history as an academic subject. It's most famous, however, for the **Courtauld Gallery**, which displays its priceless art collection. Best known for its superlative Impressionist and Post-Impressionist works, the Courtauld also owns a fine array of earlier works by the likes of Rubens, Botticelli, Bellini and Cranach the Elder and hosts regular talks throughout the year.

The displays currently start on the **ground floor** with a small room devoted to medieval religious paintings. Next, you ascend the beautiful, semicircular **staircase** to the first-floor galleries, whose exceptional plasterwork ceilings recall their original use as the learned societies' meeting rooms. This is where the cream of the Courtauld's collection is currently displayed: rehangings have become more frequent, however, so ask if you can't find a particular painting.

Mezzanine gallery

Opened in 2015, the Gilbert and Ildiko Butler Drawings Gallery is the Courtauld's first dedicated space for the display of drawings. Numbering some 7000 works and featuring artists such as Dürer, Michelangelo and Rembrandt, this is one of the most important collections of drawings in the country. A rolling programme of displays takes place throughout the year.

The first-floor galleries

To follow the collection chronologically, start in room 2, where you'll find two splendid fifteenth-century Florentine *cassoni* (chests), with their original backrests, and a large

Botticelli altarpiece commissioned by a convent and refuge for repentant prostitutes; hence Mary Magdalene's pole position below the Cross. You can also admire **Lucas Cranach the Elder's** *Adam and Eve*, one of the highlights of the collection, with the Saxon painter revelling in the visual delights of Eden. Works by **Rubens** dominate room 3, ranging from oil sketches for church frescoes to large-scale late works, plus a winningly informal portrait of his close friend Jan Brueghel the Elder and family. Further on, there are works by Goya, Reynolds, Romney, Tiepolo and an affectionate portrait by **Gainsborough** of his wife, painted in his old age.

The cream of the gallery's Impressionist works occupy the next few rooms. The gallery holds the finest group of works by Paul Cézanne in Britain, many of which hang in these rooms, featuring his characteristically lush landscapes and one of his series of *Card Players*. The works in room 6 are all by artists who took part in the first Impressionist exhibition in Paris in 1874, and include **Renoir**'s *La Loge*, a **Monet** still-life and a view of Lordship Lane by **Pissarro** from his days in exile in London. Also on display are a small-scale version of **Manet**'s bold *Déjeuner sur l'herbe*, and his atmospheric *A Bar at the Folies-Bergère*, a nostalgic celebration of the artist's love affair with Montmartre, painted two years before his death. In room 7, **Gauguin**'s Breton peasants *Haymaking* contrasts with his later Tahitian works, including the sinister *Nevermore*. And there are works by **Van Gogh** including his *Self-Portrait with Bandaged Ear*, painted shortly after his remorseful self-mutilation, following his attempted attack on his flatmate Gauguin. Look out, too, for **Picasso**'s *Child with a Dove*, from 1901, which heralded his "Blue Period".

Second floor: twentieth-century works

The **second floor** is used primarily to display the Courtauld's twentieth-century works, which bring a wonderful splash of colour and a hint of modernism to the galleries. There isn't the space to exhibit the entire collection, so it's impossible to say for definite which paintings will be on show at any one time. Room 8 is home to paintings, sketches and sculptures by **Edgar Degas**, while in room 9, you hit the bright primary colours of the Courtauld's superb collection of **Fauvist** paintings, by the likes of Derain, Vlaminck, Braque, Dufy and Matisse, which spill over into room 10. You'll also find *Yellow Irises*, a rare early Picasso from 1901, and one of **Modigliani**'s celebrated nudes.

The Courtauld owns a selection of works by **Roger Fry**, who helped organize the first Impressionist exhibitions in Britain, and went on to found the Omega Workshops in 1913 with Duncan Grant. Fry also bequeathed his private collection to the Courtauld, including several paintings by Grant, his wife Vanessa Bell and Fry himself. There's a room devoted to British artists from the 1930s like Ben Nicolson, Barbara Hepworth and Ivon Hitchens, and at least one room with works by the likes of Kokoschka, Jawlensky, Kirchner, Delaunay and Léger, and an outstanding array of works by **Kandinsky**, the Russian-born artist who was 30 when he finally decided to become a painter and move to Munich. He's best known for his pioneering abstract paintings, such as *Improvisation on Mahogany* from 1910, where the subject matter begins to disintegrate in the blocks of colour.

King's College

Strand • ☎ 020 7848 2343, ⊛ kcl.ac.uk • ⊖ Temple or Covent Garden

Adjacent to Somerset House, the ugly concrete facade of **King's College** (part of the University of London) conceals Robert Smirke's much older buildings, which date from its foundation in 1829. Rather than entering the college itself, stroll down Surrey Street and turn right down Surrey Steps, which are in the middle of the old *Norfolk Hotel*, whose terracotta facade is worth admiring. This should bring you out at one of the most unusual sights in King's College: the **"Roman" Bath**, a 15ft-long tub (actually dating from Tudor times at the earliest) with a natural spring that produces 2000 gallons a day. It was used in Victorian times as a cold bath; Dickens himself used it and

David Copperfield "had many a cold plunge" here. The bath is visible through a window (daily 9am–dusk), but you can only get a closer look by appointment (ring Westminster Council one week in advance ☎ 020 7641 5264).

St Mary-le-Strand

Strand • Tues–Thurs 11am–4pm, Sun 10am–1pm • Free • ☎ 020 7836 3126, Ⓦ stmarylestrand.org, • ⊖ Temple or Covent Garden

St Mary-le-Strand, completed in 1724 in Baroque style and topped by a delicately tiered tower, was the first public building of James Gibbs, who went on to design St Martin-in-the-Fields (see p.37). Nowadays, the church sits ignominiously amid the traffic hurtling westwards down the Strand, though even in the eighteenth century, parishioners complained of the noise from the roads, and it's incredible that recitals are still given here. The entrance is flanked by two lovely magnolia trees, and the interior has a particularly rich plastered ceiling in white and gold. It was in this church that Bonnie Prince Charlie allegedly renounced his Roman Catholic faith and became an Anglican, during a secret visit to London in 1750.

St Clement Danes

Strand • Daily 9am–4pm • Free • ☎ 020 7242 8282, Ⓦ raf.mod.uk/stclementdanes • ⊖ Temple or Covent Garden

St Clement Danes, designed by Wren, occupies a traffic island in the Strand. Badly burnt out in the Blitz (the pock marks are still visible in the exterior north wall), the church was handed over to the RAF, who turned it into a memorial to those killed in World War II. Glass cabinets in the west end of the church contain some poignant mementoes, such as a wooden cross carved from a door hinge in a Japanese POW camp. The nave and aisles are studded with over eight hundred squadron and unit badges, while heavy tomes set in glass cabinets record the 120,000 RAF service personnel who died. The church's carillon plays out various tunes, including the nursery rhyme *Oranges and Lemons* (daily 9am, noon, 3, 6 & 9pm), though St Clement's Eastcheap in the City is more likely to be the church referred to in the rhyme.

In front of the church, the statue of **Gladstone**, with his four female allegorical companions, is flanked by two air chiefs: **Lord Dowding**, the man who oversaw the Battle of Britain, and "**Bomber**" **Harris**, architect of the saturation bombing of Germany which killed five hundred thousand civilians (and over 55,000 Allied airmen commemorated on the plinth). Although Churchill was ultimately responsible, the opprobrium was left to fall on Harris, who was denied the peerage all the other service chiefs received, while his forces were refused a campaign medal. The statue was unveiled somewhat insensitively, in 1992, on the anniversary of the bombing of Cologne.

Twinings shop and museum

216 Strand • Mon–Fri 9.30am–7.30pm, Sat 10am–5pm, Sun 10.30am–4.30pm • ☎ 020 7353 3511, Ⓦ twinings.co.uk • ⊖ Temple, Chancery Lane or Covent Garden

In 1706, Thomas Twining, tea supplier to Queen Anne, bought Tom's Coffee House and began serving tea as well as coffee, thereby effectively opening the world's first tearoom. A branch of **Twinings**, which sells limited edition long leaf tea, still occupies the site and its slender Neoclassical portico features two reclining Chinese men, dating from the time when all tea came from China. At the back of the shop is a small **museum** with a fine display of ornate caddies, photos of the Twining family and some historic packaging and advertising. You can also sample teas at the *Loose Tea Bar* inside.

6

Bloomsbury and King's Cross

Bloomsbury was built over in grid-plan style from the 1660s onwards, and the formal, bourgeois Georgian squares remain the area's main distinguishing feature. In the last century, Bloomsbury acquired the reputation it continues to hold, as the city's most learned quarter, dominated by the dual institutions of the British Museum and London University. The area's unhurried, easy-going vibe ends abruptly at busy Euston Road, where the hustle and bustle of three mainline train stations make this one of the most hectic thoroughfares in central London. There are, however, good reasons to cross over to the other side other than to catch a train – and increasingly so at Euston Road's eastern end, where, around King's Cross, an exciting new city district is emerging, as pedestrian-friendly as Bloomsbury, where squares, restaurants and galleries are being sculpted out of the industrial landscape that once characterized the area.

The British Museum

With some eighty thousand exhibits ranged over several miles of galleries, the British Museum (BM) is perhaps the most complete single showcase of human culture and history anywhere. It boasts one of the largest collections of antiquities, prints and drawings housed under one roof – over thirteen million objects (and growing). Its assortment of Roman and Greek art is unparalleled; its Egyptian collection is the best outside Egypt; and there are fabulous treasures from all over the world, including Africa, China, Japan, India and Mesopotamia, as well as from Anglo-Saxon and Roman Britain. From one perspective it is the world's largest museum of plundered goods, the heart of the collection assembled during the heyday of the British Empire. The "robberies" of Lord Elgin (see p.121) are the best known, but countless others engaged in sporadic looting throughout the Empire and the museum itself commissioned archeologists to strip classical sites bare.

The origins of the BM lie in the seventy-one thousand curios – from fossils and flamingo tongues to "maggots taken from a man's ear" – collected by **Hans Sloane**, a Chelsea physician who bequeathed them to George II in 1753 for £20,000. The king couldn't (or wouldn't) pay, so the collection was purchased by an unenthusiastic government to form the world's first public secular museum, housed in a mansion bought with the proceeds of a dubiously conducted public lottery. Soon afterwards, the BM collection began to expand rapidly and a much larger space was needed. This demand was met with the creation of what remains one of London's grandest Greek Revival buildings, fronted by a giant Ionic colonnade and portico, designed by Robert Smirke in the 1820s.

The BM can get very crowded, particularly at weekends, so get here as early as possible. It's all a far cry from the museum's beginnings, when it was open for just three hours a day, entry was by written application and tickets for "any person of decent appearance" were limited to ten per hour. Nowadays, the BM can tire even the most ardent museum lover and you'll never manage to see everything in one visit. It's best to concentrate on a couple of areas of interest, perhaps focus on the **highlights** (see box, p.124) or else sign up with one of the museum's excellent guided tours of a single room.

INFORMATION AND TOURS

Opening hours Daily 10am–5.30pm, Fri until 8.30pm.

Admission Free except for large special exhibitions – for these, tickets cost £12–15 and are best bought in advance as they often sell out.

Contact details ☎ 020 7323 8000, ⊚ britishmuseum.org.

Tube Tottenham Court Road, Russell Square or Holborn.

Orientation There are two entrances: the main one on Great Russell St and a back entrance on Montague Place. You can pick up a museum plan from the main information desk in the Great Court, but even equipped with a plan, it's easy to get confused – don't hesitate to ask the helpful and knowledgeable museum staff.

Tours Regular daily guided tours, known as eye-opener tours (30–40min; free), concentrate on just one room, as do Friday evening Spotlight tours (20min; free) – visit the website for the fixed start time for each room. A Highlights tour costs £12 (Fri–Sun 11.30am & 2pm; 1hr 30min). Look out, too, for the 'Hands On' desks in some galleries, where, in the company of staff, you can handle some artefacts. Another option is to pick up a multimedia guide (available daily 10am–4.30pm, Fri till 7.30pm; £5) – you'll need to leave some ID as a deposit.

Eating The museum's best café and restaurant is the *Gallery Café* beyond room 12; the *Court Café* in the Great Court itself is more snacky, though it has a spectacular setting; the *Court Restaurant* on the upper floor is pricier, and best booked in advance (☎ 020 7323 8990).

THE GREAT COURT

At the centre of the British Museum is the spectacular **Great Court** – the largest covered square in Europe – with its startling glass-and-steel curved roof, designed in 2000 by Norman Foster. At the centre of the Great Court, newly encased in stone, is the domed, Round **Reading Room**, designed by Sydney Smirke, Robert's younger brother, in 1857 to house the British Library. Numerous writers from Oscar Wilde to Virginia Woolf have frequented the library, and it was here at padded leather desk O7 that Karl Marx wrote *Das Kapital*. Since the British Library moved out (see p.134), the BM has been using the space to stage temporary exhibitions.

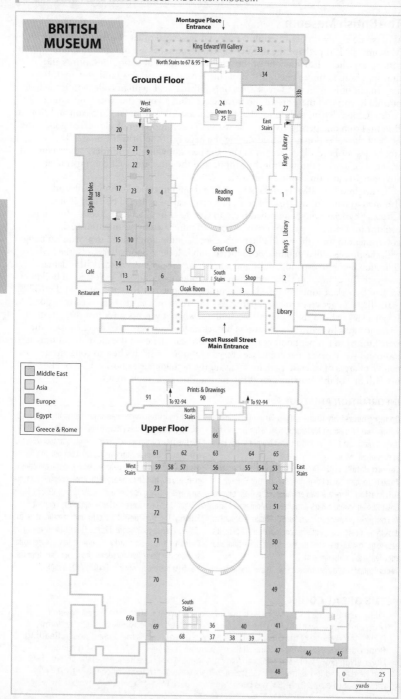

BRITISH MUSEUM

Montague Place
Entrance ↓

King Edward VII Gallery   33

North Stairs to 67 & 95 →

Ground Floor

34

33b

West
Stairs

24
Down to
25

26   27

East
Stairs

20

19   21   9

22

17   23   8   4

18

Elgin Marbles

7

15   10

14

13   6

12   11

Café

Restaurant

Reading
Room

Great Court   ⓘ

South
Stairs

Cloak Room

Shop

3

2

Library

King's Library

King's Library

1

Great Russell Street
Main Entrance

Middle East
Asia
Europe
Egypt
Greece & Rome

91   Prints & Drawings
90
To 92-94   ↑ To 92-94

North
Stairs

Upper Floor

66

61   62   63   64   65

West
Stairs   59   58   57   56   55   54   53   East
Stairs

73   52

72   51

71   50

70   49

South
Stairs

69a   69   36   40   41

68   37   38   39

47   46   45

48

0   25
yards

7

Ancient Greece and Rome

The BM's **Ancient Greece and Rome galleries** make up the largest section in the museum. The ground floor (rooms 11–23) is laid out along broadly chronological lines, from the Bronze Age to Hellenistic times; the upper floor (rooms 69–73) concentrates on the Roman Empire.

On the ground floor, don't miss the **marble relief from the Harpy Tomb**, an imposing 30ft funerary pillar from Xanthos in Turkey whose name is derived from the birdwomen which appear on two sides of the relief (room 15), nor the **sculpted column drum from the Temple of Artemis at Ephesus**, one of the Seven Wonders of the Ancient World (room 22).

Upstairs, look out for the **Warren Cup**, a silver stemmed drinking-cup whose graphic depictions of gay sex were deemed too risqué to be shown to the public until the 1990s, and the Portland Vase, made from cobalt-blue blown glass, and decorated with opaque white cameos (it was smashed into pieces by a drunken Irishman in 1845, for which he was fined £3; room 70, cabinet 12a). Nearby, check the crocodile-skin suit of armour, worn by a Roman follower of the Egyptian crocodile cult (room 70, cabinet 18).

7

Elgin Marbles

Dull is the eye that will not weep to see
Thy walls defaced, thy mouldering shrines removed
By British hands, which it had best behoved
To guard those relics ne'er to be restored.
Curst be the hour when from their isle they roved,
And once again thy hapless bosom gored,
And snatch'd thy shrinking gods to northern climes abhorred!   *Childe Harold's Pilgrimage,* Lord Byron

The large, purpose-built room 18 houses the museum's most famous relics, the **Parthenon sculptures**, better known as the **Elgin Marbles**, after Lord Elgin, who removed them from the Parthenon in Athens between 1801 and 1812. As British ambassador, Elgin claimed he had permission from the Ottoman authorities (who ruled Greece at the time) to remove them. There were justifications for Elgin's action – a Venetian missile had caused considerable damage in 1687 when it landed on a pile of gunpowder the Turks had stored there – though Byron was not the only one to protest at the time. The Greek government has asked for the sculptures to be sent back so they can be displayed, along with the rest of the sculptures, at the Acropolis Museum in Athens – so far, to no avail.

Despite their grand setting (and partly due to all the hype), first impressions of the marble friezes, carved between 447 and 432 BC under the supervision of the sculptor **Pheidias**, can be a little disappointing. The long, repetitive queues of worshippers lack the vigorous immediacy of high-relief sculptural friezes. To prepare yourself, head into the adjacent interpretive rooms to learn more about the context of the marbles. The main frieze, for example, would actually have been situated virtually out of sight behind the first set of columns, and would originally have been picked out in red, blue and gold paint.

GREEK VASES

The BM boasts an exhausting array of **Greek vases**: Mycenaean vases (1300 BC) in room 12 and Geometric (around 800 BC) and Athenian black-figure vases (around 600 BC) in room 13. Among the red-figure vases from Greece's Classical age (500 BC onwards) in rooms 14 and 15, check out the satyrs balancing wine coolers on their erect penises (room 15, cabinet 7). There are further hoards of mostly red-figure vases in room 19 and the mezzanine gallery in room 20, not to mention various examples dotted about rooms 68–73 and in the Enlightenment gallery (room 1).

Middle East

The **Middle Eastern collection** covers all the lands east of Egypt and west of India. The majority of exhibits on the ground floor (rooms 6–10) come from the Assyrian Empire, centred on modern-day Iraq; upstairs (rooms 52–59) you'll find more rich pickings from Mesopotamia and the surrounding region; in the north wing of the building, on the ground floor, is a room devoted to Islamic art (room 34).

On the ground floor, you can't miss the **Nineveh reliefs**, which decorated the palace of Assyrian king Sennacherib (704–681 BC) at Nineveh, in modern day northern Iraq (room 9). In room 10a, you'll find other Assyrian reliefs depicting the **Royal lion hunts of Assyrian King Ashurbanipal** (668–631 BC).

On the first floor, look out for the **Ram in a Thicket**, discovered in the royal cemetery at Ur (in modern-day Iraq) – its name was given by the excavator Leonard Woolley, prone to biblical allusions, but it is probably a goat (room 56, cabinet 17). Not far, don't miss the miniature four-horse chariot of the **Oxus Treasure** the most important surviving hoard of Persian goldwork from the Achaemenid Empire (550–330 BC), discovered in modern-day Tajikistan the 1870s and eventually picked up from the bazaar in Rawalpindi (room 52, cabinet 3).

Among a wide range of ceramics, glasswork and calligraphic ornaments, the Islamic collection in room 34 boasts a **brass geomantic instrument**, made by Muhammad ibn Khutlukh al-Mawsili (AD 1241-42), a **brass basin inlaid with silver and gold** made for the Mamluk Sultan al-Nasir Muhammad (AD 1320-41) and a rotating display of works on paper.

Ancient Egypt

The BM's collection of **Egyptian antiquities** is one of the finest in the world, rivalled only by the Cairo Museum's. Ranging from Pre-dynastic times to Coptic Egypt, it boasts an impressive gathering of sculptures (room 4), a surprising funerary collection (rooms 61-66) composed of numerous mummified corpses, embalmed bodies, and inner and outer coffins richly decorated with hieroglyphs as well as mummies of animals, including cats, apes, crocodiles, falcons and an eel, along with their highly ornate coffins, and amulets, *shabtis* and other pieces of funerary paraphernalia.

On the ground floor, look out for the **head of Amenhotep III** (1390–1352 BC), in the middle of the room, left of the Rosetta Stone, and for the **Gayer-Anderson Cat** (Late Period, after 600 BC), on the right of the Rosetta Stone, behind a statue of Rameses II.

Upstairs, have a look at the colourful **paintings from the tomb-chapel of Nebamun** (c.1350 BC) in room 61. In room 62, among an impressive collection of mummified corpses, don't miss the **mummies of animals** (cabinet 29), including that

THE ROSETTA STONE

There's usually a little huddle of people in the centre of the Egyptian sculpture hall crowded round the **Rosetta Stone**, officially the most visited object in the BM. This slab of dark granodiorite, found in Rashid (Rosetta) in the Nile delta in 1799 by French soldiers, is inscribed with a decree extolling the virtues of the Greek pharoah Ptolemy V in 196 BC. What made the Rosetta Stone so famous, however, was that it was the same text written in two different languages and three different scripts: Ancient Greek at the bottom, demotic Egyptian script in the middle and, most importantly of all, **Egyptian hieroglyphs** at the top. It was surrendered to the Brits in 1801, after they had defeated the French at Alexandria, and brought to the BM, where it has been on more or less continuous display since 1802. However, it was a French professor, Champollion, who eventually unlocked the secret of Egyptian hieroglyphs, and produced an accurate translation some twenty years later. A full-size replica, displayed as the Stone used to be, is in the Enlightenment gallery – it's free to touch and free from crowds.

7

of an eel, and look out for the **glazed turquoise hippo** (cabinet 23) which has become one of the museum's best-known artefacts.

Europe

The European collection displays a vast range of exhibits from Iron Age jewellery to twentieth-century objets d'art through Roman Britain, the medieval era, the Renaissance and the Enlightenment.

On the ground floor, the **Enlightenment gallery** (room 1), runs the length of the east wing. Originally built to house George III's library (now at the British Library in St Pancras), it looks like a very large cabinet of curiosities and displays an eclectic collection of artefacts ranging from a **black obsidian mirror** used by magician John Dee to conjure up spirits (case 20), to **Tipu Sultan's sword and ring** (case 23).

Don't neglect to pop into adjacent room 2, where some of the museum's oldest exhibits are usually displayed, such as the thirteen thousand-year-old ivory sculpture of a swimming reindeer.

On the first floor, starting from Prehistoric Britain, look out for the Mold Gold Cape, a gold garment from the Bronze Age (c. 1900-1600 BC) found in Wales (room 51). Progressing to Roman times, don't miss the **Lindow Man**, who may have been clubbed and garrotted during a Druid sacrificial ceremony and who, more certainly, found his way to the 1980s, when he was discovered, by being preserved in a peat bog (room 50). Entering the medieval section, check the **Lewis Chessmen**, carved from walrus ivory in the twelfth century and discovered in the Outer Hebrides (room 40). In the next room lies the **Anglo-Saxon Sutton Hoo Treasure**, buried with a forty-oar open ship in East Anglia around 625 AD and discovered when the tumulus was excavated in 1939 (room 41).

Rooms 46, 47 and 48 will take you from **Renaissance and Baroque art**, including a collection of eighteenth-century Huguenot silver, to the nineteenth-century collection, which reflects the era's eclectic tastes, and twentieth-century exhibits, which include stunning examples of iridescent Tiffany glass.

The Americas

The BM has two American galleries, in rooms 26 and 27, which display a particularly visual collection of North and South American objects.

The North American exhibits (room 26) change regularly due to the delicate, organic nature of the material used. However, you will always find feather headdresses, masks and zoomorphic stone pipes as well as Inuit furs and skins.

The Mexican gallery (room 27) covers Mexican art from the second millenium BC to the sixteenth century AD. Its centrepiece is the Aztec **double-headed fire serpent Xiuhcoatl**, carved in basalt. Also look out for the **seated figure of the Sun-God Xiuhtecuhtli** and the series of limestone **Mayan reliefs from Yaxchilan**, depicting blood-letting ceremonies, which lines one wall.

PRINTS AND DRAWINGS

The sheer volume of the BM's **prints and drawings** – two million prints and fifty thousand drawings – means there's only space for a changing display in room 90. However, with an incredible collection of drawings by Leonardo, Raphael, Michelangelo, Rubens and Rembrandt, plus prints by Dürer and works by Hogarth, Constable, Turner and Blake – to mention but a few – the exhibitions are always worth exploring.

TIME AND MONEY

The BM has a number of themed rooms, the largest of which is the Enlightenment gallery on the ground floor (see above). On the upper floor, **clocks and watches** (rooms 38 & 39) resound to the tick-tocks and chimes of every type of timepiece from pocket watches to grandfather clocks. One of the best party pieces is the Polish clock from 1600 (room 38), featuring a cow that produced liquid from its udders on the hour, and the spectacular ship from 1585 (room 39), whose concealed organ would announce a banquet.

The **money** gallery (room 68) traces the history of filthy lucre from the use of grain in Mesopotamia around 2000 BC, through the advent of coins in around 600 BC in Lydia in Asia Minor to the plastic money of today. The prize for the largest denomination bill goes to the 1946 one hundred million billion *pengö* note from Hungary (cabinet 16). In the centre of the room, there's a geometric lathe for old £1 notes (cabinet 14), a wonderful Tiffany-designed National Cash Register till (cabinet 17) and a hoard of fake Roman coins and fake £1 coins (cabinet 10). Plus ça change.

Africa

The BM's **Africa** collection is housed on the lower floor (room 25). As you enter, you'll see the "Throne of Weapons", made in Mozambique from decommissioned weapons, as is the "Tree of Life" further on. Nearby there are **woodcarvings** from a whole range of African cultures: everything from carved gods from Mali to backrests from the Congo. Further to the left, you'll find the Yoruba royal palace doors, carved in high relief and depicting, among other things, lazy British imperialists arriving on a litter to collect taxes. And don't miss the incredible display of throwing knives from central Africa in the next door gallery.

To the right, there's a section on **masquerades**, with elaborate crocodile, buffalo, warthog and hippo masks from the last two centuries, and a video of contemporary initiation ceremonies in Nigeria. Perhaps the most famous of the BM's African exhibits are the so-called "**Benin Bronzes**", looted by the British in 1897. Confusingly, these are neither bronzes (they are, in fact, brass), nor from modern-day Benin, but from the former Benin Empire within modern-day Nigeria. Among the most impressive are the fifty or so ornate sixteenth-century brass plaques, nine hundred of which once decorated the royal palace in Benin City. Other Benin exhibits, such as the eye-catching ivory leopards studded with copper gun caps, were actually commissioned by Europeans.

Asia

The Asian galleries (rooms 33, 67 and 92–95) are in the north wing, by the Montague Place entrance. They display an impressive collection of exhibits from China (room 33), South and Southeast Asia (room 33), Korea (room 67) and Japan (rooms 92-94). Room 95 is devoted to Chinese ceramics, with nearly 1700 objects on display. Dating from the third to the twentieth centuries, they once formed the largest private collection in the world, that of Sir Percival David.

In room 33, look out for the **Chinese miniature landscapes** (cabinet 56), the **Tibetan depictions of Tantric sex** (cabinet 55) and the ivory figures from Kandy (cabinet 39), which represent the local royal family and officials. Don't overlook the collection of Chinese jade in the adjacent corridor (room 33b)

In room 67, up the north stairs from room 33, don't miss the nail-free reconstruction of a **sarangbang** (a scholar's study), nor the **bamboo fans** (cabinet 21).

The sensitive materials used in Japanese art mean that the items on display in the Japan (galleries rooms 92–94) change frequently, but you can't miss the ornate suit of **samurai armour**, complete with horned helmet and mask.

South of the British Museum

Over the years, there have been moves to give the British Museum a more triumphal approach by demolishing the small grid of Georgian streets to its south. Thankfully, none have come to fruition and this small jumble of half a dozen streets, including **Museum Street** and **Bury Place,** remain a pleasure to explore, thriving on a mixture of antiquarian and secondhand print and book shops, and cafés and sandwich shops which feed the museum hordes. It's worth looking in at **Jarndyce**, the booksellers at 46 Great Russell St, whose left window is renowned for its display of bizarre antiquarian books, with titles such as *Correctly English in Hundred Days* and *The Art of Faking Exhibition Poultry.*

Cartoon Museum

35 Little Russell St • Tues–Sat 10.30am–5.30pm, Sun noon–5.30pm • £7, concessions £5, students £3, under-18s free • ☎ 020 7580 8155, ⓦ cartoonmuseum.org • ⊖ Tottenham Court Road

As well as putting on excellent temporary exhibitions, the **Cartoon Museum** has a permanent display of over two hundred works spanning two centuries, beginning with Hogarth's moralistic engravings and the caricatures of Gillray, Rowlandson and Cruickshank. The emphasis is very much on British cartoons from the likes of *Punch*, one of the earliest and longest-lasting satirical magazines, to *Private Eye*, which helped launch the careers of, among others, Ralph Steadman and Gerald Scarfe. The comic strips range from Ally Sloper, Britain's first regular comic-strip character who appeared in 1884, through to the adult comic *Viz*, the country's best-selling comic ever, full of toilet humour, filthy language and hilarious pastiches of tabloid journalism, at its peak selling over a million copies each edition.

Church of St George's Bloomsbury

Bloomsbury Way • Daily 1–4pm • Free • Guided tours by arrangement • £5 • ☎ 020 7242 1979, ⓦ stgeorgesbloomsbury.org.uk • ⊖ Tottenham Court Road or Holborn

A couple of blocks south of the British Museum is the **Church of St George's Bloomsbury**, built in 1730 to serve Bloomsbury's respectable new residents and one of six London churches designed by Nicholas Hawksmoor, the pre-eminent architect of the English Baroque style. Its main point of interest is the unusual steeple – Horace Walpole called it "a masterpiece of absurdity" – a stepped pyramid based on Pliny's description of the tomb of Mausolus at Halikarnassos (fragments of which now reside in the BM), with lions and unicorns clinging precariously to the base. The tower is topped by a statue of the unpopular German-speaking monarch, George I, dressed in a Roman toga. The interior is tall, wide and gleaming white, with a large clerestory, its best features the flaming pentecostal tongues on the keystones and the unusual semicircular apse, complete with a scallop-shell recess. There's an interesting multimedia exhibition on Hawksmoor and Bloomsbury in the crypt (Mon–Fri 10am–5pm), and, since April 2014, the **Museum of Comedy** (Mon–Wed 4–8pm, Thurs–Sat 12.30–8pm, Sun 5–8pm; ⓦ museumofcomedy.com) a collection of British stage and TV comedy memorabilia as well as a stand-up comedy venue.

Bloomsbury Square

Laid out in 1665, **Bloomsbury Square** was the first of the city's open spaces to be officially called a "square". John Evelyn thought it "a noble square or piazza – a little towne", but sadly little remains of its original or later Georgian appearance. At the south end of the square you'll find **Sicilian Avenue**, a beautifully preserved architectural set piece from 1910. This unusually continental promenade leads diagonally onto Southampton Row and is separated from the main roads by slender Ionic screens. On Southampton Row itself, you can see the only **tram lines** left uncovered in central London from what was, between World Wars I and II, the world's largest tram system: to catch a glimpse, you must dodge the traffic and peek through the wrought-iron railings to the tracks as they descend into the former Kingsway tram subway.

Bedford Square

The most handsome of Bloomsbury's squares is **Bedford Square**, to the west of the British Museum. Some of Bloomsbury's best-known publishing houses had their offices here until the 1980s – now it's home to Bloomsbury, publishers of Harry Potter. Architecturally, what you see now is pretty much as it was in the 1770s when it was built by the Russells (who still own it), though the gates which sealed the square from traffic have unfortunately been removed, as have all but one of the mews that once accommodated the coaches and servants of the square's wealthy inhabitants. Today, it's

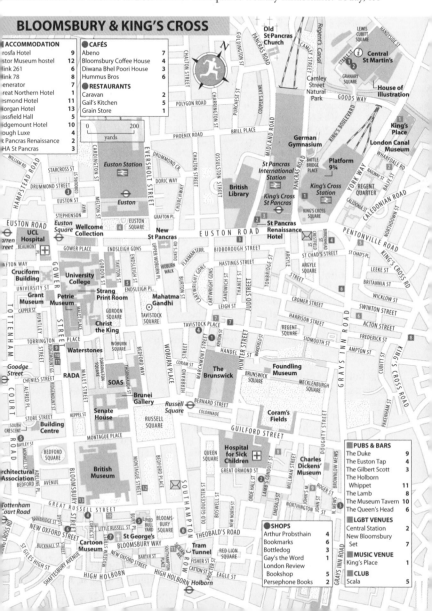

BLOOMSBURY & KING'S CROSS

◼ ACCOMMODATION
Arosfa Hotel	9
Astor Museum hostel	12
Clink 261	6
Clink 78	8
Generator	7
Great Northern Hotel	1
Jesmond Hotel	11
Morgan Hotel	13
Passfield Hall	5
Ridgemount Hotel	10
Rough Luxe	4
St Pancras Renaissance	2
YHA St Pancras	3

◼ CAFÉS
Abeno	7
Bloomsbury Coffee House	4
Diwana Bhel Poori House	3
Hummus Bros	6

◼ RESTAURANTS
Caravan	2
Gail's Kitchen	5
Grain Store	1

◼ PUBS & BARS
The Duke	9
The Euston Tap	4
The Gilbert Scott	3
The Holborn Whippet	11
The Lamb	8
The Museum Tavern	10
The Queen's Head	6

◼ LGBT VENUES
Central Station	2
New Bloomsbury Set	7

◼ MUSIC VENUE
King's Place	1

◼ CLUB
Scala	5

◼ SHOPS
Arthur Probsthain	4
Bookmarks	6
Bottledog	3
Gay's the Word	
London Review Bookshop	5
Persephone Books	2

THE BLOOMSBURY GROUP

The **Bloomsbury Group** were essentially a bevy of upper-middle-class friends who lived in and around Bloomsbury, at that time "an antiquated, ex-fashionable area", in the words of Henry James. The group revolved around siblings Virginia, Vanessa, Thoby and Adrian Stephen, who moved into 46 Gordon Square in 1904. Thoby's Thursday-evening gatherings and Vanessa's Friday Club for painters attracted a whole host of Cambridge-educated types who subscribed to Oscar Wilde's theory that "aesthetics are higher than ethics". Their diet of "human intercourse and the enjoyment of beautiful things" was hardly revolutionary, but their behaviour, particularly that of the two sisters – unmarried, unchaperoned, intellectual and artistic – succeeded in shocking London society, especially through their louche sexual practices (most of the group swung both ways).

All this, though interesting, would be forgotten were it not for their individual work. In 1922, Virginia declared, without too much exaggeration, "Everyone in Gordon Square has become famous": Lytton Strachey was the first to make his name with a series of unprecedentedly frank biographies; Vanessa, having married the art critic Clive Bell, became involved in Roger Fry's prolific design firm, **Omega Workshops**; and the economist John Maynard Keynes became an adviser to the Treasury. (He later went on to become the leading economic theorist of his day.) The group's most celebrated figure, Virginia, who by this time was married to Leonard Woolf, had become an established novelist; she and Leonard had also founded the **Hogarth Press**, which published T.S. Eliot's *Waste Land* in 1924.

Eliot was just one of a number of writers, such as Aldous Huxley, Bertrand Russell and E.M. Forster, who were drawn to the Bloomsbury set, but others, notably D.H. Lawrence, were repelled by the clan's narcissism and narrow-mindedness. Whatever their limitations, the Bloomsbury Group were certainly Britain's most influential intellectual coterie of the interwar years, and their appeal shows little sign of waning.

a perfect example of eighteenth-century symmetry and uniformity: each doorway arch is decorated with rusticated Coade stones; each palatial facade of the square is broken only by the white-stuccoed central houses; and the central garden is for residents only.

Architectural Association

36 Bedford Square • Term time Mon–Fri 9am–9pm, Sat 10am–3pm • ☎ 020 7887 4000, ⓦ aaschool.ac.uk • ➋ Tottenham Court Road

The best way to get a look inside one of Bedford Square's Georgian mansions is to head for the **Architectural Association**, which occupies eight houses on the west side of the square. The public can visit the AA's occasional exhibitions, its basement bookshop and the studenty café-bar on the first floor, with a roof terrace open in fine weather.

The Building Centre

26 Store St, entrance on South Crescent • Mon–Fri 9.30am–6pm, Sat 10am–5pm • Free • ☎ 020 7692 4000, ⓦ buildingcentre.co.uk • ➋ Goodge Street

If you've got even a passing interest in London's architecture and planning, it's a good idea to pop into the **Building Centre**, which stages topical exhibitions on London's built environment. Its centrepiece is a vast 1:1500 interactive model of London, including the latest City skyscrapers and the Olympic Park. There's a small café in the reception area.

Russell Square

The largest square in Bloomsbury – indeed one of the largest garden squares in London – is **Russell Square**, to the northeast of the British Museum. Apart from its sizeable scale, little remains of the Georgian scheme, though the gardens, with their gargantuan plane trees, are good for a picnic, and there's a café in the northeastern corner. The Bloomsbury figure most closely associated with the square is T.S. Eliot, who worked at no. 24, then the offices of Faber & Faber, from 1925 until his death in 1965. The only architectural curiosity is the **Russell Hotel**, on the eastern side; twice as high as everything around it, it's a no-holds-barred Victorian terracotta fancy, concocted in a bewildering mixture of styles in 1898 by Fitzroy Doll.

Gordon Square

Gordon Square is owned by the University of London, which surrounds it on three sides, and open to the public. With its winding paths and summer profusion of roses, it remains one of Bloomsbury's quietest sanctuaries, is predictably popular with students and is one of the nicest picnic spots among the many in Bloomsbury. Between the wars, it was at the centre of the Bloomsbury Group (see box opposite): on the east side, where the Georgian houses stand intact, plaques mark the residences of writer Lytton Strachey (no. 51) and economist John Maynard Keynes (no. 46), while another (no. 50) commemorates the group as a whole.

Church of Christ the King

Gordon Square · Mon–Fri 8am–4pm · Free · ☏ 020 7388 3588, ⦿ fifparish.com · ⊖ Euston Square or Goodge Street

7

Looking like a miniature cathedral in the southwest corner of the square stands the strangely towerless **Church of Christ the King**, built in neo-Gothic style in the 1850s. The five-bay nave is cathedralesque – the nave of Westminster Abbey is only 13ft taller – with a hammer-beam roof, full triforium and clerestory; the unbuilt spire was to have been nearly 150ft high. It was built for (and still belongs to) the Catholic Apostolic Church, a prayer sect within the Anglican Church who were utterly convinced that the Second Coming was imminent (and who were renowned for elaborate rituals, for speaking in tongues and for miraculous healing). It's currently the home of Forward in Faith, the conservative wing of the Church of England.

Tavistock Square

One block east of Gordon Square is **Tavistock Square**, laid out by Thomas Cubitt in the early nineteenth century. Though the west side of the square survives intact, the house on the south side at no. 52, where the Woolfs lived from 1924 until shortly before Virginia's suicide in 1941, and from which they ran the Hogarth Press, is no longer standing. It was here that Woolf wrote her most famous novels – *To the Lighthouse*, *Mrs Dalloway*, *Orlando* and *The Waves* – in a little studio decorated by her sister Vanessa and Duncan Grant. At the centre of the square's gardens is a statue of **Mahatma Gandhi**, who studied law at UCL, and whose presence has transformed the square into something of a garden for peace, with trees and benches dedicated to the cause. That peace, however, was shattered on the morning of **July 7, 2005**, when a suicide bomber blew himself up on bus #30 as it approached the northeast corner of the square, killing thirteen people. The blast occurred shortly after three tube trains had been hit by bombs (see p.460) – a plaque on the British Medical Association building commemorates the victims.

Woburn Walk

A short distance up Upper Woburn Place from Tavistock Square, not far from where the July 7, 2005, blast occurred, is the beautifully preserved Georgian terrace of **Woburn Walk**, designed in 1822 by Cubitt as London's first purpose-built pedestrianized shopping street. **W.B. Yeats** moved into no. 5 in 1895, shortly afterwards losing his virginity at the age of 31 to fellow writer Olivia Shakespear. He and Olivia went to Heal's to order a bed before consummating the relationship, and Yeats found the experience (of ordering the bed) deeply traumatic, as "every inch added to the expense".

Coram's Fields

Guilford Street · Daily 9am–dusk · Free · ☎ 020 7837 6138, ⓦ coramsfields.org · ⊖ Russell Square

Halfway along Guilford Street stands the old entrance to the **Foundling Hospital**, established in 1739 by **Thomas Coram**, a retired sea captain. Coram campaigned for nearly twenty years to obtain a royal charter for the hospital, having been shocked by the number of dead or dying babies left by the wayside on the streets of London during the gin craze. (At the time, 75 percent of London's children died before they were 5.) All that remains of the original eighteenth-century buildings is the whitewashed loggia which forms the border to **Coram's Fields**, an inner-city haven for children, with swings and slides, plus a whole host of hens, goats, rabbits, ducks and a sheep. There's a seasonal **café** (March–Oct daily 10am–5pm), but adults are not allowed into the grounds unless accompanied by a child.

Foundling Museum

40 Brunswick Square · Tues–Sat 10am–5pm, Sun 11am–5pm · £8.25, concessions £5.50, under-17s free · ☎ 020 7841 3600, ⓦ foundlingmuseum.org.uk · ⊖ Russell Square

The **Foundling Museum**, north of Coram's Fields, tells the fascinating story of the Foundling Hospital. As soon as it took in its first babies, in 1741, it was besieged, and forced to introduce a ballot system, with around a third of the applicants accepted. After 1801 only illegitimate children were admitted, and even then only after the mother had given a verbal statement confirming that "her good faith had been betrayed, that she had given way to carnal passion only after a promise of marriage or against her will." Among the most tragic exhibits are the tokens left by the mothers in order to identify the children should they ever be in a position to reclaim them: these range from a heart-rending poem to a simple enamel pot label reading "ale".

One of the hospital's governors – he even fostered two of the foundlings – was the artist **William Hogarth**, who established London's first-ever public art gallery at the hospital to give his friends somewhere to display their works and to attract potential benefactors. As a result the museum boasts works by artists such as Gainsborough and Reynolds, as well as Hogarth's splendid *March of the Guards to Finchley*. Upstairs, the original Georgian **Court Room**, where the governors still hold their meetings, has been faithfully reconstructed, with all its fine stuccowork. The fireplace features a wonderful relief depicting the trades of navigation and agriculture, into which the foundling boys were apprenticed at the age of 10 before being sent out to the colonies. (The girls went into service.) On the top floor, there's a room dedicated to **Georg Friedrich Handel**, who gave annual charity performances of the *Messiah*, wrote an anthem for the hospital (basically a rehash of the *Hallelujah Chorus*) and donated an organ for the chapel, the keyboard of which survives. Today, the museum continues to put on regular concerts and family events and hosts special exhibitions in the basement.

Charles Dickens Museum

48 Doughty St · Daily 10am–5pm, last admission 4pm · £8, concessions £6, under-17s £4, under-6s free · ☎ 020 7405 2127, ⓦ dickensmuseum.com · ⊖ Russell Square

Despite its plethora of blue plaques, Bloomsbury boasts just one literary museum, the **Charles Dickens Museum**, the only one of the writer's fifteen London addresses to survive intact. Doughty Street was a well-to-do gated Georgian street when Dickens – flushed with the success of his first two published works – moved here in 1837 soon after his marriage to Catherine Hogarth. The family lived in this light and airy house for two years, during which time he wrote *Oliver Twist* and *Nicholas Nickleby*. Catherine gave birth to two children in the bedroom here, and her younger sister died tragically in Dickens' arms. Presented as far as possible in its inhabited state, the idea is to give the impression that the family is still resident. Much of the house's furniture belonged, at one time or another, to Dickens, and the house also owns the earliest

CHARLES DICKENS

Few cities are as closely associated with one writer as London is with **Charles Dickens** (1812–70). The recurrent motifs in his novels have become the clichés of Victorian London – the fog, the slums and alleys, the prisons and workhouses and the stinking river. Drawing on his own personal experience, he was able to describe the workings of the law and the conditions of the poor with an unrivalled accuracy.

Born in Portsmouth, the second of eight children, Dickens spent a happy early childhood mostly in Chatham, Kent. This was cut short at the age of 12 when his father was imprisoned in Marshalsea debtors' prison, and Dickens was forced to work in a boot-blacking factory on the site of Charing Cross Station. The experience scarred him for life – he was hurt further when his mother forced him to keep the job even after his father's release – and was no doubt responsible for Dickens' strong philanthropic convictions. After two years as a solicitor's clerk at Gray's Inn, he became a parliamentary reporter and wrote *Sketches by Boz* (Dickens' journalistic pen name) and *The Pickwick Papers*, the two works that propelled him to fame in 1836.

The same year he married **Catherine Hogarth**, and there followed ten children – "the largest family ever known with the smallest disposition to do anything for themselves", as Dickens later described them – and fifteen novels, each published in monthly (or weekly) instalments, which were awaited with bated breath by the Victorian public. Then in 1857, at the peak of his career, Dickens fell in love with the actress, **Ellen Ternan**; Dickens was 45, Ternan just 18. His subsequent separation from his wife, and his insistence that she leave the family house (while her sister Georgina and most of the children stayed), scandalized society and forced the author to retreat to Kent.

Dickens died at his desk at the age of 58, while working on *The Mystery of Edwin Drood*. According to his wishes, there was no public announcement of his burial, though he was interred in Westminster Abbey (at Queen Victoria's insistence) rather than in Rochester (as he had requested). The twelve people present at the service were asked not to wear a black bow, long hatband or any other accessories of the "revolting absurdity" of Victorian mourning.

If you're on the **Dickens trail**, there are one or two other sights worth checking out: the **Old Curiosity Shop** (see p.141), on Lincoln's Inn Fields, the (possible) inspiration for Dickens' novel of the same name; the atmospheric **Inns of Court** (see p.139), which feature in several Dickens novels; "**Nancy's Steps**", where Nancy tells Rose Maylie Oliver's story in *Oliver Twist*, on the west side of London Bridge on the South Bank; and the evocative dockland area east of **Shad Thames** (see p.238), where Bill Sykes has his hide-out.

7

known portrait of the writer (a miniature painted by his aunt in 1830). The museum also owns the adjacent house, no. 49, where they stage special exhibitions, house the bookshop and have a lovely café with free wi-fi.

London University

London only organized its own **University** in 1826, but it was the first in the country to admit students regardless of race, class, religion or gender. The university started life in Bloomsbury, but it wasn't until after World War I that it really began to take over the area. Nowadays, the various colleges and institutes have spread their tentacles to form an almost continuous academic swathe from the British Museum all the way to Euston Road, occupying some 180 buildings. Despite this, the university's piecemeal development has left it with only a couple of distinguishing landmarks in the form of **Senate House** and **University College**. Several of the university departments run their own small, specialist **museums and galleries**, scattered across the campus.

Senate House

Looming over central Bloomsbury is the skyscraper of **Senate House**, a "bleak, blank, hideous" building, according to Max Beerbohm, now housing the university library. Designed with discreet Art Deco touches by Charles Holden in 1932, and austerely clad in Portland stone, it's best viewed from Malet Street. During World War II it served as the Ministry of Information, where the likes of Evelyn Waugh, Graham Greene, Dorothy L. Sayers and George Orwell worked. Orwell later modelled the Ministry of Truth in *1984* on it: "an enormous pyramidal structure of glittering white concrete, soaring up, terrace after terrace, 300 metres into the air".

SOAS (School of Oriental and African Studies)

Thornhaugh St • Galleries Tues–Sat 10.30am–5pm, Thurs till 8pm • Free • ☎ 020 7898 4046, ⓦ soas.ac.uk • ⊖ Russell Square

To the north of Senate House, the **School of Oriental and African Studies**, or **SOAS**, puts on fascinating temporary exhibitions of photography, sculpture and art at the rather snazzy **Brunei Gallery**, funded by the immensely rich Sultan of Brunei. Within the Brunei Gallery is the **Foyle Special Collections Gallery**, a space for showcasing SOAS's own impressive collection of Asian and African artworks and artefacts on a rotating basis. There's also a tiny but excellent bookshop and a café on the ground floor, and a secluded Zen-like Japanese **roof garden** dedicated to Forgiveness.

7 Petrie Museum of Egyptian Archaeology

Malet Place • Tues–Sat 1–5pm • Free • ☎ 020 7679 2884, ⓦ ucl.ac.uk/museums/petrie • ⊖ Euston Square or Goodge Street

The **Petrie Museum**, next door to the Science Library, has a handful of rooms jam-packed with Egyptian antiquities, the bulk of them from excavations carried out from the 1880s onwards by Flinders Petrie, UCL's first Professor of Egyptology. The first large room is crammed with objects, including huge slabs of stonework – look out for Min, the god of fertility, depicted with a particular type of lettuce which, when rubbed, secreted a milky substance. Other cabinets are crammed full of tiny objects including weights and measures, *shabti* figures, combs, bottle stoppers, sandals, legs from a toy table, a mummified bird and a pair of tweezers. At the back of the room is the richly decorated wooden coffin of Nairytisitnefer from 750 BC, while down the back stairs are frog amulets, ivory spoons and a giant sandstone jackal's paw. To the non-specialist, the adjacent room appears to contain little more than broken bits of pottery (a speciality of Professor Petrie's). Look more closely, however, and you'll also find the world's oldest dress, an understandably ragged, pleated garment worn by an Ancient Egyptian teenager around 3000 BC. More intriguing still is the very revealing bead-net dress made for a 12-year-old, from around 2400 BC.

Grant Museum of Zoology

21 University St • Mon–Sat 1–5pm • Free • ☎ 020 3108 2052, ⓦ ucl.ac.uk/museums/zoology • ⊖ Warren Street or Euston Square

Another museum piled high with exhibits – in this case skeletons – is the **Grant Museum of Zoology**, named after Robert E. Grant (1793–1874), the university's first Professor of Zoology and Comparative Anatomy, a pre-Darwinian transmutationist who always wore full evening dress when delivering lectures and later risked his career by teaching evolution at UCL. Among the numerous specimens here, don't miss the jar of pickled moles, the walrus penis bone and the skeletons of a dugong, a dodo, a quagga (an extinct zebra) and a thylacine (a marsupial wolf thought to have been extinct since the 1930s but which British zoologists claimed to be very much alive in 2013 after an expedition to Tasmania).

University College London (UCL)

Gower St • Art Museum Mon–Fri 1–5pm • Free • ☎ 020 7679 2540, ⓦ ucl.ac.uk • ⊖ Euston Square

The oldest part of **University College London** is the rather prosaically named **Main Building**, William Wilkins' Neoclassical edifice from the 1820s, with its handsome Corinthian portico and fine quadrangle, set back (and well hidden) from busy Gower Street. UCL is home to one of London's most famous art schools, the **Slade**, which puts on small, but excellent temporary exhibitions drawn from its collection of over ten thousand works of art, by the likes of Dürer, Rembrandt, Turner and Constable, as well as works by former students, such as Stanley Spencer, Paul Nash, Gwen John, Augustus

JEREMY BENTHAM'S SKELETON

Also in the south cloisters of UCL's Main Building is the philosopher **Jeremy Bentham** (1748–1832), one of the university's founders. Bentham bequeathed his fully clothed skeleton so that he could be posthumously present at board meetings of the University College Hospital governors, where he was duly recorded as "present, but not voting". Bentham's **Auto-Icon**, topped by a wax head and wide-brimmed hat, is in "thinking and writing" pose as the philosopher requested, and can be seen in a hermetically sealed mahogany booth. Close by is a pair of watchful Ancient Egyptian lions, reconstructed from several thousand fragments belonging to the Petrie Museum (see opposite).

John and Raymond Briggs. These are held at the **UCL Art Museum**, situated in the south cloister of the main quadrangle.

There's more artwork on display in the octagon beneath the Main Building's central dome, in an area known as the **Flaxman Gallery** – follow the signs to the library and ask the guards to let you through. John Flaxman (1755–1826) made his name producing Neoclassical funerary sculpture – his works feature prominently in Westminster Abbey and St Paul's – and the walls here are filled with scaled-down, high-relief, plaster models worked on by Flaxman himself for his marble monuments. The gallery's centrepiece is a dramatic, full-size plaster model of *St Michael Overcoming Satan*.

Euston

The northern boundary of Bloomsbury is defined by **Euston Road**, which was laid out in 1756 as part of the "New Road", the city's first bypass. This was the northern limit of London until the mid-nineteenth century when rival companies built Euston, King's Cross and St Pancras, rail termini serving the industrial boom towns of the north of England. Since those days, Euston Road has had some of the city's best and worst architecture foisted on it, which, combined with the current volume of traffic, makes this an area where it pays to be selective.

Amidst all the hubbub of Euston Road, it's easy to miss the depressingly functional **Euston Station**, descendant of London's first great train terminus, originally built with just two platforms way back in 1837. Philip Hardwick's original Neoclassical ensemble – including the famous Euston Arch – was demolished in the face of fierce protests in the 1960s – British Rail claimed it needed the space in order to lengthen the platforms, which it never did. All that remains of old Euston are the sad-looking lodge-houses, though there are moves afoot to rebuild the arch if and when the new high-speed link to Birmingham, HS2, arrives at the overstretched station.

Wellcome Collection

183 Euston Rd • Tues–Sat 10am–6pm, Thurs till 10pm, Sun 11am–6pm • Free • ☎ 020 7611 2222, ⓦ wellcomecollection.org • ⊖ Euston or Euston Square

Despite its unpromising location, the **Wellcome Collection** puts on thought-provoking temporary exhibitions on topical scientific issues on the ground floor, where there's also an excellent café and bookshop. The permanent collection, on the first floor, is also worth a visit, beginning with **Medicine Now**, which focuses on contemporary medical questions such as the body, genomes and obesity. Each subject has an "art cube" displaying contemporary artists' responses to the issues, including a giant jelly baby "clone" by Mauro Perucchetti. Next door, **Medicine Man** showcases the weird and wonderful collection of historical and scientific artefacts amassed by American-born pharmaceutical magnate Henry Wellcome (1853–1936). These range from Florence Nightingale's moccasins and Napoleon's toothbrush to a sign for a Chinese doctor's hung with human teeth, from erotic figurines and phallic amulets to Inuit snow goggles and a leper clapper – in other words, this section is an absolute must.

St Pancras New Church

Euston Rd • Mon–Fri 8am–6pm • Free • ☎ 020 7388 1461, ⓦ stpancraschurch.org • ⊖ Euston

Euston Road's oldest edifice is **St Pancras New Church**, built at enormous expense in the 1820s on the corner of Upper Woburn Place. The first Greek Revival edifice in London, it is notable for its octagonal tower, based on the Tower of the Winds in Athens, and for the caryatids, tacked onto the east end, which are modelled on the Erechtheion on the Acropolis – though the Euston Road ladies had to be truncated at the waist after they were found to be too tall. The best time to visit the interior, which features a dramatically lit Ionic colonnade in the apse, and some lovely Victorian stained glass, is during one of the free Thursday lunchtime recitals. There are also regular art exhibitions held in the atmospheric **Crypt Gallery** (ⓦ cryptgallery.org.uk), with access from Duke's Road.

King's Cross St Pancras

The area around **King's Cross** and **St Pancras** stations is always buzzing with buses, cars, commuters, tourists and, with the massive ongoing development behind King's Cross Station, construction workers. Architecturally, it's dominated by **St Pancras Station**, the most glorious of London's red-brick Victorian edifices, which overshadows its two neighbours: recently restored **King's Cross Station** and the red-brick brutalist **British Library**, one of the largest libraries in the world and home to some of the nation's most precious books and documents.

British Library

96 Euston Rd • Mon–Fri 9.30am–6pm, Tues till 8pm, Sat 9.30am–5pm, Sun 11am–5pm • ☎ 01937 546546, ⓦ bl.uk • ⊖ King's Cross St Pancras

As one of the country's most expensive public buildings, the **British Library** took flak from all sides during its tortuously long construction between 1982 and its opening in 1998: few readers wanted to move out of the splendid Round Reading Room in the British Museum, where the library had been since the 1850s; the number of extra readers' seats was negligible and the shelving inadequate; and, to top it all, the design was criticized by Prince Charles, who compared it to an academy for secret policemen. Yet, while it's true that Colin St John Wilson's penchant for red-brick brutalism is horribly out of fashion, the building was awarded Grade I listed status in 2015 and the library has proved popular both with the scholars who use it and the public who visit the superb galleries, while no one can fail to be impressed by the sheer size of its collection: 170 million items and counting.

The **piazza** features Eduardo Paolozzi's giant statue of Isaac Newton bent double over his protractor, inspired by William Blake – just one of a number of specially commissioned artworks. Look out, too, for Bill Woodrow's *Book, Ball & Chain* sofa and R.B. Kitaj's unsettling giant tapestry, *If not, not*, both in the main foyer, and Patrick Hughes' optical illusion, *Paradoxymoron*, near the basement cloakroom. The spiritual heart of the building is a multistorey glass-walled tower housing the vast **King's Library**, collected by George III and donated by George IV in 1823. The library puts on a wide variety of events, including talks, films and occasional live performances, and has several cafés, a restaurant and free wi-fi.

John Ritblat Gallery: Treasures of the British Library

The dimly lit **John Ritblat Gallery** is where the BL's ancient manuscripts, maps and precious books are permanently displayed. The sheer variety of sacred texts displayed is overwhelming, from illuminated Torahs to richly decorated Qur'ans (Korans), from a tiny palm-leaf glorification of the Hindu goddess Jagannatha in the shape of a cow to folding books on the life of the Buddha. The richly illustrated **Lindisfarne Gospels**, begun in 698 AD, is always on display, as is the fourth century AD Codex Sinaiticus, one of the earliest Greek Bibles in the world, and the thousand-year-old manuscript of the Anglo-Saxon epic poem *Beowulf*. In the section on printing, you can see the world's earliest-dated printed document, along with the **Gutenberg Bible** from 1454–55, the first Bible printed using movable type (and therefore capable of being mass-produced).

The most famous of the **historical documents** is the **Magna Carta**, King John's agreement with his rebellious barons in 1215, returned now to its own display room after starring in the 800th anniversary exhibition. In the interests of preservation, and to furnish temporary exhibitions, other exhibits in the permanent collection change from time to time, but should normally include Lenin's application for a British Library pass, Shakespeare's First Folio from 1623, Jane Austen's notebooks and writing desk and the touchingly beautiful handwritten and illustrated copy of *Alice in Wonderland* given by Lewis Carroll to Alice Liddell. You can also hear recordings of several authors reading extracts from their works. Similarly, in the **music** section, which contains oddities such as Mozart's marriage contract and Beethoven's tuning fork, you can listen to works by Bach and The Beatles while perusing Purcell's autographed score.

The other galleries

The BL has several galleries in which it stages temporary exhibitions (occasionally with an entrance charge), employing more of the library's wonderful texts, supplemented by items from the British Museum. Stamp lovers should make their way up to the BL's gargantuan **Philatelic Collections**, made up of over eight million items, eighty thousand of which are displayed in vertical pull-out drawers just outside the John Ritblat Gallery. The Tapling Collection kicks off the proceedings, as it did when it was bequeathed in 1891, and in drawer number one you'll find the famous "Penny Black", the birthmark of modern philately. After that you get a world tour of stamps from long-forgotten mini-kingdoms such as Mecklenburg-Schwerin and Nowanugger. Those with a political interest should head for the Bojanowicz Collection, which covers Polish stamps from 1939 to 1946, including ones from the German and Russian occupations, and even POW and displaced persons' camps.

St Pancras Old Church

Pancras Rd • Daily 9am to dusk • Free • ☎ 020 7387 4193, ⓦ posp.co.uk • ⊖ King's Cross St Pancras

Though allegedly the first parish church built in London, most of **St Pancras Old Church** actually dates from the nineteenth century, with only a little exposed Norman masonry and the sixth-century Roman altar stone remaining of the oldest buildings that once stood here. The interior may be a little forlorn and the location unremarkable, tucked away up the road behind St Pancras train station, but this is still a pleasant place to visit, more for the sweep of parkland around which its uncluttered **churchyard** extends. Partially destroyed by the arrival of the railway in the 1860s, many of the graves in the churchyard were heaped around an ash tree under the supervision of an architect and his apprentice Thomas Hardy, the later-to-be novelist and poet. Now known as the Hardy Tree, this quirky feature sits alongside some distinguished graves which remain in their original locations, including **John Soane's mausoleum** from 1816, to the north of the church. Also originally buried here was Britain's great protofeminist, **Mary Wollstonecraft**, who died a few days after giving birth to her daughter, Mary. At the age of 16, the younger Mary was spotted visiting her mother's grave by the poet Percy Bysshe Shelley, who immediately declared his undying love, before eloping with her to Italy – both Marys are now buried in Bournemouth. A list of the graveyard's most illustrious corpses is inscribed on the monumental sundial erected by Baroness Burdett-Coutts, below which sit four beasts, two of which are based on her collie dog – there's also a map of the prominent graves by the left-hand entrance.

St Pancras Station

Euston Rd • ☎ 020 7843 7688, ⓦ stpancras.com • Official guided tours ⓦ stpancrastours.co.uk • £9 • ⊖ King's Cross St Pancras

Among London's greatest Victorian follies is the former *Midland Grand Hotel*, whose majestic sweep of lancets, dormers and chimneypots forms the facade of **St Pancras**

THE REBIRTH OF KING'S CROSS

The King's Cross area is undergoing the largest urban redevelopment in Europe, transforming 67 acres of previously uninviting, grim industrial landscape into a completely new city quarter. This 25-year project, most of which is scheduled for completion by 2022, will put twenty new streets and ten new public squares on the London map; three new bridges will span the Regent's Canal, which cuts through this vast site, while a good chunk of canalside land has already been opened up, making the waterway more accessible and more visible; the arrival of an art college, primary school, public leisure centre, sports pitches and several small galleries and parks will ensure the site is not dominated by the inevitable corporate and retail presence here. Fifty new buildings are to be erected, many of them already in use, and although a whole host of lovely old buildings have bitten the dust, around twenty venerable structures have survived, among them the **German Gymnasium** on St Pancras Road, built in the 1860s for the German Gymnastics Society, thought to be the first purpose-built gymnasium in Britain and now housing a restaurant; and the **Great Northern Hotel**, in between the two stations, originally opened in 1854 and reopened in 2013, beautifully and painstakingly restored after over a decade lying derelict – with painfully high room prices to match.

One of the recently established streets, **King's Boulevard**, slopes up from Battle Bridge Place, between the German Gymnasium and King's Cross Station, past Google's new UK headquarters, over the canal to **Granary Square**, one of the largest of the new squares so far constructed, complete with dancing fountains. Here, in the old Granary building, is Central Saint Martins, part of the **University of the Arts**, previously housed in Holborn, several restaurants and, to the east side of the square, the House of Illustration (Tues–Sun 10am–6pm), whose three small rooms of exhibition space form the country's only gallery dedicated to illustration, occupying what used to be goods yards offices. Down the other side of the Granary building, on Stable Street is the **King's Cross Visitor Centre** (Mon–Fri 10am–5pm, Sat 10am–4pm; ☎020 3479 1795), where you can play with an interactive model of the development and from which you can take a guided tour of the area (90 mins; free; book online at ⓦ kingscross.co.uk). On the other side of Stable Street, behind a construction site fence, the blackened old Victorian coal drops, long brick buildings once used for the transfer of coal from rail wagons to road carts, are being converted into a shopping complex. Look out, too, for the brooding skeletal **gasholders**, Victorian monsters that hark back to an era when nothing was too lowly to be given Neoclassical decoration. There are four in total, over the canal from Camley Street Natural Park (see opposite), one of them destined to hold a landscaped park, the other three framing a series of apartment buildings.

One of the least expected, innovative installations on the site, just to the north of dinky Lewis Cubitt Park, behind the Granary building, is the **King's Cross Pond Club** (May–Sept Mon–Fri 6.30am–8pm, Sat & Sun 9am–7pm; Oct–March daily 10am–4pm), a work of art doubling up as an outdoor swimming pool, naturally filtered by aquatic plants. What exactly makes this novel bathing pond a piece of art is anyone's guess but, no matter, it's a great spot for a splash, atop a grassy mound, though booking is essential (£6.50/£3.50 peak/off-peak; ⓦ kingscrosspond.club) and the water pretty cold. Overlooking the pool is one of two viewing platforms (daily 8.30am–dusk; free) hereabouts, temporary scaffold structures sufficiently elevated to give half-decent views over the giant development, with everything in sight helpfully labelled on signboards. This is the south-facing platform – the north-facing one is over the road from Granary Square.

Station, London's Eurostar terminus. The hotel was completed in 1876 by George Gilbert Scott, though the station itself had been in use since 1868. This masterpiece of neo-Gothic architecture enjoyed a brief heyday in the 1890s when the ratio of staff to guests was 3:1, but with few private bathrooms and no central heating, the hotel couldn't survive long into the modern age. For fifty years from 1935, it languished as underused railway offices and, for periods, a poorly connected station until it was closed and vacated in 1985. Then in 2004 a complete renovation began, doubling the station's length, reopening in 2007 to replace Waterloo as London's direct rail link to Paris and the continent. The hotel, which enjoyed its own full refurbishment, is now the stunning *St Pancras Renaissance*, and houses private apartments as well as luxury rooms.

King's Cross Station

King's Cross Station, opened in 1852 as the terminus for the Great Northern Railway, cannot compete with the illustriousness of the St Pancras building over the road, but after a smart, imaginative refurbishment it is nonetheless both a handsome and distinct building, its new semi-circular concourse covered by a striking white, cascading roof. Legend has it that Boudicca's bones lie under platform 9 – the area used to be known as Battle Bridge, and was believed to have been the site of the final set-to between the Iceni and the Romans. More famously, the fictional **Harry Potter** and his wizarding chums leave for school on the Hogwarts Express each term from platform 9¾. (The scenes from the films were, in fact, shot between platforms 4 and 5, but a station trolley half-submerged into the wall provides a photo opportunity in the new semi-circular concourse to the west, and there's an Harry Potter shop close by.)

Camley Street Natural Park

12 Camley St • Daily except Sat: April–Sept 10am–5pm; Oct–March 10am–4pm • Free • ☎ 020 7833 2311, ⓦ wildlondon.org.uk • ⊖ King's Cross St Pancras

Pre-dating the King's Cross redevelopment but sitting very much alongside it is **Camley Street Natural Park**, transformed from a rubbish dump into a canalside wildlife haven in the 1980s, and run by the London Wildlife Trust. Pond, meadow and woodland habitats have been re-created and provide a natural environment for birds, butterflies, frogs, newts, toads and even the odd heron, plus a rich variety of plant life.

Kings Place

90 York Way • ☎ 020 7520 1490, ⓦ kingsplace.co.uk • ⊖ King's Cross St Pancras

Well established now and one of the welcome arrivals in the King's Cross redevelopment is **Kings Place**, the glassy new arts centre overlooking the Regent's Canal. As well as housing two state-of-the-art concert halls – home to the London Sinfonietta and the Orchestra of the Age of Enlightenment – the venue puts on art exhibitions, talks and events and has a swanky canalside café and restaurant to boot. The most famous residents, however, are the *Guardian* and *Observer* newspapers, which occupy the southern part of the building.

London Canal Museum

12–13 New Wharf Rd • Tues–Sun 10am–4.30pm; first Thurs in month till 7.30pm • £4, concessions £3, under-16s £2 • ☎ 020 7713 0836, ⓦ canalmuseum.org.uk • ⊖ King's Cross St Pancras

Packed with traditional narrowboats, Battlebridge Basin, behind Kings Place, is a thoroughly appropriate location for the **London Canal Museum**. The museum testifies to the hard life that boat families endured and includes a restored "butty" (an engine-less narrowboat used for storage) and some of the unusual Measham Ware pottery and crockery that was popular with canal-boat families. Other exhibits relate to the building itself, built as an icehouse by Swiss-Italian entrepreneur Carlo Gatti, London's main ice trader in the nineteenth century. Gatti single-handedly popularized ice cream in London, supplying most of the city's vendors, who became known as "Hokey-Pokey Men" – a corruption of the street cry *Ecco un poco*, "Just try a little". Upstairs there's video footage of the canal from the 1920s and the 1990s.

7

ROYAL COURTS OF JUSTICE

Holborn and the Inns of Court

Strategically placed between the royal and political centre of Westminster and the mercantile and financial might of the City, Holborn (pronounced "Ho-bun") became the hub of the English legal system in the thirteenth century. Campuses, known as Inns of Court, each with its own dining hall, library, chapel and gardens, were established where lawyers could eat, sleep and study law. Hidden away from the general hubbub of London, the Inns make for a relaxing and interesting stroll, albeit one you should take on a weekday since most of their gates are locked at weekends. Their archaic, cobbled precincts exude the rarefied atmosphere of an Oxbridge college, and shelter one of the city's oldest churches, the twelfth-century Temple Church.

Temple

Temple, the largest of the Inns of Court, was once the headquarters of the Knights Templar, a military order of monks whose job was to protect pilgrims en route to Jerusalem. The Templars became very powerful, the Crown took fright and the order was suppressed in 1307, with the land passing to another order, the Knights Hospitaller. Legal London already had a foothold here by this point, so when the monks left during the Reformation, the lawyers simply took over the whole precinct. Temple actually consists of two Inns – **Middle Temple** and **Inner Temple** – both of which lie south of the Strand and Fleet Street. Seemingly one big campus, it's difficult to tell which Inn you're in, unless you check the coat of arms on each building: the Lamb of God (for Middle Temple) and the Pegasus (for Inner Temple). Nevertheless, the maze of courtyards and passageways is fun to explore – especially after dark, when Temple is gas-lit – and a welcome haven from London's traffic. There are several points of access, simplest of which is Devereux Court, which leads south off the Strand, but at the weekend you can usually only enter from Tudor Street to the east.

Middle Temple Hall and Gardens

Hall Mon–Fri 10–11.30am & 3–4pm, though sometimes closed for events • Free • **Gardens** May–Sept Mon–Fri noon–3pm • ☎ 020 7427 4800, Ⓦ middletemplehall.org.uk • Ⓔ Temple or Blackfriars

Medieval students ate, attended lectures and slept in the **Middle Temple Hall**, on Fountain Court, and it remains the Inn's main dining room. The present building was constructed in the 1560s and provided the setting for many Elizabethan masques and plays – including Shakespeare's *Twelfth Night*, which was premiered here in 1602. The hall is worth a visit for its fine hammer-beam roof, wood panelling and decorative Elizabethan screen, and the small wooden table said to have been carved from the hatch from Francis Drake's ship, the *Golden Hind*. In the summer months you can combine a visit to the hall with a barbecue lunch (weather dependent) in gorgeous **Middle Temple Gardens** right next to the hall.

Temple Church

Mon–Fri 10am–4pm, but times and days vary • £5, concessions £3, under-19s free • ☎ 020 7353 3470, Ⓦ templechurch.com • Ⓔ Temple or Blackfriars

Despite wartime damage, the original round **Temple Church** – built by the Templars in 1185 and modelled on the Church of the Holy Sepulchre in Jerusalem – still stands. The immaculate interior features striking Purbeck marble piers, recumbent marble effigies of medieval knights and tortured grotesques grimacing in the spandrels of the blind arcading, as well as exhibitions. At the northwestern corner of the choir, behind the decorative altar tomb of Edmund Plowden, builder of Middle Temple Hall, stairs lead up to a cell, less than 5ft long, in which disobedient knights were confined. The church makes an appearance in both the book and the film of *The Da Vinci Code* by Dan Brown.

THE INNS

Even today, every aspiring barrister in England and Wales must belong to one of the four Inns – **Inner Temple**, **Middle Temple**, **Lincoln's Inn** and **Gray's Inn** – in order to qualify and be "called to the Bar". It's an old-fashioned system of patronage (you need contacts to get accepted at one of the Inns) and one that has done much to keep the judiciary overwhelmingly white, male, public school- and Oxbridge-educated. The most bizarre stipulation is that to qualify as a barrister, you must attend a dozen formal dinners. Dress code is strict – "dark lounge suit, plain collar and sober tie/white blouse" or "genuine ethnic dress" – although the meals are heavily subsidized: under £20 for a four-course meal with wine and port. Back in medieval times, aspiring lawyers would take part in mock courts and dine together in the main halls. Today, while the barristers' professional training is conducted by private law schools, the dinners live on.

8

The church has a renowned choir, who are regularly broadcast on national radio, and a concert programme which it shares with Middle Temple Hall, ranging from free lunchtime organ recitals to staged operas (ⓦ templemusic.org).

Inner Temple

Garden May–Sept: Mon–Fri 12.30–3pm • Free • ⓦ innertemple.org.uk • ⊖ Temple or Blackfriars

The millennium column, to the south of Temple Church, marks the point where the Great Fire of 1666 was extinguished; it's topped by a diminutive statue of two knights

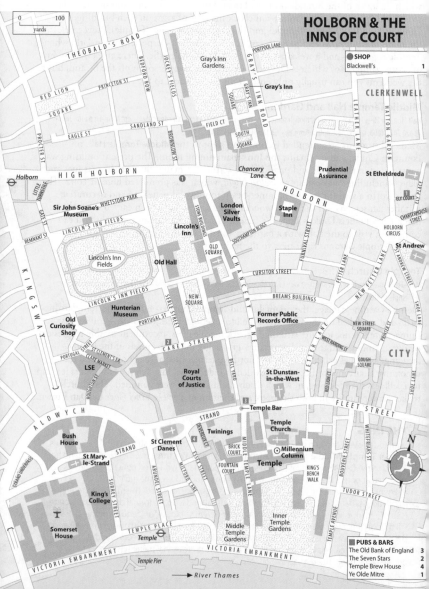

HOLBORN & THE INNS OF COURT

0   100
yards

THEOBALD'S ROAD
JOCKEY'S FIELDS
BEDFORD ROW
Gray's Inn Gardens
PORTPOOL LANE
GRAY'S INN SQUARE
Gray's Inn
GRAY'S INN ROAD
LEATHER LANE
HATTON GARDEN

● SHOP
Blackwell's 1

RED LION SQUARE
PRINCETON ST
FIELD CT
SOUTH SQUARE
CLERKENWELL

EAGLE ST
SANDLAND ST
BROWNLOW ST
Chancery Lane ⊖
Prudential Assurance
St Etheldreda
ELY COURT
CHARTERHOUSE STREET
ELY PLACE

PROCTER ST
⊖ Holborn
HIGH HOLBORN
HOLBORN
HOLBORN CIRCUS
St Andrew
ST ANDREW STREET

LITTLE TURNSTILE
GATE ST
REMNANT ST
Sir John Soane's Museum
WHETSTONE PARK
STONE BUILDINGS
London Silver Vaults
Staple Inn
FURNIVAL STREET
FETTER LANE
NEW FETTER LANE
SHOE LANE

KINGSWAY
LINCOLN'S INN FIELDS
Lincoln's Inn Fields
Lincoln's Inn
Old Hall
OLD SQUARE
SOUTHAMPTON BLDGS
CURSITOR STREET
CITY

Hunterian Museum
NEW SQUARE
BREAMS BUILDINGS
Former Public Records Office
NEW STREET SQUARE
PORTUGAL STREET
SEARLE STREET
PINFOLD
GOUGH SQUARE

Old Curiosity Shop
ST CLEMENT'S LANE
CLARE MARKET
CAREY STREET
BELL YARD
WEST HARDING ST
RED LION CT
NEPTUS

PORTUGAL STREET
HOUGHTON ST
LSE
Royal Courts of Justice
St Dunstan-in-the-West
FLEET STREET

ALDWYCH
Bush House
STRAND
St Clement Danes
Temple Bar
Temple Church
WHITEFRIARS ST
BOUVERIE STREET

St Mary-le-Strand
SURREY STREET
ARUNDEL STREET
MILFORD LANE
ESSEX STREET
Twinings
SURREY STREET
BRICK COURT
FOUNTAIN COURT
Millennium Column
Temple
KING'S BENCH WALK

N

King's College
TEMPLE PLACE
⊖ Temple
Middle Temple Gardens
MIDDLE TEMPLE LANE
Inner Temple Gardens
TEMPLE AVENUE
TUDOR STREET

Somerset House
VICTORIA EMBANKMENT
VICTORIA EMBANKMENT
Temple Pier
→ River Thames

■ PUBS & BARS
The Old Bank of England 3
The Seven Stars 2
Temple Brew House 4
Ye Olde Mitre 1

sharing a horse, emphasizing the vow of poverty taken by the Knights Templar. **Inner Temple Hall**, to the south of the column, is a postwar reconstruction, as is clear from the brickwork. This was the Inn Mahatma Gandhi belonged to in 1888, when he was studying law, living as a true Englishman, dressing as a dandy, dancing, taking elocution lessons and playing the violin, while his close associate Jawaharlal Nehru, the first Prime Minister of India, spent two years here a decade or so later, gambling, drinking and running up considerable debts. The public are also permitted to explore the **Inner Temple Garden**, which slopes down to the Embankment and is where Shakespeare set the fictional scene of the plucking of red and white roses in *Henry VI Part One*.

Royal Courts of Justice

Strand • Mon–Fri 9.30am–4.30pm; no cameras allowed • Free • Guided tours by advance booking only Mon–Fri 11am or 2pm • £12 • ☎ 020 7947 6000 • ⊖ Temple

On the north side of the Strand, the **Royal Courts of Justice** are home to the Court of Appeal and the High Court, where the most important civil cases are tried (criminal cases are heard at the Old Bailey). The main portal and steps of this daunting Gothic Revival complex, designed in the 1870s, often features in the news, as this is also where libel disputes and high-profile divorce cases are heard. In the intimidating Main Hall, where bewigged barristers are busy on their mobiles, you can pick up a plan and a short guide to the complex, while the glass cabinets in the centre of the hall list which cases are being heard and where. In the Minstrels' Gallery, there's a small exhibition on the history of legal dress codes.

8

Lincoln's Inn Fields

To the north of the Law Courts lies **Lincoln's Inn Fields**, London's largest square. Originally simply pasture land and a playground for Lincoln's Inn students, it was used as a place of execution in Tudor times; would-be assassin Anthony Babington and his Catholic accomplices were hanged, drawn and quartered here for high treason in 1586. Laid out in the early 1640s, the square's most arresting statue is that of Margaret MacDonald (wife of the first Labour prime minister Ramsay MacDonald, who lived and died at no. 3), amid a brood of nine children (she herself had six), commemorating her social work among the young. Just off the southwest corner of the square is one of London's few surviving timber-framed buildings, the sixteenth-century **Old Curiosity Shop** at 13–14 Portsmouth Street (currently a shoe shop), which claims to be the inspiration for Dickens' sentimental tale of the same name.

Hunterian Museum

Lincoln's Inn Fields • Tues–Sat 10am–5pm • Free • ☎ 020 7869 6560, ⓦ hunterianmuseum.org • ⊖ Holborn

The **Hunterian Museum** is on the first floor of the imposing Royal College of Surgeons building on the south side of Lincoln's Inn Fields. First opened in 1813, the museum contains the unique and captivating specimen collection of the surgeon-scientist John Hunter (1728–93). The centrepiece of the museum is the Crystal Gallery, a cabinet-encased room of jars of pickled skeletons and body pieces – from the gall bladder of a puffer fish to the thyroid of a dromedary – prepared by Hunter himself. Among the most prized exhibits are the skeleton of the "Irish giant" Charles Byrne (1761–83), who was seven feet ten inches tall, and the "Sicilian dwarf" Caroline Crachami (1815–24), who stood at only one foot ten and a half inches when she died at the age of 9. You'll find Crachami in the McCrae Gallery, where a series of gruesome dental instruments herald the odontological collection. Upstairs, you can have a go at simulated minimal-access surgery, and examine Joseph Lister's cumbersome carbolic-acid spray machine, known as the "donkey engine", with which he pioneered antiseptic surgery, performing operations obscured in a cloud of phenol.

Sir John Soane's Museum

13 Lincoln's Inn Fields • Tues–Sat 10am–5pm, candle-lit eve first Tues of month 6–9pm (the museum is very popular, with a maximum capacity of 80 people so you may have to queue); no large bags or prams • Free • Guided tours Tues, Thurs, Fri & Sat noon; £10 • ☎ 020 7405 2107, ⓦ soane.org • ⊖ Holborn

A group of buildings on the north side of the square houses the fascinating **Sir John Soane's Museum**. Soane (1753–1837), a bricklayer's son who rose to be architect of the Bank of England, gradually bought up three adjoining Georgian properties here between 1792 and 1824, altering them to serve not only as a home but also as a place to stash his large collection of art and antiquities. The central house at no. 13 is arranged much as it was in his lifetime, with an ingenious ground plan and an informal, treasure-hunt atmosphere. Few of Soane's projects were actually built, and his home remains the best example of what he dubbed his "poetry of architecture", using mirrors, domes and skylights to create wonderful spatial ambiguities. On the intriguing tour of the house you also encounter false walls, a wooden chamber on stilts from which Soane supervised his students, a crypt, complete with tomb, cloister and eerie medieval casts and gargoyles, and a colonnaded atrium.

Lincoln's Inn

Lincoln's Inn Fields • **Precincts** Mon–Fri 7am–7pm; Chapel Mon–Fri 9am–5pm but times vary **Gardens** Mon–Fri noon–2.30pm • Free • First and third Fri of month guided tour 2pm (no tours in August); £5 • ☎ 020 7405 1393, ⓦ lincolnsinn.org.uk • ⊖ Holborn

On the east side of Lincoln's Inn Fields, **Lincoln's Inn** is in many ways the prettiest of the Inns of Court – famous alumni include Thomas More, Oliver Cromwell and Margaret Thatcher. The oldest building is the fifteenth-century Old Hall (by guided tour only), where the lawyers used to live and where Dickens set the case Jarndyce versus Jarndyce, the opening scene in *Bleak House*.

Beyond the Old Hall is the sixteenth-century **gatehouse** – best viewed from Chancery Lane – impressive for its age and bulk, not to mention its characteristic diamond-patterned brickwork. Adjacent is the **chapel**, built in 1620, with its unusual fan-vaulted open crypt, or undercroft, at ground level; on the first floor, the nave, rebuilt in 1880, hit by a Zeppelin in World War I and much restored since, still boasts its original ornate pews. North of the chapel lie the Palladian **Stone Buildings**, best appreciated from the manicured lawns of the Inn's gardens; the strange miniature castle near the garden entrance is the gardeners' tool shed, a creation of George Gilbert Scott, designer of St Pancras Station.

Chancery Lane

Running along the eastern edge of Lincoln's Inn is legal London's main thoroughfare, **Chancery Lane**, home of the Law Society (the solicitors' regulatory body for England and Wales) and lined with shops where barristers, solicitors and clerks can buy their wigs, gowns, legal tomes, stationery and champagne.

London Silver Vaults

Chancery Lane, entrance on Southampton Buildings • Mon–Fri 9am–5.30pm, Sat 9am–1pm • Free • ☎ 020 7242 3844, ⓦ thesilvervaultslondon.com • ⊖ Chancery Lane

On the east side of Chancery Lane are the **London Silver Vaults**, which began life in 1876 as the Chancery Lane Safe Deposit for London's wealthy elite, but now house a strange, claustrophobic lair of subterranean shops selling every kind of silverware – mostly antique, mostly English and often quite tasteless.

Gray's Inn

South Square • **Precincts** Mon–Fri 6am–8pm; **Gardens** Mon–Fri noon–2.30pm • Free • ☎ 020 7458 7800, ⓦ graysinn.info • ⊖ Chancery Lane

Hidden away off High Holborn, opposite the top of Chancery Lane, is **Gray's Inn**, another of the four Inns of Court; access is from Theobald's Road, Gray's Inn Road and next to the venerable *Cittie of Yorke* pub on High Holborn. Established in the fourteenth century, the Inn took its name from the de Grey family, who owned the original mansion used as student lodgings; most of what you see today, however, was rebuilt after the Blitz. The **Hall** (by appointment only), with its fabulous Tudor screen and stained glass, witnessed the premiere of Shakespeare's *Comedy of Errors* in 1594. The north side of the Inn, taken up by the wide green expanse of **Gray's Inn Gardens**, also known as The Walks, is entirely and impressively visible through its wrought-iron railings from Theobald's Road.

Holborn

Confusingly, **Holborn** is also the name of a street – an eastern continuation of High Holborn – with two remarkable buildings, one on either side of the road. The first, on the south side, is **Staple Inn**, a former Inn of Chancery (a less prestigious version of the Inns of Court). Its overhanging half-timbered facade and gables date from the sixteenth century and are the most extensive in the whole of London; they survived the Fire, but had to be extensively rebuilt after the Blitz. More or less opposite stands the palatial, terracotta-red **Prudential Assurance Building**, begun in 1879 by Alfred Waterhouse. This fortress of Victorian capitalism has its very own Bridge of Sighs, harbours a dramatic memorial to the Prudential men who fell in World War I (plus a more sober one for World War II) and retains much of its original Doulton-tiled interior. At the eastern end of Holborn lies **Holborn Circus**, a vast traffic intersection centred on London's politest statue, in which a cheerful Prince Albert doffs his hat to passers-by.

8

Hatton Garden

ⓦ hatton-garden.net

Hatton Garden, connecting Holborn Circus with Little Italy (see p.146), is no beauty spot, but, as the centre of the city's **diamond and jewellery trade** since medieval times, it's an intriguing place to visit during the week. There are over fifty shops and, as in Antwerp and New York, Orthodox Jews dominate the business here as middlemen. In 2015 the street was the scene of a £35 million jewellery heist when thieves raided the Hatton Garden Safe Deposit vaults.

Near the top of Hatton Garden, there's a plaque commemorating **Hiram Maxim** (1840–1916), the American inventor who perfected the automatic gun named after him in the workshops at no. 57. Parallel to Hatton Garden, take a wander through **Leather Lane Market**, a weekday lunchtime market selling everything from fruit and veg to clothes and electrical gear; nowadays, there are trendy street-food vans too.

St Etheldreda's Church

14 Ely Place · Mon–Sat 8am–5pm, Sun till 12.30pm · Free · ☏ 020 7405 1061, ⓦ stetheldreda.com · ⊖ Chancery Lane

Just off Charterhouse Street, which runs northeast from Holborn Circus, is the cul-de-sac of **Ely Place**, named after the Bishop of Ely, whose London residence used to stand here from 1290 to 1772. It's from Ely Place that Shakespeare has John of Gaunt say his "this sceptre'd isle" speech in *Richard II*. All that remains of the bishop's palace now is **St Etheldreda's Church**, the bishop's former private chapel, halfway down the street on the left. Built in the thirteenth century, the chapel was bought by the Roman Catholic Rosminian Order in 1874. The Upper Church, though restored, retains much of its medieval masonry, and features two spectacularly huge postwar stained-glass windows; the west window depicts several English Catholic martyrs, including the Carthusian Prior John Haughton, whose statue also occupies the first niche on the south wall. The atmospherically gloomy medieval crypt contains a model of the pre-Reformation church complex.

CLERKENWELL GREEN

Clerkenwell

Situated slightly uphill from the City and, more importantly, outside its jurisdiction, Clerkenwell (pronounced "Clark-unwell") began life as a village serving the various local monastic foundations. In the nineteenth century, the district's population trebled, mostly through Irish and Italian immigration, and the area acquired a reputation for radicalism exemplified by the Marx Memorial Library, where the exiled Lenin plotted revolution. Nowadays, Clerkenwell is a typical London mix of Georgian and Victorian townhouses, housing estates, old warehouses, loft conversions and art studios. It remains off the conventional tourist trail, but since the 1990s, it has established itself as one of the city's most vibrant and fashionable areas, with a host of shops, cafés, restaurants and pubs bustling with activity during the week.

Following the Great Fire, Clerkenwell was settled by craftsmen, including newly arrived French Huguenots, excluded from the City guilds. At the same time, the springs that give the place its name were rediscovered (and are still visible through the window of 14–16 Farringdon Lane), and Clerkenwell became a popular **spa resort** for a century or so. During the nineteenth century, the district's springs and streams became cholera-infested sewers, and the area became an overpopulated **slum area**, home to three prisons and the setting for Fagin's Den in Dickens' *Oliver Twist*. Victorian slum clearances and wartime bombing took their toll; the population declined and by the 1980s, the area's traditional trades – locksmithing, clockmaking, printing and jewellery – had all but disappeared. Nowadays, the area is characterized by media and design companies (particularly architects), with trendy bars and restaurants catering for the area's loft-dwelling residents.

Mount Pleasant and the British Postal Museum

Rosebery Ave • Postal Museum Mon–Fri 10am–5pm, Thurs till 7pm, plus second Sat of month 10am–5pm (closed the following Mon) • Free • ℡ 020 7239 2570, ⓦ postalheritage.org.uk • ⊖ Farringdon

Halfway up Rosebery Avenue stands the **Mount Pleasant Mail Centre**, usually referred to simply as Mount Pleasant, opened in 1889 and at one time the largest sorting office in the world. A third of all inland mail passes through here, and originally much of it was brought by the post office's own underground railway network, **Mail Rail** (ⓦ mailrail .co.uk). Opened in 1927 and similar in design to the tube, the railway was fully automatic, sending driverless trucks between London's sorting offices and train stations at speeds of up to 35mph. Unfortunately, all 23 miles of this 2ft-gauge railway were mothballed in 2003, though plans have been floated to reopen sections of the rail as a tourist attraction. Philatelists, meanwhile, should head to the **British Postal Museum**, by the side of the sorting office on Phoenix Place, which puts on small exhibitions drawn from its vast archive.

Exmouth Market

Food market Mon–Fri noon–3pm • ⓦ exmouth-market.com • ⊖ Farringdon

Opposite Mount Pleasant is **Exmouth Market**, the heart of today's vibrant Clerkenwell. Apart from a surviving pie-and-mash shop, the street is now characterized by modish shops, bars and restaurants, and a small **foodie market**, at its busiest towards the end of the week. A blue plaque at no. 56 pays tribute to **Joseph Grimaldi** (1778–1837), son of Italian immigrants and the "Father of Clowns", who first appeared on stage at nearby Sadler's Wells at the age of 3. Close by, the street's **Church of the Holy Redeemer** sports a fetching Italianate campanile, while the groin-vaulted interior features a large baldachin and Stations of the Cross – yet despite appearances, it belongs to the Church of England.

Sadler's Wells

Rosebery Ave • ⓦ sadlerswells.com • ⊖ Angel

Clerkenwell's days as a fashionable spa began when Thomas Sadler rediscovered a medicinal well in his garden in 1683 and established a music house to entertain visitors. The well has since made a comeback at the **Sadler's Wells Theatre** on Rosebery Avenue, the seventh theatre here since 1683, and now one of London's main dance venues. A borehole sunk into the old well provides some of the water used in the building.

Islington Museum

245 St John St • Daily except Wed & Sun 10am–5pm • Free • ℡ 020 7527 2837, ⓦ islington.gov.uk • ⊖ Angel or Farringdon

If you're keen to learn more about Clerkenwell, Finsbury or the wider borough of Islington (see p.289), it's worth seeking out the **Islington Museum**, housed in the

9

LITTLE ITALY

In the late nineteenth century, London experienced a huge influx of Italian immigrants who created their own **Little Italy** in the triangle of land now bounded by Clerkenwell Road, Rosebery Avenue and Farringdon Road; craftsmen, artisans, street performers and musicians were later joined by ice-cream vendors, restaurateurs and political refugees. Between the wars the population peaked at around ten thousand, crammed into overcrowded, insanitary slums. The old streets have long been demolished, and few Italians live here these days; nevertheless, the area remains a focus for a community that's now spread right across the capital.

The main point of reference is **St Peter's Italian Church** (☏020 7837 1528, ⓦitalianchurch .org.uk), a surprisingly large, bright, basilica-style church built in 1863 and still the favourite venue for Italian weddings and christenings, as well as for Sunday Mass. It's rarely open outside of daily Mass, though you can view the World War I memorial in the main porch, and, above it, the grim memorial to seven hundred Anglo-Italian internees who died aboard the *Arandora Star*, a POW ship which sank en route to Canada in 1940. St Peter's is the starting point of the annual Italian Procession, begun in 1883 and a permanent fixture on the Sunday nearest July 16 (see p.26).

A few old-established Italian businesses survive, too: the Scuola Guida driving school (aka the Holborn School of Motoring) at 178 Clerkenwell Rd, and the deli, G. Gazzano & Son, at 167–169 Farringdon Rd. There's also a plaque to **Giuseppe Mazzini** (1805–72), the chief protagonist in Italian unification, above the barbers at 10 Laystall St. Mazzini lived in exile in London for many years and was very active in the Clerkenwell community, establishing a free school for Italian children in Hatton Garden.

basement of the Finsbury Library (access is down the steps on the north side). There's a dressing-up box for the kids and some fascinating sections on the area's radical politics for the adults. Highlights include the bust of Lenin, part of a memorial erected by socialist Finsbury Council in 1942 in Holford Square (see p.146), but had to be removed after the war, after it was targeted by Fascists; you can also listen to recordings of interviews with Caribbean nurses working in Islington in the 1950s and 60s and view some of the library books embellished by Joe Orton and Kenneth Halliwell (see p.293).

Clerkenwell Green

There hasn't been any green on **Clerkenwell Green** for at least three centuries and it's better described now as a square, though there's actually more road than pavement. In the nineteenth century, when poverty and overcrowding were the main features of Clerkenwell, the Green was well known in the press as "the headquarters of republicanism, revolution and ultra-non-conformity" and a popular spot for **demonstrations**. The most violent of these was the "Clerkenwell Riot" of 1832, when a policeman was stabbed to death during a clash between unemployed demonstrators and the newly formed Metropolitan Police Force. London's first **May Day** march set off from here in 1890, and the tradition continues to this day. In 1900, the Labour Party was founded at a meeting on nearby Farringdon Road; in 1903 Lenin and Stalin first met at the *Crown & Anchor* (now the *Crown Tavern*); the Communist Party had its headquarters close by on St John Street for many years; and the Party's *Daily Worker* (and later *Morning Star*), the *Guardian* and the *Observer* were all printed on Farringdon Road. Ironically, or perhaps appropriately, the grandest building on the square, a Neoclassical construction dominating the west side, is an old courthouse, the former Middlesex Sessions House, completed in 1782. The last trial here was in 1920, and today it stands largely in disuse, with plans to convert it into shops and restaurants in little evidence.

Sunk back but visible from Clerkenwell Green, the modest church of **St James** dates from 1792, the descendant of the convent church of the Benedictine nunnery of St Mary that once occupied the area north of the Green.

9

Marx Memorial Library

37a Clerkenwell Green • Mon–Thurs noon–4pm; closed Aug • Free • ☎ 020 7253 1485, ⓦ marx-memorial-library.org •
⊖ Farringdon

The oldest building on the Green is the former Welsh Charity School, at no. 37a,
built in 1738 and now home to the **Marx Memorial Library**. Headquarters of the
left-wing London Patriotic Society from 1872, and later the Social Democratic
Federation's Twentieth Century Press, this is where **Lenin** edited seventeen editions of
the Bolshevik paper *Iskra* in 1902–03. The library itself, founded in 1933 in response
to the book burnings in Nazi Germany, is open to members only. However, visitors
are welcome to view the "workerist" *Hastings Mural* from 1935, and the poky little
back room where Lenin worked on *Iskra*. Stuffed with busts, the latter is maintained
as a kind of shrine, and there's a copy of Rodchenko's red-and-black chess set for
good measure, too.

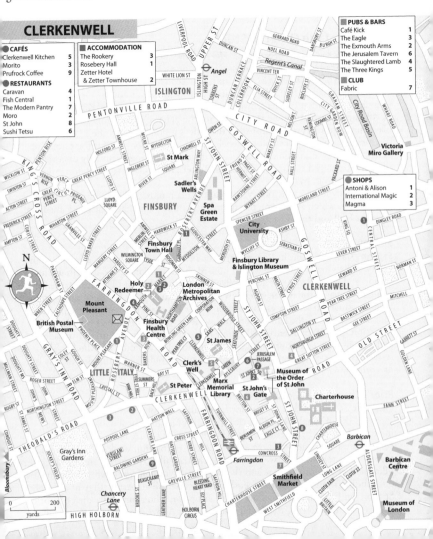

9

THE PEOPLE'S REPUBLIC OF FINSBURY

The Borough of Finsbury was subsumed into Islington in 1965, but the former **Finsbury Town Hall** (now a dance academy) still stands, an attractive building from 1899, whose name is spelt out in magenta glass on the delicate wrought-iron canopy that juts out into Rosebery Avenue. As the plaque outside states, the district was the first to boast an Asian MP, **Dadabhai Nairoji**, who was elected (after a recount) as a Liberal MP in 1892 with a majority of five. In keeping with its radical pedigree, the borough went on to elect several Communist councillors and became known popularly as the "People's Republic of Finsbury". The council commissioned Georgian-born Berthold Lubetkin to design the modernist **Finsbury Health Centre** on Pine Street, off Exmouth Market, described by Jonathan Glancey as "a remarkable outpost of Soviet thinking and neo-Constructivist architecture in a part of central London wracked with rickets and TB". Lubetkin's later **Spa Green Estate**, the council flats further north on the opposite side of Rosebery Avenue from Sadler's Wells, featured novelties such as rubbish chutes and an aerofoil roof to help tenants dry their clothes.

Museum of the Order of St John

St John's Lane and St John's Square • Mon–Sat 10am–5pm • Free • Guided tours Tues, Fri & Sat 11am & 2.30pm • £5 donation suggested • ☎ 020 7324 4005, ⓦ museumstjohn.org.uk • ❸ Farringdon

The **Museum of the Order of St John**, split between two buildings on opposite sides of Clerkenwell Road, is housed on the site of the former Priory of the Order of St John of Jerusalem, the oldest of Clerkenwell's religious establishments. The Knights of St John, or Knights Hospitaller, were responsible for the defence of the Holy Land, and the Clerkenwell priory was established as the order's headquarters in the 1140s. The priory was sacked by Wat Tyler's poll-tax rebels in 1381 on the lookout for the prior, Robert Hales, who was responsible for collecting the tax; Hales was eventually discovered at the Tower, dragged out and beheaded on Tower Hill. Following the Reformation, the Knights moved to Malta.

To view any more of the priory, beyond the main museum buildings, you must take a **guided tour**, which allows you to explore the Council Chamber, the mock-medieval Chapter Hall and the West Tower.

St John's Gate

St John's Gate was built in Kentish ragstone in 1502 as the southern entrance to the priory. Following the Reformation it housed the Master of Revels, the Elizabethan censor, and later a Latin-speaking coffee house run by Richard Hogarth, father of the painter, William. Today, the gatehouse is the headquarters of **St John Ambulance**, a voluntary first-aid service, established in 1877. The main room of the gatehouse museum, known as the **Link Gallery,** traces the development of the Order before its expulsion in 1540 by Henry VIII. There's masonry from the old priory, crusader coins and a small arms collection salvaged from the knights' armoury on Rhodes. The museum's other gallery tells the story of St John Ambulance, featuring a display of early uniforms and equipment.

Priory Church and Cloister Garden

Opposite St John's Gate, on the northern half of St John's Square, the surviving scraps of the original **Priory Church** form part of an historical patchwork that includes three of the exterior walls of the fifteenth-century church, the eighteenth-century west wall and some twentieth-century restoration work helping to hold it all together. Of the original twelfth-century church, all that remains are the bases of two pillars either side of the altar and the wonderful **Norman crypt**, which contains two outstanding monuments: a sixteenth-century Spanish alabaster effigy of a Knight of St John, and the emaciated effigy of the last prior, who supposedly died of a broken heart in 1540 following the Order's dissolution. Above ground, there's a small

LENIN IN CLERKENWELL

Virtually every Bolshevik leader spent at least some time in exile in London at the beginning of the twentieth century, to avoid the attentions of the Tsarist secret police. **Lenin** (1870–1924) and his wife, Nadezhda, arrived in April 1902 and found unfurnished lodgings at 30 Holford Square, off Great Percy Street, under the pseudonyms of Mr and Mrs Jacob Richter. Like Marx, Lenin did his studying in the British Library (see p.134) – L13 was his favourite desk.

The couple also entertained other exiles – including **Trotsky**, whom Lenin met for the first time at Holford Square in October 1902 – but Lenin's most important job was his editing of *Iskra* with Yuli Martov (later the Menshevik leader) and Vera Zasulich (one-time revolutionary assassin). The paper was set in Cyrillic script at a Jewish printer's in the East End and run off on the Social Democratic Federation presses on Clerkenwell Green.

In May 1903, Lenin left to join other exiles in Geneva, though over the next eight years he visited London on five more occasions. The Holford Square house was destroyed in the Blitz, so, in 1942, the local council erected a (short-lived) **monument** to Lenin (now in the Islington Museum). A blue plaque at the back of the hotel on the corner of Great Percy Street commemorates the site of 16 Percy Circus, where Lenin stayed in 1905.

museum gallery containing a few bits and pieces from the life of the church down the centuries, a collection of around a dozen historic paintings including portraits of some of the Knights of the Order and a lovely recreation of the **Cloister Garden**. The curve of the original church's walls – it was circular, like Temple Church – is traced out in cobblestones on St John's Square.

Charterhouse

Charterhouse Square • By guided tour only April–Aug Tues, Wed, Thurs and every other Sat • £10 • ☎ 020 7253 9503, ⓦ thecharterhouse .org • ⊖ Barbican or Farringdon

In the southeast corner of Clerkenwell lies **Charterhouse**, founded in 1371 as a Carthusian monastery. The Carthusians were the most respected of the religious orders in London and the only one to put up any significant resistance to the Dissolution of the Monasteries, for which the prior was hanged, drawn and quartered at Tyburn, and his severed arm nailed to the gatehouse as a warning to the rest of the community. The gatehouse, on Charterhouse Square, which retains its fourteenth-century oak doors, is the starting point for the excellent, exhaustive two-hour **guided tours**.

Very little remains of the original buildings, as the monastery was rebuilt as a Tudor mansion after the Dissolution. The monks lived in individual cells, each with its own garden and were only allowed to speak to one another on Sundays; three of their tiny cells can still be seen in the west wall of **Preachers' Court**. The larger of the two enclosed courtyards, **Masters' Court**, retains the wonderful Great Hall, which boasts a fine Renaissance carved screen and a largely reconstructed hammer-beam roof, as well as the Great Chamber where Elizabeth I and James I were once entertained. The **Chapel**, with its geometrical plasterwork ceiling, is half-Tudor and half-Jacobean, and contains the marble and alabaster tomb of **Thomas Sutton**, whose greyhound-head emblem crops up throughout the building. It was Sutton, deemed "the richest commoner in England" at the time, who bought the place in 1611 and converted it into a charity school for boys (now the famous public school in Surrey) and an **almshouse** for gentlemen – known as "brothers" – forty of whom continue to be cared for here.

BANK OF ENGLAND

The City

The City is where London began. It was here, nearly two thousand years ago
that the Romans first established a settlement on the Thames; later the
medieval city emerged as the country's most important trading centre; and it
remains one of the world's leading financial hubs. When you consider what's
happened here, it's amazing that anything has survived. Yet there are Roman
remains and Wren's spires still punctuate the skyline, as does his masterpiece,
St Paul's Cathedral. Other relics, such as the City's few remaining medieval
alleyways are less conspicuous, and even the locals have problems finding
the Museum of London and their way around the Barbican arts complex. The
City's modern architecture includes some of the most iconic London
buildings built in the last thirty years, from Richard Rogers' mould-breaking
Lloyd's Building to The Walkie Talkie and The Cheesegrater.

Today the City stretches from Temple Bar in the west to the Tower of London in the east – administrative boundaries only slightly larger than those marked by the Roman walls and their medieval successors. However, in this **Square Mile** (as the City is often called) you'll have to dig hard to find leftovers of London's early days: four-fifths of the area burnt down in the Great Fire. What you see on the ground is mostly the product of three fairly recent building phases: the Victorian construction boom; the rapid reconstruction that followed the Blitz; and the building frenzy that began in the late 1980s, and which has since seen over half the City's office space rebuilt.

The biggest change of all, though, has been in the City's **population**. Until the eighteenth century, the vast majority of Londoners lived and worked in or around the City; nowadays, while more than 350,000 commuters spend Monday to Friday here, only ten thousand actually live here, many cooped up in the Barbican complex. The result of this shift is that the City is only fully alive during office hours, with many pubs, restaurants and even some tube stations and tourist sights closing at the weekend.

10

Fleet Street

Fleet Street offers one of the grandest approaches to the City, thanks to the view across to Ludgate Hill and beyond to St Paul's Cathedral, but it's best known for its associations with the printed press and particularly the newspaper industry (see box, p.155). The press headquarters that once dominated the area have all now relocated, leaving just a handful of small publications and a few architectural landmarks to testify to five hundred years of printing history. The former **Daily Telegraph** building, at nos. 135–141, is one of London's few truly Art Deco edifices, built in a Greco-Egyptian style in 1928, with a striking polychrome clock and a great stone relief above the doorway depicting Mercury's messengers sending news around the world. It was upstaged a few years later, however, by the city's first glass curtain-wall construction, the former **Daily Express** building at no. 127, with its sleek black Vitrolite facade. It's worth peering inside the cinema-like foyer, which features a silver-leaf sunburst ceiling, ocean-wave floor tiles, shiny silver serpent handrails and remarkable chrome and gold relief panels extolling the British Empire.

Temple Bar

Temple Bar, at the western end of Fleet Street, is the latest in a long line of structures marking the boundary between the City of Westminster and the City of London. It began as a simple chain between two posts, but a Wren-designed triumphal arch stood here by the 1670s. The heads of executed traitors were displayed on the arch until the mid-eighteenth century – one could even rent a telescope for a closer look. Then, in 1878, the arch was removed to ease traffic and exiled for over a century to a park in Hertfordshire, only to be re-erected in 2004 at the entrance to Paternoster Square near St Paul's (see p.159). The current monument, topped by a winged dragon, marks the spot where the sovereign must ask for the Lord Mayor's permission to enter the City, a tradition that began when Elizabeth I passed through on her way to St Paul's to give thanks for the defeat of the Spanish Armada.

CITY OF LONDON INFORMATION CENTRE

Located between St Paul's Cathedral and the Millennium Bridge, **The City Information Centre** (Mon–Sat 9.30am–5.30pm, Sun 10am–4pm; ☎020 7332 1456; ⬤cityoflondon.gov.uk) is the only officially recognized Tourist Information Centre in central London. The multilingual staff can provide simple directions or detailed advice on events or suggestions for days out. They sell maps, oyster cards and fast-track tickets to London attractions (allowing you to jump queues at places like the Tower of London and St Paul's Cathedral) and you can book some very rewarding themed tours and walks here too, two of which leave from the centre itself; for more walking tours go to the Museum of London (see p.165).

THE CITY

Map labels

OLD STREET
GOSWELL ROAD
WOODBRIDGE ST
BANNER ST
GOLDEN LANE
FORTUNE ST
GREAT SUTTON STREET
AYLESBURY ST
FANN STREET
CLERKENWELL ROAD
CLERKENWELL
Charterhouse
ST JOHN STREET
CHARTERHOUSE SQUARE
BEECH STREET
Barbican Arts Centre
BARBICAN
St Giles
SAFFRON HILL
FARRINGDON ROAD
GREVILLE ST
COWCROSS ST
Farringdon
CHARTERHOUSE STREET
LONG LANE
ALDERSGATE STREET
CLOTH FAIR
St Bartholomew-the-Great
Museum of London
LONDON WA
HATTON GARDEN
LEATHER LANE
HOLBORN
HOLBORN CIRCUS
St Andrew
HOLBORN VIADUCT
SNOW HILL
COCK LANE
St Sepulchre
Smithfield Market
WEST SMITHFIELD
LITTLE BRITAIN
GILTSPUR STREET
St Bartholomew's Hospital
King Edward St
St Botolph
Postman's Park
Goldsmiths' Hall
GRESHAM STREE
ST ANDREW ST
FETTER LANE
NEW FETTER LANE
BREAM'S BUILDINGS
NEW STREET SQUARE
STONE ST
ST BRIDE STREET
FARRINGDON ROAD
City Thameslink
NEWGATE STREET
Old Bailey
WARWICK LANE
St Paul's
St Vedast
ST LA
WOOD STREET
NOBLE STREET
FOSTER LANE
GUTTER LANE
ALDERSGATE STREET
W. HARDING ST
GOUGH SQUARE
WINE OFFICE CT
Dr Johnson's House
SHOE LANE
LIMEBURNER LANE
OLD BAILEY
St Martin Ludgate
Temple Bar
PATERNOSTER SQUARE
St Paul's Cathedral
One New Change
CHEAPSIDE
St le
BRIDE LANE
St Dunstan-in-the-West
FLEET STREET
BOUVERIE ST
WHITEFRIARS ST
DORSET RISE
St Bride
LUDGATE CIRCUS
LUDGATE HILL
City Thameslink
ST PAUL'S CHURCHYARD
NEW CHANGE
WATLING STREET
Temple Bar
CREED LANE
KNIGHTRIDER ST
College of Arms
CANNON STREET
Mansion House
TEMPLE
TUDOR STREET
CARMELITE ST
TEMPLE AVENUE
CARTER LANE
BLACKFRIARS LANE
ST ANDREWS HILL
Apothecaries' Hall
Church of Scientology
Andrew-by-the-Wardrobe
GODLIMAN STREET
QUEEN VICTORIA STREET
DISTAFF LANE
St Nicholas Cole Abbey
St Benet
PETER'S HILL
LAMBETH HILL
GARLICK HILL
ST PETER'S HILL
VICTORIA EMBANKMENT
Blackfriars
Blackfriars Station
UPPER THAMES
CASTLE BAYNARD STREET
WHITE LION HILL
HIGH TIMBER ST
UPPER
Vintners' Hall
RIVERSIDE WALK
QUEENHITHE
Blackfriars Millennium Pier
BLACKFRIARS BRIDGE
River Thames
BANKSIDE
MILLENNIUM BRIDGE
Bankside Pier
SOUTHWARK BRIDGE
UPPER GROUND
Shakespeare's Globe Theatre & Sam Wanamaker Theatre
HOPTON STREET
Tate Modern
PARK STREET
BANKSIDE
STAMFORD STREET
HOLLAND STREET
SUMNER STREET
GREAT GUILDFORD ST
SOUTHWARK ST

Scale

0 ___ 200
yards

Legend

PUBS & BARS
The Black Friar	6
Jamaica Wine House	4
The Lamb Tavern/ Old Tom's Bar	5
The Viaduct Tavern	2
Ye Old Cheshire Cheese	3

LGBT VENUES
Steel Yard	8
WayOut Club	7

MUSIC VENUE
Barbican	1

ACCOMMODATION
Andaz	1
Apex City of London Hotel	4
The King's Wardrobe	3
YHA St Paul's	2

CAFÉ
Patty & Bun	2

RESTAURANTS
Duck & Waffle	3
José Pizarro	1

St Dunstan-in-the-West

186a Fleet St • Mon–Fri 9.30am–5pm • ☎ 020 7405 1929, ⓦ stdunstaninthewest.org • ⊖ Temple or Blackfriars

The church of **St Dunstan-in-the-West**, with a distinctive neo-Gothic tower and lantern, from the 1830s, dominates the top of Fleet Street. To the side is the much earlier clock temple, erected in 1671 by the parishioners in thanks for escaping the Great Fire, which stopped just short of the church; inside the temple, sculpted depictions of the legendary British giants Gog and Magog, in gilded loincloths, nod their heads and clang their bells on the hour. The statue of Queen Elizabeth I, in a niche in the vestry wall, and the crumbling statues of the legendary King Lud and his two sons in the porch, originally stood over Ludgate, the City gateway that once stood halfway up Ludgate Hill. The church's unusual, octagonal, neo-Gothic interior features a huge wooden iconostasis (altar screen), brought from a Bucharest monastery in 1966 to this Anglican church building which doubles as the home of the Romanian Orthodox Church in London.

Dr Johnson's House

17 Gough Square • Mon–Sat: May–Sept 11am–5.30pm; Oct–April 11am–5pm • £4.50, concessions £3.50, under-17s £1.50, under-5s free • ☎ 020 7353 3745, ⓦ drjohnsonshouse.org • ⊖ Blackfriars

Numerous narrow alleyways lead off the north side of Fleet Street beyond Fetter Lane, concealing legal chambers and offices. Two of the narrow alleyways that lead north off Fleet Street – Bolt Court and Hind Court – eventually open out into cobbled Gough Square, which features a statue of Dr Johnson's cat, Hodge, enjoying an oyster. The square's one authentic eighteenth-century building is **Dr Johnson's House,** where the great savant, writer and lexicographer lived from 1748 to 1759 while compiling the 41,000 entries for his very successful English dictionary.

Johnson rented the house on Gough Square with the £1575 advance he received for the dictionary. Despite his subsequent fame, Johnson was in and out of debt all his life – his bestselling romance, *Rasselas*, was written in less than a week to raise funds for his mother's funeral. The house itself is a lovely Georgian period piece peppered with quotes by the great man and portraits of his contemporaries, including Johnson's servant Francis Barber, to whom he left most of his wordly goods. On the second floor, you can watch a film on Johnson's life, after which you get to see the open-plan attic, in which Johnson and his six clerks put together the dictionary.

SAMUEL PEPYS

Born to a humble tailor and a laundress in Salisbury Court, off Fleet Street, **Samuel Pepys** (1633–1703) was baptized in St Bride's (see box opposite) and buried in St Olave's, having spent virtually his entire life in London. Family connections secured an education at St Paul's School, a scholarship to Cambridge and a career in the civil service. He was an MP, served as Secretary to the Admiralty and was instrumental in the establishment of a professional British navy. In 1679 he was imprisoned for six weeks in the Tower on suspicion of treason, but returned to office, only to be forced out again in 1689, following the overthrow of James II.

It's not Pepys' career, but his **diaries**, written between 1660 and 1669, that have immortalized him. This rollicking journal includes eyewitness accounts of the Restoration, the Great Plague and the Great Fire, giving an unparalleled insight into London life at the time. Ultimately, Pepys emerges from the pages, warts and all, as an eminently likeable character, who seems almost imperturbable – he gives as much space to details of his pub meals as he does to the Great Fire, and finishes most entries with his catchphrase "and so to bed".

Pepys was also a notorious womanizer, detailing his philanderings in his diary in a mixture of Spanish, Italian and French so as to avoid detection by his French Huguenot wife. Nevertheless he was caught *in flagrante* with their maid, and his slow reconciliation with his spouse is recorded in a novelist's detail, the diary ending in 1669 as they sail off to the Continent to patch things up. In the event, his wife died later that year and he never remarried. Pepys bequeathed his vast library to his old college in Cambridge, where his diaries lay undiscovered until the nineteenth century, when they were finally published (with the erotic passages omitted) in 1825.

THE FLEET STREET PRESS

Fleet Street's associations with the printed press began in 1500, when Wynkyn de Worde, William Caxton's apprentice (and the first man to print italics in England), moved the Caxton presses from Westminster to Fleet Street to be close to the lawyers of the Inns of Court (his best customers) and to the clergy of St Paul's, London's largest literate group. In 1702, the world's first daily newspaper, the now defunct **Daily Courant**, began publishing here, and by the nineteenth century, all the major national and provincial dailies had moved their presses to the area. Then in 1985, Britain's first colour tabloid, *Today*, appeared, using computer technology that rendered the Fleet Street presses obsolete. It was left to media tycoon Rupert Murdoch to take on the printers' unions in a bitter year-long dispute that changed the newspaper industry for ever.

There's a tiled wall in Magpie Alley, off Bouverie Street, which illustrates the history of Fleet Street's presses, and some metal information panels nearby in the windows of the old *Daily Mail* building at Ashentree Court, off Whitefriars Street. Another account of Fleet Street's history is the exhibition in the crypt of **St Bride's Church** (Mon–Fri 9am–5pm, Sat hours vary, Sun 10am–6.30pm; free; ☎ 020 7427 0133, ⓦ stbrides.com), the "journalists' and printers' cathedral", situated behind the former Reuters building. The church also boasts Wren's tallest, and most exquisite, spire (said to be the inspiration for the traditional tiered wedding cake).

Ludgate Circus

Fleet Street terminates at **Ludgate Circus**, built in the 1870s to replace a bridge over the **River Fleet**, which had already been buried under the roads after a drunken butcher got stuck in the river mud and froze to death. The Fleet originally marked the western boundary of the walled City, and was once an unmissable feature of the landscape, as the tanneries and slaughterhouses of Smithfield, to the north, used to turn the water red with entrails. The Fleet's western bank was the site of the notoriously inhumane **Fleet Prison**, where the poet John Donne was imprisoned in 1601 for marrying without his father-in-law's consent. Until 1754, Fleet Prison was renowned for its clandestine "**Fleet Marriages**", performed by priests (or impostors) who were imprisoned there for debt. These marriages, in which couples could marry without a licence, attracted people of all classes, and took place in the prison chapel until 1710, when they were banished to the neighbouring taverns, the fee being split between clergyman and innkeeper.

St Paul's Cathedral

Cathedral Mon–Sat 8.30am–4.30pm, last admission 4pm; **galleries** Mon–Sat 9.30am–4.15pm • £18, concessions £16, under-17s £8, under-6s free (£15.50, £13.50, £7 online, must be bought at least a day in advance) • ☎ 020 7236 4128, ⓦ stpauls.co.uk • ⊖ St Paul's

The enormous lead-covered dome of **St Paul's Cathedral** has dominated the City skyline since it was built after the Great Fire – and remains so despite the encroaching tower blocks. Its showpiece west facade is particularly magnificent, fronted by a wide flight of steps, a double-storey portico and two towers, among the finest examples of Baroque architecture in London. While it can't compete with Westminster Abbey for celebrity corpses, pre-Reformation sculpture, royal connections and sheer atmosphere, St Paul's is nevertheless a perfectly calculated architectural space, a burial place for captains rather than kings, artists not poets, and a popular wedding venue for the privileged few (including Charles and Diana).

The current building is the fifth on this site, its immediate predecessor being **Old St Paul's**, a huge Gothic cathedral built by the Normans, whose 489ft spire (destroyed by lightning in 1561) was one of the wonders of medieval Europe. St Paul's was just one of over fifty church commissions Christopher Wren received in the wake of the Great Fire. Hassles over his initial plans, and wrangles over money plagued the project throughout, but Wren remained unruffled and England's first Protestant cathedral was officially completed in 1710 under Queen Anne, whose statue stands below the steps. The cathedral achieved iconic status during the **Blitz**, when it stood defiantly unscathed amid the carnage (as seen in a famous wartime propaganda photo), and a monument to the south of the cathedral commemorates both the **St Paul's Watch** – volunteers who patrolled the cathedral roof every night to combat the incendiary bombs – and all those firefighters who have died since while carrying out their duties.

INFORMATION AND TOURS

Entry Admission charges are nothing new at St Paul's – they were first introduced in 1709, before the cathedral was even finished. Once inside, pick up a free plan, and simply ask the vergers or stewards if you're having trouble locating a particular monument; alternatively, multimedia guides are available free of charge.

Tours Free introductory talks run regularly throughout the day, and there are longer guided tours (1hr 30min), also free, that allow you access to one or two areas off limits to the public, setting off at 10am, 11am, 1pm and 2pm. If

you're in a group of five or more, you can also pay an extra £8 each to go on a full-on behind-the-scenes triforium tour (Mon & Tues 11.30am & 2pm, Fri 2pm; book at least a week in advance on ☏ 020 7246 8357).

Services It's worth attending one of the cathedral's services, if only to hear the choir, who perform during most evensongs (Mon–Sat 5pm), and on Sundays at 10.15am, 11.30am and 3.15pm. On Sundays St Paul's is only open for services. A full schedule of services is available on the website.

The interior

Queen Victoria thought the **nave** "dirty, dark and undevotional", though since the destruction of the stained glass in the Blitz, it is once again light and airy, as Wren intended. Burials are confined to the crypt, and memorials were only permitted after 1790 when overcrowding at Westminster Abbey had become intolerable. What followed was a series of overblown funerary monuments to the military heroes of the Napoleonic Wars. Some are simply ludicrous, like the virtually naked statue of Captain Burges, in the south aisle, holding hands with an angel over a naval cannon; others are more offensive, such as the monument to Thomas Fanshaw Middleton, first Protestant bishop of India, depicted baptizing "heathen" locals. The best of the bunch are Flaxman's **Nelson** memorial, in the south transept, with its seasick lion, and, in the north aisle, the bombastic bronze and marble monument – the cathedral's largest – to the **Duke of Wellington**, begun in 1857 but only topped with the statue of the duke astride his faithful steed, Copenhagen, in 1912. Both men are buried in the crypt.

The best place from which to appreciate the glory of St Paul's is beneath the **dome**,

---

THE CITY'S CHURCHES

The City of London is crowded with **churches**, the majority of them built or rebuilt by Christopher Wren after the Great Fire. Prompted by the decline in the City's population, the Victorians demolished a fair few, but over forty remain intact. The **opening times** given in the text should be taken with a pinch of salt, since many rely on volunteers to keep their doors open. As a general rule, weekday lunchtimes are the best time to visit, since many City churches put on free lunchtime concerts. Below is a list of the six most interesting:

St Bartholomew-the-Great Cloth Fair. This is the oldest surviving pre-Fire church in the City and by far the most atmospheric. It was also the first church in the country to charge an entrance fee. See p.163.

St Mary Abchurch Abchurch Lane. Uniquely for Wren's City churches, the interior features a huge, painted, domed ceiling, plus the only authenticated Gibbons reredos. See p.170.

St Mary Aldermary Bow Lane/Watling St. Wren's most successful stab at Gothic, with fan vaulting in the aisles and a panelled ceiling in the nave. See p.160.

St Mary Woolnoth King William St. Hawksmoor's only City church, sporting an unusually broad, bulky tower and a Baroque clerestory that floods the church with light from its semicircular windows. See p.169.

St Olave Hart Street. Built in the fifteenth century, and one of the few pre-Fire Gothic churches in the City. See p.175.

St Stephen Walbrook Walbrook. Wren's dress rehearsal for St Paul's, with a wonderful central dome and plenty of original woodcarving. See p.169.

which was decorated (against Wren's wishes) by Thornhill's monochrome trompe-l'oeil frescoes, now rather upstaged by the adjacent gilded spandrels. St Paul's most famous work of art, however, hangs in the north transept: the crushingly symbolic *Light of the World* by the Pre-Raphaelite **Holman Hunt**, depicting Christ knocking at the handleless, bramble-strewn door of the human soul, which must be opened from within. The original is actually in Keble College, Oxford, though this copy was executed by the artist himself, some fifty years later in 1900.

10

The chancel

By far the most richly decorated section of the cathedral is the **chancel**, in particular the spectacular, swirling, gilded Byzantine-style mosaics of birds, fish, animals and greenery, from the 1890s. The intricately carved oak and limewood choir stalls, and the imposing organ case, are the work of Grinling Gibbons. The north choir-aisle contains Henry Moore's *Mother and Child* sculpture and allows you to admire Jean Tijou's ornate black-and-gold **wrought-iron gates** that separate the aisles from the high altar. Behind the high altar stands the **American Memorial Chapel**, dedicated to the 28,000 Americans based in Britain who lost their lives in World War II (check out the space rocket hidden in the carved wooden foliage of the far right-hand panel, a tribute to America's postwar space exploration). Leaving via the south choir-aisle, you'll find the upstanding shroud of **John Donne**, poet, preacher and one-time Dean of St Paul's, the only complete effigy to have survived from Old St Paul's.

The galleries

From the south transept, a series of stairs lead to the dome's three **galleries**, and they're well worth the climb. The initial 257 steps take you to the **Whispering Gallery**, so called because of its acoustic properties – words whispered to the wall on one side are audible 100ft away on the other, though it's often so busy you can't hear much above the hubbub. Another 119 steps up bring you to the open-air **Stone Gallery**, around the base of the dome, while the final 152 steel steps take you inside the dome's inner structure to the **Golden Gallery**, just below the golden ball and cross which top the cathedral. The views of the City and along the Thames are surprisingly good – you should be able to identify the distinctive white facade of Wren's London house, next to the Globe Theatre, from which he could contemplate his masterpiece. Before you ascend the last flight of stairs, be sure to look through the peephole in the floor, onto the monochrome marble floor beneath the dome, a truly terrifying sight.

The crypt

The entrance to the cathedral's vast **crypt** is on your left as you leave the south choir-aisle. Brightly lit and with whitewashed walls, this is not the most atmospheric of mausoleums – a far cry from the nineteenth century, when visitors were shown around the tombs by candlelight.

THE CORPORATION

The one unchanging aspect of the City is its special status, conferred on the area by William the Conqueror to win favour with London's powerful burghers, and extended and reaffirmed by successive rulers ever since. Even today, with its own Lord Mayor, its Beadles, Sheriffs and Aldermen, its separate police force and its select electorate of freemen and liverymen, the City is an anachronistic, one-party mini-state. It's run by the **City of London Corporation** (ⓦ cityoflondon.gov.uk), an unreconstructed old-boys network whose medievalist pageantry camouflages the very real power and wealth that it holds. Its anomalous status is all the more baffling when you consider that the area was an early bastion of British democracy: it was the City that traditionally stood up to bullying sovereigns.

> ## PATERNOSTER SQUARE
> The Blitz destroyed the area immediately to the north of St Paul's, including Paternoster Row, which had been the centre of the book trade since 1500. The postwar office complex that replaced it was torn down in the 1980s and supplanted by the softer, post-classical development of **Paternoster Square**, centred on a Corinthian column topped by a gilded urn, and, since 2004, home to the London Stock Exchange. One happy consequence of the square's redevelopment is that the **Temple Bar arch**, the last surviving City gateway which once stood at the top of Fleet Street (see p.151), found its way back to London after a century of languishing in a park in Hertfordshire. Designed by Wren himself, the triumphal arch now forms the entrance to Paternoster Square from St Paul's, with the Stuart monarchs, James I and Charles II, and their consorts, occupying the niches.

10

The crypt boasts as many painters and architects as Westminster Abbey has poets, most of them stuffed into the southern aisle, known as **Artists' Corner**. Appropriately enough, it was Wren himself who started the trend with his own tomb, inscribed: "*Lector, si monumentum requiris, circumspice*" (Reader, if you seek his monument, look around). Close to Wren are the graves of Reynolds, Turner, Millais, Holman Hunt, Lord Leighton and Alma-Tadema; nearby there's a bust of Van Dyck, whose monument perished along with Old St Paul's. Over in the north aisle is the grave of Alexander Fleming, the discoverer of penicillin.

The crypt's two star tombs – those of **Nelson** and **Wellington** – occupy centre stage. Wellington's porphyry and granite monstrosity is set in its own mini-chapel, surrounded by memorials to illustrious British field marshals, while Nelson lies in a black marble sarcophagus originally designed for Cardinal Wolsey and later intended for Henry VIII and his third wife, Jane Seymour. As at Trafalgar Square, Nelson lies close to later admirals Jellicoe and Beatty. Beyond are the cathedral shop, a café and the exit.

St Paul's Churchyard Gardens
April–Oct 7am–8.30pm; Nov–March 7am–4pm

Small but artfully landscaped **St Paul's Churchyard Gardens**, encircling the eastern end of the cathedral, on the site of former burial grounds, were first established in 1878. Their most arresting feature is a column, erected in 1910, topped by a gilded statue of St Paul, and diplomatically inscribed "amid such scenes of good and evil as make up human affairs, the conscience of the church and nation through five centuries found public utterance". This is a reference to **Paul's Cross**, a polygonal open-air pulpit – its groundplan is marked out in the paving – from which official proclamations and religious speeches were made. Heretics were regularly executed on this spot, and in 1519 Luther's works were publicly burnt here, before Henry VIII changed sides and demanded the "preaching down" of papal authority from the same spot. The cross was destroyed by the Puritans in 1643.

Cheapside

It's difficult to believe that **Cheapside**, which connects St Paul's with Bank, was once London's foremost shopping street, the widest thoroughfare in the City, and site of the medieval marketplace. Nowadays only the names of the nearby streets – Bread Street, Milk Street, Honey Lane, Poultry – recall its former prominence, which faded when the shops and their customers moved to the West End from the eighteenth century onwards.

One New Change
1 New Change • **Shops** Mon–Fri 10am–7pm, Thurs until 8pm, Sat 10am–6pm, Sun noon–6pm **Roof terrace** Mon–Sat 10am–midnight, Sun 10am–8pm; restaurants and bars generally close between 9 and 11pm • ⓦ onenewchange.com • ⊖ St Paul's

Commerce has recently returned to Cheapside in the form of **One New Change**, an uncompromisingly modern building by Jean Nouvel, whose opaque brown glass facade is reminiscent of a Stealth bomber. Even if you've no interest in the formulaic franchises which fill this multistorey shopping mall, it has one great thing going for it: a sixth-floor, sun-trap roof terrace that's open to the public and has a few mosaics by Boris Anrep and views over to St Paul's, Tate Modern and the Shard. There's an upmarket restaurant and bar up here too, both facing St Paul's.

St Mary-le-Bow

Cheapside • Mon–Wed 7.30am–6pm, Thurs 7.30am–6.30pm & Fri 7.30am–4pm • ☎ 020 7248 5139, ⓦ stmarylebow.co.uk • ⊖ St Paul's

One of the distinguishing features of Cheapside is Wren's church of **St Mary-le-Bow**, whose handsome tower features a conglomeration of pilasters, a circular colonnade, a granite obelisk and a dragon weather vane. The tower also contains postwar replicas of the famous "Bow Bells", which sounded the 9pm curfew for Londoners from the fourteenth to the nineteenth centuries, and within earshot of which all true Cockneys are born. The original interior was totally destroyed in the Blitz and the present one is a postwar re-creation, but the church's medieval crypt survived and is home to the atmospheric *Café Below* (see p.377).

St Mary Aldermary

Bow Lane/Watling Street • Mon–Fri 9am–4.30pm • ☎ 020 7248 9902, ⓦ stmaryaldermary.co.uk • ⊖ Mansion House or Bank

At the southern end of Bow Lane lies the church of **St Mary Aldermary**, whose interior is a rare foray into the perpendicular Gothic style by Wren, based on the original church – the plaster fan-vaults and saucer domes in the aisles are the highlight and, as a bonus, there's a great café called *Host* in the nave. **Bow Lane** itself is a lovely, narrow, pedestrianized street redolent of the pre-Fire City, jam-packed at weekday lunchtimes with office workers heading for its sandwich bars and pubs.

Blackfriars

Most folk heading south from St Paul's are aiming for the **Millennium Bridge** (see p.228), to cross over the river to Tate Modern and Bankside. However, instead of simply heading for the bridge, it's worth taking time to venture into the backstreets and alleyways, or go for a stroll along the **Riverside Walk** which now extends all the way from Blackfriars railway bridge to Tower Bridge.

Blackfriars, the district between Ludgate Hill and the river, is named after the Dominican monastery that stood here until the Dissolution. The monks' old refectory

---

DICK WHITTINGTON

The City's Lord Mayor is elected on an annual basis, and the most famous Lord Mayor of the lot is **Dick Whittington** (c.1350–1423) of pantomime fame. The third son of a wealthy Gloucestershire family, Whittington was an apprentice mercer, dealing in silks and velvets, who rose to become one of the richest men in the City by the age of just 21. He was an early philanthropist, establishing a library at Greyfriars' monastery and a refuge for single mothers at St Thomas's Hospital, and building one of the city's first public lavatories, a unisex 128-seater known as "Whittington's Night Soil House of Easement". The pantomime story appeared some two hundred years after Whittington's death, though quite how he became the fictional ragamuffin who comes to London after hearing the streets are paved with gold, no one seems to know. Traditionally, Whittington is leaving London with his knapsack and cat, when he hears the Bow Bells ring out "Turn again, Whittington, thrice Lord Mayor of London" (he was, in fact, mayor on four occasions and was never knighted as the story claims). The theory on the cat is that it was a common name for a coal barge at the time, and Whittington is thought to have made much of his fortune in the coal trade. There's a statue on Highgate Hill commemorating the very spot where Dick allegedly heard the Bow Bells, and a stained-glass window in St Michael Paternoster Royal, on Skinner's Lane, near where he lived.

became Blackfriars Theatre, where Shakespeare and his fellow actors performed in the winter months. Although the area was destroyed in the Great Fire, it suffered little from wartime bombing and remains a warren of alleyways, courtyards and narrow streets, conveying something of the plan of the City before the Victorians, the German bombers and the 1960s brutalists did their worst. The best place to go for a taste of the monastic is *The Black Friar*, 174 Queen Victoria St, which boasts a fantastically ornate **Arts and Crafts** pub interior (see p.390).

Church of Scientology

146 Queen Victoria St · Mon–Fri 9.30am–10pm, Sat & Sun 9.30am–6pm · Free · ☎ 020 7246 2700, ⓦ scientology-london.org · ⊖ Blackfriars

Built in the 1860s for the British and Foreign Bible Society, the London headquarters of the Church of Scientology look like an Italian *palazzo*. If you're prepared to put up with the overly earnest attendants, the building itself is worth admiring, and there's a whole exhibition on **L. Ron Hubbard**, the American pulp-fiction writer and hypnotist who founded the Scientology cult.

College of Arms

130 Queen Victoria St · Mon–Fri 10am–4pm · Free · ☎ 020 7248 2762, ⓦ college-of-arms.gov.uk · ⊖ Blackfriars or Mansion House

Originally built round a courtyard in the 1670s, the red-brick mansion of the **College of Arms** was opened up to the south with the building of Queen Victoria Street in the 1870s. The college is the headquarters of heraldry in England, and even today is in charge of granting coats of arms to those who can prove they've been "a benefit to the community". The Earl Marshal's Court – featuring a portrait gallery of past Officers of Arms, copious wooden panelling and a modest throne – is the only room open to the public, unless you apply to trace your family or study heraldry in the college library.

Old Bailey

Old Bailey · Mon–Fri 10am–12.40pm & 2–3.40pm · Free · ☎ 020 7248 3277, ⓦ cityoflondon.gov.uk · ⊖ St Paul's

The Central Criminal Court is better known as the **Old Bailey**, after the street on which it stands, which used to run along the medieval city walls. The court's pompous, domed, Edwardian building – "Defend the Children of the Poor & Punish the Wrongdoer" the entrance proclaims – is topped by a gilded statue of Justice, depicted without blindfold, holding her sword and scales. The country's most serious criminal cases are heard here, and have included, in the past, the trials of Lord Haw-Haw, the Kray Twins and the Angry Brigade (see p.201), plus all Britain's multiple murderers. You can watch the proceedings from the visitors' gallery (no under-14s), but you're not allowed to take anything into the court (and that includes mobiles), you must be dressed appropriately (men, no vests or shorts; women, no low-cut tops or short skirts) and there's no cloakroom. Sadly, visitors do not get to see the Grand Hall, with its swirling marble floor and walls, succession of domes and grandiloquent frescoes.

The site of the Old Bailey was originally occupied by **Newgate Prison**, which began life as a small lock-up above the medieval gateway of Newgate. Burnt down in the 1780 Gordon Riots, it was rebuilt as "a veritable Hell, worthy of the imagination of Dante", as one of its more famous inmates, Casanova, put it. Earlier well-known temporary residents included Thomas Malory, who wrote *Le Morte d'Arthur* while imprisoned here for murder (among other things); Daniel Defoe, who was put inside for his *The Shortest Way with Dissenters*; Ben Jonson, who served time for murder; and Christopher Marlowe, who was on a charge of atheism.

Smithfield

The ground was covered, nearly ankle-deep with filth and mire; a thick steam perpetually rising from the reeking bodies of the cattle, and mingling with the fog.
Oliver Twist, Charles Dickens

Originally open ground outside the City walls, **Smithfield** is a corruption of "Smooth Field". It was used as a horse fair in Norman times, and later became the site for **Bartholomew Fair**, established in 1133 by Rahere, prior and founder of St Bartholomew's priory and hospice to raise funds. Rahere himself used to perform juggling tricks, while Pepys reports seeing a horse counting sixpences and, more reliably, a puppet show of Ben Jonson's play *Bartholomew Fair*. Predictably enough, it was the Victorians who closed it down to protect public morals.

10

Smithfield Market

Smithfield • Mon–Fri 2am–around 10am • Free • ☎ 020 7248 3151 • ⓦ smithfieldmarket.com • Guided tours once monthly; £12.50; book at ⓦ cityoflondonguides.com • ⦵ Farringdon or Barbican

The meat **market**, with which Smithfield is now synonymous, grew up as a kind of adjunct to Bartholomew Fair. Live cattle continued to be herded into Smithfield until 1852, when the fair was suppressed and the abattoirs moved out to Islington. A new covered market hall was erected in 1868, along with the "Winkle", a spiral ramp at the centre of West Smithfield, linked to the market's very own (now defunct) tube station. Smithfield subsequently tripled in size and remains London's main meat market. To see the market at its most animated and find the full range of stalls open, arrive by 7am – the action is mostly over by mid-morning.

St Bartholomew's Hospital

West Smithfield • Museum Tues–Fri 10am–4pm • Free • Guided tours Fri 2pm; £5 • ☎ 020 3465 5798 • ⓦ bartshealth.nhs.uk • ⦵ St Paul's

St Bartholomew's Hospital – affectionately known as Bart's – is the oldest hospital in London. It began as an Augustinian priory and hospice in 1123, founded by Rahere, courtier, clerk and even court jester to Henry I, on the orders of St Bartholomew, who appeared to him in a vision while he was in malarial delirium on a pilgrimage to Rome. The priory was dissolved by Henry VIII, but in 1546, with just two weeks left to live, the king agreed to re-found the hospital.

PUBLIC EXECUTIONS AND BODY SNATCHERS

After 1783, when hangings at Tyburn were stopped (see p.243), **public executions** at Newgate began to draw crowds of one hundred thousand and more. The last public beheading took place here in 1820 when five Cato Street Conspirators (see p.86) were hanged and decapitated with a surgeon's knife. It was in hanging, however, that Newgate excelled, its most efficient gallows dispatching twenty criminals simultaneously. Unease over the "robbery and violence, loud laughing, oaths, fighting, obscene conduct and still more filthy language" that accompanied public hangings drove the executions inside the prison walls in 1868. The night before an execution, a handbell was tolled outside the condemned's cell, while the jailer recited the Newgate verse that ended:

"All you that in the condemned hole do lie/Prepare you, for tomorrow you shall die… And when St Sepulchre's bell in the morning tolls/The Lord above have mercy on your souls." Until Newgate got its own bell, the "Great Bell of Old Bailey" was in the church of **St Sepulchre-without-Newgate** (Mon–Fri 11am–3pm; ⓦ stsepulchres.org), and tolled the condemned to the scaffold at eight in the morning. The handbell and verse are displayed inside the church, opposite the Old Bailey.

The bodies of the executed were handed over to the surgeons of St Bartholomew's for dissection, but body snatchers also preyed on non-criminals buried in St Sepulchre churchyard. Such was the demand for corpses that relatives were forced to pay a nightwatchman to guard the graveyard in a specially built watch-house – still visible to the north of the church – to prevent the "Resurrection Men" from retrieving their quarry. Successfully stolen stiffs were taken to the nearby *Fortune of War* tavern, which stood on Pie Corner, by Cock Lane, to be sold to the surgeons. Today, Pie Corner is marked by a gilded overfed cherub known as **Fat Boy**, who commemorates the "staying of the Great Fire" of 1666, which, when it wasn't blamed on the Catholics, was ascribed to the sin of gluttony, since it had begun in Pudding Lane and ended at Pie Corner.

BLOOD AND GUTS AT SMITHFIELD

Blood was spilled at **Smithfield** long before the meat market was legally sanctioned here in the seventeenth century. The Scottish hero, William Wallace, was dragged behind a horse from the Tower, then hanged, drawn and quartered here in 1305. Most famously, during the 1381 Peasants' Revolt, the poll-tax rebels under **Wat Tyler** assembled here to negotiate with the boy-king Richard II. At the meeting, Lord Mayor Walworth pulled Tyler from his horse and stabbed him, after which he was bustled into St Bartholomew's for treatment, only to be dragged out by the king's men and beheaded.

Smithfield subsequently became a regular venue for **public executions**. The bishop of Rochester's cook was boiled alive in 1531, after being found guilty of poisoning, but the local speciality was **burnings**. These reached a peak during the reign of "Bloody" Mary in the 1550s, when hundreds of Protestants were burnt at the stake for their beliefs, in revenge for the Catholics who had suffered a similar fate under Henry VIII and Edward VI; a plaque on the side of Bart's commemorates some of those who died.

10

The **Henry VIII Gate**, built in 1702, features a statue of the king, with a lame man on the right and a diseased man on the left lounging on the broken pediment above. Further along, you can make out shrapnel marks left from a 1916 Zeppelin air raid. Behind the Henry VIII Gate stands the church of **St Bartholomew-the-Less** (daily 7am–8pm), sole survivor of the priory's four chapels. The tower and vestry are fifteenth-century and the octagonal interior is neo-Gothic, though it does contain a Tudor memorial to Elizabeth I's surgeon. Beyond the church lies three-quarters of the **Square** created for the hospital by James Gibbs in the mid-eighteenth century, with the **Great Hall** on the north side, accessed by the **Grand Staircase**, its walls decorated with biblical murals that were painted free of charge by Hogarth, who was born and baptized nearby and served as one of the hospital's governors.

You can get a glimpse of the hospital's Grand Staircase from inside **St Bartholomew's Museum**, on the left, under the archway into the courtyard. Among the medical artefacts, there are some fearsome amputation instruments, a pair of leather "lunatic restrainers", and some great jars with labels such as "poison – for external use only". To see the Great Hall join one of the fascinating weekly **guided tours**, which take in the surrounding area as well; the meeting point is the Henry VIII Gate.

St Bartholomew-the-Great

Cloth Fair • Mon–Fri 8.30am–5pm, Sat 10.30am–4pm, Sun 8.30am–8pm; mid-Nov to mid-Feb Mon–Sat closes 4pm • £4, concessions £3.50 • ☏ 020 7606 5171, ⓦ greatstbarts.com • ⊖ Barbican

Hidden in the backstreets north of the hospital, **St Bartholomew-the-Great** is London's oldest and most atmospheric parish church. Begun in 1123 as the main church of St Bartholomew's priory and hospice, it was partly demolished in the Reformation, and gradually fell into ruins: the cloisters were used as a stable, there was a boys' school in the triforium, a coal and wine cellar in the crypt, a blacksmith's in the north transept and a printing press (where Benjamin Franklin once worked) in the Lady Chapel. From 1887, Aston Webb restored what remained, and added the chequered patterning and flintwork that now characterizes the exterior. Much beloved of film companies, it is one of the few parish churches in the country to charge an entrance fee, though there is no charge for anyone wishing to visit the church for prayer or for the café.

To get an idea of the scale of the original church, approach it through the half-timbered Tudor **gatehouse**, on Little Britain Street. A wooden statue of St Bartholomew stands in a niche; below is the thirteenth-century arch that once formed the entrance to the nave. The churchyard now stands where the nave itself would have been, and one side of the **cloisters** survives to the south, now housing the delightful *Cloister Café* (closed Sat). The rest of the church is a confusion of elements, including portions of the transepts and, most impressively, the **chancel**, where thick Norman pillars separate the main body from the ambulatory. There are various pre-Fire monuments, the most prominent being the tomb of Rahere (see p.162), which shelters under a fifteenth-century canopy north of the altar.

The Barbican

The City's only large residential complex is the concrete, brutalist maze of the Barbican estate, known simply as the **Barbican**, built on the heavily bombed Cripplegate area. It's a classic 1970s urban dystopia, a labyrinth of pedestrian walkways and similar-looking apartment buildings, pinioned by three 400ft towers. Whilst for its critics the Barbican feels like a giant prison block, it does have a much softer side and is actually one of the most vibrant cultural quarters in the city, with a fantastic arts centre set alongside a man-made oblong lake, at its heart, and home to the Guildhall School of Music and Drama as well as plenty of other welcoming features, including a number of bars, cafés and restaurants, most of them in the Barbican Centre.

The Barbican Centre

Silk St • Mon–Sat 9am–11pm, Sun 10am–11pm • Free • ☎ 020 7638 8891, ⓦ barbican.org.uk • ⊖ Barbican

The Barbican complex is synonymous with the **Barbican Centre**, one of the great cultural institutions in the capital, whose seven floors feature a concert hall, two theatres, three cinemas, a rooftop garden, and an art gallery. The events programme is jam-packed all year round and this is one of the top London venues for jazz, classical and world music plus one of the most affordable places in the city for quality theatre and dance. As well as being a champion of young and new artists, playwrights and performers and independent film, the Barbican Centre is home to the London Symphony Orchestra and the BBC Symphony Orchestra and has been the London home of the Royal Shakespeare Company for much of its existence, the company's most recent residency finishing in 2016. It also features one of the largest public libraries In London, plenty of places to eat and drink, art and design shops and, most unexpectedly, a giant conservatory (daily 11am–5pm), brimming with tropical plants.

St Giles Cripplegate

Fore St • Mon–Fri 11am–4pm • Free • ☎ 020 7638 1997, ⓦ stgilescripplegate.com • ⊖ Barbican

The Barbican's solitary prewar building is the heavily restored early Tudor church of St St Giles Cripplegate, now bracketed between a pair of artificial lakes, and overlooking

---

LONDON'S WALLS

London was a bona fide **walled city** from the time of the Romans until the Great Fire of 1666. For another hundred years, it still had its **seven gateways** – the last one, Temple Bar, was only removed in 1878, and now stands near St Paul's Cathedral. Sections of wall were still being dismantled in the eighteenth and nineteenth centuries, and, if you know where to look, there are still several substantial slices of the city walls in situ today.

In 120 AD, the Romans built a grid-plan **military fort** to house around one thousand soldiers, just east of the Museum of London – the wall is visible from the museum, and one of the corner bastions (complete with section of moat) can be seen at St Giles Cripplegate in the Barbican. However, it wasn't until 200 AD that the Romans threw up a proper two-mile long curtain wall, 20ft high and 9ft thick. The walls fell into decay in Saxon times, but were repaired and restored in the medieval and Tudor periods. On **Noble Street**, just southeast of the museum, one of the most interesting sections came to light after the Blitz, showing where the new city walls joined the older wall of the military fort.

There's an official **London Wall Walk**, which starts outside Tower Hill tube, by the remains of the medieval Postern Gate, although the only other really impressive sections of wall are in nearby Cooper's Row (see p.183).

POSTMAN'S PARK

Opposite the former General Post Office building, south of the Museum of London, lies **Postman's Park**, one of the most curious and little-visited corners of the City. Here, in 1900, in the churchyard of St Botolph, Aldersgate, the painter and sculptor George Frederick Watts paid for a national memorial to "heroes of everyday life", a patchwork wall of majolica tiles protected by a canopy and inscribed with the names of ordinary folk who had died in the course of some act of bravery. It exhibits the classic Victorian sentimental fascination with death, and makes for macabre but compelling reading: "Drowned in attempting to save his brother after he himself had just been rescued" or "Saved a lunatic woman from suicide at Woolwich Arsenal station, but was himself run over by the train". In 2009, the first new addition for 78 years was added to the wall.

10

an impressive corner bastion of the old Roman fort. It was in this church that Oliver Cromwell was married in 1620 and John Milton buried in 1674 – he was subsequently exhumed in 1793, his teeth knocked out as souvenirs and his corpse exhibited to the public until the novelty wore off.

Museum of London

150 London Wall • Daily 10am–6pm • Free • Highlights tours (40 min) daily at 11am, noon, 3pm and 4pm • Free • ☎ 020 7001 9844, ⓦ museumoflondon.org.uk • ⊖ Barbican or St Paul's

Hidden in the southwestern corner of the Barbican estate is the **Museum of London,** whose permanent galleries are basically an educational trot through London's past from prehistory to the present day, illustrated by the city's major archeological finds and some great scale models. Throughout the year the museum puts on excellent temporary exhibitions, gallery tours, lectures, and themed walks at weekends around the City and beyond.

London until 1666

The permanent displays start on floor E (where visitors enter), with a section on **London before London.** Here, you'll find a cave-bear skull from half a million years ago, Neolithic flint tools, not to mention a lion skull, a hippo's tooth, an auroch's skull and an elephant's foot. The **Roman London** section includes the Bucklersbury mosaic floor, displayed in a mock-up of a wealthy Roman dining room, gold coins, marble busts from the Temple of Mithras and mock-up Roman shop displays. Highlights in the **Medieval London** section include a reconstructed Saxon home, a model of Old St Paul's and a wonderfully over-the-top video on the Black Death. Look out, too, for the Cheapside Hoard, found by workmen in 1912, and containing the finest collection of Elizabethan and Jacobean jewels in the world.

Modern London

The museum's post-1666 galleries are all on the ground floor (L2), and begin with **Expanding City**, which includes revealing sections on how slavery helped increase the city's wealth, an original Newgate Prison door and a recreation of a pleasure garden. The **People's City** section traces the history of the suffragette movement and the political struggles of the 1930s and features one of the most popular sections, the **Victorian Walk**, with several streets of reconstructed period shops from a toyshop to a barber's. You can relax in a mock-up interwar cinema and watch old footage of prewar London, admire the wonderful Art Deco bronze lifts from Selfridges or play on the interactive Charles Booth map which plotted the city's poverty in 1889.

The postwar section features snapshots from each decade: a model of the Skylon from the 1951 Festival of Britain, some groovy Swinging Sixties clothes, punk and Silver Jubilee memorabilia from 1977. Finally, you reach the space reserved for the **Lord Mayor's Coach**, which rivals the Queen's in sheer weight of gold decoration. Built in 1757, it's still used to parade the new Lord Mayor at the annual Lord Mayor's Show (see p.27).

Guildhall

Gresham St • Daily 10am–4.30pm; Oct–April closed Sun • Free • ☎ 020 7606 3030, ⊕ guildhall.cityoflondon.gov.uk • ⊖ Bank

The seat of the City governance for over eight hundred years, the **Guildhall** complex mixes fine medieval and early modern civic and religious architecture with uninspired twentieth-century office buildings, all gathered around Guildhall Yard. The showpiece is the **Great Hall** which miraculously survived both the Great Fire and Blitz – you must approach from the reception on the west side of the courtyard, not the quasi-Indian porch, tacked on by George Dance the Elder in the eighteenth century, to the north. The hall is lined with statues of worthies and is still used for functions, though only the walls survive from the original fifteenth-century building, which was the venue for several high-treason trials, including those of Lady Jane Grey and her husband, Lord

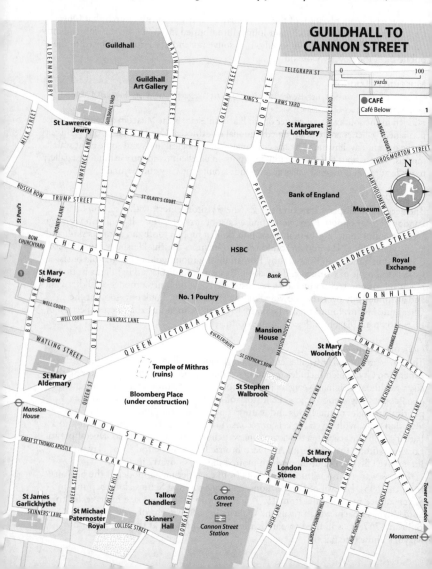

Dudley, and, three years later, Archbishop Cranmer. As you leave, be sure to check out the crazy pagan giants Gog and Magog, who look down from the minstrels' gallery, and who feature every year in the Lord Mayor's Show (see p.27).

Guildhall Art Gallery
Mon−Sat 10am−5pm, Sun noon−4pm • Free • Highlights tours (45min) Fri 12.15, 1.15, 2.15 & 3.15pm • Free • ☎ 020 7332 3700, Ⓦ cityoflondon.gov.uk • ⊖ Bank

Occupying the eastern side of Guildhall Yard is the **Guildhall Art Gallery**, displaying the City of London Corporation's art collection. First opened in 1885, the gallery was destroyed in the Second World War and this replacement building was not commissioned until 1985, the new gallery finally opening in 1999. Amongst its 4500 artworks, the collection's greatest strengths are the number and breadth of its nineteenth-century works, one of the most extensive assemblages of Victorian paintings in the UK, as well as its excellent range of paintings depicting London.

10

After a complete rehang in late 2014 to celebrate the gallery's fifteenth anniversary, the layout has been reorganized along thematic lines, with ten themes in all, including love, leisure, work and faith. Seven of these themes appear in the Main Gallery, up the stairs as you enter the building, where some of the best Pre-Raphaelite pictures are displayed. Featured here are **Rossetti**'s *La Ghirlandata*, a typically lush portrait, in intense blues and greens, of a model who's a dead ringer for Jane Morris, with whom the artist was infatuated; and **Millais**' two portraits of his daughter Effie in her Sunday best.

Downstairs, in the Undercroft Gallery, the theme is **London**, where an engaging set of pictures charts four hundred years of the city's history, many depicting views of life on and from the Thames. Waggoner's atmospheric painting of *The Great Fire of London 1666*, contrasts perfectly with Jan Griffier's captivating depiction of *The Thames During the Great Frost of 1739*, a dramatic capturing of one of over twenty occasions when the river has completely frozen over.

Roman amphitheatre
During the gallery's construction in the 1990s, a **Roman amphitheatre**, dating from around 120 AD, was discovered in the Guildhall courtyard. The foundations of the eastern entrance are all that remain, displayed to impressive effect in the basement, and giving you a hint of the vast size of the original arena, which would have held up to six thousand. The sense of scale is greatly enhanced by an illuminated outline of one end of the arena, providing some much-needed context for the small sections of wall (the outline of the amphitheatre is marked out on the pavement in the courtyard outside).

St Lawrence Jewry
Mon−Fri 8am−5pm • Recitals Mon & Tues 1pm • ☎ 020 7600 9478, Ⓦ stlawrencejewry.org.uk • ⊖ Bank

Across the courtyard from the Guildhall stands Wren's church of **St Lawrence Jewry**, whose smart interior reflects its role as the official City of London Corporation church. Opened in 1677 in the presence of Charles II, but gutted during the Blitz, the church's handsome, wide, open-plan interior is well worth a peek for its richly gilded plasterwork ceiling. The name "Jewry" recalls the site of London's **Jewish ghetto**. Old Jewry, the street two blocks east, was the nucleus of the community, who suffered a bloody expulsion on the orders of Edward I.

Bank and around
Bank lies at the heart of the City's financial district and is the busy meeting point of eight streets. It's an impressive architectural ensemble, overlooked by a handsome collection of Neoclassical buildings – among them the Bank of England, the Royal Exchange and Mansion House – each one faced in Portland stone.

10

Royal Exchange

Mon–Fri: shops 10am–6pm; cafés, bars and restaurants 8am–11pm • Ⓦ theroyalexchange.co.uk • ➌ Bank

By far the most imposing and elegant of Bank's buildings is the **Royal Exchange**, first built in 1570 at the personal expense of the fabulously wealthy businessman, Thomas Gresham (his gilded grasshopper flies from the roof), as a meeting place for City merchants. The current building, fronted by a massive eight-column portico and a very convenient set of steps for lunching office workers, is the third on the site and was built in the 1840s. Nowadays, the building is filled with expense account shops, but it's still worth exploring the inner courtyard, with its beautifully tiled floor, glazed roof and half-columns in three classical orders. The swish *Grand Café* occupies both the courtyard and the mezzanine floor, from which you can view a series of frescoes illustrating the history of the City.

Mansion House

Guided tours Tues 2pm; closed Aug • £7, concessions £5 • ☎ 020 7937 9306, Ⓦ cityoflondon.gov.uk • ➌ Bank

Mansion House, the Lord Mayor's sumptuous Neoclassical lodgings during his or – on the odd, rare occasion – her term of office, is open to the public once a week but visits

---

THE CITY LIVERY COMPANIES

The hundred or so **City Livery Companies** in the Square Mile are descended from the craft guilds of the Middle Ages, whose purpose was to administer apprenticeships and take charge of quality control, in return for which they were granted monopolies. Over time, the guilds grew prodigiously wealthy, built themselves ever more opulent halls and staged lavish banquets at which they would wear elaborate "livery" (or uniforms). Most – though not all – of the old guilds now have very little to do with their original trade, though this is not the case with the guilds that have been formed in the last hundred years. It's fair to say the livery companies remain deeply undemocratic and anomalous, but their prodigious wealth and charitable works have helped pacify the critics. As with the Freemasons, the elaborate ceremonies serve to hide the very real power that these companies still hold. Liverymen dominate the Court of Common Council, the City's ruling body, and as Aldermen, they take it in turns to be first a Sheriff, and eventually Lord Mayor – a knighthood is virtually guaranteed.

The City boasts numerous Livery Company halls, many with enticing names such as the Tallow Chandlers and Cordwainers. Few survived the Great Fire, fewer still the Blitz, but a handful are worth visiting for their ornate interiors. The problem is gaining **admission**. The City Information Centre (☎ 020 7332 1456) has tickets to some halls; other halls will allow you to join a pre-booked group tour for around £5–10 per person. It's not something you can do on the spur of the moment, though some Livery halls are used during the City of London Festival and others are open on Open House weekend (see p.27). Below is a selection of the most interesting Livery halls:

Apothecaries' Hall Blackfriars Lane ☎ 020 7236 1189, Ⓦ apothecaries.org; ➌ Blackfriars. The seventeenth-century courtyard is open to the public, but entry to the magnificent staircase and the Great Hall – with its musicians' gallery, portrait by Reynolds and collection of leech pots – is by appointment only.

Fishmongers' Hall London Bridge ☎ 020 7626 3531, Ⓦ fishhall.org.uk; ➌ Monument. A prominent Greek Revival building on the riverfront, with a grand staircase hall, and the very dagger with which Mayor Walworth stabbed Wat Tyler (see box, p.163).

Goldsmiths' Hall Foster Lane ☎ 020 7606 7010, Ⓦ thegoldsmiths.co.uk; ➌ St Paul's. One of the easiest to visit as there are regular exhibitions allowing you to see the sumptuous central staircase built in the 1830s.

Skinners' Hall 8 Dowgate Hill ☎ 020 7236 5629, Ⓦ theskinnerscompany.org.uk; ➌ Cannon Street. The seventeenth-century staircase and courtroom survive, while the wood-panelled hall contains a wonderful series of Frank Brangwyn murals from 1902. There are a couple of annual Open Day Tours here.

Tallow Chandlers' Hall 4 Dowgate Hill ☎ 020 7248 4726, Ⓦ tallowchandlers.org; ➌ Cannon Street. Set back from the street around an attractive courtyard, the Tallow Chandlers Hall retains its seventeenth-century courtroom, complete with original seating.

Vintners' Hall 68 Upper Thames St ☎ 020 7236 1863, Ⓦ vintnershall.co.uk; ➌ Mansion House. The oldest hall in the City, dating from 1671, with a period-piece staircase with "fabulously elaborate balusters".

are by guided tour only (1hr; no advance booking). Designed in 1753 by George Dance the Elder, the building's grandest room is the columned **Egyptian Hall**, with its high, barrel-vaulted, coffered ceiling. Also impressive is the vast collection of gold and silver tableware, the mayor's 36-pound gold mace and the pearl sword given by Elizabeth I and held out to the sovereign on visits to the City. Scattered about the rooms are an impressive array of Dutch and Flemish paintings by the likes of Hals, Ruisdael, Cuyp, Hobbema and de Hooch. Places on the tour are allocated on a first-come, first-served basis, so turn up at the Walbrook entrance in good time.

10

Bank of England

Threadneedle St • Museum Mon–Fri 10am–5pm • Free • ☎ 020 7601 5545, ⓦ bankofengland.co.uk • ⊖ Bank

Established by William III in 1694 to raise funds for his costly war against France, the **Bank of England** – the so-called "Grand Old Lady of Threadneedle Street" – wasn't erected on its present site until 1734. The bank was attacked during the 1780 Gordon Riots, but never sacked thanks to the bank's clerks, who melted down their inkwells into bullets. Subsequently a detachment of the Foot Guards, known as the Bank Picquet, was stationed overnight here until 1973. Security remains pretty tight at the bank, which still acts as a giant safe-deposit box, storing the official gold reserves of many of the world's central banks, as well the UK's, in its basement vaults (you can take a virtual tour of the vaults in the bank's museum).

The windowless, outer curtain wall, which wraps itself round the 3.5-acre island site, is pretty much all that remains of John Soane's late eighteenth-century design. However, you can view a reconstruction of Soane's Bank Stock Office, with its characteristic domed skylight, in the **museum**, whose entrance is on Bartholomew Lane. The interactive exhibition traces the history of the bank, banknotes and banking in general. Don't miss the small screens in the first section of the museum providing vivid virtual tours of the bank, including mesmerizing views of the cash vaults and gold vaults. Beneath a reconstruction of Herbert Baker's interwar rotunda (wrecked in the Blitz), you can caress a 13kg gold bar, worth over £250,000, and, elsewhere, view specimens of every note issued by the Royal Mint over the centuries (including a million pound note).

St Mary Woolnoth

King William St • Mon–Fri 7.15am–5.15pm • Free • ⓦ stml.org.uk • ⊖ Bank

Hidden from the bustle of Bank itself, a short distance down King William Street, stands **St Mary Woolnoth**, one of Nicholas Hawksmoor's six idiosyncratic London churches. The main facade is very imposing, with its twin turrets, Doric pillars and heavy rustication. Inside, in a cramped but lofty space, Hawksmoor manages to cram in a cluster of three big Corinthian columns at each corner, which support an ingenious lantern lit by semicircular clerestory windows. The most striking furnishing is the altar canopy, held up by barley-sugar columns and studded with seven golden cherubic faces. The church's projecting clock gets a brief mention in T.S. Eliot's *The Waste Land*, and the quote is commemorated in the southeast corner of the church.

St Stephen Walbrook

39 Walbrook • Mon–Fri 10am–4pm • Free • ⓦ ststephenwalbrook.net • ⊖ Bank

Named after the nearby shallow stream which provided Roman London with its fresh water, the church of **St Stephen Walbrook** is the Lord Mayor's official church and Wren's most spectacular after St Paul's. Faced with a fairly cramped site, no less snugly positioned today, Wren created a church of great space and light, with sixteen Corinthian columns arranged in clusters around a central coffered dome, which many regard as a practice run for his cathedral. The furnishings are mostly original, but the modern beech-wood pews jar, as does Henry Moore's altar, an amorphous blob of Travertine stone – nicknamed "The Camembert". The Samaritans were founded here

10

FROM COFFEE HOUSE TO BOARDROOM

Several of the City's most important institutions have their origins in the **coffee houses** which sprang up in the second half of the seventeenth century. The first coffee house in London was established in St Michael's Alley, off Cornhill, in 1652 by **Pasqua Rosée**, the Armenian servant of a merchant who traded in Turkey. It was an instant success, and in less than a century, there were literally hundreds of rival establishments, as the coffee house became the place the City's wheelers and dealers preferred to conduct their business. **Richard Lloyd's** coffee house – perhaps the best known – was where London's sailors, merchants and ship owners went for the latest maritime news, eventually evolving into Lloyd's Register of Shipping and Lloyd's of London insurance market. Meanwhile, **Jonathan's**, in Exchange Alley, posted up the price of stocks and commodities, attracting dealers who'd been ejected from the nearby Royal Exchange for rowdiness, and eventually became the London Stock Exchange.

by the local rector in 1953, and their first helpline telephone serves as a memorial in the church's southwest corner.

St Mary Abchurch

Abchurch Lane, off King William St • Mon–Fri 11am–3pm • ⊖ Cannon Street

St Mary Abchurch is set in its own courtyard (the paved-over former graveyard), but nothing about the dour red-brick exterior prepares you for Wren's spectacular interior, which is dominated by a vast dome fresco painted by a local parishioner and lit by oval lunettes, with the name of God in Hebrew centre stage. The lime-wood reredos, festooned with swags and garlands, and decorated with gilded urns and a pelican, is a Grinling Gibbons masterpiece.

Bishopsgate to the Tower

Financial institutions predominate in the easterly section of the Square Mile, many of them housed in the brashest of the City's new architecture. One of the main streets here, **Bishopsgate**, named after one of the seven gates in the old City walls, is dominated by bombastic skyscrapers such as the angular, glass-clad Broadgate Tower, at the northern end, Heron Tower, halfway along, and, at the southern end of the street, work resumed in 2015 on what is set to be the City's tallest skyscraper, originally dubbed the Pinnacle but renamed the Stump when construction stalled in 2012 after only seven floors had been built. The area's two most original architectural works are the groundbreaking **Lloyd's Building** and the unmissable **Gherkin**. These, plus the Victorian splendour of **Leadenhall Market**, the oldest **synagogue** in the country, several pre-Fire churches and Wren's famous **Monument** to the Great Fire make for an especially interesting sector of the City to explore.

Liverpool Street Station

Built in 1874, **Liverpool Street Station** stands on the site of the old Bethlem Royal Hospital (or Bedlam), the infamous lunatic asylum, where the public could pay a penny and laugh at the inmates. Liverpool Street is now the City's busiest terminus, renowned for its vibrantly painted wrought-iron Victorian arches. The station's Liverpool Street entrance features the **Kindertransport memorial**, erected in 2003 and depicting some of the nearly ten thousand Jewish children who arrived at the station from central Europe, without their parents, shortly before World War II broke out.

Adjoining Liverpool Street Station, to the west, are the traffic-free piazzas of the very successful 1980s **Broadgate** complex. *Fulcrum*, Richard Serra's 55ft-high rusting steel sheets, acts as a kind of gateway to the **Broadgate Circle**, whose arena is used as an open-air ice rink in winter and as a performance space in summer. Continuing north to **Exchange Square**, you'll find a cascading waterfall, the hefty *Broadgate Venus* by

Fernando Botero, and Xavier Corbero's *Broad Family* of obelisks, one of whose "children" reveals a shoe.

Bishopsgate Institute

230 Bishopsgate • Library Mon–Fri 9am–5.30pm, Wed till 8pm • Free • ☎ 020 7392 9200, ⓦ bishopsgate.org.uk • ⊖ Liverpool Street

Across the road from Liverpool Street Station is the faïence facade of the diminutive **Bishopsgate Institute**, a graceful Art Nouveau building designed by Harrison Townsend. Townsend went on to design the excellent Whitechapel Art Gallery (see p.197) and the wonderful Horniman Museum (see p.311). Opened in 1895, the institute houses a public library and puts on courses, talks and small exhibitions throughout the year.

10

St Ethelburga's

78 Bishopsgate • Fri 11am–3pm • Free • ☎ 020 7496 1610, ⓦ stethelburgas.org • ⊖ Liverpool Street

Hemmed in by office blocks on either side is the "humble rag-faced front" of the pre-Fire church of **St Ethelburga's**. All but totally destroyed by an IRA bomb in 1993, the church was rebuilt and opened as a Centre for Reconciliation and Peace in 2002, hosting regular interfaith events and workshops, and world music gigs. The bare interior retains the nineteenth-century font inscribed with the Greek palindrome "Nipson anomemata me monan opsin" ("Cleanse my sins, not just my face"). Half the tiny garden round the back houses a polygonal, multi-faith Bedouin tent covered in woven goat's hair.

St Helen's

Bishopsgate • Mon–Fri 9.30am–12.30pm and usually until 5pm on Mon, Wed & Fri • Free • ☎ 020 7283 2231, ⓦ st-helens.org.uk • ⊖ Liverpool Street, Bank, Monument or Aldgate

Another pre-Fire church that suffered extensive damage in the IRA blasts of the 1990s is the late Gothic church of **St Helen**, set back to the east of Bishopsgate. With its undulating crenellations and Baroque bell turret, it's an intriguing building, incorporating the original pre-Reformation Benedictine nunnery church and containing five grand pre-Fire tombs. Since the bomb, the floor level has been raised, the church screens shifted, a new organ gallery added and the seating rearranged to focus on the pulpit, in keeping with the church's current evangelical bent.

The Gherkin

30 St Mary Axe • ⊖ Liverpool Street or Aldgate

Completed in 2003, Norman Foster's glass-diamond-clad **Gherkin** remains one of the most popular of the rash of brash tall buildings built in the City in the last fifteen years. Most Londoners like it for its cheeky shape, though it's beginning to be hemmed in and upstaged by the skyscrapers it helped encourage. Officially known as **30 St Mary Axe**, the Gherkin sits on the site of the old Baltic Exchange, destroyed in an IRA bomb in 1992 that killed three people, commemorated on a nearby wall. At 590ft, it's actually pretty tall, but at street level it appears a very modest building – you can't go up it, but you can grab a bite to eat on the ground floor (the restaurant at the top is part of a private members' club).

LONDON STONE

Bank may have a good claim to being the heart of the City, or perhaps Guildhall as the administrative core, but London's real omphalos, its geomantic centre, is the **London Stone**, a small block of limestone lodged behind an iron grille set low into the exterior wall of 111 Cannon St, at the corner of St Swithin's Lane. Whatever your reaction to this bizarre relic, it has been around for some considerable time, certainly since the 1450 Peasants' Revolt, when the Kentish rebel Jack Cade struck it, declaring himself "Lord of the City".

10

Lloyd's Building

1 Lime St • ☎ 020 7327 6586, ⓦ lloyds.com • ⊖ Bank or Monument

Completed by Richard Rogers in 1986, the **Lloyd's Building** remains probably the City's most innovative and remarkable office block. "A living, breathing machine", it's a vertical version of Rogers' and Renzo Piano's Parisian Pompidou Centre, in which the jumble of blue-steel pipes and cables form the outer casing, with glass lifts zipping up and down the exterior. The portico of the previous, much more sedate, Lloyd's Building (c.1925) has been preserved on Leadenhall Street, so the current headquarters represented a bizarre leap into the modern by this most conservative of City institutions – the largest insurance and reinsurance market in the world. Some things never change, though, and the building is still guarded by porters in antiquated waiters' livery, in recognition of Lloyd's origins as Edward Lloyd's coffee house in 1688.

Lloyd's started out in shipping, but the famous **Lutine Bell**, salvaged from a captured French frigate in 1799 and traditionally struck once for bad news, twice for good, now only tolls once to commemorate more general disasters, twice for distinguished guests.

Leadenhall Market

Gracechurch St • Market: Mon–Fri 10am–6pm • ⓦ cityoflondon.gov.uk • ⊖ Bank or Monument

Occupying the very site where Roman London's basilica and forum once stood, **Leadenhall Market**'s graceful Victorian cast-ironwork is richly painted in cream and maroon, with each of the four entrances to the covered arcade topped by an elaborate stone arch. Inside, the traders cater mostly for the lunchtime City crowd, their barrows laden with exotic seafood and game, fine wines, champagne and caviar, while the surrounding shops and bars remain busy until the early evening.

Bevis Marks Synagogue

4 Heneage Lane • Mon, Wed & Thurs 10.30am–2pm, Tues & Fri 10.30am–1pm, Sun 10.30am–12.30pm • £5, concessions £4, children £2.50 • Guided tours Wed & Fri 11.15am, Sun 10.45am; free • ☎ 020 7626 1274, ⓦ bevismarks.org.uk • ⊖ Aldgate

Hidden away behind a red-brick office block in a little courtyard off Bevis Marks is the **Bevis Marks Synagogue**. Built in 1701 by Sephardic Jews who had originally fled the Inquisition in Spain and Portugal, this is the country's oldest surviving synagogue, and its roomy, rich interior gives an idea of just how wealthy the community was at the time. Although it seats over six hundred, it's only a third of the size of its prototype in Amsterdam, where many Sephardic Jews initially settled. The Sephardic community has since moved out to Maida Vale and Wembley, and the congregation has dwindled, though the synagogue's magnificent array of chandeliers makes it very popular for

---

CITY SKYSCRAPERS

The City skyline is continuing to sprout a whole new generation of glass-clad **skyscrapers**. From 1980, for thirty years, the City's tallest building was 600ft **NatWest Tower** (now **Tower 42**; ⓦ tower42.com) by Richard Seifert (in the shape of the bank's logo), which has a public bar on the 42nd floor (prior booking required). In 2010, this was topped by the **Heron Tower** (ⓦ herontower.com), a fairly undistinguished 660ft skyscraper with a 144ft mast at 110 Bishopsgate, designed by Kohn Pedersen Fox – on the plus side, it has a 70,000-litre aquarium in the atrium, restaurants on the 39th and 40th floors, one of them the *Duck and Waffle* (see p.377), and a rooftop bar. Rafael Viñoly's 525ft **Walkie Talkie**, 20 Fenchurch St (ⓦ 20fenchurchstreet. co.uk), so-called because it's wider at the top than the bottom, includes a free public "Sky Garden", café and restaurant on the roof. **The Cheesegrater**, Richard Rogers' 737ft tapered office block at 122 Leadenhall St (ⓦ theleadenhallbuilding.com) is remarkable not simply for its triangular shape but also for its giant steel frame and its 90ft-high ground-floor atrium, which features lawns and mature trees and is open to the public. Kohn Pedersen Fox are also responsible for **The Scalpel**, a twisted 620ft angular shard of glass in Lime Street, due for completion in 2017.

candle-lit Jewish weddings. Close by Bevis Marks, just past Creechurch Lane, a plaque commemorates the even larger **Great Synagogue** of the Ashkenazi Jews, founded in 1690 but destroyed by bombs in 1941.

St Katharine Cree

86 Leadenhall St • Mon–Fri 10.30am–4pm • Free • ⓦ sanctuaryinthecity.net • ⊖ Aldgate

The church of **St Katharine Cree**, completed in 1631, is a rare example of its period, having miraculously escaped the Great Fire of 1666. It's a transitional building with Neoclassical elements, such as the Corinthian columns of the nave and, above, a Gothic clerestory and ribbing. At the east end is a very lovely, seventeenth-century stained-glass Catherine-wheel window. The church was consecrated in 1631 by Bishop Laud, and the "bowings and cringings" he indulged in during the service, were later used as evidence of his Catholicism at his trial and execution for heresy in 1645.

London Metal Exchange

56 Leadenhall St • Mon–Fri noon–1.30pm & 3.30–5pm • Free • ☎ 020 7264 5555, ⓦ lme.com • ⊖ Aldgate

The only place in the City where you can still witness the human scrum of share dealing – known as "open-outcry" – is at the **London Metal Exchange**, where metals – and even plastic – but not silver, gold or platinum are traded. The dealing takes place within the Ring, with each metal traded in five-minute bursts. To visit the public viewing gallery you must phone ahead.

St Botolph-without-Aldgate

Aldgate High St • Mon 11am–3pm, Tues–Fri 9am–3pm • Free • ☎ 020 7283 1670, ⓦ stbotolphs.org.uk • ⊖ Aldgate

St Botolph-without-Aldgate was designed in the 1740s by George Dance the Elder, and stood beside Aldgate, one of the old City gateways, now commemorated by a modern, wooden, latticed "palace on pillars" which stands close by. The church's bizarre interior, remodelled last century, features blue-grey paintwork, gilding on top of white plasterwork, some dodgy modern art, a batik reredos and a stunning, modern stained-glass rendition of Rubens' *Descent from the Cross* on a deep-purple background. Situated at the edge of the East End, this is a famously campaigning church, active on issues like gay priests and social exclusion.

The Monument

Fish St Hill • Apr–Sept daily 9.30am–6pm; Oct–March 9.30am–5.30pm; last admission 30min before close • £4, concessions £2.70, children £2 • ☎ 020 7626 2717, ⓦ themonument.info • ⊖ Monument

In the 1670s, Robert Hooke and Christopher Wren's **Monument** commemorating the Great Fire of 1666 (see p.452) used to rise above the rooftops. No longer so prominent on the skyline, this plain 202ft Doric column, crowned with spiky gilded flames, nevertheless remains the tallest isolated stone column in the world; if it were laid out flat it would touch the site of the bakery where the fire started, east of Monument. The bas-relief on the base depicts Charles II and the Duke of York in Roman garb conducting the emergency relief operation. The 311 steps to the gallery at the top – plagued by suicides until a cage was built around it in 1842 – once guaranteed an incredible view; nowadays it's dwarfed by the surrounding buildings.

St Magnus-the-Martyr

Lower Thames St • Tues–Fri 10am–4pm • ☎ 020 7626 4481, ⓦ stmagnusmartyr.org.uk • ⊖ Monument

Not far from the Monument is another Wren edifice, the church of **St Magnus-the-Martyr**, whose octagonal spire used to greet all travellers arriving in the City across old London Bridge. Now it stands forlorn by busy Lower Thames Street, though the Anglo-Catholic interior holds, in T.S. Eliot's words, "an inexplicable splendour of Ionian white and gold". In addition, there's a wooden pier from an old Roman wharf in the porch, and a great model of the old London Bridge in the vestry.

Old Billingsgate Market

16 Lower Thames St • ☎ 020 7283 2800, ⓦ oldbillingsgate.co.uk • ⊖ Monument

Along the river from St Magnus is **Old Billingsgate Market**, a handsome Victorian market hall that once housed London's chief wholesale fish market, but has since been turned into a corporate events venue. It's difficult now to imagine the noise and smell of old Billingsgate, whose porters used to carry the fish in towers of baskets on their heads, and whose wives were renowned for their bad language even in Shakespeare's day: "as bad a tongue… as any oyster-wife at Billingsgate" (*King Lear*). Next door stands the Neoclassical **Custom House**, from 1825, which has been collecting duties from incoming ships since around 1275, and still houses a department of HM Customs and Revenue.

10

St Olave

8 Hart St • Mon–Fri 10am–5pm • Free • ☎ 020 7488 4318, ⓦ sanctuaryinthecity.net • ⊖ Tower Hill

Saved from the Fire, but left as an empty shell by the Blitz, the Kentish ragstone church of **St Olave** was dubbed "St Ghastly Grim" by Dickens after the skulls and crossbones and vicious-looking spikes adorning the 1658 entrance to the graveyard on Seething Lane, a short stroll from St Dunstan's. Samuel Pepys lived in Seething Lane for much of his life, and he and his wife, Elizabeth, are both buried here amid the pre-Fire brasses and monuments – Elizabeth's monument was raised by Pepys himself; Pepys' own is Victorian.

All Hallows-by-the-Tower

Byward St • Mon–Fri 8am–6pm, Sat & Sun 10am–5pm • Guided tours Mon–Fri Apr–Oct 2–4pm • Free • ☎ 020 7481 2928, ⓦ ahbtt.org .uk • ⊖ Tower Hill

All Hallows-by-the-Tower, another pre-Fire church, only just survived the Blitz – most of the church is a postwar neo-Gothic pastiche wrought in concrete. The furnishings are fascinating, however, and include lots of maritime memorials, model ships, two wings of a Flemish triptych from around 1500, and, best of all, the exquisitely carved Gibbons limewood font cover, in the southwest chapel. Close by is an arch from the original seventh-century church; remains of a tessellated Roman pavement can also be found in the tiny Crypt Museum. All Hallows also has some superb pre-Reformation brasses.

LONDON BRIDGE

Unreal City
Under the brown fog of a winter dawn,
A crowd flowed over London Bridge, so many,
I had not thought death had undone so many.   *The Waste Land*, T.S. Eliot

At rush hour, you can still see Eliot's "undead" trudging to work across **London Bridge**, which was, until 1750, the only bridge across the Thames. The Romans were the first to build a permanent crossing here, a structure succeeded by a Saxon version that was pulled down by King Olaf of Norway in 1014, and commemorated in the popular nursery rhyme *London Bridge is Falling Down*. It was the medieval bridge, however, that achieved world fame: built of stone and crowded with timber-framed houses, it became one of London's greatest attractions. At the centre stood the richly ornate **Nonsuch House**, decorated with onion domes and Dutch gables, and a chapel dedicated to Thomas Becket; at the Southwark end was the Great Gatehouse, on which the heads of traitors were displayed, dipped in tar to preserve them. The houses were removed in the mid-eighteenth century, and a new stone bridge erected in 1831 – that one now stands near **Lake Havasu** in the Arizona desert, having been bought in the 1960s by a guy who, so the apocryphal story goes, thought he'd purchased Tower Bridge. The present concrete structure – without doubt the ugliest yet – dates from 1972.

BEEFEATERS AT THE TOWER OF LONDON

Tower of London and around

Tower Hill is choked with tourists who flock here to see two of London's most famous landmarks, Tower Bridge and the adjacent Tower of London. Despite all the attendant hype and heritage claptrap, the Tower remains one of London's most remarkable buildings, site of some of the goriest events in the nation's history, and somewhere all visitors and Londoners should explore at least once. Sitting beside the river, at the eastern edge of the old city walls, the Tower is chiefly famous as a place of imprisonment and death, yet it's also been used as a royal residence, armoury, mint, menagerie, observatory and – a function it still serves – a safe-deposit box for the Crown Jewels. And, finally, it's easy to forget that the Tower is, above all, the most perfectly preserved (and restored) medieval fortress in the country.

Begun as a simple watchtower, built by **William the Conqueror** to keep an eye on the City, the Tower had evolved into a palace-fortress by 1100. The inner curtain wall and towers were built under Henry III, while the outer fortifications, and an even wider moat, were added by Edward I, on his return from the Crusades, which means that most of what's visible today was already in place by 1307, the year of Edward's death. The Tower has been besieged on a number of occasions – first, in 1191, when the unpopular Bishop Longchamp held out against Richard I's brother, John, but caved in after only three days – but sacked only once, during the 1381 Peasants' Revolt, when the Archbishop of Canterbury, Simon Sudbury, among others, was dragged out and lynched.

The Tower's **first prisoner**, the Bishop of Durham, arrived in 1101, imprisoned by Henry I, and promptly escaped from the window of his cell by a rope, having got the guards drunk. Gruffydd ap Llywelyn Fawr, heir to the Welsh throne, attempted a similar feat from the White Tower in 1244, with less success – "his head and neck were crushed between his shoulders… a most horrid spectacle" – the window he used was subsequently bricked up and can still be seen on the south side of the Tower. Incidentally, the **most famous escapee** from the Tower was the Jacobite 5th Earl of Nithsdale, who, the night before his execution in 1716, managed to get past the guards dressed as his wife's maid (despite his red beard), and lived in poverty and happiness for almost thirty years in exile in Rome.

Following the Restoration in 1660, the general public were admitted to the Tower for the first time to view the **coronation regalia** and the impressive displays of arms and armour – by the end of Victoria's reign, there were half a million visitors to the fortress each year. Nevertheless, during both of the world wars, the Tower was still used to hold prisoners: **Roger Casement**, the Irish nationalist, was held here briefly before his trial and hanging in 1916, and the last VIP inmate was **Rudolf Hess**, Hitler's deputy, who flew secretly into Britain to try to sue for peace in May 1941 and was held in the tower for a few days. The **last execution** took place on August 14, 1941, when Josef Jakobs, a German spy who (like Hess) had broken his ankle while parachuting into Britain, was given the privilege of being seated before the firing squad.

In 2014, to mark the centenary of the beginning of Britain's involvement in the World War I, 888,246 ceramic poppies filled the Tower's moat. The poppies were 'planted' progressively, over a period of four months, so that the moat gradually turned red, until every one of the British military fatalities in the war was represented by a poppy. The spectacle attracted huge crowds and the overall effect was very striking.

INFORMATION AND TOURS

Opening hours March–Oct Mon & Sun 10am–5.30pm, Tues–Sat 9am–5.30pm; Nov–Feb closes 4.30pm, last admission 30mins before close.

Admission £24.50, concessions £18.70, under-16s £11.

To avoid queuing (and save some money), buy your ticket online.

Contact details ☎ 0844 482 7777 or ☎ 020 3166 6000, ⊛ hrp.org.uk.

BEEFEATERS

Formed in 1485 by Henry VII as a personal bodyguard, the Tower's forty or so Beefeaters are officially known as **Yeoman Warders** – the nickname "Beefeaters" was coined in the seventeenth century, when it was a term of abuse for a well-fed domestic servant. These self-assured, eminently photogenic guards are best known for their scarlet-and-gold Tudor costumes, but unless it's a special occasion you're more likely to see them in dark-blue Victorian "undress". The Beefeaters have all done at least 22 years' military service, reached at least the rank of sergeant major and are aged between 40 and 55 on appointment. The first-ever woman Beefeater was appointed in 2007; two years on, two of her male colleagues were dismissed for harassing her. All the Beefeaters live in the Tower and one of their many duties is to give theatrically irreverent guided tours to the tourists, which many of them clearly relish.

Tube ⊖ Tower Hill.

Eating There's a spacious and fairly decent café in the New Armouries building, and plenty of benches on which to picnic. Alternatively, you can obtain a re-entry pass and have lunch outside the Tower.

Tours You can explore the Tower complex independently, or with an audioguide (£4), but it's a good idea to get your bearings by joining up with one of the free, entertaining hour-long guided tours, given at regular intervals by one of the Tower's Beefeaters – it's also the easiest way to visit the Chapel of St Peter-ad-Vincula.

Bell Tower

Visitors enter the Tower by the Middle Tower and the Byward Tower, in the southwest corner. Two of the first victims of the Reformation – Thomas More and John Fisher – were incarcerated nearby in the **Bell Tower**, from whose dinky wooden belfry a bell still signals the curfew hour (and used to toll to signal an execution). More was initially

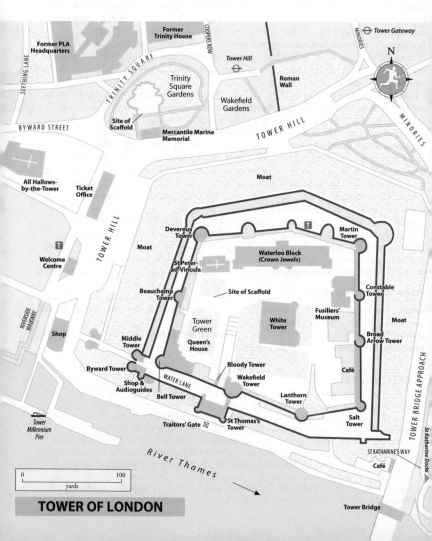

TOWER OF LONDON

allowed writing materials, but later they were withdrawn; Fisher was kept in worse conditions ("I decay forthwith, and fall into coughs and diseases of my body, and cannot keep myself in health") and was so weak that he had to be carried to the scaffold on Tower Hill. The 20-year-old future Queen Elizabeth I arrived here in 1554, while her half-sister Queen Mary tried to find incriminating evidence against her. Catholic Mass was performed daily in Elizabeth's cell for the two months of her imprisonment, but she refused to be converted.

Traitors' Gate

Most prisoners were delivered through **Traitors' Gate**, on the waterfront, which forms part of **St Thomas's Tower**, now partially reconstructed to re-create the atmosphere of Edward I's **medieval palace**. The King's Bedchamber has a beautiful little oratory in one of the turrets, while in the larger oratory of the Throne Room, in 1471, the "saintly but slightly daft" Henry VI was murdered at prayer, possibly on the orders of Edward IV or Richard III. Not long afterwards, Edward had his brother, the Duke of Clarence, executed in the Tower for high treason, drowned in a butt of malmsey wine (at his own request – according to Shakespeare).

11

Bloody Tower

The main entrance to the Inner Ward is beneath a 3.5-ton, seven hundred-year-old portcullis, which forms part of the **Bloody Tower**, so called because it was here that the 12-year-old Edward V and his 10-year-old brother, Richard, were accommodated "for their own safety" in 1483 by their uncle, Richard of Gloucester (later Richard III), following the death of their father, Edward IV. Of all the Tower's many inhabitants, few have so captured the public imagination as the **Princes in the Tower**. According to Thomas More, they were smothered in their beds, and buried naked at the foot of the White Tower. In 1674, workmen discovered the skeletons of two young children close to the Tower; they were subsequently buried in Innocents' Corner in Westminster Abbey.

The study of **Walter Raleigh** (see box below) is re-created in the lower chamber, while his sleeping quarters in the upper chamber, built to accommodate his wife, children and three servants, now house an exhibition on the Princes in the Tower and on the poisoning of the poet **Thomas Overbury**. Confined to the Bloody Tower in 1613 by James I, Overbury was slowly poisoned to death with arsenic concealed within the tarts and jellies sent by the wife of one of the king's favourites, Robert Carr, Earl of

---

WALTER RALEIGH

The Bloody Tower's most illustrious inmate – even more famous in his time than the princes – was **Walter Raleigh** (1554–1618), who spent three separate periods in the Tower. His first misdemeanour was in 1591 when he impregnated and secretly married Elizabeth Throckmorton, one of Elizabeth I's ladies-in-waiting, without the Queen's permission. A year later his crime was discovered and he was sent to the Tower (with his wife Bess); his second spell began in 1603, when he was found guilty of plotting against James I. He spent nearly thirteen years, with his wife and kids, growing and smoking tobacco (his most famous import), composing poetry, concocting potions in his distillery and writing *The Historie of the World*, which outsold even Shakespeare, despite being banned by James I for being "too saucy in censuring princes". When Raleigh complained that the noise of the portcullis kept him awake at night, he was moved to much worse accommodation. In 1616 he was released and sent off to Guyana to discover gold, on condition that he didn't attack the Spanish; he broke his word and was sent straight back to the Tower on his return in 1618. For six weeks he was imprisoned in "one of the most cold and direful dungeons", before being beheaded at Westminster.

Somerset. Three years later, Carr and his wife were themselves arrested, tried and condemned to death – in the end, they were simply incarcerated in the Tower for six years before being pardoned. The Lieutenant of the Tower was less fortunate, and was hanged for failing to protect his prisoners.

White Tower

William the Conqueror's central hall-keep, known as the **White Tower**, is the original "Tower", begun in 1076. Whitewashed (hence its name) in the reign of Henry III, it now sports a Kentish ragstone exterior thanks to Wren, who added the large windows. Of the tower's four turrets, topped by stylish Tudor cupolas, only three are square: the fourth is rounded in order to encase the main spiral staircase, and for a short while was used by Charles II's royal astronomer, Flamsteed, before he moved to Greenwich. The main entrance to the Tower is the original one, high up in the south wall, out of reach of the enemy, and accessed by a wooden staircase which could be removed during times of siege.

11

Royal Armouries

The four floors of arms and armour displayed within the tower represent a mere smidgen of the **Royal Armouries** (the majority of which resides in Leeds), originally established by Henry VIII in Greenwich and on display here since the time of Charles II. Among the most striking armour displayed on the ground floor is the colossal garniture of 1540 made for Henry VIII (and famous for its protruding codpiece, which women used to touch to boost their fertility), juxtaposed with boy king Edward VI's tiny suit of armour. Several exotic gifts presented to the royalty reside here, too, including the Japanese shogun armour presented to King James I by the East India Company. The collection takes a lurch into the present day with a polo helmet and knee pads belonging to Prince Charles.

The **Line of Kings**, on the same floor, is a display first recorded in 1660, a sort of Restoration waxworks only in wood, originally depicting the monarchs of England on horseback. Also on show here is a suit of armour for a man six feet nine inches tall

---

ROYAL MENAGERIE

The **Royal Menagerie** began in earnest in 1235 when the Holy Roman Emperor presented three "leopards" to Henry III; the keeper was initially paid sixpence a day for the sustenance of the beasts (they were, in fact, **lions**), and one penny for himself. They were joined in 1251 by a **polar bear** from the King of Norway (who was put on a leash and allowed to catch fish in the Thames) and in 1255 by an **elephant** from the King of France. From the 1330s, the lions were put on public display in the outer barbican (which became known as the Lion Tower). James I was particularly keen on the menagerie, and used to stage regular animal fights on the green, but the practice was stopped in 1609 when one of the bears killed a child. In 1704, six lions, two leopards, three eagles, two Swedish owls "of great bigness", two "cats of the mountains" and a jackal were recorded. Visitors were advised not to "play tricks" after a baboon threw a cannonball at a young boy and killed him.

The menagerie was transferred to the newly founded **London Zoo** in the 1830s, leaving the Tower with just its **ravens**, descendants of early scavengers attracted by waste from the palace kitchens. They have been protected by royal decree since the Restoration, and have their wings clipped so they can't fly away – legend says that the Tower (and therefore the kingdom) will fall if they do, the theory almost put to the test during the Second World War after the Tower suffered heavy bombing and only one raven survived, though numbers were soon brought back up. While the ravens may appear harmless, they are wild, territorial creatures best given a wide berth. They live in coops in the south wall of the Inner Ward, are fed raw meat from Smithfield Market, have individual names and even have their own graveyard in the dry moat near the main entrance.

(once thought to have been John of Gaunt) and one for a boy just three feet one and a half inches high (possibly Charles I). On the top floor, there's an interesting exhibition on the executions that have taken place within the Tower and on Tower Hill over the years – the block and axe from the last beheading are here (see box below).

Chapel of St John's

Whatever your interests, you should pay a visit to the first-floor **Chapel of St John's**, a beautiful Norman structure completed in 1080, making it the oldest intact ecclesiastical building in London. It was here that Henry VI's body was buried following his murder in 1471; that Henry VII's queen, Elizabeth of York, lay in state surrounded by eight hundred candles, after dying in childbirth, and that Lady Jane Grey came to pray on the night before her execution. Today, the once highly decorated blocks of honey-coloured Caen limestone are free of all ecclesiastical excrescences, leaving the chapel's smooth curves and rounded apse perfectly unencumbered.

Tower Green

Despite appearances, the pretty little open space of **Tower Green** was the chief place of execution within the Tower for many centuries, reserved for prestigious prisoners who were treated to their beheading away from the baying crowd – the likes of Catherine Howard, Anne Boleyn and Lady Jane Grey were executed here, their names appearing alongside the other victims on an incongruous glass monument at the centre of the green. The bloody, headless corpses of the executed (from Tower Green and Tower Hill) were buried in the Tudor **Chapel of St Peter-ad-Vincula**, to the north, accessible only during the first and last hour the Tower is open, or on the Beefeaters' tours.

On the west side of the green, the **Beauchamp Tower** houses an exhibition on the Tower's prisoners on the ground floor. Beauchamp Tower itself accommodated only the wealthiest prisoners and boasts a better class of graffiti: Lord Dudley, husband of Lady Jane Grey, even commissioned a stonemason to carve the family crest on the first floor.

In the southwest corner of the green is the sixteenth-century **Queen's House** (closed to the public), distinguished by its swirling Tudor timber frames and the most luxurious cells in the Tower. In 1688, William Penn, the Quaker and founder of Pennsylvania, was confined to the Queen's House, where he wrote his most popular work, *No Cross, No Crown*.

Jewel House

The castellated Waterloo Block or Jewel House, north of the White Tower, now holds the **Crown Jewels**, the major reason so many people flock to the Tower. The Jewels

---

THE TOWER GREEN TEN

Being **beheaded** at Tower Hill (as opposed to being hanged, drawn and quartered) was a privilege of the nobility; being beheaded on Tower Green, the stretch of lawn to the west of the White Tower, was an honour conferred on just ten people. It was an arrangement that suited both parties: the victim was spared the jeering crowds of Tower Hill, and the monarch was spared bad publicity. Among the victims were: Lord Hastings, executed immediately after his arrest on the orders of Richard III, who swore he wouldn't go to dinner until Hastings was beheaded; **Anne Boleyn** (Henry VIII's second wife), accused of incest and adultery, who was dispatched cleanly and swiftly with a French long sword rather than the traditional axe, at her own insistence; 19-year-old **Catherine Howard** (Henry VIII's fifth wife and Anne's cousin), convicted of adultery and beheaded along with her lady-in-waiting, who was deemed an accomplice; 16-year-old **Lady Jane Grey**, who was Queen for just nine days; and the Earl of Essex, one-time favourite of Elizabeth I.

> ## TOWER CEREMONIES
>
> **The Ceremony of the Keys** is a seven hundred-year-old, seven-minute floodlit ceremony. At 9.53pm daily, the Chief Yeoman Warder, accompanied by the Tower Guard, locks the Tower gates, and as he attempts to return to the Inner Ward, the following exchange then takes place: "Halt. Who comes there?" "The Keys." "Whose Keys?" "Queen Elizabeth's Keys." "Pass then, all's well." Then the Last Post is sounded and the ceremony ends. To find out how to witness this long-running drama, visit the website.
>
> **Gun Salutes** are fired by the Honourable Artillery Company at 1pm at Tower Wharf on royal birthdays and other special occasions.
>
> **The Constable's Dues** occurs once a year when a large Royal Navy ship moors alongside the Tower; the ship's captain and his escort march through the Tower and present a barrel of rum to the Constable of the Tower.
>
> **The Ceremony of the Lilies and Roses** is carried out every year on May 21 by the provosts of Eton and King's College, Cambridge, who place white lilies and roses (their respective emblems) on the spot where King Henry VI, founder of both institutions, was murdered on May 21, 1471.
>
> **The Beating of the Bounds** ceremony takes place once every three years (including in 2017) on Ascension Day (forty days after Easter), outside the walls of the Tower. It used to be little boys who were beaten, but now it's the 29 stones that mark the limits of the Tower's jurisdiction that are thrashed with willow wands by local children, while the Chief Yeoman Warder gives the order "Whack it, boys! Whack it!"

include the world's three largest cut diamonds, but only a few of the exhibits could be described as beautiful – assertions of status and wealth are more important considerations. Queues can be long, and you only get to view the rocks from moving walkways. The vast majority of exhibits postdate the Commonwealth of 1649–60, when most of the royal riches were melted down for coinage or sold off.

Before you reach the walkway, look out for the twelfth-century **Coronation Spoon**, the oldest piece of regalia. The first major piece along the walkway is the Sceptre with the Cross, which contains the world's largest colourless cut diamond, the 530-carat "First Star of Africa" or **Cullinan I**, followed by **St Edward's Crown**, used in every coronation since the Restoration. The legendary 105.6-carat **Koh-i-Nûr** (Mountain of Light) is set into the Queen Elizabeth, the Queen Mother's Crown from 1937. The last and most famous crown, set apart from the others, is the **Imperial State Crown**, worn by the Queen on state occasions, and sparkling with 2868 diamonds, 17 sapphires, 11 emeralds, 5 rubies and 273 pearls. The crown contains several very famous jewels: St Edward's Sapphire, taken from the ring of Edward the Confessor and set in the cross atop the crown; the Black Prince's Ruby, on the front cross; and Cullinan II, the 317-carat "Second Star of Africa"; the crown also contains pearls from Elizabeth I's ear-rings.

Salt Tower to the Martin Tower

Visitors can walk along the Tower's eastern walls, starting at the **Salt Tower**, which features more prisoners' graffiti, including a stunningly detailed zodiac carved by Hugh Draper, incarcerated in 1561 on a charge of sorcery. This is where Edward I kept the Scottish King John Balliol prisoner for three years from 1296. Halfway along the walls, the **Constable Tower** contains a small exhibition on the 1381 Peasants' Revolt (see opposite).

The **Martin Tower**, at the far end of the wall walk, houses a display of crowns with their gems taken out and relates the story of the most famous attempt to steal the Crown Jewels which took place here in 1671, when "Colonel" **Thomas Blood**, an Irish adventurer, made an attempt to make off with the lot, disguised as a parson. He was caught with the crown under his habit, the orb in one of his accomplices' breeches and the sceptre about to be filed in half. Charles II, good-humoured as ever, met and pardoned the felon, and even awarded him a pension and made him welcome at court.

Fusiliers' Museum

Last, and probably least, the Tower also contains the **Fusiliers' Museum** which tells the story of the Royal Fusiliers, now part of the Royal Regiment of Fusiliers. The original regiment was founded by James II in 1685 from Tower guards and was called the Ordnance Regiment, as it was their job to escort the artillery. The museum trots through the regiment's various campaigns, displays its medals and spoils from across the Empire, and lists its most famous alumni, although it neglects to mention that East End gangsters, the Kray Twins, were once Fusiliers, and were in fact held prisoner in the Tower overnight in 1952 after having failed to turn up on time for their National Service call-up.

Tower Hill

Perhaps it's fitting that traffic-blighted **Tower Hill** to the northwest of the Tower should be such a god-awful place, for it was here that the Tower's convicted "traitors" were executed. The actual spot for the executions, at what was the country's first permanent scaffold, is marked by a plaque on the west side of Trinity Square Gardens, which names a handful of the 125 executed here.

Close by stands the **Mercantile Marine Memorial**, designed by Edwin Lutyens, smothered with the names of the 12,000 merchant seamen who died in World War I, and subsequently enlarged with a vast, sprawling sunken section commemorating the 24,000 more who died in World War II.

The marine theme is continued in the buildings overlooking the gardens: at 10 Trinity Square is the gargantuan temple-like former headquarters of the **Port of London Authority**, an Edwardian edifice that exudes imperial confidence, with Neptune adorning the main tower (the building now houses unaffordable apartments and a luxury *Four Seasons* hotel); and, to the east, the elegant Neoclassical former headquarters of **Trinity House** (75min tours take place two to four times a month and must be booked; £8; ☏020 7481 6900, ⊕trinityhouse.co.uk), the organization that oversees the upkeep of the lighthouses of England, Wales, the Channel Islands and Gibraltar – check out the reliefs of mermen, cherubs and lighthouses on the main facade, and the splendid gilded nautical weather vane.

Continuing east, you'll find perhaps the most impressive remaining section of London's **Roman walls** (see p.164) behind the *Grange City Hotel*, on Cooper's Row, and in Wakefield Gardens, close to Tower Hill tube station, along with an

11

OFF WITH HIS HEAD!

During the **1381 Peasants' Revolt**, rioters broke into the Tower, dragged out the Lord High Treasurer (the man responsible for the hated poll tax), and hacked him to death on Tower Hill, along with the Archbishop of Canterbury. However, the first official beheading didn't take place until 1388 with the last one in 1747, when the 80-year-old Jacobite **Lord Lovat** was dispatched. Lovat's beheading drew such a crowd that one of the spectators' stands collapsed, killing several bystanders, at which Lovat exclaimed: "The more mischief, the better sport." The Duke of Monmouth, beheaded in 1685 for his rebellion against James II, suffered the most botched execution: it took **Jack Ketch** (who lives on in Punch & Judy shows) five blows of the axe to sever his head, and even then the job had to be finished off with a surgeon's knife. Hangings continued for another thirty-odd years, ending with the execution of two prostitutes and a one-armed soldier arrested for attacking a Catholic-run pub in the 1780 Gordon Riots.

eighteenth-century copy of a Roman statue of Emperor Trajan, saved from a Southampton scrapyard by a local vicar.

Tower Bridge

Daily: April–Sept 10am–6pm; Oct–March 9.30am–5.30pm; last admission 30min before close • £9, concessions £6.30, under-16s £3.90, under-5s free • ☎ 020 7403 3761, Ⓦ towerbridge.org.uk • ⊖ Tower Hill

Tower Bridge ranks with Big Ben as the most famous of all London landmarks. Completed in 1894, its neo-Gothic towers are clad in Cornish granite and Portland stone, but conceal a frame of Scottish steel, which, at the time, represented a considerable engineering achievement, allowing a road crossing that could be raised to give tall ships access to the upper reaches of the Thames. The raising of the bascules (from the French for "seesaw") remains an impressive sight, and an event that takes place around a thousand times a year – visit the website for "bridge lift times". If you buy a ticket for a visit, packaged as the Tower Bridge Exhibition, you get to walk across the elevated walkways linking the summits of the towers, now with glass floors for views of the bridge and traffic below, and visit the Tower's Engine Rooms, on the south side of the bridge, where you can see the now-defunct, giant coal-fired boilers which drove the hydraulic system until 1976, and play some interactive engineering games.

11

STOKE NEWINGTON ROAD

East London

Nowadays, even south, west and north Londoners will admit – albeit grudgingly – that east London's where it's at. Part of their sniffiness is down to the fact that what exactly defines that "it" is a little hazy – to a certain extent it's simply this area's self-perpetuating buzz. But chasing the scene – creative goings-on in warehouses, art previews, edgy nightlife or word-of-mouth soft openings – can be a lot of fun. Just as the traditional image of the old "East End" conjured romantic notions of togetherness and community, so today's east London is more about the people than the urban fabric, much of which is functional and industrial. East Londoners might be cut from a different (and very varied) cloth these days – you won't hear many Cockney accents – but even the appeal of the relatively short roll call of traditional sights lies in their significance to the area's peopled history.

Of course, you could say there was a buzz about the old "**East End**" too. This somewhat outdated geographical label – which, strictly speaking, refers to a four-mile stretch bounded by the City, the River Lea, the Thames and Victoria Park – was long synonymous with slums, sweatshops and crime, its dark mythology surrounding the likes of Jack the Ripper and the Kray twins (see p.198) making it a shadowy counterpoint to the glitz and bright-light theatricality out west. But with its low rents (still, arguably, the case), the East End has been the first port of call for wave after wave of **immigrants** (see box, p.189), and it preserves rich mementoes from each – with the districts of Whitechapel and Spitalfields, within sight of the City's skyscrapers, especially redolent of this heritage – and east London's East End kernel is still where most of the traditional sights are to be found.

Even as east London has ballooned beyond the old East End, this is still the part of town for fresh arrivals to try things out – a project, a business, a new start – and that means the area is thronged with creatives, egged on by the can-do, pop-up atmosphere. This impacts on the **nightlife** – particularly good around Brick Lane, Shoreditch and Dalston – which means that many an east London visit is nocturnal. But there's plenty to shake you out of bleariness the morning after, with some of the city's finest cafés, **open spaces** (often with a bracing, edgeland feel, particularly at Hackney's outer reaches) and, if you're in the mood, a whole Aladdin's Cave of eye-opening **art**. As with countless east London arrivals before you, it pays to be bold, get out there and engage with people.

12 Spitalfields

On the eastern edge of the City, **Spitalfields** is located near the site of an early cemetery that lay just outside the Roman walls. Its name derives from the medieval priory and hospital (hence "spital") of St Mary which stood here until the Dissolution – the old priory mortuary chapel has been preserved, in an underground vault, to the west of the old market. Nowadays, Spitalfields is continuing to undergo a slow but steady gentrification and is one of London's prime battlegrounds between the forces of development and those of preservation. The latter camp is spearheaded by the longstanding Spitalfields Trust (ⓦwww.thespitalfieldstrust.com), with the preservation of Norton Folgate, a stretch of road connecting Bishopsgate with Shoreditch High Street, the current focus of their efforts. Another champion for the area comes in the form of one of London's finest blogs (ⓦspitalfieldslife.com), which sees a daily post by "the Gentle Author" that covers some aspect – often with a historical slant – of east London life.

The whole area is at its busiest and buzziest on Sundays, when there are no fewer than four **markets** – Petticoat Lane, Brick Lane, Columbia Road Flower Market and Spitalfields Market – all within easy walking distance of one another.

Spitalfields Market

Market stalls: Mon–Wed 10am–5pm, Thurs & Sun 9am–5pm, Fri 10am–4pm, Sat 11am–5pm; street food traders till 9.30pm; shops till 7pm; restaurants till 11pm • ⓦoldspitalfieldsmarket.com or ⓦ spitalfields.co.uk • ⊖ Liverpool Street

Originally established back in the seventeenth century in open countryside east of the City, **Spitalfields Market** was once the capital's premier fruit and vegetable market. Since the wholesale market moved out to Stratford in 1991, Spitalfields has become something

---

The East End of London is the hell of poverty. Like an enormous, black, motionless, giant kracken, the poverty of London lies there in lurking silence and encircles with its mighty tentacles the life and wealth of the City and of the West End…

J.H. Mackay, *The Anarchists* (1891)

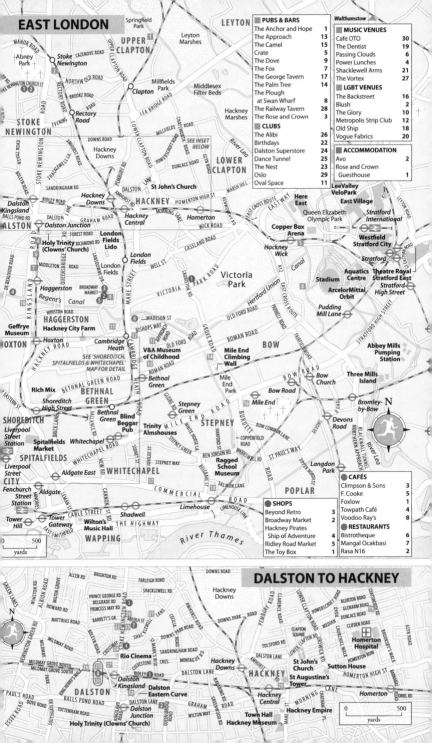

of a hybrid. In the rather lugubrious Victorian red-brick and green-gabled building, a daily market thrives, with stalls selling crafts, clothing (mostly of the vintage or quirky variety), food and gifts, with the occasional sale of old vinyl records. Thursdays sees an influx of antiques traders, while Fridays shifts the focus to independent fashion and art makers. Meanwhile, the western, 1920s half of the market has been replaced by a glass-box mixed offices and shops development designed by Norman Foster. Part of the original facade survives on the north side of Brushfield Street; on the south side, the old fruiterers' shops are occupied by modishly retro businesses, such as Verde & Co, author Jeanette Winterson's deli venture (see p.378), while as many people come to the market nowadays to eat as to shop, drawn by the market's scattering of "street food" vans and burgeoning array of small, independent restaurants such as Nuno Mendes' *Taberna do Mercado* (see p.379). A corporate and chain presence is strong now too, but thankfully the old London atmosphere is still just about managing to hold sway.

Christ Church

Commercial St • Mon–Fri 10am–4pm, Sun 1–4pm; services Sun 8.30am (first, third and fifth Sun of the month), 10.30am, 5pm & Tues 1.10pm; tours can be arranged by calling in advance, though ten people is the usual minimum number • ☎ 020 7377 2440, ⓦ ccspitalfields.org & christchurchspitalfields.org • ⊖ Liverpool Street or Shoreditch High Street

Opened in 1729, **Christ Church** is a characteristically bold church by Nicholas Hawksmoor – arguably his masterpiece – and it is a truly memorable sight, particularly when viewed front on from Brushfield Street. The church's main features are its huge 225ft-high broach spire and giant Tuscan portico, raised on steps and shaped like a Venetian window (a central arched opening flanked by two smaller rectangles), a motif repeated in the tower and doors. Inside, you'll find giant columned bays, a hexagonal, embossed ceiling, with a lion and a unicorn playing peekaboo on the top of the chancel beam. The church's slow restoration began in 1976 and saw it once more gleaming numinous and white – both inside and out – come 2004. In 2015 the church celebrated another landmark in its restoration as London's largest Georgian organ, dating from 1735 and silent since 1960, was finally restored to working order. Late 2015 saw a refectory open in the crypt.

South of Old Spitalfields Market

South of Spitalfields Market are several reminders of the old Jewish community (see box opposite): the **Soup Kitchen for the Jewish Poor**, on Brune Street, which opened in 1902 and closed in 1992 (the undulating stone lettering with the Christian and Jewish dates of its foundation are still clearly visible), a mural opposite and the **Sandys Row synagogue** (ⓦ sandysrowsynagogue.org), an old Huguenot chapel converted in 1870 for Dutch Jews and one of the few working synagogues left in the East End. The surrounding network of narrow streets is fascinating to walk around – unique survivors that give a strong impression of the old East End. From the bakery at 12 Widegate St, with its high-relief ceramic friezes, cross Sandys Row and walk down Artillery Passage into **Artillery Lane**, which boasts a superb Huguenot shop front at no. 56, occupied since 2009 by Raven Row, an art exhibition space (ⓦ ravenrow.org). Incidentally, the ballistic connection dates from the reign of Henry VIII, when the Royal Artillery used to hold gunnery practice here.

EAST LONDON HIGHLIGHTS

Christ Church, Spitalfields Arguably Hawksmoor's masterpiece. See above
Dalston Eastern Curve Garden A green oasis with an irresistible community feel. See p.201
Brick Lane Beigel Bake Legendary 24hr joint serving some of the city's best bagels. See p.378
Queen Elizabeth Olympic Park A wonderful expanse full of intriguing attractions. See p.205
Whitechapel Gallery The driving force behind the "First Thursdays" initiative. See p.197
Dalston nightlife Dalston can still lay claim to the city's hippest night out. See p.392 & p.403

Petticoat Lane (Middlesex St)

Main market Sun 9am–2pm **Wentworth St market** Mon–Fri 8am–4pm • ⊖ Liverpool Street, Aldgate or Aldgate East

Heavily bombed in the Blitz, **Petticoat Lane** is not one of London's prettiest streets, but it has a rich history. The street originally lay outside the City walls, and was called Hogs Lane; later, the area became known for its second-hand goods market, offering, among other things, petticoats, which led to the change of name. In 1830, the authorities renamed it Middlesex Street to avoid the mention of ladies' underwear – though the old name has stuck – and tried to prevent Sunday trading here (it was finally sanctioned by law in 1936). Today, the market spills into the surrounding area, with a smaller lunchtime version in the week on Wentworth Street. While it's worth a look for its sheer longevity and the glimpse of everyday east London life it affords, Petticoat Lane is hardly a place for souvenirs, with the goods on offer ranging from cheap (new) clothes to toiletries and luggage.

Dennis Severs' House

18 Folgate St • Mon noon–2pm (last admission 1.15pm) £10, Mon & Wed "Silent Night" 5–9pm £15, Sun noon–4pm (last admission 3.15pm) £10; monthly "Exclusive Silent Night" £50 • ☎ 020 7247 4013, ⓦ dennissevershouse.co.uk • ⊖ Shoreditch High Street or Liverpool Street

Just to the north of Old Spitalfields Market, you can visit one of the area's characteristic eighteenth-century terraced houses at 18 Folgate St, where the American artist **Dennis Severs** lived until 1999. Eschewing all modern conveniences, Severs lived under candlelight, decorating his house as it would have been two hundred years ago. The public were invited to share in the experience, which he described as like "passing through a frame into a painting". Today, visitors are free to explore the candle-lit rooms, with the conceit that the resident Huguenot family has literally just popped out: during these "Silent Night" explorations, you'll experience the smell of food, lots of clutter and the sound of horses' hooves on the cobbled street outside.

12

Brick Lane

⊖ Aldgate East, Shoreditch High Street, Liverpool Street

Brick Lane gets its name from the brick kilns situated here after the Great Fire to help rebuild the City. By 1900, this was the high street of London's unofficial Jewish ghetto

---

EAST LONDON'S IMMIGRANTS

The first immigrants were **Huguenots**, French Protestants fleeing from religious persecution in the 1680s, who bequeathed the word "refugee" (from the French, *réfugié*). They were welcomed by all except the apprentice weavers whose work they undercut. Some settled in Soho, but the majority settled in Spitalfields (ⓦ huguenotsofspitalfields.org), where they were operating thousands of silk looms by the late eighteenth century. Within three generations the Huguenots were almost entirely assimilated, and the Catholic **Irish** became the new immigrant population. Irish labourers, ironically enough, played a major role in building the area's Protestant churches, and were crucial to the development of the canals and docks. The threat of cheap Irish labour provoked riots in 1736 and 1769, and their Catholicism made them easy targets during the 1780 Gordon Riots.

It was the influx of **Jews** escaping pogroms in eastern Europe and Russia that defined the character of the East End in the late nineteenth century. The bishop of Stepney complained in 1901 that his churches were "left like islands in the midst of an alien sea". The same year, the MP for Stepney helped found the East End's first organized racist movement, the British Brothers League, whose ideology foreshadowed the British Union of Fascists, led by Oswald Mosley and famously defeated at the **Battle of Cable Street** (see p.456). The area's Jewish population has now dispersed throughout London, while much of east London's contemporary vibrancy – from Ridley Road Market (see p.201) to Brick Lane's curry houses and the *ocakbaşı* restaurants of Dalston and Stoke Newington – can be attributed to the rich influence of African-Caribbean, Turkish and Bangladeshi communities.

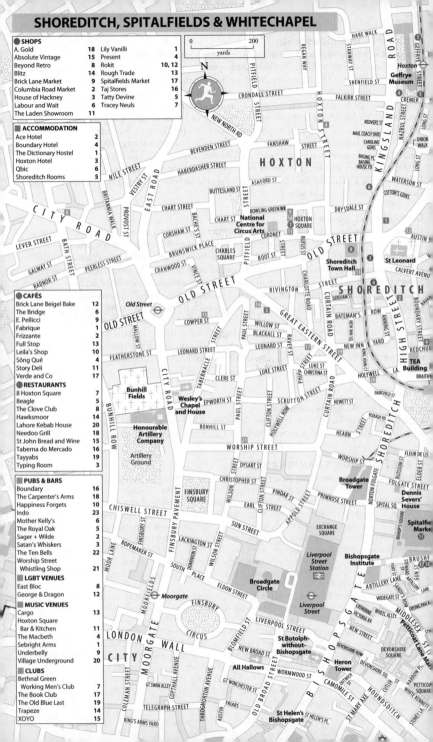

SHOREDITCH, SPITALFIELDS & WHITECHAPEL

● SHOPS
A. Gold	18	Lily Vanilli	1
Absolute Vintage	15	Present	4
Beyond Retro	8	Rokit	10, 12
Blitz	14	Rough Trade	13
Brick Lane Market	9	Spitalfields Market	17
Columbia Road Market	2	Taj Stores	16
House of Hackney	3	Tatty Devine	5
Labour and Wait	6	Tracey Neuls	7
The Laden Showroom	11		

■ ACCOMMODATION
Ace Hotel	2
Boundary Hotel	4
The Dictionary Hostel	1
Hoxton Hotel	3
Qbic	6
Shoreditch Rooms	5

● CAFÉS
Brick Lane Beigel Bake	12
The Bridge	6
E. Pellicci	9
Fabrique	2
Frizzante	1
Full Stop	13
Leila's Shop	10
Sông Quê	4
Story Deli	11
Verde and Co	17

● RESTAURANTS
8 Hoxton Square	7
Beagle	5
The Clove Club	8
Hawksmoor	14
Lahore Kebab House	20
Needoo Grill	18
St John Bread and Wine	15
Taberna do Mercado	16
Tayyabs	19
Typing Room	3

■ PUBS & BARS
Boundary	16
The Carpenter's Arms	18
Happiness Forgets	10
Indo	23
Mother Kelly's	6
The Royal Oak	5
Sager + Wilde	2
Satan's Whiskers	3
The Ten Bells	22
Worship Street	
Whistling Shop	21

■ LGBT VENUES
East Bloc	8
George & Dragon	12

■ MUSIC VENUES
Cargo	13
Hoxton Square	
Bar & Kitchen	11
The Macbeth	4
Sebright Arms	1
Underbelly	9
Village Underground	20

■ CLUBS
Bethnal Green	
Working Men's Club	7
The Book Club	17
The Old Blue Last	19
Trapeze	14
XOYO	15

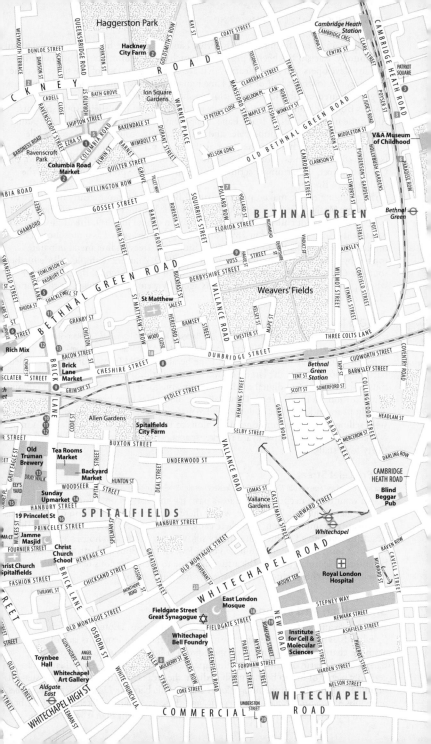

(see box, p.456), but from the 1960s, Brick Lane became the heart of the Bangladeshi community. Racism has been a problem for each wave of immigrants, but nowadays it's City developers and gentrification that are changing the face of the street. For the moment, the southern half of Brick Lane remains pretty staunchly Bangladeshi: bright-coloured sari fabrics line the clothes-shop windows, and, in the evening, waiters from the numerous curry houses try to cajole you into their establishments. Along the northern half of Brick Lane, the pavements are busy with punters heading for the vintage clothing shops, cafés and clubs that have colonized the area, while others again are just here for the street art (see box, p.194) and famous bagel shops (see p.378). The Sunday flea market (8am–3pm) occupies this stretch of the road, plus Cheshire Street, a charmingly scruffy contrast to the more polished markets in the Old Truman Brewery.

The changing ethnic make-up of this part of Brick Lane is most clearly illustrated in the **Jamme Masjid** (Great Mosque) on the corner of Fournier Street. Established in 1743 as a Huguenot church, it became a Wesleyan chapel in 1809, the ultra-Orthodox Spitalfields Great Synagogue in 1897, and since 1976 has served as a mosque – it's impossible to miss thanks to the 90ft-high luminous, freestanding metal minaret, topped by a crescent moon, that was erected in 2009. Another example, a little further south, is **Christ Church primary school**, a Church of England school the majority of whose pupils are Muslim; a hundred years ago they were mainly Jewish, as the Star of David on one of the drainpipes testifies.

The Old Truman Brewery

Brick Lane • ⓦ trumanbrewery.com • **UpMarket** Sun 10am–5pm **Backyard Market** Sat 11am–6pm, Sun 10am–5pm **Tea Rooms** Sat 11am–6pm, Sun 10am–5pm **Boiler House** Sun 11am–6pm **Vintage Market** Fri & Sat 11am–6pm, Sun 10am–5pm

A red-brick chimney halfway up Brick Lane heralds the **Old Truman Brewery**, founded back in 1666 and once the largest brewery in the world. It's now a creative centre for music, fashion, art and digital media and forms the focal point of Brick Lane's ongoing gentrification. In the brewery's **Dray Walk**, the old stables have been turned into cafés and shops for independent designers and artists; at weekends, a huge number of market stalls selling everything from one-off fashions to Polish food fill the UpMarket, Vintage Market, Tea Rooms and Backyard Market spaces, while the Boiler House hosts around thirty food stalls.

19 Princelet Street

Occasional open days • Free • ☎ 020 7247 5352, ⓦ 19princeletstreet.org.uk • ⊖ Liverpool Street

If you want to dig deeper into the area's past, try and visit on one of the open days at **19 Princelet St**, just off Brick Lane, where there's a permanent exhibition on Spitalfields' rich history of immigration – get there early, though, as it's always very popular. This beautifully preserved eighteenth-century silk-weavers' house also houses a wonderfully evocative former synagogue, built by Polish Jews in the 1860s and entirely hidden behind the Georgian facade. The attic was home to the mysterious real-life main character in Rachel Lichtenstein's *Rodinsky's Room* (see p.463).

Shoreditch and around

Home to creatives of all stripes and beloved of graffiti artists, **Shoreditch**, north of Spitalfields, is now one of the city's most design-led enclaves, despite its lack of obvious aesthetic charm – but since many of Shoreditch's visitors come out under cover of darkness, the dearth of stunning architecture really doesn't matter. While there's still certainly plenty of fun to be had in Shoreditch, the area's reputation for edgy, hipster-led **nightlife** – epitomised in the noughties by shabby chic bars like *Dream Bags Jaguar Shoes* and clubs like *Plastic People* – is long gone, and these days you're as likely to see City boys and hen parties snaking from bar to bar. Still, while less urgent than it was when the

HOXDITCH

Ever since **Shoreditch** and **Hoxton** became trendy, there's been utter confusion over the name of the area. The problem is that Shoreditch was one of the boroughs that was swallowed up into Hackney, during the local government shake-up in 1965. The old borough of Shoreditch was made up of three main areas: Shoreditch, Hoxton and Haggerston. Strictly speaking, Shoreditch is south of Old Street, and Hoxton north of it, but you'll still find the *Hoxton Hotel* in Shoreditch and the Shoreditch Electric Light Station (now the National Centre for Circus Arts) in Hoxton. Then there's the question of where Old Street fits into all this.

YBAs (Young British Artists) were strutting their Shoreditch stuff, creativity is now firmly part of the neighbourhood's fabric – Old Street roundabout is nicknamed Silicon Roundabout for the sheer number of web-based companies thereabouts. In fact, the literary and artistic have a long legacy in Shoreditch. Situated just outside the City, it was here that James Burbage established the country's **first public theatre** – called simply the Theatre – in 1576 (he later took it down and reassembled it on Bankside as the Globe). There are a couple of specific sights of interest, such as the **Geffrye Museum of the Home** and **Wesley's Chapel and House**, while you can also do a bit of an art crawl, thanks to the graffiti (see box, p.194) and raft of **galleries**, such as the David Adjaye-designed **Rivington Place** (ⓦ rivingtonplace.org), with some taking part in First Thursdays (see box, p.197).

St Leonard's, Shoreditch

Open after Sun service which takes places noon–1.30pm; tours can be arranged by emailing ⓔ events@shoreditchchurch.org.uk • Free • ⓦ shoreditchchurch.org.uk • ⊖ Old Street, Hoxton or Shoreditch High Street

12

The area's most prominent landmark is **St Leonard's**, the Neoclassical church designed by George Dance the Elder in 1740 and situated at the junction of Old Street, Shoreditch High Street and Kingsland Road. It's worth a look inside if you've ever seen the BBC sit-com *Rev*, which is filmed in the church, and also to admire the memorial to Elizabeth Benson on the southeast wall, which depicts two skeletons tearing at the Tree of Life.

Arnold Circus

ⓦ arnoldcircus.co.uk, ⓦ twitter.com/Arnold_Circus • ⊖ Shoreditch High Street

The bandstand atop landscaped **Arnold Circus** is a peaceful perch to escape from the Shoreditch hustle and bustle. All around is the **Boundary Estate**, which opened in 1900 as arguably the world's first example of social housing. The estate took the place of the Old Nichol rookery, a slum whose degradation was immortalized in Arthur Morrison's *A Child of the Jago*, though a fierce campaign had led to its demolition before the book's publication in 1896. The slum's rubble was used to build the circus and, with the surroundings' slightly gloomy feel, it can seem as if some of the old rookery's spirit imbues the modern incarnation. That said, it's all cheer at the lovely *Leila's* café (see p.377), while the Friends of Arnold Circus community group throws occasional events and street parties.

Shoreditch Town Hall

380 Old St • ⓣ 020 7739 6176, ⓦ shoreditchtownhall.com • ⊖ Old Street, Hoxton or Shoreditch High Street

The former **Shoreditch Town Hall** is a self-confident Victorian edifice, now operating as a venue for theatre and contemporary performance, and host to the Michelin-starred *Clove Club* restaurant (see p.378). The town hall's tower features a statue of Progress, torch and battle-axe in hand, and, in the pediment, Hope and Plenty, reclining beside the Shoreditch motto "More Light, More Power", adopted in recognition of the borough's progressive policy of creating power from rubbish incineration. The source of this power, the Shoreditch Electric Light Station, still stands on Coronet Street, sporting the wonderful motto *E pulvere lux et vis* (Out of the dust, light and power). The old refuse destructor now houses the National Centre for Circus Arts

BANKSY WOZ ERE

Bare, unblemished skin? Stick a tat on it. A virgin wall? You need some graffiti on there, mate. That's the Shoreditch way. Stridently countercultural in its early expressions, graffiti (like tattoos) are now part and parcel of the local identity, and the sight of a tourist with a modishly retro camera snapping wall stencils and lamppost stickers is so familiar as to be something of an east London cliché. You can blame **Banksy**, of course, for this ennobling of a protest into an art form that's now mounted as neat-and-tidy framed prints and endlessly Instagrammed. Which is not to say you should stick the blinkers on as you explore the Shoreditch area: this is where the scene exploded around the turn of the millennium and there are some truly eye-smacking works to enjoy. Local and **international artists**, stars and complete unknowns are all here, with the likes of Eine, C215, Borondo and ROA (and Banksy) represented. You might even see some art being made, since a lot of it is permissioned these days and done in broad daylight, a take-out flat white sitting next to the spray cans on the pavement.

You can easily see the local street-art sights by simply following your nose (Brick Lane, Sclater Street, Redchurch Street, Holywell Lane, Rivington Street and Curtain Road all offer rich pickings), but Shoreditch Street Art Tours (Ⓦ shoreditchstreetarttours.co.uk) lead well-established and highly recommended walks that explore everything from the artists' motives to techniques. You might also consider Alternative London (Ⓦ alternativeldn.co.uk) and Street Art London Tours (Ⓦ streetartlondon.co.uk).

(Ⓦ nationalcircus.org.uk); you'll also spot the *Electricity Showrooms* bar (Ⓦ electricityshowrooms.com) at the corner of Hoxton Street and Old Street.

Geffrye Museum of the Home

Kingsland Rd • **Museum** Tues–Sat 10am–5pm, Sun noon–5pm • Free **Almshouse tours** First Sat and first & third Wed of month • £3 • ☎ 020 7739 9893, Ⓦ geffrye-museum.org.uk • ⊖ Hoxton

Hoxton's chief attraction is the **Geffrye Museum of the Home**, housed in a grandiose enclave of eighteenth-century ironmongers' almshouses. The Geffrye explores the home – and home life – with the almshouses rigged out as period living rooms of the urban middle class, ranging from the oak-panelled seventeenth century, through refined Georgian to cluttered Victorian. You'll also pass through the original central Georgian **chapel**, with its tiny Neoclassical apse and archetypal stone-coloured wood panelling.

Further on is the museum's twentieth-century wing, with four "snapshots in time", beginning with an Edwardian drawing room in understated Arts and Crafts style, and finishing off with a minimalist 1990s loft conversion. The extension also houses a pleasant, licensed **café**. Behind the museum is a pungent, walled **herb garden** and a series of period gardens that show the transition in horticultural tastes from a seventeenth-century knot garden to an Arts and Crafts-inspired Edwardian garden (April–Oct only).

The Geffrye is currently embarked on a £15m **redevelopment** (due for completion in 2019/2020), with an additional entrance directly opposite Hoxton station.

Columbia Road

Market Sun 8am–2pm • Ⓦ columbiaroad.info • ⊖ Hoxton

Just about everywhere you go in east London on a Sunday afternoon, you'll see people toting brown paper bundles of lillies or testing their biceps getting trays of succulents home. The likely source is **Columbia Road**, home to a wildly popular Sunday flower market that turns it into the most bountifully gorgeous stretch of road in this part of town. It's not bad even when the market's not on, since the street is lined with cute cafés and shops like Lily Vanilli (see p.430). But really it's all about market day, when you should visit not just for blooms, bonsais and bagels, but for a slice of east London folklore – the stallholders still do a fine line in Cockney costermonger patter, especially when it's time to start selling off their wares towards 2pm.

CLOCKWISE FROM TOP STREET ART ON HANBURY STREET, OFF BRICK LANE (ABOVE); CHRIST CHURCH VIEWED FROM BRUSHFIELD STREET (P.188); COLUMBIA ROAD (ABOVE) >

Wesley's Chapel and House

49 City Rd • Mon–Sat 10am–4pm, Sun 12.30–1.45pm • Free • ☎ 020 7253 2262, ⓦ wesleyschapel.org.uk • ⊖ Old Street

Striking an unusual note of calm on busy City Road is the largely Georgian ensemble of **Wesley's Chapel and House** set around a cobbled courtyard and recently refurbished. A place of pilgrimage for Methodists from all over the world, the chapel was designed in 1778 by George Dance the Younger and heralded the coming-of-age of the followers of **John Wesley** (1703–91), who had started out in a small foundry east of the present building.

The **chapel** forms the centrepiece of the complex, though it is uncharacteristically ornate for a Methodist place of worship, with its powder-pink columns of French jasper and its superb, Adam-style gilded plasterwork ceiling, not to mention the colourful Victorian stained glass depicting, among other things, Wesley's night-time conversion, with his brother still in his dressing gown. The chapel has often attracted well-heeled weddings: one Margaret Hilda Roberts married divorcé Denis Thatcher here in 1951, and later paid for the new communion rail.

The **Museum of Methodism** (same hours) in the basement tells the story of Wesley and Methodism, and there's even a brief mention of Mrs Mary Vazeille, the 41-year-old, insanely jealous, wealthy widow he married, and who eventually left him. Wesley himself lived in the Georgian **house** to the right of the main gates on and off for the last twelve years of his life, and inside you can see bits of his furniture and his deathbed, plus an early shock-therapy machine with which he used to treat members of his congregation. Wesley's **grave** is round the back of the chapel, in the shadow of a modern office block.

Bunhill Fields and around

City Rd • April–Sept Mon–Fri 7.30am–7pm, Sat & Sun 9.30am–7pm; Oct–March closes 4pm • ⊖ Old Street

Appropriately enough, **Bunhill Fields**, the main burial ground for Dissenters or Nonconformists (practising Christians who were not members of the Church of England), lies across the road from Wesley's Chapel. Following bomb damage in World War II, most of the graveyard is fenced off, though you can still stroll through on the public footpaths under a canopy of giant London plane trees. The three most famous graves have been placed in the central paved area: the simple tombstone of poet and artist **William Blake** stands next to a replica of writer **Daniel Defoe**'s, while opposite lies the recumbent statue of **John Bunyan**, seventeenth-century author of *The Pilgrim's Progress*. A five-minute walk north brings you to St Luke's, another of Hawksmoor's churches (designed with John James), now used by the London Symphony Orchestra (ⓦ lso.co.uk/lso-st-lukes). It is worth a look if only for the distinctive, obelisk-like steeple, and also has a peaceful garden behind.

Whitechapel

Whitechapel High Street lies at the heart of the old East End, and – along with its extension, Whitechapel Road – follows the route of the old Roman road from London

---

JOHN WESLEY AND METHODISM

The name "**Methodist**" was a term of abuse used by John Wesley's fellow Oxford students, because of the methodical way Wesley and his followers ordered their lives. However, it wasn't until his "conversion" at a Moravian prayer meeting in Aldersgate (marked by a large memorial outside the Museum of London) in 1738, that Wesley decided to become an independent field preacher. "I felt my heart strangely warmed" was his famous description of the experience. More verbal and even physical abuse followed during which Wesley was accused of being, among other things, a papist spy and an illegal gin distiller. Yet despite his lifelong dispute with the Anglican church, despite commissioning preachers, and bequeathing more than 350 Methodist chapels serving over 130,000 worshippers, Wesley himself never left the Church of England and died within it, urging his followers, where possible, to do the same.

to Colchester. Starting in the west at Aldgate, the City's eastern gateway, the street is still a good barometer for the current East End and is worth a stroll for a glimpse of London that's only a stone's throw (and yet light years) from the City. Whitechapel Road boasts the most visible symbol of Muslim presence in the East End, the **East London Mosque** (ⓦeastlondonmosque.org.uk), a gaudy red-brick 1980s building, with a golden dome and minarets, which seats five thousand.

Whitechapel Gallery

77–82 Whitechapel High St • Tues–Sun 11am–6pm, Thurs until 9pm • Free • ☎ 020 7522 7888, ⓦ whitechapel.org • ⊖ Aldgate East

The East End institution that draws in more outsiders than any other is the **Whitechapel Art Gallery**, housed in a beautiful, crenellated 1899 Arts and Crafts building by Charles Harrison Townsend, who was also behind the Bishopsgate Institute cultural centre in Spitalfields and south London's Horniman Museum (see p.311). The gallery's facade has been embellished with a smattering of gilded leaves by the sculptor Rachel Whiteread – cast from the original arts-and-craft Tree of Life reliefs on either side – while the gallery's extension to the east into a former library (doubling the gallery's size), sports a modern copper weather vane by the artist Rodney Graham, featuring the philosopher Erasmus seated backwards reading a book. The gallery was founded by one of the East End's many Victorian philanthropists, **Samuel Barnett**. His motives may have been dubious – "The principle of our work is that we aim at decreasing not suffering but sin", he once claimed – but the legacy of his good works is still discernible across the East End. The gallery now puts on innovative exhibitions of contemporary art, and has a great bookshop and café-bar.

12

Whitechapel Bell Foundry

33–34 Whitechapel Rd • Mon–Fri 9am–5pm • Free • Guided tours Sat 10am, 1.15 & 4pm; £14; no under-14s • ☎ 020 7247 2599, ⓦ whitechapelbellfoundry.co.uk • ⊖ Whitechapel

On the south side of Whitechapel Road, the **Whitechapel Bell Foundry** occupies the short terrace of Georgian houses on the corner of Fieldgate Street. Big Ben, the Liberty Bell, the Bow Bells and numerous English church bells (including those of Westminster Abbey) all hail from the foundry, established in 1570. Inside, there's a small exhibition on the history of the foundry, which is the oldest manufacturing company in the country.

Whitechapel Market

Mon–Sat 8am–6pm • ⊖ Whitechapel

Whitechapel Road widens halfway along, at the beginning of **Whitechapel Market**, once one of the largest hay markets in London, now given over to everything from nectarines to net curtains, and including a large number of stalls catering for the local Bangladeshi and Somali communities. In the 1890s, this was where casual workers used to gather to be selected for work in the local sweatshops, earning it the Yiddish nickname *Hazer Mark*, or "pig market". The sole reminder of those days is the Edward VII monument at the centre of the market, erected by the local Jewish community in 1911.

FIRST THURSDAYS

Some 150 east London galleries small and large, from Whitechapel to Hackney, take part in the **First Thursdays** initiative, opening till 9pm (and often offering free booze) on the first Thursday of every month. It is perhaps the one evening when the east London creativity-hipster mash-up is most manifest. Whether you're an art aficionado or are just in it for the alcohol (semi-chilled bottles of beer and cheap wine, generally), this **gallery crawl** is a lot of fun and a perfect way to soak up the east London buzz. The Whitechapel Gallery (see above) is as good a place to start as any. Here you can pick up a brochure that includes a map of the galleries involved. Alternatively, hop on the bus that leaves from the Whitechapel Gallery for a whistle-stop tour of the month's highlights.

JACK THE RIPPER: THE WHITECHAPEL MURDERS

In eight weeks between August and November 1888, five prostitutes were stabbed to death in and around Whitechapel. Few of the letters received by the press and police, which purported to come from the murderer, are thought to have been genuine (including the one which coined the nickname **Jack the Ripper**), and the murderer's identity remains a mystery to this day. At the time, it was assumed he was a Jew, probably a *shochet* (a ritual slaughterman), since the mutilations on the corpses were obviously carried out with some skill. The theory gained ground when the fourth victim was discovered outside the (predominantly Jewish) Working Men's Club off Commercial Road, and for a while it was dangerous for Jews to walk the streets at night for fear of reprisals.

Ripperologists have trawled through the little evidence there is to produce **numerous suspects**, none of whom can be conclusively proven guilty. The most celebrated suspect is the Duke of Clarence, eldest son of the future Edward VII, an easy if improbable target, since he was involved in a scandal involving a male brothel and was a well-known homosexual. Crime writer Patricia Cornwell spent over a million dollars trying (and failing) to prove conclusively that the Ripper was the painter Walter Sickert, who exhibited an unhealthy fascination with the murders. The man who usually tops the lists, however, was a cricket-playing barrister named Druitt whose body was found floating in the Thames some weeks after the last murder, though, as usual, there is no evidence linking him with any of them.

The one **positive outcome** of the murders was that they focused the attention of the rest of London on the squalor of the East End. Philanthropist Samuel Barnett, for one, used the media attention to press for improved housing, streetlighting and policing to combat crime and poverty in the area. Today, the murders continue to be exploited in gory detail by the likes of Madame Tussauds and the London Dungeon, while guided walks retracing the Ripper's steps set off every week throughout the year (see p.24).

12

Royal London Hospital Museum

Newark St • Tues–Fri 10am–4.30pm • Free • ☏ 020 7377 7608 • ⊖ Whitechapel

It was on Whitechapel Road that Joseph Merrick, better known as the **Elephant Man**, was discovered in a freak show in 1884 by Dr Treves and subsequently admitted as a patient to the then **London Hospital**, which lay nearby. Merrick soon returned to the freak show life, however, travelling throughout Britain and across Europe for the next two years, before returning to London and being "rescued" by Treves, living at the hospital – thanks to money raised by its House Committee – from 1896 until his death in 1880, at the age of just 27 in the **Hospital Museum**. There's an interesting twenty-minute documentary on Merrick, and a small section displaying, among other things, the veil and hat he wore, housed in the crypt of an old church on Newark Street, the museum also covers the history of the hospital and of nursing and medicine in general, with a section on Edith Cavell, who trained here before assisting Allied soldiers to escape from occupied Belgium; she was eventually arrested and shot as a spy by the Germans in 1915.

The Blind Beggar

337 Whitechapel Rd • Mon–Sat 11am–11pm, Sun noon–10.30pm • Free • ☏ 020 7247 6195, ⓦ theblindbeggar.com • ⇌ Whitechapel

The **Blind Beggar** has been the East End's most famous pub since March 9, 1966, when Ronnie Kray walked into the crowded bar and shot gangland rival George Cornell for calling him a "fat poof". This murder spelt the end of the infamous Kray Twins, Ronnie and Reggie, both of whom were sentenced to life imprisonment, though their well-publicized gifts to local charities created a Robin Hood image that still persists, and footage of their funerals (particularly Ronnie's in 1995), available on YouTube, shows how they were regarded by many as East End royalty to the end.

Bethnal Green and Bow

Lying beyond Whitechapel are the districts of **Bethnal Green**, to the north, which is enjoying an ever-increasing number of good eating (see p.380) and drinking (see p.392) options, and **Bow**, to the northeast – tradition has it that a true Cockney must have been born within earshot of the bells of St Mary-le-Bow church. The Mile End Road is just an extension of Whitechapel Road, and easily explored on foot, but to reach more mainstream sights such as the **V&A Museum of Childhood**, you'll need to hop on public transport.

Mile End Road

The **Mile End Road** is an extension of Whitechapel Road, and the westernmost section, known as the Mile End Waste, is punctuated at the western end by a bust, and at the eastern by a more dramatic statue, of William Booth, founder of the Salvation Army (see below). There are also two unusual architectural features worth mentioning nearby. The more surprising is the **Trinity Almshouses**, a quaint courtyard of cottages with a central chapel, built in 1695 for "Twenty-eight decay'd Masters and Commanders and the widows of such". Further up, on the same side of the street, stands a large Neoclassical former department store, sporting a central domed tower, its facade of Ionic half-columns sliced in two by a small two-storey shop (currently boarded up) that used to belong to a Jewish watchmaker called **Spiegelhalter**. This architectural oddity is the result of a dispute between Spiegelhalter and his affluent Gentile neighbour, Thomas Wickham, who was forced to build his new store around the watchmaker's shop after he refused to be bought out.

Ragged School Museum

46–50 Copperfield Rd • Wed & Thurs 10am–5pm, first Sun of month 2–5pm • Free • ☎ 020 8980 6405, ⓦ raggedschoolmuseum .org.uk • ⊖ Mile End

12

South of the Mile End Road, on what is left of Copperfield Road, the **Ragged School Museum** occupies Victorian canalside warehouses, one of which was originally used to store lime juice. Accommodating more than one thousand pupils from 1877 to 1908, this was the largest of London's numerous Ragged Schools, institutions that provided free education and, often, free meals to children with no means to pay the 1d, 2d or 3d a week charged by many Victorian Board schools. This particular Ragged School was just one of innumerable projects set up by the East End's most irrepressible philanthropist, the diminutive and devout **Dr Thomas Barnardo**, whose tireless work for the children of the East End is the subject of the ground-floor exhibition. Upstairs, there's a reconstructed Victorian schoolroom, where period-dressed teachers, cane in hand, take today's schoolchildren through the rigours of a Victorian lesson – the public can experience the same treatment on Sunday openings (2.15 & 3.30pm; donation suggested).

EAST END PHILANTHROPISTS

The poverty of the East End has attracted numerous philanthropists over the years, particularly during the Victorian era, from Dr Barnardo, of Ragged School fame, to Lady Burdett-Coutts, whose fountain still stands in Victoria Park. The most famous of the lot, however, was **William Booth** (1829–1912), a pawnbroker by trade and a Methodist lay preacher. One June evening in 1865, Booth was preaching to the crowds of revellers outside *The Blind Beggar* (see opposite). Some fellow missioners were so impressed they asked him to lead a series of meetings in a tent they had set up on the Mile End Waste (see above). Booth and his wife then set up the Christian Mission, which eventually led to the foundation, in 1878, of the quasi-military Christian movement known as the **Salvation Army**. In contrast to many Victorian philanthropists, Booth never accepted the divisive concept of the deserving and undeserving poor ("if a man was poor, he was deserving") and railed against the laissez-faire economic policies of his era. He attended to the immediate demands of the poor, setting up soup kitchens and founding hostels, which, by the time of his death in 1912, had spread right across the globe. Booth is buried in Abney Park Cemetery (see p.202).

Victoria Park

Grove Rd • Daily 6am–dusk • ⊖ Hackney Wick or ⇌ Cambridge Heath; bus #277 from ⊖ Mile End or bus #8 from ⊖ Liverpool Street

London's first public park (as opposed to royal park) **Victoria Park** was opened in the heart of the East End in 1845, after a local MP presented Queen Victoria with a petition of thirty thousand signatures. The only large open space in the area, "Viccy Park" immediately became a favourite spot for **political rallies**: Chartists congregated here in their thousands in 1848; Suffragette supporters of the ELFS (East London Federation of Suffragettes) gathered here, under the leadership of Sylvia Pankhurst; it even had its own Speakers' Corner attended by the likes of George Bernard Shaw and William Morris. Since the Anti-Nazi League played here in 1978, it's probably more famous for its regular use for **music festivals** like Field Day and Lovebox (see box, p.404).

The world's oldest **model boat club**, the Victoria Model Steam Boat Club, founded in 1904, still meets on most summer Sunday mornings at the park's lakes. Look out, too, for the (replica) **Dogs of Alcibiades**, two snarling sculpted beasts based on the Molossian hounds kept by the Athenian statesman and presented by Lady Regnart in 1912. The much larger eastern section of the park contains an extraordinarily lavish Gothic-cum-Moorish **drinking fountain**, decorated with oversized cherubs and paid for by Baroness Burdett-Coutts in 1861 – it hasn't functioned for years. At the park's eastern edge are two alcoves from Old London Bridge, brought here in 1860.

V&A Museum of Childhood

Cambridge Heath Rd • Daily 10am–5.45pm • Free • ☎ 020 8983 5200, ⓦ vam.ac. uk/moc • ⊖ Bethnal Green

The elegant, open-plan wrought-iron hall that houses the **V&A Museum of Childhood** was, in fact, part of the original V&A building, and was transported to the East End from South Kensington in the late 1860s in order to bring art to the poor. The emphasis has changed since those pioneering days, and although the wide range of exhibits means that there's something here for everyone, the museum's most frequent visitors are children, with plenty of hands-on exhibits and special kids' events at weekends and during school holidays.

To the right as you enter are the clockwork and moving **toys** (you'll need a stash of 20p pieces for the bigger exhibits), with everything from classic robots to a fully functioning model railway, early computer games and wooden toys – there's often a queue for the replica Victorian rocking horse. At the back, the museum has a great collection of marionettes and puppets, which brings you into the doll and figures section, ranging from teddies and Smurfs to Inuit dolls. The most famous exhibits are the remarkable antique **dolls' houses** dating back to 1673: they are displayed upstairs, where you'll also find antique dolls and prams, a play area for very small kids, the ever-popular Wallace the Lion gobbling up the little schoolboy Albert, and a space for temporary exhibitions.

Dalston

Dalston has undergone a seismic transformation, and has now overtaken Shoreditch as London's hippest, grittiest neighbourhood (though Peckham might have something to say about that). Among the early pioneers was the excellent *Vortex Jazz Club*, on Gillett Square, followed by the Arcola Theatre, one of the city's most dynamic fringe venues, which now occupies a former paint factory on Ashwin Street, next door to *Café Oto*, avant-garde music venue by night, hub of coffee-swilling laptoppers by day. This trio has been accompanied by late-opening bar-clubs dotted up and down the high street from Dalston Junction – at times, it seems like every basement space along the road is a venue, with queues outside and a grungy list girl on the door, while some of the city's best gay venues are also to be found in these parts. The Shoreditch effect is happening here too, though, with groups of revellers now coming en masse as they would to Soho looking for a night out, rather than to a specific venue.

Kingsland High Street

Kingsland High Street had a history of entertainment long before the current crop of clubs and bars came along, with four or five cinemas in close proximity. The lone survivor is the Art Deco **Rio Cinema**, at no. 107, opened in 1937 as the Dalston Classic, replacing the 1915 Kingsland Empire, and still going strong. Dalston's other heritage sight is the *Shanghai* restaurant at no. 41 (ⓦshanghaidalston.co.uk), which preserves the 1910 decor of tiles, marble and glass from its days as an eel and pie shop, founded in 1862 by the ubiquitous Cooke family.

Ridley Road Market

Mon–Thurs 6am–6pm, Fri & Sat 6am–7pm • ⓦ www.ridleyroad.co.uk • ⊖ Dalston Kingsland or Dalston Junction

In the immediate postwar period, Dalston was a predominantly Jewish area, and **Ridley Road Market** was the scene of battles between Mosley's fascists and Jewish ex-servicemen. The market is an accurate reflection of Dalston's ethnic diversity, with Cockney fruit and veg stalls, halal butchers, a 24-hour bagel bakery, West Indian grocers and African and Asian fabric shops. A Turkish/Kurdish supermarket marks the eastern end of the market, its railings still displaying the Star of David from its original Jewish occupants.

Dalston Eastern Curve

Dalston Lane • Daily 11am–6/7pm (later in summer) • Free • ⓦ dalstongarden.org • ⊖ Dalston Junction

As close to a secret garden as you're going to find in these parts, **Dalston Eastern Curve** features a wood-chipped, gently sloping path that meanders between planting boxes and trees, their foliage splattering the ground with shadow, to – well, nothing much at all, really, beyond a child-friendly sandpit (see p.442). Above the wall at the far end rears the bulk of Kingsland Shopping Centre, yet all that urban grit feels blissfully far away. The garden has a pleasing community vibe and, on fine days, there are few better places in east London to enjoy a local ale or slice of home-made cake. Free wi-fi too.

Stoke Newington

Bus #73 or #476 from ⊖ Angel; #149, #243 or #67 from Dalston or Shoreditch; or ⇌ Stoke Newington from Liverpool St station

Though it's inconveniently off the tube map, **Stoke Newington** (or "Stokey") is probably the most immediately appealing area of the borough of Hackney. Stokey's best attribute is **Church Street**, a more or less franchise-free, former village high street of little independent shops and restaurants.

The whole area was, for several centuries, a haven for Nonconformists (Christians who were not members of the Anglican church), who were denied the right to live in the City. The most famous Dissenter to live in Stokey was **Daniel Defoe**, who wrote *Robinson Crusoe* on the corner of what is now Defoe Road and Church Street; his gravestone is displayed in the Hackney Museum – stolen from Bunhill Fields in the

---

THE ANGRY BRIGADE

On August 20, 1971, six alleged members of the **Angry Brigade** – at the time Britain's only home-grown urban terrorist group – were arrested at 359 Amhurst Rd, off Stoke Newington High Street, along with (according to the police) a small arsenal of weapons and explosives. The police attempted to link the Angries with the explosives (despite the lack of forensic evidence) and a total of 25 bomb attacks on the homes of Tory politicians and other members of the Establishment, during which one person had been slightly injured. After one of the longest criminal trials in English history, at which two other alleged members were also charged, four of the accused were sent to prison for conspiracy to cause explosions and four were acquitted.

1870s, it was discovered in Southampton in 1940. A farmers' market
(⑩growingcommunities.org) occupies the car park of St Paul's church on Saturdays
(10am–2.30pm).

Abney Park Cemetery

Stoke Newington High St • **Cemetery** 8am to dusk **Visitor Centre** Mon–Fri 10am–2pm • Free • ☎ 020 7275 7557, ⑩ abneypark.org and
⑩ twitter.com/abneyparkn16 • ⇌ Stoke Newington

When Bunhill Fields (see p.196) became overcrowded, **Abney Park Cemetery** became
the "Campo Santo of English non-Conformists", in the words of the 1903 brochure.
The most famous grave is that of **William Booth**, founder of the Salvation Army (see
p.199), by the Church Street entrance, but the romantically overrun cemetery was
originally planted as an A–Z arboretum, and is now an inner-city wildlife reserve
(not to mention a gay cruising area). A **visitors' centre** is housed in one of the
Egyptian-style lodges at the main entrance, on busy Stoke Newington High Street.

Clissold Park

Stoke Newington Church St • Daily 7.30am–dusk • Free • ☎ 020 7923 3660, ⑩ hackney.gov.uk and clissoldpark.com • ⇌ Stoke
Newington

Stoke Newington's two main churches, both dedicated to **St Mary**, stand either side of
Church Street and reflect the changes wrought on the area in the last couple of
centuries: the sixteenth-century village church firmly in the shadow of the more urbane
structure built by George Gilbert Scott in the 1850s, with a spire that outreached all
others in London in its day. This pair marks the entrance to **Clissold Park**, founded in
1889 and centred on a porticoed mansion built in the 1790s as a country house for the
Quaker Hoare banking family, now beautifully restored and housing the park café. The
duck pond in front was once part of the New River; elsewhere are goats, deer, a small
aviary, a butterfly dome and a popular paddling pool (May–Sept Tues, Wed & Fri–Sun
11am–7pm). A new orienteering course is proving popular with families (maps
available from the house or downloadable from the council website).

Stamford Hill and Clapton

In the northern tip of Hackney, **Stamford Hill** is home to a tight-knit, mostly
Yiddish-speaking, community of Hasidic Jews, one of the borough's oldest
immigrant populations. The most visually striking aspect of this ultra-Orthodox
community is the men's attire – frock coats, white stockings and elaborate headgear
– which adheres to strict dress codes that are hundreds of years old in origin. The
shops on Stamford Hill and Dunsmure Road, running west, are where the Hasidim
buy their kosher goods. Other than being one of the city's new hipster hubs, **Clapton**,
to the east of Stamford Hill, boasts lovely **Springfield Park** and the idiosyncratic
nature reserve of **Middlesex Filter Beds**.

Springfield Park

Springfield • Daily: summer 7.30am–9.30pm; winter 7.30am–4.30pm • Free • ☎ 020 8356 3000, ⑩ hackney.gov.uk/springfield-park •
⇌ Stamford Hill

On Sundays, large numbers of Hasidic families take the air at **Springfield Park**, opened
in 1905 "to change the habits of the people and to keep them out of the public
houses". The park boasts an awesome view east across the Lee Valley to the adjacent
Walthamstow Marshes, a valuable stretch of wetland that's alive with butterflies and
warblers in the summer. The park also has a decent **café** (⑩springfieldparkcafe.co.uk) in
the White Lodge Mansion by the pond.

To reach Springfield Park from Stamford Hill, walk across Clapton Common, and
down Spring Hill. En route, check out the four winged beasts (characters from the
Book of Revelation) at the base of the spire of the **Cathedral Church of the Good**

Shepherd on the corner of Rookwood Road, built for the sect of Spiritual Free Lovers, the Agapemonites, in 1892. Six thousand gathered outside here in 1902 to throw rotten tomatoes at a womanizing vicar, who had declared himself the Second Messiah, and to drive him into Clapton Pond to see if he could walk on water.

Middlesex Filter Beds

Sat & Sun: Easter–Sept 10am–6pm; Oct–Easter 10am–4pm; summer holidays also Mon–Fri 10am–5pm • Free • ⇌Clapton

If you follow the River Lea south of Walthamstow Marshes, you will eventually reach the **Middlesex Filter Beds**, originally built in 1852 on the south side of Lea Bridge Road. Closed in 1969 and mostly drained, the filter beds now serve as a nature reserve – in the spring check out the noisy frogs in the pond by the main culvert. To the south of the filter beds lie the **Hackney Marshes**, best known as the venue for Sunday League football matches, beyond which is the Queen Elizabeth Olympic Park (see p.205).

Hackney Central

The old parish of Hackney was originally centred around the dumpy fifteenth-century tower of the former parish church of **St Augustine**, and next to it, the Old Town Hall, built in 1802 (now a betting shop). At this point, Mare Street is still discernibly a village high street, and is known, for obvious reasons, as the **Narroway**. The modern borough has its headquarters further south on Mare Street around **Hackney Town Hall**, built in a very restrained 1930s Art Deco style and set back from the high street. Close by is the ornate terracotta **Hackney Empire**, one of the last surviving music halls in London, built in typically extravagant style by Frank Matcham in 1899.

12

Hackney Museum

1 Reading Lane • Tues, Wed & Fri 9.30am–5.30pm, Thurs 9.30am–8pm, Sat 10am–5pm • Free • ☎ 020 8356 3500, ⓦ hackney.gov.uk/museum • ⊖ Hackney Central

Beside the town hall stands the borough's central library and **Hackney Museum**. As well as excellent temporary exhibitions, the museum has an interesting permanent display with lots of personal accounts from local residents. Specific exhibits to look out for include the "upside-down" map of Dalston and an Anglo-Saxon log boat found in Springfield Park, thought to have been a ferry for taking folk across the River Lea.

Sutton House

2 & 4 Homerton High St • Feb to mid-Dec Wed–Sun noon–5pm; daily during August • NT • £3.50 • ☎ 020 8986 2264, ⓦ nationaltrust .org.uk/sutton-house • ⊖ Hackney Central

Hidden away, at the east end of the Georgian terrace of Sutton Place, stands **Sutton House**. Built in 1535 for Ralph Sadleir, a rising star at the court of Henry VIII, the house takes its name from Thomas Sutton, founder of Charterhouse, who lived in an adjacent building (he is buried at Charterhouse, minus his entrails, which you've probably just walked over in the graveyard by Mare Street). The National Trust has done its best to adapt to unfamiliar surroundings and has preserved not just the exquisite Elizabethan "linenfold" wooden panelling, but also a mural left by squatters in 1986. In addition to showing its rambling complex of period rooms, the site also features "Breaker's Yard", a fabulously innovative and engaging garden created on a reclaimed patch of scrubland.

Broadway Market and London Fields

Market hours: **Broadway Market** Sat 9am–5pm; **London fields farmers' Market** Sun 10am–2pm • ⓦ broadwaymarket.co.uk, ⓦ twitter .com/Broadway_Mkt, ⓦ twitter.com/lfmarkethackney, ⓦ hackney.gov.uk/cp-londonfields.htm • ⇌London Fields or Cambridge Heath

With the Regent's Canal at one end and the green expanse of **London Fields** at the other, **Broadway Market** is one of east London's most pleasantly situated old market streets. These days, the community-run Saturday market is hugely popular for its food stalls of the local-artisan-ethical (and delicious) variety, a gentrification also manifested in the types of business now lining the street, such as the coffee geek-friendly café *Climpson and Sons* (see p.379). Still, the market's original incarnation as a place of fruit, veg and Cockneys is, happily, enshrined in pie, mash and eel shop, *F. Cooke* (see p.379). With its lido (see p.439), wildflower meadow, disposable barbecue-friendly policy and bike paths, meanwhile, **London Fields** is a real east London hangout – both for families and hipsters – and rammed, music festival-style, on fine days. It also hosts a Sunday farmers' market at London Fields Primary School.

Walthamstow

East of the River Lea and the marshes (take the overland train for some pretty impressive views), the chief reason to head out to **Walthamstow** is to visit the William Morris Gallery, but there are one or two other points of interest in the district. **Walthamstow Market** (Tues–Sat 8am–5pm) stretches for almost a mile along the old High Street, north of the tube station, and claims to be the country's longest street market. For a traditional East End snack, head for *Manzes*, at no. 76, one of London's finest pie-and-mash shops, with its traditional tiled walls and ceiling.

Vestry House Museum

Vestry Rd • Wed–Sun 10am–5pm • Free • ☎ 020 8496 4391, ⓦ walthamforest.gov.uk/vestry-house or facebook.com/VestryHouse • ⊖ Walthamstow Central

12

At the peaceful heart of the old village of Walthamstow is the **Vestry House Museum**, built in 1730 and at one time the village workhouse. Later on, it became the police station, and a reconstructed police cell from 1861 is one of the museum's chief exhibits. Pride of place, however, goes to the tiny Bremer car, Britain's first-ever petrol-driven automobile, designed in 1892 by local engineer Fred Bremer, 20-year-old son of German immigrants. Victorian times are comprehensively covered, while the temporary exhibitions tend to focus on contemporary topics. The other point of interest nearby is the fifteenth-century half-timbered **Ancient House**, a short walk up Church Lane.

Civic Centre

Walthamstow's **Civic Centre** is an arresting sight, set back from Forest Road around a huge open courtyard. Designed in an unusual 1930s Scandinavian style, it is, without doubt, London's grandest town-hall complex. Indeed, there's a touch of Stalinism about the severe Neoclassical central portico and in the William Morris-inspired exhortation above the adjacent Assembly Hall (nowadays booked out for events from weddings to concerts): "Fellowship is life and the lack of fellowship is death." Sadly, construction of the law courts that would have completed the

---

WILLIAM MORRIS

Poet, artist, designer and socialist, **William Morris** (1834–96) was one of the most fascinating characters of Victorian London. Closely associated with both the Pre-Raphaelite and the Arts and Crafts movements, he set up Morris & Co, whose work covered all areas of applied art:: glasswork, tiles, furniture, woven and printed textiles, carpets and (perhaps most famously) wallpaper. As well as being a successful businessman – the company's flagship store was on Oxford Street – Morris also became one of the leading political figures of his day, active in the Socialist League with Eleanor Marx, and publishing several utopian tracts, most famously *News from Nowhere*, in which he suggested that the Houses of Parliament be used as "a storage place for manure" (you can buy a copy in the William Morris Gallery bookshop). If you like your WM, you can see more of his work elsewhere in London: at the V&A, Holy Trinity Church and the Red House.

ensemble was interrupted by the war, but this remains one of the most startling public buildings in London.

William Morris Gallery

Forest Rd • Wed–Sun 10am–5pm • Free • ☎ 020 8496 4390, ⓦ wmgallery.org.uk • ⊖ Walthamstow Central

The **William Morris Gallery** is housed in a lovely Georgian mansion with two big bay windows. This was the Morris family home from 1848, following the death of Morris's father, a wealthy businessman in the City, the previous year. The gallery has benefitted from a total refurb, and is now a very attractive museum (and café) to visit.

Ground floor displays tell the story of Morris's early life and business projects, accompanied by examples of his first wallpaper design (a rose trellis), a lovely oak settle and some glorious De Morgan animal tiles for a nursery. Upstairs, there are "Brownies" (fairies) in stained glass, and beautiful first editions from the Kelmscott Press, souvenirs from Iceland and the modest leather satchel he took everywhere with him. The contradiction between his rich clients and his socialist ideals is touched upon, and there's a copy of the anti-war song he wrote in 1878. There's also a whole room devoted to Frank Brangwyn, who trained at Morris & Co and was something of a jack-of-all-trades like Morris.

Queen Elizabeth Olympic Park

ⓦ queenelizabetholympicpark.co.uk • ⊖ Stratford, Pudding Mill Lane DLR or Hackney Wick

London is the only city in the world to have hosted the Olympics three times. In 1908, the city saved the day when Vesuvius erupted and Rome had to pull out as host. In 1948, London stepped in at short notice and staged the "Austerity Games", where the athletes were told to bring their own food and were put up in RAF camps. 2012 was an altogether more extravagant affair, with a total spend in excess of £9 billion. The focus of the 2012 Olympics was London's **Olympic Park** – officially now the Queen Elizabeth Olympic Park – situated in a most unlikely East End backwater, on a series of islands formed by the River Lea and various tributaries and canals. Since the Olympics, the whole area has been replanted with swathes of grass, trees and flowers making it a great new park in which to hang out on a sunny day, particularly with additional features such as adventure playgrounds and a climbing wall. In addition, the park is also peppered with former Olympic venues that are now open to the public, plus a number of cafés to cater for passing visitors.

The centrepiece of the park is the former **Olympic Stadium**, surrounded on three sides by the River Lea and the City Mill River. It is set to permanently reopen in 2016 as the home of West Ham United Football Club and UK Athletics, and will also serve as a major events venue. Standing close to the stadium, with a bird's-eye view of the whole site from its public observation decks, is the **ArcelorMittal Orbit** tower (ⓦarcelormittalorbit.com), a 377ft-high continuous loop of red recycled steel designed by Anish Kapoor, looking like a giant helter-skelter. The most eye-catching of the former Olympic venues is Zaha Hadid's wave-like **London Aquatics Centre** (see p.438), to the east, which is now open to the public for swimming and diving, as well as hosting elite level competition. The other truly sexy building is the curvy **velodrome**, part of Lee Valley VeloPark (see p.438), with its banked, Siberian pine track and adjacent BMX, road racing and mountain biking circuits (all open to the public). At the park's western edge, the **Copper Box Arena**, used for handball during the Olympics, is now a multi-sports centre, gym and events venue. In the north of the park, **Lee Valley Hockey and Tennis Centre** (see p.439) offers state-of-the-art playing and viewing facilities for both sports. Overlooking the whole site, the **Olympic Village** – now renamed East Village – at the eastern edge of the park, originally housed seventeen thousand athletes during the Games and has been converted into 2800 homes.

12

Three Mills Island

A short walk south of Queen Elizabeth Olympic Park, along the River Lea, you can visit the eighteenth-century architectural ensemble of **Three Mills Island**, an artificial island in the Lee Valley. Despite its name, there are now only two mills remaining, the most distinctive of which is the **Clock Mill**, with its conical oasts – kilns used to dry grain – and its pretty white clock tower. It now forms part of the 3 Mills film and TV studios. The northern section of the island has been transformed into **Three Mills Green**, an open space with play equipment and a few pieces of sculpture that kids will love.

House Mill

Three Mill Lane • May–Oct Sun 11am–4pm; March, April & Dec first Sun of month • £3 • ☎ 020 8980 4626, ⓦ housemill.org.uk • ⊖ Bromley-by-Bow

Opposite the Clock Mill stands the Dutch-style **House Mill**, built in 1776 and restored in the 1980s, around which you can take a guided tour, which explains the milling process and shows you the surviving mill wheels which were driven by the tide (this is the largest tidal mill in the world). Beyond the mills are later gin-distillery buildings, now converted into television and film studios. There's a café in the Miller's House (open when the House Mill is open and on weekdays).

Abbey Mills

Visible to the northeast of Three Mills Island is the modern **Abbey Mills Pumping Station**, sporting a gleaming metal pitched roof, and, adjacent, its much more famous Victorian predecessor, a glorious Gothic-Italianate edifice nicknamed the "Cathedral of Sewage". The latter was built in the 1860s by Joseph Bazalgette and Edwin Cooper, and was originally flanked by two twin chimneys decorated in Moorish style, which were sadly demolished during World War II. Visible to the southeast of Three Mills are seven ornate, wrought-iron **Victorian gasholders**, built on the site of a rocket factory set up in the 1820s by William Congreve.

12

CANARY WHARF

Docklands

The architectural embodiment of smash-and-grab capitalism according to its
critics or a blueprint for inner-city regeneration to its free-market supporters
– the Docklands area has always provoked extreme reactions. Despite the
catch-all name, however, Docklands is far from homogeneous. Canary Wharf,
with its skyscrapers, is the most visible landmark, but it's by no means
typical; warehouse conversions, industrial-estate sheds, council housing and
Costa del Thames apartments in a mishmash of styles, are more indicative.
Then there are the strikingly evocative remnants of a bygone era, with
atmospheric little corners such as Wapping Old Stairs worth seeking out. The
area is rarely pretty, but you're guaranteed a raft of memorable, grittily
spectacular sights here.

13

From the sixteenth century onwards the **Port of London** was the trading lynchpin of the British Empire and the key to the city's wealth. The "legal quays" – roughly the area between London Bridge and the Tower – were crowded with as many as 1400 seagoing vessels forced to wait for up to six weeks to be unloaded, with some 3500 cutters, barges and punts jostling between their hulls. It was to relieve such congestion that, from 1802 onwards, London constructed the largest enclosed **cargo-dock system** in the world. Each dock was surrounded by 40ft-high walls, patrolled by its own police force and geared towards a specific cargo. Casual dockers gathered at the dock gates each morning for the "call-on", a human scrimmage to get selected for work. This system was only stopped after World War II, when the Dock Labour Scheme was introduced, and by then it was too late. Since the mid-nineteenth century, competition from the railways eroded the river traffic, and with the development of container ships and the movement of the port to Tilbury in the 1960s, the old city docks began to wind down.

In 1981, the **London Docklands Development Corporation (LDDC)** was set up to regenerate the area. By the time it was wound up in 1998, it had achieved more than many thought possible – including the delivery of the Docklands Light Railway (DLR) and City Airport – though it had met with plenty of criticism too, accused of ad hoc planning and a lack of basic amenities, green spaces, civic architecture or public buildings. Today, construction continues apace, with the £3.5 billion Silvertown scheme the latest to tweak this patch of raw industry towards other purposes.

Wapping

Once famous for its boatyards and its 36 riverside pubs (a handful of which remain), **Wapping** changed forever with the construction of the enclosed docks. Cut off from the East End by the high dock walls, its inhabitants crowded into unsanitary housing, the area became notorious for thieves, attracted by rolling drunk sailors and poorly guarded warehouses. With the destruction wrought during the Blitz and the commercial demise of the docks, Wapping was very run down by the 1980s and an early candidate for Docklands regeneration. Restoration of existing property rather than demolition and redevelopment has been the rule, so much of Wapping's Victorian atmosphere remains, and, as it's only a short walk from the Tower, this is easily the most satisfying part of Docklands to explore.

St Katharine Docks
Ⓦ skdocks.co.uk, twitter.com/StKats or twitter.com/StKatsMarina • ⊖ Tower Hill or Tower Gateway DLR

St Katharine Docks was built in the late 1820s to a Thomas Telford design – in the process some 11,300 people were made homeless, and the medieval hospital of St Katharine demolished. The docks specialized in luxury goods such as ivory, spices, carpets and cigars, but they were very badly bombed in the Blitz and, in the early 1970s, were turned into a luxury yacht marina.

With little of the original warehouse architecture surviving, the docks' redeeming qualities are the old **swing bridges** and the central **Ivory House** warehouse, the only one remaining, with its clock tower and wrought-iron colonnade. Built in 1854, at its peak this warehouse received over 200 tons of ivory annually (that's four thousand dead elephants), plus hippopotamus and walrus teeth and even mammoth

---

THE THAMES PATH

The **Thames Path** is a 184-mile National Trail that runs along, or close to, the riverbank of the Thames from its source to the Thames Barrier. The London section exists on both banks, and is clearly signposted, so you can **walk** the two miles Docklands stretch from Tower Bridge, via Wapping and Limehouse to Canary Wharf. And if you're feeling really energetic, you can continue right round the Isle of Dogs to East India Dock near Trinity Buoy Wharf.

tusks from Siberia. Halfway along East Smithfield, you can see the original gates with (modern, fibreglass) elephants on the pillars, and on the corner of Thomas More Street, a section of the **original dock wall** survives, plus the main entrance to the former London Docks, with two Neoclassical Customs and Excise offices from 1805.

Dickens Inn, an eighteenth-century timber-framed brewery warehouse, was airlifted in 1969 from its original site several hundred yards to the east. At the centre of the docks is the squat **Coronarium chapel** (now a *Starbucks*), built for Queen Elizabeth II's Silver Jubilee, and as near as possible to the church of St Katharine, which was owned by the Crown.

St George-in-the-East
The Highway • Daily 8am–6pm • ☎ 020 7481 1345, ⓦ stgite.org.uk • ⊖ Shadwell DLR

Nicholas Hawksmoor's church of **St George-in-the-East**, built in 1726, stands on the north side of the busy Highway. As bold as any of Hawksmoor's buildings, it boasts four "pepperpot" towers above the nave, built to house the staircases to the church's galleries, and a hulking west-end tower topped by an octagonal lantern. Within, it comes as something of a shock to find a miniature modern church squatting in the nave, but that's all the parish could come up with following the devastation of the Blitz, to which the church's barren surroundings also bear witness.

Tobacco Dock
☎ 0207 680 4001, ⓦ tobaccodocklondon.com

East from St Katharine Docks down the busy Highway lies **Tobacco Dock**, a huge warehouse built in 1814 and initially used to store tobacco and wine. A fascinating combination of timber and early cast-iron framing, it was converted into a shopping complex in 1990 by postmodernist Terry Farrell, but the place closed soon afterwards and was a dead space until being relaunched as an events venue in late 2012, with a programme featuring occasional exhibitions, food and drink festivals, and dance music parties (ⓦlondonwarehouseevents.co.uk). On the south of Tobacco Dock, a tree-lined **canal walk** – all that remains of the huge Western Dock that once stood here – leads to Wapping High Street.

Wapping High Street
If you arrive on **Wapping High Street** expecting the usual parade of shops, you're in for a big surprise. Traditionally, the business of Wapping took place on the river; thus tall brick-built warehouses, most now converted into flats, line the Thames side of the street, while to the north – in a stark contrast typical of Docklands – lie the council estates of the older residents.

Five minutes' walk along the High Street will bring you to **Wapping Pier Head**, former entrance to the London Docks, now grassed over and cut off as a private garden to the grand, curvaceous Regency terraces (built for the officials of the Dock Company) that flank it. Further east is the unusual neo-Gothic former tea warehouse, **Oliver's Wharf**, a trailblazing apartment conversion from 1972, with a couple of preserved overhead gangways crossing the High Street just beyond. Beside the *Town of Ramsgate* pub (see p.393), you'll also find **Wapping Old Stairs**, one of the few intact sets of steps down to the river; at low tide you can see where pirates were tied to drown.

Wapping Police Station
Further along the High Street from Oliver's Wharf stands **Wapping Police Station**, headquarters of the world's oldest uniformed police force, the Marine Police, founded in 1798 and now a subdivision of the Met. The police boatyard is a 1960s building which features funky, abstract, vertical fibreglass friezes. Down by the riverside here, at

13

the low-water mark, was **Execution Dock**, where for four centuries pirates, smugglers and mutineers were hanged and left dangling until three tides had washed over them – the worst offenders were then tarred and gibbeted further downstream. The most famous felon to perish here was Captain Kidd, pirate-catcher-turned-pirate, hanged in 1701, and left gibbeted in an iron cage by the Thames for twenty years; the last victims were executed for murder and mutiny in 1830.

Wapping Wall

Beyond Wapping station, along **Wapping Wall**, you'll find the finest collection of nineteenth-century warehouses left in the whole of Docklands, beginning with the gargantuan Metropolitan Wharf, its wrought-iron capstan cranes and pulleys still clearly in evidence. At the far end of Wapping Wall is the venerable *Prospect of Whitby* pub (see p.393), and, opposite, the ivy-clad red-brick **London Hydraulic Pumping Station**, built in the 1890s and once chief supplier of hydraulic power to the whole of central London; it operated as arts space, **The Wapping Project**, for some 35 years until 2013, but currently awaits a new use (probably as apartments).

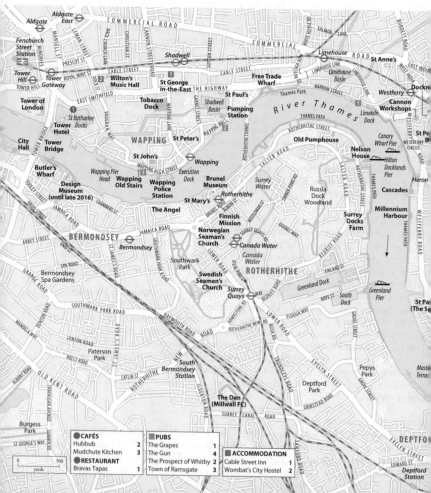

Shadwell Basin

Over the swing bridge to the north of the Pumping Station, **Shadwell Basin** is one of
the last remaining stretches of water that once comprised three interlocking docks,
known simply as London Docks and first opened in 1805. Now a watersports centre,
it's enclosed on three sides by new housing finished off in primary reds and blues.
Rising up majestically behind the houses to the north is **St Paul's** (Ⓦstpaulsshadwell
.org), the "sea captains' church", with a Baroque tower.

Limehouse

East of Wapping, **Limehouse** was a major shipbuilding centre in the eighteenth and
nineteenth centuries, hub of London's canal traffic and the site of the city's first
Chinatown, a district sensationalized in Victorian newspapers as a warren of opium
and gambling dens, and by writers such as Oscar Wilde, Arthur Conan Doyle, Sax
Rohmer and Dickens, who wrote: "Down by the docks the shabby undertaker's shop
will bury you for next to nothing, after the Malay or Chinaman has stabbed you for

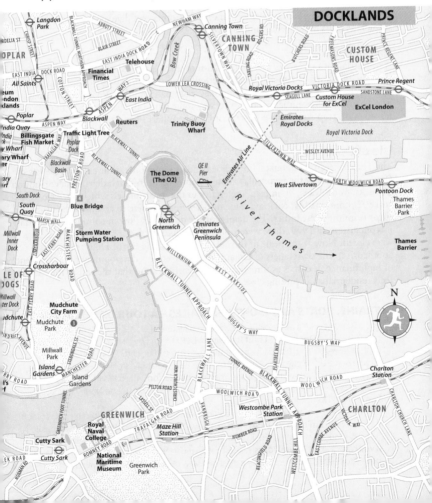

13

nothing at all." Wartime bombing and postwar road schemes all but obliterated Limehouse: the only remnants of the Chinese community are the street names: Canton, Mandarin, Ming and Pekin among them. **Narrow Street**, the main thoroughfare, is sleepier than Wapping High Street, and famous primarily for its pub *The Grapes*, currently owned by the actor Ian McKellen (see p.393). On the shoreline (and visible from the pub terrace) is one of Antony Gormley's statues, mounted on a mooring pile.

St Anne's Church

Three Colt St • Open for Sun service 10.30am • ☎ 020 7987 1502, ⊕ stanneslimehouse.org • ⊖ Limehouse DLR

Limehouse's major landmark is Hawksmoor's **St Anne's Church**, rising up just north of the DLR viaduct. Begun in 1714, and dominated by a gargantuan west tower, topped by an octagonal lantern, it boasts the highest church clock in London. The interior was badly damaged by fire in 1850, though it does contain a superb organ built for the Great Exhibition the following year. In the graveyard is a fabulously evocative pyramidal structure, carved with eroded masonic symbols and the legend "The Wisdom of Solomon". It is said to be one of what was originally a pair that were destined for the church's stubby east towers. The other was damaged, perhaps by locals suspicious of its rather pagan appearance.

Limekiln Dock

A pedestrian bridge carries the Thames Path over the entrance to Limehouse Basin and then the tidal inlet of **Limekiln Dock**, overlooked to the north by a picturesque gaggle of listed warehouses, and to the south by the gargantuan Dundee Wharf development. The Thames Path eventually ploughs its way right round the Isle of Dogs, but for now it's still a bit stop-start once you get past Canary Wharf Pier.

Isle of Dogs

The Thames begins a dramatic horseshoe bend at Limehouse, thus creating the **Isle of Dogs**. The origin of the peninsula's strange name has been much debated: a corruption of ducks, or of dykes, or, in fact, a reference to the royal kennels which once stood here. In 1802, London's first enclosed trade docks were built here to accommodate rum and sugar from the West Indies. The demise of the docks was slow in coming, but rapid in its conclusion: in 1975, there were still eight thousand job here; five years later they were closed. Now at the heart of the new Docklands, the Isle of Dogs reaches its apotheosis in the skyscrapers of **Canary Wharf**. Given this development's role as a centre of high finance, it comes as something of a surprise to find that the rest of the island feels residential and working class.

TRAINS, BOATS AND (SORT OF) PLANES – A TOUR OF DOCKLANDS

The best way to get a sense of the scale and architecture of Docklands is to use the driverless, mostly elevated **Docklands Light Railway** or DLR. Arriving by DLR at Canary Wharf (from Bank or Tower Hill) is particularly spectacular, with the rail line cutting right through the middle of the office buildings, spanned by Cesar Pelli's parabolic steel-and-glass canopy. At this point, you could switch to Canary Wharf's **tube station**, which has its Norman Foster-designed entrance on West Plaza, and take the tube one stop to North Greenwich, home of the Dome (or O2).

From close to the Dome, you can leap aboard an unusual addition to London's transport system, the £60 million **Emirates Air Line** (see p.321), a Swiss-built cable car (Mon–Fri 7am–9pm, Sat 8am–9pm, Sun 9am–9pm; £3.20 single with Oyster card), which will whisk you silently over the River Thames to the **Royal Docks**. Take the return trip to North Greenwich, and you can catch a **boat** into central London and enjoy a great river view of Docklands and Greenwich.

13

Canary Wharf

The strip of land in the middle of the former West India Docks, **Canary Wharf** was originally a destination for rum and mahogany, and later tomatoes and bananas (from the Canary Islands, hence the name). It's the easiest bit of the Isle of Dogs to explore on foot, though the whole place feels a bit like a stage-set, a spotlessly clean business quarter policed by security guards, with make-believe streets like Wren Steps and Chancellor Passage. The most famous building is Cesar Pelli's 800ft-high stainless-steel **Canary Wharf Tower** (closed to the public) – the highest building in the country for two decades after it was completed in 1991. Officially known as One Canada Square, the tower is flanked by Norman Foster's HSBC and Pelli's Citigroup skyscrapers, both of which are 656ft high, glass-clad and rather dull.

Just to the east lies Trafalgar Way where, on a traffic island near the entrance to Billingsgate Market (see box below), you'll see Pierre Vivant's **Traffic Light Tree** monument. This cluster of traffic signals all flashing madly is supposed to echo the restlessness of the financial centre that overlooks it.

West India Quay and around

North of Cabot Square, you can cross a floodlit floating bridge to **West India Quay**, probably the most pleasing development on the Isle of Dogs. Here, two Georgian warehouses (out of nine) have survived and now house flats, bars, restaurants and the Museum of London Docklands (see p.214). On the water, among other boats, is London's only floating church, **St Peter's Barge** (talks Wed & Thurs lunchtime & services on Sun; ⓦstpetersbarge.org), a Dutch freight barge that was refitted for the job by a group of churches including, St Anne's (see opposite).

Immediately to the west of the warehouses is the old entrance to the West India Docks, heralded by the **Ledger Building** (converted into an unsympathetically flash pub), which sports a dinky Doric portico and, round the corner, a splendidly pompous plaque commemorating the opening of the docks from 1800. Opposite, across Hertsmere Road, stands a small, circular, domed building, the lone survivor of two guardhouses that flanked the main entrance to the docks; behind it lies the former cooperage, now the **Cannon Workshops**.

To the northeast, behind the Ledger Building, are more little-known remnants of the old docks, among them the stately **Dockmaster's House**, built in 1809 as the Excise Office and now an Indian restaurant, with a smart white balustrade. It is sadly overshadowed by a supremely ugly Cineworld. Behind here, on Garford Street, there's a prim row of **Dock Constables' Cottages**, built in pairs in 1802. Tucked in behind them is **Grieg House**, a lovely yellow and red-brick building, built in 1903 as part of the Scandinavian Seamen's Temperance Home, with a little cupola and lovely exterior mouldings. It is now incorporated into – or rather, engulfed by – a bland, modern Salvation Army complex.

A FISHY BUSINESS

Seagulls squawk and circle, scanning for a dropped morsel, packing cases crash and traders curse – much of Docklands' buzz and clamour is a thing of the past, but things are as rowdy as ever they were at **Billingsgate Fish Market** (ⓦbillingsgatefishmarket.org), the largest inland fish market in the UK, with a history stretching back some five hundred years (though it only moved to the present location in 1982. Even if you're not buying – it's mostly a wholesale affair, anyway – Billingsgate is worth a visit for the atmosphere alone. But there's a catch! One of the reasons that the market isn't more visited, other than its less-than-touristy location, are the hours it keeps – it opens at 4am (till 8.30am Tues–Fri and 9am Sat; closed the Tuesday following a Bank Holiday Monday) – and some traders are packing up by 7am. There's a fish and seafood cookery school here (ⓦseafoodtraining.org) which offers **tours**, but note that under-12s are not permitted into the market. Wear appropriate clothes, and non-slip footwear.

13

Museum of London Docklands

West India Quay • Daily 10am–6pm • Free • ☎ 020 7001 9844, ⊕ museumoflondon.org.uk/docklands • ⊖ West India Quay DLR

If you've any interest in the history of the docks or the Thames, then a visit to the **Museum of London Docklands** is well worth it. Housed in a warehouse built in 1803 for storing rum, sugar, molasses, coffee and cotton, the museum takes a chronological approach, beginning on the top floor, where you'll find a great model of old London Bridge, one side depicting it around 1450, the other around 1600. Also here is a reproduction of the Rhinebeck Panorama, an 8ft-long watercolour showing the "legal quays" in the 1790s, just before the enclosed docks were built. On the floor below are diverse sections on slavery, frost fairs and whaling, a reconstructed warren of late nineteenth-century shops and cobbled streets called "Sailortown", plus mock-ups of a cooperage, a bottling vault and a tobacco-weighing office. Look out, too, for the model of Brunel's *Leviathan*, the fascinating wartime film reel and the excellent even-handed coverage of the docks' postwar history. Themes such as East End music hall are covered too.

Those with kids should head for Mudlarks (daily 2–5.30pm; school holidays 10am–5.30pm), where children can learn a bit about pulleys and ballast, drive a DLR train or just romp around the soft play area. It's worth booking online for this. The museum's top floor will be undergoing a refurbishment from March 2016.

Mudchute and Island Gardens

In the southeast corner of the Isle of Dogs is a hilly area called **Mudchute**, where the soil from digging out the nearby Millwall Docks was dumped in the 1860s. It's now home to **Mudchute City Farm** (see p.442), one of the largest in Europe, with a great café to boot (see p.380). From Mudchute, the DLR goes directly under the river to Greenwich, but it's worth considering getting out at **Island Gardens**, in the far south of the Isle of Dogs. From the eponymous park here, Christopher Wren used to contemplate his masterpieces, the Royal Naval College and the Royal Observatory, and you, too, can do the same, before heading across the river via the 1902 **Greenwich Foot Tunnel** (see p.314).

East of Isle of Dogs

There's not a great deal to detain you east of the island, but any journey in the direction of City Airport guarantees dramatic vistas, particularly if you're on the DLR (see box, p.212). This is London in widescreen: the route takes you across the River Lea, before treating you to monumental sights ranging from the Royal Victoria Dock and its vast ExCel exhibition centre, to Silvertown's Tate and Lyle refinery (a rare surviving site of full-force Docklands industry), Brick Lane Music Hall and the bulk of the Millennium Mills block, which is about to undergo a new lease of life as part of the Silvertown regeneration scheme, while all the while the Emirates Air Line spins out like a spider's web towards the great dome of the O2 arena across the river.

Trinity Buoy Wharf

64 Orchard Wharf • ☎ 020 7515 7153, ⊕ trinitybuoywharf.com • Daily 9am–5pm • Free • Longplayer Sat & Sun 11am–5pm • Free • ⊕ longplayer.org • ⊖ East India DLR or boat from the O2 QEII Pier (Mon–Fri 5am–7pm; £2 each way; call ☎ 07947 637 925)

Hidden to the east of East India Dock is the bizarre little enclave of **Trinity Buoy Wharf**. Built in 1803, it is home to London's only lighthouse, one of a pair built by Trinity House for experiments in optics and used by, among others, Michael Faraday. The wharf also houses offices, artists studios and flats, built out of old shipping containers, an original 1940s American mobile diner where you can get a bite to eat, and a whole array of boats. In the lighthouse itself, there's a musical installation called **Longplayer**, a twenty-minute recording of Tibetan singing bowls, manipulated to create a one

13

Nothing will convey to the stranger a better idea of the vast activity and stupendous wealth of London than a visit to these warehouses, filled to overflowing with interminable stores of every kind of foreign and colonial products; to these enormous vaults, with their apparently inexhaustible quantities of wine; and to these extensive quays and landing-stages, cumbered with huge stacks of hides, heaps of bales, and long rows of casks…Those who wish to taste the wines must procure a tasting-order from a wine merchant. Ladies are not admitted after 1pm. Visitors should be on their guard against insidious effects of "tasting" in the heavy, vinous atmosphere.
                                                    Baedeker's Handbook for London (1905)

thousand-year-long loop, and due to play until December 31, 2999. The wharf is a ten-minute walk from East India DLR station, at the end of Orchard Place, where the Bow Creek (part of the River Lea) winds its way into the Thames.

Thames Barrier Park
North Woolwich Rd • ⊖ Pontoon Dock DLR

One of London's most distinctive open spaces – and the city's first new park for some fifty years when it opened in 2001 – **Thames Barrier Park** features a striking sunken garden (dubbed the "green dock") lined with undulating topiary that leads the eye down towards the river and the metallic sleekness of the barrier itself (see p.324). There's a children's playground at the park, plus fountains and a café that, though architecturally interesting, offers mixed food and service.

Just to the north of the park, on the far side of North Woolwich Road, lies the disused London Pleasure Gardens site, an ill-fated cultural park for visitors to the 2012 Olympic Games. It is worth a peek (through the fencing) at the various sculptural installations and interventions into this otherwise barren patch – one of the Games' eerier legacies.

DECKCHAIRS OUTSIDE THE ROYAL FESTIVAL HALL

The South Bank

The South Bank has a lot going for it. As well as the massive waterside arts centre, it's home to a host of tourist attractions including the enormously popular London Eye, Europe's largest observation wheel, the London Aquarium and, further south, the impressive Imperial War Museum. With most of London's major sights sitting on the north bank of the Thames, the views from here are the best on the river, and thanks to the wide, traffic-free riverside boulevard, the area can be happily explored on foot, while for much of the year there's some kind of outdoor festival going on along the riverbank. You can continue your wanderings eastwards along the riverside towards Tate Modern and Bankside (see p.226).

For centuries London stopped southwards at the Thames; the South Bank was a marshy, uninhabitable place, a popular spot for duck-shooting, but otherwise seldom visited. Then, in the eighteenth century, wharves began to be built along the riverbank, joined later by factories, so that by 1905 the Baedeker guidebook characterized **Lambeth** and Southwark as "containing numerous potteries, glass-works, machine-factories, breweries and hop-warehouses". Slums and overhead railway lines added to the grime until 1951, when a slice of Lambeth's badly bombed riverside was used as a venue for the Festival of Britain, the site eventually evolving into the **Southbank Centre**, a vibrant arts complex, encased in a concrete shell. What helped kick-start the South Bank's twenty-first century rejuvenation was the arrival of the spectacular **London Eye**, and the renovation of **Hungerford Bridge**, which is flanked by a majestic symmetrical double-suspension footbridge, called the Golden Jubilee Bridges. **Waterloo Bridge**, famous for being built mostly by women during World War II, marks the eastern limit of the Southbank Centre, but the next stretch of riverside to Blackfriars Bridge has cultural attractions of its own: from the city's leading arts cinema, **BFI Southbank**, to the **Oxo Tower**. The bridge itself was the scene of the **assassination** of Georgi Markov, a Bulgarian dissident working at the BBC World Service, in 1978. He was shot in the leg with a ricin pellet fired from an umbrella by a member of the Bulgarian secret police and died three days later.

14

Southbank Centre

Ⓦ southbankcentre.co.uk • ⊖ Waterloo

In 1951, the South Bank Exhibition, on derelict land south of the Thames, formed the centrepiece of the national **Festival of Britain**, an attempt to boost postwar morale by celebrating the centenary of the Great Exhibition (when Britain really did rule over half the world). The most striking features of the site were the Ferris wheel (now reincarnated as the London Eye), the saucer-shaped Dome of Discovery (inspiration for the Millennium Dome), the Royal Festival Hall (which still stands) and the cigar-shaped steel and aluminium Skylon tower.

The great success of the festival eventually provided the impetus for the creation of the **Southbank Centre** comprising the Royal Festival Hall, Queen Elizabeth Hall, the Purcell Room and the Hayward Gallery, all squeezed between Hungerford and Waterloo bridges. Unfortunately, however, it failed to capture the imagination of the public in the same way, and became London's much unloved culture bunker. The low point came in the 1980s when hundreds of homeless lived under the complex in a "Cardboard City". Since then, there has been a transformation: the centre's unprepossessing appearance softened by the crowds enjoying its riverside location, its avenue of trees, fluttering banners, regular festivals and food stalls, skateboarders and, at weekends secondhand bookstalls outside nearby BFI Southbank.

Royal Festival Hall

Southbank Centre • Poetry Library Tues–Sun 11am–8pm • Free • Ⓦ poetrylibrary.org.uk • ⊖ Waterloo

The only building left from the 1951 Festival of Britain is the **Royal Festival Hall** or RFH, one of London's main concert venues, whose auditorium is suspended above the open-plan foyer – its curved roof is clearly visible above the main body of the building. The interior furnishings remain fabulously period, and exhibitions and free events in the foyer – the main space is the **Clore Ballroom**, though they can take over spaces on any of the five floors – are generally excellent, making this one of the most pleasant South Bank buildings to visit. At the little-known **Poetry Library** on Level 5, you can either browse or, by joining (membership is free), borrow from the library's vast collection of poetry accumulated since 1912. Just outside, there's a little children's reading den, and kids (big and small) might also enjoy riding the "**singing lift**"(officially Martin Creed's *Work No.409* for elevator and choir) – the glass lift on the QEH side of the building, where a recorded choir announces each floor.

THE SOUTH BANK

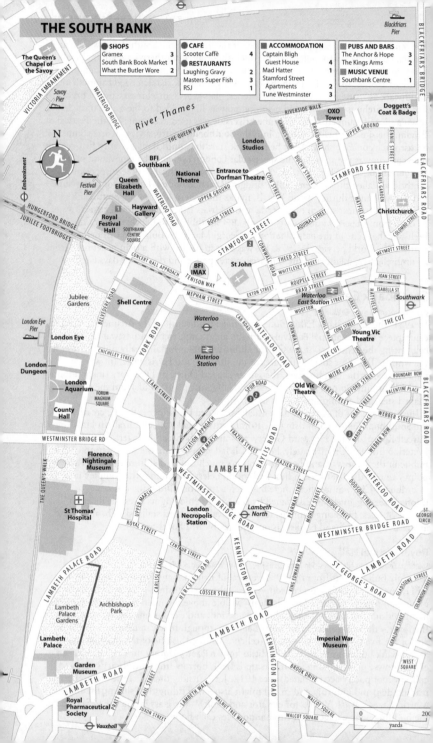

Queen Elizabeth Hall and Hayward Gallery

Hayward Gallery Mon noon–6pm, Tues, Wed, Sat & Sun 10am–6pm, Thurs & Fri 10am–8pm · Exhibitions from £10 ·
☎ 020 7960 4200 · ⊖ Waterloo

Architecturally, the most depressing parts of the Southbank Centre are the **Queen Elizabeth Hall** (QEH) and the more intimate **Purcell Room**, which share the same foyer and are built in uncompromisingly brutalist 1960s style. They have, however, proved adept at accommodating new uses, not always intended. At ground level, the graffiti-covered space known as the **undercroft** is a legendary skateboarding destination that, after a successful campaign, is now protected as a skatepark for the foreseeable future. Up above, a lovely roof garden appears each summer (see box, p.220). Immediately behind, and equally stark from the outside, is the **Hayward Gallery**, a large and flexible art gallery that puts on temporary art exhibitions, mostly (but not exclusively) modern or contemporary art. Renovation of these buildings is planned throughout 2016, after which there should be more rooftop garden spaces.

14

BFI Southbank

Belvedere Rd · Mediathèque Tues–Sat noon–8pm, Sun 12.30–8pm · Free · ☎ 020 7928 3232, ⓦ bfi.org.uk · ⊖ Waterloo

Tucked underneath Waterloo Bridge is **BFI Southbank** (operated by the British Film Institute), which screens London's most esoteric films, hosts a variety of talks, lectures and mini-festivals and also runs **Mediathèque**, where you can settle into one of the viewing stations and choose from a selective archive of British films, TV programmes and documentaries. The BFI also runs the **BFI IMAX**, housed within the eye-catching glass drum, which rises up from the centre of the old "Bullring" roundabout at the southern end of Waterloo Bridge; the underpasses here were previously home to hundreds of homeless people in the notorious "Cardboard City", of the 1980s, which was eventually cleared to make way for the cinema in 1998.

National Theatre

South Bank · **Backstage tours** normally 2–6 daily, times vary; 1hr 15min · £9 **Sherling High Level Walkway** Mon–Sat 9.30am–7.30pm · Free · ☎ 020 7452 3000, ⓦ nationaltheatre.org.uk · ⊖ Waterloo

Just east of Waterloo Bridge, looking like a multistorey car park, is Denys Lasdun's **National Theatre** (officially the Royal National Theatre). An institution first mooted in 1848, it was only finally realized in 1976, and, like the Southbank Centre, its concrete brutalism is a classic of the style, though it tends to divide critical opinion, with Prince Charles likening it to a nuclear power station. A recent revamp has opened up the foyer which has improved the public spaces. Lasdun's design is most remarkable for the way it neatly accommodates three superb auditoriums (see p.418): the 1160-seat Olivier, modelled after a Greek amphitheatre, with perfect sight-lines; the 890-seat proscenium-arch Lyttleton; and the smaller Dorfman theatre, located directly below the Olivier. The excellent **backstage tours**, led by well-informed guides, are a great way to understand how the building all slots together. Exactly what you see depends on the theatre schedules, but you're taken behind the stages and through the prop-making and set-construction areas. You can also get a glimpse of the inner workings of the theatre from the **Sherling High Level Walkway**, which runs from the first floor of the Dorfman theatre foyer out over the set-design areas. A temporary theatre in front of the National – a red-wood clad building, which looks like an upturned table – is due to remain in place until 2017.

Gabriel's Wharf

East of the National Theatre, you pass the 24-storey **London Studios**, where ITV and other companies film many of the biggest shows on telly (if you're interested in being part of a studio audience, visit: ⓦ itv.com/beontv/join-the-audience). The riverside

14

SUMMER ON THE SOUTH BANK

The multi-level modernist spaces of the South Bank make a striking canvas for an inventive and popular series of events and installations throughout the year. In particular, between May and September, promenaders descend, and open-air bars make use of the broad terraces and fantastic river views. Check ⓦ southbankcentre.co.uk for details of events, and look out for these recurring favourites:

Appearing Rooms (the fountain) Playing in Jeppe Hein's large fountain installation might be the single most popular thing to do on a hot summer's day on the South Bank, at least for the under-10s. On the Level 2 terrace between the QEH and Festival Hall (usually June or July–Sept).

Roof garden at the Queen Elizabeth Hall Designed by Eden Project gardeners and created and maintained by men and women who have experienced homelessness or mental health problems, the garden, featuring banks of wildflower and raised vegetable beds, is a popular, not-so-secret spot to relax in summer (usually from April onwards; some disruption is expected during renovation, but additional roof gardens are planned).

Southbank food market Southbank Centre Square, behind the Royal Festival Hall (usually Fri noon–8pm, Sat 11am–8pm, Sun and bank holiday Mon noon–6pm). Street food stalls and local products for sale.

Udderbelly and **Wonderground** A mini-festival site goes up in a space between the Hungerford Bridge and Jubilee Gardens, with bars and food stalls, cabaret music and comedy in two temporary venues: Udderbelly (April–July) hosts comedy in its performance tent shaped like an upturned purple cow, while Wonderground (May–Sept) is a playground of camp and cabaret, hosted in the Spiegeltent.

promenade brings you eventually to **Gabriel's Wharf**, an ad hoc collection of craft shops and cafés. It's a refreshing change from the franchises which have colonized much of the South Bank, and one for which **Coin Street Community Builders** (CSCB; ⓦcoinstreet.org) must be thanked. With the population in this bomb-damaged stretch of the South Bank down from fifty thousand at the beginning of the century to four thousand in the early 1970s, big commercial developers were keen to step in and build hotels and office blocks galore. They were successfully fought off, and instead the emphasis has been on projects that combine commercial and community interests.

OXO Tower

South Bank • **Exhibition Gallery** Daily 11am–6pm • Free **Public viewing gallery** Daily 10am–10pm • Free • ⓦ oxotower.co.uk • ⊖ Blackfriars

East of Gabriel's Wharf stands the landmark **OXO Tower**, an old power station that was converted into a meat-packing factory in the late 1920s by Liebig Extract of Meat Company, best known in Britain as the makers of OXO stock cubes. To get round the local council's ban on illuminated advertisements, the company cleverly incorporated the letters into the windows of the main tower, and then illuminated them from within. Now, thanks again to CSCB, the building contains an exhibition gallery on the ground floor, plus flats for local residents and a series of retail-workshops for designers on the first and second floors, and a swanky restaurant and bar on the top floor. To enjoy the view, however, you don't need to eat or drink here: you can simply take the lift to the eighth-floor **public viewing gallery** (not prominently signed).

Waterloo Station

Built in 1848, **Waterloo Station** is easily the capital's busiest train and tube station, serving the city's southwestern suburbs and the southern Home Counties. Easily missed, the ornate Edwardian-style facade is hidden behind the railway bridge on Mepham Street. Without doubt Waterloo's most bizarre train terminus was the former **London Necropolis Station**, whose early twentieth-century facade survives at 121

Westminster Bridge Rd, to the south of the station. Opened in 1854 following one of London's worst outbreaks of cholera, trains from this station took coffins and mourners to Brookwood Cemetery in Surrey (at the time, the world's largest cemetery). Brookwood Station even had separate platforms for Anglicans and Nonconformists and a licensed bar – "Spirits served here", the sign apparently read – but the whole operation was closed down after bomb damage in World War II.

West from the main station concourse, an overhead walkway heads off to the South Bank, passing through the Stalinist-looking **Shell Centre**. Officially and poetically entitled the Downstream Building, it was built in the 1950s – and was the tallest building in London at the time – by oil giant Shell. They have sold the building, and the main tower is set to be at the centre of a new high-rise development.

14

London Eye

Daily: April–June 10am–9pm, May & June Fri & Sat till 9.30pm; July & Aug 10am–9.30pm, Fri till 11.30pm; Sept–March 10am–8.30pm, some later opening during holidays in summer; closes for 10 days in Jan • From £19.35 online • ☎ 0871 781 3000, ⓦ londoneye.com • ⊖ Waterloo or Westminster

Having graced the skyline since the start of the twenty-first century, the **London Eye** is firmly established as one of the city's most famous landmarks. Standing an impressive 443ft high, it's the tallest Ferris wheel in Europe, weighing over 2000 tons, yet as simple and delicate as a bicycle wheel. It's constantly in slow motion, which means a full-circle "flight" in one of its 32 pods (one for each of the city's boroughs) should take around thirty minutes, which passes incredibly quickly. You can see right out to the very edge of the city – bring some binoculars if you can – where the suburbs slip into the countryside, while its river location means it still has the edge for spectacular views across to Westminster and central London. Book online (to save money) – on arrival, you'll still have to queue to be loaded on unless you've paid extra for fast track – or you'll have to buy your ticket from the box office at the eastern end of County Hall.

County Hall

The colonnaded crescent of **County Hall** is the only truly monumental building on the South Bank. Designed to house the London County Council, it was completed in 1933 and enjoyed its greatest moment of fame in the 1980s as the headquarters of the GLC (Greater London Council), under the Labour leadership of Ken Livingstone, or "Red Ken", as the right-wing press called him at the time. The Tories moved in swiftly, abolishing the GLC in 1986, and leaving London as the only European city without an elected authority. In 2000, Livingstone had the last laugh when he became London's first popularly elected mayor, and head of the new Greater London Authority (GLA), housed in City Hall, near Tower Bridge. The building's tenants are constantly changing, but it's currently home to, among other things, several hotels and fast-food restaurants, the London Dungeon, an aquarium and the new "Shrek's Adventure" experience (ⓦshreksadventure.com). None of the attractions is an absolute must, but they prosper (as do the numerous buskers) by feeding off the vast captive audience milling around the London Eye.

London Aquarium

County Hall • Daily 10am–7pm, last entry 6pm • From £20 online **Behind the scenes tours** daily hourly 10.30am–3.30pm, Fri–Sun also 4.30pm • £7.50 extra **Snorkelling with Sharks experience** £125 • ☎ 0871 663 1678, ⓦ visitsealife.com/london • ⊖ Waterloo or Westminster

The most enduring County Hall tenant is the **Sea Life London Aquarium**, housed in the basement across three subterranean levels. Impressive in scale, the largest tanks, viewable from several levels, house a wealth of large creatures, such as the extremely weird bowmouth guitar shark, one of several shark species in the biggest tank, eerie large rays that glide over the walk-through glass tunnel, a magnificent green sea turtle and, in an Antarctic area, a few slightly forlorn-looking Gentoo penguins. Dozens of smaller tanks have jellyfish, "nemo" clown fish and much more besides, with species native to the Thames housed in stylish new digs, though the greyish chub can't compete with the tanks of more colourful tropical varieties. This is an attraction that's pretty much guaranteed to please kids – especially feeding times (check online or ask for daily schedule), and activities like getting up close to stroke a starfish – albeit at a price (book online to save a few quid and avoid queuing; combination tickets with other attractions available).

London Dungeon

14

County Hall • Mon–Wed & Fri 10am–5pm, Thurs 11am–5pm, Sat & Sun 10am–6pm; school holidays closes 7pm or 8pm • From £20. 50 online (£22 on Sat) • ☎ 0871 423 2240, ⓦ thedungeons.com • ⊖ Waterloo or Westminster

Gothic horror-fest the **London Dungeon** remains one of the city's major crowd-pleasers – to shorten the amount of time spent queuing (and save money), buy your ticket online. Teenagers and the credulous probably get the most out of the ninety-minute trip through various ludicrous live action scenarios such as "Jack the Ripper", each one hyped up by the team of ham actors dressed in period garb, plus a couple of horror rides, the Henry VIII-themed "Tyrant Wrath Boat Ride" and "Drop Dead Drop Ride".

North Lambeth

Away from the river, you leave the South Bank behind (and lose the crowds) and reach what used to be the village of Lambeth (now a large borough stretching south to Brixton and beyond). Vestiges of village atmosphere are notably absent, although **Lower Marsh**, with its market (Mon–Fri 10.30am–5pm, Sat 10am–3pm), interesting, offbeat shops and a good bar or two, and **The Cut**, home to the Old and Young Vic theatres (see p.418), retain a local feel and are worth a wander. Just by Lambeth Bridge, **Lambeth Palace** is the impressive private home of the Archbishop of Canterbury, though visiting requires pre-booking. It's also from this stretch of the riverbank that you get the best views of the Houses of Parliament. Inland lies London's most even-handed military museum, the **Imperial War Museum**, which has a moving permanent exhibition devoted to the Holocaust.

Florence Nightingale Museum

Lambeth Palace Rd • Daily 10am–5pm • £7.50 • ☎ 020 7620 0374, ⓦ www.florence-nightingale.co.uk • ⊖ Lambeth North or Westminster

On the south side of Westminster Bridge, a series of red-brick Victorian blocks and modern white accretions make up **St Thomas' Hospital**, founded in the twelfth century, but only established here after being ejected from its original location by London Bridge in 1862. At the hospital's northeastern corner, off Lambeth Palace Road, is the **Florence Nightingale Museum**, celebrating the devout woman who single-mindedly revolutionized the nursing profession by establishing the first school of nursing at St Thomas' in 1860 and publishing her *Notes on Nursing*, emphasizing the importance of hygiene, decorum and discipline. The small exhibition is imaginatively set out, aided by listening posts and interactive screens. It hits just the right note by putting the two years she spent tending to the wounded of the Crimean War in the context of a lifetime of tireless social campaigning. Exhibits include the Turkish lantern she used in Scutari hospital, near Istanbul, that earned her the nickname "The Lady with the Lamp", and her pet owl, Athena (now stuffed), who used to perch on her shoulder.

Lambeth Palace

Lambeth Palace Rd • **Tours** Certain Thurs & Fri 10.30am & 2pm • £12, plus booking fee **Garden** March–Oct first Wed of Month noon–3pm • £4 • ☎ 0844 248 5134, ⓦ archbishopofcanterbury.org • ⊖ Westminster, Lambeth North or Vauxhall

A short walk south of St Thomas' stands the imposing red-brick Tudor Gate of **Lambeth Palace**, London residence of the Archbishop of Canterbury since 1197, which is well worth a visit, although guided tours need booking in advance. The most impressive room is, without doubt, the **Great Hall** (now the library), with its very late Gothic, oak hammer-beam roof, built after the Restoration by Archbishop Juxon, whose coat of arms, featuring African heads, can be seen on the bookshelves. Upstairs, the **Guard Room** boasts an even older, arch-braced timber roof from the fourteenth century, and is the room where Thomas More was brought for questioning before being sent to the Tower.

Among the numerous portraits of past archbishops, look out for works by Holbein, Van Dyck, Hogarth and Reynolds. The final point on the tour is the **palace chapel**, where the religious reformer and leader of the Lollards, John Wycliffe, was tried (for the second time) in 1378 for "propositions, clearly heretical and depraved". The door and window frames date back to Wycliffe's day, but the place is somewhat overwhelmed by the ceiling frescoes by Leonard Rosoman, added in the 1980s, telling the story of the Church of England. Best of all is the fact that you can see the choir screen and stalls put there in the 1630s by Archbishop Laud, and later used at his trial as evidence of his Catholic tendencies for which he was executed in 1645.

The elegantly landscaped palace **gardens**, planted with many mature trees, are open once a month in summer, though unfortunately not on the same day as the guided tours.

Garden Museum

Lambeth Palace Rd • Mon–Fri & Sun 10.30am–5pm, Sat 10.30am–4pm; closed for renovation until late 2016 • £7.50 • ☎ 020 7401 8865, ⓦ gardenmuseum.org.uk • ⊖ Westminster or Lambeth North

Next door to Lambeth Palace stands the Kentish ragstone church of **St Mary-at-Lambeth**, largely rebuilt in Victorian times, but retaining its fourteenth-century tower. The church is home to the **Garden Museum** which puts on excellent exhibitions on a horticultural theme, while much of its permanent exhibition is dedicated to the two John Tradescants (father and son), gardeners to James I and Charles I, who are both buried in the churchyard. The **Tradescant memorial** features several unusual reliefs: a seven-headed griffin contemplating a skull and a crocodile sifting through sundry ruins flanked by gnarled trees. The Tradescants were tireless travellers in their search for new plant species, and John the Elder set up a museum of curiosities known as "Tradescant's Ark" in Lambeth in 1629. Among the exhibits were the "hand of a mermaid… a natural dragon, above two inches long… blood that rained on the Isle of Wight… and the Passion of Christ carved very daintily on a plumstone". The less fantastical pieces formed the nucleus of Oxford's Ashmolean Museum. The Garden Museum is currently undergoing renovation, and when it reopens, some of Tradescant's collection will be displayed in a re-creation of part of this Ark, including– a "vegetable lamb" that's in fact a Russian fern. The small graveyard, currently laid out as a **seventeenth-century knot garden**, is to be surrounded by a series of new pavilions, one of which will hold the museum café. Along with the Tradescants, the other famous name resting here is **Captain Bligh** of *Mutiny on the Bounty* fame, whose sarcophagus is topped by an ornamental breadfruit.

Imperial War Museum

Lambeth Rd • Daily 10am–6pm • Free • ☎ 020 7416 5000, ⓦ iwm.org.uk • ⊖ Lambeth North

From 1815 until 1930, the domed building at the east end of Lambeth Road was the infamous lunatic asylum of Bethlem Royal Hospital, better known as **Bedlam**. (Charlie Chaplin's mother was among those confined here – the future comedian was born and spent a troubled childhood in nearby Kennington.) When the hospital was moved to Beckenham in southeast London, the wings of the 700ft-long facade were demolished, leaving just the central section, now home to the **Imperial War Museum**, by far the capital's best military museum.

The atrium and First World War galleries

The treatment of the subject is impressively wide-ranging and fairly sober – the main atrium's large exhibits are described not as weapons but as **Witnesses to War**, and the story of each piece of hardware is recounted on video screens. What could be merely a militaristic display of guns, tanks and fighter planes is thoughtfully counterbalanced with other vehicles, such as a Reuters-owned Land Rover that was shot by an Israeli helicopter in Gaza in 2006, which sits beneath a Harrier jet and a 1940 Spitfire, while the giant V-2 rocket, which landed near the museum, is used to tell the problematic tale of the relationship between these weapons and the twentieth-century space race. Off the atrium is the entrance to one of the museums most effective (and affecting) displays, the **First World War galleries**, where fourteen rooms cover the many stories of the war at home and on the front, with a reconstructed trench at the centre of the exhibition.

14

First and second floors

On the first floor, the World War II collection, under the moniker **Turning points: 1934–45**, hasn't been given the same immersive treatment, but you can see plenty of famous exhibits, among them *Tamzine*, one of the littlest of the Dunkirk Little Ships, and General Montgomery's Humber staff car. Make sure you take a look at **A Family in Wartime**, which traces the wartime lives of one local family, the Allpresses, who lived nearby in Lambeth.

The second floor picks up the story of wartime from 1945 onwards, starting with the **Shadow of the Bomb,** introduced by a casing for the "Little Boy" atomic bomb as used in Hiroshima. The **War on the Doorstep** section awkwardly combines Northern Ireland and the Falklands War into one narrative – the connection incongruously suggested by the *Spitting Image* puppet of Margaret Thatcher tucked into a corner. However, a couple of contemporary artworks are worth seeking out, including Steve McQueen's *Queen and Country* (2006), paying tribute to the service personnel killed in the second Iraq war. The floor also has sections on divided societies and terror, while the **Secret War** gallery follows the clandestine activities of MI5, MI6 and the SOE (the wartime equivalent of MI6) – expect code-making kits, trip wires and spy cameras.

The art galleries and Extraordinary Heroes

The museum's **art galleries**, on the third floor, put on superb temporary exhibitions, many taken from its own vast collection of works by war artists, official and unofficial. One painting that's on permanent display, alongside other World War I artworks, is *Gassed* by John Singer Sargent.

On the top floor, the **Extraordinary Heroes** exhibition displays the largest collection of Victoria Crosses in the world, collected by Lord Ashcroft. However, this is much more than a medal gallery as videos and artefacts tell the moving stories of each recipient.

The Holocaust Exhibition

Many people come to the Imperial War Museum specifically to see the **Holocaust Exhibition** (not recommended for under-14s), which starts on the fourth floor and continues on the third floor. The museum has made a valiant attempt to avoid depicting the victims of the Holocaust as nameless masses, by focusing on individual cases, and interspersing archive footage with accounts from survivors. The exhibition pulls few punches, bluntly stating that the pope failed to denounce the anti-Jewish **Nuremberg Laws**, that anti-Semitic views were widespread and that at the 1938 Evian Conference, the European powers refused to accept any more Jewish refugees. There are sections on the extermination of the gypsies and those with physical and mental disabilities, pre-Holocaust Yiddish culture and the persecution of the Slavs. The **genocide**, which began with the *Einsatzgruppen* and ended with the gas chambers, is catalogued in painstaking detail. The centrepiece of the museum is a vast, all-white, scale model of (what is, in fact, only a very small slice of) **Auschwitz-Birkenau**, showing what happened to the two thousand Hungarian Jews who arrived at the camp from the town of Beregovo in May 1944. This section, and sections on life and death in the camps, is especially harrowing, and it's as well to leave yourself enough time to listen to the reflections of camp survivors at the end, as they attempt to come to terms with the past.

Southwark

In Tudor and Stuart London, the chief reason for crossing the Thames, to what is now Southwark, was to visit the disreputable Bankside for its pubs, brothels and bear-baiting pits around the south end of London Bridge. Four hundred years on, Londoners have rediscovered the habit of heading for the area, thanks to the traffic-free riverside path and a wealth of top attractions, with the charge led by the mighty Tate Modern. Tourist spots now pepper the riverside from Blackfriars Bridge to Bermondsey – from the remarkable reconstruction of Shakespeare's Globe Theatre to the sublime view from the Shard. Meanwhile, the indulgences of choice for modern visitors are largely epicurean: Borough market is the biggest draw for gourmets, but Bermondsey and Maltby streets are both de rigueur destinations for foodies in the know.

Bankside

Ⓦ visitbankside.com

Bankside is dominated by the awesome **Tate Modern**, while, close by, the **Millennium Bridge** provides a wonderful pedestrian link from the City and St Paul's. To the east are two thoroughly researched reconstructions: **Shakespeare's Globe Theatre** and Drake's Tudor galleon, the **Golden Hinde**. At this point, the shops, cafés and stalls of nearby **Borough Market**, a gourmet food haven that provides a welcome refuelling stop before you check out some of the city's best-preserved Gothic architecture in **Southwark Cathedral**.

The reconstruction of Shakespeare's Globe is pretty much all there is above ground today to remind you of Southwark's pre-industrial golden age of entertainment under the Tudors and Stuarts. For centuries, however, Bankside was best known for its **brothels**, which were already doing a thriving trade under the Romans. In 1161, the brothels were licensed by royal decree, but made to adhere to various rules and restrictions: prostitutes could now be fined three shillings for "grimacing to passers-by", but were given Sunday mornings off in order to attend church. The women wore red-and-white-striped caps and white aprons, and were known as "Winchester Geese", since the land was owned by the Bishop of Winchester. The Church made a small fortune out of the rent until Henry VIII closed the bawdy houses down.

In Elizabethan times, Bankside once again became the most nefarious area in London, known as "Stew's Bank" for its brothels or "stewhouses", and was studded with **bull- and bear-pits**. Pepys recalls seeing "some good sport of the bulls tossing of the dogs; one into the very boxes", but opinion was by then inclining towards Evelyn's

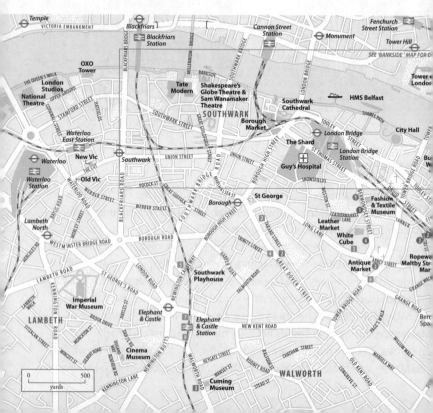

description of the sport as a "rude and dirty pastime" and in 1682 the last bear-garden was closed down. Most famous of all, however, were Bankside's **theatres** (see p.230).

Tate Modern

Bankside • Daily 10am–6pm, Fri & Sat until 10pm • Free; special exhibitions around £16 • ☏ 020 7887 8888, ⓦ tate.org.uk • ⊖ Southwark or Blackfriars

Tate Modern is an absolute must for anyone visiting or living in London. Designed as an oil-fired power station by Giles Gilbert Scott, this austere, brick-built "cathedral of power" was closed down in 1981 and reopened as a modern art gallery in 2000. The masterful conversion, by the Swiss duo Herzog & de Meuron, has left plenty of the original industrial feel, while providing wonderfully light and spacious galleries to show off Tate's impressive collection of international twentieth-century artists, including the likes of Monet, Duchamp, Hepworth, Matisse, Mondrian, Picasso, Pollock, Rothko and Warhol. More than any single artwork, however, it is the stupefying vastness of the main **Turbine Hall,** which rises to a height of 115ft from Level 0 (below the Thames), and the large-scale installations that have so captured the public's imagination.

Tate Modern receives over five million visitors a year, more than double what was envisaged. To alleviate this, it is expanding to the south. Opening in 2016, the Tate's major **new extension**, also designed by Herzog & de Meuron, is a distorted prism of latticed bricks rising to 215ft, which houses three new floors of gallery space. It sits above the old power station's subterranean oil tanks, which have been converted into rough-edged spaces for live work, video installations and performance art.

Tate's **permanent collection** dates back to 1900, but the curators have eschewed a

15

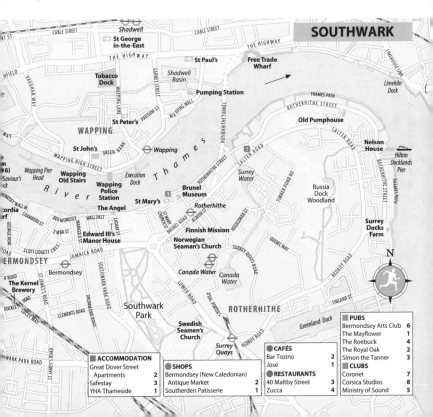

THE MILLENNIUM BRIDGE

The first bridge to be built across the Thames since Tower Bridge opened in 1894, the sleek, stainless-steel **Millennium Bridge** is London's sole pedestrian-only crossing. A suspension bridge of innovative design – the high-profile triumvirate responsible were sculptor Anthony Caro, architect Norman Foster and engineers Ove Arup – it famously bounced up and down when it first opened in 2000 and had to be closed for another two years for repairs. It still wobbles a bit, but most people are too busy enjoying the spectacular views across to St Paul's Cathedral and Tate Modern to notice.

chronological approach, and gone instead for hanging works according to themes and -isms. So in among all the attention-grabbing conceptual stuff, you'll find some early twentieth-century paintings, and each wing has a few rooms dedicated to single artists. They also change displays regularly to keep things current, so even big names may not be on show when you visit; check first if there's one thing you want to see. And remember that one of the joys of Tate Modern is coming across artists or artistic movements about which you may know very little.

ARRIVAL, INFORMATION AND TOURS

Arrival For the best views of the Tate, approach from the Millennium Bridge. The nearest entrance to the bridge is the North Entrance underneath the chimney, which brings you out at Level 1. The best entrance, however, is via the ramp at the West Entrance to the Turbine Hall on Level 0. There's also a Tate Boat, which plies between the two galleries (every 40min; 20min; £7.15; ⓦ thamesclippers.com).

Orientation Level 0 is also where you'll find the information desk, and, on the opposite side, the museum's cloakroom and giant bookshop – escalators from this floor lead straight up to Level 2. Entering from the bridge or river brings you to Level 1, linked by stairs and elevators to the other floors, but not escalators. Level 3 is used for temporary exhibitions.

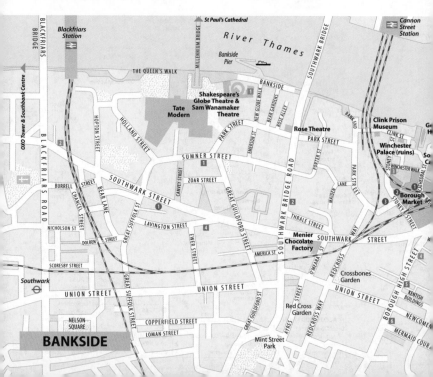

Tours There are free guided tours (daily at 11am, noon, 2 & 3pm; 45min) and multimedia guides (£4).

Eating There's a pricey restaurant and bar on Level 7, with a great view over the river, though the views are just as good from the balconies on Level 3, where there's an espresso bar. There's also a more reasonably priced café on Level 1, which offers a free kids' meal with an adult main course.

Level 2

On Level 2, **Poetry and Dream** concentrates, though by no means exclusively, on the interwar period. At the heart of the wing is a large room densely hung with works by the major Surrealists: **Miró**, **Magritte**, **Dalí** and **Ernst**, with **Picasso**'s *The Three Dancers* nearby (Tate owns works from every period of his life). Other rooms are given over to single artists, such as German artist **Joseph Beuys**, whose distinctive choice of materials derives directly from his wartime experiences, when his plane crashed in the Crimea and he was saved by local Tartars, who cocooned him in felt and fat. For those who prefer their art more representational, the **Realisms** room might appeal, with portraits by Matisse, Picasso and Lucian Freud.

In **Making Traces**, the emphasis is on the postwar decades, so there's a fairly wide selection of abstract expressionist works in all its forms, though the thematic tie is ostensibly gesture and action. At the heart of the display is Tate favourite **Mark Rothko**'s *Seagram Murals*. Commissioned by the *Four Seasons* restaurant in New York, they were withheld by Rothko, who decided he didn't wish his art to be a mere backdrop to the recreation of the wealthy. He gave them to Tate instead, and here they are displayed just as he intended, in an austere, dimly lit room. Like Rothko, **Gerhard Richter** gets an entire room in which to display his six, rather more upbeat, abstract "John Cage" paintings from 2006, as does **Rebecca Horn**, whose video performance pieces, shown alongside costumes and props used in them, are brilliantly strange.

15

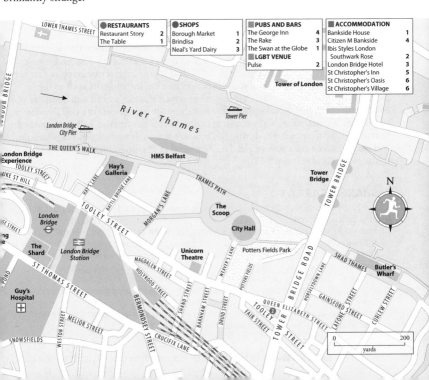

Level 4

The central room in **Structure and Clarity**, on Level 4, has an impressive collection of interwar abstract art by the likes of Kandinsky, Naum Gabo and Mondrian and, with a series of small sculptures displayed alongside, including several exquisite pieces by **Barbara Hepworth** and **Brancusi**'s beautifully simple bronze *Fish*. Picasso and Braque's **Cubism** gets a room to itself, while the **Minimalism** room is dominated by two works by **Donald Judd**.

Over in **Energy and Process**, there's a gallery devoted to the Italian art movement, *arte povera*, from the late 1960s, in which found objects played an important role. But this wing also has more recent acquisitions, and a whole room of **Cy Twombly**'s late works: bronze casts and great Bacchic explosions of paint. Other highlights include Lucio Fontana's slashed canvases, and watching other visitors' embarrassment as they look at Art & Language (Michael Baldwin)'s *Untitled Painting* (it's actually a mirror).

Shakespeare's Globe Theatre

21 New Globe Walk • Exhibition and tours daily 9am–5.30pm; summer no Globe tours Tues–Sat after 12.30pm • £13.50 • ☎ 020 7902 1500, ⓦ shakespearesglobe.com • ⊖ Southwark or London Bridge

Dwarfed by Tate Modern, but equally remarkable in its own way, **Shakespeare's Globe Theatre** is a more or less faithful reconstruction of the polygonal playhouse where most of the Bard's later works were first performed. The theatre, which boasts the first new thatched roof in central London since the Great Fire, puts on plays by Shakespeare and his contemporaries, using only natural light and the minimum of scenery. The season runs from May to September, and the performances are usually fun, historically authentic and critically acclaimed (see p.419). Round the back of the Globe, **Sam Wanamaker's Playhouse** is a faithful reconstruction of the sort of intimate, candlelit, indoor Jacobean theatre where Shakespeare's company would have performed during the winter months, and where plays are put on throughout the year.

The Globe's stylish **exhibition**, to the west of the theatre, is well worth a visit. It details the history of the Bankside theatres and the long campaign by the single-minded American actor Sam Wanamaker (1919–93) to have the Globe rebuilt. Examples of the meticulously authentic costumes on display include the one Mark Rylance wore as Cleopatra and a pearl-studded dress for Elizabeth I, worn by Jane Lapotaire for the royal gala opening in 1997. But it's the interactive exhibits that hit the spot: you can have a virtual play on period musical instruments such as the crumhorn or sackbut and there are booths in which you can record and compare your own rendition of key speeches with those of the stage greats, plus the odd live demo on the exhibition's stage. Visitors also get taken on an informative half-hour **guided tour** round the theatre itself; during the summer season, if you visit in the afternoon, you may be taken on a tour of the Sam Wanamaker Playhouse instead, or occasionally to the Rose Theatre (see p.232).

SHAKESPEARE & CO

London's first purpose-built theatres emerged in Shoreditch in the 1570s, but they flourished on Bankside, with no fewer than four during the reign of James I: the **Rose**, built in 1587, its foundations still extant on Park Street (see p.232); the **Swan**, built in 1595; the **Hope**, built in 1613, which doubled as a bear-garden and theatre; and the **Globe**, erected in 1599 on Park Street, where Shakespeare put on his greatest plays, now reconstructed on New Globe Walk. The theatres lasted barely half a century before being closed down by the Puritans, who considered them "chapels of Satan". With the Restoration, the focus of the theatre scene, and its accompanying vices, moved to Covent Garden, and Southwark faded from the limelight. Visit today, though, and the area has a couple of theatrical draws: as well as joining the groundlings at the Globe, you can catch some excellent off-West End productions at both the Menier Chocolate Factory (see p.419) and Southwark Playhouse (see p.420).

15

The Rose Theatre

56 Park St · Sat 10am–5pm · Free · ☎ 020 7261 9565, Ⓦ rosetheatre.org.uk · ⊖ London Bridge

The first purpose-built theatre on Bankside (see box, p.230), the **Rose Theatre** was founded by Philip Henslowe in 1587, with Edward Alleyn (founder of Dulwich College) as the lead actor and Christopher Marlowe as its main playwright. Shakespeare's earliest plays, *Titus Andronicus* among them, were first performed here, though Shakespeare then moved to the Rose's great rival, the Globe, just over the road. The discovery of the remains of the Rose Theatre beneath an office block on Park Street in 1989 helped enormously in the reconstruction of the Globe, and the campaign to save the site from the developers galvanized the great and the good of London's theatre world, which ensured the archeological remains were protected beneath the modern building. The outline of the theatre can clearly be traced and is marked out by red lights, but most of the site is flooded to preserve it while funds are gathered for a full excavation. The effect is eerily atmospheric, while the enthusiastic volunteers who open the site once a week, the small exhibition and short video, narrated by Ian McKellan, make it a fascinating place for anyone interested in the history of English theatre. They also use the space for theatre productions (check the website for details and wrap up warm). Close by on Park Street, there's a plaque showing where the Globe actually stood, before it was destroyed in a fire started by a spark from a cannon during a performance of Shakespeare's **Henry VIII**.

Clink Street

Clink Prison Museum 1 Clink St · Mon–Fri 10am–6pm, Sat & Sun 10am–7.30pm; July–Sept closes 9pm · £7.50 · ☎ 020 7403 0900, Ⓦ clink.co.uk · ⊖ London Bridge

Cobbled **Clink Street** is so named as it marks the site of the original **Clink Prison**, which is the origin of the expression "in the clink". The prison began in the twelfth century as a dungeon for disobedient clerics under the Bishop of Winchester's Palace – the **rose window** of the palace's Great Hall has survived here – and later it became a dumping ground for heretics, debtors, prostitutes and a motley assortment of Bankside lowlife, before being burnt to the ground during the 1780 Gordon Riots. The **Clink Prison Museum**, housed in the suitably dismal confines of an old cellar, features prison-life tableaux and dwells on the torture and grim conditions, but, given the rich history of the place, it's a disappointingly lacklustre display.

Golden Hinde

1 Pickfords Wharf, Clink St · Daily 10am–5.30pm, but phone ahead · Tour £7, otherwise £6 · ☎ 020 7403 0123, Ⓦ goldenhinde.com · ⊖ London Bridge

At the east end of Clink Street, in St Mary Overie Dock, sits an exact replica of the **Golden Hinde**, the galleon in which Francis Drake sailed around the world from 1577 to 1580. This version was launched in 1973, and circumnavigated the world for the next twenty years, before eventually settling here in Southwark. The ship is surprisingly small and, with a crew of eighty-plus, must have been cramped, to say the least. There's a refreshing lack of interpretive panels, so it's worth trying to coincide with one of the tours, during which costumed guides show you the ropes, so to speak. Always phone ahead, though, to check that a group hasn't booked the place up.

Southwark Cathedral

Mon–Fri 8am–6pm, Sat & Sun 8.30am–6pm · Free · ☎ 020 7367 6700, Ⓦ cathedral.southwark.anglican.org · ⊖ London Bridge

Built in the thirteenth century as the Augustinian priory church of St Mary Overie, it's a minor miracle that **Southwark Cathedral** survived the nineteenth century, which saw the east-end chapel demolished to make way for London Bridge, railways built within a few feet of the tower and some very heavy-handed Victorian restoration. As if in compensation, the church was given cathedral status in 1905, and has since gone from strength to strength.

Of the original thirteenth-century **interior**, only the choir and retrochoir now remain, separated by a beautiful, high, stone Tudor screen; they are probably the oldest Gothic structures left in London and were used by the Bishop of Winchester as a court – those sentenced ended up in the nearby Clink. The cathedral contains numerous intriguing **monuments**: from a thirteenth-century oak effigy of a knight, to the brightly painted tomb of poet John Gower, Chaucer's contemporary, in the north aisle, his head resting on the three books he wrote – one in Latin, one in French and one in English. The quack doctor Lionel Lockyer has a humorous epitaph in the north transept, and, nearby, there's a chapel dedicated to John Harvard, who was baptized here in 1607 and whose deathbed bequest helped found Harvard College. In the south aisle, an early twentieth-century memorial to Shakespeare (he was a worshipper in the church and his actor brother is buried here) depicts the Bard in green alabaster lounging under a stone canopy. Above the memorial is a postwar stained-glass window featuring a whole cast of characters from the plays.

Borough Market

Mon & Tues some stalls 10am–5pm, Wed & Thurs 10am–5pm, Fri 10am–6pm, Sat 8am–5pm ☎ 020 7407 1002, ⓦ boroughmarket .org.uk • ⊖ London Bridge

Medieval Southwark, also known as **The Borough**, was London's first suburb, clustered round the southern end of London Bridge, the only bridge over the tidal Thames until 1750, and thus the only route south. London Bridge was the most obvious place for the Kent farmers to sell their goods to the City grocers, and there's been a thriving market here since medieval times. The early-morning wholesale fruit and vegetable market winds up around 8am. But the market is best known nowadays for its busy specialist food market (see p.433), with stalls selling top-quality produce from around the world, along with hot food stalls (some of which operate Mon–Sat). The present **Borough Market** sprawls over a fairly large area, under the railway arches, in the Victorian market halls on Stoney Street and encroaching on Southwark Cathedral. Green Market, near the Cathedral, houses the majority of the hot food stalls, while produce – pungent cheeses, unusual wild mushrooms, oysters, game, charcuterie and far more besides – is largely concentrated on the Three Crown Square area between Stoney Street and Borough High Street and along "Middle Road", though the division is not rigid, so you're best off wandering and tasting. The swanky glass entrance foyer just by the bridge on Borough High Street hosts cooking demonstrations on Thursdays and Fridays (12.30–2pm).

15

Borough High Street

As the main road south out of the City, **Borough High Street** was for centuries famous for its **coaching inns**. Chaucer's Canterbury pilgrims set off from *The Tabard* (in Talbot Yard), but by Dickens' time "these great rambling queer old places", as he called them, were closing down. The only extant coaching inn is the **George Inn**, situated in a cobbled yard east off the High Street, dating from 1677 and now owned by the National Trust. Unfortunately, the Great Northern Railway demolished two of the three original galleried fronts, but the lone survivor is a remarkable sight nevertheless, and is still run as a pub (see p.393).

Opposite Borough tube station, at the southernmost end of Borough High Street, is **St George the Martyr**, built in the 1730s, with four clock faces: three white and illuminated at night; one black and pointing towards Bermondsey, whose parishioners refused to give money for the church. To the north of St George's, a wall survives from the **Marshalsea**, the city's main debtors' prison, where Dickens' father (and family) was incarcerated for six months in 1824.

Redcross Way

Redcross Way • **Red Cross Garden** daily 9am–dusk **Cross Bones** garden usually Fri 11am–1pm plus occasional events • ⓦ bost.org.uk & ⓦ crossbones.org.uk • ⊖ London Bridge and Borough

Running parallel with Borough High Street, one block to the west, is **Redcross Way**, a little-visited backstreet that hides a couple of remarkable sights. The first is **Red Cross Garden**, the row of cottage-style model dwellings established by the social reformer (and founder of the National Trust) Octavia Hill, to house the workers from a local rag factory. The row of houses faces onto a miniature village green, complete with village pond. Meanwhile, on the opposite side of the street, is the site of the **Cross Bones cemetery**. It was on this unconsecrated land that the prostitutes who worked on Bankside were buried, and later, the local poor were interred. Local residents have turned the gates, leading to the plot of land, into an impromptu shrine of messages and tokens to those buried, and recently created a Garden of Remembrance on the site. A short vigil is held on the 23rd of every month around 7pm outside the gates.

Old Operating Theatre Museum and Herb Garret

St Thomas St • Daily 10.30am–5pm; closed mid-Dec to early Jan • £6.50; NT members half-price • ☎ 020 7188 2679, ⓦ thegarret .org.uk • ⊖ London Bridge

The most educative and the strangest of Southwark's museums is the **Old Operating Theatre Museum and Herb Garret**. Built in 1822 in the roof of St Thomas' church, where the hospital apothecary's herbs had been stored since 1703, this women's operating theatre was once adjacent to the women's ward of St Thomas' Hospital (now in Lambeth). Despite being gore-free, the museum, reached via a narrow, spiral staircase, is as stomach-churning as the London Dungeon, for this theatre dates from the pre-anaesthetic era.

The surgeons who used this room would have concentrated on speed and accuracy (most amputations took less than a minute), but there was still a thirty percent mortality rate, with many patients simply dying of shock, and many more from bacterial infection (about which very little was known). Sawdust was sprinkled on the floor to soak up the blood and prevent it dripping onto the congregation in the church below. In the herbarium section, you view all sorts of old apothecary paraphernalia, see samples of spices that were used and read up on such delights as the recipe for snail water.

Guy's Hospital

St Thomas St • ⓦ guysandstthomas.nhs.uk • ⊖ London Bridge

Guy's Hospital was founded in 1726 by Thomas Guy, a governor of nearby St Thomas' Hospital, with the money he made in the City's South Sea Bubble fiasco. It was originally established to treat "incurables" discharged by neighbouring St Thomas' Hospital. With its 469ft-high concrete brutalist tower, Guy's is one of the tallest hospitals in the world, but it also retains several original eighteenth-century buildings: the courtyard on the south side of St Thomas Street, with a pretty little **Hospital Chapel**, on the west side of the courtyard. It's worth having a look at the interior with its cheerful light-blue paintwork, raked balconies on three sides and the giant marble and alabaster tomb of the founder, who's depicted welcoming a new patient to the hospital, though in fact Guy died a year before the first patients were admitted. To the south of the courtyard are the old cloisters, which now harbour one of the original alcoves from old London Bridge, with a statue of the poet **John Keats** (who trained as a surgeon at Guy's) seated within.

Bermondsey

Famous in the Middle Ages for its Cluniac abbey, **Bermondsey**, the area east of London Bridge, changed enormously in the nineteenth century. In 1836, the London and Greenwich Railway – the city's first – was built through the district, supported by 878 brick arches stretching for four miles. The area became famous for its wharves, its tanneries and its factories. So much of the city's food – teas, wines, grain, butter, bacon and cheese – was stored here that it was nicknamed "London's Larder". Bermondsey also became infamous for some of the worst social conditions in Victorian London, as Charles Kingsley discovered: "O God! What I saw! People having no water to drink but the water of the common sewer which stagnates full of… dead fish, cats and dogs."

Badly bombed in the Blitz, the docks had closed down by the 1960s. Undergoing extensive redevelopment in the 1980s, much of the original warehouse architecture has been preserved, particularly east of Tower Bridge, around Butler's Wharf. **HMS Belfast**, the cruiser moored near City Hall, is the only permanent maritime link. Nearby the curvaceous dock of Hay's Wharf, built to accommodate tea clippers like the *Cutty Sark*, has been filled and transformed into the **Hay's Galleria** shopping precinct. The area's most popular attraction, however, is of course **The Shard,** London's most recognizable skyscraper.

The Shard

32 London Bridge • April–Oct daily 9am–10pm; Nov–March Mon–Wed & Sun 10am–7pm, Thurs–Sat 10am–10pm • £24.95 online in advance • ☎ 0844 499 7111, Ⓦ theviewfromtheshard.com • ⊖ London Bridge

London's – and the country's – tallest building, Renzo Piano's 1016ft, tapered, glass-clad tower **The Shard** divided opinion when it went up, though in the few short years since it topped out in 2012, the consensus has shifted from it being seen as a monstrous intrusion on an historic city's skyline to being affectionately considered part of the furniture, not least because it's considerably more elegant than some of the newer towers that have shot up since. Though pricey to visit, the view from the two public galleries at the top is sublime, making everything else in London look small, from the unicycle of the London Eye to the tiny little box of St Paul's Cathedral, while the model railway that is London Bridge is played out below you. On a good day, you might see right to the edge of the city and beyond to the North Downs and out past the Thames Barrier to Tilbury Docks. Floor 69 has digital viewfinders that mean you can zoom in on the details, and you can enjoy a £10 glass of champagne while you look around (though if you want to appreciate the views with a drink, then a £16 cocktail at *Aqua Shard* on the 31st floor might be the way to go; Ⓦ aquashard.co.uk). Hair-raising platform 72 is right the top where you can feel the breeze blowing through the crowning shards. Book online; if visibility is extremely poor on the day you visit, you may be eligible for a ticket for a return visit.

London Bridge Experience

2–4 Tooley St • Mon–Fri 10am–5pm, Sat & Sun 10am–6pm • From £17 online • ☎ 020 7403 6333, Ⓦ thelondonbridgeexperience.com • ⊖ London Bridge

Horror fans might enjoy the vaguely historically pertinent **London Bridge Experience**, in the railway vaults on the north side of Tooley Street, the first part of which is a theatrical trot through the history of London Bridge, with guides in period garb hamming up the gory bits. Then, in case you're not scared enough yet, in the **London Tombs** section (no under-11s), more actors, dressed as zombies and murderers, leap out of the foggy gloom to frighten the wits out of you.

HMS Belfast

The Queen's Walk • Daily: March–Oct 10am–6pm; Nov–Feb 10am–5pm • £14.50 • ☎ 020 7940 6300, Ⓦ iwm.org.uk/visits/hms-belfast • ⊖ London Bridge

Permanently moored opposite Southwark Crown Court, the camouflage-painted **HMS Belfast** is an 11,550-ton Royal Navy cruiser. Launched in Belfast in 1938, the *Belfast* spent the first two years of World War II in the Royal Navy shipyards, after being hit by a mine in the Firth of Forth. It later saw action in the 1943 Battle of North Cape and assisted in the D-Day landings before being decommissioned after the Korean War, and becoming an outpost of the Imperial War Museum.

The fun bit is exploring the maze of cabins, workrooms and galleys, scrambling up and down the vertiginous ladders of the ship's seven confusing decks, which could accommodate a crew of over nine hundred. Be sure to check out the very top Flag Deck for the views, and the claustrophobic lowest levels, the Boiler and Engine rooms, a spaghetti of pipes and valves that descend for three levels below water level, from which there was very little chance of escape in the event of the ship being hit; similarly the heavily protected Shell Room on Level -2, where munitions were stored before being loaded onto carousels to be transported up to the guns overhead, gives you a sense of the ship's awesome firepower. Up above, the Gun Turret Experience aims to re-create what it was like when one of these shells was fired, complete with cordite smells and juddering floor.

City Hall

The Queen's Walk • Mon–Thurs 8.30am–6pm, Fri 8.30am–5.30pm • Free • **Café** Mon–Fri 8am–5pm • ☎ 020 7983 4000, ⓦ london.gov.uk • For Scoop events see: ⓦ morelondon.com • ⊖ London Bridge

East of the HMS *Belfast*, overlooking the river, is Norman Foster's startling glass-encased **City Hall**, headquarters for the Greater London Authority and the Mayor of London, which looks like a giant car headlight or fencing mask. Visitors are welcome to stroll up the helical walkway as far as the second floor and watch proceedings or visit the café. Unfortunately "London's Living Room" on the ninth floor, which boasts the best views over the Thames isn't open to the public, except for Open House weekend (see p.27). The amphitheatre outside, **The Scoop**, hosts free events – theatre, outdoor film screenings and music – between June and September. Before you leave the area, be sure to check out Fiona Banner's shiny black *Full Stops*, 3D renditions styled in different fonts and wrought in bronze.

Bermondsey Street

Once the area's high street, **Bermondsey Street** has been transformed over the last decade or so into a trendy strip of cafés, pubs, shops and art galleries. This was also once the heart of the tanning industry – hence Tanner Street, Morocco Street (where much of the leather came from) and Leathermarket Road, which leads to the former **Leather Hide and Wool Exchange** of 1878, decorated with roundels depicting the process of tanning. With Borough Market getting ever busier, an offshoot foodie market has evolved on Saturdays and Sundays under the railway arches on Ropewalk, near **Maltby Street** (see below), at the end of Tanner Street. At the far end of Bermondsey Street on Bermondsey Square, the venerable Bermondsey **antique market** takes place early on Friday mornings (6am–2pm). The market is also known confusingly as the New Caledonian Market, after the prewar flea market that used to take place off Islington's Caledonian Road.

GOURMET BERMONDSEY

The combination of overspill from **Borough Market** (see p.233), a few historic pubs ready to be given a gastro makeover, pretty narrow streets around **Bermondsey Street** and relatively affordable spaces in old warehouses and railway arches has attracted some of those at the forefront of London's gourmet scenes to the neighbourhood. Spanish chef José Pizarro, formerly of *Brindisa* in Borough Market, chose Bermondsey Street for his eponymous tapas bar and nearby restaurant (see p.381), while **Maltby Street**'s (see p.370) reputation is built on the weekend street food market (Sat 9am–4pm, Sun 11am–4pm) and a couple of excellent restaurants, such as *40 Maltby Street* (see p.381). As Maltby Street has become more street food focused, some producers and distributors have moved to the industrial units and railway arches further down in **Spa Terminus** (ⓦwww.spa-terminus.co.uk), near Dockley Road. If you're curious about the provenance of some of the craft beers you see for sale in many London pubs, you could spend a Saturday visiting several small **breweries** that have set up under the arches all along this stretch of railway (sometimes called the "**Bermondsey Beer Mile**"), which open for tastings and trade sales. Try: The Kernel (takeaway only; Spa Terminus, Unit 11, Dockley Road Industrial Estate; Sat 9am–2pm; ⓦthekernelbrewery.com); Partizan (8 Almond Rd; Sat 11am–5pm; ⓦpartizanbrewing.co.uk); and Brew by Numbers (79 Enid St; Sat 10am–5pm; ⓦbrewbynumbers.com).

Fashion and Textile Museum

83 Bermondsey St • Tues–Sat 11am–6pm; Thurs till 8pm; Sun 11am–5pm • £8.80 • ☎ 020 7407 8664, ⓦ ftmlondon.org • ⊖ London Bridge

The **Fashion and Textile Museum** is the lifelong dream of Zandra Rhodes, fashion *grande dame extraordinaire*. Designed by Mexican architect Ricardo Legorreta, and daubed in Rhodes' favourite colours of yellow, pink and orange, the museum (a former cash-and-carry warehouse) is an arresting sight on a street that is otherwise drab architecturally. Rhodes opened her first boutique in the 1960s, and reached the peak of her popularity during the punk era. Her own sartorial taste hasn't changed much in the intervening years, but thankfully FTM's exhibitions are more wide-ranging – from art textiles to 1970s fashion.

White Cube Bermondsey

144–152 Bermondsey St • Tues –Sat 10am–6pm, Sun noon–6pm • Free • ☎ 020 7930 5373, ⓦ whitecube.com

The definitive sign that the London contemporary art scene was shifting south (see box, p.310) and that Bermondsey had come of age was the arrival of an absolutely enormous branch of the high-profile **White Cube** contemporary art gallery. Owned by Old Etonian Jay Jopling, White Cube started out in Mayfair in the 1990s, championing the art of the Young British Artists, such as Damien Hirst and Tracey Emin, opening a branch in Hoxton in 2000 (now closed) and moving south of the river in 2011. Inside, you'll find changing exhibits from an international roster of artists displayed in pristine, light spaces, all polished concrete and white walls.

15

Butler's Wharf

East of Tower Bridge, **Butler's Wharf** is one of the densest networks of Victorian warehousing left in London and one of the most enjoyable parts of Docklands to explore. From Tower Bridge itself (see p.184), you can get a really good view of the old **Anchor Brewhouse**, which produced Courage ales from 1789 until 1982, a cheery, ad hoc sort of building, with a boiler-house chimney at one end and malt-mill tower and cupola at the other. Next door is the original eight-storey **Butler's Wharf**, the largest warehouse complex on the Thames when it was built in 1873. In the 1970s, it became London's largest artists' colony, home to everyone from Derek Jarman to Sid Vicious. Renovated by Terence Conran during the 1980s, the luxury flats and restaurants here came to represent the transformation the city underwent that decade. The buildings are beautifully preserved, fronted by a wide, public, riverside promenade.

Shad Thames, the narrow street at the back of Butler's Wharf, has kept the wrought-iron overhead gangways by which the porters used to transport goods from the wharves to the warehouses further back from the river; it's one of the most atmospheric alleyways in the whole of Docklands. Worth a look, two blocks south on Queen Elizabeth Street, is the **Circle**, a 1980s take on the Victorian "circus", its street facades smothered in shiny cobalt-blue tiles.

Just east of Butler's Wharf, a stylish white Bauhaus-like conversion of an old 1950s banana warehouse designed by Terence Conran, is the original home of the **Design Museum**, located here until June 2016 (daily 10am–5.45pm; £13; ☎ 020 7403 6933, ⓦ designmuseum.org), and due to move to Kensington High Street towards the end of the year (see p.274). The building has been bought by Zaha Hadid, so will retain its association with design and architecture.

St Saviour's Dock

East of Butler's Wharf, a stainless-steel footbridge takes you across **St Saviour's Dock**, a tidal inlet overlooked by swanky warehouse offices (riverside walkway daily: March–Sept 7am–11pm; Oct–Feb 7am–10pm). Spices – cinnamon, nutmeg and cloves, mostly – were stored here until the 1970s, which is reflected in some of the names around here – Java Wharf, Cinnamon Wharf and so on. The footbridge takes you over to **New Concordia Wharf** on Mill Street, one of the first warehouse conversions in the

15

THE THAMES PATH

The **Thames Path** in London runs on both sides of the river all the way from Teddington eastwards; on the south side you can follow it as far as the Thames Barrier (see p.324), with splendid views over to the north bank. It's usually fairly well marked, sticking next to the river where possible, just weaving one street back when buildings get in the way. East from Butler's Wharf, walking the next mile along makes a leisurely way to reach Rotherhithe (though starting from Rotherhithe Overground and walking westwards, means, of course, that the views of Tower Bridge get better with each turn of the path). En route you can stop at *The Angel*, a pub once frequented by Pepys and Captain Cook, which now stands all alone on Bermondsey Wall. Close by are the foundations of Edward III's moated manor house, begun in 1353, and statues of the extraordinary **Salter family**, social reformers who campaigned for the poor of Bermondsey – Ada became mayor of the borough in 1922 (the first female mayor in London), while Alfred, a doctor, provided free medical care, and was later elected MP.

East of here, past the *Mayflower* (see p.394), the path runs parallel to **Rotherhithe Street**, the longest street in London at around a mile and a half. Here you pass mainly residential properties – though there are odd remnants of the dockland past, such as the red swing bridge at the entrance to Surrey Water. It's pleasant enough to walk or cycle along, with great views over to Limehouse and Canary Wharf. You can catch a boat back into town or on to Greenwich from the **Nelson Dock Pier** beside the *Hilton* hotel, where Nelson House is a beautiful Georgian house built for one of the wealthy owners of Nelson Dock. East again, the path runs through **Surrey Docks Farm** (see p.443), when the farm is open, about halfway to the next boat stop, Greenland, by the vast **Greenland** dock (see opposite).

area, completed in 1984. Next door stands the photogenic **China Wharf**, with its stack of semicircular windows picked out in red.

This area was dubbed by the Victorian press "the very capital of cholera". In 1849, the *Morning Chronicle* described it thus: "Jostling with unemployed labourers of the lowest class, ballast heavers, coal-whippers, brazen women, ragged children, and the very raff and refuse of the river, [the visitor] makes his way with difficulty along, assailed by offensive sights and smells from the narrow alleys which branch off." This was the location of Dickens' fictional **Jacob's Island**, a place with "every imaginable sign of desolation and neglect", where Bill Sikes met his end in *Oliver Twist*.

Rotherhithe

Rotherhithe, the thumb of marshy land jutting out into the Thames east of Bermondsey, has always been slightly removed from the rest of London. It was a thriving shipbuilding centre even before the construction of the Surrey Commercial Docks in the nineteenth century. However, no other set of London dockyards took such a hammering in the Blitz, and the immediate postwar decades were years of inexorable decline. The docks have since been reclaimed for housing, and Greenland Dock is also sometimes used for windsurfing and kayaking.

Around St Mary's Church

The bit of Rotherhithe worth visiting is the heart of the old eighteenth-century seafaring village around **St Mary's Church**, which stands in its own leafy square, northwest of the Overground station. The church itself is unremarkable, but it has rich maritime associations: several of the furnishings are made from the timber of the *Fighting Temeraire*, the veteran of Trafalgar which ended its days in a Rotherhithe breaker's yard (Turner's painting of its last voyage hangs in the National Gallery), and the master of the *Mayflower* was buried here. The **Mayflower** was Rotherhithe-owned and -crewed, and set off from outside the *Mayflower* pub in 1620 to transport the

SCANDINAVIAN SEAMEN'S MISSIONS

One of the more unusual legacies of Rotherhithe's seafaring past is the trio of Scandinavian seamen's missions – a reminder of the former dominance of the timber trade in the nearby Surrey Docks – which survive to the south of the tube station, around Albion Street. The most prominent is the **Norwegian Seamen's Church**, by the approach road to the Rotherhithe Tunnel, which features a longboat atop its weather vane. Albion Street itself still has a Scandinavian bent – even the nearby public toilets are bilingual – and further down you'll find the well-maintained **Finnish Seamen's Mission**, built in modernist style in 1958, with a freestanding belfry that looks more like a fire-station practice tower. The **Swedish Seamen's Church**, further south at 120 Lower Rd, completes the trio but is architecturally undistinguished.

Pilgrim Fathers to the New World. (The ship only called in at Plymouth for repairs after being damaged in the English Channel.) The pub (see p.394), north of the church, is a rickety white weatherboarded building, badly damaged in the last war, and a minor pilgrimage site for Americans.

15

Brunel Museum

Railway Ave • Daily 10am–5pm • £3 • ☎ 020 7231 3840, ⓦ brunel-museum.org.uk • ⊖ Rotherhithe

To the northeast of St Mary's, the **Brunel Museum** is a brick-built shed that marks the site of the Thames Tunnel, the world's first under-river tunnel. It was begun in 1825 by Marc Brunel and his more famous son, Isambard, and was originally designed for horse-drawn carriages to travel between Rotherhithe and Wapping. The technology invented by Brunel senior and its basic principles have been used for all subsequent tunnelling. However, plagued by periodic flooding, labour unrest, fatalities and lack of funds, the tunnel took eighteen years to construct and was nicknamed "The Great Bore" by the press.

Funds ran out before the spiral ramps, which would have allowed horse-drawn vehicles actually to use the tunnel, could be built. Instead, in 1843, the tunnel was opened to pedestrians as a tourist attraction, pulling in two million visitors in its first year. It was visited by Queen Victoria, who knighted Brunel junior, but the tunnel soon became the haunt of whores and "tunnel thieves". In 1869 it was taken over by the East London Railway (now the Overground) and remains the most watertight of all the rail tunnels under the Thames. The small museum tells this story and displays some souvenirs from the time.

To the east of the engine house lies the circular working shaft, which now sports a lovely **garden** on its roof, and hosts the *Midnight Apothecary* cocktail bar (May–Sept Sat 5.30–10.30pm; £5 entrance; book in advance). Inside the shaft, the vast Grand Entrance Hall survives and is used to stage a wide variety of music and theatre events – you can clamber inside it on *Midnight Apothecary* nights or as part of a guided tour of the area (see website for details).

Surrey Docks

The once marshy land of Rotherhithe peninsula, east of the old village, was chosen as the site for London's first wet dock, the Howland Great Dock, built in 1696 to take on any extra repair work and refitting emanating from the Royal Dockyards in nearby Deptford. Later renamed **Greenland Dock**, it became part of the network known as **Surrey Commercial Docks**. The main trade was timber, which was piled into stacks up to 80ft high by porters nicknamed "Flying Blondins" (after the tightrope walker), who wore distinctive leather pads on their heads and shoulders to protect them from splinters. The docks took a pounding in the Blitz, and on one occasion, 350,000 tons of timber were set ablaze in one of the largest fires ever seen in Britain.

Hyde Park and Kensington Gardens

Most visitors are amazed at how green and pleasant so much of the city centre is, with three royal parks – St James's Park, Green Park and Hyde Park – forming a continuous grassy belt that stretches for nearly three miles. Hyde Park, together with its westerly extension, Kensington Gardens, is the largest of the trio, covering a distance of a mile and a half from Speakers' Corner in the northeast to Kensington Palace in the southwest. You can jog, swim, fish, sunbathe or mess about in boats on the Serpentine, cross the park on horseback or bike, or view the latest in modern art at the Serpentine Gallery. Leaving the park from the southern borders takes you into one of London's most exclusive districts, the Royal Borough of Kensington and Chelsea (see p.250).

Hyde Park

Daily 5am—midnight • ☏ 0300 061 2000, ⓦ royalparks.org.uk • ⊖ Hyde Park Corner, Marble Arch, Knightsbridge or Lancaster Gate

Seized from the Church by Henry VIII to satisfy his desire for yet more hunting grounds, **Hyde Park** was first opened to the public by James I, when refreshments available included "milk from a red cow". Under Charles II, the park became a fashionable gathering place for the beau monde, who rode round the circular drive known as the Ring, pausing to gossip and admire each other's equipages. Its present appearance is mostly due to Queen Caroline, an enthusiast for landscape gardens, who created the park's main feature, the **Serpentine** lake.

Hangings, muggings and duels, the 1851 Great Exhibition and numerous public events have all taken place here – and it's still a popular gathering point for pop concerts in the summer, Christmas markets in the winter and political demonstrations all year round. For the most part, however, Hyde Park is simply a wonderful open space that allows you to lose all sight of the city beyond a few persistent tower blocks. The southeast corner of the park contains two conventional tourist attractions: **Apsley House**, housing a museum to the Duke of Wellington, and the triumphal **Wellington Arch**, which you can now climb.

Marble Arch

Marble Arch looks rather forlorn on a ferociously busy traffic island at the west end of Oxford Street. Designed in 1828 by John Nash as a triumphal entrance for Buckingham Palace, it has suffered over the years: the sculpted friezes intended to adorn it ended up on the palace, while the equestrian statue of George IV, intended to surmount it, was carted off to Trafalgar Square. When the palace was extended in the 1840s, the arch was moved to form an entrance to Hyde Park, its upper chambers used as a police observation post. During the 1855 riot (see below), a detachment of police emerged from the arch, like the Greeks from the Trojan Horse, much to the surprise of the demonstrators. Today the arch is separated from the park proper by four lanes of traffic and has been accompanied recently by a slightly surreal 33ft-high bronze sculpture of a horse's head by Nic Fiddian-Green.

Tyburn Convent

8 Hyde Park Place • Church daily 6.30am–8.30pm • Guided tours 10.30am, 3.30 & 5.30pm • Free • ⓦ tyburnconvent.org.uk • ⊖ Marble Arch

Despite appearance, Marble Arch stands on the most historically charged spot in Hyde Park, as it marks the site of **Tyburn gallows**, also known as **Tyburn Tree,** the city's main public execution spot from at least 1196 until 1783 (when the action moved to Newgate). There's a pavement plaque on the traffic island in the middle of the junction between Edgware Road and Bayswater Road marking the approximate site of the gallows, where around fifty thousand lost their lives. Among these were the 105 Catholic martyrs who were killed here during the English Reformation, in whose memory the **Tyburn Convent** was established in 1903. It's run by a group of cloistered Benedictine nuns who are happy to show visitors round the basement shrine, underneath the convent church, which contains a mock-up of the Tyburn gibbet over the main altar, and various pictures and relics of the martyrs. The house next door to (and now part of) the convent, no. 10, is reputedly London's smallest, measuring just three and a half feet across.

Speakers' Corner

ⓦ speakerscorner.net • ⊖ Marble Arch

In 1855 an estimated 250,000 people gathered in the northeastern corner of the park to protest against the Sunday Trading Bill (Karl Marx was among the crowd and thought it was the beginning of the English Revolution), and ever since it has been one of London's most popular spots for political demos. In 1872 the government licensed free assembly at **Speakers' Corner**, a peculiarly English Sunday-morning tradition that continues to this day, featuring a motley assortment of ranters and hecklers. Despite

16

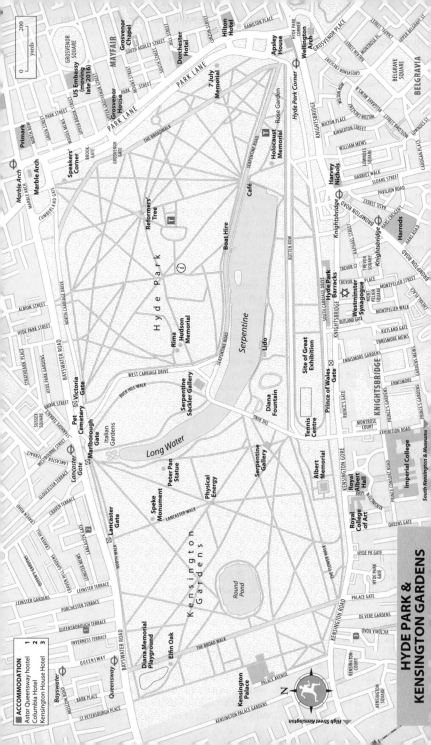

HYDE PARK & KENSINGTON GARDENS

ACCOMMODATION
Astor Queensway hostel 1
Columbia Hotel 2
Kensington House Hotel 3

the park authorities' best attempts, the largest demonstration in London's history took place in this section of the park in 2003 when over a million people turned up to try and stop the war against Iraq. For an oral and visual history of this symbol of free speech and English eccentricity, go to ⓦsoundsfromthepark.org.uk.

Hyde Park Corner

The park's southeast corner, **Hyde Park Corner,** is the site of **Wellington Arch**, which stands at the centre of London's first roundabout. A statue of Wellington no longer graces the arch, but instead stands at ground level opposite his erstwhile residence, **Apsley House** (see p.244). Wellington is depicted seated astride his faithful steed, Copenhagen, who carried the field marshal for sixteen hours during the Battle of Waterloo; the horse died in 1836 and was buried with full military honours at the duke's country pile in Hampshire.

Close by are two powerful war memorials unveiled in 1925: the first, the **Machine Gun Corps Memorial**, features the naked figure of David leaning on Goliath's sword and the chilling inscription, "Saul hath slain his thousands, but David his tens of thousands"; the larger of the two, the **Artillery Memorial**, includes a 9.2-inch howitzer rendered in Portland stone, realistic relief depictions of the brutality of war and the equally blunt, Shakespearean epitaph, "Here was a royal fellowship of death".

These two have since been joined by two much larger, very striking memorials: the **Australian War Memorial** is a gargantuan curved wall of grey granite slabs inscribed with the names of the towns in which the soldiers were born and the battles they fought; opposite stand the sixteen bronze spikes of the **New Zealand Memorial**, each of which is inscribed with text, patterns and sculptures commemorating the bonds between New Zealand and the UK.

Much more conventional in approach (and controversial in subject matter) is the gargantuan **RAF Bomber Command Memorial**, unveiled in 2012, just inside Green Park, on the eastern edge of Hyde Park Corner, as it joins Piccadilly. The tone is decidedly triumphant, with a Neoclassical portico sheltering a larger-than-life air crew amid defiant quotes from Churchill (and Pericles).

16

TYBURN GALLOWS

For nearly five hundred years, **Tyburn** was the capital's main **public execution** site, its three-legged gibbet, known as the "Tyburn Tree" or the "Triple Tree", capable of dispatching over twenty people at one go. Dressed in their best clothes, the condemned were first paraded through the streets in a cart (the nobility were allowed to travel in their own carriages) from Newgate Prison, often with the noose already in place. They received a nosegay (a small bouquet of flowers) at St Sepulchre, opposite the prison, and then a pint of ale at various taverns along the route, so that most were blind drunk by the time they arrived at Tyburn. The driver had to remain sober, however, hence the expression "on the wagon".

The condemned were allowed to make a speech to the crowd and were attended by a chaplain, though according to one eighteenth-century spectator he was "more the subject of ridicule than of serious attention". The same witness describes how the executioner, who drove the cart, then tied the rope to the tree: "This done he gives the horse a lash with his whip, away goes the cart and there swings my gentleman kicking in the air. The Hangman does not give himself the trouble to put them out of their pain but some of their friends or relations do it for them. They pull the dying person by the legs and beat his breast to dispatch him as soon as possible."

Not all relatives were so fatalistic, however, and some would attempt to support the condemned in the hope of a last-minute reprieve, or of reviving the victim when they were cut down. Fights frequently broke out when the body was cut down, between the relatives, the spectators (who believed the corpse had miraculous medicinal qualities) and the surgeons (who were allowed ten corpses a year for dissection). The executioner, known as "**Jack Ketch**" after the famous London hangman, was allowed to take home the victim's clothes, and made further profit by selling the hanging rope by the inch. Following the 1780 Gordon Riots, the powers-that-be took fright at unruly gatherings like Tyburn, and in 1783 the Tyburn Tree was demolished.

Wellington Arch

Hyde Park Corner • Daily: April–Sept 10am–6pm; Oct 10am–5pm; Nov–March 10am–4pm • EH • £4.30, concessions £3.90, under-16s £2.60 • ⊖ Hyde Park Corner

Designed by a youthful Decimus Burton in 1828 to commemorate Wellington's victories in the Napoleonic Wars, **Wellington Arch** originally served as the northern entrance to Buckingham Palace. Positioned opposite Burton's delicate Hyde Park Screen, the arch once formed part of a fine architectural ensemble with Apsley House, Wellington's London residence, and the former St George's Hospital, now the *Lanesborough Hotel*. Unfortunately the symmetry was destroyed when the arch was repositioned in 1883 to line up with Constitution Hill – named after the "constitutional" walks that Charles II used to take here. The arch's original statue was an enormous equestrian portrayal of the "Iron Duke" erected in 1846 while he was still alive. The duke was taken down in 1883, and eventually replaced by Peace and her four-horse chariot, erected in 1912. Inside, you can view a permanent exhibition on the history of the arch, and special exhibitions on England's heritage, and take a lift to the top of the monument (once London's smallest postwar police station) where the exterior balconies offer a bird's-eye view of the swirling traffic of London's first-ever roundabout, established in 1962.

Apsley House

149 Piccadilly • Wed–Sun: April–Oct 11am–5pm; Nov–March 11am–4pm • EH • £8.30, concessions £7.50, under-16s £5 • ⊖ Hyde Park Corner

Known during the Iron Duke's lifetime as "Number One, London", **Apsley House**, opposite Wellington Arch, was once an immensely desirable residence, but nowadays, overlooking a very busy roundabout, it would be poor reward for any national hero. The interior isn't what it used to be either, but in this case it's Wellington who's to blame. Built and exquisitely decorated by Robert Adam in the 1770s for Baron Apsley, it was

16

THE IRON DUKE

Perhaps if the **Duke of Wellington** had died, like Nelson, at his moment of greatest triumph, he too would enjoy an unsullied posthumous reputation. Instead, the famously blunt duke went on to become the epitome of the outmoded, reactionary conservative, earning his famous nickname, the "Iron Duke", not from his fearless military campaigning, but from the iron shutters he had to install at Apsley House after his windows were broken by demonstrators rioting in favour of the 1832 Reform Act, to which the duke was vehemently opposed.

Born **Arthur Wesley** in Dublin in 1769 – the same year as Napoleon – he never considered himself Irish: "just because you're born in a stable, doesn't make you a horse" he is alleged to have said. He was educated at (but hated) Eton and the French military academy at Angers, and campaigned out in India, helping to defeat Tipu Sultan and becoming Governor of Mysore. After continued military success in his Napoleonic campaigns, he eventually became Duke of Wellington in 1814, shortly before achieving his most famous victory of all at Waterloo.

With great reluctance he became **prime minister** in 1828, "a station, to the duties of which I am unaccustomed, in which I was not wished, and for which I was not qualified… I should have been mad if I had thought of such a thing." Despite his own misgivings, his government passed the Catholic Relief Act – allowing Catholics to sit in Parliament – thus avoiding civil war in Ireland, but splitting the Tory ranks. Accused of popery by the Earl of Winchelsea, Wellington challenged him to a duel in Battersea Park; the duke fired and missed (he was a notoriously bad shot), while the earl shot into the air and apologized for the slur.

Wellington's opposition to the 1832 Reform Act brought down his government and allowed the Whigs (under Earl Grey, of tea fame) to form a majority government for the first time in sixty years. Despite retiring from public life in 1846, he was on hand to organize the defence of the capital against the Chartists in 1848, and strolled across to the Great Exhibition every day in 1851. Two million people lined the streets for his funeral in 1852 (more than for anyone before or since), and he has more outdoor statues (and pubs named after him) in London than any other historical figure. Despite this, his greatest legacy is, of course, the **Wellington boot**, originally made of leather, now rubber.

HYDE PARK STATUES AND MEMORIALS

Hyde Park is peppered with statues, none more colossal than the 18ft-high bronze of **Achilles**, in the southeastern corner of the park, designed in 1822 by Richard Westmacott to commemorate the Duke of Wellington, and cast from captured French cannon. As the country's first public nude statue it caused outrage, especially since many thought it a portrait of the duke himself, and the chief fundraisers were "the women of Great Britain". In actual fact, it represents neither the duke nor Achilles, but is a copy of one of the Horse Tamers from the Quirinal Hill in Rome. William Wilberforce led a campaign to have the statue removed for decency's sake; a fig leaf was added in the appropriate place as a compromise.

Visible to the north is the **July 7 Memorial**, a simple, startling memorial to the 2005 London suicide bombings. The 52 stainless steel pillars stand nearly 12ft high, and each one is inscribed with the victim's time and cause of death. Only a short distance to the west, in The Dell, a couple of boulders set in gravel within a copse of silver birch, form an even more understated **Holocaust Memorial**.

To the north of the nearby Serpentine stands the park's over-manicured bird sanctuary, overlooked by the **Hudson Memorial**, sculpted by Jacob Epstein and featuring a low relief of Rima, a naked, female, South American version of Tarzan, and several exotic birds. (Rima the Jungle Girl is the main protagonist in the 1904 adventure novel *Green Mansions*, written by the naturalist and writer W.H. Hudson.) It's difficult to believe now, but when the memorial was unveiled in 1925, there was a campaign of protest against the statue, led by the *Daily Mail*. Rima was considered too butch, the art too "Bolshevist", and the memorial later became the victim of several (anti-Semitic) attacks.

16

remodelled by Benjamin Wyatt after Wellington bought the place in 1817. Wyatt faced the red-brick exterior with Bath stone and more or less got rid of the Adam interiors. As a result, the house is very much as it would have been in Wellington's day, and the current duke, Charles Wellesley, still lives with his family on the upper floors.

The art collection

The house is worth visiting for the **art collection** alone. Wellington acquired the paintings in 1813 after the Battle of Vittoria, when he seized the baggage train of Napoleon's brother, Joseph, who was fleeing for France with two hundred paintings belonging to the King of Spain. The best pieces, including works by de Hooch, Van Dyck, Goya, Rubens and Murillo, cover the red walls of the **Waterloo Gallery** on the first floor, where sliding mirrors cover the windows. The most prized works of all are a trio by Velázquez – *The Water-Seller of Seville, Portrait of a Gentleman* and *Two Young Men Eating at a Humble Table* – though Wellington preferred Correggio's *Agony in the Garden*, the key for which he used to carry round with him, so he could take the picture out of its frame and dust it fondly.

The rooms

Like several of the house's other rooms, the Waterloo Gallery was originally hung with yellow satin, which, as one of the duke's friends lamented, "is just the very worst colour he can have for the pictures and will kill the effect of the gilding". It was here that Wellington held his annual veterans' **Waterloo Banquet**, using the thousand-piece silver-gilt Portuguese service, now displayed in the rather lugubrious **Dining Room** at the other end of the house. Most of the Waterloo portraits are, in fact, hung in the adjacent **Striped Drawing Room**, which is decorated like a military tent in the manner of Napoleon's Loire chateau, Malmaison.

Canova's famous, more than twice life-sized, **nude statue of Napoleon** stands at the foot of the main staircase, having been bought by the government for the duke in 1816. It was disliked by the sitter, not least for the tiny figure of Victory in the emperor's hand, which appears to be trying to fly away. In the dimly lit **Plate and China Room**, also on the ground floor, you can view numerous gifts to the duke, including a four hundred-piece Prussian dinner service decorated with scenes of Wellington's life, and the bizarre Egyptian service, which was originally a divorce present from Napoleon to Josephine; unsurprisingly, she rejected it and Louis XVIII ended up giving it to the duke. In the basement there's plenty of Wellingtonia, a goodly selection of cruel, contemporary caricatures and a pair of the famous boots.

Rotten Row

Just inside the grand Neoclassical entrance to the park, known as the Hyde Park Screen, which stands beside Apsley House, two thoroughfares set off west to Kensington: South Carriage Drive, a road which is open to cars, and **Rotten Row**, which remains a bridle path. The name is thought to be a corruption of *route du roi* (king's way), after William III who established it as a bridle path linking Westminster and Kensington. William had three hundred oil lamps hung from the trees to try to combat the increasing number of highwaymen active in the park, thus making Rotten Row the first road in the country to be lit at night. The measure was only partly successful – George II himself was later mugged here. To the south of Rotten Row, the **Hyde Park Barracks** are difficult to miss, thanks to Basil Spence's uncompromising 308ft-tall concrete residential tower block. Early in the morning, you might catch sight of the Household Cavalry exercising in the park, and at around 10.30am daily (Sun 9.30am) they set off for the Horse Guards building in Whitehall for Changing the Guard (see p.48).

The Serpentine

16

Rowing boats and pedalos Easter–Oct; £12/hr per adult, £5/hr per child **Solarshuttle** Sat, Sun and public holidays all year; June–Aug daily every 30min noon–dusk • One way £2.50

The Serpentine, Hyde Park's curvaceous lake, was created in 1730 by damming the Westbourne, a small tributary of the Thames, so that Queen Caroline might have a spot for the royal yachts to mess about on. A miniature re-enactment of the Battle of Trafalgar was staged here in 1814, and two years later Shelley's pregnant wife, Harriet Westbrook, drowned herself after the poet had eloped with the 16-year-old Mary Wollstonecraft Godwin. The popular **Lido** (see p.439) is on the south bank, alongside its lovely café, and rowing boats and pedalos can be rented from the **Boathouse** on the north bank. The solar-powered **Solarshuttle** boat ferries folk from one bank to the other in summer.

Diana Fountain

Daily: March & Oct 10am–6pm; April–Aug 10am–8pm; Sept 10am–7pm; Nov–Feb 10am–4pm • Free • ⊖ Knightsbridge or Lancaster Gate

Close to the Lido is the **Diana Fountain**, a memorial to the Princess of Wales, which opened in 2004. Less of a fountain, and more of a giant oval-shaped mini-moat, the intention was to allow children to play in the running water, but, after three people suffered minor injuries, the fountain has been fenced off and supplied with security guards, making it rather less fun for kids, who are now officially only allowed to dabble their feet. More fun is the **Diana Memorial Playground**, in the northwest corner of Kensington Gardens, featuring a ship stuck in sand, paving gongs and other imaginative playthings (though at busy times you may have to queue to get in).

ROYAL GUN SALUTES

At noon in Hyde Park on February 6 (Accession Day), April 21 (Queen's Birthday) and November 14 (Prince of Wales's Birthday), the Royal Horse Artillery wheel out cannons and the park resounds to a 41-round **Royal Gun Salute**. If a date falls on a Sunday, then the salute takes place the next day. Further gun salutes take place in Green Park, on 2 June (Coronation Day), 10 June (Duke of Edinburgh's Birthday), at 11.08am for the State Opening of Parliament (in early May) and at 11am on the Queen's official birthday (a variable date in June), as well as for official State visits.

Kensington Gardens

Daily 6am to dusk • ☎ 020 7298 2141, Ⓦ royalparks.org.uk • ➌ Lancaster Gate, Queensway or High Street Kensington

The park's more tranquil half, west of the West Carriage Drive, is known as **Kensington Gardens**, and is, strictly speaking, separate from Hyde Park, though the only difference is that Kensington Gardens locks its gates at dusk. More exclusive because of the nearby royalty at Kensington Palace, the gardens were first opened to the public in George II's reign, but only on Sundays and only to those in formal dress, not including sailors, soldiers or liveried servants. Unrestricted access was only granted in Victoria's reign, by which time, according to the Russian ambassador's wife, the park had already been "annexed as a middle-class rendezvous. Good society no longer [went] there except to drown itself."

Long Water

The upper section of the Serpentine – beyond the bridge – is, officially, actually known as the **Long Water**, and is by far the prettiest section of the lake. It narrows until it reaches the lovely **Italian Gardens**, which boasts a group of five fountains, laid out symmetrically in the 1860s, in front of a pumphouse disguised as an Italianate loggia.

Pet Cemetery

To the east of the Italian Gardens, by Victoria Gate, lies the odd little **Pet Cemetery**, begun in the 1880s when Mr and Mrs J. Lewis Barnes buried their Maltese terrier, Cherry, here. When the Duke of Cambridge buried his wife's pet hound at the same spot after it had been run over on Bayswater Road, it became *the* place to bury your pooch; three hundred other cats and dogs followed, until the last burial in 1967. The cemetery – "perhaps the most horrible spectacle in Britain", according to George Orwell – is no longer open to the public, though you can peep over the wall.

16

THE GREAT EXHIBITION AND THE CRYSTAL PALACE

South of the Serpentine was the site of the **Great Exhibition** of the Works and Industry of All Nations, held between May 1 and October 15, 1851. The idea originated with Henry Cole, a minor civil servant in the Record Office, and was taken up enthusiastically by Prince Albert despite opposition from snooty Kensington residents, who complained it would attract an "invasion of undesirables who would ravish their silver and their serving maids". A competition to design the exhibition building produced 245 rejected versions, until Joseph Paxton, head gardener to the Duke of Devonshire, offered to build his "**Crystal Palace**", a wrought-iron and glass structure some 1848ft long and 408ft wide. The acceptance of Paxton's radical proposal was an act of faith by the exhibition organizers, since such a structure had never been built, and their faith was amply rewarded – two hundred workers completed the building in just four months.

As well as showing off the achievements of the **British Empire**, it was also a unique opportunity for people to enjoy the products of other cultures. Thousands of exhibits were housed in the Crystal Palace, including the Koh-i-Noor diamond (displayed in a birdcage), an Indian ivory throne, a floating church from Philadelphia, a bed which awoke its occupant by ejecting him or her into a cold bath, false teeth designed not to be displaced when yawning, a fountain running with eau de Cologne and all manner of china, fabrics and glass.

To everyone's surprise, **six million visitors** came, and the exhibition made a profit, which was used to buy 87 acres of land south of Kensington Road, for the creation of a "Museumland" where "the arts and sciences could be promoted and taught in a way which would be of practical use to industry and make Britain the leading country of the industrialized world". The Crystal Palace itself was dismantled after the exhibition and rebuilt in southeast London in 1854, where it served as a concert hall, theatre, menagerie and exhibition space, only to be destroyed by fire in 1936 (see p.312).

Serpentine Gallery

Tues–Sun 10am–6pm; Pavilion mid-June to mid-Oct • Free • ☎ 020 7402 6075, ⊕ serpentinegalleries.org • ⊖ Knightsbridge or South Kensington

Alongside the southern section of West Carriage Drive stands the **Serpentine Gallery**, built as a tea room in 1908 because the park authorities thought "poorer visitors" might otherwise cause trouble if left without refreshments. An art gallery since the 1960s, it has a reputation for lively, and often controversial, contemporary art exhibitions, and contains an excellent bookshop. Each year, the gallery also commissions a leading architect to indulge his or her experimental impulses and design an innovative temporary **pavilion** for its summer-only teahouse extension.

A second exhibition building, the **Serpentine Sackler Gallery**, is 300m up West Carriage Drive on the northern side of the Serpentine. It's housed in a former munitions depot, built in 1805 so that the military could arm themselves in the event of a "foreign invasion or popular uprising". The original building was designed in the style of a Palladian villa, but its restoration included an ultra-modern extension by Zaha Hadid, with an undulating roof, site of **The Magazine** restaurant (Tues–Thurs & Sun 9am–6pm, Fri & Sat 9am–11pm). The gallery is exclusively for temporary exhibitions, usually of modern avant-garde art, often installation pieces.

Albert Memorial

45min guided tours March–Dec first Sun of month, 2 & 3pm • £8, concessions £7 • ☎ 020 7495 0916, ⊕ royalparks.org.uk • ⊖ South Kensington

Completed in 1876 by George Gilbert Scott, the **Albert Memorial**, on the south side of Kensington Gardens, is as much a hymn to the glorious achievements of Britain as to its subject, Queen Victoria's husband (who died of typhoid in 1861, aged 42), who sits under its central canopy, gilded from head to toe and clutching a catalogue for the 1851 Great Exhibition. The pomp of the monument is overwhelming: the spire, inlaid with semiprecious stones and marbles, rises to 180ft; a marble frieze around the pediment is cluttered with 169 life-sized figures (all men) in high relief, depicting poets, musicians, painters, architects and sculptors from ancient Egypt onwards; the pillars are topped with bronzes of Astronomy, Chemistry, Geology and Geometry; mosaics show Poetry, Painting, Architecture and Sculpture; four outlying marble groups represent the four continents; and other statuary pays homage to Agriculture, Commerce and other aspects of imperial economics. Albert would not have been amused: "I can say, with perfect absence of humbug, that I would rather not be made the prominent feature of such a monument…it would upset my equanimity to be permanently ridiculed and laughed at in effigy", he once claimed. To get inside the memorial railings you will have to join a guided tour.

PETER PAN & CO

The best-known of all the park's outdoor monuments is **Peter Pan**, the fictional character who enters London along the Serpentine and whose statue stands by the west bank of the Long Water; fairies, squirrels, rabbits, birds and mice scamper round the pedestal. It was in Kensington Gardens that the author, J.M. Barrie, used to walk his dog, and it was here that he met the five pretty, upper-class Llewellyn Davies boys, who wore "blue blouses and bright red tam o'shanters" and were the inspiration for the "Lost Boys", and whose guardian he eventually became. Barrie himself paid for the statue, which was erected in secret during the night in 1912.

The rough-hewn muscleman struggling with his horse, to the southwest of Peter Pan, is G.F. Watts' **Physical Energy**, a copy of the Rhodes memorial in Cape Town; to the north is a granite obelisk raised to **John Hanning Speke**, who was the first non-African to find the source of the Nile, and who died in 1864 after accidentally shooting himself rather than the partridge he was aiming at. Just outside the Diana Memorial Playground is the **Elfin Oak**, a gnarled stump from Richmond Park, carved with little animals and mystical creatures by children's-book illustrator Ivor Innes in the late 1920s.

Kensington Palace

Daily: March–Oct 10am–6pm; Nov–Feb 10am–5pm; last admission 1hr before close • March–Oct £17.50, concessions £14.10; Nov–Feb £16.50, concessions £13.70; under-16s free all year • ☎ 020 3166 6000, ⚙ hrp.org.uk • ⊖ Queensway or High Street Kensington

On the western edge of Kensington Gardens stands **Kensington Palace**, a modestly proportioned, Jacobean brick mansion bought as an out-of-town residence by William and Mary in 1689. Wren, Hawksmoor and later William Kent were called in to embellish the place, though the palace was actually chief royal residence for barely fifty years.

Queen Victoria was born in Kensington Palace in 1819 and spent her dull, sad childhood cooped up here with her strict mother, the Duchess of Kent, who slept with her in the same room. According to her diary, her best friends were the palace's numerous "black beetles". Victoria's apartments have not been preserved, but you get to see the gloomy Red Saloon, where the 18-year-old queen held her first Privy Council meeting, just hours after William IV's death on June 20, 1837.

Nowadays, KP – as it's fondly known in royal circles – is the official London residence of Prince William and Kate Middleton. It's also where William's mother, **Princess Diana**, lived until her death in 1997, although there's no access to her rooms, which were on the west side of the palace, where the dukes and duchesses of Kent and Gloucester all still live.

The palace regularly displays items of dress from the **Royal Ceremonial Dress Collection**, in temporary exhibitions. Usually you get to see a few of the Queen's dresses and various other garments from the royal wardrobe.

KP's most handsome facade faces south, behind a flamboyant statue of William III, given to Edward VII by the Kaiser. The public entrance is on the east side, and is best approached from the Round Pond, where George I used to keep his edible turtles, and the Broad Walk, a favourite rollerblading avenue; both are overlooked by a flattering statue of Queen Victoria sculpted by her daughter, Princess Louise.

16

INFORMATION

Tours Some of KP's themed tours change from year to year, others, like the State Apartments, are permanent.

Eating To the north of the palace there's a lovely café in Hawksmoor's Orangery, built for Queen Anne as a summer dining room, and decorated with carving and statues by Grinling Gibbons.

King's State Apartments

The palace's most impressive rooms are in the **King's State Apartments**, beginning with the grandiose **King's Staircase**, designed by William Kent, with its Irish black marble steps, its Tijou wrought-iron balustrade and trompe-l'oeil crowds of courtiers and yeomen. Another great Kent creation is the "grotesque"-style painting on the ceiling of the **Presence Chamber**, which also features a lovely pear-wood Gibbons overmantle with weeping putti. Further on, the **Cupola Room**, with its chunky, musical clock occupying centre stage, features another wonderful trompe-l'oeil fresco, which gives the effect of a coffered dome. The palace's grandest room, the **King's Gallery**, has red damask walls hung with paintings by, among others, Tintoretto. Also of interest is the wind dial above the fireplace, connected to the palace weather vane; built for William III, it is still functioning.

Queen's State Apartments

The **Queen's State Apartments** begin with the **Queen's Gallery**, once magnificently decorated with 154 pieces of Oriental porcelain (a mere handful remain), and instead lined with royal portraits, all part of the Royal Collection and rotated periodically. The Queen's Apartments are much more modest than the King's: wood-panelled rooms hung with Dutch works reflecting the tastes of William and Mary. The **Queen's Closet** was the scene of a furious quarrel between Queen Anne and her rumoured lover, the Duchess of Marlborough, after which they never saw each other again. The best original decor is in the **Queen's Bedchamber**, which boasts a four-poster bed that belonged to Queen Mary of Modena, James II's second wife – it was here that the diminutive and corpulent Queen Anne died of gout.

ROYAL ALBERT HALL

South Kensington, Knightsbridge and Chelsea

The Royal Borough of Kensington and Chelsea has been in vogue ever since royalty moved into Kensington Palace in the late seventeenth century. The popular tourist attractions lie in South Kensington, home to three of London's top museums – the V&A, Natural History and Science museums. Chelsea, to the south, also also has royal connections, though these date mostly from Tudor times and have left only a few scant remains. From the nineteenth century, when artists and writers began to move here, Chelsea became more bohemian than its neighbours – and even developed a rebellious streak in the 1960s and 70s. Today, however, it's far from cutting edge and has become a byword for posh London.

South Kensington

17

South Kensington, with its remarkable cluster of **museums and colleges**, plus the vast Royal Albert Hall, stands as one of London's most enlightened examples of urban planning. This impressive concentration of education and culture has its origins in the 1851 Great Exhibition (see p.251), a vast demonstration of the cultural diversity and productive industry of the British Empire, which to everyone's surprise was not only an enormous success, but also actually yielded a profit. Prince Albert and his committee, the men behind the exhibition, bought 87 acres of land here with the proceeds and established a kind of "**Museumland**", whose purpose was to "extend the influence of Science and Art upon Productive Industry". Albert died of typhoid in 1861 at the age of just 42, and was not around to witness the full realization of his dream, the area sometimes referred to as "Albertopolis".

With the founding of "Museumland", the surrounding area was transformed almost overnight into one of the most fashionable in town. Fields, farms and private estates were turned into street after street of ostentatious, whitewashed Italianate terraces, grandiose red-brick mansions and mews houses. Today, the borough includes some of the world's most expensive slices of real estate, and is the heartland of London's wealthiest families and also the stamping ground of the international rich and famous.

Victoria and Albert Museum (V&A)

Cromwell Rd • Daily 10am–5.45pm, Fri until 10pm • Free • Various free tours set off regularly from the meeting point in the Grand Entrance • ☏ 020 7942 2000, ⓦ vam.ac.uk • ⊖ South Kensington

For variety and scale, the **Victoria and Albert Museum** is the world's leading museum of decorative arts and design, with significant collections of paintings and performance art too. The range of exhibits on display means that whatever your taste, there's bound to be something to grab your attention: the finest collection of Italian sculpture outside Italy, the world's largest collection of Indian art outside India, plus extensive Chinese, Islamic and Japanese galleries; a gallery of twentieth-century objets d'art; and more Constable paintings than Tate Britain. The V&A's temporary shows on art, photography and fashion – some of which you have to pay for – are among the best in Britain. As Baedeker noted in 1905, "it can hardly be claimed that the arrangements of the [museum] are specially perspicuous". Beautifully but haphazardly displayed across a seven-mile, four-storey maze of rooms, the V&A's treasures are impossible to survey in a single visit, so get hold of a **free floor plan** to help you decide which areas to focus on.

The V&A began life in 1852 as the Museum of Manufactures – it being Albert's intention to bolster Britain's industrial dominance by inspiring factory workers, students and craftspeople with examples of excellence in applied art and design. Later it was renamed the South Kensington Museum, with Queen Victoria laying the foundation stone in 1857. She was on hand again to give her blessing to the present, deeply colonial building in 1899 (her last major public engagement), after which it was known as the Victoria and Albert Museum; ten years later Aston Webb's imposing main entrance, with its octagonal cupola, flying buttresses and pinnacles, was finished. The side entrance on Exhibition Road, originally built in 1873 for the School of Naval Architects, is equally ornate, with terracotta arcading and Minton tiles.

Raphael Cartoons

The most famous of the V&A's many exhibits are the **Raphael Cartoons** (room 48a) – from the Italian *cartone* meaning a large piece of paper. They comprise seven vast, full-colour paintings in distemper, which are, in fact, designs for tapestries ordered in 1515 by Pope Leo X for the Sistine Chapel. The pictures – based on episodes from the New Testament – were bought by the future Charles I and subsequently reproduced in countless tapestries and engravings, thereby becoming more familiar and influential than any of the artist's paintings. Alongside the paintings is an example of one of the tapestries woven at Mortlake.

17

At the far end of the room stands the **Retable of St George**, a huge fifteenth-century gilded altarpiece from Valencia, centred on a depiction of James I of Aragon defeating the Moors at the Battle of Puig in 1237. More alarming, though, are the bloodthirsty side panels, which feature the gross tortures endured by St George, with him having nails driven through his body before being placed in a cauldron of molten lead, dragged naked through the streets and finally beheaded and sawn in half.

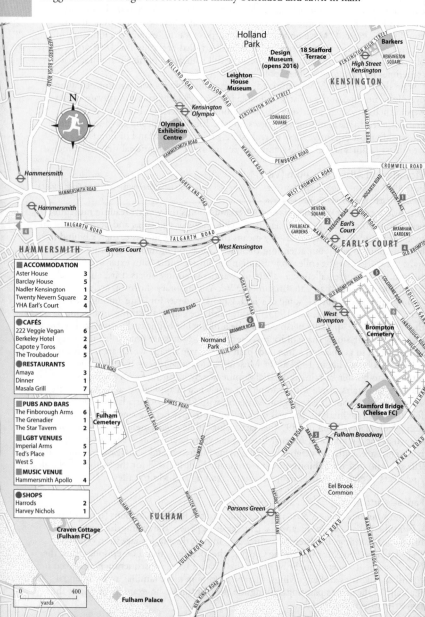

ACCOMMODATION

Aster House	3
Barclay House	5
Nadler Kensington	1
Twenty Nevern Square	2
YHA Earl's Court	4

CAFÉS

222 Veggie Vegan	6
Berkeley Hotel	2
Capote y Toros	4
The Troubadour	5

RESTAURANTS

Amaya	3
Dinner	1
Masala Grill	7

PUBS AND BARS

The Finborough Arms	6
The Grenadier	1
The Star Tavern	2

LGBT VENUES

Imperial Arms	5
Ted's Place	7
West 5	3

MUSIC VENUE

| Hammersmith Apollo | 4 |

SHOPS

| Harrods | 2 |
| Harvey Nichols | 1 |

South Asia

Such are the constraints of space that a mere fraction of the world-class **South Asia** collection is displayed (room 41), much of it derived from London's former East India Company Museum. The most popular exhibit is **Tipu's Tiger**, a life-sized wooden automaton of a tiger mauling an officer of the East India Company; the innards of the tiger feature a miniature keyboard which simulates the groans of the dying soldier. It

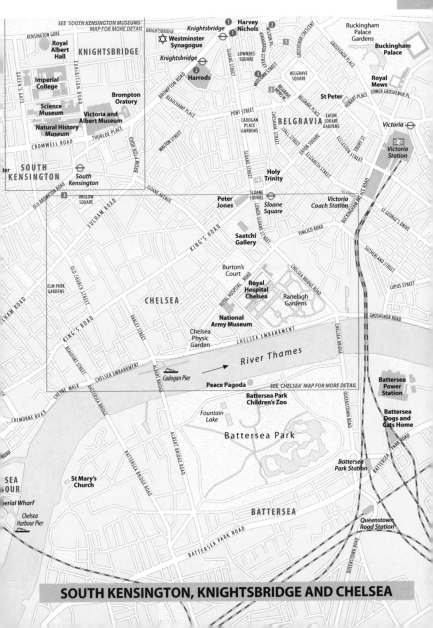

SOUTH KENSINGTON, KNIGHTSBRIDGE AND CHELSEA

17

was made for the amusement of Tipu Sultan, who was killed when the British took Seringapatam in 1799, and whose watch, telescope, brooch and sword are also displayed here. Close by is the **Golden Throne**, revered by the Sikh community as it belonged to **Ranjit Singh**, the first and last Sikh emperor, and was taken by the British when they annexed the Punjab in 1849. Next to it is a conical turban decorated with quoits, which can be taken off and hurled at your enemy. Elsewhere, there's a superb white nephrite-jade wine cup, carved in the shape of a shell, made for the Mogul emperor Shah Jahan.

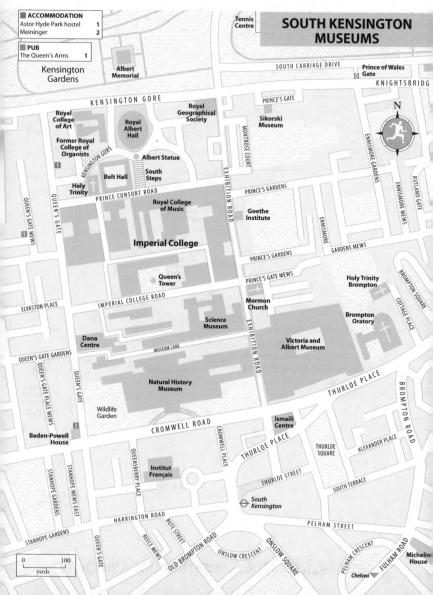

Islam

The **Islamic Middle East** gallery (room 42), next door, has, as its centrepiece, the silk-and-wool **Ardabil Carpet**, the world's oldest dated Persian carpet, from 1540: copies have variously adorned the floors of 10 Downing Street and Hitler's Berlin office. Unusually, on the west side of the gallery, there are several oil paintings of female acrobats, a harem tea party and several full-length portraits from the Qajar dynasty in nineteenth-century Iran.

China and Japan

In the **China** gallery (room 44), the range of materials, from jade to ceramic, lacquer to lapis lazuli, is more striking than any individual piece, though the pair of top-hatted gentlemen carved in marble stand out in the parade of Buddhas near the entrance – they are thought to represent Korean envoys. There's a surprising range, from a sixteenth-century Ming cupboard that's so minimalist, it could be modernist, to a great Art Deco clock from fashionable interwar Shanghai.

The adjacent **Japan** gallery (room 45) shows a wealth of silk, lacquer and samurai armour; look out for the tiny, elaborately carved, jade and marble *netsuke* (belt toggles) portraying such quirky subjects as "spider on aubergine", "starving dog on a bed of leaves" and "badger dressed in a lotus leaf".

Cast Courts

Two enormous **Cast Courts** (rooms 46a & 46b), one of which, the Weston Cast Court (46b), was reopened after renovation in 2014, are filled with plaster casts of famous works of art and architecture. Created at the outset of the V&A, the courts allowed ordinary Londoners to experience the glories of classical and ancient art. In room 46a, a copy of the colossal Trajan's Column, sliced in half to fit in the room, towers over the rest of the plaster casts, while over in room 46b, a life-sized replica of Michelangelo's *David* stands among the pulpits of Pisa cathedral and baptistry, and Ghiberti's celebrated bronze doors for the baptistry in Florence.

Sculpture

Along the south side of the central garden (rooms 21–24), in the V&A's showpiece **Sculpture** display, you'll find **Bernini**'s life-sized fountain sculpture, *Neptune and Triton*, amid a whole series of top-notch Italian pieces. Other highlights include Canova's depiction of Theseus astride the Minotaur, and his head of Helen of Troy about which Byron wrote an eight-line paean. **Auguste Rodin** donated several sculptures to the V&A in 1914, including his beautifully wrought *The Fallen Angel*, a swirling mass of rippling bronze, and his sensuous *Cupid and Psyche*, in which the lovers emerge half-hewn from the white marble. Look out, too, for a torso by Meštrovic, several strikingly simple works by Eric Gill and an Art Deco fireplace with a relief depicting society gossip.

RECENT AND FUTURE DEVELOPMENTS

Like most big museums, the V&A is in a constant state of flux. It is currently in the midst of an ambitious programme of renovation and transformation to provide new exhibition spaces and facilities for visitors as well as to restore original architectural elements to historic galleries. The most ambitious of these transformations is the Exhibition Road project, providing a new entrance, courtyard and purpose-built subterranean gallery for temporary exhibitions, all due to open to the public in early 2017. These changes form part of the V&A's extensive and ongoing FuturePlan renovation programme, which started in 2001. Since then, 27,000 square metres of public space has been restored and redesigned and 5000 square metres of back of house space has been transformed and brought into the public domain, creating new and renovated Furniture galleries and Fashion galleries as well as the Weston Cast Court and, most recently, having reopened at the end 2015, the new Europe 1600–1800 collections spaces.

17

There's also a bridge room with **small-scale sculpture** on Level 3 (room 111) which reveals a marvellous view into the Cast Courts. The display ranges from medieval religious ivories and English alabaster relief panels to German lime-wood masterpieces and a whole collection of works by Gilbert Bayes, who worked at Doulton, the ceramics company (Bayes' Art Deco Doulton frieze from the company's headquarters in Lambeth is displayed in room 127).

Medieval & Renaissance 300–1600

To visit the V&A's outstanding **Medieval & Renaissance** galleries chronologically, head for the lower-level galleries (Level 0, room 8–10c), where the highlights include the **Gloucester Candlestick**, a mass of gilded foliage and figures commissioned for the city's Benedictine abbey around 1104, and the **Becket Casket**, a Romanesque reliquary in Limoges enamel designed to house the English saint's relics. Don't miss the German altarpiece, painted around 1400 and decorated with 45 vivid scenes from the Apocalypse.

The collection continues into the Renaissance upstairs (Level 2, rooms 62–64b), where you'll find the **Burghley Nef**, a slightly ludicrous sixteenth-century French gilded silver salt cellar in the shape of a ship. Even more incredible craftsmanship is on view in the Italian carved pearwood altarpiece, which features a complex crucifixion scene. Other highlights include a Tintoretto self-portrait, one of Leonardo's tiny notebooks and Donatello's *Chellini Madonna*, a bronze roundel given by the artist to his doctor in lieu of payment – the reverse was designed to cast replicas in glass, and a bronze of the good doctor stands close by.

The galleries to the right of the information desk (Level 1, rooms 50a–50d) display the large-scale **Renaissance sculptures** such as Giambologna's expressively brutal *Samson Slaying a Philistine*. Passing through the immense marble and alabaster choir-screen from 's-Hertogenbosch cathedral, you'll find a series of full-scale altarpieces and an entire Florentine chapel, plus a new ambulatory-cum-treasury of monstrances, fold-away croziers, crosses and chalices.

British Galleries 1500–1760

The superbly designed **British Galleries** are a joy to visit. The first series of rooms covers **Britain 1500–1760** (Level 2, rooms 52–58b), and begins in room 58 with Tudor times. Highlights include Torrigiani's bust of Henry VII, Holbein's miniature of Anne of Cleves, with its original ivory case, and the **Howard Grace Cup**, a medieval ivory cup associated with Thomas Becket, but given a Tudor silver-gilt makeover and crowned by a tiny St George and dragon. Other specific items to look out for include the **Dark Jewel** given to Francis Drake by Queen Elizabeth I, the tapestries embroidered by **Mary, Queen of Scots** during her incarceration, James II's wonderfully camp wedding suit and the amazing high-relief lime-wood *Stoning of St Stephen* by Grinling Gibbons.

The galleries also contain a number of **period interiors** saved in their entirety from buildings that have since been demolished. These include a Jacobean panelled room from Bromley-by-Bow, a Georgian parlour from Henrietta Street in Covent Garden and the heavily gilded Rococo **Norfolk House Music Room** from St James's Square (where concerts are held on occasional Fridays at 6.30pm). Towards the end, you should pass Roubiliac's marble statue of **Handel**, carved in 1738 and the first statue in Europe of a living artist. It originally stood in the then-fashionable Vauxhall Gardens in south London, and caused a great stir in its day, with the composer depicted as Apollo slouching in inspired disarray, one shoe dangling from his foot.

British Galleries 1760–1900

Upstairs, **Britain 1760–1900** (Level 4, rooms 118–125) kicks off with a Chippendale four-poster made for the actor David Garrick, paintings by Gainsborough and Constable and Canova's *Three Graces*. Again, period interiors are a big feature of the collection: Adam's Venetian-red Glass Drawing Room from Northumberland House

17

THE WORLD'S FIRST MUSEUM CAFÉ

Whatever you do, make sure you pay a visit to the *V&A Café* in the museum's original refreshment rooms, the **Morris, Gamble & Poynter Rooms**, at the back of the main galleries.
   Embellished by Edward Poynter with a wash of decorative blue tiling depicting the months and seasons of the year, the eastern **Poynter Room**, where the hoi polloi ate, was finished in 1881 and originally known as the Grill Room – the grill, also designed by Poynter, is still in place and was in use until 1939.
   On the opposite side, the dark-green **Morris Room** (William Morris's first public commission), completed in 1868, accommodated a better class of diner. The decorative detail is really worth taking in – gilded Pre-Raphaelite panels and Burne-Jones stained glass, embossed olive-branch wallpaper and a running cornice frieze of dogs chasing hares.
   The largest and grandest of the rooms lies between the two. The **Gamble Room**, completed in 1878 by the museum's own team of artists, boasts dazzling, almost edible decor, with mustard, gold and cream-coloured Minton tiles covering the walls and pillars from floor to ceiling. Fleshy Pre-Raphaelite nudes hold up the nineteenth-century chimneypiece from Dorchester House, while a ceramic frieze of frolicking cherubs accompanies a quote from Ecclesiastes, spelt out in decorative script around the cornice.

and the fan-vaulted Strawberry Room from Lee Priory in Kent, which was inspired by Walpole's Gothic Revival masterpiece in Twickenham, Strawberry Hill. You'll also find plenty of outpourings from the **Arts and Crafts movement**, starting with a cabinet painted with medieval scenes by William Morris, inspired by Walter Scott's novels. Other highlights to look out for include *La Belle Iseult*, Morris's only known painting (of his future wife), and a whole room on the Scottish School, including several tables and chairs from Glasgow tearooms designed by Charles Rennie Mackintosh.

Silver, Gold, Mosaics and Ironwork

The vast **Silver** galleries (Level 3, rooms 65–70a) are almost overwhelming. More manageable is the wonderful nearby gallery of **Sacred Silver and Stained Glass** (rooms 83–84). The stained glass, all beautifully backlit, dates from around 1140 to the present day, while the silver includes reliquaries, crosses, crowns and medieval shrines from every era and from all over Europe.
   Somewhat off the beaten path, it's worth persevering to find the V&A's **Ironwork** collection, a display of keys, locks, gates and grilles, ranged along a vast corridor (Level 3, rooms 113–114e via room 111). At the centre is George Gilbert Scott's Hereford Screen, an eight-ton neo-Gothic monster of copper and ironwork that was pulled out of the city's cathedral in 1967. Nearby, there are two great cabinets filled with every kind of tin, from a Huntley & Palmers biscuit-dispensing machine to a money box in the shape of a tea caddy.

Paintings

The V&A's collection of **Paintings** (Level 3, rooms 81, 82, 87–88a) includes minor works by Blake, Corot, Delacroix, Rembrandt, Tintoretto and Botticelli, a study for Ingres' *Odalisque*, a Tiepolo sketch, some Fantin-Latour flowers and several Pre-Raphaelite works, the best of which is Rossetti's verdant, emerald-green *The Day Dream*, one of his last great works. The V&A owns over four hundred works by John Constable, bequeathed by his daughter, including famous views of Salisbury Cathedral (in the British Galleries) and Dedham Mill, and full-sized preparatory oil paintings for *The Hay Wain* and *The Leaping Horse*, plus a whole host of his alfresco cloud studies and sketches. There are also several works by Turner, including a dreamy view of East Cowes Castle, painted for the castle's owner, John Nash, and **Gainsborough's Showbox**, in which he displayed the oil-on-glass landscapes he executed in the 1780s. Room 90 is used for temporary exhibitions of prints and drawings, and room 90a displays **portrait miniatures** by Holbein, Hilliard and others.

17

V&A'S HIDDEN GEMS

The V&A is so vast, it's very easy to miss one or two of its hidden gems. While you're on Level 3, make sure you see the spectacular Minton tiles of the **Ceramic Staircase**, designed by Frank Moody. Note the ceramic memorial to Henry Cole, the work of his niece, who has rendered her uncle in mosaic with "Albertopolis" in relief above. Make sure, too, that you get a close look at the grandiose **Leighton Frescoes** (Level 3, rooms 102 & 107), which used to look down onto the Cast Courts from on high.

The V&A's **20th Century** collection (Level 3, rooms 7 & 76) is stuffed with high-quality artefacts: furniture by Otto Wagner, Charles Rennie Mackintosh, Bauhaus and the Wiener Werkstätte co-op; Constructivist fabrics and crockery; and a range of works by Finnish modernist supremo Alvar Aalto. Postwar design classics, from plywood chairs and melamine tableware to Olivetti typewriters and Dyson vacuum cleaners, are displayed in one half of the adjacent National Art Library. For the story of furniture design and production continue to the Furniture galleries (room 133–135, level 6) to see over two hundred outstanding pieces.

Theatre

The display areas of the **Theatre & Performance** galleries (Level 3, rooms 103–106) are divided into themes and cover every theatrical genre from music hall to theatre itself, plus a surprisingly large amount of pop memorabilia. See some great individual exhibits, ranging from Joey, the life-size puppet from *War Horse* to Shakespeare's First Folio from 1623; the rotating hook, tunic and shorts used by Pansy Chinery in her teeth-spinning act to Pink Floyd's Azimuth Co-ordinator, which could produce an early form of surround sound. Perhaps the best section is "costume and make-up" where you can examine General Tom Thumb's waistcoat, Adam Ant's self-made Prince Charming get-up, Elton John's lurex Bicycle John outfit from the height of glam rock and an exact replica of Kylie Minogue's dressing room from 2007. Look out for the engaging temporary displays too.

Jewellery

The justifiably popular **Jewellery** galleries (Level 3, rooms 91–93) display everything from a Bronze Age gold collar from Ireland to contemporary jewellery made from recycled materials. Among the earlier pieces, there are some pretty impressive gold papal rings – giant knuckle-dusters made from rock crystal – and some lovely gilded pomanders used to ward off evil. Specific highlights to look out for, further on, include the emeralds and diamonds given by Napoleon to his adopted daughter in 1806 (cabinet 15), the emeralds and rubies captured from Seringapatam in 1799 and the rare Siberian amethysts given by Tsar Alexander I to the wife of the Third Marquess of Londonderry (all in cabinet 24). Elsewhere, there are Art Nouveau pieces by René Lalique (cabinet 26), Arts and Crafts works by May Morris (cabinet 29) and the ostentatious personal jewellery of the eccentric Edith Sitwell (cabinet 30). Check out cabinet 56, too, for the Fabergé cigarette cases, the spectacular Manchester Tiara from 1903 (cabinet 55a) and the whole series of semiprecious carved animals that belonged to Queen Alexandra (cabinet 56).

Architecture, Glass and Ceramics

The V&A's **Architecture** gallery (Level 4, rooms 127–128) puts on special exhibitions, but also has a permanent display of architectural models in room 128. It's an eclectic array of realized and unrealized projects – everything from a fifteenth-century mosque and a Le Corbusier villa, to Spiral (Daniel Libeskind's now-shelved extension for the V&A) and Bluewater, Britain's fourth largest mall. Beyond, lies the relatively small **Glass Gallery** (Level 4, room 131), with its spectacular modern glass staircase and balustrade. The beauty and variety of the glass on display is staggering, and ranges from the Greek and Roman world to objets d'art by contemporary artists.

17

For those with stamina, or who wish to lose the crowds, there's the vast ceramics study collection (Level 6, rooms 136–146) on the top floor. You'll find work by the Wiener Werkstätte and the Omega Workshops, Clarice Cliff crockery, a Suffragette tea-set and Communist ceramics in room 140. The contemporary pieces in room 141 range from manga to mad, while room 142 features one-off modern pieces by everyone from Picasso to Grayson Perry. And for a global overview of ceramics through the ages, continue to room 145, which has everything from Greek black-figure vases to Victorian de Morgan tiles.

Finally, if you persevere, you'll make it to the museum's fabulous new **Furniture** galleries (Level 6, rooms 133–135), which tell the story of furniture over the past six hundred years, from an Isokon bookshelf and the UFO-like 1960s Garden Egg Chair to contemporary designers like Stephen Richards and the computer-aided designs of Jeroen Verhoeven.

Science Museum

Exhibition Rd • Daily 10am–6pm, last entry 5.15pm & till 7pm during school holidays • Free • ☎ 020 7942 4000, ⓦ sciencemuseum .org.uk • ⊖ South Kensington

The **Science Museum** is undeniably impressive, filling seven floors with items drawn from every conceivable area of science, with hands-on galleries that appeal to adults and kids. It once formed part of the South Kensington Museum which, in 1909, split into two, marking the beginnings of the Science Museum as a separate institution and removing the science collections from what had already been renamed the Victoria and Albert Museum. Since 2000, when the spectacular **Wellcome Wing** opened, the museum began to reconfigure its collection, creating new themes and concepts for its galleries. Most of the old galleries have now been replaced but the renovation continues, with two new galleries in 2016, the Mathematics and Interactive galleries, and, by 2019, the complete transformation of the first floor which will house the museum's medicine collections, doubling the size of what was previously on display.

INFORMATION AND TOURS

Tours and events Your first stop should be the information desk, in the Energy Hall, where you can pick up a museum plan and find out about the day's events and demonstrations; you can also sign up for a free guided tour on a specific subject. **Exhibitions** The museum stages populist special exhibitions (for which you have to pay) and has flight simulators and a 3D IMAX cinema (£11, children £10). **Eating** Refreshment pit-stops include the *Energy Café* off the Energy Hall, and the funky *Deep Blue Café* in the Wellcome Wing, plus several picnic areas.

The ground floor

The largest exhibit in the **Energy Hall**, by the entrance, is the bright red Burnley mill engine, whose enormous wheel used to drive 1700 looms and still works today. To the side is an exhibition on **James Watt** (1736–1819), the Scot who was instrumental in kick-starting the Industrial Revolution in Britain. As well as inspecting examples of his inventions, you can view the perfectly preserved garret room workshop that Watt used in his retirement.

Beyond lies the **Exploring Space** exhibition, which follows the history of rockets from tenth-century China and Congreve's early nineteenth-century efforts, through the V-1 and V-2 wartime bombs, right up to the Apollo landings. There's a great, full-size replica of the Apollo 11 landing craft which deposited US astronauts on the moon in 1969.

Beyond, **Making the Modern World** displays iconic inventions of modern science and technology. These include *Puffing Billy*, the world's oldest surviving steam locomotive, used for hauling coal in 1815, and Robert Stephenson's *Rocket* of 1829, which won the competition to haul the Manchester–Liverpool passenger service. Other ground-breaking inventions on display include the Apollo 10 Command Module, a Ford Model T, the world's first mass-produced car, and a gleaming aluminium Lockheed

17

10A Electra airliner from 1935, which signalled the birth of modern air travel. Less glamorous discoveries, such as the brain scanner, occupy the sidelines, along with disasters such as the drug thalidomide.

Wellcome Wing

The darkened, ultra-violet **Wellcome Wing** beckons you on from Making the Modern World. The **Antenna** displays, on the ground floor, change regularly in order to cover contemporary science issues while they are topical. **Pattern Pod**, meanwhile, is for under-5s, and is basically a lot of interactive hi-tech fun. Kids can experiment with water ripples, footprints and the Penrose tessellation, and groove away in the multicoloured human shadow box.

On Floor 1, **Who am I?** is a guaranteed winner, as it concentrates on humans themselves. You can morph yourself into the opposite sex, watch a sperm race and test the gender of your brain. **Atmosphere**, on Floor 2, is a touch-screen exhibition exploring the causes and effects of climate change, and the possibilities for reducing carbon emissions. Floor 3 contains **Engineer Your Future**, where you can play frivolous but fun multi-player educational games, and vote on contemporary socio-scientific questions, such as "Should you be able to choose the gender of your child?"

The basement

As well as a café and terrace picnic area the basement also houses **The Garden**, misleadingly entitled but perfect for children, where 3- to 6-year-olds don waterproofs to experiment with lock gates, and hard hats to play with pulleys.

Floor 1

The **Challenge of Materials**, ranged around the balcony on the first floor, is an extremely stylish exhibition – the glass-floored suspension bridge is particularly cool – covering the use of materials ranging from aluminium to zerodur (used for making laser gyroscopes). As well as the excellent hands-on displays, there are aesthetically pleasing exhibits as diverse as a Bakelite coffin and an Axminster-carpet morning gown designed by Vivienne Westwood.

Further on, you'll find a very old-fashioned, little-visited section on **Agriculture**, perfect for those with a penchant for ploughs and tractors. Beyond lies **Cosmos & Culture**, which explores our relationship with the universe through astronomy, and features objects from the 7ft telescope used by William Herschel to discover Uranus in 1781, to DRIFT I, with which scientists attempted (and failed) to detect the invisible "dark matter" that's thought to make up around a quarter of the universe.

Floor 2

The most popular section on Floor 2 is **Energy**, with its "do not touch" electric-shock machine that fascinates kids. Much of it is thought-provoking stuff – you can play computer games to learn how to reduce your carbon emissions – and the rest comprises more conventional displays, everything from a bird oil lamp to a clay stove from contemporary Kenya.

Floor 2 also houses the largest gallery in the museum, **Information Age**, opened in October 2014. Charting more than two hundred years of communication and information technology, the six zones explore events and inventions that shaped our technological age, from the development of the telegraph cable to the World Wide Web.

Floor 3

On Floor 3, **Launchpad**, enormously popular with kids who have lots of fun experimenting with water, waves, light and sound, is closed until late 2016 and will reopen as the **Interactive Gallery**.

CLOCKWISE FROM TOP LEFT SCIENCE MUSEUM (P.259); V&A (P.251); NATURAL HISTORY MUSEUM INTERIOR AND EXTERIOR (P.262) >

17

If you're looking for peace and quiet, head next door for the exquisite scientific instruments, chiefly created by George Adams for George III, in **Science in the Eighteenth Century**. Close by, **Health Matters** dwells thoughtfully on modern medical history from the introduction of mass vaccination to the challenge of finding a cure for HIV.

Heading towards the Wellcome Wing, you eventually reach the giant hangar of **Flight**, festooned with aircraft of every description from a Spitfire to a modern executive jet. Look out for the scaled-down model of the Montgolfier balloon which achieved the first human flight in 1783, and the full-size model of the flimsy contraption in which the Wright brothers made their epoch-making power-assisted flight in 1903.

Floors 4 and 5
Medical science is the focus on the top two floors but the main galleries closed in late 2015, with temporary exhibitions occupying the space up here until the new Medicine Galleries open in 2019.

Natural History Museum
Cromwell Rd • Daily 10am–5.50pm, last entry 5.30pm • Free • ☎ 020 7942 5000, ⓦ nhm.ac.uk • ⊖ South Kensington

Alfred Waterhouse's purpose-built mock-Romanesque colossus, with its 675ft terracotta facade built in 1880, ensures the status of the **Natural History Museum** as London's most handsome museum. Its vast collections derive from a bequest by Hans Sloane to the British Museum, separated off in the 1860s after a huge power struggle. The founding director, Richard Owen, was an amazing figure, who arranged expeditions around the globe to provide everything from butterflies to dinosaurs for the museum's cabinets.

Nowadays, the museum copes manfully with the task of remaining an important resource for serious zoologists, and a major tourist attraction for the families with kids who flock here to check out the dinosaur collection. The central **Hintze Hall** is dominated by "Dippy", a replica **Diplodocus** skeleton, 85ft from tip to tail, while the "side chapels" are filled with "wonders" of the natural world – a model of a sabre-toothed tiger, a stuffed Great Bustard, a dodo skeleton and so on. It's also worth pausing here to take in the architecture of this vast "nave", whose walls are decorated with moulded terracotta animals and plants.

INFORMATION AND TOURS

Arrival If the queues are long for the main entrance, you're better off heading for the Red Zone's side entrance on Exhibition Rd. The museum is divided into four colour-coded zones, but all you really need to know is that the Red Zone is the old Geology Museum linked to the rest of the museum by the Birds section, and the Orange Zone is the Darwin Centre.

Tours The museum puts on free tours or you can download the free visitor app from the website and use that to navigate around the collections.

Activities and exhibitions As well as large, very popular special exhibitions (for which there's a charge), there are lots of free talks, discussions, workshops and performances, and in the winter there's an ice rink in front of the building.

Eating There's a restaurant and three cafés plus a picnic area in the basement, or you can head out to the Wildlife Garden (April–Oct), west of the entrance.

Blue Zone
In **Dinosaurs**, a raised walkway leads straight to the highlight for many kids, the grisly life-sized animatronic dinosaur tableau, currently a roaring *Tyrannosaurus rex*. The rest of the displays are less theatrical and more informative, with massive-jawed skeletons and more conventional models.

The old-fashioned **Mammals** section is filled with stuffed animals and plastic models and dominated by a full-sized model of a blue whale juxtaposed with its skeleton. It usually goes down well enough with younger children, but it's showing its age somewhat.

Green Zone

The other firm favourite with kids is the arthropod room, known as **Creepy Crawlies**. Filled with giant models of bugs, arachnids and crustaceans, plus displays on spiders, mites and other unlovely creatures, it's here that you'll find the museum's only live exhibits, a colony of leaf-cutter ants from Trinidad, which feed on a fungus that they grow on the leaves they've gathered.

Meanwhile down in the basement is the excellent futuristic **Investigate** (Mon–Fri 2.30–5pm, Sat & Sun 11am–5pm; during school holidays daily 11am–5pm), aimed at children aged 7 to 14 – in school term time, public visits are restricted to the afternoon and at busy times, you may need to obtain a timed ticket. Kids get to choose a tray of specimens and then play at being scientists, using microscopes, scales, a computer and various tools of the trade to examine and catalogue the items before them. There are one or two simpler hands-on exhibits too, as well as several plant species to look at.

Up on the first floor, **Minerals** features serried ranks of glass cabinets, culminating in a darkened chamber called **The Vault**. Here, the cream of the museum's rocks reside: a meteorite from Mars, a golden nugget weighing over 1000lb, one of the largest uncut emeralds in the world and the Star of South Africa, found in 1869, which triggered the South Africa diamond rush. Don't miss the 1300-year-old slice of **Giant Sequoia**, on the top floor, and while you're there, admire the view down onto Hintze Hall, the moulded monkeys clinging to the arches and the ceiling panels depicting plant specimens.

Orange Zone

Little visited, compared to the rest of the museum, the **Orange Zone** is also known as the **Darwin Centre**, dominated by the giant concrete **Cocoon**, encased within the centre's glass-fronted atrium like a giant egg and home to over twenty million specimens. Visitors can take the lift to the seventh floor and enter the Cocoon to learn more about the history of the collection, about taxonomy and the research and field trips the museum funds.

In the nearby **Zoology spirit building**, you can view a small selection of bits and bobs pickled in glass jars, everything from silkworm larvae and a peculiar venomous snail that's killed more than one unwary collector, to a jar of parasitic worms from a sperm whale's stomach and a brown rat found during the building's construction. To join one of the **guided tours** that take you behind the scenes and allow you to talk to the museum's scientists, you need to book on the day at the information desk in Hintze Hall.

Red Zone

If you enter the museum from Exhibition Road, you enter the vast, darkened hall of the **Red Zone**, with the solar system and constellations writ large on the walls. Boarding the central escalator will take you through a partially formed globe to the top floor and **The Power Within**, an exhibition on volcanoes and earthquakes. The most popular section is the 1995 Kobe earthquake simulator, where you can enter a mock-up of a Japanese supermarket and see the soy sauce bottles wobble, while watching an in-store video of the real event. On the same floor is **Restless Surface**, an interactive display on the earth's elements, soil and rock erosion and, of course, global warming.

Down one floor, **From the Beginning** covers the geological history of the planet from the Big Bang to the present day. The display ends with a crystal ball, which predicts the earth's future (bleak, but probably not within our lifetime). More alluring is **Earth's Treasury**, a dimly lit display of lustrous minerals and crystals, gemstones and jewels. Exhibits include rocks that shine in UV light, carved artefacts such as a lapis lazuli necklace, and even some recently discovered kryptonite (the mineral that weakens Superman).

Finally, **Earth Today and Tomorrow** (on the ground floor) is a look at how we are running down the earth's non-renewable natural resources, and polluting the planet in the process.

17 **Brompton Oratory**

Brompton Rd • Mon–Fri 6.30am–8pm, Sat 6.30am–7.45pm, Sun 7.30am–8pm • Free • ☎ 020 7808 0900, Ⓦ bromptonoratory.com •
⊖ South Kensington

London's most flamboyant and atmospheric Roman Catholic church, the **Brompton Oratory** stands just east of the V&A. The first large Catholic church to be built since the Reformation, it was begun by the young and unknown Herbert Gribble in 1880 and modelled on the Gesù church in Rome, "so that those who had no opportunity of going over to Italy to see an Italian church had only to come here to see a model of one". The ornate Italianate interior, financed by the Duke of Norfolk, is filled with gilded mosaics and stuffed with sculpture, much of it genuine Italian Baroque from the Gesù church and Siena cathedral, notably the seventeenth-century apostles in the nave and the main altar, and the reredos of the Lady Chapel. The pulpit is a superb piece of neo-Baroque from the 1930s, with a high cherub count on the tester. True to its architecture, the church practises a "rigid, ritualized, smells-and-bells Catholicism", as one journalist put it, with daily Mass in Latin, a top-notch choir on Sundays and some very high-society weddings throughout the year.

Royal Albert Hall

Kensington Gore • Guided tours depart from Door 12 • £12.25 • ☎ 0845 401 5045, Ⓦ royalalberthall.com • ⊖ South Kensington or High Street Kensington

The funds raised on the death of the Prince Consort in 1861 were squandered on the nearby Albert Memorial (see p.248), and it took considerable effort by Henry Cole, his collaborator on the Great Exhibition, to get funding to complete the **Royal Albert Hall**. Plans for this splendid iron- and glass-domed auditorium had been drawn up during the prince's lifetime, with an exterior of red brick, terracotta and marble that was already the hallmark of South Ken architecture. Completed in 1871, the hall has hosted everything from Miss World to pop gigs, and is the main venue for London's most democratic classical music festival, the annual Henry Wood Promenade Concerts, better known as the **Proms** (see p.413).

Several other educational institutions congregate around the Albert Hall, as was Albert's intention. The most striking architecturally is the former **Royal College of Organists** to the west of the Albert Hall, a strange neo-Jacobean confection, designed for free in 1875 by Henry Cole's eldest son and laced with cream, maroon and sky-blue sgraffito.

Also on the west side of the Albert Hall is the headquarters of the **Royal College of Art**, founded back in 1837 but now housed in a seven-storey concrete block, designed in the 1960s by RCA staff. A postgraduate art college, the RCA's past students range from Henry Moore and David Hockney to Adam Ant and Tracey Emin; student art exhibitions are held during term-time on the ground floor.

Royal College of Music

Prince Consort Rd • Term-time Tues–Fri 11.30am–4.30pm • Free • ☎ 020 7591 4842, Ⓦ rcm.ac.uk • ⊖ South Kensington

Behind the Albert Hall, flanked by the monumental **South Steps**, is a memorial to the

---

FRENCH CONNECTIONS

Part of South Ken's cachet is thanks to its **French connections**, with a French school and creche, a couple of bookshops, a deli and several genuine patisseries and brasseries, as well as the French Consulate, clustered around the **Institut Français** (Ⓦ institut-francais.org.uk) on Queensberry Place, which itself maintains an interesting programme of theatre, cinema and exhibitions. The French Embassy is a mile away in Knightsbridge.

A further French sight worth checking out is the gorgeous Art Deco **Michelin House**, a short walk to the south down Brompton Road. Faced in white faïence and decorated with tyres and motoring murals by French artists in 1911, its ground floors now house the shop, café, oyster bar and restaurant of *Bibendum* (Ⓦ bibendum.co.uk), all run by Terence Conran.

Great Exhibition, featuring the Prince Consort. Predating the Royal Albert Hall (which Albert turns his back on), it originally stood amid the gardens and pavilions of the Royal Horticultural Society, which were replaced in the 1880s by the colossal **Imperial Institute** building. Of this only the 287ft **Queen's Tower** (closed to the public) remains, stranded amid the modern departments of Imperial College.

Instead, Albert now stands facing the splendid, neo-Gothic **Royal College of Music**, whose students have included Ralph Vaughan Williams and Benjamin Britten. The college houses a **museum** containing a collection of over eight hundred instruments, dating from the fifteenth to the twentieth centuries, including the world's oldest surviving keyboard instrument.

Royal Geographical Society

1 Kensington Gore • Mon–Fri 10am–5pm • Free • ☎ 020 7591 3000, ⓦ rgs.org • ⊖ South Kensington

East of the Albert Hall is the **Royal Geographical Society**, a wonderful brick-built complex in the Queen Anne style, with statues of two of the society's early explorers, David Livingstone and Ernest Shackleton, occupying niches along the outer wall. The society gives regular talks, maintains a remarkable library and map room and puts on excellent special exhibitions in the Pavilion (entrance on Exhibition Road).

Sikorski Museum

20 Prince's Gate • Tues–Fri 2–4pm, first Sat of month 10.30am–4pm • Free • ☎ 020 7589 9249, ⓦ pism.co.uk • ⊖ South Kensington

South Ken's Polish connections are exemplified by the **Sikorski Museum** and Polish Institute, east of the Royal Geographical Society. World War II militaria form the bedrock of the museum, along with the personal effects of General Wladyslaw Sikorski, the prewar prime minister who fled to London in 1939, only to die in a mysterious plane accident in 1943. The absence of a non-Communist leader of Sikorski's standing after the war was lamented by exiled Poles for the next forty years.

Czech Memorial Scrolls Museum

Kent House, Rutland Gardens • Tues & Thurs 10am–4pm & by appointment • Free • ☎ 020 7584 3741, ⓦ memorialscrollstrust.org • ⊖ Knightsbridge

One of South Kensington's East European connections is contained within the **Westminster Synagogue** in Kent House, a spacious Victorian mansion in Rutland Gardens, off Kensington Road. The synagogue occupies the first floor, while the third floor houses the **Czech Memorial Scrolls Museum**, which tells the miraculous story of 1564 Torah scrolls which were gathered from all over Bohemia and Moravia by the Nazis, possibly for their planned "Museum of an Extinct Race"; they survived the Holocaust, and were purchased from the Communist government in 1964 and brought here. The shelves have been gradually emptying as the scrolls are restored and sent out to Jewish communities all over the world, but there are still some 150 displayed here, as well as a display of some of the embroidered fabric 'binders' that housed the scrolls and held them intact.

Knightsbridge

Knightsbridge is irredeemably snobbish, revelling in its reputation as the swankiest shopping area in London, with designer stores all the way down **Sloane Street**, and its pretty little mews streets, built to house servants and stables, but now inhabited by the rich themselves. However, most people come to Knightsbridge for just one reason: to visit **Harrods**, London's most famous department store. **Belgravia**, over to the east and strategically close to Buckingham Palace, is London's chief embassy land, with at least 25 scattered among the grid-plan stuccoed streets. All in all, it's a pretty soulless place, although there are one or two lovely pubs hidden in the various mews.

17 Harrods

87–135 Brompton Rd • Mon–Sat 10am–9pm, Sun 11.30am–6pm • ☎ 020 7730 1234, ⓦ harrods.com • ⊖ Knightsbridge

Housed in a grandiose 1905 terracotta building, which turns into a palace of fairy lights at night, **Harrods** has come a long way since it started out as a family-run grocer's in 1849. Nowadays, it is the UK's largest shop, spread over seven floors, five acres, with over 5000 staff, and over 15 million customers a year. If you are coming to visit, note that a "clean and presentable" **dress code** is enforced and backpacks either have to be carried in the hand or placed in the store's left luggage (£10, includes a £10 voucher to spend in the store). Once here, however, you can avail yourself of the first-floor "luxury washrooms" and splash on a range of perfumes for free.

Even if you don't want one of the distinctive olive-green Harrods carrier bags, the store has a few sections and features that are sights in their own right. Chief among these are the **Food Halls**, on the ground floor, with their exquisite Arts and Crafts tiling. Nearby is the Egyptian Hall, between Doors 7 and 8, with pseudo-hieroglyphs and sphinxes, and, running from the Lower Ground Floor all the way to the Fifth Floor near the centre of the store, an Egyptian Escalator. At the foot of the escalator is the **Dodi and Diana Memorial**. Here you can contemplate a fountain shrine to Lady Diana and Dodi Fayed, topped with photos of the ill-fated couple. The shrine also features a used wine-glass from the couple's last evening and the engagement ring Dodi allegedly bought for Di the previous day. Alongside is a life-size bronze statue entitled *Innocent Victims*, depicting the couple dancing on a beach and clutching an albatross, while a Book of Condolence allows the shopping public to express their ongoing grief. Dodi's father, Mohamed Al-Fayed, sold Harrods to the Qatari royal family for £1.5 billion in 2010, but so far the memorials are still *in situ*.

Chelsea

Until the sixteenth century, **Chelsea** was nothing more than a tiny fishing village on the banks of the Thames, centred around Chelsea Old Church. It was Thomas More who started the upward trend by moving here in 1520, followed by members of the nobility, including Henry VIII himself. In the eighteenth century, Chelsea acquired its riverside houses along Cheyne Walk, which gradually attracted a posse of literary and intellectual types. However, it wasn't until the late nineteenth century that the area began to earn its reputation as London's very own Left Bank.

In the 1960s, Chelsea was at the forefront of "Swinging London", with the likes of David Bailey, Mick Jagger, George Best and the "Chelsea Set" hanging out in the boutiques and coffee bars. Later, the **King's Road** became a catwalk for hippies and in the late 1970s it was the unlikely epicentre of the punk explosion. Men wearing red trousers is about as countercultural as it gets in Chelsea nowadays, with franchise fashion rather than cutting-edge couture the order of the day, though some of its residents like to think of themselves as a cut above the purely moneyed types of Kensington. That said, King's Road remains one of the better, more interesting shopping streets outside the West End and is well stocked with restaurants, while at its eastern end are two champions of contemporary and undiscovered art and theatre, the Saatchi Gallery and Royal Court Theatre respectively. The area's other aspect, oddly enough considering its reputation, is a **military** one, with the former Chelsea Barracks, the Royal Hospital and the National Army Museum.

Sloane Square

A leafy nexus on the very eastern edge of Chelsea, **Sloane Square** is centred on a modern Venus fountain, featuring a relief of Charles II and Nell Gwynne. On the east side of the square, beside the tube station, stands the Victorian **Royal Court Theatre**, a bastion of new theatre writing since John Osborne's *Look Back in Anger* sent tremors through the establishment in 1956. On the opposite side is **Peter Jones**, a John Lewis

CHELSEA

CAFÉ		
Bibendum Oyster Bar	1	

RESTAURANTS		
Hunan	2	
Medlar	3	

SHOPS		
John Sandoe	1	
Limelight Movie Art	3	
The Shop at Bluebird	2	
Vivienne Westwood/		
Worlds End	4	

ACCOMMODATION		
Myhotel Chelsea	1	

PUBS		
The Anglesea Arms	2	
The Cooper's Arms	3	
The Fox and Hounds	1	

17

department store housed in London's finest glass-curtain building, built in the 1930s, which curves its way seductively into the King's Road.

Holy Trinity, Sloane Square

Sloane St • Mon–Sat 8.30am–5.30pm, Sun 8.30am–1.30pm • ☎ 020 7730 7270, ⓦ holytrinitysloanesquare.co.uk • ⊖ Sloane Square

Just off Sloane Square is **Holy Trinity**, created in 1890, and probably the finest Arts and Crafts church in London. The east window is the most glorious of the furnishings, a vast 48-panel extravaganza designed by Edward Burne-Jones, and the largest ever made by Morris & Co. Despite the smell of incense, statues of the Virgin Mary and even confession booths, Holy Trinity is simply High Church Anglican, not Roman Catholic.

King's Road

The **King's Road**, Chelsea's main artery, was designed as a royalty-only thoroughfare by Charles II, in order – so the story goes – to avoid carriage congestion en route to Nell Gwynne's house. Lesser mortals could travel down it on production of a special copper pass but it wasn't opened to the public until 1830. This prompted a flurry of speculative building that produced the series of elegant, open-ended squares – Wellington, Markham, Carlyle and Paultons – which still punctuate the road. If you don't fancy walking down the King's Road, hop on a bus: #11 and #22 run the length of it, and buses #19 and #319 run from Sloane Square partway down and then south across Battersea Bridge.

Saatchi Gallery

King's Rd • Daily 10am–6pm • Free • ☎ 020 7823 2363, ⓦ saatchi-gallery.co.uk • ⊖ Sloane Square

Set back from the King's Road, a short stroll from Sloane Square, is the former **Duke of York's HQ**, built in 1801 and fronted by a solid-looking Tuscan portico. The building is now the unlikely home of the **Saatchi Gallery**, which puts on changing exhibitions of contemporary art, much of it by largely unknown young artists, in its fifteen equally proportioned, whitewashed rooms. Charles Saatchi, the collector behind the gallery, was the man whose clever advertising campaigns helped keep Mrs Thatcher in power in the 1980s and who introduced Young British Artists (YBAs) like Damien Hirst, Sarah Lucas and Rachel Whiteread to the world in the 1990s, and he remains a hugely influential figure in contemporary British art. One of the most remarkable works Saatchi bought is Richard Wilson's *20:50*, the giant sump oil reservoir, first displayed in 1987 and now installed in the gallery's basement.

Royal Avenue

The first of the picturesque squares that open out onto the King's Road is **Royal Avenue**, on the south side. This particular one is rather like a Parisian *place*, with plane trees and gravel down the centre, and was originally laid out in the late seventeenth century as part of William III's ambitious (and unrealized) scheme to link Kensington Palace with the Royal Hospital to the south. The next square along is Wellington Square, suspected fictional London address of James Bond; Ian Fleming lived, on and off, in Chelsea, and no. 30 is thought to have been the location of Bond's "comfortable ground-floor flat".

World's End

The stretch of the King's Road beyond Beaufort Street, known as **World's End**, was the fulcrum of Chelsea's Swinging Sixties scene, with boutiques like Granny Takes a Trip and hippie shops like Gandolf's Garden and the Sweet Shop. In 1971, Malcolm McLaren and his schoolteacher girlfriend, Vivienne Westwood, opened a Teddy Boy-revival store called Let It Rock, located, with a neat sense of irony, right next door to the Chelsea Conservative Club, at no. 430. In 1975 they changed tack and renamed the shop SEX, stocking it with proto-punk fetishist gear, with simulated burnt limbs in the window. It became a magnet for the likes of John Lydon and John Simon Ritchie,

17

better known as Johnny Rotten and Sid Vicious, and was renamed Seditionaries – the rest, as they say, is history. Now known as World's End, the shop, with its landmark backward-running clock, continues to flog Westwood's eccentric designer clothes.

Royal Hospital Chelsea

Royal Hospital Rd · **Grounds** Daily: May–Sept 10am–8pm; Oct–April 10am–4.30pm · Free **Great Hall & Chapel** Mon–Sat 11am–noon & 2–4pm, Sun 2–4pm · Free **Museum** Mon–Fri 10am–4pm · Free **Guided tours** Book at least 4 weeks in advance (minimum 4 people) Mon–Fri 10am & 1.30pm (90min) · £10, under-16s £7 · ☎ 020 7881 5516, ⓦ chelsea-pensioners.co.uk · ⊖ Sloane Square

Among the most nattily attired of all those parading down the King's Road are the scarlet- or navy-blue-clad Chelsea Pensioners, army veterans from the nearby **Royal Hospital** founded by Charles II in 1682. Designed by Wren, the hospital's plain, red-brick wings and grassy courtyards became a blueprint for institutional and collegiate architecture across the Empire. On Founder's Day (May 29), the Pensioners, wearing their traditional tricorn hats, festoon Grinling Gibbons' gilded statue of Charles with oak leaves to commemorate the day after the disastrous 1651 Battle of Worcester, when the future king hid in an oak tree to escape his pursuers.

The public are welcome to visit the hospital's austere **chapel**, with its huge barrel vaulting and Sebastiano Ricci's colourful apse fresco *Resurrection*, in which Jesus patriotically bears the flag of St George. Opposite lies the equally grand, wood-panelled **Great Hall**, where the three hundred or so Pensioners still eat under portraits of the sovereigns and Antonio Verrio's vast allegorical mural of Charles II and his hospital. In the Secretary's Office, designed by John Soane, on the east side of the hospital, there's a small **museum** (Mon–Fri only), displaying Pensioners' uniforms, medals and two German bombs. Beyond this are picturesque Ranelagh Gardens, by far the most attractive part of the grounds, enclosed by and full of clusters of handsome trees, with paths winding around the gently undulating landscaped lawns. Here and the adjacent playing fields, from which you get the finest view of the hospital, are the venue for the annual **Chelsea Flower Show** (see p.26). Entrance to the grounds and museum is via London Gate, on Royal Hospital Road opposite the turning onto Franklin's Row.

National Army Museum

Royal Hospital Rd · Free · ☎ 020 7730 0717, ⓦ nam.ac.uk · ⊖ Sloane Square

The concrete bunker next door to the Royal Hospital houses the **National Army Museum.** Charting the history of the British Army, from the English Civil War to the present day, and its role in the shaping of the Empire and every major conflict involving the Army over the last 300 years, the museum has been closed since May 2014 and is currently undergoing a major redevelopment; it is set to reopen in mid-2016.

LONDON'S PLEASURE GARDENS

"…the fragrancy of the walks and bowers, with the choirs of birds that sung upon the trees, and the loose tribe of people that walked under their shades, I could not but look upon the place as a kind of Mahometan paradise."   The Spectator, May 20, 1712

London's pleasure gardens were among the city's chief entertainments in the eighteenth century. **Vauxhall Gardens**, open from around 1660, on the south bank, provided the blueprint: formal, lantern-lit gardens, musical entertainments and "dark walks", perfect for secret assignations. Of Vauxhall, there is now no trace, but its nearest rival was **Ranelagh Gardens**, now a pleasant little landscaped park near the Royal Hospital. A couple of information panels in the gardens' Soane-designed shelter show what the place used to look like when Canaletto painted it in 1751. The main feature was a giant Rotunda, where the beau monde could promenade to musical accompaniment – the 8-year-old Mozart played here. Shortly after it opened in 1742, Walpole reported that "you can't set your foot without treading on a Prince or Duke." Fashion is fickle, though, and the Rotunda was eventually demolished in 1805.

17 Chelsea Physic Garden

66 Royal Hospital Rd • April–Oct Tues–Fri & Sun 11am–6pm; late openings July & Aug Tues & Wed until 10pm; Nov–March Mon–Fri 9.30am–4pm • £9.90, concessions and under-16s £6.60 • ☎ 020 7352 5646, Ⓦ chelseaphysicgarden.co.uk • ⊖ Sloane Square

Founded in 1673 by the Royal Society of Apothecaries, the **Chelsea Physic Garden** is the oldest botanical garden in the country after Oxford's: the first cedars grown in this country were planted here in 1683, cotton seed was sent from here to the American colonies in 1732, England's first rock garden was constructed here in 1773, and the walled garden contains Britain's oldest olive tree. Unfortunately, it's a rather small garden, and a little too close to Chelsea Embankment to be a peaceful oasis, but keen botanists will enjoy it nevertheless. A statue of Hans Sloane, who presented the Society with the freehold, stands at the centre of the garden; behind him there's a licensed café (closed Nov–March), serving afternoon tea and delicious home-made cakes.

Cheyne Walk

Chelsea Physic Garden marks the beginning of **Cheyne Walk** (pronounced "chainy"), whose quiet riverside locale and succession of Queen Anne and Georgian houses drew artists and writers here in great numbers during the nineteenth century. Since the building of the Embankment in the 1870s and the increase in traffic, however, the character of this peaceful haven has been lost. Novelist Henry James, who lived at no. 21, used to take "beguiling drives" in his wheelchair along the Embankment; today, he'd be hospitalized in the process. An older contemporary of James, Mary Ann Evans (better known under her pen name George Eliot), moved into no. 4 – the first blue plaque you come to – in December 1880, five months after marrying an American banker 21 years her junior. Three weeks later she died of a kidney disease. Composer Ralph Vaughan Williams lived at no. 13; thirty or so years later, composers Mick Jagger and Keith Richards followed suit, at no. 48 and no. 3 respectively.

Chelsea Old Church

64 Cheyne Walk • Tues–Thurs 2–4pm • ☎ 020 7795 1019, Ⓦ chelseaoldchurch.org.uk • Bus #19 or #319 from ⊖ Sloane Square

At the end of Cheyne Walk's gardens, there's a garish, gilded statue of **Thomas More**, "Scholar, Statesman, Saint", a local who used to worship in nearby **Chelsea Old Church** where he built his own private chapel in the south aisle (the hinges for the big oak doors are still visible). More is best known for his martyrdom in 1535, though he himself showed little mercy to heretics – he even had some tied to a tree in his Chelsea back garden and flogged. Badly bombed in the last war, the church nevertheless contains an impressive number of monuments. Chief among them is Lady Cheyne's memorial (possibly by Bellini) and More's simple canopied memorial to his first wife, Jane, in which he himself hoped to be buried. In the event, his torso ended up in the Tower of London, while his head was stuck on a pike on London Bridge, but later saved and secretly buried in Canterbury by his adopted daughter, Margaret Roper. More's second wife, Alice, is also buried here.

Crosby Hall

You can get a flavour of Chelsea in Thomas More's day from **Crosby Hall**, part of a fifteenth-century wool merchant's house on Cheyne Walk once owned by More; it was transferred in 1910 bit by bit from Bishopsgate in the City to the corner of Danvers Street, west of Chelsea Old Church, on the site of More's gardens. Once occupied by the future Richard III (and used as a setting by Shakespeare), it's now a private residence, so you can admire its brick exterior, but not the great hall's fine hammer-beam roof.

Lindsey House and around

The continuation of **Cheyne Walk**, beyond Crosby Hall, is no less rich in cultural associations. Mrs Gaskell was born in 1810 at no. 93, while the painter James Whistler,

17

WILDE ABOUT CHELSEA

John Singer Sargent, Augustus John, James Whistler and Bertrand Russell all lived at one time or another in Tite Street, which runs alongside the National Army Museum, but the street's most famous resident was writer and wit **Oscar Fingal O'Flahertie Wills Wilde** (1856–1900), who moved into no. 1 in 1880 with an old Oxford chum, Frank Miles, only to be asked to leave the following year by the latter (under pressure from his father, Canon Miles), after the hostile reception given to Wilde's recently published poetry. Four years later, Wilde moved back into the street, to no. 34, with his new bride Constance Lloyd. By all accounts he was never very good at "playing husband", though he was happy enough to play father to his two boys (when he was there). It was in Tite Street, in 1891, that Wilde first met **Lord Alfred Douglas**, son of the Marquis of Queensberry and known to his friends as "Bosie", who was to become his lover, and eventually to prove his downfall.

At the height of Wilde's fame, in 1895, just four days after the triumphant first night of *The Importance of Being Earnest*, the marquis left a visiting card for Wilde, on which he wrote "To Oscar Wilde, posing as a somdomite [sic]". Urged on by Bosie, Wilde unsuccessfully sued Queensberry, losing his case when the marquis produced incriminating evidence against Wilde himself. On returning to the *Cadogan Hotel* on Sloane Street, where Bosie had rooms, Wilde was arrested by the police, taken to Bow Street police station, charged with homosexual offences and eventually sentenced to **two years' hard labour**. Bankrupt, abandoned by Bosie and separated from his wife, he served his sentence in Pentonville, Wandsworth and later Reading jail. On his release he fled abroad, travelling under the pseudonym of Sebastian Melmoth, and died three years later from a syphilitic infection. He is buried in Paris's Père Lachaise cemetery.

who lived at ten different addresses in the 41 years he spent in Chelsea, lived for a time at no. 96, the house where the Provisional IRA and the British government met secretly in 1972, to discuss peace, some five months after Bloody Sunday. The Brunels, Marc and Isambard, both lived at no. 99, which form part of **Lindsey House**, built in 1674 on the site of Thomas More's farm – it's occasionally possible to visit the entrance hall, garden room and gardens (phone ☎020 7447 6605 for more details). Last but not least, the reclusive J.M.W. Turner lived at no. 119 for the last six years of his life under the pseudonym Booth, and painted many a sunset over the Thames.

Carlyle's House

24 Cheyne Row • March–Oct Wed–Sun 11am–4.30pm • ⓦ nationaltrust.org.uk • £5.10, under-16s £2.60 • ☎ 020 7352 7087 • Bus #19 or #319 from ⊖ Sloane Square

Scottish historian **Thomas Carlyle** (1795–1881) set up home here with his wife, Jane, in 1834. Carlyle's full-blooded and colourful style of writing brought him great fame during his lifetime – a statue was erected to the "Sage of Chelsea" on Cheyne Walk less than a year after his death in 1881, and the house became a museum just fifteen years later. That said, the intellectuals and artists who visited Carlyle – among them Dickens, Tennyson, Chopin, Mazzini, Browning and Darwin – were attracted as much by the wit of his strong-willed wife, with whom Carlyle enjoyed a famously tempestuous relationship. The house itself is a typically dour Victorian abode, kept much as the Carlyles would have had it – the historian's hat still hangs in the hall. Among the artefacts are a letter from Disraeli offering a baronetcy and Carlyle's reply, refusing it. The top floor contains the garret study where Carlyle tried in vain to escape the din of the street and the neighbours' noisy roosters, in order to complete his final magnum opus on Frederick the Great.

Brompton Cemetery

210 Old Brompton Rd • Daily: summer 8am–8pm; winter 8am–4pm • Free • Guided tours May–Aug Sun 2pm; Sept–April every other Sun • £6 donation requested • ☎ 020 7352 1201, ⓦ brompton-cemetery.org • ⊖ West Brompton

Brompton Cemetery is the least overgrown of London's "Magnificent Seven" Victorian graveyards. Laid out on a grid plan in 1840 and now overlooked by the east stand of

17 Chelsea Football Club, the cemetery's leafy central avenue leads south to an octagonal chapel. Here, you'll find the grave of Frederick Leyland, president of the National Telephone Company: designed by Edward Burne-Jones, it's a bizarre copper-green jewel box on stilts, smothered with swirling wrought-ironwork. Before you reach the chapel, eerie colonnaded catacombs, originally planned to extend the full length of the cemetery, open out into the Great Circle, a forest of tilted crosses.

Few really famous corpses grace Brompton, but enthusiasts might like to seek out Suffragette leader **Emmeline Pankhurst**; Henry Cole, the man behind the Great Exhibition and the V&A; Fanny Brawne, the love of Keats' life; and John Snow, Queen Victoria's anaesthetist, whose chloroform-fixes the monarch described as "soothing, quieting and delightful beyond measure". **Long Wolf**, a Sioux Indian chief, was a temporary resident here, after he died while on tour entertaining the Victorian masses with Colonel "Buffalo Bill" Cody. His body has since been returned to his descendants in America.

Fulham Palace

Bishop's Ave • **Museum** Summer Mon–Thurs 12.30–4.30pm & Sun noon–5pm; Winter Mon–Thurs 12.30–3.30pm & Sun noon–4pm • Free **Gardens** Daily dawn–dusk • Free **Walled Garden** Summer daily 10.15am–7pm; Winter 10.15am–3.45pm • Tours most Sundays at 2pm • £5 ☎ 020 7736 3233, ⍟ fulhampalace.org • ⊖ Putney Bridge

It's worth venturing as far as the New King's Road by Putney Bridge in order to visit **Fulham Palace**, in Bishop's Park. Once the largest moated site in England, it was the residence of the Bishop of London from 704 to 1973. The oldest section of the present-day complex is the modestly scaled Tudor courtyard, patterned with black diamonds; the most recent is William Butterfield's neo-Gothic chapel. You can also visit the small **museum** which traces the building's complex history, and displays a few archeological finds, including a mummified rat. In the palace grounds there's a lovely walled herb garden, with a Tudor gateway and a maze of miniature box hedges, but sadly no sign of the moat, which was filled in in 1921.

NOTTING HILL CARNIVAL

High Street Kensington to Notting Hill

Despite the presence of royalty in Kensington Palace, the village of Kensington remained surrounded by fields until well into the nineteenth century. The village has disappeared entirely now in the busy shopping district around Kensington High Street, and the chief attractions are the wooded Holland Park and the former artists' colony clustered around the exotically decorated Leighton House. Bayswater and Notting Hill were for many years the bad boys of the borough, dens of vice and crime comparable to Soho. Gentrification has changed them beyond all recognition, though they remain more cosmopolitan districts, with a strong Arab presence and vestiges of the Afro-Caribbean community who initiated and still run the Notting Hill Carnival.

18

High Street Kensington

The village of Kensington was centred on Kensington Church Street, but once the area was transformed into a residential suburb in the nineteenth century, the commercial centre shifted to **Kensington High Street** – better known as **High Street Ken**. The street is dominated architecturally by the twin presences of George Gilbert Scott's neo-Gothic church of **St Mary Abbots** (whose 250ft spire makes it London's tallest parish church) and the Art Deco colossus of what used to be **Barkers** department store, remodelled in the 1930s and now occupied by several retail chains, most prominently a branch of the Whole Foods supermarket, though the huge block lettering remains on the sides of the building. The rest of the street is nothing special, but in the quieter backstreets you'll find one or two hidden gems like **Holland Park**, the former gardens of an old Jacobean mansion, and **Leighton House**, the perfect Victorian artist's pad.

Kensington Roof Gardens

99 Kensington High St • ☎ 020 7937 7994 for opening hours, ⓦ virginlimitededition.com • ⊖ High Street Kensington

A little-known feature of the High Street is Europe's largest **Roof Gardens**, first opened in 1938, topping the former Derry & Toms department store, another monster 1930s building. Virgin, who now own the gardens, use them for private hire and public events including a summer cinema (ⓦ rooftopfilmclub.com), live music and DJ nights – check the website for schedules. When there is no event on there is free public access to the gardens and taking a wander around the three themed areas (Spanish Garden, Tudor Garden and English Woodland), complete with four pink flamingoes, sundry ducks and views across the rooftops is a surreal but delightful experience. There's a popular restaurant and terrace-bar overlooking the gardens from the central building so to guarantee at least a sight of the greenery, book a table. Access is via the reception on Derry Street; call ahead to check there isn't a private event on.

Kensington Square

On the south side of the High Street lies **Kensington Square**, laid out in 1685. Royalty moved into Kensington Palace shortly after its construction, and the square soon became so fashionable that it was dubbed the "old court suburb". By the nineteenth century, the courtiers had moved out and the bohemians had moved in: *Vanity Fair* author William Makepeace Thackeray, philosopher John Stuart Mill, the Pre-Raphaelite painter Edward Burne-Jones and Hubert Parry, composer of *Jerusalem*, all lived on the square.

Holland Park

Daily 7.30am to dusk • Free • ⓦ rbkc.gov.uk • ⊖ Holland Park or High Street Kensington

Sinking back into the backstreets north of High Street Kensington, with an entrance right on it, is the densely wooded **Holland Park**, popular with the neighbourhood's army of nannies and au pairs who take their charges to the excellent adventure playground. To get there from the Kensington end, take one of the paths off the High Street along the east side of the former **Commonwealth Institute** – a bold 1960s building with a startling tent-shaped Zambian copper roof – which will house the **Design Museum** (see p.237) from late 2016. The park is laid out in the former grounds of **Holland House** – only the east wing of the Jacobean mansion could be salvaged after World War II, but it gives an idea of what the place used to look like. The garden ballroom houses the spectacular *Belvedere* restaurant; and throughout the summer **outdoor performances** take place (ⓦ www. operahollandpark.com), continuing a tradition which stretches back to the first Lady Holland, who put on plays here in defiance of the puritanical laws of Cromwell's Commonwealth. Several formal **gardens** are laid out before the house, drifting down in terraces to the arcades, the orangery and the ice house, which have been converted into a café and an art gallery. The most unusual of the formal gardens, which are peppered with modern sculpture, is the **Kyoto Garden**, a Japanese-style sanctuary to the northwest of the house, built in 1991 to celebrate the Japan Festival in London, complete with koi carp and peacocks.

Holland Park artists' colony

Several wealthy Victorian artists rather self-consciously founded an **artists' colony** around the fringes of Holland Park, and a number of their highly individual mansions are still standing. First and foremost is **Leighton House**, now a museum (see below). Leighton's neighbours included G.F. Watts and Holman Hunt, Marcus Stone, illustrator of Dickens, and, in the most outrageous house of all, architect William Burges, who designed his own medieval folly, the **Tower House**, at 29 Melbury Rd. Slightly further afield, at 8 Addison Rd, is the Arts and Crafts **Debenham House**, designed by Halsey Ricardo in 1906 for the department-store Debenham family. The exterior is covered with peacock-blue and emerald-green tiles and bricks; the interior, which features a wonderful neo-Byzantine domed hall, is even more impressive. Sadly, both houses are closed to the public.

18

Leighton House Museum

12 Holland Park Rd • Daily except Tues 10am–5.30pm • £7, concessions and under-17s £5 • Guided tours Wed & Sun 3pm; (free with entry fee) • ☎ 020 7602 3316, ⓦ rbkc.gov.uk • ⊖ High Street Kensington

Leighton House, the "House Beautiful", was built for Frederic Leighton, president of the Royal Academy and the only artist to be made a peer (albeit on his deathbed). "It will be opulence, it will be sincerity", the artist opined before starting work on the house in the 1860s.

The entrance hall, with its walls of peacock-blue de Morgan tiles, is wonderfully lugubrious, but the star attraction is the remarkable domed **Arab Hall**, built in 1877. Based on a Moorish palace in Palermo, it resounds to the trickle of a central black marble fountain, and is decorated with Saracen tiles, gilded mosaics and latticework drawn from all over the Islamic world. The other rooms are less spectacular in comparison, but are hung with excellent paintings by Lord Leighton and his Pre-Raphaelite friends, Burne-Jones, Alma-Tadema, Watts and Millais – there's even a Tintoretto. Skylights brighten the upper floor, which contains a lovely gilded boudoir looking down onto the Arab Hall and Leighton's vast studio, where he used to hold evening concerts.

18 Stafford Terrace

18 Stafford Terrace • Wed, Sat & Sun 2–5.30pm • £7, concessions £5, under-17s £3, under-5s free • Guided tours (£10, concessions £8, under-17s £5, under-5s free; booking essential) Wed, Sat & Sun 10.15am & 11.30am • ☎ 020 7602 3316, ⓦ rbkc.gov.uk/museums • ⊖ High Street Kensington

18 Stafford Terrace is where the successful *Punch* cartoonist, Linley Sambourne, lived until his death in 1910. A grand, though fairly ordinary stuccoed terrace house by Kensington standards, it's less a tribute to the artist (though it does contain a huge selection of Sambourne's works) and more a showpiece for late Victorian taste, complete with stained glass, heavy furnishings and richly decorative William Morris wallpaper. The seventy-five-minute guided tours are great fun, and, on Saturdays, are led by an actor in period garb.

Bayswater and Paddington

It wasn't until the removal of the gallows at Tyburn (see p.243) that the area to the north of Hyde Park began to gain respectability. The arrival of the Great Western Railway at Paddington in 1838 further encouraged development, and the gentrification of **Bayswater**, the area immediately north of the park, began with the construction of

SHOPS

Books for Cooks	7
Honest Jon's	3
Idler Academy	5
Kokon to Zai	2
Lutyens & Rubinstein	8
Paddington Bear Shop	9
Paul Smith	11
Portobello Market	4
Rellik	1
Rough Trade	6
Stumper and Fielding	12
Wolf and Badger	10

PUBS & BARS

The Churchill Arms
The Cow
The Elgin
Paradise by Way
of Kensal Green
The Union Tavern
The Victoria
The Westbourne
The Windsor Castle

CLUB

Notting Hill Arts Club

MUSIC VENUES

Bush Hall
Shepherd's Bush Empire

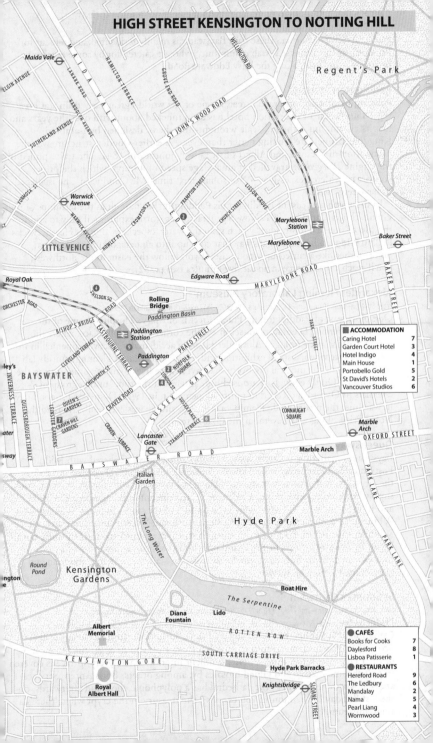

HIGH STREET KENSINGTON TO NOTTING HILL

Regent's Park

Maida Vale

Warwick Avenue

LITTLE VENICE

Royal Oak

BAYSWATER

Baker Street

Marylebone Station

Marylebone

Edgware Road

MARYLEBONE ROAD

Rolling Bridge

Paddington Basin

Paddington Station

Paddington

Lancaster Gate

Marble Arch

OXFORD STREET

Marble Arch

BAYSWATER ROAD

Italian Garden

Hyde Park

The Long Water

Kensington Gardens

Round Pond

Boat Hire

The Serpentine

Lido

Diana Fountain

ROTTEN ROW

Albert Memorial

SOUTH CARRIAGE DRIVE

KENSINGTON GORE

Royal Albert Hall

Knightsbridge

■ ACCOMMODATION	
Caring Hotel	7
Garden Court Hotel	3
Hotel Indigo	4
Main House	1
Portobello Gold	5
St David's Hotels	2
Vancouver Studios	6

● CAFÉS	
Books for Cooks	7
Daylesford	8
Lisboa Patisserie	1
● RESTAURANTS	
Hereford Road	9
The Ledbury	6
Mandalay	2
Nama	5
Pearl Liang	4
Wormwood	3

an estate called Tyburnia. These days Bayswater is mainly residential, and a focus for London's widely dispersed Arab community, who are catered for by some excellent restaurants and cafés along the busy **Edgware Road**.

Paddington Station

Paddington Station, on Praed Street, is one of the world's great early train stations: the 1850s facade of the station hotel has been mucked about with over the years and lost its charm, but cathedral-scale wrought-iron sheds, designed by Isambard Kingdom Brunel, are looking better than ever. An earlier wooden structure was the destination of Victoria and Albert's first railway journey in 1842. The train, pulled by the engine *Phlegethon*, travelled at an average speed of 44mph, which the prince consort considered excessive – "Not so fast next time, Mr Conductor", he is alleged to have remarked.

To the north and east of Paddington is **Paddington Basin**, built as the terminus of the Grand Union Canal in 1801. Now regenerated, it's worth exploring if only to admire the trio of unusual footbridges which span the water, especially Thomas Heatherwick's **Rolling Bridge**, a hydraulic gangway that coils up into an octagon (every Friday at noon) rather like a curled-up woodlouse. If you follow the basin to the northwest, you'll reach Little Venice in about five minutes (see p.282).

Alexander Fleming Laboratory Museum

Praed St • Mon–Thurs 10am–1pm • £4, concessions £2 • ☎ 020 3312 6528, ⓦ imperial.nhs.uk • ⊖ Paddington

One block east of Paddington up Praed Street is St Mary's Hospital, home of the **Alexander Fleming Laboratory Museum**, on the corner of Norfolk Place, where the young Scottish bacteriologist Alexander Fleming accidentally discovered penicillin in 1928. A short video, a small exhibition and a reconstruction of Fleming's untidy lab tell the story of the medical discovery that saved more lives than any other during the last century. Oddly enough, it aroused little interest at the time, until a group of chemists in Oxford succeeded in purifying penicillin in 1942. Desperate for good news in wartime, the media made Fleming a celebrity, and he was eventually awarded the Nobel Prize, along with several of the Oxford team.

Queensway

Bayswater's main drag is **Queensway**, a cosmopolitan street peppered with Middle Eastern cafés. Queensway is best known, however, for **Whiteley's**, opened in 1885 as the city's first real department store or "Universal Provider" with the boast that it could supply "anything from a pin to an elephant". The present building opened in 1907, and in the same year was the scene of the murder of the store's founder, William Whiteley, by a man claiming to be his illegitimate son. Hitler planned to make Whiteley's his British HQ once the invasion was over and ordered the Luftwaffe not to bomb it. The store closed in 1981, and now houses shops, restaurants and a multiscreen cinema, but the original wrought-iron staircase, centaurs' fountain and glass-domed atrium all survive.

St Sophia's Cathedral

Moscow Rd • Tues–Fri 11am–2pm • Free • ☎ 020 7229 7260, ⓦ stsophia.org.uk • ⊖ Queensway or Bayswater

Hidden away up Moscow Road, off Queensway itself, is the Greek Orthodox **Cathedral of St Sophia**, built in 1882 by John Oldrid Scott (son of George Gilbert Scott of St Pancras fame). From the red-brick exterior, you only get the merest hint of the richly decorated, atmospheric, candlelit interior, where every surface is covered in polychrome marble and gilded mosaics by, among others, Boris Anrep. Services are well worth attending as the cathedral has a polyphonic choir and afterwards, on the last Sunday of the month, you can visit the treasury in the crypt where there's a small museum.

Notting Hill

Notting Hill is home to one of London's most popular markets, **Portobello Road**, and its most famous annual street festival, the **Notting Hill Carnival**. It's also one of the city's most affluent neighbourhoods, characterized by leafy avenues, private garden squares, trendy shops and white stuccoed mansions. Back in the 1950s, however, it was described as "a massive slum, full of multi-occupied houses, crawling with rats and rubbish". Along with Brixton in south London, it was one of the main neighbourhoods settled by Afro-Caribbean immigrants, invited over to work in the public services. Tensions between the black families who'd moved into the area and the young white working-class "Teddy Boys" were exploited by far-right groups. And for four days in August 1958, Pembridge Road became the focal point of the UK's first **race riots**.

The following year, the **Notting Hill Carnival** (see box below) was begun as a response to the riots; in 1965 it took to the streets and has since grown into one of Europe's biggest street festivals. In the 1970s and early 1980s, tensions between the black community and the police came to a head at carnival time, but strenuous efforts on both sides have meant that such conflict has generally been avoided in the last two decades.

18

Portobello Road

Portobello Road is a meandering, beguiling street that starts just up Chepstow Road from the tube and is famed for its market (see p.434), at its busiest on Saturdays. A short distance up the road stands the **Electric Cinema** (see p.421), London's oldest movie house, which opened in 1910 on the corner of Blenheim Crescent. Portobello Road is the chief location in the movie *Notting Hill*: Hugh Grant's travel bookshop is at 142 Portobello Rd (now a tacky gift shop), though the real travel bookshop is actually round the corner at 13 Blenheim Crescent, his house is nearby at 280 Westbourne Park Rd and the private gardens he and Julia Roberts break into are on Rosmead Road.

NOTTING HILL CARNIVAL

When it emerged in the 1960s, **Notting Hill Carnival** was little more than a few church-hall events and a carnival parade by Trinidadians. Today Carnival, held over the August Bank Holiday weekend, still belongs to West Indians (from all parts of the city), but there are participants too from London's Latin American and Asian communities, and Londoners of all descriptions turn out to watch the bands and parades, drink Red Stripe, eat curry goat, hang out and dance.

The main sights of Carnival are the **costume parades**, which take place on the Sunday (for kids) and Monday (for adults) from around 9am until 7pm. The parade makes its way around a three-mile route, and consists of big trucks which carry the soundsystems and *mas* (masquerade) bands, behind which the masqueraders dance in outrageous costumes. Most of the *mas* bands play a variety of soca or calypso featuring steel bands – the "pans" of the **steel bands** are one of the chief sounds of Carnival and have their own contest on the Saturday at Horniman's Pleasance, off Kensal Road by the canal. As well as the parade, there are several stages for live music and numerous soundsystems where you can catch reggae, ragga, drum'n'bass, jungle, garage, house and much more.

Over the last decade or so, the Carnival has generally been fairly relaxed, considering the huge numbers of people it attracts but is nevertheless big on loud music and crowds – around a million people attend the festival each year and you can be wedged stationary during the parades. The static soundsystems are switched off at 7pm each day – if there's going to be any trouble it tends to come after that point.

Getting to and from the Carnival is quite an event in itself. Ladbroke Grove tube station is closed for the duration, while other stations have restricted hours or are open only for incoming visitors. The event's website ⓦ thenottinghillcarnival.com provides helpful advice on how to plan your journey to and from the carnival.

Trellick Tower

Passing under the **Westway** flyover and east into Golborne Road, you come face-to-face with the awesome **Trellick Tower**, a 31-floor high-rise block of flats designed by Ernö Goldfinger in 1973. The separate service tower has arrow slits and an overhanging boiler tower, yet despite its uncompromising concrete brutalist appearance, it remains popular with its residents. Golborne Road itself is known for its Portuguese and Moroccan cafés, giving the road some of the bohemian feel of old Notting Hill and making it the perfect place to wind up a visit to the market.

18

Museum of Brands, Packaging and Advertising

London Lighthouse building, 111–117 Lancaster Rd • Tues–Sat 10am–6pm, Sun 11am–5pm • £7.50, concessions £5, under-17s £3 • ☎ 020 7908 0880, Ⓦ museumofbrands.com • ⊖ Ladbroke Grove

Despite its rather unwieldy title, it's definitely worth popping into the **Museum of Brands, Packaging and Advertising**, half a block west of Ladbroke Grove, whose popularity saw it move to these new larger premises in 2015. The museum houses an awesome array of old British shop displays through the decades, based on the private collection of Robert Opie, a Scot whose compulsive collecting disorder has left him with ten thousand yoghurt pots alone. From Victorian ceramic pots of anchovy paste to the alcopops of the 1990s, the displays provide a fascinating social commentary on the times. Look out for the militarization of marketing during the two world wars, with their bile beans "for radiant health and a lovely figure" and V for Victory mugs, and clock the irony of the glamorous early cigarette adverts.

Kensal Green Cemetery

Entrance gates on Harrow Road, 100m & 800m west of Ladbroke Grove • April–Sept Mon–Sat 9am–5.50pm, Sun 10am–5.30pm; Oct–March closes 4.30pm • Free • Guided tours (2hrs) March–Oct Sun 2pm; Nov–Feb first & third Sun 2pm • £7 donation suggested • ☎ 020 8969 0152, Ⓦ kensalgreen.co.uk • ⊖ Kensal Green

Beside the gasworks, the Great Western Railway and the Grand Union Canal, lies **Kensal Green Cemetery**, the first of the city's commercial graveyards, opened in 1833 to relieve the pressure on overcrowded inner-city churchyards. Highgate may be the most famous of the "Magnificent Seven" Victorian cemeteries, but Kensal Green has by far the best funerary monuments. It's still owned by the founding company and remains a functioning cemetery, though the central Greek Revival Anglican chapel, completed in 1838 and where services were held until 2003, has been closed for years, awaiting restoration. The excellent **guided tours** of the cemetery allow a peak inside and also include a visit to the **catacomb** below the Dissenters' Chapel, itself restored over a decade ago.

The graves of the more famous incumbents – Thackeray, Trollope and the Brunels – are less interesting architecturally than those arranged on either side of the Centre Avenue, which leads from the entrance on Harrow Road nearest Ladbroke Grove. Vandals have left numerous headless angels and irreparably damaged the beautiful Cooke family monument, but still worth looking out for are Major-General Casement's bier, held up by four grim-looking turbaned Indians, circus manager Andrew Ducrow's conglomeration of beehive, sphinx and angels and artist William Mulready's neo-Renaissance extravaganza. Other interesting characters buried here include: Walter Clopton Wingfield, who invented lawn tennis; Marcus Garvey, the black nationalist (until exhumed and taken to Jamaica in 1964); Carl Wilhelm Siemens, the German scientist who brought electric lighting to London; and "James" Barry, Inspector-General of the Army Medical Department, who, it was discovered during the embalming of the corpse, was in fact a woman. Playwright Harold Pinter was buried here and Queen singer Freddie Mercury was cremated here, but his ashes were scattered in Mumbai. Mary Seacole, the "black Florence Nightingale", is buried in the adjacent St Mary's Catholic Cemetery.

KENWOOD, HAMPSTEAD HEATH

North London

A potent combination of political dissent, bohemian intellectualism and jaw-droppingly expensive real estate has led north London to become a byword for middle-class privilege – just check out satirical paper *Private Eye*'s cartoon strip "It's Grim Up North London", peopled by bearded creatives Quin and Jez brunching and blogging their way through First World nightmares. And while you will undoubtedly spot Quins and Jezes in the cafés of Islington and the pubs of Primrose Hill, on the paths of Hampstead Heath and in the bookshops of Highgate village, to write off this varied, vibrant and historically rich swathe of London would be a huge mistake. From the willow-lined banks of the Regent's Canal to the rock'n'roll markets of Camden, north London is an unmissable destination.

North London officially begins at the **Regent's Canal**, which on its completion in 1820 delineated the city's northern periphery. Today it passes along the north side of **Regent's Park**, one of London's finest, framed by elegant Nash-designed architecture and home to **London Zoo**. The canal then cuts through **Camden**, a rakish place even today, whose market is one of the city's big attractions – a warren of stalls selling a mishmash of vintage fashion, street food, furniture, hippie crafts, jewellery and vinyl.

Neighbouring **Islington** has its own flourishing antiques alley, a few quirky sights and lots of good pubs and restaurants. The real highlights of north London, though, for visitors and residents alike, are leafy **Hampstead** and **Highgate**, pretty, largely eighteenth-century neighbourhoods that still feel like the villages they once were. They have the added advantage of proximity to one of London's wildest patches of greenery, **Hampstead Heath**, where you can enjoy stupendous views, fly kites, swim outdoors and admire high art at the Neoclassical mansion of **Kenwood House**.

A handful of sights in more far-flung suburbs are also worth seeking out: the nineteenth-century utopia of **Hampstead Garden Suburb**; the Orthodox Jewish suburb of **Golders Green**; the **RAF Museum** at Hendon; and the spectacular **Swaminarayan temple** in Neasden.

Note that, unlike some other areas of the city, most of north London is easily accessible by **tube**; in fact, it was the expansion of the Underground network that enabled the relentless forward march of bricks and mortar in London's outer suburbs.

Little Venice

⊖ Warwick Avenue

The Regent's Canal starts out from the west in the triangular leafy basin known as **Little Venice**, a nickname coined by one-time resident and poet Robert Browning. The title may be far-fetched, but the willow-tree Browning's Island is one of the prettiest spots on the canal, and the houseboats and barges moored hereabouts are brightly painted and strewn with tubs of flowers. While you're here, try and catch a marionette performance on the **Puppet Theatre Barge** (see p.441), moored on the Blomfield Road side of the basin, a unique and unforgettable experience; performances take place every weekend at 3pm, and daily throughout the school holidays (except Aug & Sept). You can also catch a **canal boat** to Camden (see p.288), or walk south to the Paddington Basin (see p.278).

St John's Wood

The wealthy residential district of **St John's Wood** was built over in the nineteenth century by developers hoping to attract a moneyed clientele with a mixture of semi-detached Italianate villas, multi-occupancy Gothic mansions and white stucco terraces. Edwin Landseer (of Trafalgar Square lions fame), novelist George Eliot and Mrs Fitzherbert, the uncrowned wife of George IV, all lived here; more recently its

---

NORTH LONDON HIGHLIGHTS

Camden nightlife Gritty and edgy, Camden transports you to a pre-hipster London. See p.404

Hampstead Heath London's favourite spot for kite flying and bracing walks. See p.299

Highgate Cemetery A veritable who's who of artists, writers and revolutionaries. See p.302

Open Air Theatre, Regent's Park New takes on old classics in a lovely alfresco arena. See p.419

Regent's Canal See the city from an unfamiliar angle on a lazy narrowboat trip. See opposite

Union Chapel This glorious Gothic auditorium hosts live music. See p.292

REGENT'S CANAL

The **Regent's Canal**, completed in 1820, was constructed as part of a direct link from Birmingham to the newly built London Docks in the East End. After an initial period of heavy usage it was overtaken by the railway, and never really paid its way as its investors had hoped. By some miracle, however, it survived, and its nine miles, 42 bridges, twelve locks and two tunnels stand as a reminder of another age. The lock-less stretch of the canal **between Little Venice and Camden Town** is the busiest, most attractive section, tunnelling through to Lisson Grove, skirting Regent's Park, offering back-door views of Lord Snowdon's famous aviary at London Zoo and passing straight through the heart of Camden Market. You can walk, jog or cycle along the towpath, but this section of the canal is also served by scheduled narrowboats. Beyond, the canal takes you to Camley Street Natural Park (see p.137) and the newly regenerated King's Cross.

Three companies run daily **boat services** between Camden and Little Venice, passing through the 270-yard-long Maida Hill tunnel. Whichever you choose, return trips take around ninety minutes and you can board at either end.

Jenny Wren ☎ 020 7485 4433, ⓦ walkersquay .com. The narrowboat *Jenny Wren* gives narrated tours, starting off at Camden, travelling through a canal lock (the only company to do so) and heading for Little Venice. Two/three trips daily; £12.50. March Sat & Sun only; April–Oct daily.

Jason's Trip ⓦ jasons.co.uk. This one-hundred-year-old traditional narrow boat has been running trips since 1951. There are three (weekdays) or four (weekends) services a day between Little Venice and Camden. Cash only, no commentary. Return trips £14. April–early Nov daily.

London Waterbus Company ☎ 020 7482 2550, ⓦ londonwaterbus.com. Four working canal boats offer trips (seven daily in summer, fewer at other times) from Camden and Little Venice; some call in at London Zoo en route, picking up people who are already there. No commentary. Return £12; with zoo stop-off £24 from Camden, £25 from Little Venice. No booking required. April–Sept daily; Oct Thurs–Sun only; Nov to mid-Dec & Jan–March Sat & Sun only, weather permitting.

19

celeb-studded roll call of residents has included knights Richard Branson and Paul McCartney, singer Lily Allen, cricketer Imran Khan and comedian/actor Eric Idle.

Lord's Cricket Ground

St John's Wood Rd • **Museum** Enter via Grace Gate, southwest corner • Non-match days daily 10am–4.30pm • £7.50 • ☎ 020 7616 8658
Guided tours 4–6 daily • £18 (includes museum admission) • ☎ 020 7616 8500 • ⓦ lords.org • ⊖ St John's Wood

The arrival of the Regent's Canal was bad news for Thomas Lord, who had only recently been forced to shift his cricket ground due to the construction of Marylebone Road. In 1813, with the canal coming, he once more upped his stumps and relocated, this time to St John's Wood Road, where **Lord's**, as the ground is now known, remains to this day. Lord's is home to the **MCC** (Marylebone Cricket Club), founded in 1787, and the most hallowed institution in the game, boasting a very long members' waiting list (unless you're exceptionally famous or stinking rich). Its politics were neatly summed up by UKIP stalwart Viscount Monckton of Brenchley, who said, "I have been a member of the Committee of the MCC and of a Conservative cabinet, and by comparison with the cricketers, the Tories seem like a bunch of Commies."

Lord's is home to the **MCC Museum**, which started out in 1953 as a memorial to cricketers who had died in battle. Today its collection, arranged thematically, covers around four hundred years and houses the minuscule urn containing the Ashes (along with the complex tale of this odd trophy), numerous historic balls, bats and bails and a sparrow (now stuffed) that was "bowled out" by Jehangir Khan at Lord's in 1936; you can also watch footage of staggering cricket performances through the years. The museum is the starting point for, and included in, the ground's 1hr 40min **guided tours**, which also cover the famous Long Room (from where the players walk onto the pitch), dressing rooms, stands and the futuristic aluminium Media Centre.

NORTH LONDON

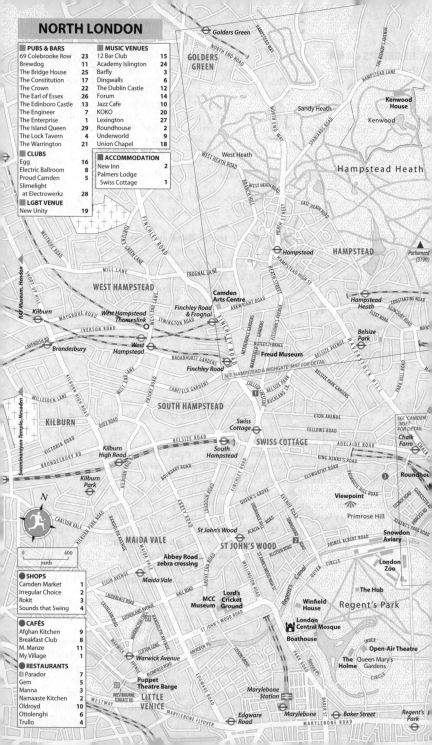

Regent's Park

Daily 5am to dusk • ☎ 0300 061 2300, ⓦ royalparks.org.uk • ⊖ Regent's Park, Baker Street, Great Portland Street, St John's Wood or Camden Town

Regent's Park is one of London's smartest parks, with a boating lake, ornamental ponds and waterfalls and wonderful gardens all enclosed in a ring of magnificent nineteenth-century mansions. As with almost all of London's royal parks, we have Henry VIII to thank for this one, which he confiscated from the Church in order to create yet more hunting grounds. However, it wasn't until the reign of the Prince Regent (later George IV) that the park began to take its current form – hence its official title, "The Regent's Park". According to John Nash's 1811 master plan, the park was to be girded by a continuous belt of terraces, and sprinkled with a total of 56 villas, including a magnificent pleasure palace for the prince himself, linked by Regent Street to Carlton House, George's palace in St James's. The plan was never fully realized, but enough was built to create something of the idealized garden city that Nash and the Prince Regent envisaged; the public weren't allowed in until 1845 (and even then for just two days of the week).

The eastern terraces

Nash's terraces form a near-unbroken horseshoe of cream-coloured stucco around the Outer Circle. By far the most impressive are the eastern terraces, especially **Cumberland Terrace**, completed in 1826, and intended as a foil for George IV's planned pleasure palace and tea pavilion. Its 800ft-long facade, hidden away on the eastern edge of the park, is punctuated by Ionic triumphal arches, peppered with classical alabaster statues and centred on a Corinthian portico with a pediment of sculptures set against a vivid sky-blue background. In 1936 an angry crowd threw bricks through the windows of no. 16, which belonged to American divorcée Mrs Wallis Simpson, whose relationship with Edward VIII was seen as a national calamity, and eventually led to his abdication.

Fifty-two more statues depicting British worthies were planned for the even longer facade of **Chester Terrace**, to the south, but Nash decided the ridicule they provoked was "painful to the ears of a professional man" and ditched them. Nevertheless, Chester Terrace is worth walking down if only to take in the splendid triumphal arches at each end, which announce the name of the terrace in bold lettering; the northern one features a bust of Nash.

To the north of Cumberland Terrace, the neo-Gothic **St Katharine's Precinct** provides a respite from the Grecian surroundings, though not one Nash was happy with. The central **church** (Tues–Fri 9am–1pm, Sat noon–3pm, Sun 10am–3pm; ⓦ danskekirke. org) serves the Danish community, who have erected a copy of the huge **Jelling Stone** – an imposing runic stone dating back to the tenth century – on the grounds.

The Inner Circle

Of the numerous villas Nash planned for the park itself, only eight were actually built, and of those just two originals have survived around the **Inner Circle**: St John's Lodge, built in 1812 and now owned by the Sultan of Brunei, and **The Holme**, Decimus Burton's first-ever work (the Nash protégé was just 18 at the time), picturesquely sited by the Y-shaped **Boating Lake** (April–Sept 10.30am–6pm; boats £8/30min), and now owned by a Saudi prince. Within the Inner Circle is the Open Air Theatre (see p.419), and **Queen Mary's Gardens**, by far the prettiest section of the whole park. A large slice of the gardens is taken up with a glorious rose garden, featuring some 12,000 flowers and hundreds of varieties, surrounded by a ring of ramblers; they're at their most beautiful in early June.

London Central Mosque

146 Park Rd • Daily 9am–10pm • Free • ☎ 020 7724 3363, ⓦ iccuk.org • ⊖ Marylebone or St John's Wood

The skyline of Regent's Park is punctuated by the shiny copper dome and minaret of the **London Central Mosque** (also known as the Islamic Cultural Centre). The foundation stone for the building was laid in 1944, after which the site served as a

THE BEATLES IN LONDON

Since the Fab Four lived in London for much of the 1960s, it's hardly surprising that the capital is riddled with Beatles associations. The prime landmark is, of course, the **Abbey Road zebra crossing** featured on the eponymous album cover, located near the EMI studios where the group recorded most of their records. The nearest tube is St John's Wood – remember to bring three friends (one barefoot), plus another to take the photos. Incidentally, Paul McCartney still owns the house at 7 Cavendish Ave, which he bought in 1966, two blocks east of the zebra crossing.

One (short-lived) nearby curiosity was the three-storey **Apple Boutique**, opened by The Beatles at 94 Baker St (⊖ Baker Street), in December 1967, as a "kind of psychedelic Garden of Eden for lovers of hippy gear with all the trappings of beautiful living", as George Harrison put it. The psychedelic murals that covered the entire corner building were whitewashed over after a lawsuit by the neighbours, and eight months later The Beatles caused even more pandemonium when, having made a huge loss on the venture, they gave the shop's entire stock away in the closing-down event – a blue plaque commemorates the shenanigans.

Other Beatles locations include the old Apple headquarters at 3 Savile Row, Mayfair, where the impromptu 1969 rooftop concert – their final live performance – took place, while Macca has his current office on Soho Square (see p.100). Real devotees of the group should sign up for a Beatles tour, run by The Original London Walks (twice weekly; 2hr; £10; ☎020 7624 3978, ⓦwalks.com).

community hub until the mosque was constructed thirty years later. Non-Muslim visitors are welcome to visit the information centre and to glance inside the hall of worship, which can hold one thousand worshippers and which is dominated by an enormous, sparkling central chandelier.

Winfield House

On the opposite side of the road from the London Central Mosque is **Winfield House**, a dull 1930s replacement for Decimus Burton's Hertford House, built by the heiress to the Woolworth chain, Countess Haugwitz-Reventlow (better known as Barbara Hutton), who gifted Winfield House to the US government during World War II and went on to marry Cary Grant; it's now the American ambassador's residence, and tends to be where the US President stays when he visits London.

London Zoo

Outer Circle, Regent's Park • **Zoo** Daily March–Aug 10am–6pm (5pm during Sunset Safaris); Sept & Oct 10am–5pm; Nov–Feb 10am–4pm • £22.50 peak season online; book online to avoid queuing **Sunset Safaris** June to mid-July Fri 6–10pm • £20.80 peak season online • ☎020 7722 3333, ⓦzsl.org/zsl-london-zoo • ⊖ Camden Town

The lion sits within his cage,
Weeping tears of ruby rage,
He licks his snout, the tears fall down
And water dusty London town.

The Zoo, Stevie Smith

The northeastern corner of Regent's Park is occupied by **London Zoo**, founded in 1826 with the remnants of the royal menagerie (see p.180). Perhaps the biggest hits here today are Animal Adventure – the children's petting zoo-cum-adventure playground – the invertebrate house (B.U.G.S), and the regular live shows, but Gorilla Kingdom and Butterfly Paradise are also winners, along with the walk-through Rainforest Life, Meet the Monkeys and lemur enclosures. On some summer evenings, Sunset Safaris allow you to encounter the animals as night falls, with acoustic music and food stands – after reports of drunken visitors in previous years upsetting or proving a danger to the animals, these evening events are now firmly family affairs.

The zoo boasts some striking architectural features, too, not least the 1934 spiral-ramped, concrete former **penguin pool** (where Penguin Books' original colophon was sketched), designed by the Tecton partnership under modernist architect Berthold Lubetkin; Tecton were also responsible for the Round House (1932). The Giraffe House (1836), by contrast, was designed in Neoclassical style by Decimus Burton, proving so fit for purpose that the zoo's giraffes still call it home today. Other landmark features are the mountainous Mappin Terraces (1913) and the vast tetrahedral aluminium-framed tent of Lord Snowdon's 1962 **aviary**.

Primrose Hill

The small northern extension of Regent's Park, known as **Primrose Hill**, commands a great view of central London from its modest summit. And it lends its name to the much sought-after residential area, to the northeast, which has attracted numerous successful literati, artists, bohemians and luvvies over the years: H.G. Wells, W.B. Yeats, Friedrich Engels, Kingsley Amis, Alan Bennett and Morrissey have all lived here, along with all the great and the good of the 1990s Britpop scene, rubbing shoulders with the likes of Gwyneth Paltrow and Kate Moss. Ted Hughes and Sylvia Plath lived in a flat at 3 Chalcot Square, just east of Regent's Park Road, which skirts Primrose Hill to the east, and it was nearby at 23 Fitzroy Rd, the house where Yeats once lived, that Plath committed suicide in 1963. Primrose Hill is swiftly being bought up by oligarchs and bankers, but you may still catch media darlings such as Jamie Oliver or David Walliams as you browse its boutiques, bakeries and bookstores.

Camden Town

Until the canal arrived, **Camden Town** wasn't even a village, but by Victorian times it had become a notorious slum area, an image it took most of the twentieth century to shed. In the meantime, it attracted its fair share of artists, most famously the Camden Town Group formed in 1911 by Walter Sickert, later joined by the likes of Lucian Freud, Frank Auerbach and Leon Kossoff. These days, you're more likely to bump into young foreign tourists heading for the market, and as-yet-unknown bands on the lookout for members of the local music industry.

For all the gentrification of the last thirty years, Camden retains a gritty edge, compounded by the various railway lines that plough through the area, the canal and the homeless shelter on Arlington Road. Its proximity to three mainline stations also made it an obvious point of immigration over the years, particularly for the Irish, but also for Greek Cypriots during the 1950s. Nowadays, the **market** overwhelms the area, especially at weekends; that, along with some genuinely mixed, unpretentious and rollicking pubs and music venues (see p.400), make it a corner of London well worth visiting.

Camden Lock

If you've seen enough market stalls for one day, stand on the bowed iron footbridge by **Camden Lock** itself, and admire the castellated former lock-keeper's house, to the west. You can catch a boat to Little Venice (see p.282); the flight of three locks to the east begins the canal's descent to Limehouse and the Thames. To the south are the covered basins of the Interchange Warehouse, linked by a disused railway line to the **Camden Catacombs**, built in the nineteenth century as stables for the pit ponies that used to shunt the railway wagons.

Roundhouse

Chalk Farm Road · ☎ 0844 482 8008, ⓦ roundhouse.org.uk · ⊖ Chalk Farm

Camden's brick-built **Roundhouse**, on Chalk Farm Road, is now a performing arts venue (see p.400), but was originally built in 1846 as an engine repair shed for 23

CAMDEN MARKET

Camden Market was confined to Inverness Street until the 1970s, when the focus shifted to the disused warehouses around Camden Lock. The tiny crafts market which began in the cobbled courtyard by the lock has since mushroomed out of all proportion, with stalls on both sides of Camden High Street and Chalk Farm Road. More than one hundred thousand shoppers turn up here each weekend, and **Camden Lock** and the vast labyrinth of the **Stables Market** now stay open all week long (see p.434). For all its tourist popularity, Camden remains a genuinely offbeat place. To avoid the crowds, which can be overpowering in the summer, aim to come either early (before noon) or late (after 4pm), or on a Friday. The nearest tube is Camden Town, though this is exit-only at peak times; Chalk Farm tube is only ten minutes' walk up Chalk Farm Road from Camden Lock.

---

goods engines, arranged around a central turntable. Within fifteen years the engines had outgrown the building, and for the next century it was used for storing booze. In 1964, Arnold Wesker established the place as a political theatre venue, and two years later, the Roundhouse began to stage rock gigs – everyone from Hendrix and The Doors to The Ramones and Kraftwerk – and counter-cultural happenings. In 1966, it held a launch party for the underground paper, *International Times*, at which Pink Floyd and Soft Machine both performed, later hosting a Dialectics of Liberation conference organized by radical psychologist R.D. Laing, not to mention performances by the anarchist Living Theatre of New York, featuring a naked cast.

19

Jewish Museum

129 Albert St • Mon–Thurs, Sat & Sun 10am–5pm, Fri 10am–2pm • £7.50 • ☎ 020 7284 7384, ⓦ jewishmuseum.org.uk • ⊖ Camden Town

Despite having no significant Jewish associations, Camden is home to London's purpose-built **Jewish Museum**. The Welcome Gallery, on the ground floor, features ten extremely varied accounts of what it's like to be Jewish in contemporary London, from a teenager at the JFS (Jewish Free School) to an Orthodox rabbi – you also get to see a thirteenth-century ritual bath (*mikveh*) from the City. On the first floor, there's an engaging exhibition explaining Jewish practices and illustrated by cabinets of Judaica from all over Europe, including a seventeenth-century Venetian Ark of the Covenant and treasures from London's Great Synagogue in the City, burnt down by Nazi bombers in 1941. The second floor has an interactive display on the history of British Jews from 1066 onwards, with good sections on Yiddish theatre, boxing and tailoring, plus a special Holocaust gallery that focuses on Leon Greenman (1920–2008), one of only two British Jews who suffered and survived Auschwitz. The museum also puts on a lively programme of special exhibitions on the top floor, as well as various talks, films, discussions and concerts, and has a café on the ground floor.

Islington

Since the 1960s, **Islington**'s picturesque but dilapidated Regency and early Victorian squares and terraces have been snapped up by professionals and City types and comprehensively renovated. The impact of this gentrification, however, has been relatively minor on the borough as a whole, which stretches as far north as Highgate Hill, and remains one of the city's most mixed. **Chapel Market** (Tues–Sun), to the west of Upper Street, selling cheap clothes, fruit and veg and Arsenal football memorabilia, is a salutary reminder of Islington's working-class roots. For more on the history of Islington, visit the borough's museum (see p.145).

There's little evidence of those roots on the glossy main drag, **Upper Street**. Its well-established antique market – along a pedestrianized lane confusingly known as **Camden Passage** – regularly brings an influx of wealthy customers, and its pubs and **restaurants** are filled night after night with young professionals splashing the cash. It's a

DANCING ON GRAVES

Iconic nineteenth-century clown Joseph Grimaldi (1778–1837), whose annual remembrance service at Holy Trinity Church in Dalston has become a cult event among hipsters and circus performers alike, is buried in the otherwise unremarkable **Joseph Grimaldi Park**, just off Pentonville Road. His real grave is set back behind respectful railings, but a modern memorial nearby allows a more irreverent homage. Two bronze casket shapes set into the ground, one dedicated to Grimaldi and the other Charles Dibdin, who employed him at Sadler's Wells, lie side by side. Against all instincts, just take the leap and dance on Grimaldi's "grave" – the pressure of your footsteps sets off his trademark tune *Hot Codlins*. Less Rest in Peace than Rest in Play, it's a fitting, and poignant, celebration of one of the world's wisest fools.

19

popular place to come in the evening – a kind of off-West End – boasting the long-established *King's Head* **pub theatre**, the Little Angel **puppet theatre** and the ever-popular Almeida, plus several live music venues (see p.400).

Upper Street

Looking at the traffic hurtling – or crawling – along **Upper Street** today, it's hard to believe that "merry Islington", as it was known, was in the seventeenth and eighteenth centuries a spa resort where people would come to drink the clear water and breathe lungfuls of clean, pure air. Today this broad, bustling thoroughfare has something of a mini-West End feel about it, lined with chichi boutiques, cool design stores and an ever-increasing roster of restaurants that bring in punters from all over north London and give the area a distinct buzz after dark. Look out for the raised pavements along stretches of this and surrounding streets: in the nineteenth century Islington was a grazing halt for livestock en route to the local **Royal Agricultural Hall** or nearby Smithfield, and those high sidewalks protected pedestrians from being splattered with mud.

Royal Agricultural Hall

52 Upper St • ⊖ Angel

The modern glass frontage of the **Business Design Centre** hides the former **Royal Agricultural Hall**, Islington's finest Victorian building, completed in 1862, and known locally as the "Aggie". As well as putting on agricultural and livestock exhibitions, the hall hosted the Royal Tournament, the first Crufts dog show and even such wonders as Urbini's performing fleas. During World War II, however, it was requisitioned by the government for use by the Post Office, who remained in residence until 1971. The interior is still magnificent, even if the exhibitions now held there are more prosaic – think greetings card conferences and stamp fairs, with January's **London Art Fair**, a prestigious contemporary art show, being one high spot.

Islington Green to Cross Street

Today, Islington has fewer green spaces than any other London borough – one of the few being the little **Islington Green**, just up from Angel tube. Five days a week (antiques Wed, Sat & Sun; books Thurs & Fri), the pavements to the east of the green are occupied by the antique stalls of **Camden Passage market** (ⓦcamdenpassageislington.co.uk); the antique and design shops in the market's narrow namesake and the surrounding streets, along with a number of good cafés and restaurants, stay open all week.

Just north of the green stands **St Mary's Church** (ⓦstmaryislington.org), built in the 1750s. Only the steeple survived the Blitz, though the light, spacious 1950s interior is an interesting period piece, with six fluted Egyptian-style columns framing the sanctuary. The churchyard opens out into Dagmar Passage, where in 1961 a former temperance hall was converted into the **Little Angel Puppet Theatre** (see p.441). The

THE NEW RIVER

In 1613, **Hugh Myddelton** (1560–1631), Royal Jeweller to James I, revolutionized London's water supply by drawing fresh water direct from the River Lea, 38 miles away in Hertfordshire, via an aqueduct known as the **New River**. A weathered statue of Myddleton, unveiled by Gladstone in 1862, stands at the apex of Islington Green. Right up until the late 1980s the New River continued to supply most of north London with its water – the original termination point was at **New River Head**, near Sadler's Wells theatre (see p.145); the succession of ponds to the northeast of Canonbury Road is a surviving fragment of the scheme. It is possible to follow the channel by foot from Islington all the way to Hertfordshire – the three-mile walk from New River Head via Canonbury and Clissold Park to the "Castle" pumping station in Stoke Newington (now a climbing centre and café) is particularly pleasant; north of here much of the river remains *in situ*. You can download maps on ⓦthameswater.co.uk.

19

archway at the end of Dagmar Terrace brings you out onto chichi **Cross Street**, with elegant eighteenth-century houses and raised pavements (see p.416) on both sides.

Union Chapel

Compton Terrace • ☎ 020 7226 1686, ⓦ unionchapel.org.uk • ⊖ Highbury and Islington

Built in 1888, at the height of the Congregationalists' popularity, the fancifully extravagant **Union Chapel** remains a church, but is now also an innovative independent live music venue (see p.400). Its lugubrious, spacious, octagonal interior is designed like a giant Gothic auditorium, with raked pew seating and galleries capable of holding 1650 rapt worshippers (or concert goers), and the pulpit centre stage.

Highbury Fields

⊖ Highbury and Islington

At the top of Upper Street, across the busy Holloway Road junction, lies the largest open space in the borough, **Highbury Fields**, where more than two hundred thousand people gathered in 1666 to escape (and watch) the Great Fire. Now overlooked on two sides by splendid Georgian and Victorian terraces, and fringed with plane trees, it's one of Islington's more elegant green spaces. A plaque on the park's public toilets commemorates the country's first-ever gay rights demonstration (against police harassment), which took place here in 1970. Highbury itself is also world famous as the former home of **Arsenal Football Club**, who now play at the modern sixty-thousand-seat Emirates Stadium, ten minutes' walk away (see p.436).

Canonbury Square

Islington's most perfect Regency set piece, **Canonbury Square** is centred on a smartly maintained flower garden, somewhat blighted by traffic ploughing up Canonbury Road. In 1928, **Evelyn Waugh** moved into the first floor of no. 17 with his wife Evelyn Gardiner (they called themselves "He-Evelyn" and "She-Evelyn"). In those days, the square was nothing like as salubrious as it is now. In fact, it was precisely the square's squalor that appealed to **George Orwell**, who moved into the top floor of no. 27 in 1944, with his wife and son, having been bombed out of his digs in St John's Wood; he later used it as the prototype for Winston Smith's home in *1984*. Immediately northeast of the square stands the last remaining relic of Islington's bygone days as a rural retreat, the red-brick **Canonbury Tower** (not open to the public) originally part of a Tudor mansion and occupied variously by figures such as Renaissance man Francis Bacon and writer Oliver Goldsmith.

Estorick Collection of Modern Italian Art

39 Canonbury Square • Wed–Sat 11am–6pm, Sun noon–5pm, first Thurs of month until 9pm • £5 • ☎ 020 7704 9522, ⓦ estorickcollection.com • ⊖ Highbury & Islington

Islington's most intriguing attraction is the **Estorick Collection of Modern Italian Art**, which occupies a Georgian mansion on Canonbury Square, with the entrance on Canonbury Road. The most exciting works here are those of the early Italian Futurists, whose founding manifesto of 1909 urged followers to "divert the canals to flood the museums". Futurism's mouthpiece was the fascist Filippo Marinetti, a rich boy with a penchant for crashing fast cars, and, as evidenced by the photos on show in the gallery, an eye for natty waistcoats.

The permanent collection, spread out over the two upper floors, ranges from the rainbow colours of *Music* (1911) by Luigi Russolo (inventor of the *intonarumori* – a sort of avant-garde hurdy-gurdy), which is firmly Futurist, to a Modigliani self-portrait and Symbolist paintings from Giorgio de Chirico. One of the most intriguing pieces is Medardo Rosso's wax sculpture *Woman with a Veil* (1893), which had a profound influence on the Futurists. Other highlights include Giacomo Balla's *Hand of the Violinist* (1912), a classic Futurist study of movement, speed and dexterity. The gallery also features paintings by lesser-known Italian artists such as Giorgio Morandi, Massimo Campigli, Mario Sironi and Zoran Music, as well as by Italy's two leading postwar sculptors, Emilio Greco and Marino Marini. There are excellent temporary exhibitions and a good little Italian café that spills out into the back garden in nice weather.

19

Hampstead

Perched on a hill to the west of Hampstead Heath, **Hampstead** village developed into a fashionable spa in the eighteenth century, and was not much altered thereafter. Its sloping site, which deterred Victorian property speculators and put off the railway companies, saved much of the Georgian village from destruction. Later, it became one of the city's most celebrated literary *quartiers* and even now it retains its reputation as a bolt hole for high-profile intelligentsia and discerning pop stars – the local Labour MP for many years was the actress Glenda Jackson.

The steeply inclined **High Street**, lined with posh shops and arty cafés, flaunts the area's ever-increasing wealth without completely losing its charm, though the most appealing area is the extensive, picturesque and precipitous network of alleyways, steps and streets east and west of Heath Street. Proximity to **Hampstead Heath** is, of course, the real joy of the area, for this mixture of woodland, smooth pasture and landscaped garden is quite simply the most exhilarating patch of greenery in London.

ORTON IN ISLINGTON

Controversial playwright **Joe Orton** and his lover **Kenneth Halliwell** lived together for sixteen years, spending the last eight years of their lives in a top-floor bedsit at 25 Noel Rd, to the east of Upper Street, where the Regent's Canal emerges from the Islington tunnel. It's ironic that the borough council has seen fit to erect a plaque on the house commemorating the couple, when it was instrumental in pressing for harsh prison sentences after both men were found guilty of stealing and defacing local library books in 1962. A few of the wittily doctored books are now on display at the **Islington Museum** (see p.145).

Six months in prison worked wonders for Orton's authorial skills, as he himself said: "Being in the nick brought detachment to my writing." It also brought him success, with irreverent comedies like *Loot*, *Entertaining Mr Sloane* and *What the Butler Saw* playing to sell-out audiences in the West End and on Broadway. Orton's meteoric fame and his sexual profligacy drove Halliwell to despair, however, and on August 9, 1967, the latter finally cracked – beating Orton to death with a hammer and then killing himself with a drug overdose. Their ashes were mixed together and scattered over the grass at **Golders Green Crematorium** (see p.304). Apart from the nearby public toilets, Orton's favourite local hangout was the appropriately entitled *Island Queen* pub (see p.397), at the end of Noel Road.

Holly Bush Hill

If you wander into the backstreets north of Hampstead tube, you will probably end up at the small triangular green on **Holly Bush Hill**, where the white weatherboarded **Romney House** stands (closed to the public). In 1797, painter George Romney converted the house and stables into London's first purpose-built artist's studio house, though he spent only two years here before returning to the Lake District and the wife he had abandoned thirty years earlier. Later, it served as Hampstead's Assembly Rooms, where Constable used to lecture on landscape painting.

Fenton House

Hampstead Grove • March–Oct Wed–Sun 11am–5pm • NT • House £6.50 • ☎ 020 7435 3471, ⓦ nationaltrust.org.uk/fenton-house • ⊖ Hampstead

Fenton House, a seventeenth-century merchant's house set grandly behind wrought-iron gates, houses a collection of **European and Oriental ceramics**, a smattering of British twentieth-century paintings by the likes of Walter Sickert, Duncan Grant and Spencer Gore, and a superb collection of **early musical instruments** – all displayed on the top floor, from which you can see right across London. Among the spinets, virginals and clavichords is an early Broadwood grand piano and an Unverdorben lute from 1580 (one of just three in the world). Don't miss the beautiful walled **garden**, with an orchard, a kitchen garden and a formal garden.

Admiral's Walk

Up Hampstead Grove, beyond Fenton House, is **Admiral's Walk**, so-called after its most famous building, **Admiral's House**, a vast whitewashed Georgian mansion whose top storey resembles a quarterdeck. Once painted by Constable, it was later lived in by Victorian architect George Gilbert Scott, of Albert Memorial and St Pancras fame. Until his death in 1933 John Galsworthy lived in the adjacent cottage, **Grove Lodge** – "[it] wasn't cheap, I can tell you", he wrote to a friend on arrival – where he completed *The Forsyte Saga* and received the 1932 Nobel Prize, which was presented to him here since he was too ill to travel abroad. Opposite is **The Mount**, a gently sloping street descending to Heath Street, which has changed little since it was depicted in *Work* by Pre-Raphaelite artist (and local resident) Ford Madox Brown.

St John-at-Hampstead and around

Church Row • Daily 9am–5pm • Free • ☎ 020 7794 5808, ⓦ hampsteadparishchurch.org.uk • ⊖ Hampstead

The Georgian terraces of tree-centred **Church Row**, at the south end of Heath Street, are where City gents would stay for the week when Hampstead was a thriving spa. The street forms a grand approach to **St John-at-Hampstead**, which has an attractive period-piece Georgian interior and a romantically overgrown cemetery. **John Constable** is buried in the southeastern corner; Hugh Gaitskill, Labour Party leader from 1955 until his death in 1963, lies in the Churchyard Extension to the northeast. If you continue up Holly Walk, you'll come to **St Mary's Church**, whose Italianate facade is squeezed into the middle of a row of three-storey cottages. This was one of the first Catholic churches built in London after the Reformation; the original facade from 1816 was much less conspicuous.

Hampstead Cemetery

Fortune Green Rd • Mon–Fri 7.30am–dusk, Sat 9am–dusk, Sun 10am–dusk • Free • ☎ 020 7527 8300, ⓦ islington.gov.uk • ⊖ Hampstead or Finchley Road & Frognal Overground

A good selection of Hampstead luminaries is buried in the neatly maintained **Hampstead Cemetery**, half a mile west of central Hampstead, on the west side of Finchley Road, and founded in 1876 when St John's Churchyard Extension was full. The pioneer of antiseptic surgery Joseph Lister, music-hall star Marie Lloyd and children's book illustrator Kate Greenaway are among those buried here. The full-size stone organ monument to the obscure Charles Barritt is the most unusual piece of funerary art, while the most unlikely occupant is Grand Duke Mikhail Mikhailovitch, uncle to the last Russian tsar, Nicholas II.

Freud Museum

20 Maresfield Gardens • Wed–Sun noon–5pm • £7 • ☎ 020 7435 2002, ⓦ freud.org.uk • ⊖ Finchley Road

One of the most poignant of London's house museums is the **Freud Museum** in the leafy suburban streets of south Hampstead. Having fled Vienna after the Anschluss, **Sigmund**

HAMPSTEAD WHO'S WHO

Over the years, countless writers, artists and politicos have been drawn to Hampstead, which has more blue plaques commemorating its residents than any other London borough. **John Constable** lived here in the 1820s, trying to make ends meet for his wife and seven children and painting cloud formations on the Heath, several of which hang in the V&A. **John Keats** moved into Well Walk in 1817, to nurse his dying brother, then moved to a semi-detached villa, fell in love with the girl next door, bumped into Coleridge on the Heath and in 1821 went to Rome to die; the villa is now a museum (see p.298). In 1856, **Karl Marx** finally achieved bourgeois respectability when he moved into Grafton Terrace, a new house on the south side of the Heath. **Robert Louis Stevenson** stayed here when he was 23 suffering from tuberculosis, and thought it "the most delightful place for air and scenery".

Author **H.G. Wells** lived on Church Row for three years just before World War I. In the same period, the photographer **Cecil Beaton** was attending a local infants' school, and was bullied there by author **Evelyn Waugh** – the start of a lifelong feud. The composer **Edward Elgar**, who lived locally, became a special constable during the war, joining the Hampstead Volunteer Reserve. **D.H. Lawrence**, and his German wife Frieda, watched the first major Zeppelin raid on London from the Heath in 1915 and decided to leave. Following the war, Lawrence's friend and fellow writer, **Katherine Mansfield**, lived for a couple of years in a big grey house overlooking the Heath, which she nicknamed "The Elephant". Actor **Dirk Bogarde** was born in a taxi in Hampstead in 1921. **Stephen Spender** spent his childhood in "an ugly house" on Frognal, and went to school locally. **Elizabeth Taylor** was born in Hampstead in 1932, and came back to live here in the 1950s during her first marriage to Richard Burton.

In the 1930s, Hampstead's modernist Isokon building, a block of flats on Lawn Road, became something of an artistic hangout, particularly its drinking den, the *Isobar*: architect **Walter Gropius** and artists **Henry Moore**, **Barbara Hepworth** and her husband **Ben Nicholson** all lived here (Moore moved out in 1940, when his studio was bombed, and retired to Herefordshire); another tenant, **Agatha Christie**, compared the exterior to a giant ocean liner. Architect **Ernö Goldfinger** built his modernist family home at 2 Willow Road, now a museum, (see p.298) and local resident **Ian Fleming** named James Bond's adversary after him. **Mohammed Ali Jinnah** abandoned India for Hampstead in 1932, living a quiet life with his daughter and sister, and working as a lawyer. **George Orwell** lived rent-free above Booklovers' Corner, a bookshop on South End Road, in 1934, in return for services in the shop in the afternoon; *Keep the Aspidistra Flying* has many echoes of Hampstead and its characters. **Sigmund Freud** spent the last year of his life in Hampstead, having reluctantly left Austria, following the Nazi Anschluss; his house is now a museum (see above). Artist **Piet Mondrian** also escaped to Hampstead from Nazi-occupied Paris, only to be bombed out a year later, after which he fled to New York. Nobel Prize-winning writer **Elias Canetti** was another refugee from Nazi-occupied Europe, as was painter/poet **Oskar Kokoschka** who, along with photomontage artist John Heartfield, was given assistance by the Hampstead-based Artists' Refugee Committee, set up by local Surrealist artist Roland Penrose. **General de Gaulle** got first-hand experience of Nazi air raids when he lived on Frognal with his wife and two daughters.

Ruth Ellis, the last woman to be hanged in Britain in 1955, shot her lover outside the *Magdala Tavern* by Hampstead Heath train station. **Sid Vicious** and **Johnny Rotten** lived in a squat on Hampstead High Street in 1976. **John le Carré** lived here in the 1980s and 1990s and set a murder in *Smiley's People* on Hampstead Heath. **Michael Foot**, the former Labour leader, lived in a house he bought in 1945 with his redundancy cheque from *The Evening Standard* until the age of 96. Today comedian **Ricky Gervais**, director **Ridley Scott**, footballer **Thierry Henry** and pop stars **Boy George** and **Harry Styles** have homes here.

19

Alexandra Palace ▲

HAMPSTEAD & HIGHGATE

■ **ACCOMMODATION**
Hampstead Village
Guesthouse **1**

● **CAFÉS**
Brew House **1**
Lauderdale House **2**
Louis Patisserie **4**

● **RESTAURANT**
Jin Kichi **3**

■ **PUBS & BARS**
The Bull and Last **7**
The Duke's Head **5**
The Red Lion and Sun **4**
The Southampton Arms **9**
The Spaniards Inn **1**
The Stag **8**

■ **LGBT VENUES**
Boogaloo **3**
The Dome **10**
Exilio **6**
Jackson's Lane Arts Centre **2**

Highgate
Wood

Queen's
Wood

Highgate

SHELDON AVENUE
NORTH HILL
CHURCH ROAD
VIEW ROAD
GRANGE ROAD
TALBOT ROAD
BISHOPS ROAD
ARCHWAY ROAD
MUSWELL HILL ROAD
WOOD LANE
PRIORY GARDENS
SHEPHERD'S HILL
DENEWOOD ROAD
STORMONT ROAD
BROADLANDS ROAD
COMPTON AVENUE
HAMPSTEAD LANE
BISHOPSWOOD ROAD

Highpoint 1 & 2

JACKSON'S LANE

2
3

H I G H G A T E

SOUTHWOOD LANE
SOUTHWOOD AVENUE
SOUTHWOOD LAWN ROAD
HIGHGATE AVENUE
HOLMESDALE ROAD
NORTHWOOD ROAD
NORTH ROAD
4

CHOLMELEY CR.
CAUSTON ROAD
ARCHWAY ROAD

Highgate
Village
Green
FITZROY PARK
THE GROVE
HIGHGATE WEST HILL
PONO
SQUARE
**Highgate
School**
CHOLMELEY PARK
CROMWELL AVE

SOUTH GROVE
**Highgate
Society** **5**
HIGHGATE HIGH STREET
BISHAM GDNS

**St Michael's
Church** ✝

Ladies'
Bathing
Pond

**West
Cemetery**

**Lauderdale
House** **2**

HORNSEY LANE
The Archway

MERTON LANE
HILLWAY
SWAIN'S LANE

St Joseph ✞

Waterlow
Park

OAKESHOTT AVENUE
MAKE PEACE AVENUE
LANGBOURNE AVENUE
HIGHGATE WEST HILL
MILLFIELD LANE
HIGHGATE HILL
DARTMOUTH PARK HILL
ARCHWAY ROAD

Men's
Bathing
Pond

**East
Cemetery**

**Whittington
Stone**

MAGDALA AVENUE

RAYDON STREET
CHESTER ROAD
ST ALBAN'S RD
ST ALBAN'S ROAD
BROOKFIELD PARK
CROFTDOWN ROAD

MACDONALD RD
VORLEY RD
TOLLHOUSE WAY
Archway
ST JOHN'S WAY
HOLLOWAY ROAD
6

BREDGAR ROAD
HARGRANE PARK
BICKERTON ROAD
ST JOHN'S GROVE
PEMBERTON GARDENS
HARGRANE ROAD

Upper Holloway

WOODSOME ROAD
BOSCASTLE ROAD
YORK RISE
LAURIER ROAD
DARTMOUTH PARK AVE
DARTMOUTH PARK HILL
DARTMOUTH PARK ROAD
JUNCTION ROAD
PEMBERTON TERR.

7
HIGHGATE ROAD

(i)

Lido

CATHCART HILL
MONNERY RD
MONERY RD

CHETWYND ROAD
SPENCER RISE
CHURCHILL ROAD
STATION ROAD
MIDDLETON GROVE
FOXHAM ROAD

Gospel Oak
GORDON HOUSE ROAD
INGESTRE ROAD
BURGHLEY ROAD
LAMBLE STREET
...FIELD ROAD
...AKE ROAD
9

10
Tufnell Park

0   400
yards

N

Freud arrived in London in the summer of 1938, and was immediately Britain's most famous Nazi exile. He had been diagnosed as having cancer way back in 1923 (he was an inveterate cigar-smoker) and given just five years to live. He lasted sixteen, but was a semi-invalid when he arrived in London, and rarely left the house except to visit his pet dog, Chun, who was held in quarantine for nearly a year. On September 21, 1939, Freud's doctor fulfilled their secret pact and gave his patient a lethal dose of morphine.

The ground-floor study and library look exactly as they did when Freud lived here (they are modelled on his flat in Vienna); the large collection of antiquities and the psychiatrist's couch, sumptuously draped in an opulent Iranian rug, were all brought here from Vienna in 1938. Upstairs, there's some old footage of the family, while another room is dedicated to his favourite daughter, Anna, herself an influential child analyst, who lived in the house until her death in 1982. Sigmund's architect son, Ernst, designed a loggia at the back of the house so that Freud could sit out and enjoy the garden; it has since been enclosed and serves as the museum shop, which flogs merchandise from silk scarves inspired by his patients' artworks to novelty "Freudian slippers", plus a good selection of books.

19

Burgh House

New End Square • Wed–Fri & Sun noon–5pm; Sat café only • Free • ☎ 020 7431 0144, ⓦ www.burghhouse.org.uk • ⊖ Hampstead

The Queen Anne mansion of **Burgh House** dates from Hampstead's halcyon days as a spa – known briefly as Hampstead Wells – and was at one time occupied by Dr Gibbons, the physician who discovered the spring's medicinal qualities. Today the house hosts exhibitions of local art – along with regular talks, music recitals and theatre pieces – and its attractive wood-panelled Music Room is a popular wedding venue. You can see fascinating old photos in the modest on-site museum of local history, along with some fine modernist Isokon plywood furniture, including a long chair by Marcel Breuer, found in a Hampstead skip. The *Buttery* café has lovely garden seating in summer.

2 Willow Road

2 Willow Rd • March–Oct Wed–Sun 11am–5pm; note that before 3pm, visits are by hourly guided tour • NT • £6 • ☎ 020 7435 6166, ⓦ nationaltrust.org.uk/2-willow-road • ⊖ Hampstead

Designed as his own family home by **Ernö Goldfinger** – the Budapest-born architect best known for his brutalist concrete high-rises, such as Trellick Tower (see p.280) – **2 Willow Road** is the central house in a modernist red-brick terrace. At the time of its completion in 1939 this was state-of-the-art stuff, its open-plan rooms flooded with natural light and much of the ingenious furniture designed by Goldfinger himself. The family altered very little during the fifty years they lived here, so what you see is a 1930s avant-garde dwelling preserved in aspic, a house at once both modern and old-fashioned. An added bonus is that the rooms are packed with the Goldfingers' extensive art collection: Surrealist *objets trouvés* and works of art by the likes of Max Ernst, Bridget Riley, Henry Moore and Man Ray.

Keats House

10 Keats Grove • March–Oct Tues–Sun 1–5pm; Nov–Feb Fri–Sun 1–5pm; free tours 3pm (30min) • £5.50 • ☎ 020 7332 3868, ⓦ cityoflondon.gov.uk/keats • ⊖ Hampstead

Hampstead's most illustrious figure is celebrated at **Keats House**, an elegant, whitewashed Regency double villa. The consumptive poet lodged here with his friend Charles Brown in 1818, after his brother Tom had died of the same illness. Inspired by the tranquility of Hampstead, and by his passion for girl-next-door Fanny Brawne (whose house is also part of the museum), Keats wrote some of his most famous works here before leaving for Rome, where he died in 1821 aged just 25.

In the pretty front garden a diminutive plum tree stands on the site of the much larger specimen in whose shade Keats is said to have sat for two or three hours before composing *Ode to a Nightingale*. The simple interior contains books and letters, an anatomical notebook from Keats' days as a medical student at Guy's Hospital, Fanny's engagement ring and the four-poster bed in which the poet first coughed up blood, and proclaimed "that drop of blood is my death warrant." Check the website for regular poetry readings, performances and talks.

Hampstead Heath

Ⓦ cityoflondon.gov.uk • ⊖ Hampstead or Hampstead Heath and Gospel Oak Overground

Hampstead Heath is hands down London's most enjoyable public park. Little of the original heathland survives, but this green swath nevertheless packs in a wonderful variety of bucolic scenery, from the formal **Hill Garden** and rolling pastures of **Parliament Hill** to the dense woodland of **West Heath** and the landscaped grounds of **Kenwood**. As it is, the Heath was lucky to survive the nineteenth century intact, for it endured more than forty years of campaigning by the Lord of the Manor, Thomas Maryon Wilson, who introduced no fewer than fifteen parliamentary bills in an attempt to build over it. It wasn't until after Wilson's death in 1871 that 220 acres of the Heath passed into public ownership. The Heath now covers more than eight hundred acres, and is run by the Corporation of London (see p.158).

19

Parliament Hill

Parliament Hill, the Heath's southernmost ridge, is perhaps better known as Kite Hill; this is north London's premier spot for **kite flying**, especially at weekends when some serious equipment takes to the air. The "parliamentary" connection is much disputed by historians, so take your pick: a Saxon parliament met here; Guy Fawkes' cronies gathered here (in vain) to watch the Houses of Parliament burn; the Parliamentarians placed cannon here during the Civil War to defend London against the Royalists; the Middlesex parliamentary elections took place here in the seventeenth century. Whatever the reason for the name, the view over the London skyline is unrivalled, a sweeping panorama that takes in the City's ever-spreading rash of corporate towers and the dome of St Paul's Cathedral, among other landmarks.

Boudicca's Mound to Viaduct Pond

To the northwest of Parliament Hill is a fenced-off tumulus, known as **Boudicca's Mound**, where, according to tradition, the warrior queen was buried after she and ten thousand other Brits had been massacred at Battle Bridge; another legend says she's buried under Platform 10 in King's Cross Station. Due west lies the picturesque **Viaduct Pond**, named after its red-brick bridge, which is also known as Wilson's Folly. It was built as part of Thomas Maryon Wilson's abortive plans to drive an access road through the middle of the Heath to his projected estate of 28 villas.

Vale of Health

West of Viaduct Pond, an isolated network of streets nestles in the wonderfully named **Vale of Health**, an area that was, in fact, a malarial swamp until the late eighteenth century. Literary lion Leigh Hunt moved to this quiet backwater in 1816, after serving a two-year prison sentence for calling the Prince Regent "a fat Adonis of fifty", among other things; Hunt was instrumental in persuading Keats to give up medicine for poetry. Other artistic residents have included Nobel Prize-winner Rabindranath Tagore, who lived here in 1912, and painter Stanley Spencer, who stayed here with the Carline family and married their daughter Hilda in the 1920s. Author D.H. Lawrence spent a brief, unhappy period here in 1915: in September of that year his novel *The Rainbow* was banned for obscenity, and by December, Lawrence and his wife, Frieda von Richthofen, whose German origins were causing the couple immense problems with the authorities, had resolved to leave the country.

POND DIPPING

The Heath is the source of several of London's lost rivers – the Tyburn, the Westbourne and the Fleet – and home to some 28 natural ponds, many of which are fishing ponds and three of which are used as **Bathing Ponds**. These are very popular in good weather: the single-sex men's and ladies' ponds, on the Highgate side, are open all year; mixed bathing, on the Hampstead side, is in summer only (see p.439).

West Heath

The busy road junction around **Whitestone Pond**, west of the Vale of Health, marks the highest point in this part of north London (440ft), overlooked by the faux-ancient *Jack Straws Castle* apartments. To the west lies **West Heath**, a densely wooded, boggy area with a thick canopy of deciduous trees sloping down towards the suburban neighbourhood of Childs Hill; it's a very peaceful place for a stroll and doubles as a popular gay cruising area. A track leads northwest from *Jack Straws Castle*, across West Heath, over to **Hill Garden** (daily 8.30am to dusk), the Heath's most secretive and romantic little gem. Originally an extension to the grounds of nearby Hill – or Inverforth – House, built by Lord Leverhulme in 1906 (and now converted into flats), the garden's most startling feature is the 800ft-long **Pergola**, whose Doric columns support a host of climbers including a wonderfully gnarled wisteria. The pergola is elevated some 15ft above the ground in order to traverse a public footpath that Lord Leverhulme tried in vain to have removed.

Golders Hill Park

West Heath Ave • Daily 7.30am–dusk • Free • ☎ 020 7332 3511, ⓦ cityoflondon.gov.uk • ⊖ Golders Green

Adjacent to the West Heath are the landscaped gardens of **Golders Hill Park**. Near the main entrance is the park café, serving Italian ice cream, and close by, a beautifully kept walled garden and pond. The central section of the park is taken up by a **zoo** containing alpacas, red-legged seriemas, ring-tailed lemurs and a series of impeccably maintained aviaries, home to white-naped cranes and other exotic birds.

Kenwood

Hampstead Lane • **Gardens** Daily summer 8am–8pm; winter 8am–4pm • Free **House** Daily 10am–5pm • Free • ☎ 020 8348 1286, ⓦ www.english-heritage.org.uk/visit/places/kenwood • Bus #210 from ⊖ Archway or Golders Green

Hampstead Heath's most celebrated sight is **Kenwood**, the former private estate whose beautiful white Neoclassical mansion faces south to catch the sun. The house dates from the seventeenth century, but was later remodelled by Robert Adam for the Earl of Mansfield, the most powerful judge in the country. Mansfield, who sent 102 people to the gallows and sentenced another 448 to transportation, was a deeply unpopular character and one of the prime targets of the 1780 Gordon Riots. He and his wife also raised **Dido Elizabeth Belle**, the illegitimate mixed-race daughter of his nephew and an African slave, at Kenwood, along with their adopted niece. Mansfield went on to make some important, if pragmatic, rulings that influenced the eventual abolition of the slave trade; Belle herself lived at Kenwood, ostensibly as a free woman, for thirty years.

Nowadays, with its free art collection and magnificently landscaped grounds, Kenwood is deservedly popular. The **gardens**, to the west of the house, boast splendid azaleas and rhododendrons and are dotted with **sculptures** by Henry Moore, Barbara Hepworth and Eugène Dodeigne; to the south, rolling green lawns slope down to a lake. The whole area is something of a suntrap and a favourite picnic spot; the provision-less can head for the *Brew House* café (see p.384) in the old coachhouse, which has some wonderful garden seating.

Kenwood House

Kenwood House is home to a superb seventeenth- and eighteenth-century **art collection** from the English, Dutch and French schools. First off, head for the Dining Room, where an eminently moving late self-portrait by **Rembrandt** (1665) shares space with marvellous portraits by Franz Hals, Van Dyck, Sir Joshua Reynolds and Ferdinand Bol and **Vermeer**'s delicate *Guitar Player* (1672). The Music Room holds more masterful portraits by **Gainsborough**, most strikingly the diaphanous *Countess Howe* (1764) caught up in a bold, almost abstract landscape, and the ghostly *Lady Brisco* (1776). Of the house's many wonderful period interiors, the most spectacular is Adam's Wedgwood-blue and rose pink **Library**, its book-filled apses separated from the central area by paired columns. The *pièce de résistance* is the tunnel-vaulted ceiling, decorated by Antonio Zucchi, who married Kenwood's other ceiling painter, Angelica Kauffmann.

Upstairs, you'll find more paintings, including William Larkin's full-length portraits of the arrogant Richard Sackville, a dissolute aristocrat resplendent in pompom shoes, and his much nicer brother, Edward, also sporting some fine pompoms plus earrings festooned with ribbons.

Highgate

19

Northeast of Hampstead Heath, **Highgate** lacks the literary cachet of Hampstead, but makes up for it with London's most famous **cemetery**, resting place of, among others, Karl Marx. It also retains more of its village origins, especially around **The Grove**, Highgate's finest row of houses, set back from the road in pairs overlooking the village green, and dating back to 1685. Their most famous one-time resident, the poet **Samuel Taylor Coleridge**, lived at no. 3 from 1816, with a certain Dr Gillman and his wife. With Gillman's help, Coleridge got his opium addiction under control and enjoyed the healthiest, if not necessarily the happiest, period of his life, until his death here in 1834.

Coleridge was initially buried in the local college chapel, but in 1961 his remains were reburied in **St Michael's Church**, in South Grove. Its spire is a landmark, but St Michael's is much less interesting architecturally than the grandiose, late seventeenth-century Old Hall next door, or the two tiny ramshackle cottages opposite, built for the servants of one of the luxurious mansions that once characterized Highgate. Arundel House, which stood on the site of the Old Hall, was where **Francis Bacon**, the Renaissance philosopher and statesman, is thought to have died, having caught a chill while trying to stuff a chicken full of ice for an early experiment in refrigeration.

Highgate High Street

Highgate gets its name from the tollgate – the highest in London and the oldest in the country – that stood where the *Gatehouse* pub now stands on **Highgate High Street**. The High Street itself, though architecturally pleasing, is packed out with franchises and estate agents, and marred by heavy traffic, as is its northern extension, North Road. If you persevere with North Road, however, you'll pass **Highgate School**, founded in 1565 for the local poor but long since established as an exclusive fee-paying public school, housed in suitably impressive Victorian buildings. T.S. Eliot was a master here for a while, and famous poetical alumni, known as Cholmeleians after the founder Sir Roger Cholmeley, include Gerard Manley Hopkins and John Betjeman.

Highpoint 1 and 2

At the top end of North Road, on the left, are the whitewashed high-rises of **Highpoint 1** and **2**, seminal early essays in modernist architecture designed by Berthold Lubetkin and his Tecton partnership from the late 1930s. Highpoint 1, the more northerly of the two blocks, was conceived as workers' housing, with communal roof terraces and a tearoom. The locals were outraged so Highpoint 2 ended up being luxury apartments, the caryatids at the entrance a joke at the expense of his anti-modernist critics. Lubetkin also designed himself a penthouse apartment on the roof in the style of a Georgian dacha, with views right across London, where he lived until 1955.

Waterlow Park and Lauderdale House

Highgate Hill • **Park** Daily 8am–6pm • Free • ⓦ waterlowpark.org.uk **Lauderdale House** Wed–Fri 11am–4pm, Sun 10am–5pm, closed Sat • Free **Café** Daily 9am–5pm • ☏ 020 8348 8716, ⓦ lauderdalehouse.org.uk • ⊖ Archway

On the west side of Highgate Hill lies charming **Waterlow Park**, named after Sydney Waterlow, who donated it in 1889 as "a garden for the gardenless". Waterlow also bequeathed **Lauderdale House**, a much-altered sixteenth-century building, on the eastern edge of the park, which is thought to have been occupied at one time by Nell Gwynne and her infant son. The house is now a vibrant cultural centre, staging events – including poetry, jazz, cabaret and kids' shows – and exhibitions; it's also home to a decent **café** that spills out into the terraced gardens. The park itself, occupying a dramatic sloping site, is an amalgamation of several house gardens, and one of London's finest landscaped parks, providing a through route to Highgate Cemetery. Not far away, down Highgate Hill, you'll find the **Whittington Stone**, with cat, marking the spot where Dick Whittington miraculously heard the Bow Bells chime (see p.160).

19

Highgate Cemetery

Swain's Lane • **East Cemetery** March–Oct Mon–Fri 10am–5pm, Sat & Sun 11am–5pm; Nov–Feb closes 4pm; guided tours Sat 2pm • £4, guided tours £8 **West Cemetery** Guided tours only: March–Oct Mon–Fri 1.45pm, Sat & Sun every 30min 11am–3pm; Nov–Feb Sat & Sun hourly 11am–3pm; £12; no under-8s • ☏ 020 8340 1834, ⓦ highgatecemetery.org • ⊖ Archway

Ranged on both sides of Swain's Lane, **Highgate Cemetery** is London's most famous graveyard. Opened in 1839, it quickly became the preferred resting place of wealthy Victorian families, who could rub shoulders with numerous intellectuals and artists. As long as prime plots were available, business was good and as many as 28 gardeners were employed to beautify the place.

But as the plots filled, funds dried up and the place fell prey to **vandalism**. The cemetery, which had provided inspiration for Bram Stoker's *Dracula*, found itself at the centre of a series of bizarre incidents in the early 1970s. Graves were smashed open, cadavers strewn about, and the High Priest of the British Occult Society, Allan Farrant, was arrested, armed with a stake and crucifix with which he hoped to destroy "the Highgate Vampire". He was eventually sentenced to four years' imprisonment, after being found guilty of damaging graves, interfering with corpses and sending death-spell dolls to two policemen.

In 1975, the old (West) cemetery was closed completely and taken under the wing of the Friends of Highgate Cemetery. Nowadays, you have to take a guided tour to visit it, though you can still wander freely around the less dramatic East Cemetery.

West Cemetery

The old, overgrown and ivy-tangled **West Cemetery** is one of London's most affecting sights. While trees are being lopped and paths cut through the undergrowth in order to return it more closely to its original state, it remains a wild, otherworldly place, and gloomily beautiful with its huge vaults and eerie, crumbling statuary.

This being Highgate, there are countless artists, eccentrics and revolutionaries buried here, and several oddities among the familiar Celtic crosses and draped urns. Guides may well point out the lion that snoozes above the tomb of menagerist George Wombwell, and the faithful dog that lies patiently on bare-knuckle fighter Thomas Sayers' grave. Another popular sight is the **Rossetti family tomb**, resting place of Elizabeth Siddall, Pre-Raphaelite model and wife of Dante Gabriel Rossetti, who buried the only copy of his love poems along with her. Seven years later he changed his mind and had the poems exhumed and published. The poet Christina Rossetti, Dante's sister, is also buried in the vault.

The cemetery's spookiest section is around **Egyptian Avenue**, entered through an archway flanked by Egyptian half-pillars, known as the "Gateway to the City of the Dead". The avenue slopes gently upwards to the Circle of Lebanon, at the centre of which rises a giant cedar. The circular Egyptian-style sunken catacombs here include the tomb of the lesbian novelist Radclyffe Hall. Above are the **Terrace Catacombs**, and the cemetery's most ostentatious mausoleums, some of which hold up to fifteen coffins; the largest – based on the tomb of Mausolus at Halicarnassus – is that of Julius Beer, one-time owner of the *Observer* newspaper.

East Cemetery

What the **East Cemetery** lacks in spooky atmosphere, it makes up for by the fact that you can wander at will through its maze of circuitous paths. The most publicized occupant is **Karl Marx** who spent more than half his life in London, much of it in bourgeois Hampstead. Marx asked for a simple headstone, but ended up with this lumpen bronze bust and granite plinth bearing the words "Workers of all lands, unite", from *The Communist Manifesto*. He was visited here by Khrushchev, Brezhnev and just about every postwar Communist leader in the world, and lesser-known Communists such as Yusef Mohamed Dadoo, chairman of the South African Communist Party until his death in 1983, cluster around him.

Nearby is **George Eliot**'s grave and, behind it, that of her lover, George Henry Lewes. **Malcolm McLaren**'s headstone is typically defiant – "Better a spectacular failure, than a benign success" – while a shelf of supersized stone books gives an unexpectedly learned air to the resting place of TV prankster **Jeremy Beadle**, "Writer, Presenter, Curator of Oddities". Perhaps most striking, however, is **Patrick Caulfield**'s stark, self-designed stone, crowned with one simple word: D-E-A-D.

19

Alexandra Palace

Alexandra Palace Way · ☎ 020 8365 2121, ⓦ alexandrapalace.com · Bus #W3 from Alexandra Palace train station or walk from ⊖ Wood Green

Since its more famous rival, Crystal Palace, burnt down in 1936 (see p.312), **Alexandra Palace**, built in 1873 on the commanding heights of Muswell Hill, is London's only surviving example of a Victorian "People's Palace". Sixteen days after the official opening, "Ally Pally" itself burnt down and, despite being rebuilt within two years and boasting a theatre, a reading room, an exhibition hall and a concert room with one of the world's largest organs, it was a commercial failure. During World War I more than seventeen thousand German POWs passed through its gates, and in 1936 the world's first television transmission took place here, launched by the BBC. It was the venue for the *International Times'* "14 Hour Technicolour Dream" in 1967, which featured performances by, among others, Pink Floyd and Soft Machine. The palace was rebuilt again after another devastating fire in 1980, and there are major Lottery-funded plans to restore the Victorian theatre and BBC studios for visitors. Meanwhile, the annual round of trade shows, funfairs, festivals and gigs continues, with an indoor ice rink, a boating lake, a pitch and putt course and a garden centre.

Golders Green

If the East End is the spiritual home of London's working-class Jews, **Golders Green** and the suburbs to the northwest of Hampstead are its middle-class equivalent. A little over a hundred years ago this whole area was open countryside but, like much of suburbia, it was transformed overnight by the arrival of the tube in 1907. Before and after World War II, the area was heavily colonized by Jews moving out of the old East End ghetto around Spitalfields or fleeing as refugees from the Nazis. Nowadays, Golders Green, along with Stamford Hill, is one of the most distinctively Jewish areas in London. The Orthodox community has a particularly strong presence here and there's a profusion of kosher shops beyond the railway bridge on Golders Green Road, at their busiest on Sundays.

Hampstead Garden Suburb

W hgs.org.uk • ⊖ Golders Green

Much of Golders Green is architecturally bland, the one exception being **Hampstead Garden Suburb**, begun in 1907. This model housing development was the Utopian dream of **Henrietta Barnett**, who believed the key to social reform was to create a mixed social environment where "the poor shall teach the rich, and the rich, let us hope, shall help the poor to help themselves." Yet from the start the suburb was socially segregated, with artisan dwellings to the north, middle-class houses to the west and the wealthiest villas overlooking the Heath to the south. As a social engineering experiment it was a failure – the area has remained a middle-class ghetto – but as a blueprint for suburban estates it was enormously influential.

The suburb's formal entrance is the striking Arts and Crafts gateway of shops and flats on Finchley Road. From here, ivy-strewn houses, each with its own garden encased in privet, yew and beech hedges, fan out eastwards along tree-lined avenues towards **Central Square**, laid out by Edwin Lutyens in a neo-Georgian style he dubbed "Wren-aissance". (Pubs, shops, cinemas and all commercial buildings were, and still are, excluded from the suburb.) Lutyens also designed the square's twin churches: the Nonconformist **Free Church**, with an octagonal dome, and the Anglican **St Jude's-on-the-Hill** with its steeply pitched roof and spire, and unusual 1920s murals. East of Central Square is the Lutyens-designed **Institute**, with its clock tower, now occupied by an adult education centre.

Golders Green Crematorium

62 Hoop Lane • Daily: April–Sept 9am–6pm; Oct–March 4pm • ☎ 020 8455 2374 • ⊖ Golders Green

More than 320,000 Londoners have been cremated at **Golders Green Crematorium** since it opened in 1902. The city's oldest crematorium, it's a secular space (there's even a special Communist corner), and more famous names have been scattered over the unromantically named Dispersal Area than have been buried at any single London graveyard: Enid Blyton, Charles Rennie Mackintosh, Ernö Goldfinger, Joe Orton, Peter Sellers, Joyce Grenfell, Sid James, Marc Bolan, Keith Moon, Bram Stoker and Doris Lessing among them. Finding a particular memorial plaque among the serene red-brick chapels and arcades is not easy, so it's best to ask at the office in the main courtyard. Other luminaries – including Anna Pavlova, Sigmund Freud and his wife and daughter – are in the columbaria, which you can only enter with an attendant.

Golders Green Jewish Cemetery

Hoop Lane • Daily except Sat: summer 8.30am–5pm; winter 8.30am–4pm • ☎ 020 8455 2569, W hooplanecemetery.org.uk •
⊖ Golders Green

Golders Green Jewish Cemetery was founded in 1897, before the area was built up. The eastern section is for Orthodox Sephardic Jews, whose tombs are traditionally laid flat with the deceased's feet pointing towards Jerusalem. On the west are the upright headstones of Reform Jews, including the great cellist Jacqueline du Pré, and Lord Hore-Belisha, Minister of Transport in the 1930s, who gave his name to "Belisha beacons" (the yellow flashing globes at zebra crossings for pedestrians).

Hendon: the RAF Museum

Grahame Park Way • Daily 10am–6pm • Free; simulators £3; 4D theatre shows £4 • ☎ 020 8205 2266, W rafmuseum.org.uk • ⊖ Colindale

One of the world's most impressive collections of historic military aircraft is lodged at the **RAF Museum**, in the former Hendon Aerodrome. The most obvious place to start is in the **Historic Hangars**, dominated by a vast 1920s Southampton reconnaissance flying boat. Highlights here include the Hoverfly, the first really effective helicopter; the clinically white Valiant, the first British aircraft to carry thermonuclear bombs; and, of course, the most famous British plane of all time, the Spitfire.

Of the museum's other halls, **Milestones of Flight** displays a century's worth of aircraft from an early airship gondola to the state-of-the-art Eurofighter Typhoon, while the **Grahame-White Factory**, the UK's first aircraft factory, purpose-built in Hendon in 1917, is filled with displays on aviation during World War I. Most chilling of all is the **Bomber Hall**, where you're greeted by a colossal Lancaster bomber, similar to those used in Operation Chastise, the mission carried out by Squadron 617 (and immortalized in the film *The Dambusters*). The **Battle of Britain Hall**, which contains a huge Sunderland flying boat, a V-1 flying bomb and a V-2 rocket, is another hit, featuring *Our Finest Hour*, an unashamedly jingoistic fifteen-minute audiovisual show on the crucial aerial battle between the RAF and the Luftwaffe during the autumn of 1940.

A number of 4D shows evoke various thrilling aeronautical experiences, while **simulators** allow you to experience anything from a WWI dogfight to a Red Arrows flight. The kid-friendly interactive **Aeronauts** gallery teaches the basic principles of flight and airplane construction, and lets you take the controls of a helicopter.

19

Neasden: the Swaminarayan temple

105–119 Brentfield Rd • **Temple** Daily 9am–6pm • Free **Understanding Hinduism** Mon–Fri 9am–5pm, Sat & Sun 9am–6pm • £2 • ☎ 020 8965 2651, Ⓦ mandir.org • ⊖ Neasden

The lotus blooms in splendour, but its roots lie in the dirt.

Hindu proverb

One of the most remarkable buildings in London lies just off the busy North Circular, in the glum suburb of Neasden. Rising majestically above the dismal interwar housing like a mirage, the **Shri Swaminarayan mandir** is a traditional Hindu temple topped with domes and *shikharas*, erected in 1995 in a style and scale unseen outside of India for more than a millennium. The building's vital statistics are incredible: 3000 tons of Bulgarian limestone and 2000 tons of Carrara marble were shipped out to India, carved by over 1500 sculptors, and then shipped back to London and assembled in a matter of weeks. Even more surprising is the fact that **Lord Swaminarayan** (1781–1830), to whom the temple is dedicated, is a relatively obscure and very recent Hindu deity. Note that shoulders, upper arms and legs must be covered when visiting.

The Mandir (temple)

To reach the temple, you must enter through the adjacent **Haveli**, or cultural complex, with its intricately carved wooden portico and balcony, and twin covered, carpeted courtyards. Having placed your shoes in the appropriate alcove, you can then proceed to the **Mandir**. The temple is carved out of marble, with every surface transformed into a honeycomb of arabesques, flowers and seated gods. Pillars are decorated with figures of gods and goddesses, while alcoves shelter **Murti** (idols), serene figures in resplendent clothes representing, among others, Rama, Sita, Ganesh the elephant god, Hanuman the monkey god and Shri Swaminarayan himself. The shrines are only open during darshan – or viewing – periods; check the website for timings. Visitors are welcome to attend the midday Rajbhog Arti ceremony, when candles are lit and musical prayers are offered to the deities.

Understanding Hinduism exhibition

Beneath the mandir, an **exhibition** explains Hinduism's basic tenets, extols the virtues of vegetarianism and details the life of Lord Swaminarayan, who became a yogi at the age of 11, and stood naked on one leg for three months amid snowstorms and "torturing weather". There's also a short documentary about the temple's history.

BRIXTON VILLAGE ARCADE

South London

Spreading out from the river that marks the city's great divide – both real and imagined – south London has many scattered points of interest. Greenwich, with its glorious views, Baroque architecture and Royal Observatory, stands head and shoulders above the rest as a tourist attraction, though other highlights include Dulwich Picture Gallery and, on the edge of London, the Medieval–Art Deco mash-up Eltham Palace. But south London is more than a hotchpotch of sights, incorporating such diverse neighbourhoods as Brixton, with its African-Caribbean roots, and Woolwich, with its military past. Add in some of the city's most delightful green spaces, riverside enclaves like Battersea and Greenwich Peninsula; and some of London's best emerging art and live music scenes, and this side of the Thames provides an irresistible mix.

Brixton

Brixton is a classic Victorian suburb, transformed from open fields into bricks and mortar in a couple of decades following the arrival of the railways in the 1860s. The viaducts dominate the landscape of central Brixton, with shops and arcades hidden under their arches, but it's the West Indian community, who arrived here in the 1950s and 1960s, who still define the character of the place – Notting Hill may have Carnival, but it's Brixton that has the most upfront African-Caribbean consciousness. Brixton once suffered from a reputation for violence, earned during the 1981, 1985 and 1995 riots when tensions between the police and the local youth came to a head. Now, however, it stands at the frontline of debates that rage across the city about property ownership and gentrification, as its revived and expanding markets attract increasing numbers of visitors to a plethora of small restaurants and bars, making an always busy, noisy neighbourhood even more frenetic.

Brixton's main axis is the junction of Brixton Road, Acre Lane and Coldharbour Lane, south of the tube station and overlooked by the slender clock tower of the immense Edwardian **Lambeth Town Hall**. Opposite, the large, incoherent pedestrianized plaza of **Windrush Square** is looked over by the Ritzy cinema, which opened in 1911 as the Electric Pavilion; Tate Library, built in 1892; and and the **Black Cultural Archives**. At the point where Brixton Road splits into Effra Road and Brixton Hill stands the Neoclassical church of **St Matthew**, from 1824, with its grandiose Doric portico. A short walk up Effra Road brings you to Brixton's main green space, hilly **Brockwell Park**, beloved for its lido (see p.439), and venue for July's Lambeth Country Show, a celebration of *rus in urbe* (see p.26).

20

Brixton Market

Street stalls Mon–Sat 8am–6pm, Wed closes 3pm **Brixton Village and Market Row** Mon 8am–6pm, Tues–Sun 8am–11.30pm (shops shut earlier, check individual café and restaurant times) **Farmers' market** Sun 10am–2pm • ⓦ brixtonmarket.net **Pop Brixton** Mon–Wed & Sun 9am–11pm, Thurs–Sat 9am–midnight • ⓦ popbrixton.org • ⊖ Brixton

The commercial lifeblood of Brixton pulses most strongly through **Brixton Market**, whose stalls spread out through the warren of streets and covered arcades east of Brixton Road. **Electric Avenue** – made famous by Eddy Grant's 1983 hit single – runs behind the tube station, and is so called as it was one of the first London shopping streets to be lit by electricity in the 1880s. A network of three sets of interwar arcades connect the streets, creating a complicated maze of activity: **Market Row** runs parallel with Electric Avenue, with entrances on Atlantic Road, Electric Lane and Coldharbour Lane; **Brixton Village** (originally Granville Arcade), its main entrance past the bridge on Coldharbour Lane, is along with Market Row, the hub of Brixton's foodie scene; while a third small arcade, **Reliance Arcade**, runs from Brixton Road to Electric Lane. The whole area harbours a unique mixture – butchers, fishmongers, stalls selling Caribbean fruit and veg, bold African fabrics, cheap clothes, homeware and religious artefacts – interspersed with newer cafés and bars, some of which are pioneers of London's street food scene (see p.370). You can find everything from divine ice cream and posh coffee to Thai food and Japanese

---

SOUTH LONDON HIGHLIGHTS

Brixton's markets Witness wonderful arcaded markets and changing street scenes. See above
Dulwich Picture Gallery A fine old collection plus well-curated temporary exhibitions. See p.310
Horniman Museum Delightful gardens, eclectic collections and a stuffed walrus. See p.311
Taking the boat to Greenwich Arrive by river for sublime views of the royal borough. See p.314
The Cutty Sark Clamber aboard the immaculately restored tea clipper. See p.315
Eltham Palace A famous Art Deco spectacle See p.324

Okonomiyaki, all following in the wake of the famous *Franco Manca* (see p.385) in Market Row. North of the railway tracks, the market continues along **Brixton Station Road** where there are food stalls (Wed–Fri lunchtime), craft and vintage stalls (Fri), rotating Saturday markets, such as a monthly makers' market, and a Sunday farmers' market.

With the success of Brixton Village, Lambeth Council has set up **Pop Brixton** (see p.385), on the corner of Pope's Road and Brixton Station Road, a shipping container-built mini village of local businesses, including designers, yet more street food, bars and an events space.

Black Cultural Archives

1 Windrush Square • Gallery Tues–Sat 10am – 6pm, café till 5pm; **archive and reference library** By appointment Wed–Fri 10am–4pm, library also Sat 1–4pm • ☏ 0203 757 8500, ⓦ bcaheritage.org.uk • ➔ Brixton

Founded in 1981, the **Black Cultural Archives** moved into its new home in 2014, the restored early nineteenth-century Raleigh Hall, which had been derelict for over a decade. The archive has gathered together the foremost collection of historical material

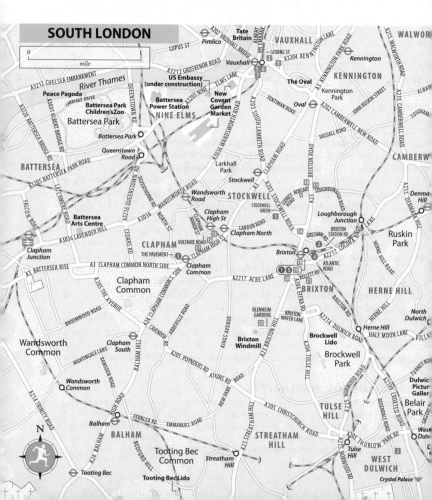

on Black people in Britain, which you can visit by appointment, while the small gallery in the modern extension hosts interesting temporary exhibitions and the courtyard café is a lovely spot looking out on Windrush Square.

Brixton Windmill

Windmill Gardens, end of Blenheim Gardens • April–Oct tours, usually second weekend of month Sat & Sun, book online in advance •
Ⓦ brixtonwindmill.org • ⊖ Brixton

Brixton is about the last place in London you'd expect to find a fully functioning **windmill**, but if you duck down Blenheim Gardens, off Brixton Hill, past the venue of the same name (see p.401), you'll see a tower mill nearly 40ft high, built in 1816, with its sails restored and a fetching weatherboarded "hood". Wind power drove the mill until 1862 when the area became too built-up, then steam and gas followed until the mill fell into disuse in the 1930s. Now restored, it's open sporadically and you need to book in advance. In the 1820s, the mill gained another source of power for its corn-grinding: the country's first **treadmill**, designed by William Cubitt and worked by inmates of Brixton Prison.

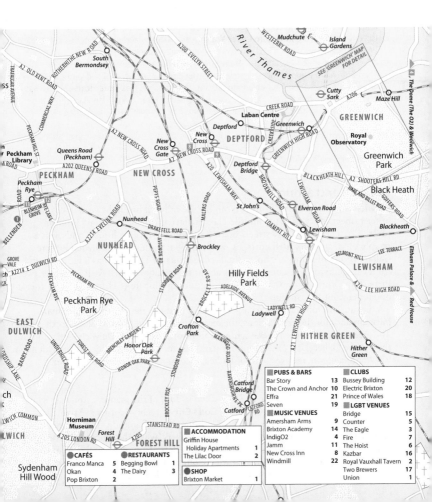

● CAFÉS		● RESTAURANTS	
Franco Manca	5	Begging Bowl	1
Okan	4	The Dairy	3
Pop Brixton	2		

■ ACCOMMODATION	
Griffin House Holiday Apartments	1
The Lilac Door	1

● SHOP	
Brixton Market	1

■ PUBS & BARS		■ CLUBS	
Bar Story	13	Bussey Building	12
The Crown and Anchor	10	Electric Brixton	20
Effra	21	Prince of Wales	18
Seven	19		
■ MUSIC VENUES		■ LGBT VENUES	
Amersham Arms	9	Bridge	15
Brixton Academy	14	Counter	5
IndigO2	4	The Eagle	3
Jamm	11	Fire	7
New Cross Inn	8	The Hoist	6
Windmill	22	Kazbar	16
		Royal Vauxhall Tavern	2
		Two Brewers	17
		Union	1

SOUTH LONDON'S ART SCENE

In recent years, the focus of London's art scene has moved southwards, concentrated on a few southeast London suburbs. The south London Art Map (SLAM; ⓦ southlondonartmap.com) features galleries in Bankside and Bermondsey, where White Cube is the big name (see p.237), Deptford, Greenwich and Peckham, a busy neighbourhood not dissimilar to Brixton, though it's the Black African communities here that have long had the largest presence. On the last Friday of the month many featured galleries open late and SLAM organize a walking tour of one of the neighbourhoods (£10; book in advance).

PECKHAM ART HIGHLIGHTS

A good place to start a gallery tour is **South London Gallery**, 65–67 Peckham Rd, between Peckham and Camberwell (Tues–Sun 11am–6pm, Wed & last Fri of month till 9pm; free; ❶020 7703 6120, ⓦ southlondongallery.org; ⊖⇌ Peckham Rye, bus #345 from Brixton). A gallery to bring art to the masses has been on this site (next to Camberwell College of Art) since 1891; now it's known for showcasing emerging artists, and has a great café. Hard to miss in the centre of Peckham, the striking Will Alsop-designed **Peckham Library**, 122 Peckham Hill St, won the Stirling Price for Architecture in 2000, while nearby **Peckham Platform** (89 Peckham High St; Wed–Fri 11am–6pm, Sat & Sun 10am–5pm; ❶020 7358 9645, ⓦ peckhamplatform.com), is a bright gallery space and educational project – in the week you may find school groups visiting. Directly opposite, the **Peckham Peace Wall** is a mural that reproduces the post-it notes stuck up on a boarded-up Poundland shop window in the aftermath of the 2011 riots.

A few minutes' walk away, attractive **Bellenden Road** has long been the posher end of Peckham, with the added cache of bollards designed by Antony Gormley and lampposts by local artist Tom Phillips. At no. 210, artist John Latham's former home, **Flat Time House** (Thurs–Sun noon–6pm during exhibitions; ❶020 7207 4845, ⓦ flattimeho.org.uk) – identifiable from the installation of oversize books protruding from the windows – exhibits his and others' work. Finally, finish the day on Rye Lane at the *Bussey Building* (see p.404), or in summer at the popular **Frank's Café** rooftop bar, part of an art project that takes over the top of the local car park (10th floor, 95a Rye Lane; June–Sept Tues & Wed 5–11pm, Thurs–Sun 11am–11pm; ⓦ boldtendencies.com, ⓦ frankscafe.org.uk).

Dulwich and around

Dulwich is just two stops from Brixton on the railway, but light years away in every other respect. This affluent, middle-class enclave is one of southeast London's prettier patches – its leafy streets boast handsome Georgian houses and even a couple of weatherboarded cottages, while the Soane-designed **Dulwich Picture Gallery** is one of London's finest small collections. If Dulwich has a fault, it's the somewhat cloying self-consciousness about its "village" status, with its rather twee little shops, rural signposts and fully functioning tollgate (£1) from 1789 – the only one remaining in London.

A day out in Dulwich can be combined with a visit to the charming **Horniman Museum** and, for the very curious, the remnants of the old **Crystal Palace**, further south. The green spaces between these sights are also worth exploring. **Dulwich Park**, opposite the Picture Gallery, is a pleasant public park, but for something a bit wilder, **Sydenham Hill Wood**, a nature reserve south of Dulwich Common, is the one to head for.

Dulwich College

Dulwich came to prominence in 1619 when its lord of the manor, actor-manager Edward Alleyn, founded the **College of God's Gift** as a school for twelve poor boys on the profits of his whorehouses and bear-baiting pits on Bankside. The original buildings and chapel stand to the north of the Picture Gallery, while the school is housed in a fanciful Italianate complex designed by Charles Barry (son of the architect of the Houses of Parliament), south of Dulwich Common. Now a large, fee-paying, independent boys' school, its impressive roll call of old boys includes Raymond

Chandler, P.G. Wodehouse and Ernest Shackleton, although they tend to keep quiet about World War II traitor Lord Haw-Haw. More recent alumni include rightwing populist politician Nigel Farage and the Oscar-nominated actor Chiwetel Ejiofor.

Dulwich Picture Gallery

Gallery Rd • Tues–Sun & bank hols 10am–5pm • Permanent collection £6; exhibitions around £12.50 • Guided tours Sat & Sun 3pm; free
• ☎ 020 8693 5254, ⓦ dulwichpicturegallery.org.uk • ⇌ West Dulwich (from Victoria) or North Dulwich (from London Bridge); buses #3 or #P4 from Brixton

Dulwich Picture Gallery, the nation's oldest public art gallery, was designed by John Soane in 1814, and houses, among other bequests, the collection assembled in the 1790s by the French dealer Noel Desenfans on behalf of King Stanislas of Poland, who planned to open a national gallery in Warsaw. In 1795, Poland disappeared from the map of Europe, Stanislas abdicated and Desenfans was left with the paintings. Neither the British nor Russians would buy the collection, so Desenfans proposed founding a national gallery. In the end it was left to his business partner, the landscape painter Francis Bourgeois, and Desenfans' widow, to complete the task and open the gallery in 1817. Soane, who worked for no fee, created a beautifully spacious building, awash with natural light, and added a tiny **mausoleum** at the centre for the sarcophagi of the Desenfans family and of Francis Bourgeois. Based on an Alexandrian catacomb, it's suffused with golden-yellow light from the mausoleum's coloured glass – a characteristic Soane touch.

The paintings

The gallery is crammed with superb paintings – elegiac landscapes by **Cuyp**, one of the world's finest **Poussin** series and splendid works by Murillo and Rubens. There's an unusually cloudy **Canaletto** of Walton Bridge on the Thames, **Rembrandt**'s beautiful *Girl at a Window*, a top-class portrait of poet, playwright and Royalist George Digby, the second Earl of Bristol, by **Van Dyck**, and a moving one of his much lamented kinswoman by marriage, Venetia Stanley, on her deathbed (and painted after she had died). Among the gallery's fine array of **Gainsborough** portraits are his famous *Linley Sisters*, sittings for which were interrupted by the elopement of one of them with the playwright Sheridan, and a likeness of Samuel Linley that's said to have been painted in less than an hour. There are regular special exhibitions, for which there is an extra charge.

20

Horniman Museum

100 London Rd • **Museum** daily 10.30am–5.30pm • free; aquarium £3.85 **Gardens** Mon–Sat 7.15am–dusk, Sun 8am–dusk, Animal Walk daily 12.30pm–4pm, nature trail daily 9am–4pm • Free • ☎ 020 8699 1872, ⓦ horniman.ac.uk • ⊖⇌ Forest Hill; bus #P4 from Brixton and Dulwich

The wonderful **Horniman Museum** was purpose-built in 1901 by Frederick Horniman, a tea trader with a passion for collecting. The building itself is a striking edifice designed by Charles Harrison Townsend, architect of the Whitechapel Gallery. Its most arresting features are the massive clock tower, with its smoothly rounded bastions and circular cornice, and the polychrome mosaic of allegorical figures in classical dress on the facade.

Entry to the museum is from the **gardens** to the west, where you'll see a graceful Victorian conservatory, brought here from the Horniman mansion in Croydon. Spreading out over a hill, with sublime views across the city, the gardens are a joy, with plenty for children to explore. They are planted for maximum educational benefit, so the Arts and Crafts sunken garden features plants that are used as dyes, and there are some oversized musical instruments to bash away on. A small animal enclosure, home to a couple of sheep, two alpaca and an exceedingly large rabbit, and a half-mile nature trail complete the picture.

The collections

The main **Natural History** gallery of stuffed animals and birds – everything from humming birds, puffins and an ostrich to large primates – and their skeletons, attracts the most visitors, with pride of place going to the splendid overstuffed Horniman Walrus (the taxidermist didn't know he was supposed to have wrinkles, so stuffed him to capacity). In one corner the **Nature Base** includes a Perspex beehive, so you can watch the honeybees at work. On the lower ground floor, head first for the dimly lit **Centenary Gallery**, which contains an eclectic ethnographic collection, much of it gathered by Horniman, from the precious butterflies that started his obsession at the age of 8 to a papier-mâché figure of Kali dancing on Shiva. Equally arresting are later acquisitions like the Nigerian puppets of Charles, Di and a British bobby.

The **African Worlds** gallery contains a wide-ranging anthropological collection from African masks – including the vast Igbo Ijele mask – and voodoo altars to some fine "Benin Bronzes", much like those at the British Museum (see p.125). In the **Music Gallery** you can see and hear more than 1500 instruments including Chinese gongs and beautiful clavichords, or have a go at some of the instruments in the hands-on room. There's a small charge for special exhibitions and for the **Aquarium** in the basement.

Crystal Palace

Anerley Hill • **Park** Daily 7.30am–dusk • Free **Museum** Sat & Sun 11am–4pm; ☎ 020 8676 0700, ⓦ crystalpalacemuseum.org.uk • ⊖≈Crystal Palace

After the 1851 Great Exhibition (see p.247), the **Crystal Palace** was enlarged and re-erected on the commanding heights of Sydenham Hill, to the south of Dulwich, affording spectacular views over London, Kent and Surrey. A fantastic pleasure garden was laid out around this giant glasshouse, with a complex system of fountains, some of which reached a height of 250ft. Exhibitions, funfairs, a pneumatic railway and a whole range of events were staged here. Despite its initial success, though, the palace soon became a financial liability – then, in 1936, the structure burnt to the ground overnight.

All that remains now are the stone terraces, the triumphal staircase and a few sphinxes, all in desperate need of renovation; a small **museum** on Anerley Hill tells the history of the place. Nowadays, the **park** is identified by a TV transmitter, visible from all over London, while the **National Sports Centre** in the centre of the park, whose tartan athletics track (Europe's first) was opened in the 1960s. The stadium stands on the site of the old Crystal Palace football ground, where the FA Cup Final was held from 1895 to 1914. For families, the best part of the park is the eastern section, particularly around **Lower Lake**, with further reminders of the park's Victorian heyday. The lake's islands feature around thirty life-sized **dinosaurs** (and other prehistoric creatures) lurking in the

---

ROAR! THE DINOSAURS OF CRYSTAL PALACE

Competing with the Horniman Walrus (see above) for best-loved Victorian curiosity in south London, the dinosaurs of Crystal Palace may look like extras from a 1970s sci-fi film, but they have an illustrious place in the history of the public understanding of paleontology. Created by animal sculptor Benjamin Waterhouse Hawkins in 1854, he consulted the experts of the day, in particular Richard Owen who had coined the term "dinosaur" in 1842. Though most are wildly inaccurate according to our current understanding of dinosaur anatomy, at the time it was an ambitious project to show to the public the latest scientific discoveries, and the models were based on recent fossil discoveries and comparing those bones with existing creatures. When Hawkins didn't know how they looked – or if the scientists disagreed – he had to be a little creative. For the Iguanodon he produced two sculptures, one standing like a pachyderm – as Owen envisaged it – and one slithering like a lizard, closer to the version of Gideon Mantell (who had found the first Iguanodon tooth). The dinosaurs were a sensation, the public drawn in by such publicity stunts as Owen and Hawkins hosting a New Year's Eve dinner party inside the cast of the Iguanodon during its construction. Visit on a busy weekend and you'll see they've lost none of their appeal. They are, however, in need of repair, but they do have friends: see ⓦ cpdinosaurs.org.

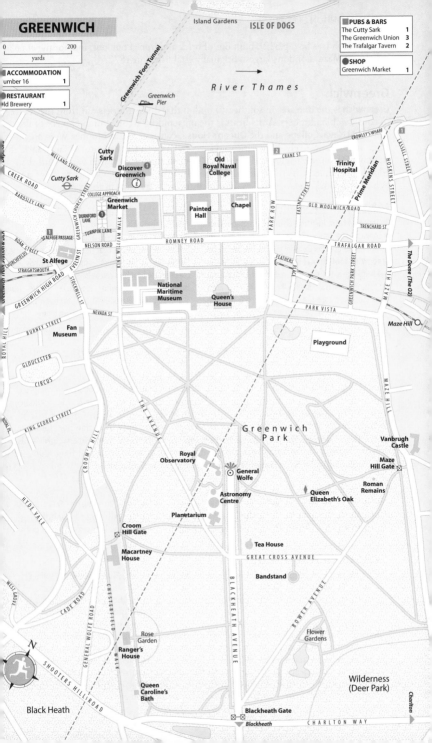

GREENWICH

0   200
yards

ACCOMMODATION
umber 16   1

RESTAURANT
ld Brewery   1

PUBS & BARS
The Cutty Sark   1
The Greenwich Union   3
The Trafalgar Tavern   2

SHOP
Greenwich Market   1

Island Gardens   **ISLE OF DOGS**

Greenwich Foot Tunnel

Greenwich Pier

River Thames

Crowley's Wharf

LASSELL STREET

HOSKINS STREET

DEPTFORD

WELLAND STREET

CREEK ROAD

BARDSLEY LANE

Cutty Sark

Cutty Sark

Discover Greenwich

Greenwich Market

COLLEGE APPROACH

GREENWICH CHURCH STREET

DURNFORD LANE

TURNPIN LANE

NELSON ROAD

ST ALFEGE PASSAGE

ROAN STREET

CHURCHFIELDS

St Alfege

STRAIGHTSMOUTH

GREENWICH HIGH ROAD

EVELYN ST

STOCKWELL ST

KING WILLIAM WALK

Old Royal Naval College

Painted Hall

Chapel

ROMNEY ROAD

CRANE ST

PARK ROW

EASTNEY STREET

OLD WOOLWICH ROAD

Trinity Hospital

Prime Meridian

TRENCHARD ST

TRAFALGAR ROAD

MAZE HILL

The Dome (The O2)

GREENWICH PARK STREET

FEATHERS

National Maritime Museum

Queen's House

PARK VISTA

NEVADA ST

BURNEY STREET

Fan Museum

GLOUCESTER

CIRCUS

ROYAL HILL

ROAN PL

KING GEORGE STREET

Maze Hill

Playground

G r e e n w i c h
P a r k

THE AVENUE

CROOM'S HILL

HYDE VALE

Royal Observatory

General Wolfe

Astronomy Centre

Planetarium

Croom Hill Gate

Macartney House

Vanbrugh Castle

Maze Hill Gate

Roman Remains

Queen Elizabeth's Oak

MAZE HILL

Tea House

GREAT CROSS AVENUE

Bandstand

BLACKHEATH AVENUE

BOWER AVENUE

WEST GROVE

CADE ROAD

GENERAL WOLFE ROAD

CHESTERFIELD WALK

SHOOTERS HILL ROAD

Rose Garden

Ranger's House

Queen Caroline's Bath

Flower Gardens

Wilderness (Deer Park)

Charlton

Blackheath Gate

Blackheath

CHARLTON WAY

Black Heath

N

undergrowth (see box, p.312), built out of brick and iron. Look out, too, for the circular hornbeam **Maze**, London's largest, originally established in 1872.

Greenwich

Greenwich is the one area in southeast London that draws tourists out from the centre in considerable numbers. At its heart is the outstanding architectural set piece of the **Old Royal Naval College** and the **Queen's House**, courtesy of Christopher Wren and Inigo Jones respectively. Most visitors, however, come to see the restored **Cutty Sark**, the **National Maritime Museum** and the **Royal Observatory** in Greenwich Park. With the added attractions of its riverside pubs and walks – plus startling views across to Canary Wharf and Docklands – it makes for one of the best day-trips in the capital.

ARRIVAL AND INFORMATION

By DLR and train Train from Charing Cross, Waterloo East or London Bridge (every 15–30min) to Greenwich station; DLR from Bank or Tower Gateway to Cutty Sark DLR station.

Greenwich foot tunnel For the best view of the Wren buildings across the river, get out of the DLR at Island Gardens, and then walk through the Greenwich Foot Tunnel under the Thames (open 24hr; lifts at both end). No cycling – and don't take a Boris Bike through with you, there are no docks in Greenwich.

By boat The most scenic and leisurely way to reach Greenwich is to take a boat from central London (every 20–30min). At busy times – summer weekends – the queue for the boat back can be long.

Information Greenwich information centre (daily 10am–5pm; ☎ 0870 608 2000, ⓦ visitgreenwich.org.uk) is in Pepys House in the Discover Greenwich centre.

20

Greenwich Market

Greenwich Church St • Tues–Sun 10am–5.30pm; April–Sept also Mon; generally: antiques and crafts Tues, Thurs & Fri; art, crafts and furniture Wed & Fri–Sun • ⓦ greenwichmarketlondon.com • ⊖ Cutty Sark DLR

Greenwich town centre was laid out in the 1820s, hence the Nash-style terraces of Nelson Road, College Approach and King William Walk, and is now a one-way system plagued with traffic. However, at the centre of these busy streets, filled with craft shops, bookshops, small galleries and sweet shops, stands **Greenwich Market**, an old covered market that has been sensitively restored, where you can still see the wonderfully Victorian inscription on one of the archways: "A false balance is abomination to the Lord, but a just weight is his delight." Stalls differ each day, with a changing array of generally excellent food stalls and some craft stalls all week, though the market is biggest at weekends.

St Alfege's Church

Greenwich Church St • Mon–Fri 11am–4pm, Sat 10am–4pm, Sun noon–4pm • ☎ 020 8853 0687, ⓦ st-alfege.org • ⊖ Cutty Sark DLR

Rising above the town centre is the Doric portico and broken pediment of Nicholas Hawksmoor's **St Alfege's Church**, built in 1712–18 to replace a twelfth-century structure in

---

GREENWICH RIVERSIDE

A fine vantage point for viewing the Old Royal Naval College is the **Five-Foot Walk**, which squeezes between the college railings and the riverbank. It was here that George I, Elector of Hannover (and a Protestant), landed to take the throne on September 18, 1714. If you're in need of riverside refreshment, drop into the Regency-style **Trafalgar Tavern** (see p.398), at the east end of the walk. Just beyond the pub, down Crane Street, is the **Trinity Hospital**, founded in 1613 by the Earl of Northampton for 21 pensioners; the entry requirements declared the hospital would admit "no common beggar, drunkard, whore-hunter, nor unclean person… nor any that is blind… nor any idiot". The cream-coloured mock-Gothic facade and chapel (which contains the earl's tomb) date from the nineteenth century, but the courtyard of almshouses remains much as it was at its foundation. Beyond the Trinity Hospital, the Thames Path continues along the river, past a few more pubs, and eventually all the way to the O2. In the other (western) direction you reach Deptford Creek.

which Henry VIII was baptized and Thomas Tallis, the "father of English church music", was buried. The church was flattened in the Blitz, but its lovely wooden galleries and its trompe-l'oeil coffered apse, originally by Thornhill, have since been magnificently restored.

Cutty Sark

Greenwich Church St • Daily 10am–5pm • £13.50; combined ticket with Observatory £18.50 • ☎ 020 8312 6608, ⓦ rmg.co.uk • ⊖ Cutty Sark DLR

Launched from the Clydeside shipyards in 1869, the majestic **Cutty Sark** is the world's last surviving tea clipper, which would race to get the tea harvest to Britain in the shortest possible time, with a dividend being paid to the ship that won. In actual fact, the *Cutty Sark* spent more time as a wool clipper, returning from Australia in just 72 days.

The ship suffered a devastating fire in 2007, while mid-restoration, but has risen from the ashes, beautifully restored and with interactive displays to engage children and adults alike. First off, you get to inspect below decks, where every single bit of space would have been taken up with cargo, leaving most of the thirty-strong crew to sleep in bunkhouses on deck – only the officers' quarters provide any privacy and creature comforts. The stunning hull clad in Muntz (a brass-like alloy) has been lifted up off the ground to allow space underneath for a café, and an impressive display of multi-coloured figureheads beneath the ship's prow, itself adorned with Nannie, the angry witch (who wears a "cutty sark", a short nightdress) from Robbie Burns' poem *Tam O'Shanter*. The lower hold is sometimes used as a small studio theatre for comedy and music (check the website for details).

Old Royal Naval College

20

Cutty Sark Gardens • Daily: grounds 8am–6pm; buildings 10am–5pm; June–Sept till 6pm • Free • ☎ 020 8269 4747, ⓦ ornc.org • ⊖ Cutty Sark DLR

It's entirely appropriate that the one London building that makes the most of its riverbank location should be the **Old Royal Naval College**, a majestic Baroque ensemble which opens out onto the Thames. Despite the symmetry and grace of the four buildings, which perfectly frame the Queen's House beyond, the whole complex has a strange and piecemeal history.

The first of the four blocks was built in the 1660s as a **royal palace** for Charles II, but the money ran out. William and Mary preferred Hampton Court and turned Greenwich into a **Royal Hospital for Seamen**. Wren, working for nothing, had his original designs vetoed by the queen, who insisted the new development must not obscure the view of the river from the Queen's House – what you see now is Wren's revised plan, augmented by, among others, Hawksmoor and Vanbrugh. The naval hospital moved out in 1869, replaced by the **Royal Naval College**, which, in turn, was supplanted by the current incumbents, the **University of Greenwich** and **Trinity College of Music**. The two grandest rooms, situated underneath Wren's twin domes, are open to the public and well worth visiting, and there's an excellent exhibition, **Discover Greenwich.**

Painted Hall

The magnificent **Painted Hall**, in the west wing, is dominated by James Thornhill's gargantuan allegorical ceiling painting, which depicts William and Mary enthroned, with a vanquished Louis XIV clutching a broken sword. Equally remarkable are Thornhill's trompe-l'oeil fluted pilasters and decorative detailing, while on the far wall, behind the high table, Thornhill himself appears (bottom right) beside George I and family, with St Paul's in the background. Designed as the sailors' dining hall, it was later used for Nelson's lying-in-state in 1806 and then as a naval art gallery.

Chapel

The **Chapel** (service Sun 11am), in the east wing, was designed by James Stuart after a fire in 1779 destroyed its predecessor. However, it is Stuart's assistant, William Newton, whom we have to thank for the chapel's exquisite pastel and sky-blue plasterwork and spectacular decorative detailing, among the finest in London. The altarpiece, by Benjamin West, depicts St Paul wrestling with the viper that leapt out of the fire after he was shipwrecked off Malta.

Discover Greenwich

If you're interested in Greenwich's rich history, you can get a good overview at **Discover Greenwich**, in the Pepys Building, which has a permanent exhibition on the area. Among the museum's prize possessions are *Beer* and *Gin*, two oak sculptures dating from around 1550–1580 from the buttery screen of old Greenwich Palace, while the centrepiece is a scale model of Greenwich which lights up to tell the history of the borough. The building also contains a tourist information office and the Royal Hospital's old brewhouse, which used to supply a ration of three pints to each seaman, and has now been revived and turned into a café-bar and microbrewery run by Greenwich Meantime (see p.385).

National Maritime Museum

Romney Rd • Daily 10am–5pm; Ahoy! and All Hands Tues, Sat, Sun & hols 10am–5pm, Mon & Wed–Fri 2–5pm, other times if no school groups • Free; charge for special exhibitions • ☎ 020 8858 4422, 🖰 rmg.co.uk • ⊖ Cutty Sark DLR

The main building of the **National Maritime Museum** occupies the west wing of the former Naval Asylum, and has two separate entrances: from Romney Road you enter a glass-covered courtyard, while from the park, you enter the Sammy Ofer Wing, with *Nelson's Ship in a Bottle* by Yinka Shonibare, first shown on the Fourth Plinth (see p.37), displayed at the entrance. The museum's permanent galleries are ranged over three floors – in a layout that can be slightly confusing at first – and there are several hands-on areas for children.

Ground floor: Royal Barge and Voyagers

If you enter via the Sammy Ofer Wing, you'll find **Voyagers** straight ahead, with a complex projection "The Wave" showing archive images from the collection and some remarkable objects in the cabinets, such as John Franklin's snow goggles, Captain Cook's fly whisk and a musical pig that survived the *Titanic*. The main building's covered courtyard displays some of the museum's largest artefacts, among them the

20

ROYAL GREENWICH

The history of Greenwich is replete with **royal connections**. Edward I appears to have been the first of the English kings to have stayed here, though there was nothing resembling a palace until Henry V's brother, the Duke of Gloucester, built **Bella Court** (later known as the Palace of Placentia) in 1447. Henry VI honeymooned here with his new wife, Margaret of Anjou, and eventually took over the place and rebuilt it in her honour. However, it was under the Tudors that the riverside palace enjoyed its royal heyday. **Henry VIII** was born there and made it his main base, pouring even more money into it than into Hampton Court. He added armouries, a banqueting hall and a huge tiltyard, hunted in the extensive grounds and kept a watchful eye over proceedings at the nearby **Royal Dockyards** in Deptford. His daughters, Mary and Elizabeth, were both born here.

Edward VI came to Greenwich in 1553 to try to restore his frail health, but died shortly afterwards. Mary came here rarely as queen, and on one of her few visits had the wall of her personal apartment blasted away by a cannonball fired in salute. For Elizabeth, Greenwich was the **chief summer residence**, and it was here in 1573 that she revived the Maundy Ceremony, washing the feet of 39 poor women (though only after three others had washed them first). The royal palace fell into disrepair during the 1650s Commonwealth, when it was turned into a biscuit factory, and was finally torn down by Charles II to make way for a new edifice, which eventually became the Royal Naval College.

splendid 63ft-long **Royal Barge**, a gilded Rococo confection designed by William Kent for Prince Frederick, the much-unloved eldest son of George II. In the centre are a couple of galleries: **Maritime London from 1700** and a room set aside for Turner's *Battle of Trafalgar, 21st October, 1805*, his largest work and only royal commission, which was intended for St James's Palace. To one side, **Ahoy!** is a nautically themed play area for under-7s, with model boats to clamber on and vaguely educational activities.

Floor one: The Great Map, the Atlantic and Traders

The museum's **Great Map** is displayed on the Upper Deck – kids can pick up a tablet device to sail their own personal boats (while parents relax in the adjacent café). The nearby **Traders** gallery tells the story of the all-important East India Company, which was given a monopoly on British trade with the East, and ended up taking over and more or less running India until the 1857 Rebellion.

The Atlantic focuses on the history of the trade links with the New World, from slavery to whaling. While you're here, don't miss the **stained glass** from the **Baltic Exchange**, a colourful 1920s memorial salvaged from the Baltic Exchange in the City, after it was blown up by the IRA in 1992.

Floor two: Nelson, World War I and Children's Gallery

The **Nelson, Navy, Nation** exhibition does exactly what it says on the tin, focusing on Nelson the man, the navy during his time and the wider context. Of all the Nelson memorabilia and model ships, it's the coat he wore at Trafalgar, with bullet hole, that stands out. **Forgotten Fighters** covers World War I, with a display of model ships and medals of some of those who fought at sea. Also on this floor, the **All Hands** children's gallery gives kids a taste of life on the seas, firing a cannon and so forth. Older children and adults will enjoy the **Ship Simulator** in which you have to demonstrate your boat handling skills.

Queen's House

Daily 10am–5pm; closed for renovation until July 2016 • Free • ☎ 020 8858 4422, ⓦ rmg.co.uk • ⊖ Cutty Sark DLR

Inigo Jones's **Queen's House**, originally built on a cramped site amid the Tudor royal palace, is the focal point of the Greenwich ensemble. As royal residences go, it's an unassuming little Palladian country house, "solid… masculine and unaffected" in Jones's own words. Its significance in terms of British architecture, however, is immense. Commissioned in 1616, it was the first Neoclassical building in the country, signifying a clear break with all that preceded it. The interior, exterior and setting of the Queen's House have all changed radically since Jones's day, making it difficult to imagine the impact the building must have had when it was built. The house is now linked to its neighbouring buildings by open colonnades, added in the early part of the nineteenth century.

Inside, few features survive from Stuart times. The **Great Hall**, a perfect cube, remains, but Orazio Gentileschi's ceiling paintings were removed to Marlborough House by the Duchess of Marlborough during the reign of Queen Anne; to celebrate the building's four-hundredth anniversary, Gentileschi's *Joseph and Potiphar's Wife* will be displayed here from 2016 onwards (it was removed in 1650), on loan from the Royal Collection. The southeastern corner of the hall leads to the beautiful **Tulip Staircase**, Britain's earliest cantilevered spiral staircase, whose name derives from the floral patterning in the wrought-iron balustrade. Upstairs, the **Queen's Presence Chamber**, designed for Henrietta Maria, retains its rich ceiling decoration from the 1630s. The **King's Presence Chamber**, originally the Queen's Withdrawing room, before it became part of the king's quarters in 1662, will be similarly restored. The remaining rooms of the Queen's House show pieces from the maritime museum's vast **art collection**, illustrating the history of royal Greenwich along with naval battles, portraits of admirals and so on. The museum owns works by the likes of Reynolds and Hogarth, as well as twentieth-century pieces by official war artists.

20

Greenwich Park

Daily 6am to dusk • Ⓦ royalparks.org.uk • ⊖ Cutty Sark or Greenwich DLR

Greenwich Park is one of the city's oldest royal parks, having been enclosed in the fifteenth century by the Duke of Gloucester, who fancied it as a hunting ground. Henry VIII was particularly fond of the place, introducing deer in 1515, as well as archery and jousting tournaments and sword-fighting contests. The park was opened to the public in the eighteenth century, but it was only after the arrival of the railway in 1838 that it began to attract Londoners in great numbers. In 1894, a young **French anarchist** called Martial Bourdin was killed in the park, outside the Royal Observatory, when the bomb he was carrying in a brown-paper bag exploded. Joseph Conrad used the unexplained incident as the inspiration for his novel *The Secret Agent*.

The descendants of Henry's deer are now safely enclosed within **The Wilderness**, a fenced area in the southeast corner where they laze around "tame as children", in Henry James's words. Don't miss **Vanbrugh Castle**, halfway down Maze Hill, on the east side of the park, England's first mock-medieval castle, designed by the architect John Vanbrugh as his private residence in 1726. Note, too, **Queen Caroline's Bath**, by the park's southern wall, which is all that remains of the house where the queen used to hold her famous orgies – the rest of the house was destroyed by her estranged husband George IV after she left the country in 1804. If you're heading for the Ranger's House, the best approach is via the semicircular **Rose Garden**, laid out in front of it, which is worth a visit itself from June to August.

One of the park's chief delights is the view over to the Isle of Dogs from the steep hill crowned by the observatory and a statue of **General James Wolfe** (1727–59), who spent part of his childhood in Greenwich, lived near the park and is buried in St Alfege's. Wolfe is famed for the audacious, successful campaign to capture Quebec from the French in 1759, a battle in which he and his opposite number, General Montcalm, were both mortally wounded. Victory celebrations took place throughout England, but were forbidden in Greenwich out of respect for Wolfe's mother.

Royal Observatory

Blackheath Ave • **Astronomy Centre** Daily 10am–5pm • Free **Flamsteed House** Daily 10am–5pm • £9.50; combined ticket with Cutty Sark £18.50 **Planetarium** shows every 45min • £7.50; combined ticket with Flamsteed House £12.50 • ☎ 020 8858 4422, Ⓦ nmm.ac.uk • ⊖ Greenwich DLR

Established by Charles II in 1675, the **Royal Observatory** is the longest-established scientific institution in Britain. The chief task of John Flamsteed, the first Astronomer Royal, was to study the night sky in order to discover an astronomical method of finding the longitude of a ship at sea, the lack of which was causing enormous problems for the emerging British Empire. Astronomers continued to

---

THE PRIME MERIDIAN AND GREENWICH MEAN TIME

Greenwich's greatest claim to fame is as the home of the **Prime Meridian** – a meridian being any north–south line used as a basis for astronomical observations, and therefore also for the calculation of longitude and time. In 1884, the International Meridian Conference in Washington DC agreed to make Greenwich the Prime Meridian of the World – in other words, **zero longitude**. As a result, the longitude of the entire world is fixed as either east or west of Greenwich. Unfortunately for Greenwich, more and more people use **Global Positioning System (GPS)**, which makes its calculations from the centre of the earth, not the surface, and places the meridian approximately 336ft to the east of the observatory's strip.

The world also used to set its clocks according to **Greenwich Mean Time (GMT)**. However, in many spheres of life, GMT has been usurped by **Coordinated Universal Time (UTC)**, which is basically the same as GMT, except that it is more accurately calculated using atomic clocks and therefore better for sub-second precision.

work here at Greenwich until the postwar smog and light pollution forced them to decamp to Herstmonceux Castle in Sussex; the observatory, meanwhile, is now a very popular museum.

Flamsteed House

The oldest part of the observatory is **Flamsteed House**, designed by Wren (himself an astronomer) "for the observator's habitation and a little for pompe". The northeastern turret sports a bright-red **Time Ball** that climbs the mast at 12.58pm and drops at 1pm GMT precisely; it was added in 1833 to allow ships on the Thames to set their clocks. The strip in the observatory's main courtyard is the **Meridian Line**, and at night a green laser beam shines northwards along the meridian. On the house's balcony overlooking the Thames, you can take a look at a **Camera Obscura** of the kind Flamsteed used to make safe observations of the sun. Inside, beyond the **Astronomers' apartments** you eventually reach the impressive **Octagon Room**, built so that the king could show off his astronomical toys to guests. There are replicas (and some original sections) of the precision clocks installed behind the walnut panelling in 1676.

Time galleries

The **Time and Longitude** gallery focuses on the search for longitude and displays the first four marine chronometers built by **John Harrison**. Harrison eventually won the £20,000 **Longitude Prize** in 1763 with his giant pocket watch, H4, after much skulduggery against his claims, most notably by the Astronomer Royal at the time, Nevil Maskelyne (a story wonderfully told by Dava Sobel in her book *Longitude*). Downstairs, in **Time and Greenwich**, you can learn about the story of GMT, UTC and GPS and listen to three generations of the speaking clock.

Meridian Observatory

Flamsteed carried out more than thirty thousand observations – "nothing can exceed the tediousness and ennui of the life" was his dispirited description of the job – in a small building outside Flamsteed House. Later Astronomers Royal used different parts of the **Meridian Observatory** building. Edmond Halley, who succeeded Flamsteed, bought more sophisticated quadrants, sextants, spyglasses and telescopes, which are among those displayed in the **Halley Quadrant Room**. With the aid of his 8ft iron quadrant, he predicted the next appearance of the eponymous comet – though he never lived to see it. Next door, you'll find **Bradley's Meridian**, used for Ordnance Survey maps since 1801, followed by a room that's sliced in two by the present-day Greenwich Meridian, fixed by the cross hairs in "Airy's Transit Circle", the astronomical instrument that dominates the room. Finally, go through the shop and up the stairs through the Time and Society display to reach the **Great Equatorial Telescope** dating from 1893 (free entry).

Astronomy Centre and Planetarium

Housed in the fanciful, domed terracotta South Building, built in the 1890s, the **Astronomy Centre** houses hi-tech galleries giving a brief rundown of the Big Bang theory of the universe, and with hands-on exhibits exploring concepts such as dark matter. You can also watch one of the thirty-minute presentations in the **Planetarium**.

Ranger's House

Chesterfield Walk · Guided tour only April–Sept Mon–Wed & Sun 11am & 2pm (1hr 30min); advance booking recommended · EH · £7.20 · ☎ 020 8294 2548 · ⊖ Greenwich DLR or ⇌ Blackheath

In the southern corner of Greenwich Park stands the **Ranger's House**, a red-brick Georgian villa looking out over Blackheath. Built as a private residence, it became the official residence of the park ranger (hence its name), a sort of top-notch grace-and-favour home. The house is used to display the private collection of **Julius Wernher**

(1850–1912), an Edwardian German-born millionaire who made his money by exploiting the diamond deposits of South Africa, and at his death was one of the world's richest men. He amassed a vast collection of largely Medieval and Renaissance works, partly as he was interested in craftsmanship – he was definitely a man who placed technical virtuosity above artistic merit – and he acquired some very rare objects, and a few grotesque horrors. Highlights on the top floor include the cabinet of exquisite Renaissance jewellery, an intricate sixteenth-century German carved boxwood triptych altarpiece and the pair of sixteenth-century maiolica dishes decorated with mythological scenes for Isabella d'Este, wife of the Marchese of Mantua and a great patron of the arts.

Downstairs, rooms are set out to replicate the entertaining rooms of the Wernhers' house, Luton Hoo in Bedfordshire, for which most of these works were bought. There's a sparkling Reynolds portrait of Lady Caroline Price and, in the main gallery, a series of seventeenth-century French tapestries depicting life in the court of the Emperor of China. At the far end of the main gallery is Bergonzoli's striking *Love of Angels*, a highly charged marble sculpture that, despite weighing two tons, succeeds in appearing light and ethereal.

THE O2 AND GREENWICH PENINSULA

Clearly visible from Greenwich's riverside and park is the marquee-like former **Millennium Dome**: over half a mile in circumference and 160ft in height, it's the world's largest dome, held up by a dozen, 300ft, yellow steel masts. Built in 2000 at a cost of £800 million, it housed the Millennium Experience exhibition, which was panned by critics and dismantled after one year.

Since then entertainment giant AEG spent another £600 million turning it into **The O2** (wtheo2.co.uk), a mall of restaurants and bars, a nightclub, a multiplex cinema, bowling and, occupying forty percent of the Dome, the 23,000-seat **O2 Arena**, venue for sports events and big-name gigs, plus a smaller venue, Indigo. Meanwhile, the land all around continues to be developed, with numerous upmarket riverside flats going up on the peninsula.

The easiest way to get here is to take the tube to **North Greenwich**. It's also possible to walk or cycle the mile and a half along the riverside pathway from Greenwich – you can also walk the **Thames Path** in the other direction all the way to the Thames Barrier (about 1hr); past the ecology park the feel is very industrial. From the barrier (see p.324) you can get the bus back or on to Woolwich. The most enjoyable ways to reach the O2, though, are by boat to the **QEII Pier**, or by **cable car** across the Thames from Royal Victoria DLR (see p.211). Nearby are two intriguing works of art: Antony Gormley's very busy *Quantum Cloud* by the pier and Richard Wilson's *Slice of Reality*, the bridge of a boat cut away from its mother ship on the Thames to the west.

THINGS TO SEE AND DO AT THE O2

Greenwich Peninsula Ecology Park Thames Path, John Harrison Way (Wed–Sun 10am–5pm; free; 020 8293 1904, wgreenwichecologypark.com). A bucolic mini-wetlands just off the Thames Path, fifteen minutes' walk from the O2.

Up at the O2 (mid-Feb till Dec: generally Mon–Fri noon–dusk, Sat & Sun 10am–dusk; July–Sept & hols daily 10am–dusk; £28–£35; wtheo2.co.uk). Don an astronaut suit, attach your carabiner and you can "climb" the outside of the O2, along a bouncy walkway. The sense of achievement is more memorable than the view – particularly as the new InterContinental Hotel limits visibility to Canary Wharf.

The cable car (April–Sept Mon–Thurs 7am–10pm, Fri 7am–11pm, Sat 8am–11pm, Sun 9am–10pm; Oct–March Mon–Fri 7am–8pm, Sat 8am–8pm, Sun 9am–8pm; £3.40 single with Oyster). Spectacular views over the docks and City Airport.

Emirates Aviation Experience (daily 10am–7pm; general entrance £3; flight simulator £45; waviation-experience.com). Airline themed displays and activities, just by the cable car base, with the highlight the pricey flight simulators. One for aeroplane enthusiasts, though the "Be the Baggage" film is mesmerizing.

Boat to Trinity Buoy Wharf (Mon–Fri 5am–7pm; £2; 07947 637 925) See p.214. Call for the *Predator II* boat to collect you from the pier and shuttle you across the river to the old wharves on the north bank.

20

Fan Museum

12 Crooms Hill • Tues–Sat 11am–5pm, Sun noon–5pm • £4 • ☎ 020 8305 1441, ⓦ thefanmuseum.org.uk • ⊖ Greenwich DLR

At the bottom of Crooms Hill, you'll find the **Fan Museum**. It's a fascinating little place (and an extremely beautiful house), revealing the importance of the fan as a social and political document. The permanent exhibition on the ground floor traces the history of the fan and the materials employed, from peacock feathers to straw, with a fan painted by Sickert and a fan-shaped work by Gauguin particular highlights. Temporary exhibitions upstairs are drawn from the museum's large collection. Outside, there's a tearoom, housed in the hand-painted orangery, with afternoon tea served (Tues & Sun sittings 1.45– 3.45pm, booking essential; Fri & Sat 12.30–4.30pm, no bookings).

Blackheath

South of Greenwich lies the well-to-do former village of **Blackheath** (so-called because of the colour of the soil), whose bleak, windswept heath, crisscrossed with busy roads, couldn't be more different from the adjacent royal park. Nonetheless, with its heath-side pubs it can be pleasant on a summer afternoon, and the odd fair takes place here on public holidays.

Lying on the main road to Dover, Blackheath was a convenient spot on which to pitch camp, as the Danes did in 1011, having kidnapped St Alfege. During the **1381 Peasants' Revolt**, Wat Tyler's rebels were treated to a rousing revolutionary sermon by John Bull, which included the famous lines "When Adam delved and Eve span, who was then the gentleman?" **Henry V** was welcomed back from the Battle of Agincourt here in 1415, while Henry VII fought the Cornish rebels here in 1497. It was at Blackheath, also, that Henry VIII suffered disappointment on meeting his fourth wife, **Anne of Cleves**, in 1540; he famously referred to her as "the Flanders mare" and filed for divorce after just six months.

From Blackheath station walk up through the village-like centre and the charmingly named Tranquil Vale to reach the heath itself, with the *Hare and Billet* pub opposite a pond to the left. The heath's chief landmark is the rugged Kentish ragstone **All Saints' Church**, a Victorian church nestled in a slight depression in the south corner. The most striking building on the heath, though, is **The Paragon**, to the east, a crescent of four-storey Georgian mansions linked by Doric colonnades.

DOWN IN DEPTFORD

Deptford, just west of Greenwich, might not be high up on most people's list of places to visit, but it does have a proper south London market along Deptford High Street and Douglas Way (Wed, Fri & Sat 9am–6pm), the Laban Dance centre (see p.416) and a few emerging art galleries (see box, p.310), plus great live music venues like the *Amersham Arms* (see p.400) in neighbouring New Cross. Before all this, though, the area had a rich history thanks to the **Royal Dockyards**, which existed here (and at Woolwich) from 1513 until 1869. It was at Deptford in 1581 that Francis Drake moored the *Golden Hinde* (see p.332) after circumnavigating the globe, had Elizabeth I on board for dinner, and was knighted for his efforts. And it was in Deptford that the playwright **Christopher Marlowe** was murdered (possibly) in the company of three men who had links with the criminal underworld and the Elizabethan intelligence service.

All that remains of the old dockyards today are a few officers' quarters hidden in the Pepys housing estate, and the (not visible) **Master Shipwright's House** of 1708 at the bottom of Watergate Street. A little downstream, towards Greenwich, there's even a waterfront statue of Peter the Great (flanked by a dwarf and an empty chair), who came to Deptford in 1798 to learn about shipbuilding. You can get an idea of how prosperous the area once was just off the High Street at **St Paul's Church**, the local architectural gem, designed by Thomas Archer in 1720, whose interior Pevsner described as "closer to Borromini and the Roman Baroque than any other English church".

20

Woolwich

In 1847, a visitor to **Woolwich** commented that it was the "dirtiest, filthiest and most thoroughly mismanaged town of its size in the kingdom". With its docks and factories defunct, Woolwich remains one of the poorest parts of the old Docklands. However, if you have an interest for military history, it's worth exploring the old dockyards and arsenal, for their architecture and the **Firepower** artillery museum. The other reason to come to Woolwich is to visit the **Thames Barrier**, an awesome piece of modern engineering and the largest movable flood barrier in the world.

ARRIVAL AND DEPARTURE

By DLR and train DLR from Canning Town or train from London Bridge to Woolwich Arsenal.

By boat During the week, there's a limited commuter boat service to and from Woolwich Arsenal (approx 6–9.30am & 5.40–8pm, last departure from Woolwich), and at the weekend a more regular service, usually changing boat at the O2 (every 30min; boats are timed to connect with the ones from the centre); there are also boat trips that cruise round the barrier (May–Oct; £7 from Westminster; ⓦ thamesriverservices.co.uk).

Royal Arsenal

Close to Woolwich Arsenal DLR station, on the market square, is **Beresford Gateway**, built in 1828 as the Arsenal's main entrance, but now separated from the rest of the complex to the north by busy Beresford Street/Plumstead Road.

Across the road, you enter **Dial Square**, overlooked by some of the Arsenal's most historic buildings, built by the likes of Vanbrugh, Wren and Hawksmoor: the Main Guard House, with its eighteenth-century Doric portico; Verbruggen's House, opposite, begun in 1772, and former residence of the Master Founder; and the Royal Brass Foundry, made of wood, but encased in brick, from 1717. To the north, the **Dial Arch Block**, now a pub, is distinguished by its central archway, sporting a sundial, pillars and a pile of cannonballs. A football on a plinth commemorates the fact that it was here in 1886 that a group of machinists formed Dial Square Football Club, later Woolwich Arsenal FC, and then just **Arsenal FC**, eventually moving to Highbury in north London. The team used to get changed in the toilets of the *Royal Oak* (now the Woolwich Arsenal DLR station).

20

Firepower: Royal Artillery Museum

Royal Arsenal • Tues–Sun 10am–5pm • £5.30 • ☏ 020 8855 7755, ⓦ firepower.org.uk • ⊖ Woolwich Arsenal DLR

If you head down Number One Street, towards the river, you'll come to **Firepower**, the Royal Artillery Museum, housed in part of the old Arsenal. Inevitably, there's a propaganda video on today's Royal Artillery, along with a twenty-minute multimedia show, *Field of Fire*, concentrating on the chief conflicts of the twentieth century. The main **Gunnery Hall** features World War I field guns, old and new howitzers, anti-tank guns and 1960s Thunderbird guided-missile launchers. You can watch wartime film clips and there's a nice video about the use of firepower technology in film special effects. Upstairs, the **History Gallery** takes you through the history of artillery, with one of the earliest pieces a Tudor bronze saker, and includes the Medals Gallery. Ask at reception about a tour of the **Cold War** store, which they run several times a day. The former factory building over the road houses some of the big beasts of twentieth-century weaponry and the guides take you through the successes and many expensive, sometimes farcical failures of weapon design.

Greenwich Heritage Centre

Artillery Square • Tues–Sat 9am–5pm • Free • ☏ 020 8854 2452, ⓦ www.royalgreenwich.gov.uk • ⊖ Woolwich Arsenal DLR

Opposite Firepower (and sharing a building with the Cold War store) **Greenwich Heritage Centre** displays a small informative permanent exhibition on the history of the Arsenal. Next door is the distinctive eighteenth-century, brown-brick building that served as the Royal Military Academy, from 1741 until 1806, when new barracks were built.

MILITARY WOOLWICH

Woolwich, like Deptford, owes its existence to its **Royal Dockyards**, founded here in 1513 by Henry VIII. The men-of-war that established England as a world naval power were built in these dockyards: the *Great Harry*, the largest ship in the world, was launched from here in 1514; Walter Raleigh and Captain Cook set out from Woolwich on their voyages of discovery. The docks closed in 1869, and the area is better known for the **Royal Arsenal**, which reached its heyday during World War I, when it stretched for three miles along the Thames, employed nearly one hundred thousand workers (half of whom were women) and had its own internal railway system. The ordnance factories were closed altogether in 1967, and council housing built over much of the site. However, a fine collection of mostly eighteenth-century buildings survives and has been converted into flats, plus a couple of museums.

The **Royal Artillery Barracks**, half a mile to the south of the Royal Arsenal, are still seen as the spiritual home of the Royal Artillery, even though the last artillery regiment moved out in 2007. Completed in 1802 by James Wyatt, the barracks' three-storey Georgian façade runs for an amazing 1080ft. Appropriately enough, the barracks hosted the shooting competition during the 2012 Olympics. The barracks face south onto the grassy parade ground, to the east of which lies the husk of the **Garrison Church of St George**, built in neo-Romanesque style in 1863. Gutted in the last war, fragments of its colourful interior decor survive.

On the south side of Woolwich Common stands James Wyatt's former **Royal Military Academy**, completed in 1806 in an imposing mock-Tudor style. The 720ft facade faces onto a parade ground, with an imitation of the Tower of London's White Tower as its centrepiece.

Thames Barrier

Unity Way • Thurs–Sun 10.30am–5pm • £3.75 • ☎ 020 8305 4188, ⓦ www.gov.uk/the-thames-barrier • ⇌ Charlton or Woolwich Dockyard; or buses #472 or #161 from either ⊖ North Greenwich or Woolwich Arsenal DLR

London has been subject to flooding from surge tides since before 1236, when it was reported that in "the great Palace of Westminster men did row with wherries in the midst of the Hall". A flood barrier was advocated as far back as the 1850s, but it was only after the 1953 flood that serious consideration was given to defences. Opened in 1982, the **Thames Barrier** is a mind-blowing feat of engineering, with its gleaming fins and movable steel gates weighing 3300 tons. The best way to view it is, undoubtedly, from a boat from the O2 to Woolwich. If you want to find out more, head for the small **information centre** where a working model and macho videos help explain the basic mechanism of the barrier (by no means obvious). Times and dates of the monthly test are posted on the website.

Eltham Palace

Court Yard • April–Sept Mon–Thurs & Sun: 10am–6pm; Oct Mon–Thurs & Sun 10am–5pm; Nov–March Sun 10am–4pm (daily during half-term hols) • EH • £13 • ☎ 020 8294 2548, ⓦ elthampalace.org.uk • ⇌ Eltham from Victoria, London Bridge or Charing Cross, then 15min walk

Eltham Palace was one of the country's foremost medieval royal residences and even a venue for Parliament for some two hundred years from the reign of Edward II. All that remains now is the fifteenth-century **bridge** across the moat, and the **Great Hall**, built by Edward IV in 1479, with a fine hammer-beam roof and two fan-vaulted stone oriels.

Somewhat incredibly, in the 1930s, millionaire **Stephen Courtauld** (of art-collecting fame) got permission to build his own "Wrenaissance"-style house on the site, renovating the Great Hall, and incorporating it into the new house. He lavished a fortune on the place, creating a movie star's palace for his glamorous half-Italian, half-Hungarian wife, Virginia. The house was designed by **Seely and Paget**, furnished by the best Swedish and Italian designers, and kitted out with the latest mod cons: underfloor heating, a centralized vacuum cleaner and ten en-suite bedrooms. Then, shortly before the end of the war, the family left for Rhodesia, taking most of the furniture with them, though English Heritage have restored many rooms, and some furniture and paintings have been loaned back or reproduced. The result is a cruise-liner style Art Deco masterpiece, with acres of exotic veneer, lavish bathrooms, such as Virginia's gold-mosaic one, and lots of quirky **Art Deco** touches. Most spectacular is the circular entrance hall, lined with veneer and panels of marquetry and flooded with light from a glazed dome, though each of the dozen or so rooms you see has some unusual design detail. The excellent multimedia guides detail the family's eccentricities, which included keeping a **pet ring-tailed lemur** called Mah-Jongg, which had its own bedroom and was notorious for biting disliked male visitors. Such was their devotion to him that he crops up in numerous artworks, such as the mural by Mary Adshead in the billiard room in the basement, which is set out as it would have been during the Blitz, when the family, staff and visitors sheltered there.

Leave time to explore the **gardens**, again an idiosyncratic mix of medieval – the moat from which you can best appreciate the original bridge, a few remains of the old palace – and the latest in 1930s fashions, such as Stephen's rock garden.

Red House

Red House Red House Lane, Bexleyheath · Mid-Feb till Oct Wed–Sun 11am–5pm; Nov & Dec Fri–Sun 11am–5pm; pre-booked tours only, every 30min before 1.30pm · NT · £8· ☎ 020 8304 9878, ⓦ nationaltrust.org.uk · ⇌ Bexleyheath from Victoria, Charing Cross or London Bridge; the nearest place to park is Danson Park

Hidden among the nondescript suburbia of **Bexleyheath**, three miles east of Eltham, lies **Red House**, a wonderful red-brick country house designed by Philip Webb in 1859 for his friend **William Morris**, following Morris's marriage to Pre-Raphaelite heart-throb Jane Burden. The mock-medieval exterior features pointed brick arches, steep gables, an oriel windows and even a turreted well in the garden, and the whole enterprise stands as the embodiment of the Arts and Crafts movement. Sadly, after just five years, with "Janey" conducting an affair with Dante Gabriel Rossetti, the couple were forced to leave their dream home due to financial difficulties and move to Kelmscott in Oxfordshire. The interior, half-finished even in Morris's time, only has a few of the larger interior furnishings still in place, but it is slowly being restored, a process that has revealed a delightful original painted ceiling in the hallway and several wall paintings by Morris's set, which included Edward Burne-Jones. The morning tours are excellent at pointing out architectural details and bringing the place to life, thanks to the various anecdotes about Morris and his entourage.

20

Down House

Luxted Rd, Downe · April–Sept daily 10am–6pm; Oct daily 10am–5pm; Nov–March Sat & Sun 10am–4pm (daily half-term hols) · EH · £11.70 · ☎ 01689 859119, ⓦ www.english-heriage.org.uk · Bus #146 Bromley South or #R8 from Orpington

Down House was the home of the scientist **Charles Darwin** (1809–82). Born in Shrewsbury, Darwin showed little academic promise at Cambridge. It was only after returning from his five-year tour of South America aboard HMS *Beagle* – when he visited the Galapagos Islands – that he began work on the theory he would publish in 1859 as *On the Origin of Species*. Darwin moved to Down House in 1842, shortly after marrying his cousin Emma Wedgwood, who nursed the valetudinarian scientist here until his death. The house is set in lovely grounds, and is stuffed with Darwin memorabilia, including his journal, though there's no sign (or smell) of the barnacles which he spent eight years dissecting. He later moved on to the study of orchids, several examples of which you can find in the glasshouse.

Battersea

Sometimes seen as a southern extension of Chelsea (see p.266), attractive to those who want but can't afford to live there, **Battersea**, on the river west of Vauxhall, was originally a village and market garden, centred on **St Mary's Church**, half a mile upstream from Battersea Park, where William Blake married in 1775. Turner also used to visit the church, sitting in the oriel vestry window to paint the clouds and sunsets. With the arrival of industry and the railway in the nineteenth century, Battersea became a staunchly working-class enclave. In 1913 it elected the country's first black mayor, John Richard Archer, and in the 1920s returned Shapurji Saklatvala as its MP – first for the Labour Party, then as a Communist. These days, Battersea is primarily known for two things: **Battersea Dogs and Cats Home**, established in 1871 as the "Home for Lost Dogs and Cats" (ⓦbattersea.org.uk); and the mighty **power station**.

Battersea Power Station
Kirtling St • ⓦ batterseapowerstation.co.uk • ⭢Battersea Park

Physically, Battersea is dominated by the presence of **Battersea Power Station**, Giles Gilbert Scott's awesome cathedral of power from 1933, which looks like an upturned table and featured (along with an inflatable flying pig) on the Pink Floyd album cover *Animals*. Closed down in 1983, it is finally being renovated and will house offices, shops, a large venue and some extraordinarily expensive apartments, surrounded by huge residential developments. Until the work is completed (scheduled for 2020 for the power station phase) access to the building is very limited. In the meantime, if you spot the power station without its four famous chimneys don't be too alarmed: the developers are taking them down and rebuilding them, and they even promise to put a public viewing platform at the top of one of them.

Battersea Park
Park Daily 6.30am–10.30pm• Free • ⓦ batterseapark.org Zoo Daily 10am–5.30pm; closes 4.30pm or dusk in winter • £8.95 adult, £6.95 child • ☎ 020 7924 5826, ⓦ batterseaparkzoo.co.uk • ⭢Battersea Park

Battersea being a place of great poverty, the Victorians decided, in the 1850s, to do something to help ameliorate the social conditions by establishing **Battersea Park**. Today, the park is best known for its two-tier **Peace Pagoda**, erected in 1985 by Japanese Buddhists. Made from a combination of reconstituted Portland stone and Canadian fir trees, the pagoda shelters four large gilded Buddhas. The park's **fountain lake** is impressive in summer, and there's a small family-run **Children's Zoo**, established during the 1951 Festival of Britain, and home to monkeys, lemurs, emus and otters.

VAUXHALL, NINE ELMS AND BATTERSEA

The stretch of the south bank of the Thames that runs west from Vauxhall to Battersea is currently one of London's biggest building sites. With the new **US Embassy**, a sturdy (and secure) cube designed by Kieran Timberlake, scheduled to open in Nine Elms in 2017, and the redevelopment of **Battersea Power Station**, the area has attracted legions of developers, who aim to create one of the fanciest new quarters in London. It says something about the scale of the project that the development around the power station features statement apartment buildings by both Frank Gehry and Foster + Partners, while a cluster of largely residential skyscrapers is under construction at the Vauxhall end; around 18,000 new homes are planned in total, plus hotels, offices and shops. A new spur to the northern line will add **tube stations** at Battersea and Nine Elms by 2020; Thames Clipper **boats** will stop near the power station; and there are even plans for a pedestrian and cycle **bridge** from Nine Elms to Pimlico. The developers promise to add green spaces and make an accessible **Thames Path** along this stretch, as well as helping to fund a revamp of the New Covent Garden wholesale market near Vauxhall. The wholesale **flower market** is currently the most fragrant destination hereabouts, which you can visit if you get up early enough (Nine Elms Lane; Mon–Sat 4–10am; ⓦ newcoventgardenmarket.com).

HAMPTON COURT PALACE

West London: Hammersmith to Hampton Court

Hammersmith to Hampton Court – a distance of some seven miles overland (more by the river) – takes you from the traffic-clogged western suburbs of London to the royal outpost of Hampton Court. This is the greenest side of London, with splashes of countryside increasing as you head westwards, the leafy expanses of the fabulous Kew Gardens and the two old royal hunting parks, Richmond and Bushy Park of particular note – though, as one nineteenth-century visitor observed, they are "no more like the real untrimmed genuine country than a garden is like a field". Taking a boat along the river Thames, once known as the "Great Highway of London", is still the most pleasant way to travel in these parts during the summer.

21

Aside from the river and the parks, the chief attractions of west London are the royal palaces and lordly mansions that pepper the riverbanks: textbook Palladian style at **Chiswick House**, unspoilt Jacobean splendour at **Ham House** and Tudor and Baroque excess (and the famous maze) at **Hampton Court**. For riverside walks and pubs, you can't beat the stretch of the river from **Hammersmith** – London's gateway to the west, by road or tube – and neighbouring **Chiswick**, to **Kew**, **Richmond** and **Twickenham** beyond.

Hammersmith

Blighted by constant traffic **Hammersmith** is among west London's largest and busiest transport interchanges and many visitors arriving here tend to be switching tube lines only to head on elsewhere. There are some good reasons to stick about though, including an excellent riverside cinema and performing arts centre (Riverside Studios, closed until late 2017 for redevelopment), one of London's most renowned concert venues, the Hammersmith Apollo, and, arguably, the city's top Italian restaurant, *The River Café*. Hammersmith tube station is also the nearest to the Wetland Centre (see p.330) and gives easy access to the riverside walk to Chiswick. The riverside walk begins a short way southwest of the tube, down Queen Caroline Street. First off, you pass underneath **Hammersmith Bridge**, a graceful green-and-gold suspension bridge from the 1880s that the IRA have tried to blow up three times: first in 1939, as part of their attempt to disrupt the British war effort, secondly by the Provisional IRA in 1996 and finally four years later by the Real IRA. From the bridge, you can walk all the way to Chiswick along one of the most picturesque stretches of riverbank in the whole of London, much of it closed to traffic (the path on the southern bank goes all the way to Richmond).

The riverside

The first section of the riverside, just west of the bridge, known as **Lower Mall**, is a mixture of Victorian pubs, boathouses, Regency verandas and modern flats. An interesting array of boats huddle around the marina outside the *Dove*, an atmospheric seventeenth-century riverside pub (see p.398). This started out as a coffee house and has the smallest back bar in the country, copious literary associations – regulars have included Graham Greene, Ernest Hemingway and William Morris – and a canopied balcony overlooking the Thames.

Kelmscott House

26 Upper Mall • Thurs & Sat 2–5pm • Free • ☎ 020 8741 3735, ⓦ williammorrissociety.org • ⊖ Ravenscourt Park

It's strange to think that this genteel part of the Thames was once a hotbed of radicals, who used to congregate at **Kelmscott House**, where **William Morris** lived and worked

---

WEST LONDON BY BOAT

From **Westminster**, from April to October, Westminster Passenger Services (☎ 020 7930 2062, ⓦ wpsa.co.uk) run a scheduled service from Westminster Pier to Kew, Richmond and Hampton Court. Departure times vary but the first boat from Westminster is usually around 10.30am and the last around 2pm; your last chance to get back from Kew to Westminster is usually 5.30pm. The trip to Kew takes about 90 minutes and all the way to Hampton Court takes around three hours, though times vary significantly depending on the direction of the tide (check website for latest departure times). Adult single and return fares from Westminster are £12 and £15 to Kew; £18 and £22.50 to Hampton Court. In addition, Turks (☎ 020 8546 2434, ⓦ turks.co.uk) runs a regular service from **Richmond** to **Hampton Court** (April to mid-Sept Tues–Sun; Aug daily; journey time 1hr 45min) which costs £8.10 single or £9.60 return. For the latest on **boat services** on the Thames, see ⓦ tfl.gov.uk.

from 1878 until his death in 1896. (Morris used to berate the locals from a soapbox on Hammersmith Bridge.) From 1885 onwards, the local socialists used to meet here on a Sunday evening, with Labour leader Keir Hardie, anarchist Prince Kropotkin, writer George Bernard Shaw and Fabian founders the Webbs among the speakers – their photos now line the walls.

21

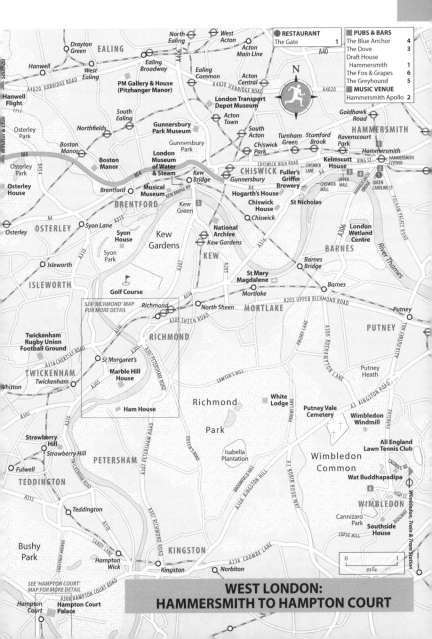

● RESTAURANT	
The Gate	1

▮ PUBS & BARS	
The Blue Anchor	4
The Dove	3
Draft House Hammersmith	1
The Fox & Grapes	6
The Greyhound	5
▮ MUSIC VENUE	
Hammersmith Apollo	2

WEST LONDON: HAMMERSMITH TO HAMPTON COURT

21

7 Hammersmith Terrace

7 Hammersmith Terrace • ☎ 020 8741 4104, ⓦ emerywalker.org.uk • ⊖ Stamford Brook

A socialist mate of William Morris, the printer Emery Walker lived just down the riverbank at **7 Hammersmith Terrace**, one of a line of tall Georgian houses built facing the river sometime before 1755. The house has a well-preserved Arts and Crafts interior and contains lots of Morris memorabilia as well as de Morgan ceramics and furniture by Philip Webb, architect of Morris's Red House in Bexleyheath (see p.325). It is closed to the public until early 2017 while it undergoes thorough repairs and renovations.

London Wetland Centre

Queen Elizabeth's Walk • Daily: April–Oct 9.30am–6pm; Nov–March 9.30am–5pm • Adults £11.59, concessions £8.64, under-17s £6.36 • Free guided tours daily 11.30am & 2.30pm • Duck feeding daily, 3pm • ☎ 020 8409 4400, ⓦ wwt.org.uk • Bus #283 from ⊖ Hammersmith or ⇌ Barnes Bridge from Waterloo and 15min walk

For anyone interested in wildlife, the **London Wetland Centre**, in well-to-do Barnes, is an absolute must. The Wildfowl & Wetlands Trust (WWT) has created a mosaic of wetland habitats on the site of four disused reservoirs. On arrival – unless it's raining – skip the introductory audiovisual, and head straight out to the ponds. If the weather's bad, head for the **Discovery Centre**, where kids can take part in a swan identification parade, or take a duck's-eye view of the world. You can also look out over the wetlands from the glass-walled **Observatory** next door, or from the tables of the *Water's Edge Café*. Visitors with children should make their way to **Explore**, a nature-themed adventure playground, while the **Pond Zone** gives younger children a chance to do some pond-dipping.

The centre basically serves a dual function: to attract native species of bird to its watery lagoons, and to assist in the WWT's programme of breeding rare wildfowl in captivity. The **World Wetlands** area harbours a variety of extremely rare wildfowl – from White-faced Whistling Ducks to the highly endangered Blue Duck – whose wetland habitats have been re-created in miniature (3pm is feeding time). In the **Wildside** are the reedbeds and pools that attract native species, such as lapwings, sand martins, water rails and, if you're lucky, even the odd wintering bittern, all of which you can view from a moss-roofed hide. At the far end is the **Peacock Tower**, the mother of all hides: a triple-decker octagonal one with a lift, allowing views over the whole of the reserve.

Chiswick

The old riverside village of **Chiswick** was centred on the church of St Nicholas from medieval times until the Victorian period, when the action moved north to **Chiswick High Street**, near the tube. **Church Street**, leading down to the riverfront but cut off rudely from modern Chiswick by the traffic-choked, arterial Great West Road, was the medieval village high street, and its oldest building today is the Old Burlington, originally a sixteenth-century inn, and now a private residence. The most picturesque approach is to walk along the river from Hammersmith. If you do so, you'll soon come to **Chiswick Mall**, which continues for a mile or so along the river to the church. A riotous ensemble of seventeenth- and eighteenth-century mansions lines the north side of the Mall, which cuts them off from their modest riverside gardens. Halfway along, a particularly fine trio ends with **Walpole House**, once the home of Barbara Villiers, who was the Duchess of Cleveland, Countess of Castlemaine and one of Charles II's many mistresses.

Church of St Nicholas

Church St • Visiting hours vary but generally Mon–Fri 9.30am–6pm & Sun 2.30–5pm • ☎ 020 8995 7876, ⓦ stnicholaschiswick.org • ⊖ Turnham Green

At the very western end of Chiswick Mall stands the church of **St Nicholas**, rebuilt in the 1880s, but still retaining its original fifteenth-century ragstone tower. Lord

Burlington and his architect friends William Kent and Colen Campbell are all buried in the graveyard, as is the aforementioned Barbara Villiers, though only the painters William Hogarth and James Whistler are commemorated by gravestones, the former enclosed by wrought-iron railings.

Fuller's Griffin Brewery

Chiswick Lane South • Mon–Fri guided tours hourly 11am–3pm • £10; booking essential and online only • ☎ 020 8996 2063, ⊛ fullers. co.uk • ⊖ Turnham Green

Wedged between Chiswick Mall and the Great West Road is **Fuller's Griffin Brewery**, dating back to the seventeenth century and still going strong. You can book yourself onto one of the ninety-minute **guided tours**, which include the inevitable tasting session, and also give visitors the chance to see the country's oldest wisteria, which has clung to the brickwork for over 180 years. Fuller's brew the ubiquitous London Pride, one of the country's most popular ales, as well as plenty of other successful and lesser known beers, and Fuller's pubs, of which there are over 400 in London and southeast England, are generally among the more agreeable big-brewery boozers.

Chiswick House

Great Chertsey Rd • House Sun–Wed and bank holidays 10am–6pm • EH • £6.30, concessions £5.70, under-16s £3.80 **Gardens** Daily 7am–dusk • Free • ☎ 020 8995 0508, ⊛ chgt.org.uk • ⇌ Chiswick from Waterloo or ⊖ Turnham Green

Chiswick House is a perfectly proportioned classical villa, designed by Richard Boyle, third Earl of Burlington, in the 1720s, and set in a beautifully landscaped garden. Like its prototype, Palladio's Villa Capra near Vicenza, the house was purpose-built as a "Temple to the Arts" – an extension to Burlington's adjacent Jacobean mansion (which was torn down in 1788). Here, amid his fine art collection, Burlington used to entertain such friends as Swift, Handel and Pope, who lived in nearby Twickenham.

Guests and visitors (who could view the property on payment of an admission fee even in Lord Burlington's day) would originally have ascended the quadruple staircase and entered the *piano nobile* through the magnificent Corinthian portico. The public entrance today is via the **lower floor**, where the earl had his own private rooms and kept his extensive library. Here, you can pick up an audioguide, watch a short video and peruse an exhibition on the history of the house and grounds.

Entertaining took place on the **upper floor**, a series of cleverly interconnecting rooms, each enjoying a wonderful view out onto the gardens – all, that is, except the **Tribunal**, the domed octagonal hall at the centre of the villa, where the house's finest paintings and sculptures are displayed, just as they would have been in Burlington's day. The other rooms retain much of their rich decor, in particular the ceilings, designed by William Kent. The most sumptuous is the **Blue Velvet Room**, decorated in a deep Prussian blue, with eight pairs of heavy gilded brackets holding up the ceiling.

The gardens

Like the villa, the house's extensive **gardens** were influenced by descriptions of the gardens of classical Rome and, in their turn, became the inspiration for the **English landscape garden**. You can admire the northwest side of the house from the stone benches of the exedra, a set of yew-hedge niches harbouring lions and copies of **Roman statuary**, and overlooking a smooth carpet of grass, punctuated by urns and sphinxes, that sit under the shadow of two giant cedars of Lebanon. Other highlights include England's first **mock ruin** – the Kent-designed cascade – and the network of narrow yew-hedge avenues, each one ending at some diminutive building or statue. One of the most remarkable focal points is the grassy **amphitheatre**, by the side of the lake, centred on an obelisk in a pond and overlooked by an Ionic temple. To the north of the villa, beside a section of the gardens' old **ha-ha**, stands a grand stone gateway designed by Inigo Jones, with a **café** close by. Beyond lies a large **conservatory**, built to grow peaches, grapes and pineapples and now stuffed with camellias. It looks out onto the formal

21 Italian Garden, laid out in the early nineteenth century by the sixth Duke of Devonshire, who also established a zoo (now gone) featuring an elephant, giraffes, elks and emus.

Hogarth's House

Hogarth's Lane, Great West Rd • Tues–Sun noon–5pm • Free • ☎ 020 8994 6757, ⓦ hounslow.info • Free • ⇌ Chiswick from Waterloo or ⊖ Turnham Green

Hogarth's House, where William Hogarth spent each summer with his wife, sister and mother-in-law from 1749 until his death in 1764, sits by the thunderous A4 road. Nowadays it's difficult to believe that the artist came here, from Leicester Square, for "peace and quiet", but in the eighteenth century the house was almost entirely surrounded by countryside. Compared to nearby Chiswick House, whose pretentious Palladianism and excess epitomized everything Hogarth loathed the most, the domesticity here is a marked contrast. Among the scores of Hogarth's engravings, you can see copies of his satirical series – *An Election, Marriage à la Mode, A Rake's Progress* and *A Harlot's Progress* – and compare the modern view from the parlour with the more idyllic scene in *Mr Ranby's House*.

Brentford

Named after the River Brent, which empties into the Thames, just west of Chiswick, **Brentford** was the first point at which you could ford the tidal river in ancient times, and (very possibly) the place where Julius Caesar crossed in 54 BC. Nowadays, it's worth visiting, not for its humdrum high street, but for its various scattered historic landmarks, from the conspicuous campanile of the **London Museum of Water and Steam** to the discreet charm of the aristocratic estate of **Syon**.

Gunnersbury Park

Daily: park 8am–dusk; museum April–Oct 11am–5pm; Nov–March closes 4pm • Free • ☎ 020 8992 1612, ⓦ hounslow.info • ⊖ Acton Town

Like Chiswick Park, **Gunnersbury Park** used to have a Palladian villa at its centre, in this case designed by Inigo Jones' son-in-law, John Webb, for George II's favourite daughter, Princess Amelia. Amelia used the place as a summer retreat and also erected the Neoclassical temple that overlooks the boating lake to this day. At one time, the temple was used as a private synagogue by the Rothschilds, the last owners of the estate, who sold it to the local council in the 1920s. The park has plenty of history – but it could do with some love and attention, too. The **Gunnersbury Park Museum**, housed in the Rothschilds' former double mansion, is closed for renovation and refurbishment until spring 2017.

Kensington Cemetery

143 Gunnersbury Ave • Daily 9am–dusk • Free • ☎ 020 8992 2924, ⓦ rbkc.gov.uk • ⊖ Gunnersbury

There are actually three cemeteries in this neck of the woods sometimes known as **Kensington Cemetery**, all owned and managed by the Royal Borough of Kensington and Chelsea and set up to provide space for Kensington's clog-poppers after that borough's cemeteries reached saturation point. This one, also known as **Gunnersbury Cemetery** (the other two are on Uxbridge Road and are both also known as Hanwell Cemetery) was established in 1929. West London, and the borough of Ealing in particular, has a large Polish community, and the cemetery contains a black marble obelisk erected in 1976 to the 14,500 **Polish POWs** who went missing in 1940, when the Nazi–Soviet Pact carved up Poland. A mass grave containing 4500 bodies was later discovered by the advancing Nazis at Katyn, near Smolensk, but responsibility for the massacre was denied by the Russians until fifty years later, as a plaque bitterly records. Fifty yards to the south is the grave of **General Komorowski**, leader of the Polish Home Army during the ill-fated 1944 Warsaw Uprising, who lived in exile in Britain until his death in 1966. Also buried here is the film director **Carol Reed**, best known for *The Third Man*. There's no direct access to the graveyard from the park, only from Gunnersbury Avenue.

London Museum of Water and Steam

Green Dragon Lane • Daily 11am–4pm • £11.50, concessions £10, under-16s £5 • ☎ 020 8568 4757, ⓦ waterandsteam.org.uk • Bus #237 or #267 from ⊖ Gunnersbury or ⇌ Kew Bridge from Waterloo

Difficult to miss thanks to its stylish, tapered, Italianate standpipe tower, the **London Museum of Water and Steam**, until 2014 known as the **Kew Bridge Steam Museum,** occupies an old pumping station, 100m west of Kew Bridge. At the heart of the museum is the **Steam Hall**, which contains a collection of steam pumping engines, including the gigantic nineteenth-century Cornish beam engines and rotative engines, which you can see in action most weekends.

The steam engines may be things of great beauty, but they are primarily of interest to enthusiasts. However, the museum's wonderfully imaginative and educational **Waterworks** gallery, situated in the basement and overlooked by a vast bank of ancient boilers, baths, sinks, taps and kettles, has universal appeal. The exhibition tells the history of the capital's water supply: the section on rats and cockroaches goes down particularly well with kids, while the tales of the Victorian "toshers", who had to work the sewers in gangs of three to protect themselves from rat attacks, will make adults' stomachs turn. The best time to visit is at weekends, when not only are the museum's industrial dinosaurs put through their paces, but a narrow-gauge **steam railway** runs back and forth round the yard.

Musical Museum

399 Brentford High St • Fri–Sun all year plus Tues in July & Aug 11am–5pm, last entry 4pm • £10, concessions £7.50, under-17s £4 • ☎ 020 8560 8108, ⓦ musicalmuseum.co.uk • Bus #237 or #267 from ⊖ Gunnersbury or ⇌ Kew Bridge from Waterloo

The **Musical Museum** is stuffed with the world's largest collection of self-playing instruments. The best time to come is for the noisy hour-long live demonstrations (phone ahead for times) when the enthusiastic staff put all the mechanical music-making machines through their paces, from cleverly crafted music boxes, through badly tuned barrel organs, to the huge orchestrions that were once a feature of London cafés. The museum also boasts one of the world's finest collections of player-pianos, which can reproduce live performances of the great pianists. In addition, regular concerts, tea dances and silent films are put on to the accompaniment of the museum's enormous Art Deco Wurlitzer, which once graced the Regal cinema in Kingston upon Thames.

Boston Manor

Boston Manor Rd • Park daily 8am–dusk; house April–Oct Sat & Sun noon–5pm • Free • ☎ 020 8568 2818, ⓦ hounslow.info • ⊖ Boston Manor

Built by a wealthy widow who married into the Spencer family, the Jacobean **Boston Manor House** was bought by James Clitherow, a City merchant, in 1670 and remained in the family until taken over by the local council in the 1920s. With magnificent cedar trees and ornamental flowerbeds, the grounds are well worth a visit, despite the nearby presence of the M4. The highlight of the house is the Drawing Room on the first floor, which retains a sumptuous mantelpiece and an extraordinarily elaborate, original Jacobean plaster ceiling. In an unusual break with protocol, William IV and Queen Adelaide paid a visit to the Clitherows (mere commoners), and dined in the Dining Room, which also boasts a fine plaster ceiling, in 1834.

Syon Park

House Mid-March to Oct Wed, Thurs & Sun 11am–5pm, last entry 4pm • £12, concessions £10.50, under-17s £5 (price includes gardens) **Gardens** Mid-March to Oct daily 10.30am–5pm; Nov–Feb Sat & Sun 10.30am–5pm, last entry 4pm • £7 concessions £5.50, under-17s £3.50 • ☎ 020 8569 7497, ⓦ syonpark.co.uk • Bus #237 or #267 to Brent Lea bus stop from ⊖ Gunnersbury or ⇌ Kew Bridge, or 15min walk from ⇌ Syon Lane

Syon Park sits directly across the Thames from Kew Gardens, and is one of the few aristocratic estates left intact in London, with a fantastically lavish stately home, Syon House, at its heart. It has been in the hands of the Percy family since Elizabethan times,

21

although these days it's more of a working commercial concern than a family retreat, with a garden centre, an indoor adventure playground and various other attractions on offer. The main reason to come here, though, is to view the magnificent house and its accompanying gardens. Syon started out as one of the richest monasteries in the country, established by Henry V after the Battle of Agincourt. Dissolved by Henry VIII, who incarcerated his fifth wife, Catherine Howard, here shortly before her execution in 1542, it was eventually granted to the Percys, earls (and later dukes) of Northumberland.

Syon House

From its rather plain castellated exterior, you'd never guess that **Syon House** contains the most opulent eighteenth-century interiors in London. The splendour of Robert Adam's refurbishment is immediately revealed, however, in the pristine **Great Hall**, where you can pick up the excellent audioguide. An apsed double cube with a screen of Doric columns at one end and classical statuary dotted around the edges, the hall has a chequered marble floor that cleverly mirrors the pattern of the coffered ceiling. It was in the hall's Tudor predecessor that Henry VIII's body lay in state en route to Windsor, and was discovered the next morning surrounded by a pack of hounds happily lapping the blood seeping from the coffin.

The state apartments

From the austerity of the Great Hall you enter the lavishly decorated **Ante Room**, with its florid scagliola floor and its green-grey Ionic columns topped by brightly gilded classical statues. Here, guests could mingle before entering the **State Dining Room**, a compromise between the two preceding rooms, richly gilded with a double apse but otherwise calm in its overall effect. The remaining rooms are warmer and softer in tone, betraying their Elizabethan origins much more than the preceding ones. The **Red Drawing Room** retains its original red-silk wall hangings from Spitalfields, upon which are hung portraits of the Stuarts by Lely, Van Dyck and others, and features a splendid ceiling studded with over two hundred roundels set within gilded hexagons. Looking out to the Thames, the **Long Gallery** – 136ft by just 14ft – stretches the entire width of the house, decorated by Adam's busy pink and gold plasterwork and lined with 62 individually painted pilasters. It was in the Long Gallery that Lady Jane Grey was formally offered the crown by her father-in-law, John Dudley, the owner of Syon at the time; nine days later they were arrested and eventually beheaded.

The private apartments

The private apartments pale in comparison with the first five rooms. However, there are still one or two highlights to look out for: more works by Lely and Van Dyck, as well as Gainsborough and Reynolds in the **Print Room**; a superb Adam fireplace and ornate fan-patterned ceiling, plus portraits by Holbein and Reynolds, in the **Green Drawing Room** – still used by the family; and a monster golden Sèvres vase at the foot of the modest principal **staircase**. Upstairs, past the delicate thousand-piece Sèvres dinner service, there are several plush bedrooms, including two refurbished in 1832 for the future Queen Victoria and her mother, the Duchess of Kent, with magnificent canopied beds, blue silk outside and yellow within.

The gardens

While Adam beautified Syon House, Capability Brown laid out its **gardens** around an artificial lake, surrounding it with oaks, beeches, limes and cedars. Since then, the gardens have been further enhanced by still more exotic trees, ranging from an Indian bean tree to a pagoda tree. Beside the lake, there's a stretch of lawn overlooked by a Doric column topped by a fibreglass statue of Flora, but the gardens' real highlight is the crescent-shaped **Great Conservatory**, an early nineteenth-century addition which is said to have inspired Joseph Paxton, architect of the Crystal Palace.

Osterley Park

Jersey Rd • **Park** Daily April–Sep 7am–7.30pm; Oct–March 7am–6pm • Free **House** April –Sept Wed–Sun 11am–5pm; Oct Wed–Sun noon–4pm; Nov–March Sat & Sun noon–4pm • NT • £9.90, under-16s £4.95 • ☎ 020 8232 5050, Ⓦ nationaltrust.org.uk • ⊖ Osterley

Robert Adam redesigned another colossal Elizabethan mansion three miles northwest of Syon at **Osterley Park** – one of London's largest surviving estate parks, which still gives the impression of being in the middle of the countryside, despite the M4 motorway to the north of the house. The main approach is along a splendid avenue of sweet chestnuts to the south, past the National Trust-sponsored **farmhouse** (whose produce you can buy all year round). The driveway curves past the southernmost of the park's three lakes, with a Chinese pagoda at one end. Cedars planted in the 1820s and oaks planted in Victorian times stand between the lake and the house, and to the north are the grandiose Tudor stables of first owner Thomas Gresham, now converted into a **café**.

Osterley House

Unlike Syon, **Osterley House** was built with mercantile rather than aristocratic wealth: it was erected in 1576 by Thomas Gresham, the brains behind the City's Royal Exchange. Later it was bought by another City gent, the goldsmith and banker Francis Child, who used it merely as a kind of giant safe-deposit box – it was his grandsons who employed Robert Adam to create the house as it is today. From the outside, Osterley bears some similarity to Syon, the big difference being the grand entrance portico, with a broad flight of steps rising to a tall, Ionic colonnade, which gives access to the central courtyard.

The interior

From the central courtyard, you enter Adam's characteristically cool **Entrance Hall**, a double-apsed space decorated with grisaille paintings and classical statuary. The finest rooms are the State Rooms of the south wing, where the nouveaux riches Childs hoped, in vain, to entertain royalty as Gresham had once done. The **Drawing Room** is splendid, with Reynolds portraits on the damask walls and a coffered ceiling centred on a giant marigold, a theme continued in the lush carpet and elsewhere in the house. The **Tapestry Room** is hung with Boucher-designed Gobelins tapestries, while the silk-lined **State Bedchamber** features an outrageous domed bed designed by Adam. Lastly, there's the **Etruscan Dressing Room**, in which every surface is covered in delicate painted trelliswork, sphinxes and urns, dubbed "Etruscan" by Adam (and Wedgwood), though it is in fact derived from Greek vases found at Pompeii.

The **Long Gallery** is much broader, taller and plainer than the one at Syon and, like much of the house, features Adam-designed furniture, as well as some fine chinoiserie. In the north wing, the whitewashed Library is worth a quick peek, as is the Neoclassical **Great Staircase**, with its replica Rubens ceiling painting.

Pitzhanger Manor House and Gallery

Mattock Lane • ☎ 020 8567 1227, Ⓦ pitzhanger.org.uk • ⊖ Ealing Broadway

Closed for major renovations and repairs until 2018, **Pitzhanger Manor House**, in the northeast corner of attractive Walpole Park, was designed in 1770 by George Dance, but later bought and extensively remodelled by John Soane, architect of the Bank of England. Once returned to its former glory, the house – with a gallery for art, design and architecture attached (also under renovation) – will doubtless be worth a visit.

Kew

Kew is famous for its **Royal Botanic Gardens**, which manage the extremely difficult task of being both a world leader in botanic research and an extraordinarily beautiful and popular public park at the same time. Kew began life in the eighteenth century as the pleasure gardens of two royal estates, but it was Princess Augusta, the widow of Prince Frederick, eldest son of George II, who turned the estate into the first botanic gardens in the 1750s, with the help of her paramour, the Earl of Bute. Some of the earliest specimens were brought back from the voyages of Captain Cook, instantly establishing Kew as a leading botanical research centre. From its original eight acres the gardens have grown into a 300-acre site in which more than 33,000 species are grown in plantations and glasshouses, a display that attracts nearly two million visitors annually, most of them with no specialist interest at all. The only drawbacks with Kew are the hefty entry fee, and the fact that it's on the main flight path to Heathrow. That aside, it's a wonderful place, with something to see whatever the season. Apart from the gardens, there's not much reason to linger in Kew, although Kew Green, to the north of the gardens, is quite pretty, and the National Archives lurks in the backstreets.

Royal Botanic Gardens

There are four entrances; Victoria Gate is a short walk from the tube down Lichfield Rd • April–Aug Mon–Fri 10am–6.30pm, Sat & Sun 10am–7.30pm; Sept–Oct daily 10am–6pm; Nov–March daily 10am–4.15pm; at weekends arrive early to avoid the queues • £16.50, concessions £15.50 • ☎ 020 8332 5000, ⓦ kew.org • ⊖ Kew Gardens

Most folk arrive at **Kew Gardens** by tube and enter via the **Victoria Gate**, where you'll find the main shop and visitor centre, and the distinctive **campanile**, which originally served as the chimney for the furnaces below the glasshouses. Beyond lies the **Pond**, home to two ten-ton Ming lions, and the best vantage point from which to appreciate Kew's magnificent **Palm House**, which is a great place to start any visit to Kew.

The glasshouses

A curvaceous mound of glass and wrought iron, designed by Decimus Burton in the 1840s, the **Palm House** is the most distinctive of Kew's glasshouses. It nurtures most of the known palm species in its drippingly humid atmosphere, while in the basement there's a small, but excellent, tropical aquarium. From the Palm House, head north to the diminutive **Waterlily House**, where a canopy of plants and creepers overhangs a circular pond boasting spectacular, giant water lilies.

Further north still, is the rather less graceful **Princess of Wales Conservatory**, opened in 1987. However, the cacti collection here is awesome, as are the giant koi fish that swim stealthily beneath the pathways – look out, too, for the bizarre plants in the insectivorous section. Immediately east, set amid Kew's gargantuan Rock Garden, is the extraordinary **Alpine House**, a glasshouse shaped like the sail on the back of a dimetrodon. Twice the size (and to the south) of the Palm House, and almost forty years in the making, Decimus Burton's **Temperate House** is the largest glasshouse in the world and is currently under restoration until at least 2018.

The eighteenth-century gardens

His mosque, waxworks, observatory and House of Confucius may be gone, but several of the buildings William Chambers created in the 1760s for the amusement of Princess Augusta remain dotted about the gardens. The most famous is his ten-storey, 163ft-high **Pagoda**, Kew's most distinctive landmark, albeit minus the eighty enamelled dragons that used to adorn it. Standing nearby in a sort of miniature tea

---

KEW FOR KIDS

If it's raining, the **aquarium** beneath the Palm House usually goes down well with kids, while under-10s will enjoy the indoor interactive play area, **Climbers & Creepers**. If the weather's good, there's the **Treetop Walkway**, **Treehouse Towers** – an outdoor play area full of ropes and ladders – a giant **Badger Sett** and the **Stag Beetle Loggery**, home to stag beetles and the like.

21

garden is the ornate **Japanese Gateway**, a scaled-down version of the one in Kyoto and a legacy of the 1910 Japan–British Exhibition, built in cedarwood and topped by a copper roof.

North of the pagoda, you can walk through Chambers' **Ruined Arch**, purpose-built with sundry pieces of Roman masonry strewn about as if tossed there by barbarian hordes. Chambers is also responsible for the classical temples, the most picturesque being the **Temple of Aeolus**, situated on one of Kew's few hillocks near Cumberland Gate, surrounded in spring by a carpet of bluebells and daffodils.

Capability Brown's horticultural work has proved more durable than Chambers': his lake remains a focal point of the Syon vista from the Palm House, and the hidden **Rhododendron Dell** he devised survives to the south of it. More recent nearby additions include the **Bamboo Garden**, laid out in 1891, and the **Minka House**, a thatched wooden farmhouse built in the suburbs of Okazaki in Japan, and transferred here in 2001. Even more recent is the **Treetop Walkway**, in the centre of the gardens – not a thing of beauty in itself, but the views are good and it's quite novel to be 60ft in the air among the tree canopy.

Queen Charlotte's Cottage

April–Sept Sat & Sun 10am–4pm • Free

The thickly wooded, southwestern section of Kew Gardens is the bit to head for if you want to lose the crowds, few of whom ever make it to **Queen Charlotte's Cottage**, a fairly substantial thatched summerhouse built in brick and timber in the 1770s as a royal picnic spot for George III's wife. The cottage was adjacent to a mini royal menagerie, which featured England's first kangaroos and the now extinct, zebra-like, quagga. Today, there's very little to see inside, beyond a room of Hogarth prints and a trompe-l'oeil pergola (possibly painted by one of the Queen's daughters), but the surrounding native woodland is very peaceful and carpeted with bluebells in spring.

The museum and art galleries

Kew's **Museum No. 1**, designed by Decimus Burton across the Pond from the Palm House, provides an excellent wet-weather retreat. Inside, an exhibition called **Plants and People** shows the myriad uses to which humans have put plants, from food and medicines to clothes and tools. Along with the usual static glass-case displays, there are also touch-screen computers to hand, a scent station and various hands-on exhibits which should keep younger visitors happy. There's also a great 1886 model of an Indian indigo factory, with over one hundred clay figures and one colonial overseer in a pith helmet.

Kew also boasts three art galleries (closed Mondays and daily 1–2pm). To the south of Victoria Gate is the **Shirley Sherwood Gallery of Botanical Art**, a modern space that displays the most exquisitely executed botanical art from the last three centuries. Next door stands the resolutely old-fashioned **Marianne North Gallery**, purpose-built in 1882 to house the prolific output of the self-trained artist Marianne North. Over eight hundred paintings, completed in fourteen years of hectic world travel, are displayed end to end, filling every single space in the gallery. Finally, **Kew Gardens Gallery**, the largest of the lot, in Cambridge Cottage, in the northeastern corner of the gardens, puts on temporary exhibitions often on more general botanical themes.

Kew Palace

April–Sept daily 10.30am–5.30pm • Free with entrance to gardens • ☎ 020 8332 5655, ⓦ hrp.org.uk

In the north of the gardens stands the country's smallest royal residence, **Kew Palace**, a three-storey red-brick mansion measuring a mere 70ft by 50ft, and commonly known as the "Dutch House", after its fancy Flemish-bond brickwork and its curly Dutch gables. It's the smallest (and sole survivor) of Kew's three former royal residences and was bought from a City merchant by George II as a nursery and schoolhouse for his umpteen children.

The only king to live here was **George III**, confined to the palace from 1801 onwards and subjected to the dubious attentions of doctors who attempted to find a cure for his "madness" by straitjacketing him and applying poultices of mustard and Spanish fly – only his strong constitution helped him to pull through.

Inside the palace, there are one or two bits and bobs belonging to the royals, like the much-loved doll's house, on the ground floor, which belonged to George III's daughters. Upstairs, you can view the chair in which Queen Charlotte passed away in 1818, while the top floor has been left pretty much untouched since those days. You also get to visit the **Royal Kitchens** for a glimpse into Georgian life below stairs. Take time, too, to explore the secluded **Queen's Garden**, behind the palace, set out in a formal late seventeenth-century style, with a pleached hornbeam avenue and a lovely sunken nosegay garden.

Kew Green

Kew's majestic **Main Gates**, designed by Decimus Burton, fulfilled their stated function until the arrival of the railway at Kew. Nowadays, you only get to see them if you're walking from Kew Bridge or exploring **Kew Green**, once an archetypal English village green; though still very pleasant it's now sliced in half by busy Kew Road. Lined with Georgian houses, the green is centred on the delightful church of **St Anne** (for opening times, visit ⓦ saintanne-kew.org.uk), an unusual building sporting a Victorian polygonal clock turret at one end and a peculiar Georgian octagonal cupola at the other; the painters Gainsborough and Zoffany lie in the churchyard. Inside, there's a royal Georgian gallery, held up by Tuscan columns, while at the east end is a rather fine late-Victorian chancel with scagliola columns and a top-lit dome. There are music recitals, tea and cakes on summer Sunday afternoons.

The National Archives

Off Mortlake Rd, down Ruskin Ave • Tues & Thurs 9am–7pm, Wed, Fri & Sat 9am–5pm • Free • ☎ 020 8876 3444, ⓦ nationalarchives .gov.uk • ⊖ Kew Gardens

Hidden in the residential backstreets of Kew are the brutish-looking beige and green premises housing **the National Archives**, whose uninviting facade is softened considerably by the surrounding leafy park and ponds. Its research rooms are full of academics and family historians consulting primary source materials, while its exhibition gallery displays a changing rota of fascinating artefacts ranging from the likes of the Domesday Book and the trial record of Charles I, to Queen Victoria's 1851 census return and Elton John's Deed Poll certificate changing his name (wisely) from Reginald Kenneth Dwight.

Richmond

Richmond, upstream from Kew, basked for centuries in the glow of royal patronage, with Plantagenet kings and Tudor monarchs frequenting the riverside Palace of Shene, as Richmond Palace was then called. In the eighteenth century Richmond enjoyed a brief life as a spa, and its agreeable locale began to attract City merchants, as well as successful artists, actors and writers: Pope, Gainsborough, Garrick and Reynolds are just some of the plaque-worthy names associated with the place. Although most of the courtiers and aristocrats have gone, as has the Tudor palace on the green, Richmond is still a wealthy district, with two theatres and highbrow pretensions. To appreciate its attractions fully, you need to visit the old village green, take in the glorious view from **Richmond Hill** and pay a visit to the vast acreage of **Richmond Park**, the old royal hunting grounds, still wild and replete with deer, and walk along the riverside to the nearby Jacobean mansion of **Ham House**.

Richmond Green

George Street, Richmond's main street, is traffic-clogged and dominated by chain stores, but take one of the narrow pedestrianized alleyways, lined with arty shops and

21

tearooms, and you'll emerge onto the wonderful open space of **Richmond Green**, one of London's finest village greens, and one of the most peaceful, except for the planes overhead on the main flight path into Heathrow. Handsome seventeenth- and eighteenth-century houses line the southwest and southeast sides of the green, with the most striking building of all, the flamboyant **Richmond Theatre**, designed by the great Frank Matcham in terracotta and brick in 1899, in the northeast corner.

Richmond Museum

Whittaker Ave • Tues–Fri 11am–5pm, Sat until 4pm • Free • ☏ 020 8332 1141, Ⓦ museumofrichmond.com • ⊖ Richmond

The old town hall, set slightly back from the riverside, now houses the library and, on the top floor, the **Richmond Museum**. The museum contains a small permanent exhibition on the history of the town, plus the lowdown on (and a model of) the old royal palace.

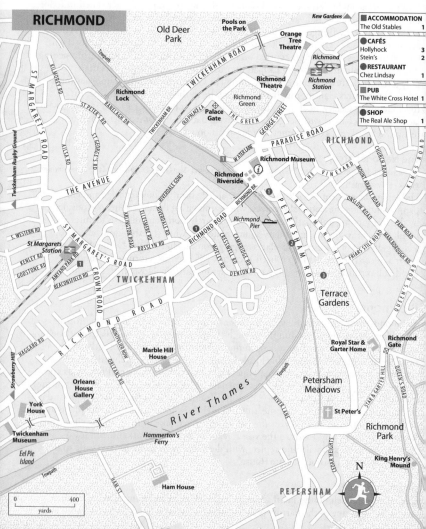

21

Richmond Riverside

To the untrained eye, the buildings that form the backdrop to the pedestrianized terraces of **Richmond Riverside** look Georgian, but closer inspection reveals the majority to be a sham: the cupolas conceal air vents, the chimneys are decorative and the facades hide offices and flats. Still, Quinlan Terry's pastiche from the late 1980s has proved very popular. One of the few originals is **Heron House**, a narrow three-storey building where Lady Hamilton and her daughter Horatia came to live shortly after Trafalgar, the battle in which the girl's father died.

To the south of the modern riverside development lies **Richmond Bridge**, an elegant span of five arches made from Purbeck stone in 1777, and cleverly widened in the 1930s, thus preserving London's oldest extant bridge. From April to September you can rent bikes or rowing boats from the nearby jetties, or take a boat trip to Hampton Court or Westminster (see p.328). If you continue along the towpath beyond Richmond Bridge, you will pass the cows grazing on **Petersham Meadows**, and leave the rest of London far behind, before eventually coming to Ham House.

Ham House

Ham St • **House** March to Oct daily noon–4pm • NT • £10, under-17s £5 **Gardens** daily 10am–5pm • NT • £4, under-17s £2 • ☎ 020 8940 1950, ⓦ nationaltrust.org.uk • Bus #371 or #65 from ↔ Richmond

Hidden in the woods that line the south bank of the Thames lies the red-brick Jacobean mansion of **Ham House**, home to the earls of Dysart for nearly three hundred years. The first Earl of Dysart was Charles I's childhood whipping boy (he literally received the punishment on behalf of the prince when the latter misbehaved), but it's his ambitious daughter, **Elizabeth**, the second Countess – a Royalist spy and at one time Oliver Cromwell's lover – who's most closely associated with the place. With the help of her second husband, the First Duke of Lauderdale, one of Charles II's Cabal Ministry, she added numerous extra rooms, "furnished like a great Prince's" according to diarist John Evelyn, and succeeded in shocking even **Restoration** society with her extravagance.

Elizabeth's profligacy, and a ruinous legal battle over her husband's inheritance, meant she died penniless in 1698, having not ventured out of the house for eight years. She also left the family heavily in debt, so they could afford to make few alterations to one of the finest **Stuart interiors** in the country, prompting Horace Walpole (who lived across the river at Strawberry Hill) to describe Ham as a "Sleeping Beauty". The Great Staircase, off the Central Hall, is stupendously ornate, featuring huge bowls of fruit at the newel posts and trophies of war carved into the balustrade. The rest of the house is equally sumptuous, with lavish plasterwork, silverwork and parquet flooring, **Verrio ceiling paintings** and rich hangings, tapestries, silk damasks and cut velvets. The Long Gallery, in the west wing, features a Van Dyck self-portrait, a portrait of Elizabeth Dysart and six "Court Beauties" by **Peter Lely**.

> ## RICHMOND'S LOST PALACE
>
> Richmond Palace was acquired by Henry I in 1125, when it was still known as **Shene Palace**. The first king to frequent the place was Edward III, who lay dying here in 1377 while his mistress urged the servants to prise the rings from his fingers. Seventeen years later a grief-stricken Richard II razed the place to the ground after his wife, Anne of Bohemia, died here of the plague. Henry V had it restored and Edward IV held jousting tournaments on the green, but it was Henry VII who, in an atypical burst of extravagance, constructed the largest complex of all, renaming it **Richmond Palace** after his Yorkshire earldom. Henry VIII granted the palace to his fourth wife, Anne of Cleves, as part of their divorce settlement. Queen Mary and Philip of Spain spent part of their honeymoon here and Elizabeth I came here to die in 1603. A lot of history is attached to the place, but very little of Richmond Palace survived the Commonwealth and even less is visible now. The most obvious relic is the unspectacular red-brick **Tudor Gateway**, in the southwest corner of Richmond Green.

21

The gardens

Ham House's formal seventeenth-century **gardens** have been beautifully restored to something like their former glory. To the east of the house lies the Cherry Garden, laid out with a pungent lavender parterre, and surrounded by yew hedges and pleached hornbeam arbours. On the south terrace, the Lauderdales would display their citrus trees, considered the height of luxury at the time, while across the lawn lies the "Wildernesse" of hornbeam hedges and maple trees. Finally, to the west, you'll find the partially resurrected kitchen garden, overlooked by the Orangery – the oldest in Britain – which serves as a tearoom.

Richmond Hill

If you're still wondering what's so special about Richmond, take a hike up **Richmond Hill**. To get there, head up Hill Rise from the top of Bridge Street, passing between the eighteenth-century antique shops and tearooms on your left, and the small sloping green on your right. Eventually you come to the **Terrace Gardens**, celebrated for the view up the thickly wooded Thames valley. Turner, Reynolds, Kokoschka and countless other artists have painted this view, which remains relatively unchanged and takes in six counties from Windsor to the North Downs. Richmond's wealthiest inhabitants have flocked to the hill's commanding heights over the centuries. The future George IV is alleged to have spent his secret honeymoon at **3 The Terrace**, after marrying Mrs Fitzherbert; twice divorced and a Catholic to boot, she was never likely to be Queen, though she bore the prince ten children.

Further along, on the opposite side of the street, William Chambers built **Wick House** in 1772 as a summer residence for the enormously successful Joshua Reynolds. The building currently houses the nurses who work at the nearby **Royal Star & Garter Home**, a rest home for war veterans built shortly after World War I, and now the dominant feature of the hillside. Disabled war veterans are also among the workforce at Richmond's **Poppy Factory** (ⓦ poppyfactory.org), who produce the thousands of poppies, petals and wreaths used during the build-up to Remembrance Day in November; the factory welcomes visitors and conducts regular ninety-minute guided tours.

Richmond Park

Daily March–Sept 7am–dusk; Oct–Feb 7.30am–dusk • Free • ☏ 0300 061 2200, ⓦ royalparks.org.uk • Bus #371 from ⊖ Richmond to Richmond Gate or #65 from ⊖ Richmond to Petersham Gate

Richmond's greatest attraction is the enormous **Richmond Park**, at the top of Richmond Hill – 2500 acres of undulating grassland and bracken, dotted with coppiced woodland and as wild as anything in London. A royal hunting ground since the thirteenth century (when it was known as Shene Chase), this is Europe's largest city park – four miles across at its widest point. It's famous for its red and fallow deer, which roam freely – and breed so successfully, they have to be culled twice a year – and for its ancient oaks. Though for the most part untamed, there are a couple of deliberately landscaped plantations which feature splendid springtime azaleas and rhododendrons.

From Richmond Gate, at the top of Richmond Hill, it's a short walk south along the crest of the hill to **Pembroke Lodge** (originally known as The Molecatcher's), the childhood home of the philosopher Bertrand Russell. Set in its own lovely garden, the house is now a tearoom with outdoor seating and more spectacular views up the Thames valley. Close by, to the north, is the highest point in the park, known as **King Henry VIII's Mount**, where tradition has it the king waited for the flare launched from the Tower of London, which signalled the execution of his second wife, Anne Boleyn, though historians believe he was in Wiltshire at the time.

Exploring the Park

For a longer stroll through the park, head east from Pembroke Lodge into **Sidmouth Wood**, whose sweet chestnuts, oaks and beeches were planted during the nineteenth century. Originally established as pheasant cover, the wood is now a bird sanctuary, and walkers must keep to the central path, known as the Driftway. A little further east lie the **Pen Ponds**, the largest stretches of water in the park and a good spot for birdwatching. To the south is the park's extremely popular **Isabella Plantation**, a carefully landscaped woodland park, with a little rivulet running through it, two small artificial ponds and spectacular rhododendrons and azaleas in the spring. The round trip from Richmond Gate is about four miles.

The two most important historic buildings in the park are both closed to the public. Of the two, the **White Lodge**, to the east of the Pen Ponds, is the more attractive, a Palladian villa commissioned by George II, and frequented by his wife, Queen Caroline, and their daughter, Princess Amelia. Much altered over the years, it was also the birthplace of the ill-fated Edward VIII, and it was home to the Duke and Duchess of York (later George VI and Queen Elizabeth); it currently houses the Royal Ballet School. The **Thatched House Lodge**, in the southernmost corner of the park, was built in the 1670s for the park's rangers, and gets its name from the thatched gazebo that can be found in the garden. General Eisenhower hung out in the lodge during World War II, and it's now home to Princess Alexandra.

Twickenham

Twickenham, on the opposite side of the river from Richmond, is best known as the home of English rugby – there's a museum if you're really keen (see p.344) – but it also conceals a cluster of lesser-known sights close to the river, all of which repay a brief visit. Most sights are by the river, and, if you want to learn a bit more about the local area, pop into the **Twickenham Museum** (Tues & Sat 11am–3pm, Sun 2–4pm; free; ☏ 020 8408 0070, ⓦ twickenham-museum.org.uk), 25 The Embankment, which puts on changing historical exhibitions.

ARRIVAL AND DEPARTURE

By ferry The most picturesque approach to Twickenham is to walk along the towpath from Richmond Riverside to Hammerton's Ferry, which takes people (and bicycles) over to the Twickenham side (March–Oct Mon–Fri 10am–6pm, Sat & Sun 10am–6.30pm; Nov–Feb Sat & Sun 10am–dusk; £1; ☏ 020 8892 9620, ⓦ hammertonsferry.com).

Marble Hill House

Richmond Rd • By guided tour only April–Oct Sat 10.30am & noon, Sun 10.30am, noon, 2.15 & 3.30pm • EH • £6.20, concessions £5.60, under-16s £3.70 • ☏ 020 8892 5115, ⓦ english-heritage.org.uk • ⇌ St Margarets from Waterloo

A stuccoed Palladian villa set in rolling green parkland, **Marble Hill House** was completed in 1729 for Henrietta Howard, Countess of Suffolk, mistress of George II for some twenty years and, conveniently, also a lady-in-waiting to his wife, Queen Caroline (apparently "they hated one another very civilly"). She was renowned not just for her "long chestnut tresses", but also for her wit and intelligence and she entertained the Twickenham Club of Alexander Pope, John Gay and Horace Walpole.

The few original furnishings in the house are enhanced with reproductions giving the place something of the feel of a fashionable Georgian villa. The Great Room, on the *piano nobile*, is a perfect cube whose coved ceiling carries on up into the top-floor apartments. Copies of Van Dycks decorate the walls as they did in Lady Suffolk's day, but the highlight is Lady Suffolk's Bedchamber, with its Ionic columned recess – a classic Palladian device – where she died in 1767 at the age of 79. There's a **café** in the coach house open daily and open-air concerts in the surrounding park on occasional summer evenings.

Orleans House Gallery

Riverside • Tues–Sun 10am–5pm • Free • ☏ 020 8831 6000, ⓦ richmond.gov.uk • ⇌ St Margarets from Waterloo

Set in a small wood to the west of Marble Hill Park is the **Orleans House Gallery**, in what began life as a retirement villa built in 1710 for James Johnston, who had been Secretary of

21

State for Scotland under William III. It was most famously occupied in 1815–17 by Louis-Philippe, the exiled Duke of Orléans (and future King of the French), who referred to it as "dear quiet Twick". In 1926, it was all but entirely demolished – all, that is, except for the **Octagon**, designed for Johnston by James Gibbs in 1720 in honour of a visit by Queen Caroline. The café and the exhibitions staged in the old stables and the modern extension are appealing enough, but it's the Octagon that steals the limelight, an unusually exuberant Baroque confection celebrated for its masterly Italian stucco decoration.

York House Gardens

Sion Rd • Daily 9am to dusk • Free • ⇌ St Margarets from Waterloo

The early seventeenth-century, Twickenham riverside residence **York House** has had a series of illustrious residents including Prince Philippe, Count of Paris and grandson of Louis-Philippe. The house itself is now owned by the local council and is used for weddings, but the **gardens**, laid out by the last private owner, the Indian businessman Ratan Tata, are open to the public. The bit to head for is the riverside section – a great picnic spot – that lies beyond the sunken garden, on the other side of the delicate arched bridge spanning the road. Here, in among the yew hedges, you'll find the gardens' celebrated "**naked ladies**", seven larger-than-life marble nymphs frolicking in the water lilies of an Italian fountain, above which Venus rises up at the head of two winged horses.

World Rugby Museum

200 Whitton Rd • Tues–Sat 10am–5pm, Sun 11am–5pm • £8, concessions £7, under-16s £6 museum only; £20, concessions £15, under-16s £12 with stadium tour • ☎ 020 8892 8877, ⓦ englandrugby.com • ⇌ Twickenham from Waterloo

The English Rugby Union fan's number-one pilgrimage site is the national stadium at Twickenham, and the **World Rugby Museum** is in the East Stand. The exhibition is full of video footage and lots of memorabilia from the sport, which was famously invented in 1823, when W.W. Ellis picked up and ran with the ball during a game of football at Rugby School. There's not much here for the nonspecialist, however, save for the Calcutta Cup, an object of supreme beauty, having been made from 270 silver rupees, with great cobra handles and an elephant lid. You can also sign up for a **stadium tour**, which allows you to see the dressing rooms and walk onto the pitch itself, and includes a visit to the museum. Note that on match days the museum is only open to match ticket-holders.

Strawberry Hill

268 Waldegrave Rd **House** March–Oct Mon–Wed 2–5.30pm, Sat & Sun noon–5.30pm (last admission 4pm) • £10.80, concessions £5.40, under-16s free **Guided tour** Wed 10am & Sat 10.30am • £11.70, under-16s £5.85 **Garden** Daily 10am–6pm • Free • ☎ 020 8744 1241, ⓦ strawberryhillhouse.org.uk • ⇌ Strawberry Hill from Waterloo

One last oddity well worth making the effort to visit is **Strawberry Hill**. In 1747 writer, wit and fashion queen Horace Walpole, youngest son of former prime minister Robert

---

ISLANDS IN THE THAMES

If you take the boat upriver (see p.328), or walk along the towpath, you'll pass a number of islands in the middle of the Thames. Several were used in the past to grow grass and willows for basketry, but most now act as formal or informal nature reserves, like **Brentford Ait** – "ait" or "eyot" is the word used on the Thames to denote an island – which supports a large heronry. There's even a makeshift raft floating mid-river, near Marble Hill House, where a local eccentric has lived for over 25 years. The only inhabited island on the tidal Thames is **Eel Pie Island**, connected to the bank near York House by a pedestrian bridge. Tea dances began at the island's *Eel Pie Hotel* back in the 1920s; bawdy jazz nights were the staple diet in the 1950s; Pink Floyd, the Rolling Stones and the Who all played there in the 1960s. The hotel burnt down in 1971 and the island is now better known for its eccentric community of independent-spirited artists and artisans (ⓦ eelpieislandartists.co.uk), among them Trevor Baylis, inventor of the clockwork radio.

Walpole, bought this "little play-thing house…the prettiest bauble you ever saw…set in enamelled meadows, with filigree hedges", renamed it Strawberry Hill and set about inventing the most influential building in the Gothic Revival. Walpole appointed a "Committee of Taste" to embellish his project with details from other Gothic buildings: screens from Old St Paul's and Rouen cathedrals, and fan vaulting from Henry VII's Chapel in Westminster Abbey.

The house quickly became the talk of London, a place of pilgrimage for royalty and foreign dignitaries alike. Walpole was forced to issue tickets in advance (never more than four and no children) to cut down the number of visitors. Those he wished to meet he greeted dressed in a lavender suit and silver-embroidered waistcoat, sporting a cravat carved in wood by Grinling Gibbons and an enormous pair of gloves that once belonged to James I. When he died in 1797, he left the house to his friend, the sculptor Anne Damer, who continued to entertain in the same spirit, giving lavish garden parties dressed in a man's coat, hat and shoes. Walpole wanted visits of Strawberry Hill to be a theatrical experience, and, with its eccentric Gothic decor, it remains so to this day. There's a *Committtee of Taste* **café** in the Great Cloister, open slightly earlier hours than the house.

Wimbledon

Wimbledon is a dreary, high, bleak, windy suburb, on the edge of a threadbare heath.　　　　Virginia Woolf

Nowadays, of course, **Wimbledon** is best known for its tennis tournament, the Wimbledon Championships, held every year in the last week of June and the first week of July, on the grass courts of the All England Lawn Tennis and Croquet Club – to give the ground its grand title. For the rest of the year, Wimbledon's vast **common** is its most popular attraction, worth a visit for its **windmill** and for the remarkable **Southside House**.

Wimbledon Lawn Tennis Museum

Gate 4, Church Rd **Museum** daily 10am–5pm • £13, concessions £11, under-16s £8 **Guided tours of grounds** book online • £24, concessions £21, under-16s £15 • ☎ 020 8946 2244, Ⓦ wimbledon.com • Bus #493 from ⊖ Southfields

If you've missed the tournament itself (see p.437), the next best thing for tennis fans is a quick spin around the state-of-the-art **Wimbledon Lawn Tennis Museum**. It traces the history of the game, which is descended from the *jeu de paume* played by the French clergy from the twelfth century onwards. The modern version, though, is considered to have been invented by a Victorian major, who called it "Sphairstike", a name that, not surprisingly, failed to stick. The new sport was initially seen as a genteel pastime, suitable for both gentlemen and ladies, and its early enthusiasts hailed almost exclusively from the aristocracy and the clergy – the museum's Edwardian dressing room is the epitome of upper-class masculinity. As well as the historical and fashion angles and the tennis-star memorabilia, there's also plenty of opportunity for watching vintage game footage.

Wimbledon Common and Windmill

Wimbledon Rd • **Common** open 24hrs • **Museum** April–Oct Sat 2–5pm, Sun 11am–5pm • £2, concessions and under-16s £1 • ☎ 020 8947 2825, Ⓦ wimbledonwindmill.org.uk • Bus #93 from ⊖ Wimbledon

With none of the views of Richmond, **Wimbledon Common** can appear rather bleak from the southeast corner, where you are likely to arrive first if you have come up the hill from Wimbledon tube station. The rough grass, bracken and scrappy playing fields here are, however, a little misleading: pleasantly natural-feeling pathways snake into and around some 800 acres of semi-wooded interior, though the greens of a golf course break up the trees in places. In the northern half of the common, situated at the end of Windmill Road, is **Wimbledon Windmill**, with conveniently placed tearooms nearby. Built in 1817, the mill was closed down in 1864, and converted into cottages, one of which was home to Baden-Powell when he began writing his *Scouting for Boys* in 1908. Subsequently restored and turned into a museum, the windmill is the last remaining hollow-post flour mill in the country; you can also climb into the first section of the wooden cap and see the giant chain wheel.

Putney Vale Cemetery

Stag Lane • Mon–Sat 8am–dusk, Sun 10am–dusk • Free • ☎ 020 8871 7820, ⓦ wandsworth.gov.uk • Bus #85 or #265 from ➜ Putney Bridge

Sandwiched between Wimbledon Common and Richmond Park, by the busy A3, is **Putney Vale Cemetery**, worth a visit for its wonderful array of Victorian angels and peaceful Gardens of Remembrance, at their best in early summer. Once you enter, turn right, and head to the end of Richards Way, where you'll find the nautical grave of Bruce Ismay, *Titanic* survivor and chairman of the ill-fated White Star Line; close by lies Sandy Denny, lead singer of Fairport Convention. The cemetery's most illustrious incumbent is Alexander Kerensky, along Alexander Way, who died in New York, but was refused burial there by the Russian Orthodox Church. Kerensky was the leader of the Russian Revolution of February 1917, which overthrew the tsar, but was himself ousted by the Bolshevik Revolution of October 1917.

Cannizaro Park

West Side Common • Mon–Fri 8am–dusk, Sat & Sun 9am–dusk • Free • ☎ 020 8946 7349, ⓦ cannizaropark.com • Bus #93 from ➜ Wimbledon

Cannizaro Park is a small, sheltered, wooded public park, made up of the grounds of Cannizaro House (now a hotel frequented by the tennis glitterati), and entered from Wimbledon Common. Within its walls are a grotesque teapot fountain, a lovely stretch of lawn for picnicking, a maze of paths, an aviary, an Italian garden and a wonderful array of rhododendrons, azaleas and magnolias. The park also stages occasional student art shows and has an open-air music and theatre festival every July.

Wat Buddhapadipa

14 Calonne Rd • Daily 9am–6pm • Free • ☎ 020 8946 1357, ⓦ buddhapadipa.org • Bus #93 from ➜ Wimbledon

Probably the most unusual and intriguing sight in Wimbledon is the **Wat Buddhapadipa**, a startling, white-washed and gabled Thai Buddhist temple, the first built in the UK, with a richly decorated red and gold roof, moved here in 1976 from its original site in Richmond and formally consecrated in 1982. You can visit the temple grounds any day of the week, and there are classes, courses and ceremonies throughout the year, but the temple itself is only accessible at the weekend.

Southside House

3–4 Woodhayes Rd • Guided tours Easter–Sept Wed, Sat & Sun 2, 3 & 4pm • £9, concessions £6 • ☎ 020 8946 7643, ⓦ southsidehouse .com • Bus #93 from ➜ Wimbledon

Hidden from the road behind high walls is the Dutch-Baroque mansion of **Southside House**, built in the late seventeenth century, and now hemmed in by Wimbledon's King's College School. Visiting the house is an unforgettable experience, not least because you may be guided round, and fed with anecdotes, by the eccentric descendants of the Pennington-Mellor-Munthe family who first built the house – several of whom still live here in a kind of time warp, using only candles for light and open fires for warmth, surrounded by the house's rich and slowly disintegrating decor, and the family's ancestral hangings, many of which are extremely valuable.

Inside, the place has a ramshackle feel, partly because at heart it's still an old Tudor farmhouse, onto which a Dutch facade has been added. Nevertheless, virtually every room is stuffed to the rafters with artworks and other sundry heirlooms. In the Dining Room alone, there are no fewer than 34, mostly full-length, portraits, including three by Van Dyck, one each by Hogarth and Goya, and a depiction of St George by Burne-Jones. Other treasures on show include the sapphire worn by the last king of Serbia on the day of his assassination, and, in a cabinet of curiosities in the royal bedroom upstairs, you can see the pearl necklace worn by Marie Antoinette on the day of her execution. Finally, in the Music Room, there's a portrait of Angelica Kauffmann, a Reynolds self-portrait, a Fragonard and one of George Romney's famous portraits of Emma, Lady Hamilton, who used to strike her "attitudes" in that very room.

Hampton Court Palace

Daily April–Oct 10am–6pm; Nov–March closes 4.30pm; last entry 1hr before close • £17.50, concessions £14.50, under-16s £8.75 (tickets 50p–£1 cheaper Nov–Feb) • ☎ 0844 482 7777, ⓦ hrp.org.uk • ⇌ Hampton Court from Waterloo

Hampton Court Palace, a sprawling red-brick ensemble on the banks of the Thames, thirteen miles southwest of London, is the finest of England's royal abodes. And it's up

HAMPTON COURT

21

there with the Tower of London when it comes to the variety of attractions on offer: not only does it boast Tudor halls and kitchens, it's got some fabulous Baroque interiors in the wings designed by Wren, superb works of art, a beautiful riverside setting, a yew hedge maze, a Real Tennis court, impressive formal gardens and a vast royal park. If your time is limited, the most rewarding sections are Henry VIII's Apartments, William III's Apartments and Henry VIII's Kitchens – and be sure to leave time for the Maze.

Brief history

The present building was begun in 1516 by the upwardly mobile **Cardinal Wolsey**, Henry VIII's high-powered, fast-living Lord Chancellor. Wolsey fell from favour when he failed to secure a papal annulment for Henry's marriage to Catherine of Aragon, and Hampton Court (and his palace in Whitehall) fell to the king in 1528.

Like Wolsey, **Henry VIII** spent enormous sums of money on the palace, enlarging the kitchens, rebuilding the chapel and altering the rooms to suit the tastes of the last five of his six wives. Under Elizabeth I and James I, Hampton Court became renowned for its masques, plays and balls; during the Civil War, it was a refuge and then a prison for Charles I. The palace was put up for sale during the Commonwealth, but, with no buyers forthcoming, Cromwell decided to move in and lived here on and off until his death in 1658. Charles II laid out the gardens, inspired by what he had seen at Versailles, but it was **William and Mary** who instigated the most radical alterations, hiring Christopher Wren to remodel the buildings. Wren was told to tear down the whole palace and build a new Versailles, but, in the end, had to content himself with rebuilding the east and south wings, adding the Banqueting House on the river and completing the chapel for Queen Anne.

George III eschewed the place, apparently because he associated it with the beatings he received here from his grandfather. Instead, he established grace-and-favour residences for indigent members of the royal household, which still exist today. The palace was opened to the public in 1838, and, along with the vast expanse of **Bushy Park**, it's now a major tourist attraction.

INFORMATION AND TOURS

Admission Tickets to the Royal Apartments cover entry to everything in the palace and grounds – to save money and avoid queuing, buy your tickets online. If you don't want to visit the apartments, you can buy a separate ticket for the gardens (April–Sept; £5.80) and the Maze (£4.40).

Tours The State Apartments are divided into six thematic walking tours, which are numbered and colour-coded. There's not a lot of information in the rooms, but guided tours, lasting half an hour or so, are available at no extra charge; all are led by period-costumed historians, who do a

fine job of bringing the place to life. In addition, audioguides are available from the information centre on the east side of Clock Court.

Events The Hampton Court Palace Flower Show takes place in early July; it rivals Chelsea for sheer snob factor, and is likewise organized by the Royal Horticultural Society (⟨w⟩rhs.org.uk). The Hampton Court Palace Festival (⟨w⟩hamptoncourtpalacefestival.com) features stars from the classical and pop music worlds, and takes place each year in June.

The Palace

The Tudor west front may no longer be moated but it positively prickles with turrets, castellations, chimneypots and pinnacles. The **Great Gatehouse** looks suitably imposing, but was in fact five storeys high until George III's reign. The first and largest courtyard, **Base Court**, is reminiscent of an Oxbridge college and features another Tudor gateway known as Anne Boleyn's Gateway, though it too dates from the time of Wolsey. Beyond lies **Clock Court**, which has none of the uniformity of the other two quadrangles: to the north rises the Tudor Great Hall, to the south Wren's colonnade, announcing the new State Apartments, and to the east a fairly convincing mock-Tudor gateway by William Kent. Originally centred on a large fountain which was equipped by Elizabeth I with a nozzle that soaked innocent passers-by, the courtyard gets its current name from the **astronomical clock** on the inside of the Anne Boleyn Gateway,

THE GHOST OF CATHERINE HOWARD

Henry VIII married his fifth wife, **Catherine Howard**, in July 1540, just weeks after having annulled his six-month marriage to Anne of Cleves. Unfortunately, despite being less than 20, Catherine had already had sexual relations with her music tutor, **Henry Mannox**, was pre-contracted to marry her lover, another courtier named **Francis Dereham**, and began an affair with another courtier named **Thomas Culpeper**. Her ambitious family – who were out of favour since the execution of Anne Boleyn, Catherine's cousin – somewhat optimistically hoped to conceal these inconvenient truths from Henry, and to restore their influence at court.

It took until November 1541 for Henry to find out he'd been duped. Seated in the Royal Pew at Hampton Court, he was passed the note from Thomas Cranmer, the Archbishop of Canterbury, alleging that Catherine was not in fact a virgin when he married her. Catherine was arrested a few days later, but is alleged to have given her guards the slip and run down the **Haunted Gallery** in an attempt to make a final plea for mercy to the king, who was praying in the chapel. Henry refused to see her, and she was dragged kicking and screaming back to her chambers. To this day, a ghost can be heard re-enacting the scene – or so the story goes.

made in 1540 for Henry VIII, which was used to calculate the high tide at London Bridge (and thus the estimated time of arrival of palace guests travelling by boat). The last and smallest of the three courtyards is Wren's **Fountain Court**, which crams in more windows than seems possible.

Henry VIII's Apartments

Henry VIII lavished more money on Hampton Court than on any other palace except Greenwich (which no longer exists). The only major survival from Tudor times, however, is his **Great Hall**, completed with remarkable speed in 1534, with Henry having made the builders work day and night – a highly dangerous exercise in candlelight. The ornate double hammer-beam roof would originally have been painted blue, red and gold and featured a louvre to allow the smoke to escape from the central hearth. Later, the hall served as the palace theatre, where theatrical troupes, among them Shakespeare's, entertained royalty. Even Cromwell had an organ installed here so he and his family could enjoy recitals by John Milton, an accomplished musician as well as a poet.

Passing through the Horn Room, you enter the **Great Watching Chamber**. The gilded oak-ribbed ceiling is studded with leather-mâché Tudor insignia, and hung with tapestries that were part of Wolsey's vast collection. Up to eighty yeomen would have been stationed here, guarding the principal entrance to the king's private chambers, which William and Mary found "old-fashioned and uncomfortable" and consequently demolished.

From here you reach the **Haunted Gallery**, built by Wolsey to connect his apartments to the chapel, and home to the ghost of Catherine Howard (see box above). The gallery gives access to the Royal Pew, where you can see a replica of **Henry VIII's Crown of State**, a magnificent piece of imperial Tudor pomp used for all royal coronations until the Commonwealth. From the Royal Pew you can look down on the **Chapel Royal**, and admire the colourful false-timber Tudor vaulting wrought in plaster, heavy with pendants of gilded music-making cherubs – one of the most memorable sights in the whole palace. It was here that Henry married the sixth of his wives (and the only one to outlive him), Catherine Parr.

Mary II's Apartments

The Queen's apartments remained unfinished at Queen Mary's death in 1694, and weren't fully furnished and decorated until the time of Queen Caroline, George II's wife. The main approach is via the grandiose **Queen's Staircase**, splendidly decorated with trompe-l'oeil reliefs and a coffered dome by William Kent.

21

One of the finest rooms here is the **Queen's Drawing Room**, decorated top to bottom with trompe-l'oeil paintings depicting Queen Anne's husband, George of Denmark – in heroic naval guise, and also, on the south wall, riding naked and wigless on the back of a "dolphin". Queen Anne takes centre stage on the ceiling as Justice, somewhat inappropriately given her habit of not paying her craftsmen, including Verrio, the painter of this room. After Anne's death in 1714, the Prince and Princess of Wales (later George II and Queen Caroline) took over the Queen's Apartments, though they hated the trompe-l'oeil paintings and hung Mantegna's works over the top of them. In 1717, the couple fell out with the king and moved to Kew; the ceiling painting in the **Queen's Bedroom** by James Thornhill predates the quarrel, with four portraits of a seemingly happy Hanoverian family staring at one another from the coving.

The **Queen's Gallery** features one of the most ornate marble fireplaces in the palace – originally intended for the King's Bedchamber – with putti, doves and Venus frolicking above the mantelpiece; the walls, meanwhile, are hung with Gobelin tapestries depicting Alexander the Great's exploits and lined with Chinese vases and Delftware.

Georgian Private Apartments

The **Georgian Private Apartments** begin with the rooms of the **Cumberland Suite**, lived in by George II before his accession, then by his eldest son, Prince Frederick, and redesigned for William, Duke of Cumberland, Frederick's brother and better known as "Butcher Cumberland" for his ruthless suppression of the Jacobites in Scotland. The rooms were decorated by Kent, who added Gothic touches to the first two rooms and a grandiose Neoclassical alcove in the bedchamber.

Beyond here you'll find the tiny **Wolsey Closet**, which, although a Victorian invention, gives a tantalizing impression of the splendour of Wolsey's original palace. It's a jewel of a room – though at 12ft square it's easily missed – with brightly coloured early sixteenth-century paintings set above exquisite linenfold panelling and a fantastic gilded ceiling of interlaced octagons.

Next is the **Communication Gallery**, constructed to link the King's and Queen's apartments, now lined with Lely's "Windsor Beauties", flattering portraits of the best-looking women in the court of Charles II. The **Cartoon Gallery** was purpose-built by Wren to display the Raphael Cartoons – the originals are in the V&A, and what you see are late seventeenth-century oil painting copies. Tapestries made from the cartoons are scattered throughout William and Mary's apartments.

The next sequence of rooms is of minor interest, though they do include an excellent Gibbons overmantle in the Queen's Private Bedchamber (which, unusually, could be locked from the inside). Last of all, you enter the **Queen's Private Oratory**, used by Queen Caroline for private worship – it's one of the few windowless rooms, hence the octagonal dome and skylight.

William III's Apartments

William III's Apartments are approached via the **King's Staircase**, the grandest of the lot thanks chiefly to Verrio's busy, militaristic trompe-l'oeil paintings glorifying the king, depicted here as Alexander the Great. The **King's Guard Chamber** is notable chiefly for its three thousand-piece display of arms, arranged as they were laid out in the time of William III. William's rather modest throne still stands in the **King's Presence Chamber**, under a canopy of crimson damask. The sixteenth-century Brussels tapestries in the room were originally commissioned by Henry VIII for Whitehall Palace.

Further on, in the **King's Privy Chamber**, there's a much grander throne used by William, with a silk and gold lace canopy that still retains its original ostrich feathers. The most impressive room here is the **Great Bed Chamber**, which boasts a superb vertical Gibbons frieze and ceiling paintings by Verrio – just as you're leaving this floor, you'll catch a glimpse of a splendidly throne-like velvet toilet. Ground-floor highlights

include a semi-nude portrait by Van Dyck of his mistress Margaret Lemon, in the East Closet, the **Lower Orangery**, built to house the queen's orange trees during the winter. Past here is the **King's Private Dining Room**, its table laden with pyramids of meringues and fruit and its walls hung with eight full-length portraits of Queen Mary's favourite ladies-in-waiting (known as the "Hampton Court Beauties"), for which the German-born painter Godfrey Kneller received a knighthood.

Young Henry VIII's Story

Several early Tudor rooms, with striking linenfold panelling and gilded strapwork ceilings, are now used to display **Young Henry VIII's Story**. This is a worthy attempt by the palace to portray Henry in his virile youth, during his happy, twenty-year marriage to his first wife, Catherine of Aragon. Interactive screens help tell the story of the Battle of the Spurs at Guinegate in 1613, when Henry led his troops from the front, and of the Field of the Cloth of Gold, Henry's famous meeting with the French king, François I, in 1620.

Henry VIII's Kitchens

After a surfeit of opulent interiors, the workaday **Tudor Kitchens** come as something of a relief. Henry VIII quadrupled the size of the kitchens, large sections of which have survived to this day and have been restored and embellished with historical reconstructions. Past the Boiling Room and Flesh Larder (not for squeamish vegetarians) you come to the **Great Kitchen**, where a fire is still lit in the main hearth every day. This kitchen is only one of three Henry built to cope with the prodigious consumption of the royal court – six oxen, forty sheep and a thousand or more larks, pheasants, pigeons and peacocks were an average daily total. The tour ends in Henry's vast **Wine Cellar**, where the palace's Rhineland wine was stored. At each main meal, the king and his special guests would be supplied with eight pints of wine; courtiers had to make do with three gallons of beer.

The Gardens

The gardens' magnificent **Broad Walk** runs for half a mile from the Thames past Wren's austere East Front to the putti-encrusted Flower Pot Gate, and is lined with some of the country's finest Victorian herbaceous borders. Halfway along lies the indoor **Royal Tennis Court**, established here by Wolsey (a keen player of Real Tennis himself), but extensively restored by Charles II. If you're lucky, you might even catch a game of this arcane precursor of modern tennis, though the rules are incredibly tricky.

Fanning out from the Broad Walk is William's **Fountain Garden**, a grand, semicircular parterre, which in William's day featured box hedges, thirteen fountains and dwarf yew trees pruned to look like obelisks. A fair number of these "black pyramids", as Virginia Woolf called them, have been reduced to chubby cone shapes, while a solitary pool stands in place of the fountains, and the box hedges have become plain lawns. A semicircular canal separates the Fountain Garden from the Home Park beyond, its waters feeding Charles II's **Long Water**, Hampton Court's most Versaillean feature, which slices the Home Park in two.

Privy Garden

Overlooked by Wren's magnificent South Front is the formal **Privy Garden**, laid out as it would have been under William III; the twelve magnificent wrought-iron panels at the river end of the garden are the work of Jean Tijou. To the west, you can peek into the **Pond Gardens**, which were originally constructed as ornamental fish ponds stocked with freshwater fish for the kitchens, and feature some of the gardens' most spectacularly colourful flowerbeds. Further along, protected by glass, is the palace's celebrated **Great Vine**, grown from a cutting in 1768 by Capability Brown and averaging about seven hundred pounds of Black Hamburg grapes per year (sold at the palace in September).

Close by stands the **Lower Orangery**, designed by Wren and used as a dimly lit gallery for *The Triumphs of Caesar*, a series of heroic canvases by **Andrea Mantegna**, bought by Charles I in 1629 and kept here ever since. Painted around 1486 for the Ducal Palace in Mantua, Mantegna's home town, these nine richly coloured paintings, depicting the general's victory parade, are among his best works, characterized by his obsessive interest in archeological and historical accuracy. Beyond the South Gardens, beside the river, is William III's dinky little red-brick **Banqueting House**, built for intimate riverside soirees, with castellations and mouldings by Gibbons and exuberant paintings by Verrio.

The Maze

To the north of the palace, Henry VIII laid out a **Tiltyard** with five towers for watching jousting tournaments, one of which survives near the garden restaurant. William III transformed the tiltyard into a **Wilderness** – an informal park of evergreens – which now contains the most famous feature of the palace gardens, the deceptively tricky trapezoidal **Maze**, laid out in 1714. Mazes, or labyrinths as they were called at the time, were used by pilgrims, who used to crawl along on hands and knees reciting prayers, as penance for not making a pilgrimage to the Holy Land. They were all the rage among the eighteenth-century nobility, who used them primarily for amusement, secret conversations and flirtation. The maze was originally planted with hornbeam but, with the onset of the tourist boom in the 1960s, the hornbeam had to be replaced with yew.

Bushy Park

Beyond the Lion Gates, to the north of the Maze, across Hampton Court Road, lies **Bushy Park**, the palace's semi-wild enclosure of over a thousand acres, which sustains copious herds of fallow and red deer. Wren's mile-long royal road, Chestnut Avenue, cuts through the park, and is at its best in May when the trees are in blossom. The main architectural feature of the park is the **Diana Fountain**, situated a third of the way along the avenue to help break the monotony. The statue – which, in fact, depicts Arethusa – was commissioned by Charles II from Francesco Fanelli and originally graced the Privy Garden; stranded in the centre of this vast pond, she looks ill-proportioned and a bit forlorn.

Off to the west, a little further up the avenue, you'll come upon the **Waterhouse Woodland Gardens**, created in 1949, and at their most colourful each spring when the rhododendrons, azaleas and camellias are in bloom. The crowds are fairly thin even here, compared with the crush around the palace, but if you really want to seek out some of the park's abundant wildlife head for its wilder western section, where few visitors venture.

ZETTER TOWNHOUSE

Accommodation

Accommodation in London is expensive. Compared with most European cities, you pay top dollar in every category from the cheapest hostel to the swankiest five-star. Add to that the fact that most B&Bs and many of the more affordable hotels are housed in historic, formerly residential properties – so rooms tend to be small, bathrooms tiny and lifts rare – and it's understandable that some unprepared visitors come away feeling short-changed. With a little savvy, however, you can get some great deals – just don't expect a mansion for the price of a garret. Remember that rooms with shared facilities may be larger than en-suites, where showers and loos are often shoehorned into tiny corners. In some of the emerging breed of boutique guesthouses, small needn't mean inconvenient anyhow – bijou can be great fun when delivered with wit and style in a buzzy location.

Talking of location, bear in mind that travelling around London is not that difficult with an Oyster card and a tube map. While the central London hotels tend to have the biggest wow factor, the prices reflect this, and it may suit you better to head out of zone 1, especially if you're not short of time.

Demand for beds is so great that the city doesn't really have a low season, though things do slacken off a little in the months just after Christmas.

ESSENTIALS

Costs With hotels charging as much as £300 per luxurious night, and even the most basic B&Bs struggling to bring their tariffs below £90 for a double with shared facilities, it's no surprise that many visitors head for the budget chain hotels (see p.356) – even those, however, are not actually all that inexpensive. For a decent double room, as a rule, you shouldn't expect much change out of £110 a night. That said, even the basic places tend to have TVs and tea- and coffee-making facilities, and breakfast is usually included in the price. Note, too, that a lot of the more upmarket hotels quote expensive walk-in or rack rates, but there are usually deals to be had online and there may be additional weekend or holiday discounts – it is always worth shopping around. You'll get the best prices by booking online well in advance.

Useful websites You can book accommodation for free online at ⓦ londontown.com, which often offers good discounts. Other useful websites for last-minute offers include ⓦ laterooms.com and ⓦ lastminute.com.

Alternative accommodation If you want to live like a local, try the network of rooms and flats, often in

interesting locations, offered via ⓦ airbnb.co.uk. ⓦ couchsurfing.com puts travellers in touch with people to stay or hang out with for free; rather more upmarket ⓦ onefinestay.com offers posh private houses and apartments with all manner of guest services thrown in (note that this will probably be more expensive than staying in a very upmarket hotel).

We Know London If you arrive without having made plans (which is *not* a good idea), you could try the We Know London desks at Heathrow airport (terminals 1–5) and St Pancras and Victoria train stations (☎ 020 7592 3055, ⓦ bhrc.co.uk; roughly 6am–11pm/midnight at Heathrow, 7am–11pm/midnight at St Pancras and Victoria). There's no booking fee and they can get good discounts at the more upmarket hotels.

Wi-fi Free wi-fi is almost universally standard in hotels – except at the very top of the range – though reception can be patchy whether you're in a cheap B&B or a swish hotel. In the following reviews, wi-fi is free unless stated otherwise.

22

HOTELS AND B&BS

The bulk of the recommendations here cost between £110 and £170 a double, though there are some good basic options for under £100. Prices listed are the quoted rack rates for the **cheapest double room** in the most expensive, mid-summer, period; even these should be taken as a rule of thumb, however – you may be able to get cheaper rooms if booked at the last minute, or well in advance.

WHITEHALL AND WESTMINSTER

★**Artist Residence** 52 Cambridge St, SW1V 4QQ ☎ 020 7931 8946, ⓦ artistresidence.co.uk; ⊖ Pimlico; map p.36. With branches in Brighton and Cornwall, this is a boutique guesthouse offering relaxed luxury and location-shoot style. The ten rooms – all exposed brick, bare wood, cool prints and quirky vintage furnishings – are gorgeous (though the cheapest are quite small), with fluffy robes, fab toiletries and luxury tea and coffee. There's a Modern British on-site restaurant, too. **£200**

B&B Belgravia 64–66 Ebury St, SW1W 9QD ☎ 020 7259 8570, ⓦ bb-belgravia.com; ⊖ Victoria; map p.36. Welcoming, good-value B&B close to Victoria train and coach stations. Though they're small, the seventeen simple rooms are comfortable, with original features and some contemporary styling; those on the ground floor can get street noise, so ask for a garden-facing room if you want quiet. They also offer self-catering studios,

sleeping two to five, for around £140. There's a lounge with tea, coffee and a guest laptop, plus a garden and bike loan. **£130**

★**Cherry Court Hotel** 23 Hugh St, SW1V 1QJ ☎ 020 7828 2840, ⓦ cherrycourthotel.co.uk; ⊖ Victoria; map p.36. This family-owned mid-terrace Victorian guesthouse on a quiet street is a good budget option, with amiable staff, twelve clean, comfy (and quite pink) rooms, and a small garden. Rooms are tiny, but all are en suite, with tea- and coffee-making facilities – and a minimal in-room breakfast. Also triples (£110) and a family room sleeping five (£135). **£75**

Luna Simone Hotel 47–49 Belgrave Rd, SW1V 2BB ☎ 020 7834 5897, ⓦ lunasimonehotel.co.uk; ⊖ Victoria; map p.36. Family-run guesthouse with spruce, well-maintained, if unexciting en-suite rooms, including triples (£200) and quads (£230), with tea- and coffee-making facilities. The hearty full English breakfasts are a bonus, and it sees a lot of repeat custom. **£145**

22

Sanctuary House Hotel 33 Tothill St, SW1H 9LA ☎ 020 7799 4044, ⊛ sanctuaryhousehotel.co.uk; ⊖ St James's Park; map p.36. Fuller's Brewery runs a number of hotels in London; this one has a terrific location by St James's Park. The 34 rooms, despite being above the drinking action, are quiet enough, decked out in uncontroversial contemporary styling. Breakfast is extra, and served in the pub. **£150**

Z Hotel Piccadilly 2 Orange St, WC2H 7DF ☎ 020 3551 3720, thezhotels.com/z-piccadilly; ⊖ Piccadilly Circus; map p.36. While, as the name suggests, this modern hotel – housed in a restored office block – is convenient for Piccadilly, it's also a hop away from Trafalgar Square. The Z chain, with properties in Soho (see opposite), Victoria and Shoreditch, specializes in pod-like rooms, the cheapest of which don't have windows (window-endowed doubles will cost about £15 more). It's spotless, comfortable and efficient, and the nightly free wine and cheese receptions are a nice touch. **£160**

ST JAMES'S

41 Hotel 41 Buckingham Palace Rd, SW1W 0PS ☎ 020 7300 0041, ⊛ 41hotel.com; ⊖ Victoria; map p.67. Intimate boutique chic opposite the Royal Mews with thirty impeccable rooms – lots of black, white and dark wood – and a cosy lounge with endless complimentary snacks (ice cream, afternoon tea, canapés, fresh bread with cheese). Some rooms are tiny,

some have open fires, but each is sumptuous and service is incredibly attentive – it's not a place for anyone who values anonymity. **£450**

MAYFAIR AND MARYLEBONE

Sumner Hotel 54 Upper Berkeley St, W1H 7QR ☎ 020 7723 2244, ⊛ thesumner.com; ⊖ Marble Arch; map p.89. A spruce, friendly guesthouse in a Georgian terrace. The twenty rooms vary – the best are light and modern, some are very small, some have tiny balconies, some have baths and showers, those at the back are quieter – but all are tasteful, with stylish touches, and there's a guest sitting room. Rates include hot buffet breakfast. **£170**

SOHO AND FITZROVIA

Charlotte Street Hotel 15–17 Charlotte St, W1T 1RJ ☎ 020 7806 2000, ⊛ firmdale.com; ⊖ Goodge Street or Tottenham Court Road; map p.97. Swanky Georgian townhouse hotel in a restaurant-filled street just north of Oxford St. It's from the designer boutique hotel stable *Firmdale*, which has gorgeous properties in Covent Garden (see opposite) and throughout London. Public spaces are lined with Bloomsbury Set originals, while the 52 quiet, whimsical and decidedly un-minimal rooms come complete with fresh flowers and pretty details. There's a gym, a restaurant and a cinema that hosts popular movie/dinner deals on Fri and Mon. **£330**

BUDGET CHAINS

Chain hotels have pretty much got the **budget hotel** market sewn up. B&Bs may be able to offer a more personal touch and more character, but the franchises are often – though not always, and not always by that much – cheaper, in convenient central locations and guarantee clean, no-surprises rooms.

Bumping along at the bottom is *easyHotel* (⊛ easyhotel.com), whose prices start at around £60 in mid-summer for a en-suite double cubbyhole with no window – if you want a window, wi-fi, TV use or room cleaning, it's extra, but the earlier you book the less you pay. There are properties in South Ken, Paddington, Victoria, Earl's Court and Barbican, as well as at Heathrow (which is cheapest). Working in a similar way, offering a base rate with add-ons, the Asian *Tune* chain offers minimal and teensy rooms in Westminster (see p.360) and Paddington, plus Liverpool Street, King's Cross and Canary Wharf; prices at the latter three tend to be a fraction cheaper than the other two, starting at around £60 in summer.

It's worth checking rates at *Travelodge* (⊛ travelodge.co.uk), which can be found all over town, with handy locations in Covent Garden, King's Cross, Euston, the City, Old Street, Waterloo, Marylebone and Southwark; rooms are utilitarian, but if you book online well in advance, en-suite doubles can cost less than £60. *Premier Inn* (⊛ premierinn.com) is generally considered a cut above *Travelodge*, with prices starting at around £80 in summer, but rising to as much as £180 in the most central properties; locations are good, too, with branches in Leicester Square (quite expensive), by County Hall, near Tate Modern, by the Tower of London, in Hampstead and King's Cross, among many others. If you want a quick nap at the airport – either Heathrow or Gatwick – *Yotel* (⊛ yotel.com) cabin rooms are handy. You pay by the hour for as long as you stay, which can work out as little as £70 per night – for this you get an adjustable bed (or a bunk) in a capsule, complete with tiny toilet and monsoon shower, foldout desk, TV, free wi-fi and complimentary coffee and tea. The rest of the budget chain gang aren't worth considering – you can get better value elsewhere.

Dean Street Townhouse 69–71 Dean St, W1D 3SE ☎020 7434 1775, ⓦdeanstreettownhouse.com; ⊖Tottenham Court Road or Leicester Square; map p.101. One of a set of hotels owned by the trendy Soho House members' club – staff can be a little too cool for some – this 1730s beauty is in a fabulous location. The split-level "broom cupboard" is manageable if you're just staying one night – and there are "small" (from £220), "medium" and "bigger" (£320) options. All are luxurious, with nice touches including fresh home-made biscuits; many have standalone tubs, some of them in the bedrooms themselves. **£170**

Every Hotel Piccadilly Coventry St, W1D 6BZ ☎0845 305 8330, ⓦevery-hotels.com; ⊖Piccadilly Circus; map p.97. You're right in the heart of things here, opposite the Trocadero on Piccadilly – in a no-surprises hotel that offers modern, quiet, well-equipped rooms with free (soft drink) minibars and Nespresso machines, and a gym on site. **£225**

Grange Langham Court Hotel 31–35 Langham St, W1W 6BU ☎020 7436 6622, ⓦgrangehotels.com; ⊖Oxford Circus; map p.97. Rooms may be tiny at this friendly 56-room hotel in a striking black and white building on a quiet Fitzrovia street, but they're clean and very comfortable, and the price is good for this part of town. **£130**

★**Hazlitt's** 6 Frith St, W1D 3JA ☎020 7434 1771, ⓦhazlittshotel.com; ⊖Tottenham Court Road; map p.101. Off the south side of Soho Square, this early eighteenth-century building hides a hotel of character and faded charm. Creaky, crooked old stairs lead up to romantic en-suite rooms, quirkily decorated with period furniture and old books. A continental breakfast (not included) is served in your room; there's also a small library, with real fire, and an honesty bar. **£280**

Nadler Soho 10 Carlisle St, W1D 3BR ☎020 3697 3697, ⓦthenadler.com; ⊖Tottenham Court Road; map p.101. They pay attention to details here (pillow menu, goodie bags for kids), and prices are reasonable for this fantastic location. The decor in the modern rooms is unremarkable (the cheapest are small), but each has a microwave, fridge and kettle – along with coffee machine – so you could effectively self-cater. **£180**

Z Hotel Soho 17 Moor St, W1D 5AP ☎020 3551 3701, ⓦthezhotels.com/z-soho; ⊖Leicester Square; map p.101. You'll feel at home at this welcoming 85-room hotel – part of the small Z chain, which also has properties near Piccadilly (see opposite), Shoreditch and Victoria – with pre-dinner cheese and wine receptions and very helpful staff. Rooms are modern, clean, quiet and comfy, but you're paying for the location rather than linger-awhile lodgings – they're tiny, and the cheapest, rather like cabins, have no windows (you'll pay around £10 more per night for that privilege). **£140**

TOP 5 HIDEAWAYS

Cable Street Inn Docklands. See p.360
The Fielding Covent Garden. See below
Hazlitt's Soho. See below
The King's Wardrobe The City. See p.359
The Rookery Clerkenwell. See p.358

22

COVENT GARDEN AND THE STRAND

Covent Garden Hotel 10 Monmouth St, WC2H 9LF ☎020 7806 1000, ⓦfirmdalehotels.com/hotels/london/covent-garden-hotel; ⊖Covent Garden or Leicester Square; map p.108. A beautiful, luxurious boutique hotel from the *Firmdale* group, with 58 pretty rooms in an old French hospital on a lively Seven Dials street. This one feels cosier and a little less avant-garde than the others, without losing the so-called "Modern English" designer details; there's an upmarket brasserie and Saturday brunch/movie deals at the in-house cinema. **£384**

The Fielding 4 Broad Court, Bow St, WC2B 5QZ ☎020 7836 8305, ⓦthefieldinghotel.co.uk; ⊖Covent Garden; map p.108. On a pedestrianized court behind the Royal Opera House, this friendly hotel is delightfully quiet for central London. The en-suite rooms are simple, but clean – the refurbished ones are better – and good value for this location. No breakfast, but there's tea and coffee in the rooms. Rates increase by £20 at the weekend. **£140**

Hospital Club 24 Endell St, WC2H 9HQ ☎020 7170 9100, ⓦthehospitalclub.com; ⊖Covent Garden; map p.108. This private club/work hub for media types has opened its portals to non-members with fifteen plush, colourful rooms. It's a business hotel with edge – a bit Mid Century here, a little 1970s there – and quirky luxury touches including a nightly (complimentary) cocktail trolley brought to your room. Overnighters also get access to the club, including modish meeting areas and admission to live music and movie screenings. The cheapest "sleeper" rooms have no windows; the next size up, with windows, costs £50 more. **£180**

Hoxton Holborn 199 High Holborn, WC1V 7BD ☎020 7661 3000, ⓦthehoxton.com; ⊖Holborn; map p.108. The *Hoxton Hotel* (see p.359), a trailblazer in bringing (just about) affordable cool to east London accommodation, has moved west with this hip hotel in a brutalist building on the Holborn/Covent Garden borders. The 174 rooms are good-looking and comfortable, all soothing colours and retro styling, with Roberts radios, vintage paperbacks and mini fridges stocked with fresh milk and water – beware, though: the smallest "Shoebox" and "Snug" (£129) options are just as they sound. Rates include a mini breakfast delivered to your room in a bag, or you can eat at the coffee shop and bar-restaurant downstairs – and, extra kudos, there's a popular restaurant, *Chicken Shop* (see p.374), in the basement. **£109**

The Savoy Strand, WC2R 0EU ☎0800 0441 1414, ⓦfairmont.com/savoy-london; ⊖Covent Garden or

22

Charing Cross; map p.108. This iconic Art Deco hotel, dripping with history, is glamorous and flashy, with classic bars and gorgeously comfortable rooms. Even if you can't afford to stay you might splash out on a classic afternoon tea (a cool £50). **£470**

Seven Dials Hotel 7 Monmouth St, WC2H 9DA ☎020 7240 0823, ⓦsevendialshotellondon.com; ⊖Covent Garden; map p.108. Welcoming, eighteen-room B&B brilliantly located on one of Covent Garden's nicest streets. It's in no way fancy: the staircase is narrow and steep (no lift) and the basic en-suite rooms (from singles to quads) are very small, but all are clean and comfy, and you're made to feel at home. **£150**

BLOOMSBURY

Arosfa Hotel 83 Gower St, WC1E 6HJ ☎020 7636 2115, ⓦarosfalondon.com; ⊖Goodge Street or Euston Square; map p.127. The fifteen en-suite rooms in this popular, friendly B&B aren't large, but have been recently upgraded, so all are clean and comfortable, with contemporary touches and excellent bathrooms. There's a guest lounge and a pretty garden out back – and the huge breakfast buffets are great. **£125**

Jesmond Hotel 63 Gower St, WC1E 6HJ ☎020 7636 3199, ⓦjesmondhotel.org.uk; ⊖Goodge Street; map p.127. Good-value, family-run Bloomsbury B&B with a peaceful walled garden. Rooms are clean and simple, if old-fashioned, some with period features; staff are unfailingly friendly. Six of the fifteen rooms (from singles to quins) have shared facilities – you'll pay £120 for an en-suite. Full breakfast; laundry £7.50. **£90**

Morgan Hotel 24 Bloomsbury St, WC1B 3QJ ☎020 7636 3735, ⓦmorganhotel.co.uk; ⊖Tottenham Court Road; map p.127. A reliable, homely guesthouse, right by the British Museum, with functional, clean and comfortable rooms – and a few apartment suites (from £175) – a secluded garden, and a full breakfast included. **£145**

★Ridgemount Hotel 65–67 Gower St, WC1E 6HJ ☎020 7636 1141, ⓦridgemounthotel.co.uk; ⊖Goodge Street; map p.127. This old-fashioned, friendly and popular family-owned B&B, faded but clean, offers a variety of rooms. Around half of the 33 have washbasins but shared facilities, which are spotless, and sizeable; en-suites cost about £20 more. The smallest

rooms (very small!) are cosy; family rooms sleep up to five. Full breakfast included. **£86**

KING'S CROSS

★Great Northern Hotel Pancras Rd, N1C 4TB ☎020 3388 0800, ⓦgnhlondon.com; ⊖King's Cross St Pancras; map p.127. The *Great Northern* builds upon the success of its stately neighbour *St Pancras Renaissance* (see below), another lovely old Victorian railway hotel, but offers a fresher, hipper vibe, with a vaguely Deco feel. They're generous with the extras, too – including Nespresso coffee, pastries and fresh fruit in the "pantries" on each floor. All the 91 boutique rooms have style; the smallest, called "couchettes", evoke the romance of a train sleeper, while others are tucked beneath the eaves. There's a good Modern European restaurant, *Plum + Spilt Milk*, on site. **£200**

Rough Luxe 1 Birkenhead St, WC1H 2BA ☎020 7837 5338, ⓦroughluxe.co.uk; ⊖King's Cross St Pancras; map p.127. This ten-room hotel offers comfort and warmth, but really it's all about the shabby chic. Each room is different (some share bathrooms, some are minuscule), but the arty, nostalgic aesthetic – ripped wallpaper and peeling plaster, the odd vintage TV, original artworks, creaky old floorboards – runs throughout, in some places more successfully than others. A posh continental breakfast is included in the rates. **£200**

St Pancras Renaissance Euston Rd, NW1 2AR ☎020 7841 3540, ⓦmarriott.co.uk/hotels/travel/lonpr-st-pancras; ⊖King's Cross St Pancras; map p.127. George Gilbert Scott's Gothic Revival masterpiece (see p.135), now a five-star *Marriott*, is certainly a thrilling spectacle – the lofty public spaces and colossal lobby evoke the golden era of railway travel, and old-style glamour seeps from every surface. It's only worth staying in the main building, though – the suites, with their arched windows and high ceilings, might justify the prices (from £340). The others are in an annexe, and better value can be found elsewhere. Online deals and *Marriott* promotions can halve the rack rates. Wi-fi £15/day (free for *Marriott* reward card holders). **£230**

CLERKENWELL

★The Rookery 12 Peter's Lane, Cowcross St, EC1M 6DS ☎020 7336 0931, ⓦrookeryhotel.com; ⊖Farringdon; map p.147. A rambling Georgian townhouse, all panelled walls, flagstoned floors and creaky timeworn floorboards, which makes a charming bolthole in trendy Clerkenwell. Rooms, some of which are a little dark, offer faded Baroque glam, with antique fittings and superb bathrooms. Breakfast, not included in the price, is served in your room, though there's a comfy conservatory and an honesty bar. **£260**

Zetter Hotel & Zetter Townhouse 86–88 Clerkenwell Rd, EC1M 5RJ ☎020 7324 4567, ⓦthezetter.com; ⊖Farringdon; map p.147. This 59-room hotel, in a stylishly converted warehouse, leads the way when it comes to affordable boutique. Rooms are simple, colourful and bold; the bistro, helmed by Bruno Loubet, is buzzy and popular. If you can afford it, splash out on a rooftop studio; they come with their own balcony terraces. Bijou hotels *Zetter Townhouse* (opposite, on St John's Square) and the new *Zetter Townhouse Marylebone* are, if anything, even more whimsical in style. Hotel **£160**, Townhouse **£200**

THE CITY

Andaz 40 Liverpool St, EC2M 7QN ☎ 020 7961 1234, ⓦ london.liverpoolstreet.andaz.hyatt.com; ⊖ Liverpool Street; map pp.152–153. The venerable 1884 *Great Eastern Hotel* by Liverpool Street Station is now one of the *Hyatt*'s swish worldwide *Andaz* hotel group. The 267 rooms – each with a complimentary (non-alcoholic) minibar – are unfussy, plush and kitted out for business travellers, and the seven restaurants and bars keep the place buzzing. **£170**

Apex City of London Hotel 1 Seething Lane, EC3N 4AX ☎ 020 7977 9593, ⓦ apexhotels.co.uk; ⊖ Tower Hill; map pp.152–153. A sleek and nicely appointed modern hotel on a secluded City street near the Tower of London. It's geared towards a corporate clientele, but everyone feels welcome and it has a variety of rooms – the priciest have balconies. Book early for the best deals. **£145**

The King's Wardrobe 6 Wardrobe Place, Carter Lane, EC4V 5AF ☎ 020 7792 2222, ⓦ bridgestreet.com; ⊖ St Paul's; map pp.152–153. In a courtyard behind St Paul's Cathedral, these seventy studios and one- to three-bedroom apartments prove good value, especially for families. It's a favourite with business visitors – kitchens, concierge service and housekeeping are standard, and some have fabulous views. Though housed in a fourteenth-century building, the interiors are modern. **£225**

EAST LONDON

Ace Hotel 100 Shoreditch High St, E1 6QJ ☎ 020 7613 9800, ⓦ acehotel.com/london; ⊖ Liverpool Street; map pp.190–191. The *Ace* has brought its uber-hipster brand over from the US to – where else? – Shoreditch. Keen to plug itself as a lifestyle experience – "a collection of individuals – multiple and inclusive, held together by an affinity for the soulful", as it says, bafflingly, on its site – it's a good place if you're out to enjoy the local nightlife. Hosting art and music events, DJ nights and pop ups, it also offers various artisan coffee and snack bars and a Modern Britsh restaurant, with a club in the basement. The rooms aren't bad, either, all subdued dark colours and quirky touches – the suites include record players and vinyl. Ask for one at the back if you want peace and quiet. **£180**

Avo 82 Dalston Lane, E8 3AH ☎ 020 3490 5061, ⓦ avohotel.com; ⊖ Dalston Junction; map p.187. Offering friendly boutique comforts in the heart of urban Dalston, this family-owned guesthouse offers modern rooms, which are small but comfortable, with swish shower rooms, plush robes and tea- and coffee-making facilities. It's all very sociable and cosy, and makes a welcoming base. **£94**

★ **Boundary Hotel** 2–4 Boundary St, E2 7DD ☎ 020 7729 1051, ⓦ theboundary.co.uk; ⊖ Shoreditch High Street; map pp.190–191. A Conran creation, this slick Shoreditch hotel offers twelve rooms and suites, each themed on different art or design styles, from Heath Robinson to YBAs. Most of them offer ample space, with lovely bathrooms and little extras including tea-time cakes. There are two good places to eat on site – the *Albion* (British café and bakery), and the *Boundary* (French), plus a stunning rooftop bar (see p.391). **£190**

Hoxton Hotel 81 Great Eastern St, EC2A 3HU ☎ 020 7550 1000, ⓦ hoxtonhotels.com; ⊖ Old Street; map pp.190–191. "The Hox" was one of the first hotels to emerge in this nightlife neighbourhood, and despite a change in ownership it goes from strength to strength, with buzzy communal areas – all exposed brick, dark wood and burnished metal, with an open fire for cold nights – and 210 attractive rooms. Downstairs, the *Hoxton Grill* and the DJ bar are popular hangouts – there's a party vibe and it can be noisy, so ask for a quiet room if you value your sleep. A light breakfast is delivered to your room. **£160**

Qbic 42 Adler St, E1 1EE ☎ 020 3021 3300, ⓦ london .qbichotels.com; ⊖ Aldgate East; map pp.190–191. Everything is funky and fresh at this bright new budget hotel – the flashpacker aesthetic, "witty" aphorisms, eye-popping colour blocks and kitschy photos are not for everyone, but if you leap in this is a great inexpensive choice, even for geriatric travellers aged 29 and above. Rooms are spick and span, with fab bathrooms and comfortable beds; the cheapest are very small, though, and have no windows, for which you'll pay around £15 more. Tea and coffee facilities on each floor. **£101**

★ **Rose and Crown Guesthouse** 199 Stoke Newington Church St, N16 9ES ☎ 020 7923 3337, ⓦ roseandcrownn16.co.uk; ⊖ Manor House or Arsenal; map p.187. Superbly placed above a splendid neighbourhood pub opposite Clissold Park, on a lively street lined with quirky shops, restaurants and bars, the boutique rooms here are chic and luxurious, and – factoring in the home-made breakfasts and the chilled-out roof terrace – well worth the price. **£132**

TOP 5 UNDER £100

Captain Bligh Guest House The South Bank. See p.360
Caring Hotel Paddington. See p.362
Cherry Court Hotel Victoria. See p.355
Portobello Gold Notting Hill. See p.362
Ridgemount Hotel Bloomsbury. See opposite

22

22

Shoreditch Rooms Shoreditch House, Ebor St, E1 6AW ☎020 7739 5040, ⓦshoreditchhouse.com/bedrooms; ⊖Shoreditch High Street; map pp.190–191. Linked to the Shoreditch House members' club, and from the same Soho House stable as the *Dean Street Townhouse* (see p.357) this hip, sophisticated little place has the same no-nonsense room-naming policy, with options from "Tiny" up to "Small-plus", which have minuscule balconies. Rooms may be small but they're gorgeous, with lots of tongue-and-groove, fresh, sun-bleached colours and vintage tiled bathrooms; there's a spa, rooftop pool and restaurants at the adjoining members' club, where you can hang out with the beautiful media types and where, refreshingly, no mobile phones are allowed. **£190**

DOCKLANDS

Cable Street Inn 232 Cable St, E1 0BL ☎020 7790 4019 ⓦcablestreetinn.co.uk; ⊖Shadwell DLR and overground; map pp.210–211. Artistic, quiet B&B in a beautifully restored eighteenth-century pub building on the Docklands/East End borders. The three en-suite doubles, decorated with antiques and contemporary art, are homely, with fresh flowers and vintage-style bathrooms; a continental breakfast is served on the roof terrace or in the gorgeous lounge, where you can help yourself to snacks all day and use the fridge, oven and kettle. **£130**

THE SOUTH BANK

★**Captain Bligh Guest House** 100 Lambeth Rd, SE1 7PT (no phone), ⓦcaptainblighhouse.co.uk; ⊖Lambeth North; map p.218. Captain Bligh's former residence can now be your home from home – a charming, cosy Georgian building, opposite the Imperial War Museum, run by a friendly, though unobtrusive, couple. The five rooms (including one single) are more like suites, with kitchenettes – they're all very different, varying in size, but each is comfortable and homely. Fantastic value – the four-night minimum may be the only snag. No cards. **£95**

Mad Hatter 3–7 Stamford St, SE1 9NY ☎020 7401 9222, ⓦmadhatterhotel.co.uk; ⊖Southwark or Blackfriars; map p.218. Good-value, friendly Fuller's hotel with thirty clean and comfy en-suite rooms, above a Fuller's pub (which serves food – including breakfast, though this is not included in the rates), in an old hat factory. This is a good location, a short walk from Tate Modern and the South Bank. **£150**

Tune Westminster 118–120 Westminster Bridge Rd, SE1 7RW ☎020 7633 9317, ⓦtunehotels.com; ⊖Lambeth North or Waterloo; map p.218. The first London branch of the Malaysian chain (see p.356), whose minimal rooms and down-to-earth pricing policy have made it a budget favourite. It's a clever idea: by doing away with niceties like tables, chairs and closets, prices stay low

and you simply opt to pay for extras, including towels, TV, hairdryers and wi-fi, on the easy-to-use booking site. Rooms are capsule-style, but well designed, with comfy beds and spotless showers; the cheapest are windowless and minuscule. **£70**

SOUTHWARK

Citizen M Bankside 20 Lavington St, SE1 0NZ ☎020 3519 1680, ⓦcitizenm.com/london-bankside; ⊖Southwark; map pp.228–229. Though the high-design concept may jar – guests are "citizens" and staff are "ambassadors" – this is a good option, part of a growing European chain, with 192 small rooms with a modern, pod-like design, touch tablet room controls and big beds. The public spaces tick all the lifestyle mag choices – Eames chairs, original artworks, coffee-table books – and the buzzing canteen/bar is handy, too. **£160**

Ibis Styles London Southwark Rose 43–47 Southwark Bridge Rd, SE1 9HH ☎0871 702 9469, ⓦibis.com; ⊖London Bridge; map pp.228–229. The *Southwark Rose* has some little design touches that raise the rooms a little above the bland chain hotels in the area, and rooms are clean, comfortable and generally spacious. Don't expect much more (and avoid the restaurant), though a good (continental) buffet breakfast is included in rates, which vary wildly depending on availability. **£130**

London Bridge Hotel 8–18 London Bridge St, SE1 9SG ☎020 7855 2200, ⓦlondonbridgehotel.com; ⊖London Bridge; map pp.228–229. Perfectly placed for Southwark and Bankside or the City, this is a contemporary, independent hotel in a Victorian building in the heart of things right by the station and the Shard. The rooms in the annexe are less good. Geared towards business travellers, it's more expensive during the week. **£175**

HYDE PARK AND KENSINGTON GARDENS

Columbia Hotel 95–99 Lancaster Gate, W2 3NS ☎020 7402 0021, ⓦcolumbiahotel.co.uk; ⊖Lancaster Gate; map p.242. A large, old-fashioned hotel, once five Victorian houses, with a variety of en-suite rooms, from singles to quads, some large, with views over Hyde Park, others rather poky. It's all quite dated, with a certain faded charm, but everything's spotless and for this price the facilities are good. Rates include continental breakfast. **£108**

Kensington House Hotel 15–16 Prince of Wales Terrace, W8 5PQ ☎020 7937 2345, ⓦkenhouse.com; ⊖High Street Kensington; map p.242. This independent hotel, in a nineteenth-century townhouse on a quiet street near Kensington Gardens, is a dependable option, with friendly staff. The en-suite rooms are smallish, and worn in places, but they're clean, comfy and light; one has a tiny balcony. Good continental breakfast included. **£147**

CLOCKWISE FROM TOP LEFT ACE HOTEL (P.359); BEAUFORT BAR, SAVOY (P.357); THE FIELDING (P.357); THE ZETTER TOWNHOUSE(P.358) >

22

SOUTH KENSINGTON AND CHELSEA

Aster House 3 Sumner Place, SW7 3EE ☎020 7581 5888, ⓦasterhouse.com; ⊖South Kensington; map pp.252–253. Friendly, quiet B&B, with a great setting on a luxurious South Ken white-stuccoed street; one of the thirteen rooms opens out onto the back garden (complete with little pond), and there's a conservatory, where the copious buffet breakfast is served. **£240**

Myhotel Chelsea 35 Ixworth Place, SW3 3QX ☎020 7225 7500, ⓦmyhotels.com; ⊖South Kensington; map p.267. Though the slightly cheap-looking decor isn't to everyone's taste, the 45 rooms (which vary wildly in size) are well equipped, and the atmosphere is generally peaceful. Above all, though, the prices are not to be sniffed at in this area, and there are excellent online deals. **£170**

EARL'S COURT AND FULHAM

Barclay House 21 Barclay Rd, SW6 1EJ ☎07767 420943, ⓦbarclayhouselondon.com; ⊖Fulham Broadway; map pp.252–253. Small Fulham B&B – just three rooms, one of them a single (from £110) – in a quiet street near the tube. Though quite luxurious – rooms have oak flooring and fancy Philippe Starck-designed bathrooms – it's relaxed, run by friendly hosts; there's a small shared kitchen area, filled with home-made pastries, bread, tea and coffee. Usually a three- or four-night minimum. **£150**

★Nadler Kensington 25 Courtfield Gardens, SW5 0PG ☎020 7244 2255, ⓦthenadler.com/kensington. shtml; ⊖Earl's Court; map pp.252–253. Excellent-value contemporary accommodation, with no fussy extras. The 65 smartly designed rooms range from bijou singles via "luxury bunks" to deluxe; all are spotless and quiet, with mini-kitchens and a choice of pillows. Well set up for self-catering, and a particularly good choice for families. **£165**

Twenty Nevern Square 20 Nevern Square, SW5 9PD ☎020 7565 9555, ⓦ20nevernsquare.co.uk; ⊖Earl's Court; map pp.252–253. In an area of bog-standard B&Bs, this is a more upmarket alternative, a small hotel strewn with Oriental and European antiques. Rooms (which vary considerably in size) are en suite, comfortable and clean – it can be noisy, however, particularly in the Mezzanine room. Tea and coffee on request, and continental buffet breakfast included. **£130**

PADDINGTON

Caring Hotel 24 Craven Hill Gardens, W2 3EA ☎020 7262 8708, ⓦcaringhotel.com; ⊖Paddington, Bayswater or Lancaster Gate; map pp.276–277. This large, handsome building, in a leafy residential street, is a popular, reliable budget hotel with great customer service. The 25 rooms are clean, comfortable and functional, if unexciting: some have shared facilities, some showers only and others are full en-suites (£106). Continental breakfast included. **£80**

Hotel Indigo 12–20 London St, W2 1HL ☎0871 423 4901, ⓦihg.com; ⊖Paddington; map pp.276–277. One of the more upmarket options in this area, near Paddington station: swish, efficiently run and friendly, with contemporary, colourful rooms (some of them tiny), well equipped and with modern bathrooms. There's an on-site gym, too. **£220**

St David's Hotels 14–20 Norfolk Square, W2 1RS ☎020 7723 3856, ⓦstdavidshotels.com; ⊖Paddington; map pp.276–277. Pleasantly located on a hotel-fringed square near Paddington station, this no-frills budget guesthouse offers a full English breakfast (included). Rooms range from singles to family options; all are pretty small and many are tired, but they're clean, and some (around £10 more) are en suite. **£85**

BAYSWATER, WESTBOURNE GROVE AND NOTTING HILL

Garden Court Hotel 30–31 Kensington Gardens Square, W2 4BG ☎020 7229 2553, ⓦgardencourthotel .co.uk; ⊖Bayswater or Queensway; map pp.276–277. Unfussy, friendly family-owned hotel on a nice street close to Portobello Market; some rooms (from singles to triples) are past their best, but they're clean and do the job. Buffet breakfast included. **£129**

★Main House 6 Colville Rd, W11 2BP ☎020 7221 9691, ⓦthemainhouse.co.uk; ⊖Ladbroke Grove or Notting Hill Gate; map pp.276–277. You get total privacy in this guesthouse, which manages to be both homely and a tad bohemian. The suites (one with two bedrooms) are huge, covering a whole floor each. There's no breakfast, but there's a fridge for guests' use (along with umbrellas, mobile phones and all manner of extras) and you can have tea/coffee brought to your room; a couple of good local cafés offer discounts for guests. Three-night minimum. **£130**

Portobello Gold 95–97 Portobello Rd, W11 2QB ☎020 7460 4910, ⓦportobellogold.com; ⊖Notting Hill Gate or Holland Park; map pp.276–277. Location, in the heart of Portobello Rd, is key at this boho budget place above a lively pub/restaurant. The eleven rooms are basic but clean and some are tiny, with miniature en-suite bathrooms. There's also an apartment (sleeps six – at a pinch) with a roof terrace, for £165. Continental breakfast included. **£85**

★Vancouver Studios 30 Prince's Square, W2 4NJ ☎020 7243 1270, ⓦvancouverstudios.co.uk; ⊖Bayswater; map pp.276–277. Comfortable, luxurious and well-equipped self-catering suites (from singles to quads, some with balconies) in a grand old Victorian townhouse with maid service and a pretty walled garden. Rooms at the back are quietest. Apartments, too, from £210 sleeping two, nearby and on site. **£149**

NORTH LONDON

Hampstead Village Guesthouse 2 Kemplay Rd, NW3 1SY ☎ 020 7435 8679, ⓦ hampsteadguesthouse.com; ⊖ Hampstead; map pp.296–297. On a quiet back street between Hampstead Village and the Heath, this is an unconventional guesthouse in a large Victorian house. Rooms (en-suite £125) are full of character, crammed with books, pictures and handmade and antique furniture – one has a freestanding antique steel bathtub. This is very much a family home, with all the warmth and charm that implies. Breakfast costs £10. The garage apartment, sleeping five and starting at £150 for two people (£200 for five), is a bargain. Bang an extra £5 (Mon–Fri)/£10 (Sat) on to the rates for stays of less than two nights. **£105**

New Inn 2 Allitsen Rd, NW8 6LA ☎ 020 7722 0726, ⓦ newinnlondon.co.uk; ⊖ St John's Wood; map pp.284–285. Comfortable, clean and contemporary rooms above a pub with food, just a few minutes' walk from the north edge of Regent's Park. Two of the five en-suite rooms are surprisingly large for the price, so ask when you book – and bathrooms are sizeable. Breakfast £7.50–11.50. **£130**

SOUTH LONDON

The Lilac Door 140 Rosendale Rd, West Dulwich, SE21 8LG ☎ 020 8761 8218, ⓦ lilacdoor.co.uk; ⇌ West Dulwich; map pp.308–309. Behind the pretty exterior of this elegant Edwardian house – flowers tangled around the eponymous lilac door – are three sleek, light B&B rooms. Robes and glamorous toiletries are included, and rates include a good continental breakfast. No children under 12. Add £10 (Sun–Thurs)/£20 (Fri/Sat) to the price for one- night occupancy. **£110**

Number 16 16 St Alfeges Passage, SE10 9JS ☎ 020 8853 4337, ⓦ st-alfeges.co.uk; ⊖ Cutty Sark DLR; map p.313. Tucked behind Hawksmoor's St Alfege church, this welcoming Greenwich B&B – owned by a flamboyant ex-antique dealer/actor – offers a warm welcome, offbeat design flair and the feel of being in a slightly eccentric home from home. One small single/double and two larger doubles. No cards. **£125**

RICHMOND

The Old Stables 1 Bridle Lane, Twickenham, TW1 3EG ☎ 020 8892 4507, ⓦ oldstables.com; ⇌ St Margarets from Waterloo; map p.340. Three spruce bedrooms and one studio apartment (sleeping three) on a quiet street right by the train station, walking distance to Richmond and the Thames. No on-site staff, which means you get a lot of privacy, but the friendly, efficient manager is a phone call away, and they provide a complimentary continental breakfast plus use of a small fridge, kettle and toaster. Rates drop the longer you stay. No cards. Doubles **£88**, apartment **£140**

22

HOSTELS

Hostels run the gamut from the efficient and occasionally rather institutional YHA establishments to funkier and more relaxed independent hostels, some of which have a serious party vibe. Virtually all offer free wi-fi and some of the independent hostels include breakfast in the price. ⓦ hostellondon.com is a good website for booking online.

YHA HOSTELS

London's Youth Hostel Association (YHA; ⓦ yha.org.uk) hostels are generally safe bets, and good options for families. Rates depend on availability, special events and the like; advance booking is recommended. You don't have to be a member of the YHA or an affiliated hostel association to stay (membership costs £20/year), but non-members are charged a £3 surcharge per night. Rates quoted below are for members.

★ **Central** 104 Bolsover St, W1W 5NU ☎ 0845 371 9154, ⓦ yha.org.uk/hostel/london-central; ⊖ Great Portland Street; map p.97. Excellent, secure and clean 300-bed hostel, in a surprisingly quiet West End location, with a kitchen, 24hr café and bar. No groups; families welcome. Most dorms (4–8 beds) are en-suite; others have showers next door. Dorms **£23**

Earl's Court 38 Bolton Gardens, SW5 0AQ ☎ 0845 371 9114, ⓦ yha.org.uk/hostel/london-earls-court; ⊖ Earl's Court; map pp.252–253. Buzzy, busy 186-bed hostel with small kitchen, café and patio garden. No groups. Dorms **£24**, doubles **£79**

Oxford Street 14 Noel St, W1F 8GJ ☎ 0845 371 9133, ⓦ yha.org.uk/hostel/london-oxford-street; ⊖ Oxford Circus or Tottenham Court Road; map p.97. The Soho location and modest size (around 95 beds) mean this hostel tends to be full year-round. The atmosphere can be party central, but it's pretty family friendly. There's a café, kitchen, dining room and lounge, and everything is colourful and clean. No groups. Dorms **£34**, doubles **£80**

St Pancras 79–81 Euston Rd, NW1 2QE ☎ 0845 371 9344, ⓦ yha.org.uk/hostel/london-st-pancras; ⊖ King's Cross St Pancras; map p.127. This hostel, on the busy Euston Rd, has nearly 200 beds. Rooms are clean, bright and double-glazed. No kitchen, but there's a café. No groups. Dorms **£28**, doubles **£80**

St Paul's 36 Carter Lane, EC4V 5AB ☎ 0845 371 9012, ⓦ yha.org.uk/hostel/london-st-pauls; ⊖ St Paul's; map pp.152–153. A 213-bed hostel in a superb location opposite St Paul's Cathedral. There's a restaurant and café bar, but no kitchen. Groups allowed. Popular with families. Dorms **£20**, doubles **£65**

Thameside 20 Salter Rd, SE16 5PR ☎ 0845 371 9756, ⓦ yha.org.uk/hostel/london-thameside; ⊖ Rotherhithe; map pp.226–227. London's largest purpose-built hostel, with 320 beds, is in a quiet spot near

22

the river, 15min from the nearest tube. It can feel a bit of a trek, but often has space when more central places are full. Self-catering available, and a café serving breakfast and dinner. Groups allowed. Dorms **£19**, doubles **£49**

INDEPENDENT HOSTELS

While the grotty flophouses of yesteryear are slowly losing ground to a slicker breed of places that have seriously upped their game, it's worth noting that private double rooms in many of the independent hostels can actually be more expensive (and worse value) than in the budget hotels. If you're keen to hang out with other travellers, however, paying for a room in a hostel might still be worth the extra cost.

Astor hostels Astor Queensway, 45 Queensborough Terrace, W2; map p.242; Astor Hyde Park, 191 Queen's Gate, SW7; map p.254; Astor Victoria, 71 Belgrave Rd, SW1; map p.36; Astor Museum, 27 Montague St, WC1; map p.127; ⓦastorhostels.com. They only take guests aged between 18 and 35, so there's quite a party atmosphere at these four central hostels. All except the *Museum* have at least some en-suite dorms, and the *Museum* and the *Victoria* have female dorms available. There are private rooms at all four; only those at the *Hyde Park* are en suite. Inexpensive continental breakfasts available, plus use of kitchens. Dorms (4–16 beds) **£24**, twins/doubles **£118**

Clink 261 261–265 Gray's Inn Rd, WC1X 8QT ☏020 7833 9400, ⓦclinkhostels.com; ⊖King's Cross; map p.127. This 170-bed hostel, in a converted office block near King's Cross/St Pancras, has laundry, kitchen facilities and a tiny lounge. Dorms – including two female-only dorms (4-bed & 10-bed) – have 4–18 beds and there are private twins/doubles with shared facilities. Breakfast is included, and you can use the facilities in the larger *Clink 78* down the road. Dorms **£23.50**, doubles **£75**

Clink 78 78 King's Cross Rd, WC1X 9QG ☏020 7183 9400, ⓦclinkhostels.com; ⊖King's Cross; map p.127. Occupying a Victorian magistrates' court – Dickens once worked here; a century later the Clash were put on trial here for bothering pigeons – this funky, friendly (and huge) party hostel, run by the same folk as *Clink 261*, has plenty of jazzed-up period features (you can even stay in one of the tiny old prison cells). It can get crowded and noisy, but it's fun if you're feeling sociable and there's a lively, late-opening bar along with a TV and film lounge. Dorms (4–16 beds, some pod beds; some en-suite) include special "girls-only" options (hairdryers, hangers, mirrors), and there are private doubles/twins (some en-suite). Kitchen facilities, internet lounge and travel shop, plus free continental breakfast. Dorms **£28**, doubles **£90**

The Dictionary Hostel 10–20 Kingsland Rd, E2 8DA ☏020 7613 2784, ⓦthedictionaryhostel.com; ⊖Old Street; map pp.190–191. This is a party hostel, as you'd expect from its Shoreditch location, and for those who want to socialize it ticks all the boxes – there's a café, bar, self-catering kitchen and roof terrace, plus a good free breakfast. The dorms (4–16 beds) and rooms look good, with whitewashed walls, timber floors, plants and pictures on the walls – some are en suite, and there's one six-bed en-suite option for women only. Dorms **£20**, doubles **£100**

Generator 37 Tavistock Place, WC1H 9SE ☏020 7388 7666, ⓦgeneratorhostels.com; ⊖Russell Square or Euston; map p.127. One of a European chain, this huge party hostel, in a converted police barracks, is friendly and good value. Dorms (some women-only) have 4–12 beds, and there are private twins, doubles, triples and quads – en-suites are available in all categories. There's a young, lively atmosphere with games nights, DJs and karaoke nights in the late-night bar. Laundry, but no kitchen; a continental breakfast buffet is served in the café. Dorms **£20**, doubles **£85**

★**Meininger** 65–67 Queen's Gate, SW7 5JS ☏020 3318 1407, ⓦmeininger-hostels.com; ⊖Gloucester Road or South Kensington; map p.254. Cheery, secure and high-quality modern hostel near the South Ken museums, run by a German chain. The 48 rooms include dorms (4–12 beds), some women-only, plus singles and doubles (some with TV). Children and groups welcome. No kitchen; buffet breakfast available. There's a laundry. Dorms **£18**, doubles **£120**

★**Palmers Lodge Swiss Cottage** 40 College Crescent, NW3 5LB ☏020 7483 8470, ⓦpalmerslodges.com; ⊖Swiss Cottage; map pp.284–285. A decent, clean and safe backpackers' lodge in a vast Victorian mansion in South Hampstead with period features galore in the public rooms. Many of the dorms (mixed or female-only; 4–28 beds) have beds with curtains and reading lights for added privacy; there are also twins, some en suite. You can get cheap meals (including breakfast) in the restaurant, and a drink at the bar. There's another branch, *Hillspring Lodge*, in Willesden Green. Groups welcome. Dorms **£23**, doubles **£95**

Safestay 144–152 Walworth Rd, SE17 1JL ☏020 7703 8000, ⓦsafestay.co.uk; ⊖Elephant and Castle; map pp.226-227. The Elephant and Castle location may not be the loveliest in town, but this is a reliable hostel in a handsome Georgian building – clean and tidy, with good beds (with curtains) and showers, and spacious common areas. Some of the four- to eight-bed dorms are en suite, and there is also a three-bed en-suite private room. Groups welcome. Dorms **£21**, triple (two people) **£90**

St Christopher's Inns ☏020 8600 7500, ⓦst-christophers.co.uk; map pp.228–229. *St Christopher's* runs seven party hostels in six buildings across London, with three on Borough High Street near London Bridge, and branches in Camden, Greenwich, Shepherd's Bush and Hammersmith. The vibe is upbeat, with most people out to socialize and hang at the hostel bars. The *Village* hostel (Borough High St) has a bar, cinema and comedy club; in the same building, the *Oasis* is women-only, while the smaller *Inn*, up the road, sits above a pub. Free breakfast, no kitchens. Dorms **£27**, doubles **£88**

★**Wombat's City Hostel** 7 Dock St, E1 8LL ☎ 020 7680 7600, ⓦ wombats-hostels.com; ⊖ Tower Hill; map pp.210–211. In a Victorian building that began its days as a sailors' hostel, this big new East End place (more than 500 beds) has light, spacious communal areas, a large kitchen and a popular, big bar. There are lots of doubles, which, along with the dorms – four to eight beds – are en suite, with one six-bed dorm for women. Dorms **£25**, doubles **£90**

STUDENT HALLS

Outside term-time, it's possible to stay in **student halls of residence**. The quality of the rooms varies enormously, but they tend to be small, neat and basic and get booked up quickly. Some have shared kitchens, some offer B&B – student and senior discounts are often available.

22

International Students House 229 Great Portland St, W1W 5PN ☎ 020 7631 8300, ⓦ ish.org.uk; ⊖ Great Portland Street; map p.89. Hundreds of hostel-style beds in a vast student complex, with two sites near Regent's Park. Rooms are light, spacious and clean. Open all year, though with variable availability. Dorms (8–10 beds), including some women-only, plus singles, twins, triples and quads, some en-suite. Dorms **£24**, twins **£72**

KING'S COLLEGE

Great Dover Street Apartments 165 Great Dover St, SE1 4XA ☎ 0844 472 1800, ⓦ greatdoverstreetapartments. com; ⊖ Borough; map pp.226–227. Huge Victorian building not far from Bankside, with modern en-suite rooms with fridges plus communal kitchens. Breakfast available. July & Aug. Singles **£55**, twins **£88**

Stamford Street Apartments 127 Stamford St, SE1 9NQ ☎ 020 7848 1700, ⓦ www.kingsvenues.com; ⊖ Waterloo; map p.218. Purpose-built block close to the South Bank, with en-suite single rooms with fridges, and kitchens. Breakfast available. July & Aug. Singles **£55**

LSE

Bankside House 24 Sumner St, SE1 9JA ☎ 020 7107 5750, ⓦ lsevacations.co.uk ⊖ Southwark; map pp.228–229. En-suite B&B singles, twins, triples and quads – plus some singles with shared facilities – near Tate Modern. There's also a bar and restaurant. July–Sept. Twins **£91**

Carr-Saunders Hall 18–24 Fitzroy St, W1T 4BN ☎ 020 7107 5888, ⓦ lsevacations.co.uk; ⊖ Warren Street; map p.97. In an office block north of Oxford Street, the B&B rooms here – singles, twins and doubles – have shared facilities. There's a kitchen. Mid-Aug to mid-Sept & Dec. Doubles **£70**

Grosvenor House 141–143 Drury Lane, WC2B 5TB ☎ 020 7107 5950, ⓦ lsevacations.co.uk; ⊖ Covent Garden; map p.108. Well situated in Covent Garden, offering self-catering en-suite single, double and twin studios with the option of B&B. Mid-Aug to mid-Sept. Doubles **£102**

High Holborn Residence 178 High Holborn, WC1V 7AA ☎ 020 7107 5737, ⓦ lsevacations.co.uk; ⊖ Tottenham Court Road; map p.108. A modern block on a busy central street, offering B&B singles, twins and doubles with shared facilities plus some en-suite triples, and shared kitchens. Mid-Aug to mid-Sept. Doubles **£97**

Northumberland House 8a Northumberland Ave, WC2N 5BY ☎ 020 7107 5603, ⓦ lsevacations.co.uk; ⊖ Charing Cross; map p.46. Self-catering en-suite singles, twins and doubles in a grandiose building near Trafalgar Square. Aug & Sept. Doubles **£102**

Passfield Hall 1–7 Endsleigh Place, WC1H 0PW ☎ 020 7107 5925, ⓦ lsevacations.co.uk; ⊖ Euston; map p.127. These attractive, late Georgian buildings in Bloomsbury hold a variety of B&B rooms, from singles to triples, some en-suite, along with shared kitchens and a garden. Mid-Aug to mid-Sept & Dec. Twins **£82**

Rosebery Hall 90 Rosebery Ave, EC1R 4TY ☎ 020 7107 5850, ⓦ lsevacations.co.uk; ⊖ Angel; map p.147. B&B singles, twins and triples, some en-suite, all with shared kitchens, near Sadler's Wells. Mid-Aug to end Sept & mid-Dec to mid-Jan. Twins **£82**

CAMPSITES

Abbey Wood Federation Rd, Abbey Wood, SE2 0LS ☎ 020 8311 7708, ⓦ caravanclub.co.uk; ⇌ Abbey Wood. Spacious, woody, well-equipped Caravan Club site, ten miles southeast of central London and near the train station, with 156 pitches and room for fifty tents, plus wooden "camping pods" – cosy huts – that sleep up to three. Open all year. Two adults plus pitch **£28.20**, pods **£40**

Crystal Palace Crystal Palace Parade, SE19 1UF ☎ 020 8778 7155, ⓦ caravanclub.co.uk; ⇌ Crystal Palace. A decent site on south London's most famous woody hill, best suited for caravans and campervans, but with eighteen tent pitches. The station is a 5min walk away, and there's a bus stop nearby with connections into Central London. Open all year. Two adults plus pitch **£28.60**

Lee Valley Camping & Caravan Park Meridian Way, Edmonton N9 0AR ☎ 020 8803 6900, ⓦ leevalleypark .org.uk; ⇌ Ponders End. Well-equipped site on the River Lea, backing onto a vast reservoir. There's an ice rink and eighteen-hole golf course, in addition to some bracing inner-city countryside, on your doorstep. Also pods sleeping two and cabins sleeping four. Open all year. Two adults plus pitch **£44**, pods **£40**, cabins **£55**

STEIN'S, RICHMOND

Cafés and restaurants

London's dining scene is among the best in the world. You can sample pretty much any kind of cuisine here, and standards – and creativity – are increasing year on year. The city boasts examples of the best British cooking it's possible to eat, from Michelin-starred Modern affairs to eel-and-pie caffs, with world food ranging from simple Cantonese, Indian and Bangladeshi diners to Spanish, Middle Eastern, Italian and Japanese restaurants, among countless others – and many that offer innovative global fusion. Street food and pop-ups, meanwhile, are going from strength to strength, many of them spawning bricks-and-mortar restaurants that focus on doing just one thing – be it burgers, bao or pizza – very well.

We cover the full range of eating options from cheap-and-cheerful pit-stops via a few enduring favourites to London's smartest destination restaurants. Among the **cafés**, you'll find bakeries, brasseries, chippies, tapas bars, coffee shops and several places where speedy service and low prices are the priority, whether you're grabbing a quick lunch or a late-night snack. In any of these, you should be able to fill up for under £15. Our **restaurant** listings, meanwhile, concentrate on places where you can get a sit-down meal, with full service and all the trimmings. We've also provided a list of the top **gastropubs** where you can eat great, modern food in relaxed surroundings, and a run-down of **specialist food stores** for top-notch picnic supplies (see p.430).

ESSENTIALS

Costs It is possible to pay an awful lot for a meal in London, but, compared with many European cities, you can get considerable value in the mid-range places. Even in the most expensive restaurants, set menus (most often served at lunch) can be a great deal, and, as "sharing plates" are all the rage, you can – if you rein in your appetite – eat for a reasonable price in some very smart venues.

Tipping Tipping 12.5 to 15 percent for service is usually discretionary, but considered normal practice. Some restaurants will add a service charge automatically to the bill, so it's always worth checking.

23

WHITEHALL, WESTMINSTER AND ST JAMES'S

CAFÉS

Café in the Crypt St Martin-in-the-Fields, Duncannon St, WC2N 5DN ☎ 020 7766 1158, ⓦ stmartin-in-the-fields .org; ⊖ Charing Cross; map p.46. This handy café – below the church on Trafalgar Square, in the eighteenth-century crypt – is a nice spot to fill up cheaply before hitting the West End. The daily changing selection consists of homely British comfort food, plus soups, salads and puds. Jazz nights Wed 8pm. Mon & Tues 8am–8pm, Wed 8am–10.30pm (jazz ticket holders only after 6.30pm), Thurs–Sat 8am–9pm, Sun 11am–6pm.

Inn the Park St James's Park, SW1A 2BJ ☎ 020 7451 9999, ⓦ www.innthepark.com; ⊖ St James's Park; map p.67. Park café/restaurant in a stylish curving wooden building overlooking the lake. It can get chaotic, and the Modern British food is a little pricey, but the cheaper self-service café section is a handy pit-stop. Daily 8am–11pm.

★ **Regency Café** 17–19 Regency St, SW1P 4BY; ⊖ St James's Park; map p.36. A rare gem in London, and much beloved: an old-fashioned, family-owned, busy caff, its highly prized postwar exterior and retro fittings still intact, dishing up enormous fry-ups, pies, pastas and jacket spuds – and strong, strong builders' tea – at low prices. Mon–Fri 7am–2.30pm, Sat 7am–noon.

RESTAURANTS

Quilon 41 Buckingham Gate, SW1E 6AF ☎ 020 7821 1899, ⓦ quilon.co.uk; ⊖ St James's Park; map p.36. This Indian restaurant has won a Michelin star for its delicately stylish, contemporary southern Indian and Goan food. The menu focuses on fish and seafood, from crispy calamari to baked black cod, with some splendid veggie choices (try the raw jackfruit pulaou) and a couple of tasty meat options. The £24/£27 lunch menus are good value. Mon–Fri noon–2.30pm & 6–11pm, Sat 12.30–3.30pm & 6–11pm, Sun 12.30–3.30pm & 6–10.30pm.

The Vincent Rooms 76 Vincent Square, SW1P 2PD ☎ 020 7802 8391, ⓦ www.westking.ac.uk/about-us/

GREAT GASTROPUBS

Gone are the days when eating in a pub meant settling for a Ploughman's and a packet of pork scratchings – the following places, reviewed in our Pubs and bars chapter, offer gourmet food to rival some of the city's best restaurants, in laidback, friendly surroundings.

Anchor & Hope South Bank. See p.393
The Cow Notting Hill. See p.396
The Dove Hackney. See p.392
The Eagle Clerkenwell. See p.390
The Elgin Notting Hill. See p.396
Greenwich Union Greenwich. See p.398
The Greyhound Kew. See p.398

The Gun Docklands. See p.393
Island Queen Islington. See p.397
Paradise by Way of Kensal Green Notting Hill. See p.396
The Stag Hampstead. See p.397
The Westbourne Notting Hill. See p.396

23

vincent-rooms-restaurant; ⊖Victoria or St James's Park; map p.36. A changing menu of French food – duck egg *en cocotte*, pot-roasted rabbit *jambon*, double-baked cheese soufflé – cooked and served by the student chefs of Westminster Kingsway College (where Jamie Oliver and Ainsley Harriott, among others, learnt their craft) in this excellent-value dining room. Mains £8–12. Reservations essential. Mon & Fri noon–3pm, Tues–Thurs noon–3pm & 6–9pm; closed Easter, summer & Christmas holidays.

MAYFAIR

CAFÉS

Tibits 12–14 Heddon St, W1B 4DA ☎020 7758 4112, ⓦtibits.co.uk; ⊖Piccadilly Circus; map p.78. Modern, rather glam veggie café (Tuesdays are totally vegan) in this restaurant-packed lane, offering more than forty seasonal self-service salads, sandwiches and hot dishes from around the world. You pay by weight (£2.30/100g before 6pm, £2.60/100g after). Mon–Wed 9am–10.30pm, Thurs–Sat 9am–midnight, Sun 11.30am–10.30pm.

★**The Wolseley** 160 Piccadilly, W1J 9EB ☎020 7499 6996, ⓦthewolseley.com; ⊖Green Park; map p.78. The lofty and stylish 1920s interior (built as the showroom for Wolseley cars) is a major draw at this opulent café/restaurant. The Viennese-inspired comfort/bistro food is good, if pricey – come for a big breakfast (haggis with fried duck egg, perhaps?), a bowl of chicken soup with dumplings, or a simple half-dozen oysters. Afternoon tea is good, too (see p.378) Mon–Fri 7am–midnight, Sat 8am–midnight, Sun 8am–11pm.

RESTAURANTS

Kiku 17 Half Moon St, W1 7BE ☎020 7499 4208, ⓦkikurestaurant.co.uk; ⊖Green Park; map p.78. Simple Japanese place serving up top-quality sushi and sashimi at good prices (from £4), along with authentic grills, soups, noodles, porridge and hotpots. Good-value set lunches start at £20. Mon–Sat noon–2.30pm & 6–10.15pm, Sun 5.30–9.45pm.

Little Social 5 Pollen St, W1S 1NE ☎020 7870 3730, ⓦlittlesocial.co.uk; ⊖Oxford Circus; map p.78. Opposite its sister restaurant, the Michelin-starred *Pollen Street Social*, chef Jason Atherton's *Little Social* offers classy British/French food, for lower prices, in a retro bistro-style space. The gutsy food – braised Irish ox cheeks with roast bone marrow and sourdough crumb, perhaps, or roasted sea bass "BLT" – focuses on the best seasonal ingredients. Mains from £18.50; two-/three-course lunch £21/£25. Mon–Sat noon–2.30pm & 6–10.30pm.

Rasa W1 6 Dering St, W1S 1AD ☎020 7629 1346, ⓦrasarestaurants.com; ⊖Oxford Circus or Bond Street; map p.78. This Indian restaurant, one of the excellent *Rasa* family (see p.380), doles out tasty, subtle South Indian veggie dishes from £6.25 – try the *bagar baingan* (aubergine in a cashew sauce) or the *beet cheera pachadi*, sweetly fragrant with beetroot. There are meat dishes available, but the vegetarian options are best. Mon–Sat noon–3pm & 6–11pm, Sun 1–3pm & 6–9pm.

Wild Honey 12 St George St, W1S 2FB ☎020 7758 9160, ⓦwildhoneyrestaurant.co.uk; ⊖Oxford Street or Bond Street; map p.78. Seasonal French-influenced food in a mellow oak-panelled dining room. Everything, from a salad of peas, quinoa and courgette flowers, via lamb sweetbreads with caramelized cauliflower to their signature wild honey ice cream with honeycomb, is delicious. Mains from £24, with good-deal fixed-price menus (from £29.50 at weekday lunch, £25 on Saturday). Mon–Fri noon–2.30pm & 6–10.30pm, Sat noon–3pm & 6–10.30pm.

MARYLEBONE

CAFÉS

Comptoir Libanais 65 Wigmore St, W1U 1JT ☎020 7935 1110, ⓦlecomptoir.co.uk; ⊖Marble Arch; map p.89. With Lebanese kitsch splashed across everything from the cutlery cans to the wallpaper, this colourful Middle Eastern deli/restaurant – one of a small chain – ticks the boxes for a quick, casual meal. Food is simple and tasty, from crunchy falafels to oven-warm flatbreads, *kibbeh* and *kofta*. Meze from £5, mains from £8. Mon–Sat 8am–11pm, Sun 9am–10pm.

Golden Hind 73 Marylebone Lane, W1U 2PN ☎020 7486 3644; ⊖Bond Street; map p.89. Marylebone's heritage fish-and-chip restaurant, founded in 1914, serves classic cod and chips from around £7, as well as slightly fancier fish offerings and a moreish deep-fried feta starter, in a pared-down retro space. Mon–Fri noon–3pm & 6–10pm, Sat 6–10pm.

Patisserie Valerie 105 Marylebone High St, W1U 4RS ☎020 7935 6240, ⓦpatisserie-valerie.co.uk; ⊖Bond Street; map p.89. Founded as Swiss-run *Maison Sagne* in the 1920s, and preserving its glorious decor, the café is now run by Soho's fab patissiers (see p.370). They do light

---

TOP 5 BRUNCH SPOTS

Beagle Hoxton. See p.378
Caravan King's Cross. See p.375
Kopapa Shoreditch. See p.375
The Lockhart Mayfair. See opposite
Towpath Café Hoxton/Dalston. See p.379

VEGGIE LONDON

Vegetarians are well served in London. Below is a list of exclusively veggie cafés and restaurants.

222 Veggie Vegan Kensington. See p.382
Diwana Bhel Poori House Bloomsbury. See p.375
The Gate Hammersmith. See p.385
Hollyhock Richmond. See p.385
Manna Camden. See p.384

Mildred's Soho. See p.372
My Village Camden Town. See p.383
Nama Notting Hill. See p.383
Poetry Café Covent Garden. See p.374
Rasa N16 Stoke Newington. See p.380
Tibits Mayfair. See opposite

lunches and brunch dishes (from £7), but the plump, creamy cakes are the big draw. Mon–Fri 7am–8pm, Sat 8am–8pm, Sun 8.30am–7pm.

★**Paul Rothe & Son** 35 Marylebone Lane, W1U 2NN ☎020 7935 6783, ⓦpaulrotheandsondelicatessen .co.uk; ⊖ Bond Street; map p.89. Deliciously old-fashioned deli/corner shop established in 1900, selling traditional "English & Foreign Provisions" and serving inexpensive breakfasts, toasties and sandwiches – filled with anything from hummus to ox tongue – to order. Take away, or eat in at formica tables. Mon–Fri 8am–6pm, Sat 11am–5pm.

RESTAURANTS

★**The Lockhart** 22–24 Seymour Place, W1H 7NL ☎0203 011 5400, ⓦlockhartlondon.com; ⊖Marble Arch; map p.89. Combining an airy, elegant ambience with an easy rustic style, this American restaurant stands head and shoulders above London's countless dude food pretenders, offering accomplished Deep South favourites with the odd contemporary twist. From the catfish to the crawfish, the cheddar grits to the buttermilk-fried chicken, it all tastes amazing – and the Sunday brunch, featuring smoked pork hash, house-cured bacon and that delectable chicken, is among London's best. Mains from £15. Tues–Sat noon–3pm & 6–10pm, Sun 11am–3pm.

The Providores and Tapa Room 109 Marylebone High St, W1U 4RX ☎020 7935 6175, ⓦtheprovidores .co.uk; ⊖ Baker Street or Bond Street; map p.89. A double whammy from genius New Zealand chef Peter Gordon. The splendid fusion restaurant serves lunch mains from £17 – pan-fried gilt-head bream with prawn bisque and charred bok choi, say – and dinner menus from £33; downstairs, the casual *Tapa Room* (no reservations) wine bar/café offers small plates, from miso broccoli to chorizo burgers, for £5–17. Providores: Mon–Fri noon–3pm & 6–10.30pm, Sat 10am–3pm & 6–10.30pm, Sun 10am–3pm & 6–10pm. Tapa Room: Mon–Fri 9am–10.30pm, Sat 9am–3pm & 4–10.30pm, Sun 9am–3pm & 4–10pm.

Twist at Crawford 42 Crawford St, W1H 1JW ☎020 7723 3377, ⓦtwistkitchen.co.uk; ⊖Edgware Road; map p.89. Don't come starving, or you may end up spending more than you bargained for at this rustic-chic restaurant – the Mediterranean/Eastern fusion tapas (£3–10), from raw Japanese scallops via fried courgette flowers to Toulouse sausage, are too tempting to resist. Charcuterie, cheeses and Josper-grilled steaks round off the menu. Mon–Thurs noon–3pm & 6–11pm, Fri noon–3pm & 6–11.30pm, Sat noon–midnight, Sun noon–10pm.

23

SOHO

CAFÉS

BAO 53 Lexington St, W1F 9AS ⓦbaolondon.com; Piccadilly Circus; ⊖ map p.97. It can be difficult wading your way through the hype when it comes to the ever-increasing crowd of contemporary Asian restaurants in Central London, but the coolly minimalist *BAO* is a safe bet, setting the bar high when it comes to authentic Taiwanese food – share a selection of side dishes and pillowy-soft steamed buns with meat fillings, and save room for the sweet fried ice cream buns for afters. No reservations. Mon–Sat noon–3pm & 5.30–10pm.

★**Bar Italia** 22 Frith St, W1D 4RF ☎020 7437 4520, ⓦbaritaliasoho.co.uk; ⊖Leicester Square; map p.101. Tiny, family-owned coffee bar that's been a Soho institution since the 1950s, keeping many of its original features and its iconic neon sign. A happy crowd of

clubbers, Italian soccer fans, tourists and locals fill the place more or less around the clock for espressos, croissants, beers and sandwiches. A real slice of old Soho life. Daily 7am–5pm.

★**Fernandez & Wells** 73 Beak St, W1F 9SR ☎020 287 8124, ⓦfernandezandwells.com; ⊖ Piccadilly Circus or Oxford Circus; map p.97. This outstanding café, with its battered urban-rustic ambience, is home from home to a cool

TOP 5 BUDGET BLOWERS

The Clove Club Shoreditch. See p.378
Dabbous Fitzrovia. See p.373
Dinner Knightsbridge. See p.382
The Ledbury Notting Hill. See p.383
St John Clerkenwell. See p.376

STREET LIFE

London's dynamic **street food** scene is exploding. You'll find excellent street food stalls at the city's markets (see p.433), and in particular, of course, at the food markets – **Borough**, **Broadway** and **Brixton Village** are the biggies, but London gourmands also make a beeline for the **Kerb** markets (🖰kerbfood.com), a loose collective of traders and trucks who pop up at seven locations around town; the **Real Food Market** in King's Cross (Wed–Fri; 🖰realfoodfestival.co.uk); and **Maltby Street** in Bermondsey (Sat 9am–4pm, Sun 11am–4pm; 🖰maltby.st), whose food stalls spread along Maltby and Druid streets down to the Spa Terminus (🖰www.spa-terminus.co.uk), with most action on the Ropewalk.

Perhaps inevitably, the roaring success of the street food concept has led to the growth of a lively **night market** scene; the monthly, community-focused 🖰brixtonnightmarket.co.uk is a firm fixture on Brixton's foodie landscape, while booze and DJs play a big part of the fun at hipster favourites Urban Food Feast in Shoreditch (🖰urbanfoodfest.com) and Streetfeast in Lewisham and Dalston (summer only; 🖰streetfeastlondon.com).

23

crowd of Soho creatives and caffeine heads – great coffee, amazing cakes and fresh sandwiches (around £5) to take away or eat in. Their wine bar/deli/tapas bar around the corner at 43 Lexington St does small plates/sandwiches made with the best Iberian ingredients – and there are four more branches around Central London. Beak St: Mon–Fri 7.30am–6pm, Sat & Sun 9am–6pm. Lexington St: Mon–Fri 11am–11pm, Sat noon–11pm, Sun noon–10pm.

Gaby's 30 Charing Cross Rd, WC2H 0DE ☏020 7836 4233; ⊖Leicester Square; map p.97. You won't eat gourmet food at this no-nonsense deli, one of a dying breed in Central London, but it remains beloved by loyal Londoners for its home-cooked (non-kosher) Jewish/ Middle Eastern specialities – falafels in pitta, latkes, salt beef bagels – and its defiantly unreconstructed ambience. Mon–Sat 11am–midnight, Sun 11am–9pm.

★**Maison Bertaux** 28 Greek St, W1 ☏020 7437 6007, 🖰maisonbertaux.com; ⊖Leicester Square; map p.101. Open since 1871, this charmingly old-fashioned, slightly ramshackle and *très* French patisserie, with a handful of cosy rooms and a couple of outdoor tables, is an unmissable Soho experience. The decor is simple and bohemian, with art on the walls and fresh flowers on every table. The cakes, tarts and croissants are to die for. Mon–Sat 9am–10pm, Sun 9am–8pm.

Patisserie Valerie 44 Old Compton St, W1 ☏020 7437 3466, 🖰patisserie-valerie.co.uk; ⊖Leicester Square; map p.101. Beloved patisserie, dating back to the 1920s, and always full with a local crowd enjoying irresistible cakes – as well as light meals – in a historic, elbow-to-elbow dining room. Takeaway available. Many other branches, including in Marylebone (see p.368). Mon & Tues 7.30am–9pm, Wed–Fri 7.30am–11pm, Sat 8am–11pm, Sun 9am–9pm.

RESTAURANTS

★**Andrew Edmunds** 46 Lexington St, W1F 0LP ☏020 7437 5708, 🖰andrewedmunds.com; ⊖Piccadilly Circus;

map p.97. Relaxed, romantic dining room in a crooked Regency townhouse, candlelit at night, with a neighbourhood feel and tasty food. Mains (£13–17) on the short, daily-changing menu might include guinea fowl with rainbow chard and chickpeas or line-caught cod with fregola, clams and wild garlic, while starters (from £5) range from dressed crab to gull's egg with celery salt. Bar food and wine is available all day. No mobile phones. Mon–Fri noon–3.30pm & 5.30–10.45pm, Sat 12.30–3.30pm & 5.30–10.45pm, Sun 1–4pm & 6–10.30pm.

Bar Shu 28 Frith St, W1D 5LF ☏020 7287 8822, 🖰barshurestaurant.co.uk; ⊖Leicester Square or Tottenham Court Road; map p.101. One of the first places to introduce fiery Szechuan cuisine to a city far more familiar with Cantonese food, offering complex dishes – like fish-fragrant pork slivers or boiled sea bass with sizzling chilli oil – to an appreciative crowd. Mains £9–30. Sun–Thurs noon–11pm, Fri & Sat noon–11.30pm.

★**Bocca di Lupo** 12 Archer St, W1D 7BB ☏020 7734 2223, 🖰boccadilupo.com; ⊖Piccadilly Circus; map p.101. Rustic Italian specialities are served in this lively contemporary take on a traditional trattoria, where you can order dishes as "large" (mains) or "small" (to share). Typical offerings might include fennel sausage with lentils, gnocchi with buffalo mozzarella and wild garlic pesto, or broad bean purée with smoked ricotta and chilli. With small dishes at £2.50–16, costs can creep up, but one-dish offers (12.30–3pm & 5.30–7pm) from around £12 are a good deal. Head over to the *Gelupo* gelateria opposite, owned by the same people, to round things off with a gourmet ice cream. Mon–Sat 12.15–3pm & 5.30–midnight, Sun 12.15–3.15pm & 5.15–11pm.

Brasserie Zédel 20 Sherwood St, W1F 7ED ☏020 7734 4888, 🖰brasseriezedel.com; ⊖Piccadilly Circus; map p.97. It's hard to resist the theatrical opulence of this huge Art Deco brasserie, where the simple all-day *prix fixe* menus – £9.75/£12.50/£19.75 – offer accomplished food

CLOCKWISE FROM TOP LEFT THE BREAKFAST CLUB (ANGEL) (P.384); BAR ITALIA (P.369); DISHOOM (P.374) >

at amazing prices. Perfectly executed Gallic dishes include onion soup, rabbit in cider and *escargots* – or simply stop by for coffee and patisserie in their street-level café. Mon–Sat 11.30am–midnight, Sun 11.30am–11pm.

Ceviche 17 Frith St, W1D 4RG ☎020 7292 2040, ⓦ cevicheuk.com; ⊖ Tottenham Court Road; map p.101. Peruvian food has taken London by storm in recent years, and while some might complain that this relaxed, noisy Soho joint is not entirely authentic, it has some very tasty offerings, from the zingy namesake raw fish dishes (£9–11) to the quinoa salad, steamed buns and grilled meats, all served sharing-plate style and washed down with plenty of Pisco Sours. There's another branch near Old St. Mon–Sat noon–11.30pm, Sun noon–10.15pm.

Mildred's 45 Lexington St, W1F 9AN ☎020 7494 1634, ⓦ mildreds.co.uk; ⊖ Oxford Circus or Piccadilly Circus; map p.97. This vegetarian restaurant, serving home-made world cuisine – nothing too adventurous (Sri Lankan curries, burritos, stir-fired Asian veg, pastas), but all tasty – is an old Soho standby. It's small, and can get busy, but takes no bookings. Mains £8.50–12. Mon–Sat noon–11pm.

The Palomar 34 Rupert St, W1D 6DN ☎0207 439 8777, ⓦ thepalomar.co.uk; ⊖ Piccadilly Circus; map p.101. Contemporary Jerusalem food in a noisy, buzzy, slick space, with super-friendly service, packed-in counter seating around the busy kitchen and a more intimate dining room at the back. Expect a sociable sharing-plate experience, full of hefty flavours – polenta with asparagus, mushroom ragout, parmesan and truffle oil; grilled octopus with chickpea msabacha – and reckon on around £40 a head. Mon–Thurs noon–2.30pm & 5.30–11pm, Fri & Sat noon–2.30pm & 5.30–11.30pm, Sun noon–3.30pm.

Pizza Pilgrims 11 Dean St, W1D 3RP ☎020 7287 8964, ⓦ pizzapilgrims.co.uk; ⊖ Tottenham Court Road; map p.101. Neapolitan pizza like mamma used to make (£5–10), served on checked tablecloths – but brought to you by two enthusiastic Brit brothers whose wildfire success serving regional recipes using fine ingredients (*fior di latte*, nduja sausage, truffle oil) from a food truck led them to expand into this bricks-and-mortar restaurant. Another branch on Kingly St, off Carnaby St. Takeaway available. Mon–Sat 11.30am–10.30pm, Sun noon–9.30pm.

★**Polpo** 41 Beak St, W1F 9SB ☎020 7734 4479, ⓦ polpo.co.uk; ⊖ Piccadilly Circus; map p.97. The *Polpo* brand, helmed by restaurateur Russell Norman, has taken London by storm. Here, at the original dining room, reminiscent of a cosy Venetian wine bar, the ambience is typically welcoming and warm. Food is tapas-style, with *cicheti* (bar snacks) and small plates from £3 to £10 – try the octopus and fennel carpaccio, pizzette or any of the *polpette* (meatballs). Reservations are taken for lunch only. The five other *Polpos* – in Covent Garden (two branches), Chelsea, Notting Hill and Smithfield – along with, from the same team, *Polpetto* on Berwick St, headed by star chef Florence Knight; *Spuntino*, a hip take on American diner food on Rupert St; and *Mishkin's*, an upmarket Jewish deli near the Strand, are all highly recommended. Mon–Sat noon–11pm, Sun noon–10pm.

Stockpot 18 Old Compton St, W1D 4TN ☎020 7287 1066; ⊖ Leicester Square; map p.101. You get (very) cheap and cheerful comfort food at this old Soho institution. It's in no way gourmet, but the long menu – heaped plates of pasta, liver and bacon, omelettes, crumble with custard and the like, with strong cups of builders' tea to wash it all down – keeps hungry, and frugal, punters happy. Mains from £5, set menus from £8.50. Mon–Thurs 9am–11.30pm, Fri & Sat 9am–midnight, Sun noon–11.30pm.

Tonkotsu 63 Dean St, W1D 4QG ☎020 7437 0071, ⓦ tonkotsu.co.uk; ⊖ Tottenham Court Road; map p.101. If you're craving ramen, head here to slurp silky home-made noodles and rich, savoury stocks. Ramen – with pork belly, smoked haddock or veggies – from £10, plus gyoza and sides, and cold ramen salad in summer. No reservations. Two more branches in Hackney. Mon–Fri noon–3pm & 5–10.30pm, Sat noon–10.30pm, Sun noon–10pm.

Yauatcha 15 Broadwick St, W1F 0DL ☎020 7494 8888, ⓦ yauatcha.com; ⊖ Piccadilly Circus; map p.101. Sleek, contemporary Chinese teahouse-restaurant serving top-notch dim sum (£5–12; tasting plates £28.88 for two Mon–Thurs 2–6pm) and ravishing patisserie (with a separate cake counter for takeaway) – try the ruby-red raspberry delice. There's a second branch near Liverpool Street. Mon–Sat noon–11.30pm, Sun noon–10.30pm.

CHINATOWN

RESTAURANTS

Four Seasons 12 Gerrard St, W1D 5PR ☎020 7494 0870, ⓦ fs-restaurants.co.uk; ⊖ Leicester Square; map p.101. There's just one dish you need to order here – the roast duck (£12.50 for a half), which even has the likes of Heston Blumenthal raving. All the barbecued and roast meats are good but they're merely supporting players. The original *Four Seasons* is in Bayswater, and there's another on Wardour St, but this location has the edge. Dishes from £6. Mon–Thurs noon–11.30pm, Fri & Sat noon–midnight, Sun 11am–11pm.

★**Mr Kong** 21 Lisle St, WC2H 7BA ☎020 7437 7341, ⓦ mrkongrestaurant.com; ⊖ Leicester Square; map p.101. Late-opening Chinatown stalwart, with a long menu of tasty Cantonese food – don't miss the fried mussels in black bean sauce – and good range of veggie dishes. Mains £7–14. Mon–Sat noon–2.45am, Sun noon–1.45am.

★**New World** 1 Gerrard Place, W1 ☎020 7434 2508; ⊖ Leicester Square; map p.101. Outstanding dim sum (Mon–Fri noon–6pm, Sat & Sun 11am–5pm, from £4) is the star attraction in this large old dining hall, with steaming, laden trolleys – don't miss the cheung fun and the glutinous rice. Mon–Fri noon–11.45pm, Sat 11am–midnight, Sun 11am–11pm.

Rasa Sayang 5 Macclesfield St, W1D 6AY ☎020 7734 1382, ⊛rasasayangfood.com; ⊖Leicester Square;

map p.101. Cheap restaurant specializing in Peranakan (a kind of Chinese/Malaysian fusion) food, and offering a solid selection of halal dishes – *nasi goreng*, *rendang*, *char kway teow* – from £5; three-course menu £13.90. Mon–Thurs noon–11pm, Fri & Sat noon–midnight, Sun 11.30am–9.30pm.

FITZROVIA

CAFÉS

Indian YMCA 41 Fitzroy Square, W1T 6AQ ☎020 7387 0411; ⊖Warren Street; map p.97. This basic student canteen, which has a cultish following, is open to all; just press the bell and pile in. The food is filling and prices low; simply collect what you want from the counter and pay at the till. Dishes from £2. Mon–Fri noon–2pm & 7–8.30pm, Sat & Sun 12.30–1.30pm & 7–8.30pm.

RESTAURANTS

Barrica 62 Goodge St, W1T 4NE ☎020 7436 9448, ⊛barrica.co.uk; ⊖Goodge Street or Tottenham Court Road; map p.97. Be transported to Spain in this cosy tapas restaurant complete with hanging hams, dark wood furnishings and yellow walls. Top tapas (£4–15) include smoked trout with apple and grapes, or sweet potato with sugarcane molasses and almonds; drinks range across Iberian favourites from Asturian cider to Pacharán liqueurs. Mon–Fri noon–11.30pm, Sat 1–11.30pm.

Dabbous 39 Whitfield St, W1T 2SF ☎020 7323 1544, ⊛dabbous.co.uk; ⊖Goodge Street; map p.97. Light, modern cuisine in a warmly distressed industrial-style space. Every dish, while practically bite-sized, is exquisitely presented, scattered with sprigs and tiny blossoms, but it's the fresh, clean flavours – mixed alliums in chilled pine infusion; raw beef with cigar and rye – that hit the spot. It's pricey, for sure, but a four-course lunch menu for £35 allows you to taste the best creations. Just don't turn up with a rumbling tum. Mon–Fri noon–2.30pm & 5.30–11.30pm, Sat noon–2.30pm & 6.30–11.30pm.

Hakkasan 8 Hanway Place, W1T 1HD ☎020 7927 7000, ⊛hakkasan.com; ⊖Tottenham Court Road; map p.97. Swanky, long-established designer restaurant with a cocktail bar attached. The novel Cantonese dishes are expensive, but you can cut costs by sticking with the tasty dim sum. Mains

from £15. They have another branch in Mayfair. Mon–Wed noon–3.15pm & 5.30–11.15pm, Thurs & Fri noon–3.15pm & 5.30pm–12.15am, Sat noon–4.15pm & 5.30pm–12.15am, Sun noon–4.15pm & 5.30–11.15pm.

Honey and Co 25a Warren St, W1T 5LZ ☎020 7388 6175, ⊛honeyandco.co.uk; ⊖Warren Street; map p.97. Simple, tiny, crowded dining room run by an Israeli husband-and-wife team with splendid credentials in home and restaurant cooking. The menu of flavour-packed Middle Eastern food changes, but you'll find delicately spiced meze, rainbow-coloured salads, comforting couscous and tasty breakfasts (toasted fig, orange and walnut loaf, for example, or "burned" potato and feta *boureka*). Mains £14.50 (from £5.50 at breakfast); set sharing menus £26.50. Mon–Fri 8am–10.30pm, Sat 9.30am–10.30pm.

Portland 113 Great Portland St, W1W 6QQ ☎0207 436 3261, ⊛portlandrestaurant.co.uk; ⊖Great Portland Street; map p.97. Everything at this upbeat, buzzy, hot-ticket restaurant is on trend, not least the short, regularly changing menu of original, umami-packed fusion dishes (pig's head croquette with fermented chilli and radish, say, or grilled heritage courgette with nasturtiums and yoghurt). Prices aren't bad for the creativity on show here. Mains from £13. Mon–Sat noon–2.30pm & 6–11pm.

Yalla Yalla 12 Winsley St, W1W 8HQ ☎020 7637 4748, ⊛yalla-yalla.co.uk; ⊖Oxford Circus; map p.97. The name is Lebanese for "hurry, hurry!", but the ambience in this spacious Beirut-style street-food restaurant is pretty relaxed. Options include good-value veggie meze – falafel, cheese parcels and the like – savoury pastries, baked dishes, spiced skewered meats and fig-stuffed patisserie. Meze from £4.50, mains from £10.50, lunch deals £4–8. Takeaway available. There's another, tiny, branch in Soho. Mon–Fri 10am–11.30pm, Sat 11am–11.30pm.

COVENT GARDEN AND HOLBORN

CAFÉS

★Battersea Pie Station/The Pie Shop Lower ground floor, 28 The Market, WC2E 8RA ☎0207 240 9566, ⊛batterseapiestation.co.uk; ⊖Covent Garden; map p.108. A cupboard of a café hidden in the heart of Covent Garden Piazza that serves delicious pie and mash (from £6) made with the finest British ingredients. Choose steak and Meantime stout or butternut squash with goat's

cheese, and add a side of fresh veggies. Cold pork pies, pasties and puds on offer, too. Mon–Thurs & Sun 11am–7pm, Fri & Sat 11am–8pm.

Homeslice Pizza 13 Neal's Yard, WC2H 9DP ☎020 3151 7488, ⊛homeslicepizza.co.uk; ⊖Covent Garden; map p.108. This rustic-cool pizza joint, which started out as a street-food star, offers thin-crust wood-fired pizzas piled high with gourmet toppings, from goat, Savoy cabbage and sumac

23

23

to celeriac, wild garlic, roasted hazelnuts and ricotta; it's de rigueur to wash them down with sparkling wine (on tap). £4 per slice, £20 for a 20" pizza. Mon–Sat noon–10.30pm, Sun noon–9pm; slices and drinks available even later.

★**Kastner & Ovens** 52 Floral St, WC2E 9DA ☎020 7836 2700; ⊖ Covent Garden; map p.108. Tiny gourmet takeaway where the emphasis is on top-quality fresh salads and heart-warming savoury pies, quiches and sausage rolls, plus soups and hot specials, and an amazing selection of cakes, all made on the premises. You'll pay around £6 for three salads. Mon–Fri 8am–4pm.

Monmouth Coffee Company 27 Monmouth St, WC2H 9EU ☎020 7232 3010; ⒲monmouthcoffee.co.uk; ⊖ Covent Garden or Leicester Square; map p.108. The marvellous aroma is the first thing that greets you when you walk in to this cosy coffee house run by the quality Monmouth Coffee roasters. Pick your coffee from a fine selection (or buy the beans to take home) and grab a pastry to go with. Branches in Borough Market and Bermondsey. Mon–Sat 8am–6.30pm.

Poetry Café 22 Betterton St, WC2H 9BX ☎020 7420 9888, ⒲poetrysociety.org.uk; ⊖ Covent Garden or Holborn; map p.108. This simple veggie café, which has been around for years, is a pleasant place to relax, with light meals and cakes on offer; mains £5–7. Evenings see esteemed poetry readings and open mic nights. Mon–Fri 11am–11pm, Sat 7–11pm.

Rock & Sole Plaice 47 Endell St, WC2H 9AJ ☎020 7836 3785, ⒲rockandsoleplaice.com; ⊖ Covent Garden; map p.108. No-nonsense, venerable fish-and-chip shop where they do all the staples just right; eat in or at one of the pavement benches, or take away. It's not cheap, mind; cod and chips costs around £15. Mon–Sat 11.30am–11.30pm, Sun noon–10pm.

RESTAURANTS

Chicken Shop 199 High Holborn, WC1V 7BD ☎020 7661 3040, ⒲chickenshop.com/holborn; ⊖Holborn; map p.108. Born in the residential neighbourhood of Kentish Town in 2012, the *Chicken Shop* has since flown the coop, with five branches in London and one in Chicago. This central branch offers the trademark menu of lip-smacking free-range

rotisserie chicken (£6 for a quarter, £18 for a whole), fries and a couple of sides in a hip, rustic-retro-cosy dining room beneath the *Hoxton Holborn* hotel. Save room if you can for the giant American-style puds. Takeaway available. Mon–Thurs noon–11pm, Fri & Sat noon–midnight.

Dishoom 12 Upper St Martin's Lane, WC2 ☎020 7420 9320, ⒲dishoom.com; ⊖Leicester Square or Covent Garden; map p.108. Re-creating the atmosphere of the Persian cafés of Old Bombay, complete with arcane "rules of the house" signs and faded movie posters, *Dishoom* is buzzy and stylish but, most importantly, serves great food – don't miss the filling black dhal. Their breakfasts, especially the bacon *naan* roll (£5.20), are a hit too. Mains from £6.50. Branches in Shoreditch and King's Cross. Mon–Thurs 8am–11pm, Fri 8am–midnight, Sat 9am–midnight, Sun 9am–11pm.

★ **Flesh & Buns** 41 Earlham St, WC2H 9LX ☎020 7632 9500, ⒲bonedaddies.com; ⊖Leicester Square or Covent Garden; map p.108. Gluttony could get the better of you at this upbeat basement diner, based on Japanese *izakaya* (bars with food) – the cloud-soft rice buns (two for £2) plus succulent toppings (crisp piglet belly £14.50; duck leg £13.50; miso-grilled aubergine £9.30) are staggeringly moreish – and then there's the fried squid, BBQ wings and sushi. Two-/three-course express menus £19/£22 (noon–6pm and after 10pm) are great value. Mon & Tues noon–3pm & 5–10.30pm, Wed–Fri noon–3pm & 5–11pm, Sat noon–11pm, Sun noon–9.30pm.

Hawksmoor 11 Langley St, WC2H 9JG ☎020 420 9390, ⒲thehawksmoor.com; ⊖ Covent Garden; map p.108. Covent Garden branch, in a historic old brewery, of this group of six contemporary steak restaurants – the original is in Spitalfields (see p.379). You could spend well over £50 per head on the best British beef and flavoursome extras, including roast bone marrow, beef dripping fries and mac 'n' cheese, but there's a two-/three-course express menu (£24/£27; not served 6–10pm), which includes rump steak, and you can eat burgers for £15 in the bar. Mon–Thurs noon–3pm & 5–10.30pm, Fri & Sat noon–3pm & 5–11pm, Sun noon–9.30pm.

J. Sheekey 28–35 St Martin's Court, WC2N 4AL ☎020 7240 2565, ⒲j-sheekey.co.uk; ⊖Leicester Square; map

---

COFFEE AND LUNCH CHAINS

Although London's old-fashioned caffs of the 1950s and 1960s have all but died a death, the city today has a number of reliable home-grown **chains** where you can grab a coffee and a sandwich. Three are particularly worthy of mention, offering healthy and well-priced food to grab and go.

Sandwich chain **EAT** (⒲eat.co.uk) produces reliable day-time food, with good home-made sandwiches, salads, hot dishes and cakes. The ubiquitous **Pret à Manger** (⒲pret.com) is slightly more gourmet, with organic coffee and sushi, among its offerings, and is beginning to open, café-style, in the evenings. Also providing some evening service, **Leon** (⒲leonrestaurants.co.uk), meanwhile, is a rapidly expanding, family-owned chain that does delicious coffee, juices and breakfasts, with healthy Mediterranean-influenced food including wraps, hot dishes and salads.

p.108. A *grande dame* of London's dining scene – established in 1896 in the heart of theatreland – this old-school seafood restaurant is a special-occasion kind of place. Price-wise, the weekend lunch three-course menu, at £28.75, is your best bet, along with the oyster bar. Mains from £16. Mon–Fri noon–3pm & 5pm–midnight, Sat noon–3.30pm & 5.30pm–midnight, Sun noon–3.30pm & 5.30–10.30pm.

Kopapa 32–34 Monmouth St, WC2H 9HA ☎ 020 7240 6076, ⓦ kopapa.co.uk; ⊖ Covent Garden; map p.108. Friendly fusion restaurant from Kiwi chef Peter Gordon, offering fresh, complex flavours in sharing plates such as steamed "pie" of shiitake, tempeh and edamame with chickpea pastry and spinach; the starters are particularly adventurous (beetroot and buttermilk gazpacho, for exaample) and breakfasts and weekend brunches – from chorizo hash to soft-shell crab burgers – are great. Small plates from £7, large plates from £14; two/three-course pre-/post-theatre menu £18.95/£21.95; sharing menus from £34.50. Mon–Fri 8–11pm, Sat 9am–11pm, Sun 9.30am–9.45pm.

Masala Zone 48 Floral St, WC2E 9DA ☎ 020 7379 0101, ⓦ masalazone.com; ⊖ Covent Garden; map p.108. Attractive, reliable restaurant, decorated with Rajasthani puppets, serving modern Indian food, including a fair few veggie options. The well-balanced, richly flavoured curries are a cut above, and the thalis (£12–15) very satisfying. Branches

in Soho, Camden, Islington, Earl's Court and Bayswater. Dishes from £4.50. Mon–Sat noon–11pm, Sun 12.30–10.30pm.

Opera Tavern 23 Catherine St, WC2B 5JS ☎ 020 7836 3680, ⓦ operatavern.co.uk; ⊖ Covent Garden; map p.108. The *Salt Yard* team – who, along with their namesake restaurant on Goodge St, are behind *Dehesa*, on Carnaby St, and *Ember Yard* near Oxford St, all of which are splendid – have cornered the market in classy Spanish-Italian tapas eating, offering sharing plates of the best produce and fine wines by the glass in a reconditioned old pub. Star dishes in this lovely spot include a mini foie gras and Iberico burger – indeed, anything featuring the Iberico ham or cooked on the charcoal grill is worth a try. Charcuterie and tapas from £4. Mon–Fri noon–3pm & 5–11.30pm (bar snacks, charcuterie and cheese 3–5pm), Sat noon–11.30pm, Sun noon–5pm.

★**Terroirs** 5 William IV St, WC2N 4DW ☎ 0207 036 0660, ⓦ terroirswinebar.com; ⊖ Charing Cross; map p.108. Great wines – including "natural", additive-free vintages – and seasonal Mediterranean/Modern British food at this excellent wine bar-restaurant. Small plates (from £7.50) – smoked eel with celeriac perhaps, or artichoke, radish and anchovy – plus French-accented *plats du jour* (from £16.50), home-made charcuterie, cheese and bar snacks. Mon–Sat noon–11pm (charcuterie and cheese 3–5.30pm).

23

BLOOMSBURY

CAFÉS

Abeno 47 Museum St, WC1 1LY ☎ 020 7405 3211, ⓦ abeno.co.uk; ⊖ Tottenham Court Road or Holborn; map p.127. Small, basic Japanese place that specializes in hearty and fresh *okonomiyaki* (£10–25), a cabbage, egg and ginger pancake stuffed with pork, kim chi, seafood, cheese, tofu. Noodles and good-value set menus, too. Another branch near Leicester Square. Daily noon–10pm.

Bloomsbury Coffee House 20 Tavistock Place, WC1H 9RE ☎ 020 7837 2877, ⓦ bloomsburycoffeehouse.co.uk; ⊖ Russell Square; map p.127. This basement café, a popular place for local students to chill out, study and chat, is a cosy little hideaway and a good spot for breakfast. Savoury dishes are healthy and comforting, and the Allpress coffee and home-made cakes are great. Mon–Fri 8am–6pm (4.30pm in summer), Sat & Sun 8am–1.30pm.

Diwana Bhel Poori House 121–123 Drummond St, NW1 2HL ☎ 020 7387 5556, ⓦ diwanabph.com; ⊖ Euston; map p.127. On a street lined with cheap Indian restaurants, this South Indian veggie diner wins out for its scrumptious, enormous all-you-can-eat lunchtime buffet (£7; served till 4pm Sat & Sun) – evening meals are not nearly as good value. Mon–Sat noon–11.30pm, Sun noon–10.30pm.

Hummus Bros Victoria House, 37–63 Southampton Row, WC1B 4DA ☎ 020 7404 7079, ⓦ hbros.co.uk; ⊖ Holborn; map p.127. Tiny, functional takeaway doling

out fresh hummus and a choice of toppings, with warm pitta bread, feta, tzatziki, garlic sauce and the like (plates from £5). Branches in the City, Soho and Clerkenwell. Mon–Fri 11am–9pm, Sat noon–5pm.

RESTAURANTS

Caravan 1 Granary Square, N1C 4AA ☎ 020 7101 7661, ⓦ caravankingscross.co.uk; ⊖ King's Cross; map p.127. A lynchpin of the increasingly foodie corner next to St Martin's School of Art, this buzzy fusion hot spot, in a lofty old granary building, offers breakfast (coconut bread with lemon cream cheese and rhubarb, perhaps), weekend brunch (prawn and chorizo omelette, say) and an all-day menu of small plates, gourmet pizza and heartier dishes. The priciest mains are around £16, but you can spend as little as £5 for a snack. Takeaway available. There's another branch on Exmouth Market (see p.376). Mon & Tues 8am–10.30pm, Wed & Thurs 8am–11pm, Fri 8am–midnight, Sat 10am–midnight, Sun 10am–4pm.

Gail's Kitchen 11 Bayley St, WC1B 3HD ☎ 020 7323 9694, ⓦ gailskitchen.co.uk; ⊖ Goodge Street; map p.127. Wholesome, creative food, from challa bread with mushroom ragu to sticky chicken with roasted garlic, in this relaxed restaurant offshoot of the *Gail's* artisan bakery chain; sharing plates from £7. Takeaway baked goods and salads available. Mon–Fri noon–3pm & 5.30–10pm, Sat

10am–3pm & 5.30–10pm, Sun 10am–3pm.

Grain Store Granary Square, N1C 4AB ☎020 7324 4466, ⊛grainstore.com; ⊖King's Cross; map p.127. This lively (read noisy) warehouse-style spot offers an eclectic menu, with a strong focus on fresh veg. Try the

butternut squash ravioli with mustard, apricots, rocket and pumpkin seeds or the hot seaweed sushi with hake, glazed pak choi and black garlic purée. Mains from £12, small plates (£6) served all day. Mon–Wed 10am–11.30pm, Thurs–Sat 10am–midnight, Sun 11am–4pm.

CLERKENWELL

CAFÉS

Clerkenwell Kitchen 27–31 Clerkenwell Close, EC1R 0AT ☎020 7101 9959, ⊛theclerkenwellkitchen.co.uk; ⊖Farringdon or Angel; map p.147. Bright, airy place serving a short, daily-changing menu, using sustainably sourced and organic ingredients in dishes like devilled crab or shallot and thyme tart. The open-plan kitchen serves everything from breakfast through to tea and cakes, with deli sandwiches (from £4.50), soups and savoury tarts to take away. There's a courtyard for outdoor dining. Mains £8–14. Mon–Fri 8am–5pm.

Morito 32 Exmouth Market, EC1R 4QE ☎020 7278 7007, ⊛morito.co.uk; ⊖Angel or Farringdon; map p.147. An offshoot of *Moro* next door (see below), this long, skinny tapas bar allows you to enjoy the same fabulous flavours and fine wines in more casual surrounds. Don't think of it as a cheap option, however – though the most expensive dish (chipirones and sumac) is just £9.75, everything is tiny and wickedly moreish, and what with all the great wines costs can mount. Tapas from £4.50. Reservations for lunch only. Daily noon–4pm & 5–11pm, Sun noon–4pm.

Prufrock Coffee 23–25 Leather Lane, EC1N 7TE ☎020 7242 0467, ⊛prufrockcoffee.com; ⊖Chancery Lane or Farringdon; map p.147. A contemporary shrine to the coffee bean, brainchild of world barista champion Gwilym Davies, and the HQ of an esteemed barista training centre. The coffee, of course, is superb – what with this and the *Department of Coffee & Social Affairs* down the road, Leather Lane has become quite the caffeine-fiend's haven – and there's a short menu of breakfast, lunch and pastries. Mon–Fri 8am–6pm, Sat & Sun 10am–5pm.

RESTAURANTS

Caravan 11–13 Exmouth Market, EC1R 4QD ☎020 7833 8115, ⊛caravanonexmouth.co.uk; ⊖Farringdon; map p.147. True to its Kiwi roots, this Exmouth Market favourite is great for coffee (roasted on site) and brunches (Sat & Sun 10am–4pm) – try the baked eggs with tomato, pepper and Greek yoghurt. Otherwise the fusion menu might feature anything from massaman goat curry to grilled octopus with paprika or Welsh lamb with butternut hummus. Small and large plates £5–17. Mon–Fri 8am–10.30pm, Sat 10am–10.30pm, Sun 10am–4pm.

Fish Central 149–155 Central St, EC1V 8AP ☎020 7253 4970, ⊛fishcentral.co.uk; ⊖Old Street; map p.147. Straddling the Barbican/City and Clerkenwell's council estates, this friendly chippie/fish restaurant attracts

hungry diners from both. The cod or haddock with chips is pretty good, but it's the likes of chargrilled squid, fresh scallops and oysters that give this place the edge. Mains £8–20. Mon–Thurs 11.30am–2.30pm & 5–10.30pm, Fri until 11pm, Sat noon–10.30pm.

The Modern Pantry 47–48 St John's Square, EC1V 4JJ ☎020 7553 9210, ⊛themodernpantry.co.uk; ⊖Farringdon; map p.147. A brace of Georgian townhouses make an elegant setting for this contemporary café with a smart dining room upstairs. Kiwi chef Anna Hansen brings Pacific Rim and fusion flavours to accomplished dishes from pan-fried pollock with cassava and green chilli hash browns to wild garlic, pea, leek and pecorino fritters. The excellent breakfasts won't hit £20, and there are weekday two-/three-course lunch menus for £22.50/£27.50. Café: Mon 8am–11am & noon–10pm, Tues–Fri 8am–11am & noon–10.30pm, Sat 9am–4pm & 6–10.30pm, Sun 10am–4pm & 6.30–10pm; restaurant: Tues–Fri noon–3pm & 6–10.30pm, Sat 9am–4pm & 6–10.30pm, Sun 10am–4pm.

★ Moro 34–36 Exmouth Market, EC1R 4QE ☎020 7833 8336, ⊛moro.co.uk; ⊖Farringdon or Angel; map p.147. This lovely, lively and warmly decorated restaurant has become a place of pilgrimage for disciples of Sam and Sam Clark's Moorish/Mediterranean/Middle Eastern cuisine. The daily-changing menus are outstanding, especially the lamb dishes and their speciality yoghurt cake; it's best to book well in advance. Mains £16.50–24; tapas (from £3.50) are served at the bar all day Mon–Sat. Mon–Sat noon–2.30pm & 6–10.30pm (plus tapas 2.30–6pm), Sun 12.30–2.45pm.

St John 26 St John St, EC1M 4AY ☎020 7251 0848, ⊛stjohnrestaurant.com; ⊖Farringdon; map p.147. Former smokehouse near Smithfield meat market that's become famous for Fergus Henderson's perfect, simple, execution of traditional British "nose to tail" dishes – often involving unfashionable animal parts – on a menu that's pared down as the dining room itself. There's a less expensive sister restaurant in Spitalfields (see p.379). Mains £17–25. Mon–Fri noon–3pm & 6–11pm, Sat 6–11pm, Sun 1–3pm.

Sushi Tetsu 12 Jerusalem Passage, EC1V 4JP ☎020 3217 0090, ⊛sushitetsu.co.uk; ⊖Farringdon; map p.147. You can believe the hype about this terrific sushi place, which turns out super-fresh *nigiri* sushi, sashimi and hand rolls from £4; there's a £30/person minimum for lunch, £45 at dinner, and you can order *omakase* (chef's choice) a day in advance for £60. It seats fewer than ten, so reservations are essential and must be made (by phone only) on two specified days per month for the weeks ahead

(see website for details). Tues–Fri 11.45–2pm (last seating noon) & 5.30–10pm (last seating 7.45pm), Sat 5–9.30pm (last seating 7.30pm).

THE CITY

CAFÉS

Café Below Church of St Mary-le-Bow, Cheapside, EC2V 6AU ☎ 020 7329 0789, ⊕ cafebelow.co.uk; ⊖ St Paul's or Bank; map p.166. A rare City gem: a cosy, inexpensive café/restaurant, in a Norman church crypt, serving home-cooked bistro-style dishes – squash, red pepper and nettle curry; pan-fried sea bass; cheese soufflé and salad – on changing menus with good veggie choices (lunch mains from £8.25). Tasty hot breakfasts, too, plus two-/three-course candlelit dinners (£15/£20). Mon & Tues 7.30–10.30am & 11.30am–2.45pm, Wed–Fri 7.30–10.30am, 11.30am–2.45pm & 5.30–9pm.

Patty & Bun 22/23 Liverpool St, EC2M 7PD ☎ 0207 621 1331, ⊕ pattyandbun.co.uk; ⊖ Liverpool Street; map pp.152–153. London's dude food frenzy has calmed down somewhat in recent years, but this joint – spawned from a raved-about food truck – continues to fly the flag, turning out succulent burgers on brioche buns from £7.50, with carb-packed sides and breakfasts. Two more branches on James St off Oxford St and London Fields in Hackney. Mon–Wed 7.30am–9.30am & 11.30am–10pm, Thurs & Fri 7.30am–9.30am & 11.30am–11pm, Sat 11.30am–9pm, Sun 11.30am–6pm.

RESTAURANTS

Duck and Waffle Heron Tower, 110 Bishopsgate, EC2N 4AY ☎ 020 3640 7310, ⊕ duckandwaffle.com; ⊖ Aldgate; map pp.152–153. The improbable juxtaposition of swanky City location – the view, from forty floors up, is amazing – and hipster comfort food (the signature dish features waffles, duck confit, fried duck egg and mustard maple syrup, while other hits include spicy ox cheek doughnuts, roasted octopus with chorizo, and bacon-wrapped dates) somehow works. For this setting the prices (small plates £9–15; duck and waffle £17) aren't too bad, and the hours make it a useful late-night, or breakfast, destination. Daily 6am–5am.

José Pizarro 36 Broadgate Circle, EC2M 1QS (no phone), ⊕ josepizarro.com; Liverpool Street; map p.152–153. Broadgate Circle is emerging into a restaurant zone, featuring new branches of *Franco Manca* (see p.385) and *Yauatcha* (see p.372) among others. This smart, City-slick spot builds on the success of Spanish chef Pizarro's Bermondsey restaurant and nearby tapas bar, with simple tapas, charcuterie, small and large plates, with the addition here of breakfasts – *sobrasada* sausage on toast with honey and Mahon cheese, for example. Mon–Fri 8am–11pm, Sat 11am–11pm.

SHOREDITCH AND HOXTON

CAFÉS

The Bridge 15 Kingsland Rd, E2 8AE (no phone); ⊖ Old Street; map pp.190–191. Designers get paid a mint to put together the kind of Miss Havisham mish-mash that comes naturally to this eccentric little Shoreditch coffee house/bar. The downstairs room, crammed with vintage Americana and London bric-a-brac, has an appealing dive-bar ambience, and you could lose hours nursing a coffee and a cake in the kitsch Baroque boudoir upstairs. Prices are high, though, so stick to coffee and snacks. Occasional live music. Mon–Wed noon–1am, Thurs–Sat noon–2.30am, Sun 1pm–1.30am.

★**Fabrique** Arch 385, Geffrye St, E2 8HZ ☎ 020 7033 0268, ⊕ fabrique.co.uk; ⊖ Hoxton; map pp.190–191. This Scandinavian-style artisan bakery – the Hoxton outpost of a Stockholm chain – keeps it simple but utterly delicious (and a tad pricey), serving spicy cinnamon and cardamon buns, stone-oven-baked sourdough breads and Johan & Nyström coffee. The white-tile and unvarnished wood space, tucked into a railway arch by Hoxton station, is lovely. Mon–Fri 8am–6pm, Sat & Sun 10am–6pm.

★**Leila's Shop** 17 Calvert Ave, E2 7JP ☎ 020 7729 9789; ⊖ Shoreditch High Street; map pp.190–191. Relaxed neighbourhood café, linked to an artlessly

nostalgic and appealing little deli/grocers/farm shop, using the freshest ingredients to serve creative, healthy Mediterranean-tinged breakfasts, brunches and light meals to a devoted Shoreditch crowd. Good biodynamic wines, too. Wed–Sat 10am–6pm, Sun 10am–5pm.

Sông Que 134 Kingsland Rd, E2 8DY ☎ 020 7613 3222, ⊕ songque.co.uk; ⊖ Hoxton; map pp.190–191. In a Hoxton street heaving with budget Vietnamese restaurants, this basic, busy place is a reliable stalwart, offering steaming *phô* (from £8.40) and lip-tinglingly spicy seafood dishes. Mon–Fri noon–3pm & 5.30–11pm, Sat noon–11pm, Sun noon–10.30pm.

RESTAURANTS

★**8 Hoxton Square** 8 Hoxton Square, N1 6NU ☎ 020 7729 4232, ⊕ 8hoxtonsquare.com; ⊖ Old Street; map pp.190–191. Welcoming restaurant whose easy-going vibe and reasonable prices belie the serious skill in the kitchen. Small plates (£3–7) and mains (£10–20) present Modern fusion flavours – *zepellos* (savoury fried buns); gorgonzola custard; smoked duck, runner beans and sour cherries – with creative veggie choices and deliciously simple weekend breakfasts. Mon–Fri noon–11pm, Sat 10am–11pm, Sun 10am–5pm.

23

23

TOP 5 AFTERNOON TEAS

The classic English **afternoon tea** – sandwiches, scones and cream, cakes and tarts, and, of course, pots of tea – is available all over London. The most popular venues are the capital's top hotels and swankiest department stores; a selection of the best is given below. To avoid disappointment, book well in advance, and leave your jeans and trainers at home, as most hotels will expect at least "smart casual" attire. Prices quoted here are for the standard teas; most places offer champagne teas, or more substantial high teas, for a higher price.

Berkeley Hotel Wilton Place, SW1X 7RL ☎020 7235 6000, ⓦthe-berkeley.co.uk; ⊖Knightsbridge; map pp.252–253. Something different: the "Pret-a-Portea" is a whimsical fashionista spread with taster spoons, sandwiches, canapés and cakes and biscuits based upon the latest couture designs. £45. Daily 1–5.30pm.

Claridge's Brook St, W1K 4HR ☎020 7107 8886, ⓦclaridges.co.uk; ⊖Bond Street; map p.78. More than twenty fine teas, sandwiches and pastries in stunning Art Deco surrounds. £55. Daily seatings every 15min 2.45–3.30pm & 4.45pm–5.30pm.

Fortnum & Mason 181 Piccadilly, W1A 1ER ☎020 7734 8040, ⓦfortnumandmason.com; ⊖Green Park or Piccadilly Circus; map p.78. Take tea in this glorious old store's *Diamond Jubilee Tea Salon*; they have savoury, vegetarian, vegan, dairy-free, gluten-free and diabetic-friendly options. £40; £44 with single estate tea. Mon–Sat noon–7pm, Sun noon–6pm.

The Ritz 150 Piccadilly, W1J 9BR ☎020 7300 2345, ⓦtheritzlondon.com; ⊖Green Park; map p.78. Seriously posh teas, with piano, harp or string quartet accompaniment, in the hotel's opulent Palm Court – gents must wear a jacket and tie. £50. Daily 11.30am, 1.30pm, 3.30pm, 5.30pm & 7.30pm.

The Wolseley 160 Piccadilly, W1J 9EB ☎020 7499 6996, ⓦthewolseley.com; ⊖Green Park; map p.78. The atmosphere is grand without being intimidating at this Viennese-style café (see p.368), where the sumptuous European pastries are the speciality. £23.75. Mon–Fri & Sun 3–6.30pm, Sat 3.30–5.30pm.

Beagle 397–400 Geffrye St, E2 8HZ ☎020 7613 296, ⓦbeaglelondon.co.uk; ⊖Hoxton; map pp.190–191. Occupying a couple of brick railway arches, this Hoxton joint has more than proved itself a grown-up dining destination. From smoked ham hock with broad beans to wild sea trout with samphire, the changing menu of seasonal Modern British food is always appealing, with tempting cocktails and popular weekend brunches. Buzzing with a youngish crowd, the vaulted space can get noisy, but there's a terrace too. Mains £13.50–20; two-/three-course express lunch £15/£18. Mon–Fri noon–3pm & 6.30–10.30pm, Sat 11am–3pm & 6.30–10.30pm, Sun 11am–5pm.

The Clove Club Shoreditch Town Hall, 380 Old St, EC1 ☎020 7729 6496, ⓦthecloveclub.com; ⊖Old Street or Shoreditch High Street; map pp.190–191. While you can opt for a more informal experience at the bar (snacks and sharing plates from 6pm; £4–25), you'll otherwise pretty much eat what you're given at this Michelin-starred restaurant – three or five courses at lunch (£35/£65), five or nine at dinner (£65/£95; vegetarian menu same price), and, with the controversial "ticketing" system, you'll pay in advance for dinner. The innovative menu – parsley root *croustillant* with chestnuts and cavolo nero; buttermilk-fried chicken with pine salt – is fabulous and uses impeccably sourced ingredients. Mon 6.30–9.30pm, Tues–Sat noon–2.30pm & 6.30–9.30pm.

SPITALFIELDS, BRICK LANE AND WHITECHAPEL

CAFÉS

Brick Lane Beigel Bake 159 Brick Lane, E1 ☎020 7729 0616; ⊖Shoreditch High Street; map pp.190–191. Fresh bagels baked on the spot in a basic shop in the heart of the East End. They're delicious, and astonishingly cheap; by far the priciest is the hot salt beef (£3.70), and even smoked salmon and cream cheese is a mere £1.60. A big hit late at night and in the early mornings. Daily 24hr.

Full Stop 202 Brick Lane, E1 6SA ☎020 7739 7086; ⊖Shoreditch High Street; map pp.190–191. Relaxed Brick Lane spot where you can linger in the retro ambience over excellent coffee from esteemed London roaster Square Mile – try their home-made cold brews – plus healthy salads, sandwiches, brunches and fresh juices. At night it segues into more of a bar scene, with lots of lively events, including open mic nights. Mon & Tues 9am–5pm, Wed & Thurs 9am–10pm, Fri & Sat 9am–midnight, Sun 9am–9pm.

Verde and Co 40 Brushfield St, E1 6AG ☎020 7247 1924, ⓦverdeandco.co.uk; ⊖Liverpool Street; map pp.190–191. Author Jeanette Winterson, who owns this Spitalfields deli/grocer's/café, has preserved the original eighteenth-century shopfront and bareboard interior; an adorable setting for classy and quirky deli goods, with some seating for excellent coffee, gourmet salads, sandwiches, soups and quiche (£4–6). Mon–Fri 8am–5.30pm, Sat & Sun 10am–5.30pm.

RESTAURANTS

Hawksmoor 157 Commercial St, E1 6BJ ☎ 020 7426 4850, ⓦ thehawksmoor.com; ⊖ Liverpool Street or Shoreditch High Street; map pp.190–191. Carnivores drool at the very mention of this steakhouse, with its huge, succulent charcoal-grilled cuts. The Sunday roasts are fantastic, naturally; a full meal could cost well over £50, but the two-/three-course lunch/afternoon menu cuts costs at £24/£27. Branches in Covent Garden, Mayfair, Knightsbridge and the City. Mon–Sat noon–2.30pm & 5–10.30pm, Sun noon–4.30pm.

Lahore Kebab House 2–10 Umberston St, E1 1PY ☎ 020 7481 9737, ⓦ lahore-kebabhouse.com; ⊖ Aldgate East; map pp.190–191. A legendary Pakistani kebab house, just off Commercial Rd. Go for the lamb cutlets and roti, and turn up hungry. BYOB. Mains £7–13. Daily noon–1am.

Needoo Grill 87 New Rd, E1 1HH ☎ 020 7247 0648, ⓦ needoogrill.co.uk; ⊖ Whitechapel; map pp.190–191. Run by a *Tayyabs* alumnus (see below), this lively Punjabi restaurant maintains its forerunner's standards – the grills are excellent, and they have some good veggie options, too – in the face of increasing popularity. Mains from £6. BYOB. Daily noon–11.30pm.

St John Bread and Wine 94–96 Commercial St, E1 6LZ ☎ 020 7251 0848, ⓦ stjohnbreadandwine.com; ⊖ Liverpool Street; map pp.190–191. A simpler offshoot of *St John* (see p.376) with the same superlative British food on a changing menu of sharing dishes – featuring offal, pig's skin and the like, but with tasty fish and veg options, plus breakfasts (try the Old Spot bacon sandwich). Dishes £5–21. Mon 9–11am, noon–3pm & 6–9pm, Tues–Fri 9–11am, noon–3pm & 6–11pm, Sat & Sun 9–11am, noon–4pm & 6–11pm.

★ **Taberna do Mercado** 107b Commercial St, E1 6BG ☎ 0207 375 0649, ⓦ tabernamercado.co.uk; ⊖ Shoreditch High Street; map pp.190–191. Stellar chef Nuno Mendes – he of celeb-studded *Chiltern Firehouse* – brings his amazing food to a wider audience at this Portuguese restaurant, serving authentic, often unfamiliar dishes at surprisingly low prices (from £5). Everything is tapas sized, which is a blessing given how irresistible it all is – hits include runner bean fritters, pork bifana sandwiches and the cuttlefish and pig trotter broth. No reservations for dinner. Mon–Sat noon–9.30pm, Sun noon–7.30pm.

Tayyabs 83–89 Fieldgate St, E1 1JU ☎ 020 7247 9543, ⓦ tayyabs.co.uk; ⊖ Whitechapel; map pp.190–191. Opened in 1974, *Tayyabs* has smartened itself up over the years but still offers the same straightforward Punjabi food: tasty, meat-heavy dishes, freshly cooked and without pretension, with flavoursome breads. The grilled lamb chops are the big hit. Prices are low, booking is essential, it gets noisy and service is speedy. BYOB. Mains from £7. Daily noon–11.30pm.

STOKE NEWINGTON, DALSTON AND LONDON FIELDS

CAFÉS

Climpson & Sons 67 Broadway Market, E8 4PH ⓦ climpsonandsons.com; ⇌ London Fields; map p.187. The go-to coffee shop in these parts, *Climpsons* was a trailblazer in London's coffee revolution, still turning out expert brews using beans from their own roastery. Mon–Fri 7.30am–5pm, Sat 8.30am–5pm, Sun 9am–5pm.

F. Cooke 9 Broadway Market, E8 4PH ☎ 020 7254 6458; ⇌ London Fields; map p.187. In the heart of foodie Broadway Market, where hip indie cafés now rule the roost, this eel-and-pie shop, in the same family for generations and on this spot since 1900, remains resolutely old school, with its 1930s interior intact. Order pie, mash, liquor (parsley gravy) and a side of jellied eels and enjoy a nostalgic taste of East End history. Mon–Thurs 10am–7pm, Fri & Sat 10am–8pm.

Foxlow 71–73 Stoke Newington Church St, N16 0AS ☎ 020 7481 6377, ⓦ foxlow.co.uk; ⇌ Stoke Newington; map p.187. Offshoot of steak maestros *Hawksmoor* (see above) *Foxton* brings on-trend, grown-up food to this gentrifying neighbourhood. Juicy burgers, crispy fried chicken and steaks are winners, of course, but the menu roams through the Mediterranean to the Middle East, with a couple of veggie choices (poblano mac cheese, for example), in a relaxed, stylish dining room filled with happy locals. Mains from £10. Mon–Fri 10am–3pm & 5–10.30pm, Sat 10am–10.30pm, Sun 10am–10pm.

★ **Towpath Café** Whitmore Bridge, 42 De Beauvoir Crescent, N1 5SB ☎ 020 7254 7606; ⊖ Haggerston; map p.187. With colourful outdoor seating by the Regent's Canal, this is a lovely, sunny spot serving good coffees, fresh home-made juices, interesting booze and quietly gourmet, seasonal food – great for brunch – truffle and parmesan buns, perhaps – a simple Mediterranean salad or Italian-influenced desserts. Dishes from £3; no cards. March–Nov Tues & Wed 9am–5pm, Thurs–Sun 9am–dusk.

Voodoo Ray's 95 Kingsland High St, E8 ☎ 020 7249 7865, ⓦ voodoorays.co.uk; ⊖ Dalston Junction; map p.187. Grungy late-night drinking dens come and go in Dalston like a rash, but *Voodoo Ray's* seems set to stay – a late-night pizza/Margarita joint where the pizzas (from

23

£3.30/slice) are huge and flavourful, and the Margaritas – usually being necked by a crowd who've had quite enough already – are cold and strong. Mon–Thurs & Sun 5pm–midnight, Fri 5pm–3am, Sat 5pm–midnight.

RESTAURANTS

Mangal Ocakbasi 10 Arcola St, E8 2DJ ☎020 7275 8981, Ⓦmangal1.com; ❺Dalston Junction; map p.187. Generally agreed to be the best of the excellent Turkish diners in a neighbourhood that's spilling over with them, *Mangal* is renowned for its grills and skewered meats, many of them served with yoghurt sauce; the veggie mezes and fresh breads are good, too. At its sister restaurant, *Mangal II*, around the corner on Stoke Newington High St, you will join artists Gilbert and George, who eat here nightly, for similarly simple food and friendly service. Dishes from £5. Daily noon–midnight.

★**Rasa N16** 55 Stoke Newington Church St, N16 0AR ☎020 7249 0344, Ⓦrasarestaurants.com; ⇌Stoke Newington; map p.187. Cosy Keralan restaurant, the first in London's *Rasa* family, with amazingly good and very inexpensive South Indian vegetarian specialities – go for any of the curries or the enormous dosas. The equally fine *Rasa Travancore* across the road specializes in Syrian Christian cooking, serving some meat and fish. Mains £4.50–6.50. Mon–Thurs 6–10.45pm, Fri 6–11.30pm, Sat noon–3pm & 6–11.30pm, Sun noon–3pm & 6–10.45pm.

23 BETHNAL GREEN

CAFÉS

★**E. Pellicci** 332 Bethnal Green Rd, E2 0AG ☎020 7739 4873; ❺Bethnal Green; map pp.190–191. London's old Italian-owned caffs are dropping like flies, and *Pellicci's* (open since 1900) is a rare jewel: an iconic, family-owned and jubilantly friendly East End institution with its stunning 1940s decor intact, serving great fry-ups and good home-made Anglo-Italian grub at low prices. Mon–Sat 7am–4pm.

Frizzante 1a Goldsmith's Row, E2 8QA ☎020 7739 2266, Ⓦfrizzanteltd.co.uk; ❺Bethnal Green; map pp.190–191. Hackney City Farm's rustic, family-friendly, Italian café serves home-made breakfasts, lunches, cakes and Sunday roasts, all using local, seasonal ingredients, for less than a tenner. Live music and "agriturismo" menu on Thurs evenings. Tues, Wed & Fri–Sun 10am–4.30pm, Thurs 10am–4.30pm & 7–10pm.

★**Story Deli** 123 Bethnal Green Rd, E2 7DG ☎07918 197352, Ⓦstorydeli.com; ❺Shoreditch High Street; map pp.190–191. Funky little ex-scout hut, all soothing whitewash and bare wood, serving excellent, organic, flatbread-style pizza. Topped with interesting herbs, pestos, cheeses and hams, they all cost £17, from the *fico*, made with goat's cheese, figs, capers, thyme and Parma ham, to the chilli-hot Fast Eddie with spicy sausage and chorizo. No cards. Daily noon–10.30pm.

RESTAURANTS

Bistrotheque 23–27 Wadeson St, E2 9DR ☎020 8983 7900, Ⓦbistrotheque.com; ❺Cambridge Heath; map p.187. Listing Modern British food, fusion dishes and bistro staples – cod and chips or steak *tartare* with frites? West Mersea oysters or avocado on toast? – and adding a dash of Manhattan-style sass, this huge monochrome brasserie is a particular hit for its cocktails and buzzy weekend brunches. Mains from £10, brunch dishes from £6. Mon–Thurs 6–10.30pm, Fri 6–11pm, Sat 11am–4pm & 6–11pm, Sun 11am–4pm.

Typing Room Patriot Square, E2 9NF ☎020 7871 0461, Ⓦtypingroom.com; ❺Bethnal Green; map pp.190–191. Based in Bethnal Green's hip *Town Hall Hotel*, the elegant *Typing Room* – backed by Jason Atherton, London's restaurateur *du jour* – offers a short, seasonal menu of beautifully presented Modern European food focusing on fresh local produce (sea trout, gooseberries, chard and smoked eel, for example, or yeasted cauliflower with raisins, capers and mint). It's not overly expensive, either, for this standard: two/three-course lunches £24/£29; five-or seven-course dinner tasting menus £60/£75. Tues 6–10pm Wed–Sat noon–2.30pm & 6–10pm.

DOCKLANDS

CAFÉS

Hubbub 269 Westferry Rd, E14 3RS ☎020 7515 5577, Ⓦhubbubcafebar.com; ❺Mudchute DLR; map pp.210–211. A creative oasis in the Docklands desert, this attractive café-bar is housed in a former Victorian church, now an arts centre, and does decent breakfasts (till 4pm), burgers, wraps and tasty daily specials from lamb skewers and steaks to aubergine parmigiana (from £9). Mon–Wed 11am–11pm, Thurs & Fri 11am–midnight, Sat 10am–midnight, Sun 10am–10.30pm.

Mudchute Kitchen Mudchute City Farm, Pier St, E14 3HP ☎020 3069 9290, Ⓦmudchute.org; ❺Mudchute DLR; map pp.210–211. Satisfying, home-made food – great cooked breakfasts, panini, jacket spuds, gelato – and farmside courtyard seating keep the kiddie-focused crowd very happy. Tues–Fri 9.30am–3pm, Sat & Sun 9.30am–5pm.

RESTAURANTS

★**Bravas Tapas** St Katharine Docks, E1W 1AT ☎0207 481 1464, Ⓦbravastapas.co.uk; ❺Tower Hill; map pp.210–211. While the rustic, shabby chic interior is appealing, you'll feel most pleased with yourself if you bag a table on the sunny dockside terrace: the perfect place to enjoy terrific, deceptively simple

modern tapas (spiced lamb chops, smoked sardines, cuttlefish croquettes; £5–20) and great Spanish wines. Mon–Sat noon–10.30pm, Sun noon–1pm.

SOUTH BANK

CAFÉS

Scooter Caffè 132 Lower Marsh, SE1 7AE ☎ 020 7620 1421; ⊖ Waterloo; map p.218. Quirky little coffee house – half old-school Italian caff, half Kiwi-run hipster hangout, filled with bric-a-brac and scooter memorabilia and prowled by a resident cat. It's a friendly, relaxed spot where locals gather to drink good coffee and linger; at night it morphs into a cocktail bar. Mon–Thurs 8am–11pm, Fri 8am–midnight, Sat 10am–midnight, Sun 10am–11pm.

RESTAURANTS

Laughing Gravy 154 Blackfriars Rd, SE1 8EN ☎ 020 7998 1707, ⓦ thelaughinggravy.co.uk; ⊖ Southwark; map p.218. There's a cosy, neighbourhood vibe at this popular, upmarket brasserie, which serves English and Mediterranean bistro food in a gorgeous brick-walled dining room. Mains £11.50–24. Mon–Thurs noon–3pm

& 5–10pm, Fri noon–3pm & 5–10.30pm, Sat noon–4pm & 5–10.30pm, Sun noon–4.30pm.

Masters Super Fish 191 Waterloo Rd, SE1 8UX ☎ 020 7928 6924; ⊖ Waterloo; map p.218. This old-school fish-and-chip restaurant serves huge portions of the classics (cod, haddock) with all the trimmings (gherkins, pickled onions, coleslaw and a few complimentary prawns) – plus some fancier options. Mains £7.50–13; lunch deal £7. Mon 4.30–10.30pm, Tues–Sat noon–3pm & 4.30–10.30pm.

RSJ 33 Coin St, SE1 9NR ☎ 020 7928 4554, ⓦ rsj.uk.com; ⊖ Waterloo; map p.218. High standards of Anglo-French cooking (mains from £12; two/three-course menus £16.95/£19.95) make this independent corner restaurant a popular spot for a pre- or post-theatre meal. It can get noisy, but the friendly atmosphere and neighbourhood feel more than make up for it. Mon–Fri noon–2.30pm & 5.15–11pm, Sat 5.15–11pm.

SOUTHWARK

CAFÉS

★Bar Tozino Ropewalk, Maltby St, SE1 3PA ⓦ bartozino.com; ⊖ London Bridge; map pp.226–227. Glorious Spanish wines and the finest acorn-fed ham, along with a couple of cheeses and tapas (£3–15), are all you'll get at this cosy *jamón bodega* under the arches in foodie Maltby St. Dark, friendly and redolent with the aroma of sweet ham, it's a welcome slice of Spain in southeast London. Wed & Thurs 5–10pm, Fri noon–10pm, Sat 10am–10pm, Sun noon–5pm.

José 104 Bermondsey St, SE1 3UB ⓦ josepizarro .com; ⊖ London Bridge; map pp.226–227. This sherry and tapas bar, run by José Pizarro, one of London's finest Spanish chefs – his more formal restaurant, *Pizarro*, nearby at no.194, is also terrific – is at the heart of Bermondsey's burgeoning foodie scene. Unfussy but beautifully executed tapas, on a regularly changing list, cost just £3–9, and the Spanish wines and sherries come by the reasonably priced glass. No reservations; it gets packed. Mon–Sat noon–10.15pm, Sun noon–5.15pm.

RESTAURANTS

★40 Maltby Street 40 Maltby St, SE1 3PA ☎ 020 7237 9247; ⊖ Bermondsey; map pp.226–227. This unpretentious wine bar, selling natural wines to drink in or take away, has the feel of a European market bar, serving simple plates of rustic, creative and delicious French-influenced food (mussel, pea and saffron rice; rabbit and bacon pie with braised radish) to go with the wine. Dishes £6–15. No reservations. Wed & Thurs 5.30–10pm, Fri

12.30–2pm & 5.30–10pm, Sat 11am–10pm (Sat food served noon–3.30pm & 6–9.30pm).

Restaurant Story 199 Tooley St, SE1 2JX ☎ 020 7183 2117, ⓦ restaurantstory.co.uk; ⊖ London Bridge; map pp.228–229. Theatrical, yes; expensive, certainly, but this restaurant deserves the accolades for its wildly imaginative tasting menus (dinner £75/£95); molecular cuisine based on the best British produce – check out the melting "candle" of dripping for your sourdough, or the heritage potato, asparagus and coal – in an unhurried dining room on a dreary street. Reservations essential. Tues–Thur 12–5pm & 6.30–9.30pm, Fri & Sat 12–5pm & 6–9.30pm

The Table 83 Southwark St, SE1 0HX ☎ 020 7401 2760, ⓦ thetablecafe.com; ⊖ Southwark or London Bridge; map pp.228–229. Contemporary, canteen-style restaurant, handy for the Tate, serving creative, seasonal food – burgers, salads, and, the highlight, fabulous all-day breakfasts – using ethically sourced ingredients. Mains £6–16. Mon 7.30am–4.30pm, Tues–Fri 7.30am–10.30pm, Sat & Sun 8.30am–4pm.

Zucca 184 Bermondsey St, SE1 3TQ ☎ 020 7378 6809, ⓦ zuccalondon.com; ⊖ London Bridge; map pp.226–227. This modern Italian restaurant sat here long before Bermondsey got trendy, serving excellent food on daily-changing menus. Fresh pasta; octopus with chickpeas and polenta; burrata with salt-baked onions; lamb belly with wild garlic and nettle – all of it is seasonal, made with the freshest, simplest ingredients. Mains £12–19. Tues–Fri noon–3pm & 6–10pm, Sat noon–3.30pm & 6–10pm, Sun noon–4pm.

23

SOUTH KENSINGTON & KNIGHTSBRIDGE

CAFÉS

222 Veggie Vegan 222 North End Rd, W14 9NU ☎020 7381 2322, ⓦ222veggievegan.com; ⊖West Kensington; map pp.252–253. It may be a mouthful, but the name says it all – this is a homely vegan place, and it attracts carnivores too for its fresh flavours and excellent prices (the lunchtime buffet is a snip at £7.50). Dinner mains – oyster mushroom and spinach raclette, perhaps, or pumpkin and courgette noodles with grated coconut – from £9. Daily noon–3.30pm & 5.30–10.30pm.

Capote y Toros 157 Old Brompton Rd, SW5 0LJ ☎020 7373 0567, ⓦcambiodetercio.co.uk; ⊖Gloucester Road or South Kensington; map pp.252–253. The emphasis at this authentic tapas bar is on Spain's sherries, with more than forty available by the glass, along with interesting modern tapas (£4.50–12). Nightly flamenco guitar. Tues–Sat 6–11.30pm.

The Troubadour 263–267 Old Brompton Rd, SW5 9JA ☎020 7341 6333, ⓦtroubadour.co.uk; ⊖Earl's Court; map pp.252–253. A classic 1950s folk bar, this quirky, cluttered boho café/club is a nostalgic slice of London history, having hosted the likes of Hendrix, Bob Dylan and Joni Mitchell. It still offers nightly folk and blues, and dishes up bistro classics, burgers, pasta and great breakfasts. Check out the pretty back garden. Daily 9am–midnight.

RESTAURANTS

Amaya Halkin Arcade, Motcomb St, SW1X 8JT ☎020 7823 1166, ⓦwww.amaya.biz; ⊖Knightsbridge; map pp.252–253. The creative contemporary Indian food served in this smart dining room – delicate, finely flavoured grills, prepared in front of you in the open kitchen – well deserves its Michelin star. Dishes, served as sharing plates, change regularly and cost from £12, with lunch menus at £24/£29. Mon–Sat 12.30–2.15pm & 6.30–11.30pm, Sun 12.45–2.45pm & 6.30–10.30pm.

Dinner Mandarin Oriental Hotel, 66 Knightsbridge, SW1X 7LA ☎020 7201 3833, ⓦdinnerbyheston.com; ⊖Knightsbridge; map pp.252–253. You know what to expect from Heston – imaginative, witty food that gives you a once-in-a-lifetime experience. That said, Blumenthal doesn't actually cook in this swish restaurant – the head chef worked with him at the *Fat Duck* – and there is less emphasis on flashy molecular cuisine. Instead, dishes are taken from British culinary history right through from medieval times, and some are marvellously odd – salamagundy, "meat fruit", frumenty. The sky's the limit as far as costs go, but there's a three-course weekday lunch menu for £38, and the atmosphere is gratifyingly unintimidating. Mains £28–42. Daily noon–2.30pm & 6.30–10.30pm.

CHELSEA

CAFÉS

Bibendum Oyster Bar 81 Fulham Rd, SW3 6RD ☎020 7589 1480, ⓦbibendum.co.uk; ⊖South Kensington; map p.267. If you can't afford a meal at the beautiful, buzzy *Bibendum* restaurant, occupying the old Art Deco Michelin headquarters and attached to the Conran Shop, head instead to its oyster bar – equally pretty but less formal – for a glass of wine and a light meal (from around £6). Mon–Fri 8am–11pm, Sat 9am–11pm, Sun noon–11pm.

RESTAURANTS

★Hunan 51 Pimlico Rd, SW1W 8NE ☎020 7730 5712, ⓦhunanlondon.com; ⊖Sloane Square; map p.267. Don't go too much by its name – rather than Hunanese cuisine, this classy restaurant serves creative Taiwanese/Chinese fusion food. There's no menu: tell them how spicy you like things, and any other preferences, and they'll bring you an array of delicious small dishes that they select. Reservations essential.

Lunch £38.80, dinner £58.80. Mon–Sat 12.30–2pm & 6.30–11pm.

Masala Grill 535 King's Rd, SW10 0SZ ☎020 7351 7788, ⓦmasalagrill.co; ⊖Fulham Broadway; map pp.252–253. Beautiful Indian restaurant offering delicious gourmet grills, street food and seafood – complicated, subtle dishes with modern twists – plus curries at surprisingly reasonable prices. Mains £15–20; Sun buffet £26. Mon–Fri 6.30–11.15pm, Sat 6.30–10.30pm, Sun 12.30–3pm & 6.30–11.15pm.

Medlar 438 Kings Rd, SW10 0LJ ☎020 7349 1900, ⓦmedlarrestaurant.co.uk; ⊖Fulham Broadway; map p.267. Really good, French-influenced Modern British food with deceptively simple dishes, the like of duck egg tart with red wine sauce or Anjou pigeon with mint and coriander pesto, served in a relaxed, welcoming dining room. It's *prix fixe*, and excellent value: three-course lunch £28 Mon–Fri, £30 Sat, £35 Sun, three-course dinner £46 (£35 on Sun). Daily noon–3pm & 6.30–10.30pm.

HIGH STREET KENSINGTON TO NOTTING HILL

CAFÉS

★Books for Cooks 4 Blenheim Crescent, W11 1NN ☎020 7221 1992, ⓦwww.booksforcooks.com; ⊖Ladbroke Grove; map pp.276–277. Cute dining area inside London's top cookery bookshop (see p.429). Conditions are cosy, to say the least, but it's a great little find. Get there early to grab a seat for the three-course set lunch (£7), which tests out recipes from one of the books in the store. Tues–Sat 10am–6pm; food served noon–1.30pm.

Daylesford 208–212 Westbourne Grove, W11 2RH ☎020 7313 8050, ⊛daylesford.com; ⊖Notting Hill Gate; map pp.276–277. This light, airy, farm shop/deli dishes up organic breakfasts, brunches and cakes made with fresh produce grown and reared on their own Gloucestershire farm. It's all rather slick, and prices mount up (scrambled eggs on toast £7, quiche and salad £12.50), reflecting its provenance and its Notting Hill location. Two more branches in Marylebone and Pimlico. Mon 8am–7pm, Tues–Sat 8am–9.30pm, Sun 10am–4pm.

Lisboa Patisserie 57 Golborne Rd, W10 5NR ☎020 8968 5242; ⊖Ladbroke Grove; map pp.276–277. Authentic Portuguese *pastelaria*, a perfect Portobello Rd pit-stop, with coffee, croissants and the best *pasteis de nata* (custard tarts) this side of Lisbon. *Café O'Porto* at 62a Golborne Rd is a good fall-back if this is full. Daily 7.30am–7.30pm.

RESTAURANTS

Hereford Road 3 Hereford Rd, W2 4AB ☎020 7727 1144, ⊛herefordroad.org; ⊖Queensway or Notting Hill Gate; map pp.276–277. The contemporary dining room, with bustling open kitchen, is a smart setting for the accomplished English cooking from St John alumnus Tom Pemberton. You'll find the same emphasis on simple, old-fashioned excellence – ham hock with white cabbage and chervil, devilled lamb's kidneys, and the like; the set meals are an astonishing bargain. Mains £11.50–24. Two-/three-course weekday lunch menu £13.50/£15.50, or an "express lunch" for £9.50. Mon–Sat noon–3pm & 6–10.30pm, Sun noon–4pm & 6–10pm.

★**The Ledbury** 127 Ledbury Rd, W11 2AQ ☎020 7792 9090, ⊛theledbury.com; ⊖Westbourne Park; map pp.276–277. Australian Brett Graham has scooped two Michelin stars for his French-inspired food – elegant, confident, a bit nouvelle and packed with flavour. Typical dishes include aged pigeon with beetroot, cherries, red leaves and pickled wild rose. Four-course menus (lunch £50 or £85, dinner £95), with tasting menus only for Fri–Sun dinner (£105/£115). Mon 6.30–9.45pm, Tues–Sat noon–2pm & 6.30–9.45pm, Sun noon–2.30pm & 6.45–9.45pm.

Mandalay 444 Edgware Rd, W2 1EG ☎020 7258 3696, ⊛mandalayway.com; ⊖Edgware Road; map pp.276–277. Authentic Burmese cuisine – a melange of Thai, Malaysian, a bit of Chinese and a lot of Indian. Portions are huge, the service friendly and the prices low. Mains £6–9. Mon–Sat noon–2.30pm & 6–10.30pm.

★**Nama** 110 Talbot Rd, W11 1JR ☎020 7313 4638, ⊛namafoods.com; ⊖Westbourne Park; map pp.276–277. An unusual spot, offering creative raw veggie food, mainly organic, ranging from walnut pancakes with banana ice cream for breakfast to zucchini spaghetti with celeriac and white wine sauce for supper. Lots of juices, smoothies and infusions, of course, with prosecco and a couple of wines to boot. Mains around £13. Mon–Wed 9am–5pm, Thurs & Fri 9am–10pm, Sat 10am–10pm, Sun 10am–6pm.

Pearl Liang 8 Sheldon Square, W2 6EZ ☎020 7289 7000, ⊛pearlliang.co.uk; ⊖Paddington; map pp.276–277. The setting, in a soulless development near Paddington station, is unpromising, but it's worth the trek to this upmarket Cantonese/Szechuan spot for extremely good dim sum (around £3.50 at lunch, £5 in the evening) – try the wasabi prawn dumplings. Dim sum; takeaway available. Daily noon–11pm.

Wormwood 16 All Saints Rd, W11 1HH ☎020 7854 1808, ⊛wormwoodrestaurant.com; ⊖Ladbroke Grove; map pp.276-277. Innovative Mediterranean-Middle Eastern-North African-French fusion, with flavour-packed dishes – piglet belly with apple and potato puree and ras el-hanout; squid croquettes with confit garlic; lobster couscous – served in beautifully presented meze portions (around £11–21). The £35 lunch menu (Tues–Sat) is superb value. Mon 6–9.30pm, Tues & Wed noon–2pm & 6–9.30pm Thurs–Sat noon–2pm & 6–10pm.

23

CAMDEN TOWN

CAFÉS

★**My Village** 37 Chalk Farm Rd, NW1 8AJ ☎020 3489 2293, ⊛myvillagecafebar.co.uk; ⊖Chalk Farm; map pp.284–285. There aren't many places like this left in London nowadays: a funky, ramshackle café whose bare-brick walls, handpainted glass, battered furniture, books, games and fairy lights welcome you in to hang out for hours. Stop for a coffee, fresh juice or a glass of wine, or tuck into the veggie and vegan Middle Eastern food – you'll get a heaped plate for £8. Mon–Fri 9am–9pm, Sat & Sun 10.30am–9pm.

RESTAURANTS

★**El Parador** 245 Eversholt St, NW1 1BA ☎020 7387 2789, ⊛elparadorlondon.com; ⊖Mornington Crescent; map pp.284–285. Though there's little fuss here, the tapas (£4.60–8.70), served in a small, simple dining room with a friendly neighbourhood buzz, are some of London's best. The veggie selection is particularly good – try the roast beet and puy lentil salad or the chargrilled broccoli with chilli and garlic. Mon–Thurs noon–3pm & 6–11pm, Fri noon–3pm & 6–11.30pm, Sat 6–11.30pm, Sun 6.30–9.30pm.

23

Manna 4 Erskine Rd, NW3 3AJ ☎020 7722 8028, ⓦmannav.com; ⊖Chalk Farm; map pp.284–285. Smart veggie restaurant, full of Primrose Hill yoga types, serving mostly organic food, much of it vegan, from around the world. Mains £12–22. Tues–Fri noon–3pm & 6.30–10pm, Sat noon–3pm & 6–10pm, Sun noon–8.30pm.

Namaaste Kitchen 64 Parkway, NW1 7AH ☎020 7485 5977, ⓦnamaastekitchen.co.uk; ⊖Camden Town;

map pp.284–285. The modern Pakistani and Indian food in this contemporary restaurant – cooked with flair in an open kitchen – well deserves its many accolades. Some dishes are deliciously unfamiliar, and even the more familiar options, like chicken tikka, are given a fresh twist, with coriander, lime and asparagus. Mains £12–23; thalis from £7.50; one-/two-/three-course lunch menus £8/£10/£12.50. Takeaway available. Mon–Thurs noon–2.30pm & 5.30–11.30pm, Fri–Sun noon–11.30pm.

ISLINGTON

CAFÉS

Afghan Kitchen 35 Islington Green, N1 8DU ☎020 7359 8019; ⊖Angel; map pp.284–285. Unadorned, simple and sleek café with bare bench seating, featuring a short menu of tasty spiced stews (try the chicken with yoghurt), dished up with hot, fresh bread. Tues–Sat noon–3.30pm & 5.30–11pm.

Breakfast Club 31 Camden Passage, N1 8EA ☎020 7226 5454, ⓦthebreakfastclubcafes.com; ⊖Angel; map pp.284–285. With its dog-eared, retro decor, this youthful place is a fun spot to linger over big all-day breakfasts and brunches (from £6 for a posh sausage sarnie) and to pop into for burgers, burritos and the like as the day progresses. Other branches around town. Sun–Wed 8am–10pm, Thurs–Sat 8am–11pm.

M. Manze 74 Chapel Market, N1 9ER ☎020 7837 5270; ⊖Angel; map pp.284–285. With its gleaming tiled walls, marble tables, wooden booths and unchanging menu, this traditional, friendly eel, pie and mash shop offers a uniquely nostalgic experience (not least in the prices – pie and mash costs around £6). Mon 11am–3pm, Tues–Sat 11am–5pm, Sun 10.30am–4pm.

RESTAURANTS

Gem 265 Upper St, N1 2UQ ☎020 7359 0405, ⓦgemrestaurant.org.uk; ⊖Highbury & Islington; map pp.284–285. This welcoming Turkish and Kurdish restaurant specializes in charcoal-grilled dishes, but ordering a selection of meze (from £3.75) will get you a good, inexpensive meal. Mop it all up with the smoky

Turkish bread that's baked on site. Mon–Thurs noon–11pm, Fri & Sat noon–midnight, Sun noon–10.30pm.

★**Oldroyd** 344 Upper St, N1 0PD ☎020 8617 9010, ⓦoldroydlondon.com; ⊖Angel; map p.284–285. Cosy up with a lively crowd of locals in this tiny, effortlessly stylish little spot, and enjoy phenomenal northern Italian/Mediterranean/Modern European food from a *Polpo* (see p.372) alumnus. It's supposedly sharing-plate style, but portions are huge and prices low – £9 for a heaped plate of crab tagliarini; £11 for the signature squid, confit rabbit and broad bean paella; £3 for a bucket of zucchini fries. A real winner. Mon–Thurs noon–11pm, Fri noon–midnight, Sat 10am–midnight, Sun 10am–10pm.

Ottolenghi 287 Upper St, N1 2TZ ☎020 7288 1454, ⓦottolenghi.co.uk; ⊖Highbury & Islington; map pp.284–285. Yotam Ottolenghi's vibrant Mediterranean food was a game-changer on London's dining scene, and this café/restaurant, with long communal tables, is a buzzy spot to enjoy his trademark imaginative salads (three for around £12), fusion-tinged mains (from £12) and fantastic desserts. Mon–Sat 8am–10.30pm, Sun 9am–7pm.

Trullo 300 St Paul's Rd, N1 2LH ☎020 7226 2733, ⓦtrullorestaurant.com; ⊖Highbury & Islington; map pp.284–285. Traffic-choked Highbury Corner is an unexpected spot for this upscale little restaurant, offering relaxed, warm elegance and simple, seasonal contemporary Italian food. Mains from £14. Mon–Sat 12.30–2.45pm & 6–10.15pm, Sun 12.30–3pm.

HAMPSTEAD AND HIGHGATE

CAFÉS

Brew House Kenwood House, Hampstead Lane, NW3 7JR ☎020 8348 4073, ⓦsearcys.co.uk; ⊖Highgate; map pp.296–297. This park café, in the servants' wing of the Robert Adam mansion, is recommended more for its surroundings than its food, though the simple soups, sausages and cakes are fine. Lots of seating in the sunny garden courtyard. Daily: Feb, March, Oct & Nov 9am–5pm; April–Sept 9am–6pm; Dec & Jan 9am–4pm.

Lauderdale House Waterlow Park, Highgate Hill, N6 5HG ☎020 8341 4807, ⓦlauderdalehouse.org.

uk; ⊖Archway; map pp.296–297. Fill up on home-made comfort food in this relaxed arts centre café, or simply enjoy a cuppa and a slab of cake. On sunny days the terrace, overlooking the park, is a great spot. Daily 8am–6pm.

Louis Patisserie 32 Heath St, NW3 6TE ☎020 7435 9908; ⊖Hampstead; map pp.296–297. Coffee house trends may come and go, but for more than fifty years now this tiny, understated and gloriously old-fashioned Hungarian tearoom/patisserie has been serving sticky cakes, tea and coffee to a mixed local crowd. Daily 9am–6pm.

RESTAURANTS

★**Jin Kichi** 73 Heath St, NW3 6UG ☎ 020 7794 6158, ⓦjinkichi.com; ⊖ Hampstead; map pp.296–297. Book ahead for this tiny, homely and busy neighbourhood Japanese diner, which specializes in charcoal-grilled *yakitori* (skewers). The sushi, noodles and other Japanese staples are great, too. Dishes from £4. Tues–Sat 12.30–2.10pm & 6–11pm, Sun 12.30–2.10pm & 6–10pm.

SOUTH LONDON

CAFÉS

Franco Manca 4 Market Row, SW9 8LD ☎ 020 7738 3021, ⓦfrancomanca.co.uk; ⊖ Brixton; map pp.308–309. This tiny gourmet pizza joint in Brixton Market may have spawned more than a dozen branches around town, but here at the original site they continue to turn out delicious, inexpensive sourdough pizzas (£4.50–7) – there are just six options, all wood-fired and made with the finest ingredients – to a loyal local crowd. Takeaway available. Mon noon–5pm, Tues–Sat noon–11pm, Sun noon–10.30pm.

Okan Unit 39, Brixton Village SW9 8PR ⓦokanbrixtonvillage.com; ⊖ Brixton; map pp.308–309. A tiny, unpretentious star dishing up authentic Osaka street food – yakisoba noodles, a few sides, and the sizzling *okonomiyaki* pancakes, topped with anything from *mochi* (sticky rice) and cheese to prawn, squid, kimchi and sweetcorn. Japanese teas, beers and wines, too. Mains from £7.50. Tues–Sun noon–11pm.

Pop Brixton 53 Brixton Station Rd, SW9 8PQ ⓦpopbrixton.org; ⊖ Brixton; map pp.308–309. The agglomeration of shipping containers that makes up this community hub is the latest addition to the neighbourhood's ever-expanding foodie scene, with scores of choices for inexpensive takeaway street food and a few sit-down dining spaces – try *Zoe's Ghana Kitchen* for tasty home-cooked specialities. Opening hours vary.

RESTAURANTS

Begging Bowl 168 Bellenden Rd, SE15 4BW ☎ 020 7635 2627, ⓦthebeggingbowl.co.uk; ⊖⇌Peckham Rye; map pp.308–309. Peckham is scooping up foodie accolades left, right and centre, and this lively little restaurant leads the way with its authentic Thai street food. These are exciting, often unfamiliar dishes – hot and sour soup of smoked trout and sorrel, perhaps, or a green curry of rabbit. Mains from £5.25. No reservations. Mon–Sat noon–2.30pm & 6–10pm, Sun noon–3pm & 6–9.30pm.

The Dairy 15 The Pavement, SW4 0HY ☎ 0207 622 4165, ⓦthe-dairy.co.uk; ⊖ Clapham Common; map pp.308–309. It's all about local, seasonal produce nowadays, and at this good-looking Clapham restaurant they really do it right. Short, simple menus list irresistible sharing plates, from Jerusalem artichoke with aged Comte and onion treacle to lamb with smoked aubergine and miso. Four-course lunch Wed–Fri £25; tasting menu £45. The same people run the equally terrific *Manor*, nearby, a modern haute cuisine dining experience. Tues 6–10pm, Wed–Sat noon–3pm & 6–10pm, Sun noon–4pm.

Old Brewery Pepys Building, The Old Royal Naval College, SE10 9LW ☎ 020 3327 1280, ⓦoldbrewerygreenwich.com; ⊖ Cutty Sark DLR; map p.313. The daytime café of the Meantime microbrewery, all bare brick and gleaming copper vats, serves bar snacks and gastropub lunches and tea and cakes before transforming with aplomb into a Modern British restaurant at night. Snacks from £6.50; mains from £13. Mon–Thurs 10am–9.30pm, Fri & Sat 10am–10pm, Sun 10am–9pm; bar snacks only 5–6pm.

HAMMERSMITH, KEW AND RICHMOND

CAFÉS

Hollyhock Terrace Gardens, Petersham Rd, TW10 6UX ☎ 020 8948 6555; ⊖ Richmond; map p.340. This laidback fairtrade veggie café, hidden away in Richmond's flower-filled Terrace Gardens, is a wonderful find – perfect for light lunches or coffee and cakes on the terrace overlooking the gardens and the river. Daily 9am–5pm or later in sunny weather and at weekends.

Stein's Richmond Towpath, Richmond, TW10 6UT ☎ 020 8948 8189, ⓦstein-s.com; ⊖ Richmond; map p.340. A Bavarian-style riverside beer garden, serving wurst, wiener, schnitzel and sauerkraut washed down with *echt* beers and strudel to finish. Outdoor seating only; it's likely to be closed in bad weather. Summer daily noon–10pm; rest of year Sat & Sun noon–dusk.

RESTAURANTS

Chez Lindsay 11 Hill Rise, Richmond, TW10 6UQ ☎ 020 8948 7473, ⓦchezlindsay.co.uk; ⊖ Richmond; map p.340. Small, bright, riverside Breton restaurant, with a loyal local following. There's a wide choice of galettes, crêpes and more formal French main courses including steak frites or moules. Galettes from £5, mains £12–23. Mon–Sat noon–11pm, Sun noon–10pm.

The Gate 51 Queen Caroline St, W6 9QL ☎ 020 8748 6932, ⓦthegaterestaurants.com; ⊖ Hammersmith; map p.329. In a converted church with a courtyard, *The Gate* has been serving excellent and original vegetarian and vegan dishes – largely Arabic/Mediterranean but with many global influences – for around 25 years, offering intense and satisfying tastes. Mains around £13. Branch in Islington. Mon–Fri noon–2.30pm (till 3pm Sat, 7pm Sun) & 6–10.30pm.

23

THE GRAPES, DOCKLANDS

Pubs and bars

London is a great drinking city, offering an extraordinary range of venues. And with its handsome Victorian gin palaces and creaking riverside taverns, just stepping inside one is often a treat – never mind the alcoholic concoctions on offer. Charming, historic pubs can be found all over the city, often in the backstreets, while many of the capital's best bars – serving everything from fine wine, artisan gin and craft beers to cocktails that test the boundaries of mixology – are clustered around buzzy nightlife zones like Soho and Shoreditch. Wherever you drink, decent (often excellent) food – from Modern British to knowingly "dirty" US-style finger-lickers – is now the rule rather than the exception. Indeed, the term "gastropub", coined for those pioneering pubs that made eating as important as drinking, has become almost old hat in London.

Most pubs serve at least three **real ales** and often a few **craft** options these days too (see box, p.388), as well as the usual array of drinks. We've also reviewed some of the capital's bars, which go in and out of fashion with incredible speed. Note that, while food standards in pubs and bars are generally high, there are still those places where food will be slammed straight from freezer to oven (a quick glance at the care taken over the menu should tell you all you need to know) and others where the food is so centre-stage that drinkers might not feel as welcome as they would like to. Be aware too that food is often not served all day long and that Sunday roasts – perennially popular – can run out before the end of the stated serving time. London also boasts numerous pubs that are primarily live music venues (see p.400), and gay and lesbian pubs and bars (see p.407). Prices can be steep, with the £4 pint common, though once you're into craft ale territory, anything goes. A good cocktail, meanwhile, will set you back at least £8. However, prices drop a little out of the centre, while many bars run weekday happy hours, usually 5–7pm, when drinks are usually half-price.

WHITEHALL, WESTMINSTER AND ST JAMES'S

The Chandos 29 St Martin's Lane, WC2N 4ER ☎ 020 7836 1401; ⊖ Charing Cross; map, p.46. If you can get one of the booths downstairs, or the leather sofas upstairs in the more relaxed Opera Room Bar, you'll find it difficult to leave this well-worn Sam Smith's pub. Mon–Sat 11am–11pm, Sun noon–10.30pm.

The Red Lion 23 Crown Passage, SW1Y 6PP ☎ 020 7930 4141; ⊖ Green Park; map p.67. Hidden away in a passageway off Pall Mall, this pub is a warm and cosy local with super-friendly bar staff, well-kept beer and good

sandwiches. Mon–Sat 11.30am–11pm.

St Stephen's Tavern 10 Bridge St, SW1A 2JR ☎ 020 7925 2286, ⓦ ststephenstavern.co.uk; ⊖ Westminster; map p.46. Opulent Victorian pub opposite the Houses of Parliament and wall to wall with civil servants and MPs (the so-called "Division Bell" sounds when the latter have to go and vote). Good real ales, plus fish and chips and pies. Mon–Thurs & Sat 10am–11.30pm, Fri 10am–midnight, Sun noon–10.30pm.

MAYFAIR

The Windmill 6–8 Mill St, W1S 2AZ ☎ 020 7491 8050, ⓦ windmillmayfair.co.uk; ⊖ Oxford Circus; map p.78. Convivial pub just off Regent St, and a perfect retreat for exhausted shoppers. The Young's beers are top-notch, as are the traditional pies, which have won numerous awards. Mon–Fri 11am–11pm, Sat noon–4.30pm.

Ye Grapes 16 Shepherd Market, W1J 7QQ ☎ 020 7493 4216; ⊖ Green Park or Hyde Park Corner; map p.78. Sited in Shepherd Market, a charming corner of Mayfair hidden away to the north of Piccadilly, it's the location that really makes this pub. If the *Grapes* is too busy, try the *King's Arms*, also in Shepherd Market. Mon–Sat noon–11pm, Sun noon–10pm.

MARYLEBONE

The Golden Eagle 59 Marylebone Lane, W1U 2NY ☎ 020 7935 3228; ⊖ Bond Street; map p.89. Proper old one-room, neighbourhood pub – a delight in this swanky area – with a good range of real ales, and regular singalongs on the old Joanna (piano). Mon–Sat 11am–11pm, Sun noon–7pm.

The Gunmakers 33 Aybrook St, W1U 4AP ☎ 020 7487 4937; ⊖ Bond Street; map p.89. Tucked away to the west of Marylebone's high street, this place is all wood panelling, Churchill memorabilia and an awful lot of framed bullets. Decent range of ales (including a few crafts) while food is very much in the pub grub vein. Mon–Sat 11am–midnight, Sun 11am–10.30pm.

SOHO

The Blue Posts 28 Rupert St, W1B 5PX ☎ 020 7437 1415; ⊖ Leicester Square; map p.101. This is our favourite of the area's numerous (unconnected) *Blue Posts*, a raffish, shabby and convivial bolthole on Soho's less trendy fringes, with live jazz on Sundays. Mon–Thurs 11am–11.30pm, Fri & Sat 11am–midnight, Sun noon–10.30pm.

The Dog & Duck 18 Bateman St, W1D 3AJ ☎ 020 7494 0697; ⊖ Tottenham Court Road; map p.101. Tiny

Nicholson's pub that retains much of its old character, beautiful Victorian tiling and mosaics, a good range of real ales and a loyal clientele. If it gets too busy downstairs, head upstairs to the George Orwell Bar (he used to drink here). Daily 10am–11pm.

★**The French House** 49 Dean St, W1D 5BG ☎ 020 7437 2799, ⓦ frenchhousesoho.com; ⊖ Leicester Square; map p.101. This cosy French pub has been a boho

24

Soho institution since Belgian Victor Berlemont bought the place shortly before World War I. Free French and literary associations galore, and half-pints, bottled beers, wine and champagne only at the bar (no real ale). Strictly no music, no televisions and no mobile phones. Mon–Sat noon–11pm, Sun noon–10.30pm.

The Lyric 37 Great Windmill St, W1D 7LT ☎020 7434 0604, ⓦlyricsoho.co.uk; ⊖Piccadilly Circus; map p.101. The venue-size to beer-range ratio is quite remarkable here, with a very impressive rota of craft and real ales for such a dinky pub. It is otherwise traditional, buzzy (and often very busy), absolutely plastered with beer mats like badges of honour. Mon–Thurs noon–11.30pm, Fri 11am–midnight, Sat noon–midnight, Sun noon–10.30pm.

Phoenix Artist Club 1 Phoenix St, WC2H 8BU ☎020 7836 1077, ⓦphoenixartistclub.com; ⊖Leicester Square; map p.101. This members' bar, tucked away beneath a theatre, has been hosting high-spirited ne'er-do-wells since way before London's Prohibition/members' club scene became trendy. And trendy this place is not – it's a high-spirited dive, with theatrical types of all stripes making merry. Non-members need to arrive before 8pm. Mon–Sat 5pm–2.30am, Sun 5pm–1am (roughly).

Two Floors 3 Kingly St, W1B 5PD ☎0207 439 1007, ⓦtwofloors.com; ⊖Oxford Circus or Piccadilly Circus; map p.97. An unlikely combo: craft ales-and-cocktails in the pubby street-level bar (well-worn wooden tables and fun illustrations on the walls), and dimly lit tiki bar in the basement – yet this place pulls it off with aplomb. Mon–Thurs noon–11.30pm, Fri & Sat noon–midnight, Sun noon–10.30pm.

FITZROVIA

Bourne & Hollingsworth 28 Rathbone Place, W1T 1JF ☎020 7636 8228, ⓦbourneandhollingsworth .com; ⊖Goodge Street; map p.97. One of the first, and still one of the best, of London's Prohibition-style vintage cocktail bars, offering creative gin cocktails and punches served in jars, tin mugs and tea cups, in a delicately shabby subterranean granny's parlour. Mon–Wed 5pm–1am, Thurs–Sat 5pm–1.30am.

Bradley's Spanish Bar 42–44 Hanway St, W1T 1UT ☎020 7636 0359; ⊖Tottenham Court Road; map p.97. Appealingly unpretentious backstreet bar with a mixed, merry clientele, a variety of Spanish beers and an excellent vinyl jukebox. When the doors close the diehards tumble out into *Sevilla Mia*, another tiny, shabby and good fun Spanish bar a couple of doors down (opens late; closed Sun). Mon–Thurs noon–11.30pm, Fri & Sat noon–midnight, Sun 3–10.30pm.

Draft House Charlotte 43 Goodge St, W1 1TA ☎0207 323 9361, ⓦdrafthouse.co.uk; ⊖Goodge Street; map p.97. This tiny craft ale-centric place is rowdy with

---

THE CAPITALE CITY

The **Campaign for Real Ale** (CAMRA; ⓦcamra.org.uk) got the ball rolling in the 1970s – and to look at the London beer scene today, you might think their work is done. As with almost everything comestible in the capital, standards are as high as they've ever been, and the selection dizzying (literally), with just about every pub, bar and restaurant now offering beers – by keg, cask (often still reasonably priced) and interestingly labelled bottle – from small (or smallish) **independent breweries** that work traditionally and with artisanal passion. The city's taste for craft ale is such that there's even a number of small chains that focus on the stuff: BrewDog (see p.396) has four bars in London, Craft Beer Co. (ⓦthecraftbeerco.com) has five and Draft House (see p.388) has eight. If you find one seemingly independent pub where you like the selection, it's worth asking if they have any **sister pubs** (they often do, and we've mentioned a handful of such relationships in this chapter), while a feature of the pubs run by the Antic group (ⓦanticlondon.com) is its focus on craft ale (as well as often unusual premises, such as a former "job centre" in Deptford). If you really want to get the lowdown, consider downloading the "Craft Beer London" app for your smartphone.

One way of experiencing some of the capital's finest **craft breweries** is to hit the popular **Bermondsey Beer Mile** (see p.236), which takes place on Saturdays. Many people start in the morning (check the brewery websites for their opening times), with the full, Dionysian experience taking in some eight venues, many housed in railway arches. Below are some more recommended London brewers that you can visit and/or take a guided tour – and liberally sample while you're at it.

Beavertown (Tottenham; affiliated venue Dukes Brew and Que in De Beauvoir; ⓦbeavertownbrewery.co.uk)

Camden Town Brewery (Kentish Town; ⓦcamdentownbrewery.com)

Hammertown (Islington; ⓦhammertonbrewery.co.uk)

London Fields Brewery (London Fields; ⓦlondonfieldsbrewery.co.uk)

Meantime (Greenwich; ⓦmeantimebrewing.com)

Sambrooks (Battersea; ⓦsambrooksbrewery.co.uk)

rock'n'roll and roistering drinkers. Food is of the slightly ironic snack variety, from foot-long scratchings to jerky, as befits a pub with a fine line in American Pale Ales. Mon–Thurs & Sat noon–11pm, Fri noon–midnight.

The Green Man 36 Riding House St, W1W 7EP ☎ 020 7580 9087, ⓦ thegreenmanw1.co.uk; ⊖ Oxford Circus; map p.97. Slightly more offbeat than most pubs this close to Oxford and Regent streets, *The Green Man* is a real find, with an excellent range of craft beers, ciders and cask ales.

Mon–Sat noon–11pm, Sun noon–10.30pm.

★ **The Newman Arms** 23 Rathbone St, W1T 1NG ⓦ newmanarmspub.com; ⊖ Tottenham Court Road or Goodge Street; map p.97. Changed hands in recent times and gone down a distinctly craft ale route, with excellent, sustainable food by the Cornwall Project (ⓦ thecornwallproject.co.uk). You might actually feel like you're in an old Cornish smuggling inn, what with the pub's dark slate floor and cottage-style windows. Mon–Sat noon–11pm.

COVENT GARDEN AND THE STRAND

The 10 Cases 16 Endell St, WC2H 9BD ☎ 020 7836 6801, ⓦ 10cases.co.uk; ⊖ Covent Garden; map p.108. A vibrant, classy (and quite pricey) little spot for wine and tapas, cheese and charcuterie. The wine selection changes regularly (they only keep ten cases on site at any one time). Mon–Thurs noon–3pm & 6–11pm, Fri & Sat noon–11pm.

The Cross Keys 31 Endell St, WC2H 9BA ☎ 020 7836 5185, ⓦ crosskeyscoventgarden.com; ⊖ Covent Garden; map p.108. You'll do well to find a seat in this Covent Garden favourite, which is stuffed with copper pots, brass instruments, paintings and memorabilia. Mon–Sat 11am–11pm, Sun noon–10.30pm.

Gordon's 47 Villiers St, WC2N 6NE ☎ 020 7930 1408, ⓦ gordonswinebar.com; ⊖ Charing Cross or Embankment; map p.108. Cavernous, shabby, darkly atmospheric old wine bar, open since 1890 and specializing in ports, sherries and Madeiras. The wine's hit and miss but *Gordon's* is perennially popular. Good food, too, especially the cheese platters. Mon–Sat 11am–11pm, Sun noon–10pm.

★ **The Harp** 47 Chandos Place, WC2N 4HS ☎ 020 7836 0291, ⓦ harpcoventgarden.com; ⊖ Leicester Square; map p.108. You'll get excellent and unusual real ales and ciders at this brilliant little pub. The tiny bar

is invariably packed; there's more room in the comfortably battered upstairs. Mon–Sat 10am–11pm, Sun noon–10.30pm.

The Lamb & Flag 33 Rose St, WC2E 9EB ☎ 020 7497 9504, ⓦ lambandflagcoventgarden.co.uk; ⊖ Leicester Square; map p.108. More than three hundred years old, this agreeably tatty Fuller's pub, tucked down an alley between Garrick and Floral streets – where John Dryden was attacked in 1679 (see p.110) – is perennially popular. Mon–Sat 11am–11pm, Sun noon–10.30pm.

★ **The Princess Louise** 208 High Holborn, WC1V 7EP ☎ 020 7405 8816, ⓦ princesslouisepub.co.uk; ⊖ Holborn; map p.108. This Sam Smith's pub features six rooms of gold-trimmed mirrors, gorgeous mosaics and fine moulded ceilings – even the toilets are listed. Mon–Fri 11.30am–11pm, Sat noon–11pm, Sun noon–10pm.

The Salisbury 90 St Martin's Lane, WC2N 4AP ☎ 020 7836 5863; ⊖ Leicester Square; map p.108. This Taylor Walker's pub is one of the capital's most beautifully preserved Victorian taverns, with etched and engraved windows, bronze figures and Art Nouveau light fittings. Mon–Thurs 11am–11pm, Fri 11am–midnight, Sat noon–midnight, Sun noon–10.30pm.

BLOOMSBURY

The Duke 7 Roger St, WC1N 2PB ☎ 020 7242 7230, ⓦ dukepub.co.uk; ⊖ Russell Square; map p.127. Lovely little neighbourhood pub with an unusual, unforced Art Deco flavour and lots of interwar design details. Its discreet location keeps the crowd in the small bar manageable; simple, good food, too. Mon–Sat noon–11pm.

★ **The Euston Tap** 190 Euston Rd, NW1 2EF ☎ 020 3137, ⓦ eustontap.com; ⊖ Euston; map p.127. Crammed into a tiny Victorian gatehouse outside the railway station, this is a sociable and high-spirited micropub for serious ale lovers. Regularly changing cask, keg and bottle beers and ciders and perries on tap. Daily noon–11.30pm.

The Gilbert Scott St Pancras International, Euston Rd, NW1 2AR ☎ 020 7278 3888, ⓦ thegilbertscott.co.uk/bar; ⊖ King's Cross; map p.127. There's no finer way to begin or end a Eurostar journey than with a glass of fizz in this opulent hotel bar. With its golden-hued decor and impeccable table service, it feels like you've stepped into some dreamy

bygone era – until you see the prices, which are very, very now. Mon–Fri 11am till late, Sat & Sun 10am till late.

The Holborn Whippet 25–29 Sicilian Ave, WC1A 2QH ☎ 020 3137 9937, ⓦ holbornwhippet.com; ⊖ Holborn; map p.127. A fantastic selection of real and craft ales pulled from taps that poke out of what looks like a brick chimney. The small-ish space's clean, pared-back decor makes a nice change from the more old-fashioned sort of pub, while the big, curved windows make for good people-watching at this busy corner. Mon–Sat noon–11.30pm, Sun noon–10.30pm.

The Lamb 94 Lamb's Conduit St, WC1N 3LZ ☎ 020 7405 0713; ⊖ Russell Square; map p.127. Well-preserved Victorian pub with mirrors, polished wood, leather banquettes and etched glass "snob" screens. Rather peaceful, as there's no music or TV. Mon–Wed noon–11pm, Thurs–Sat noon–midnight, Sun noon–10.30pm.

The Museum Tavern 49 Great Russell St, WC1B 3BA ☎ 020 7242 8987; ⊖ Tottenham Court Road or Russell

24

Square; map p.127. The erstwhile drinking hole of Karl Marx is a handsome, quite touristy, old pub opposite the main entrance to the British Museum. A range of ales and British spirits available. Mon–Thurs 11am–11.30pm, Fri & Sat 11am–midnight, Sun 10am–10pm.

The Queen's Head 66 Acton St, WC1X 9NB ☎ 020 7713 5772, ⓦ queensheadlondon.com ⊖ King's Cross; map

p.127. Attractive and laidback Victorian local, modernized but not to within an inch of its life, offering cheese, chunky pies and charcuterie alongside craft beers and ciders. Occasional live jazz and piano music. Has sister pubs in *Simon the Tanner* (see p.393) and *Mother Kelly's* (see p.392). Mon noon–11pm, Tues–Sat noon–midnight, Sun noon–11pm.

HOLBORN AND THE INNS OF COURT

The Old Bank of England 194 Fleet St, EC4A 2LT ☎ 020 7430 2255, ⓦ oldbankofengland.co.uk; ⊖ Temple or Chancery Lane; map p.140. Not the actual Bank of England, but in the Law Courts' branch, this imposing High Victorian banking hall is now an opulent Fuller's ale-and-pie pub. Unusually for this area, there's courtyard seating, too. Mon–Fri 11am–11pm.

★**The Seven Stars** 53–54 Carey St, WC2A 2JB ☎ 020 7242 8521; ⊖ Holborn; map p.140. This diminutive boozer dates from 1602 and oozes quirky charm – there's even a sleepy pub cat. It's a friendly spot, attracting a surprisingly mixed clientele. Real ales and home-made food. Mon–Fri 11am–11pm, Sat noon–11pm, Sun noon–10.30pm.

Temple Brew House 46 Essex St, WC2R 3JF ☎ 020 7936 2536, ⓦ templebrewhouse.com; ⊖ Temple; map p.140.

Hasn't quite grown into itself yet, and the enormous screens showing sport can be a little off-putting, but the beer's the real deal – which will be patently obvious from the moment you arrive, as you pass great brewing vats on the way down to a subterranean space of stripped wood, bare brick and industrial touches. Also does good grub, leaning towards American comfort food. Mon–Wed noon–11pm, Thurs noon–11.30pm, Fri & Sat noon–midnight, Sun noon–10.30pm.

Ye Olde Mitre 1 Ely Court, EC1N 6SJ ☎ 020 7405 4751, ⓦ yeoldemitreholburn.co.uk; ⊖ Farringdon; map p.140. Hidden down a tiny alleyway between Ely Place and Hatton Garden, this Fuller's pub dates back to 1546, although it was rebuilt in the eighteenth century. The low-ceilinged, wood-panelled rooms are packed with history and the real ales are excellent. Mon–Fri 11am–11pm.

CLERKENWELL

Café Kick 43 Exmouth Market, EC1R 4QL ☎ 020 7837 8077, ⓦ cafekick.co.uk; ⊖ Farringdon or Angel; map p.147. This chaotic, shabbily cool French-style café-bar is a great spot for a beer, usually accompanied by high-spirited table-football games. There's another branch (*Bar Kick*) at 127 Shoreditch High St. Mon–Thurs 11am–11pm, Fri & Sat 11am–midnight, Sun noon–10.30pm.

★**The Eagle** 159 Farringdon Rd, EC1R 3AL ☎ 020 7837 1353; ⊖ Farringdon; map p.147. The first (and still one of the best) of London's gastropubs, serving truly excellent Mediterranean food, prepared in a "kitchen" that's really just one strip of the space behind the bar – a very impressive operation. The beer selection is fairly limited. Mon–Sat noon–11pm, Sun noon–5pm.

The Exmouth Arms 23 Exmouth Market, EC1R 4QL ☎ 020 3551 4772, ⓦ exmoutharms.com; ⊖ Farringdon or Angel; map p.147. With its gorgeous exterior green tiling, from the outside this place looks every inch the classic, traditional London pub. Step inside though and all is light, fun and hip, with a young crowd and seemingly even younger staff. The range of beers is enormous, there's late opening at weekends and the table service-only cocktail bar upstairs is

good for escaping the crowds. Mon–Thurs 11am–midnight, Fri & Sat 11am–1.30am, Sun noon–11.30pm.

★**The Jerusalem Tavern** 55 Britton St, EC1M 5UQ ☎ 020 7490 4281; ⊖ Farringdon; map p.147. Tiny, converted Georgian coffee house – the frontage dates from 1810 – that has a raffish, sociable character. The excellent draught beers are from St Peter's Brewery in Suffolk (ⓦ stpetersbrewery.co.uk). Mon–Fri 11am–11pm.

The Slaughtered Lamb 34–35 Great Sutton St, EC1V 0DX ☎ 020 7253 1516, ⓦ theslaughteredlambpub.com; ⊖ Barbican or Farringdon; map p.147. Lots of live music and events downstairs, with gutsy pub grub served in the spacious upstairs room. Mon–Thurs 11.30am–midnight, Fri 11.30am–1am, Sat noon–1am, Sun 12.30–10.30pm.

★**The Three Kings** 7 Clerkenwell Close, EC1R 0DY ☎ 020 7253 0483; ⊖ Farringdon; map p.147. Unimprovable Clerkenwell favourite tucked away just north of Clerkenwell Green, with an eclectic interior, big windows and two small rooms upstairs perfect for lingering. Interesting craft beers and food, too. It's next to *The Crown*, which is also worth a trip. Mon–Fri noon–11pm, Sat 5.30–11pm.

THE CITY

The Black Friar 174 Queen Victoria St, EC4V 4EG ☎ 020 7236 5474; ⊖ Blackfriars; map pp.152–153. Quirky, relaxing place to drink, now a Nicholson's pub, with Art Nouveau marble friezes of boozy monks and a highly

decorated alcove – all original, dating from 1905. Mon–Thurs 10am–11.30pm, Fri & Sat 10am–midnight, Sun 10am–11pm.

Jamaica Wine House St Michael's Alley, EC3V 9DS

☎020 7929 6972, ⊕jamaicawinehouse.co.uk; ⊖Bank; map pp.152–153. The "Jam Pot", in a narrow alleyway on the site of London's first coffee house (1652), is an old City institution, now owned by Shepherd Neame. It's divided into four large "snugs" by original, high wood-panelled partitions. Mon–Fri 11am–11pm.

The Lamb Tavern/Old Tom's Bar 10–12 Leadenhall Market, EC3V 1LR ☎020 7626 2454, ⊕lambtavernleadenhall.com; ⊖Monument; map pp.152–153. In the middle of Leadenhall Market, this historic Young's pub offers almost exclusively standing room only (both inside and out) for a suited local crowd. The basement bar, *Old Tom's*, is a little more on-trend, serving London beers and artisan cheese and meat platters. Mon–Fri 11am–11pm.

The Viaduct Tavern 126 Newgate St, EC1A 7AA ☎020 7600 1863, ⊕viaducttavern.co.uk; ⊖St Paul's; map pp.152–153. A fuller's pub, on the site of an old jail across from the Old Bailey, with a glorious Victorian interior from 1869. Check out the amazing ceiling, the faded oils of comely women representing Commerce, Agriculture and the Arts, and the old cells in the basement. Mon–Fri 8.30am–11pm.

★**Ye Olde Cheshire Cheese** 145 Fleet St, EC4A 2BU ☎020 7353 6170; ⊖Temple or Blackfriars; map pp.152–153. A famous – chiefly because of its historic literary associations, with patrons including Dickens and Dr Johnson – seventeenth-century watering hole. Its dark-panelled bars and real fires make it a cosy maze, popular with tourists and locals alike. Mon–Fri 11am–11pm, Sat noon–11pm.

SPITALFIELDS AND WHITECHAPEL

★**The Carpenter's Arms** 73 Cheshire St, E2 6EG ☎020 7739 6342, ⊕carpentersarmsfreehouse.com; ⊖Shoreditch High Street; map pp.190–191. Iconic East End pub – the Kray twins bought it for their dear old mum, supposedly because the lone door meant they could keep a close eye on comings and goings – with an excellent range of craft lagers and ales, good home-made food and a tiny courtyard. A friendly, relaxed, low-lit place that feels wonderfully set apart from the sometimes hectic neighbourhood surrounding it. Mon–Wed 4–11.30pm, Thurs & Sun noon–11.30pm, Fri & Sat noon–12.30am.

★**The George Tavern** 373 Commercial Rd, E1 0LA ☎020 7790 7335, ⊕thegeorgetavern.co.uk; ⊖Whitechapel; map p.187. Arty, shabby, dilapidated pub, packed with history and all sorts of lovely period detail. There's a bohemian theatre space, and regular, very cool, live music. It's under

threat from developers so enjoy it while you can. Mon–Thurs 4pm–midnight, Fri & Sat 4pm–3am, Sun 4pm–midnight.

Indo 133 Whitechapel Rd, E1 1DT ☎020 7247 4926; ⊖Aldgate East or Whitechapel; map pp.190–191. Tiny, dark, grungy bar, with good pizzas, interesting music and a decent range of beers, all enjoyed by a laidback and generally non-hipster crowd. Mon–Thurs & Sun noon–1am, Fri & Sat noon–3am.

The Ten Bells 84 Commercial St, E1 6QG ☎020 7366 1721; ⊖Shoreditch High Street; map pp.190–191. Stripped-down pub (with Jack the Ripper associations), with some great Victorian tiling. The hip, young, local crowd is joined nowadays by foodies here for the superb restaurant, the brainchild of alumni from destination restaurants *St John*, *The Ledbury* and *Clove Club*. Mon–Wed & Sun noon–midnight, Thurs–Sat noon–1am.

SHOREDITCH AND HOXTON

Boundary 2–4 Boundary St, E2 7DD ☎020 7729 1051, ⊕theboundary.co.uk; ⊖Shoreditch High Street; map pp.190–191. The rooftop bar at this hip hotel (see p.359) is a gorgeous spot, complete with its own olive tree and grapevines, a covered area for when the weather's bad and blankets to snuggle under when it's chilly. You pay for the setting – cocktails start at £8.50 – but the views are

unbeatable. Daily 10am–11pm.

Happiness Forgets 8–9 Hoxton Square, N1 6NU ☎020 7613 0325, ⊕happinessforgets.com; ⊖Old Street; map pp.190–191. Candlelit, bare-brick Hoxton bar with a Hoxton-via-New York vibe, serving fashionably obscure, serious cocktails to a cool crowd. Mon–Sat 5.30–11pm.

The Royal Oak 73 Columbia Rd, E2 7RG ☎020 7729 2220 (before 6pm), ⊕royaloaklondon.com; ⊖Hoxton; map pp.190–191. This pub's beautifully preserved and unadorned interior has seen it feature in many a period drama, and the exterior isn't bad either, set as it is on impossibly cute Columbia Road. Staff and punters are hip, but there's a gritty down-to-earth vibe all the same, especially on flower market day (see p.434). The food's good too, and there's a dedicated dining room upstairs. Mon–Fri 4–11pm, Sat & Sun noon–11pm.

TOP 5 HISTORIC PUBS

The George Inn Southwark. See p.393
The Jerusalem Tavern Clerkenwell. See opposite
The Mayflower Rotherhithe. See p.394
The Princess Louise High Holborn. See p.384
Ye Olde Cheshire Cheese Fleet Street. See above

24

★**Sagar + Wilde** 193 Hackney Rd, E2 8JL ☎ 020 8127 7330, ⓦ sagerandwilde.com; ⊖ Hoxton; map pp.190–191. Gentrification doesn't get much starker than this. What was formerly an England flag-draped, locals-only boozer is now this sleek, pricey wine bar that makes for a lovely stop after visiting Columbia Road flower market (see p.434). The cheese and charcuterie boards are as good as the wine, and look out for what must be one of London's finest bar tops, made from an old pavement light. Mon–Fri 5pm–midnight, Sat & Sun noon–midnight.

Worship Street Whistling Shop 63 Worship St, EC2A 2DU ☎ 020 7247 0015, ⓦ whistlingshop.com; ⊖ Old Street; map pp.190–191. This theatrical, shabbily opulent cocktail bar looks set to outlive London's current gin craze, chiefly because the drinks, composed with unusual and creative ingredients are works of art, made in their gothic in-house lab. Mon & Tues 5pm–midnight, Wed & Thurs 5pm–1am, Fri & Sat 5pm–2am.

HAGGERSTON, DALSTON, STOKE NEWINGTON AND CLAPTON

The Anchor and Hope 15 High Hill Ferry, E5 9HG ☎ 020 8806 1730, ⓦ anchor-and-hope-clapton.co.uk; ⇌ Clapton; map p.187. You feel like you're on the edge of things here at this little locals' pub on the River Lea, which makes a fine stop-off if you're visiting Springfield Park or Walthamstow. Basic food and drink but the views over the marshes can be dreamy. Mon–Thurs 1–11pm, Fri & Sat noon–11pm, Sun noon–10.30pm.

The Dove 24–28 Broadway Market, E8 4QJ ☎ 020 7275 7617, ⓦ dovepubs.com; ⇌ London Fields or Cambridge Heath from Liverpool Street station; map p.187. Cosy, low-lit and plant-filled, this characterful pub, a friendly stalwart on trendy Broadway Market, offers a stupendous selection of Belgian beers, and specializes in excellent home-made food. Mon–Thurs noon–11pm, Fri & Sat noon–midnight, Sun noon–10.30pm.

The Fox 372 Kingsland Rd, E8 4DA ☎ 07807 217734, ⓦ thefoxe8.com; ⊖ Haggerston; map p.187. An excellent choice of craft beers, real ales and ciders along with "dirty" food are the big appeal at this bare-bones, on-trend pub, along with the flower-bedecked roof terrace, which is a fabulous spot for a summer tipple.

The Railway Tavern 2 St Jude St, N16 8JT ☎ 020 0011 1195 ⓦ facebook.com/RailwayTavernAleHouse; ⊖ Dalston Junction or Dalston Kingsland; map p.187. In a, village-like corner of Dalston, this place has a wonderfully executed railway theme, with its rickety wooden chairs upholstered like train carriage seats, Tube adverts and old-fashioned luggage on shelves. The beer selection is beyond reproach, and the spicy Thai food works well with it. Note that there's another pub of the same name near Dalston Kingsland station. Mon–Thurs 4–11pm, Fri & Sat noon–midnight, Sun noon–10.30pm.

The Rose and Crown 199 Stoke Newington Church St, N16 9ES ☎ 0207 254 7297, roseandcrownn16.co.uk; ⇌ Stoke Newington or buses 476 or 73 from Angel; map p.187. In a gorgeous spot right by Clissold Park, this pub is all wood-panelled loveliness, with a nice, spacious feel even when busy, plus a few tables on the pavement outside. Guest ales are shy of £4, while food mains, from goat's cheese tart to burgers are all around the £10 mark. Mon–Fri 5pm–12.30am, Sat & Sun noon–1am.

MILE END AND BETHNAL GREEN

The Approach 47 Approach Rd, E2 9LY ☎ 020 8980 2321; ⊖ Bethnal Green; map p.187. One of the best pubs in an area becoming increasingly well stocked, with a local, unaffected feel. Cosy and spacious, it offers food and a fine range of beers, and there's an art gallery of the same name attached. Mon–Sat noon–11pm, Sun noon–10.30pm.

★**The Camel** 277 Globe Rd, E2 0JD ☎ 07535 779229; ⊖ Bethnal Green; map p.187. Beer and pies – the great British combination. This neighbourhood favourite serves pies that are a cut above – from steak with chorizo, olives and beans to goat's cheese, sweet potato and spinach – along with real ales. Mon–Thurs 4–11pm, Fri & Sat noon–11pm, Sun noon–10.30pm.

Mother Kelly's 251 Paradise Row, E2 9LE ☎ 020 7012 1244, ⓦ motherkellys.co.uk; ⊖ Bethnal Green; map pp.190–191. One of a number of exciting venues in this little strip of railway arches, this place is all bare floorboards, barrels for tables, corrugated ceiling and industrial lighting with an array of craft-ale taps poking through a plain black-painted wooden wall. Mon 4–11pm, Tues–Thurs & Sun noon–11pm, Fri & Sat noon–midnight.

The Palm Tree Haverfield Rd, E3 5RP ☎ 020 8980 2918; ⊖ Bow Road; map p.187. The canal-side location, on a slightly desolate patch of Mile End Park, is rough-and-ready memorable, as is the dim interior, with its well-worn wooden benches and bunches of dried hops. Occasional live jazz. Mon–Thurs noon–midnight, Fri & Sat noon–2am, Sun noon–1am.

Satan's Whiskers 343 Cambridge Heath Rd, E2 9RA ☎ 020 7739 8362, ⓦ satanswhiskersblr.tumblr.com;

TOP 5 RIVERSIDE DRINKS

Dove Hammersmith. See p.398
The Gun Docklands. See above
The Mayflower Rotherhithe. See p.394
Prospect of Whitby Docklands. See above
Trafalgar Tavern Greenwich. See p.398

⊖ Bethnal Green; map pp.190–191. From the people behind excellent east London pubs *The Hunter S* and *The Hemingway*, this cocktail bar combines an intimate atmosphere (and some obscene taxidermy) with superb mixology. The most expensive concoction, the £10 "Hurricane", is justly named. Daily 5pm–midnight (sometimes later).

HACKNEY WICK

★ **Crate** Unit 7, Queen's Yard, E9 5EN ☎ 078 3427 5687, ⓦ cratebrewery.com; ⊖ Hackney Wick; map p.187. An achingly hip brewery, pizzeria and bar that feels on the very edge of the city but is handy for the Queen Elizabeth Olympic Park. The interior is great, with lots of recycled materials used (such as railway sleepers for the bar) but it's even better if you can find an outside spot, beside the River Lea; there's even an old boat or two to sit in. Mon–Thurs & Sun noon–11pm, Fri & Sat noon–midnight.

The Plough at Swan Wharf 60 Dace Rd, E3 2NQ ☎ 020 8525 9541, ⓦ hackneyplough.co.uk/swan-wharf; ⊖ Hackney Wick; map p.187. Sister pub to Homerton's excellent *Plough*, this café-bar on the River Lea offers excellent local and international craft ales. The big quayside decking terrace affords views of the former Olympic Stadium. Mon–Thurs & Sun 9am–11pm, Fri & Sat 9am–1am, Sun 10am–11pm.

DOCKLANDS

The Grapes 76 Narrow St, E14 8PB ☎ 020 7987 4396, ⓦ thegrapes.co.uk; ⊖ Westferry DLR; map pp.210–211. A lovely, narrow little pub, dating from around 1583 and featuring in Dickens's *Our Mutual Friend*. Ales all hover about £4 and the upstairs restaurant area is very popular for Sunday lunch (around £10). If you can bag a spot on the slip of a riverside balcony, you'll have the Thames sloshing about beneath you. Mon–Wed noon–3.30pm & 5.30–11pm, Thurs–Sat noon–11pm, Sun noon–10.30pm.

The Gun 27 Coldharbour, E14 9NS ☎ 020 7515 5222, ⓦ thegundocklands.com; ⊖ Canary Wharf, South Quay or Blackwall DLR; map pp.210–211. Legendary dockers' pub, once the haunt of Lord Nelson, *The Gun* is now a classy gastropub, with a cosy back bar and a deck offering unrivalled views. Mon–Sat 11am–midnight, Sun 11am–11pm.

★ **The Prospect of Whitby** 57 Wapping Wall, E1W 3SH ☎ 020 7481 1095; ⊖ Wapping; map pp.210–211. Steeped in history, this is London's most famous riverside pub, with a pewter bar, flagstone floor, ancient timber beams and stacks of maritime memorabilia. Decent beers and terrific Thames views. Mon–Thurs noon–11pm, Fri & Sat noon–midnight, Sun noon–10.30pm.

Town of Ramsgate 62 Wapping High St, E1W 2PN ☎ 020 7264 0001; ⊖ Wapping; map pp.210–211. Dark, narrow, medieval pub located by Wapping Old Stairs, which once led down to Execution Dock. Captain Blood was discovered here with the Crown Jewels under his cloak. Fairly standard ales all upwards of £4 but the food is reasonably priced food and it's popular for Sunday lunch. Mon–Sat noon–midnight, Sun noon–10.30pm.

24

SOUTH BANK

The Anchor & Hope 36 The Cut, SE1 8LP ☎ 020 7928 9898, ⓦ anchorandhopepub.co.uk; ⊖ Southwark; map p.218. This gastropub dishes up excellent, comforting grub – the likes of slow-cooked pork with *choucroute*, rabbits' livers, asparagus soup – and mouthwatering puds. You can't book (except on Sundays), so the bar is basically the waiting room. Mon 5–11pm, Tues–Sat 11am–11pm, Sun 12.30–5pm.

★ **The Kings Arms** 25 Roupell St, SE1 8TB ☎ 020 7207 0784; ⊖ Waterloo; map p.218. On a quiet terraced street, this terrific local is divided into two parts: in the front, a traditional drinking area, in the rear a tastefully cluttered,

conservatory-style space with a large open fire and long wooden table. Real ales and good Thai food. Mon–Fri 11am–11pm, Sat noon–11pm, Sun noon–10.30pm.

The Swan at the Globe 21 New Globe Walk, SE1 9DT ☎ 0843 636 2507, ⓦ swanlondon.co.uk; ⊖ London Bridge; map pp.228–229. Don't be fooled by the "ye olde tavern" name – this is a pretty sophisticated take on the pub genre, affording lovely views of the river, plus local craft ales and seasonal cocktails. One of the South Bank's nicest spots for a drink, affiliated to the theatre (see p.230). Mon–Wed 8am–11pm, Thurs 8am–midnight, Fri 8am–12.30am, Sat 10am–12.30am, Sun 10am–10.30pm.

SOUTHWARK

The George Inn 77 Borough High St, SE1 1NH ☎ 020 7407 2056, ⓦ nationaltrust.org.uk/george-inn; ⊖ Borough; map pp.228–229. London's only surviving galleried coaching inn (see p.233), dating from the seventeenth century and owned by the National Trust; it serves a good range of real ales, and is very popular with tourists. Daily 11am–11pm.

The Rake 14 Winchester Walk, SE1 9AG ☎ 020 7407 0557, ⓦ utobeer.co.uk; ⊖ London Bridge; map pp.228–229. Bright, tiny real ale bar – note the "No crap on tap" sticker – with regularly changing draught beers from Germany, America, Belgium and Holland, as well as more than a hundred bottled beers. There's an outdoor deck. Mon–Fri noon–11pm, Sat 10am–11pm, Sun noon–10pm.

★ **The Roebuck** 50 Great Dover St, SE1 4YG ☎ 0207 357 7324, ⓦ theroebuck.net; ⊖ Borough; map pp.226–227. A big, light and airy pub with artfully unfinished plasterwork complemented by colourful graphic prints on the walls. An excellent range of beers and a real mix of drinkers, not least thanks to the pub's popularity with *Canterbury Tales* walking tour groups. The upstairs room – where Charlie Chaplin performed as a boy – is used for various events from quizzes to film nights, there's sustainably sourced pub grub at good prices (£10–14) and lots of pavement seating for fine weather. Mon–Thurs noon–midnight, Fri & Sat noon–1am, Sun noon–11pm.

ROTHERHITHE AND BERMONDSEY

Bermondsey Arts Club 102 Tower Bridge Rd, SE1 4TP ☎ 020 7237 9552, ⓦ bermondseyartsclub.co.uk; ⊖ Bermondsey or Borough; map pp.226–227. A cool, atmospheric cocktail bar occupying what was once called a "public convenience" (a few of the, ahem, original fittings survive). Gin fans might also try *214 Bermondsey* (ⓦ 214-bermondsey.co.uk) a few minutes' walk away on Bermondsey Street. Tues–Sat 6pm–2am.

SOUTH KENSINGTON

The Anglesea Arms 15 Selwood Terrace, SW7 3QG ☎ 020 7373 7960; ⊖ South Kensington; map p.267. Charmingly tatty little local, with dark wooden tables and green leather benches inside, and hanging baskets and lots of tables outside. There are half a dozen first-class ales on offer. Mon–Sat 11am–11pm, Sun noon–10.30pm.

KNIGHTSBRIDGE, EARL'S COURT AND FULHAM

The Finborough Arms 118 Finborough Rd, SW10 9ED ⓦ finboroughams.co.uk ⊖ West Brompton; map pp.252–253. This beautifully restored Victorian pub takes its beer very seriously. The interior is light and airy with a swathe of beautiful green tiling and there's a theatre upstairs too (ⓦ finboroughtheatre.co.uk). Mon–Fri 5–11pm, Sat & Sun noon–11pm.

The Grenadier 18 Wilton Row, SW1X 7NR ☎ 020 7235 3074; ⊖ Hyde Park Corner or Knightsbridge; map pp.252–253. Hidden away in a private mews, this

CHELSEA

The Cooper's Arms 87 Flood St, SW3 5TB ☎ 020 7376 3120, ⓦ coopersarms.co.uk; ⊖ Sloane Square; map p.267. This revamped pub is bright and airy with Mediterranean tiles behind the bar, little framed ornithological paintings everywhere and gramophone horns for light shades. There's a decent range of ales, and pies are a speciality. The crowd can be pretty young but all are made to feel welcome. Daily noon–10pm.

The Royal Oak 44 Tabard St, SE1 4JU ☎ 020 7357 7173; ⊖ Borough; map pp.226–227. Lovingly restored Victorian pub that eschews jukeboxes and one-armed bandits and opts simply for serving well-kept real ales from Harvey's brewery in Sussex. Mon–Fri 11am–11pm, Sat noon–11pm, Sun noon–6pm.

Simon the Tanner 231 Long Lane, SE1 4PR ☎ 0207 357 8740, ⓦ simonthetanner.co.uk; ⊖ Borough; map pp.226–227. Renowned for their scotch eggs, excellent range of ales and dog-friendly policy, this pub, with a pared-back interior, occupies a discreet spot on a leafy road. Mon 5–11pm, Tues–Sat noon–11pm, Sun noon–10.30pm.

The Mayflower 117 Rotherhithe St, SE16 4NF ☎ 020 7237 4088, ⓦ themayflowerrotherhithe.com; ⊖ Rotherhithe; map pp.226–227. This eighteenth-century pub, in a peaceful spot in the heart of old Rotherhithe, is all blackened brick walls, wonky timber frames and creaky floorboards, while the terrace offers splendid Thames views. Mon–Sat 11am–11pm, Sun noon–10.30pm.

The Queen's Arms 30 Queens Gate Mews, SW7 5QL ☎ 020 7823 9293, ⓦ thequeensarmskensington.co.uk ⊖ Gloucester Road; map p.254. Brilliantly located in a quiet mews around a 10min walk from the Royal Albert Hall, this pub's buzziness seems almost uncouth in this neighbourhood of posh, wedding cake-style houses. Mon–Sat noon–11pm, Sun noon–10.30pm.

charming little pub was Wellington's local and his officers' mess; the original pewter bar survives, and there's plenty of military paraphernalia on display. Daily noon–11pm.

The Star Tavern 6 Belgrave Mews West, SW1X 8HT ☎ 020 7235 3019, ⓦ star-tavern-belgravia.co.uk; ⊖ Knightsbridge; map pp.252–253. Quiet and traditional two-storey mews pub with a large open sitting room and a murky past: allegedly, it was from here that the Great Train Robbery was planned. Fuller's beer and traditional pub grub. Mon–Sat 11am–11pm, Sun noon–10.30pm.

The Fox and Hounds 29 Passmore St, SW1W 8HR ☎ 020 7730 6367; ⊖ Sloane Square; map p.267. With its open fire, faux books, oil paintings, red banquettes and flagstone floor, not to mention its hunting memorabilia, this little Young's pub is as cosy as a ship's cabin and practically creaks as you walk in. No music or TVs, and a friendly buzz. Daily noon–11pm.

CLOCKWISE FROM TOP THE JERUSALEM TAVERN (P.390); THE LAMB (P.389); THE PROSPECT OF WHITBY (P.393) >

THE
PROSPECT OF WHITBY

PADDINGTON

★**The Victoria** 10a Strathearn Place, W2 2NH ☎ 020 7724 1191, ⓦvictoriapaddington.co.uk; ⊖ Lancaster Gate or Paddington; map pp.276–277. Beautiful, unspoilet Victorian Fuller's pub, with green-and-gold wallpapered walls enclosing a long bar with fine mirrors and elaborate carvings. There's a little outdoor space, too. An especially valuable find so near Paddington station. Mon–Sat 11am–11pm, Sun noon–10.30pm.

NOTTING HILL

The Churchill Arms 119 Kensington Church St, W8 7LN ☎ 020 7227 4242, ⓦ churchillarmskensington.co.uk; ⊖ Notting Hill Gate; map pp.276–277. Justifiably popular, flower-festooned local serving Fuller's beers, Guinness and passable Thai food in a quirky, eclectic space. Mon–Wed 11am–11pm, Thurs–Sat 11am–midnight, Sun noon–10.30pm.

★**The Cow** 89 Westbourne Park Rd, W2 5QH ☎ 020 7221 0021, ⓦ thecowlondon.co.uk; ⊖ Westbourne Park or Royal Oak; map pp.276–277. This gastropub pulls in a cool, slightly raffish crowd. Tasty British food, including oysters (£12 for six), is served in the bar and in a more formal dining room. Mon–Thurs noon–11pm, Fri & Sat noon–midnight, Sun noon–10.30pm.

The Elgin 96 Ladbroke Grove, W11 1PY ☎ 020 7229 5663; ⊖ Ladbroke Grove; map pp.276–277. Enormous pub with a riot of original features as well as modish decorative touches. Buzzy, with regular live music. Mon–Wed 11am–11pm, Thurs–Sat 11am–midnight, Sun noon–10.30pm.

Paradise by Way of Kensal Green 19 Kilburn Lane, W10 4AE ☎ 020 8969 0098, ⓦ theparadise.co.uk; ⊖ Kensal Green; map pp.276–277. Big gastropub near the Kensal Green Cemetery, with a theatrically dishevelled interior and a young west London crowd. Mon–Wed 4pm–midnight, Thurs 4pm–1am, Fri 4pm–2am, Sat noon–2am, Sun noon–11.30pm.

The Union Tavern 45 Woodfield Rd, W9 2BA ☎ 020 7286 1886, ⓦ union-tavern.co.uk; ⊖ Westbourne Park; map pp.276–277. A craft and real ale haven in an area of town not overburdened with the stuff, this Fuller's pub's focus is London-created beer (both cask and keg). The canal-side location is lovely. Mon–Thurs noon–11pm, Fri & Sat noon–midnight, Sun noon–10.30pm.

The Westbourne 101 Westbourne Park Villas, W2 5ED ☎ 020 7221 1332, ⓦ thewestbourne.com; ⊖ Westbourne Park or Royal Oak; map pp.276–277. This popular gastropub has an elegantly ramshackle interior and lots of space outside at the front. There's a tapas menu and bar snacks available. Mon 4.30–11pm, Tues–Sat 11am–11pm, Sun noon–10.30pm.

★**The Windsor Castle** 114 Campden Hill Rd, W8 7AR ☎ 020 7243 8797, ⓦ thewindsorcastlekensington.co.uk; ⊖ Notting Hill; map pp.276–277. More like something you'd find in the country than in the backstreets of one of London's poshest neighbourhoods, this is a pretty, popular, early Victorian wood-panelled pub with a great courtyard. Craft beers and fine pub grub. Mon–Sat noon–11pm, Sun noon–10.30pm.

ST JOHN'S WOOD

The Bridge House 13 Westbourne Terrace Rd, W2 6NG ☎ 020 7266 4326, ⓦ thebridgehouselittlevenice.co.uk; ⊖ Warwick Avenue; map pp.284–285. A bohemian theatre pub right by the canal, with excellent real ales and good food. Mon–Thurs noon–11pm, Fri & Sat noon–11.30pm, Sun noon–10.30pm.

The Warrington 93 Warrington Crescent, W9 1EH ☎ 020 7286 8282, ⓦ faucetinn.com/warrington; ⊖ Maida Vale; map pp.284–285. Grand Victorian pub with a flamboyant Art Nouveau interior that is worth a visit for the architecture and decor alone. Rooms available. Mon–Thurs 11am–11pm, Fri & Sat 11am–midnight, Sun 11am–10.30pm.

PRIMROSE HILL, CAMDEN TOWN AND AROUND

BrewDog 113 Bayham St, NW1 0AG ☎ 020 7284 4626, ⓦ brewdog.com; ⊖ Camden Town; map pp.284–285. Spacious and comfy bar owned by the Scottish microbrewery, with hot dogs, burgers and beer-matched cheese too, perfect to pick at as you chill out on the squidgy sofas. There's a second *BrewDog* in Shoreditch, and they also run BottleDog off-licence in King's Cross (see p.431). Mon–Thurs noon–11.30pm, Fri & Sat noon–midnight, Sun noon–10.30pm.

★**The Constitution** 42 St Pancras Way, NW1 0QT ☎ 020 7380 0767, ⓦ conincamden.com; ⊖ Camden Town or Camden Road; map pp.284–285. With its big windows, light seems to pour into this canal-side pub, while the beer garden overlooking the water is ideal for fine weather. Its lovely location makes it ripe for gentrification but, for now, it's very much a traditional, locals' place. Mon–Thurs 11am–midnight, Fri & Sat 11am–1am, Sun 11am–11pm.

The Edinboro Castle 57 Mornington Terrace, NW1 7RU ☎ 020 7255 9651, ⓦ edinborocastlepub.co.uk; ⊖ Camden Town; map pp.284–285. The main draw at this large, high-ceilinged pub, despite its glammed-up interior, is the leafy beer garden which hosts summer weekend barbecues and hog roasts. Good selection of draught continental lagers and a couple of real ales. Mon–Fri noon–11pm, Sat 11am–11pm, Sun noon–10.30pm.

The Engineer 65 Gloucester Ave, NW1 8JH ☎ 020 7483 1890, ⓦ theengineerprimrosehill.co.uk; ⊖ Chalk Farm

24

or Camden Town; map pp.284–285. An elegant pub with a good range of craft beers, many locally brewed. The food experience is mixed, however. Mon–Fri noon–11pm, Sat 10am–11pm, Sun 10am–10.30pm.

The Enterprise 2 Haverstock Hill, NW3 2BL ☎ 020 7485 2659, ⓦ camdenenterprise.com; ⊖ Chalk Farm; map pp.284–285. Chalk Farm institution, almost opposite the tube, with an unmatched atmosphere and live gigs/DJs at night. Sun–Thurs 11am–11pm, Fri & Sat 11am–1am.

The Lock Tavern 35 Chalk Farm Rd, NW1 8AJ ☎ 020 7482 7163, ⓦ lock-tavern.co.uk; ⊖ Chalk Farm; map pp.284–285. Archetypal Camden cool at this rambling music and DJ pub, with large, battered wooden tables, comfy sofas, a leafy upstairs terrace and beer garden down below. Music can be anything from punk funk and electro to rock; the pub grub is mainly dude food. Very busy on gig nights. Mon–Thurs noon–midnight, Fri & Sat noon–1am, Sun noon–11pm.

ISLINGTON

69 Colebrooke Row 69 Colebrooke Row, N1 8AA ☎ 07540 528593, ⓦ 69colebrookerow.com; ⊖ Angel or Highbury & Islington; map pp.284–285. This supercool cocktail bar – all old-school Hollywood glamour – was at the vanguard of London's craft cocktail scene – and has deservedly stayed the course. Sun–Wed 5pm–midnight, Thurs 5pm–1am, Fri & Sat 5pm–2am.

The Crown 116 Cloudesley Rd, N1 0EB ☎ 020 7837 7107; ⊖ Angel; map pp.284–285. Refined Fuller's pub, with lots of Victorian fixtures and fittings. Generally calmer than the pubs and bars closer to Upper St, and serves upmarket food. Mon–Sat noon–11pm, Sun noon–10.30pm.

★**The Earl of Essex** 25 Danbury St, N1 8LE ☎ 020 7424 5828, ⓦ earlofessex.net; ⊖ Angel; map pp.284–285. A wonderful brew pub with the rotating

craft ale options marked up like destinations on a train station departure board, and the brewing equipment smack-bang in the middle of the space. Has a punchy, beer-paired food menu and a nice garden. Mon–Thurs noon–11.30pm, Sat noon–midnight, Sun noon–11pm.

★**The Island Queen** 87 Noel Rd, N1 8HD ☎ 020 7354 8741, ⓦ theislandqueenislington.co.uk; ⊖ Angel or Highbury & Islington; map pp.284–285. Beautiful, weathered, wood-panelled Victorian pub in the backstreets, with lovely etched glass, high ceilings and eccentric bits and bobs all over the place. Good range of beers and decent pub food. A real gem. Sun–Thurs noon–11.30pm, Fri noon–midnight, Sat 11am–midnight.

HAMPSTEAD AND HIGHGATE

The Bull and Last 168 Highgate Rd, NW5 1QS ☎ 020 7267 3641, ⓦ thebullandlast.co.uk; ⊖ Gospel Oak and Tufnell Park; map pp.296–297. This heath-hugging pub offers some really excellent (and quite pricey) food. That "gastro" side of things is undoubtedly a focus but drinkers should not be put off. Mon–Fri noon–11pm, Sat 9am–midnight, Sun 9am–10.30pm.

The Duke's Head 16 Highgate High St, N6 5JG ☎ 020 8341 1310, ⓦ thedukesheadhighgate.co.uk; ⊖ Archway or Highgate; map pp.296–297. A stab at knowingly cool in this rather unhip area of the city. Beers are determinedly craft (a fair few under £4) and the menu is on-message "dirty" American diner (smoked chicken tacos £7). Mon–Wed noon–midnight, Thurs–Sat noon–1am, Sun noon–11.30pm.

The Red Lion and Sun 25 North Rd, N6 4BE ☎ 020 8340 1780, ⓦ theredlionandsun.com; ⊖ Highgate; map pp.296–297. Prettily set in chichi Highgate Village, this place is popular with locals for its ales and its whiskies, its modern British food with a French accent and, unusually, its good takeaway food. There's loads of space, with two gardens. Mon–Sat noon–midnight, Sun noon–11pm.

★**The Southampton Arms** 139 Highgate Rd, NW5 1LE ⓦ thesouthamptonarms.co.uk; ⊖ Kentish Town; map pp.296–297. They keep things simple but spot-on in this big old place, with a fabulous, rotating range of real ales and ciders, all British, along with scotch eggs, pork baps and the like to snack on. Daily noon–11pm/midnight.

The Spaniards Inn Spaniards Rd, NW3 7JJ ☎ 020 8731 8406, ⓦ thespaniardshampstead.co.uk; ⊖ Hampstead; map pp.296–297. Rambling sixteenth-century coaching inn near Kenwood and the Heath, frequented by everyone from Dick Turpin to John Keats. With a huge garden and good food, it gets extremely busy on Sun afternoons. Sun–Tues noon–11pm, Wed–Fri noon–midnight, Sat 11am–midnight.

The Stag 67 Fleet Rd, NW3 2QU ☎ 020 7722 2646, ⓦ thestaghampstead.com; ⊖ Belsize Park; map pp.296–297. Welcoming gastropub with a varied and unusual beer selection, good British food, a big garden with weekly live music and summer barbecues, and a merry mix of locals and pre- or post-Heath ramblers. Mon–Thurs noon–11pm, Fri & Sat noon–midnight, Sun noon–10.30pm.

BRIXTON AND CLAPHAM

The Crown and Anchor 246 Brixton Rd, SW9 6AQ ☎ 020 7737 7915, ⓦ crownandchorbrixton.co.uk; ⊖ Brixton or Stockwell; map pp.308–309. This sister

pub to Stoke Newington's excellent *Jolly Butchers* (ⓦ jollybutchers.co.uk) follows in its sibling's footsteps, with a superb offering of beers and ciders, to which food is

24

matched. The decor is muted – the drinks are the thing. Mon–Thurs 4.30pm–midnight, Fri 4.30pm–1am, Sat noon–1am, Sun noon–11pm.

Effra 38A Kellet Rd, SW2 1DF ☎020 7274 4180; ⊖ Brixton; map pp.308–309. An unreconstructed slice of old Brixton, with a friendly crowd of old and new regulars enjoying Red Stripe and Caribbean food, along with frequent live jazz. Mon–Thurs noon–11pm, Fri noon–midnight, Sat 10am–midnight, Sun 10am–10.30pm.

Seven Unit 7, Market Row, SW9 8LB ☎020 7998 3309, ⓦ sevenatbrixton.com; ⊖ Brixton; map pp.308–309. Though the shabby-chic decor is verging on squat-chic, this Spanish cocktail and tapas bar is still the best place for a drink in the new social hub that is Brixton Market (especially if you're a sherry fan). Nearby sister venue, cocktail bar *Three Eight Four* (ⓦ threeeightfour.com), is worth a look too. Mon 9am–6pm, Tues–Sat 9am–11.30pm, Sun 10am–11.30pm.

PECKHAM

Bar Story 213 Blenheim Grove, SE15 4QL ☎020 7635 6643, ⓦ barstory.co.uk; ⊖≋Peckham Rye; map pp.308–309. Along with seasonal rooftop bar *Frank's* (ⓦ frankscafe.org.uk), this is a Peckham must. Set in a railway arch, the vibe is young, arty and hip and the drink options excellent, with craft beers and nicely priced cocktails (even better value during happy hour, daily 6–7pm). Mon–Thurs 4–10pm, Fri 4–11pm, Sat 2–11pm, Sun 2–9pm.

GREENWICH

The Cutty Sark Ballast Quay, off Lassell St, SE10 9PD ☎020 8858 3146, ⓦ cuttysarkse10.co.uk; ⊖ Cutty Sark DLR or ≋Maze Hill from Charing Cross; map p.313. This three-storey Georgian pub, much less touristy than the *Trafalgar Tavern* (see below), is another good place for a riverside pint. Mon–Sat 11am–11pm, Sun noon–10.30pm.

The Greenwich Union 56 Royal Hill, SE10 8RT ☎020 8692 6258, ⓦ greenwichunion.com; ⊖≋Greenwich; map p.313. A modern, laidback pub, owned by the local Meantime brewery but also featuring guest ales, with a youthful feel, gastro grub and a garden. Mon–Fri noon–11pm, Sat 11am–11pm, Sun 11.30am–10.30pm.

The Trafalgar Tavern 5 Park Row, SE10 9NW ☎020 8858 2909, ⓦ trafalgartavern.co.uk; ⊖ Cutty Sark DLR or ≋Maze Hill from Charing Cross; map p.313. A commanding riverside location and a mention in Dickens' *Our Mutual Friend* have made this large Regency-style inn a firm tourist favourite. Mon–Thurs noon–11pm, Fri & Sat noon–midnight, Sun noon–10.30pm.

HAMMERSMITH AND CHISWICK

The Blue Anchor 13 Lower Mall, W6 9DJ ☎020 8748 5774, ⓦ blueanchorlondon.com; ⊖ Hammersmith; map p.329. A good riverside pub, with a maritime theme and a beautiful pewter bar; the upstairs room offers good views of Hammersmith Bridge, or you can sit outside to enjoy the river. Mon–Sat 11am–11pm, Sun noon–10.30pm.

★ **The Dove** 19 Upper Mall, W6 9TA ☎020 8748 9474, ⓦ dovehammersmith.co.uk; ⊖ Ravenscourt Park; map p.329. Very old, low-beamed, riverside pub with literary associations – Ernest Hemingway and Graham Greene used to drink here – the smallest bar in the UK (4ft by 7ft), popular Sunday roasts, and riverside terrace. Continue along Upper Mall for other riverside pubs. Mon–Sat 11am–11pm, Sun noon–10.30pm.

Draft House Hammersmith 238 Shepherds Bush Rd, W6 7NL ☎020 7042 5109, ⓦ drafthouse.co.uk; ⊖ Hammersmith; map p.329. The Draft House mini-chain – which has a number of sister pubs in the capital, including *Draft House Charlotte* (see p.388) – took over *The Laurie Arms* in 2015 to bring some craft ale goodness to this part of town. Their creative rota of interesting beers quickly made it one of the area's most popular pubs. Mon–Wed & Sun noon–11pm, Thurs noon–midnight, Fri & Sat noon–1am.

KEW, RICHMOND AND WIMBLEDON

The Fox & Grapes 9 Camp Rd, SW19 4UN ☎020 8619 1300, ⓦ foxandgrapeswimbledon.co.uk; ⊖ Wimbledon; map p.329. Right on the edge of Wimbledon Common, this place is great in the summer, when you can sit outside on the grass with a pint of well-pulled real ale. Mon–Sat 11am–11pm, Sun 11am–10.30pm.

The Greyhound 82 Kew Green, Richmond, TW9 3AP ☎020 8332 9666, ⓦ thegreyhoundkew.co.uk; ⊖ Kew Gardens; map p.329. One of a handful of good options on Kew Green – the *Botanist* and *Coach and Horses* are also worth a try – this gastropub offers tasty food and real ales. Daily 9am–11.30pm.

The White Cross Hotel Water Lane, Richmond, TW9 1TH ☎020 8940 6844, ⓦ thewhitecrossrichmond.com; ⊖ Richmond; map p.340. With a longer pedigree and more character than its rivals, the *White Cross* has a very popular, large garden overlooking the river. In winter, you can decamp to the lounge with its bay windows and open fire. Better for drinking than eating. Mon–Sat 10am–11pm, Sun 10am–10.30pm.

24

FABRIC

Live music and clubs

Genres, venues, fashions and intoxicants come and go, but London's nightlife – sprawling, chaotic and impossibly varied – carries on regardless. Clubs play everything from pop to house, techno to punk and drum'n'bass to r'n'b on virtually any night of the week. Gigs are equally wide ranging, encompassing rock, roots, jazz, hip-hop and world music. We've carved up venues into categories to make them easier to navigate, but the scene is far more mixed then these genres suggest: club nights take over music venues, DJ sets are lifted by live percussion, gay venues (see p.405) host mixed nights and jazz acts play at rock venues. Virtually all venues listed have events' calendars on their websites – keep your eyes peeled and your dancing shoes ready.

25

Clubs and venues tend to cluster together, but despite its hedonistic reputation, central London has hemorrhaged music destinations. Venture out of zone 1 to find decent gigs. North London, especially Camden, is still the place to rock; the once-cool Shoreditch still has its moments but is generally going mainstream, chasing the best club nights up the road to Dalston; or you can head south to Brixton, Peckham and New Cross for something edgier.

LIVE MUSIC

From grimy pub back rooms, through O2's franchise venues and on to the mega-stadiums, talent can play out their entire careers in London's venues. If you are after those that have already made it, check the listings for Wembley (Ⓦ wembley .co.uk) and the O2 Dome (Ⓦ theo2.co.uk). The Royal Albert Hall (Ⓦ royalalberthall.com) – traditionally a classical music venue (see p.413) – and summer concerts in the beautiful courtyard at Somerset House (Ⓦ somersethouse.org.uk) are more atmospheric alternatives. Pricewise, you might get in free to see an unknown band or pay £80 for a visiting legend. Most acts will set you back £10–30. **Booking tickets** online for anything but the smallest gigs is standard – the biggest websites are Ⓦ seetickets.com, Ⓦ ticketweb.co.uk, Ⓦ ticketmaster.co.uk and Ⓦ wegottickets.com.

GENERAL VENUES

Academy Islington N1 Centre, N1 0PS ☎ 020 7288 4400, Ⓦ o2academyislington.co.uk; ⊖ Angel; map pp.284–285. One of the better O2 venues, despite being wedged in a shopping centre, with two rooms showcasing a guitar-led programme of good up-and-coming bands. Home to long-running Saturday cheese night, Club De Fromage.

Brixton Academy 211 Stockwell Rd, SW9 9SL ☎ 020 7771 3000, Ⓦ o2academybrixton.co.uk; ⊖ Brixton; map pp.308–309. Balancing its size with some classy curation, the Academy has seen them all, from mods and rockers to Chase and Status. The 4900-capacity Victorian hall's sound quality isn't immaculate, but it makes up for it with great atmosphere and a diverse array of local bars for before and after the gig.

Cargo 83 Rivington St, EC2A 3AY ☎ 020 7739 3440, Ⓦ cargo-london.com; ⊖ Old Street or Shoreditch High Street; map pp.190–191. Mixed line-up of live acts, including jazz, hip-hop, indie and folk.

Forum 9–17 Highgate Rd, NW5 1JY ☎ 020 7428 4080, Ⓦ theforumlondon.com; ⊖ Kentish Town; map pp.284–285. Mid-sized venue. The programming has moved towards a reliance on nostalgia acts, but it still occasionally surprises with special events.

Hammersmith Apollo 45 Queen Caroline St, W6 9QH ☎ 020 8563 3800, Ⓦ eventimapollo.com; ⊖ Hammersmith; map pp.252–253. The former Hammersmith Odeon is a cavernous space (downstairs can be seating or standing), with the nostalgia circuit sharing the bill with the arts.

★ **Roundhouse** Chalk Farm Rd, NW1 8EH ☎ 0300 678 9222, Ⓦ roundhouse.org.uk; ⊖ Chalk Farm; map pp.284–285. Magnificent Victorian-era steam-engine shed turned performing arts centre. It pulls in huge names like Bob Dylan alongside more eclectic choices, but whatever the act, they always make a hell of a show.

Shepherd's Bush Empire Shepherd's Bush Green, W12 8TT ☎ 020 8354 3300, Ⓦ o2shepherdsbushempire .co.uk; ⊖ Shepherd's Bush; map pp.276–277. Great mid-league bands play here. Good news if you want to watch from seating in the vertigo-inducing balconies, but downstairs lacks atmosphere if you're not right at the front.

★ **Union Chapel** Compton Terrace, N1 2UN ☎ 020 7226 1686, Ⓦ unionchapel.org.uk; ⊖ Highbury & Islington; map pp.284–285. Intimate venue that doubles as a church, hence the pew-style seating; the array of artists ranges from contemporary stars to world-music legends, and there are free Saturday lunchtime sessions.

ROCK, BLUES AND INDIE

100 Club 100 Oxford St, W1D 4DJ ☎ 020 7636 0933, Ⓦ the100club.co.uk; ⊖ Tottenham Court Road; map p.97. Retaining a few jazz gigs from its jazz club heritage, this dinky club now veers to a more varied, rock-led but often surprising rota under its Converse sponsorship.

12 Bar Club Holloway Road, N7 8DL ☎ 020 7619 9428, Ⓦ 12barclub.com; ⊖ Holloway Road; map pp.284–285. One of many exiles from London's old musical heart, Tin Pan Alley (Denmark Street), the new Islington home still schedules rock, indie and blues for the scuzzy sneaker brigade.

★ **Amersham Arms** 388 New Cross Rd, SE14 6TY ☎ 020 8469 1499, Ⓦ theamershamarms.com; ⊖ New Cross; map pp.308–309. The backroom line-up covers everything from guitary album launches to cabaret and club nights (check Friday's bargain Whip It!), catering for whatever takes the whims of the local art student crowd.

Barfly 49 Chalk Farm Rd, NW1 8AN ☎ 020 7688 8994, Ⓦ thebarflylondon.com; ⊖ Chalk Farm; map pp.284–285. Barfly splits its nightly offerings between a relentless roster of rock, punk and metal and guitar-led club nights.

Borderline Orange Yard, Manette St, W1D 4JB ☎ 020 7734 5547, Ⓦ theborderlinelondon.com; ⊖ Tottenham Court Road; map p.101. One of the last central venues still standing, with a guitar-infused music rota and good sound. Indie club nights include Wednesday's Cheap$kates.

★ **The Dentist** 33 Chatsworth Rd, E5 0LH no telephone, Ⓦ facebook.com/33ChatsworthRd; ⊖ Homerton; map p.187. The only dentist in town you'll fun at. Tasteful guitars, experimental music, cool crowds and a laidback atmosphere are all to be found in a barely-renovated old surgery that puts you and the musicians face to face.

Dingwalls Middle Yard, Camden Lock, NW1 8AB ☎020 7428 5929, ⓦdingwalls.com; ⊖Camden Town; map pp.284–285. Split-level music/club venue for indie and rock, with live music nights Friday and open mic nights Monday.

The Dublin Castle 94 Parkway, NW1 7AN ☎07949 575149, ⓦthedublincastle.com; ⊖Camden Town; map pp.284–285. Guitar, typically post-punk gigs in a pub that relives the best of old Camden.

Hoxton Square Bar & Kitchen 2–4 Hoxton Square, N1 6NU ☎020 7613 0709, ⓦhoxtonsquarebar.com; ⊖Old Street; map pp.190–191. The bar is self-conscious and unexceptional, but it gets some fine guitar and electronic talent through its doors, and the occasional secret gig.

KOKO 1a Camden High St, NW1 7JE ☎020 7388 3222, ⓦkoko.uk.com; ⊖Mornington Crescent; map pp.284–285. An atmospheric Camden institution, hosting gigs and weekend club nights, with a cracking assortment of Radio 1-friendly types, recently including the likes of Rhodes and Mercury prize-winning Young Fathers, dominating proceedings for young crowds.

Lexington 96–98 Pentonville Rd, N1 9JB ☎020 7837 5371, ⓦthelexington.co.uk; ⊖Angel; map pp.284–285. Above the bourbon-packed downstairs lounge bar is a two hundred-capacity venue with good sound, a hip but relaxed vibe and a solid, guitar music-dominated roster.

★**The Macbeth** 70 Hoxton St, N1 6LP ☎020 7749 0600, ⓦthemacbeth.co.uk; ⊖Old Street; map pp.190–191. Beautiful venue, good soundsystem and great nights, from buzzing gigs to imaginative club nights. Try the awesome roof terrace if you need a break from the dancefloor.

Oslo 1a Amhurst Rd, E8 1LL ☎020 3553 4831, ⓦoslohackney.com; ⊖Hackney Central; map p.187. Bringing bands and DJs together with excellent food, Oslo's considered schedule runs from pop-rock to soul and beyond.

New Cross Inn 323 New Cross Rd, SE14 6AS ☎020 8355 4976, ⓦnewcrossinn.com; ⊖New Cross Gate; map pp.308–309. Relaxed boozer that's the best place to see unsigned guitar bands playing an art student crowd.

★**Power Lunches** 446 Kingsland Rd, E8 4AE ☎020 7998 1997, ⓦpowerlunchesltd.co.uk; ⊖Dalston Junction; map p.187. Want hardcore? Power Lunches is beloved by bands for its broad booking policy and DIY music ethos that's taken over where 2012's ban on squats left off.

Sebright Arms 31–35 Coate St, E2 9AG ☎020 7729 0937, ⓦsebrightarms.co.uk; ⊖Bethnal Green; map pp.190–191. Basement venue that hosted everyone from The XX to Laura Marling before they made it.

Shacklewell Arms 71 Shacklewell Lane, E8 2EB ☎020 7249 0810, ⓦshacklewellarms.com; ⊖Dalston Kingsland; map p.187. Genre-bending live music venue for Dalston's cool kids; worth a visit for the free gigs early in the week.

Underbelly 11 Hoxton Square, N1 6NU ☎020 7613 1988, ⓦunderbellyhoxton.com, ⊖Old Street; pp.190–191. Not to be confused with summer's South Bank arts venue, the punkish venue does a fine programming line in guitars from funk to rock.

Underworld 174 Camden High St, NW1 0NE ☎020 7482 1932, ⓦtheunderworldcamden.co.uk; ⊖Camden Town; map pp.284–285. Shouty, scruffy, tattoo-packed warren under the *World's End* pub that's great for metal, hardcore and heavy rock bands and rocking weekend club nights.

Village Underground 54 Holywell Lane, EC2A 3PQ ☎020 7422 7505, ⓦvillageunderground.co.uk; ⊖Old Street; map pp.190–191. More varied and sometimes experimental line-ups than most places in this part of town, playing host in a beautiful site – there are even abandoned tube carriages.

Windmill 22 Blenheim Gardens, SW2 1XN ☎020 8671 0700, ⓦwindmillbrixton.co.uk; ⊖Brixton; map pp.308–309. A fine, leftfield mix of bands play at this poky pub halfway up Brixton Hill. Entry for everything from swirly electronica to throbbing post-punk is rarely much over £5.

SECRET NIGHTS AND SPECIAL EVENT SPACES

The last few years have seen a revival in nights where you only discover the venue at the last minute, especially for big warehouse parties. The good news is that the most likely spaces are great sites, with several venues around that just host others' special events. The best bet for finding out what's on is Resident Advisor (ⓦresidentadvisor.net).

Many are spaces in Hackney and other hot spots in northeast London: **Netil House** has hosted all sorts of great after-parties and events (ⓦnetil360.com) near London Fields train station, while **Bloc** is a fun one-room studio behind the Olympic site run by the major UK promoters of the same name. Several also turn up in the hectic schedules of nearby basement space **The Laundry** (ⓦthelaundrye8.com).

Off the Hackney map and all the more special for it are **Loft Studios**, a fantastic space bringing house music to parties in northwest London, near Willesden Junction.

25

JAZZ

Jazz Cafe 5 Parkway, NW1 7PG ☎020 7485 6834, ⓦthejazzcafelondon.com; ⊖Camden Town; map pp.284–285. There's the odd cheesy pop night, but a combination of big names (at big prices) and clubbier acts from jazz, soul and beyond keep the dancefloor and balcony buzzing.

Jazz@PizzaExpress 10 Dean St, W1D 3RW ☎0845 602 7017, ⓦpizzaexpresslive.com; ⊖Tottenham Court Road; map p.101. Small basement of this branch of the pizza chain hosts consistent quality, with established and new jazz artists.

King's Place 90 York Way, N1 9AG ☎020 7520 1490, ⓦkingsplace.co.uk; ⊖St Pancras International; map p.127. Two halls host classical and jazz gigs at this rather swish development – the acoustics are excellent and the acts class.

★ Ronnie Scott's 47 Frith St, W1D 4HT ☎020 7439 0747, ⓦronniescotts.co.uk; ⊖Leicester Square; map p.101. The most famous jazz club in London plays host to the big names as part of its considered but ambitious programme. The sell-out Sunday Jazz lunches are worth trying.

The Vortex 11 Gillett Square, N16 ☎020 7254 4097, ⓦvortexjazz.co.uk; ⊖Dalston Kingsland; map p.187. The small venue is a serious player on the live jazz scene, managing to combine a touch of urban style with a cosy, friendly atmosphere.

URBAN

IndigO2 The O2, SE10 0DX ☎020 8463 2700, ⓦtheo2 .co.uk; ⊖North Greenwich; map pp.308–309. Mixed in among the old pop acts you'll find big-name r'n'b stars at The O2's smaller (well, 2500 capacity) sister venue. Also look out for commercial urban/BME club nights.

Jamm 261 Brixton Rd, SW9 6LH ☎020 7274 5537, ⓦbrixtonjamm.org; ⊖Brixton; map pp.308–309. Two big rooms and a great courtyard (expect a barbecue) with reggae, drum'n'bass and UKG all featuring.

WORLD MUSIC, FOLK AND ROOTS

Barbican Silk St, EC2Y 8DS ☎020 7638 8891, ⓦbarbican.org.uk; ⊖Barbican; map pp.152–153. It's easy to lose yourself in the Barbican, the largest arts centre in Europe and a focal point for the best world music bands, orchestras and singer-songwriters. It also hosts contemporary music events, and free music in the foyer.

Bush Hall 310 Uxbridge Rd, W12 7LJ ☎020 8222 6955, ⓦbushhallmusic.co.uk; ⊖Shepherd's Bush; map pp.276–277. Acoustic performers, folk and blues artists play beneath the cool chandeliers of this elegant former dancehall – it gets the odd rock band too.

★ Cafe OTO 18–22 Ashwin St, E8 3DL ☎020 7923 1231, ⓦcafeoto.co.uk; ⊖Dalston Kingsland; map p.187. London's most innovative folk, classical and electronica are on offer here – along with a café vibe and intelligent crowd.

Passing Clouds 1 Richmond Rd, E8 4AA ☎020 7241 4889, ⓦpassingclouds.org; ⊖Haggerston; map p.187. Charismatic world music and beats are the focus alongside arts and club nights in a socially conscious setting.

Southbank Centre South Bank, SE1 8XX ☎020 7960 4200, ⓦsouthbankcentre.co.uk; ⊖Waterloo; map p.218. The all-seater auditoriums of the Royal Festival Hall, Queen Elizabeth Hall and Purcell Room host imaginative programmes of world music, classical, jazz and folk.

CLUBS

Disco tunnels, sticky-floored rock clubs and epic house nights: London has it all. While the capital has lost most of its superclubs, the current spread of mid-sized venues gives more choice than ever. **Opening time** for most is between 10pm and midnight – check online before you go and treat our listed timings as a rough guide. **Admission prices** have dropped in recent years, so while anywhere with a dress code and all-nighters will still cost, £5–£10 is more standard, and finding somewhere free to dance midweek isn't too hard – but bear in mind that prices at the bar can be outrageous. Some things are common to all London clubs: security can be enthusiastic and deserve treating with respect if you want to get in; make sure you have ID; and if you're heading to an up-and-coming area, work out a route home beforehand. London's scene is fairly **dressed down** – West End clubs may want you to wear smart shoes, but trainers are often fine.

VICTORIA

The Qube Project 191 Victoria St, SW1E 5NE ☎020 3753 0468, ⓦthequbeproject.com; ⊖Victoria; map p.36. Feel the old school vibes as heavy-duty headliners from across house and techno perform at this shadowy venue. Fri & Sat 11pm–3am.

SOHO AND AROUND

Café de Paris 3 Coventry St, W1D 6BL ☎020 7734 7700, ⓦcafedeparis.com; ⊖Piccadilly Circus; map p.101. Velvet drapes and blood-red beds would be gaudy if they weren't carried off with Moulin Rouge-esque (pricey)

gusto. Check for times but typically Fri & Sat 6pm–3am.

★ The Phoenix 37 Cavendish Square, W1G 0PP ☎020 7493 8003, ⓦphoenixcavendishsquare.co.uk; ⊖Oxford Street; map p.89. You can find a few great club nights in this pub basement: monthly Feeling Gloomy is dedicated to sad music, Four Weddings has the cheesiest music in town and monthly How does it feel to be loved? is a top night of indie pop and Sixties soul. Club nights from around 10pm.

The Roxy 3–5 Rathbone Place, W1T 1HJ ☎020 255 1098, ⓦtheroxy.co.uk; ⊖Tottenham Court Road; map p.97. One of very few surviving student nights in town, this is a broadly indie/pop club that's a decent enough West End

GETTING THE LOWDOWN

Feeling overwhelmed by London's music choice? **Resident Advisor** (🕸residentadvisor.net) is best known for its exhaustive dance music event listings, while **Fact** (🕸factmag.com) can provide more context on what's getting played in the clubs. Tune into **NTS** (🕸ntsradio.co.uk) for the best in dance and more. **London Gigs** (🕸londongigs.net) provides no-nonsense listings for guitar music, while the broad remits of both the **NME** (🕸nme.com) and **Drowned In Sound** (🕸drownedinsound.com) steer towards rock and guitar music. **The Wire** (🕸thewire.co.uk) helps to map out experimental and leftfield acts and provides excellent listings too. More generally, **Time Out** (🕸timeout.com/london) provides great recommendations, although its listings can be difficult to browse if you're after a specific musical style.

bet. Not many places still do student discount – here does, plus there's a lengthy (very) happy hour. Mon–Thurs 5pm–3am, Fri 5pm–3.30am, Sat 6.30pm–3.30am.

CLERKENWELL

Fabric 77a Charterhouse St, EC1M 6HJ ☎020 7336 8898, 🕸fabriclondon.com; ⊖Farringdon; map p.147. Despite big queues (you're best buying tickets online) and a confusing layout, this 1600-capacity club gets in the big names. Genres booming from the devastating soundsystem include drum'n'bass (most Fri) and techno and house (most Sat). Fri 11pm–7am, Sat 11pm–8am, Sun 11pm–5.30am.

SHOREDITCH, WHITECHAPEL AND BETHNAL GREEN

★**Bethnal Green Working Men's Club** 42–44 Pollard Row, E2 6NB ☎020 7739 7170, 🕸workersplaytime.net; ⊖Bethnal Green; map pp.190–191. Postwar kitsch sets the backdrop for some serious playtime: choose from Fifties dress-up, burlesque, disco, rock'n'roll and cheese. Thurs–Sat 9pm–2am, check listings for other days.

The Book Club 100–106 Leonard St, EC2A 4RH ☎020 7684 8618, 🕸wearetbc.com; ⊖Old Street; map p.190–191. Artfully selected line-up in the cute and popular basement. The most dancefloor-friendly bet in Shoreditch.

The Old Blue Last 38 Great Eastern St, EC2A 3ES ☎020 7739 7033, 🕸theoldbluelast.com; ⊖Old Street; map pp.190–191. Vice-owned definitive Shoreditch pub and venue, with hip gigs and semi-ironic dancefloor upstairs and energetic hipsters everywhere, many complaining that it isn't as cool as it used to be. Some charges for bands, otherwise free. Daily noon–midnight, Fri–Sat till 2am.

Trapeze 89 Great Eastern St, EC2A 3HX ☎020 7739 6747, 🕸trapezebar.com; ⊖Old Street; map pp.190–191. Keeping the same space and music programmer as previous beloved occupant East Village, this is a big, fun, bolshy basement and lounge. Bar daily, club Fri & Sat 9pm–3.30am.

★**XOYO** 32–37 Cowper St, EC2A 4AP ☎020 7354 9993, 🕸xoyo.co.uk; ⊖Old Street; map pp.190–191. This 900-capacity venue and club has an annoying layout with convoluted corridors, but the programming is big-time fun, often delivered by Radio 1's roster of dance DJs. Club nights until 4am.

DALSTON AND HACKNEY

The Alibi 91 Kingsland High St, E8 2PB ☎020 7249 2733, 🕸thealibilondon.co.uk; ⊖Dalston Kingsland; map p.187. The outside doesn't look like much, but there's fun, hip DJ nights in the basement – all with nightly free entry. Sun–Wed 8pm–3am, Thurs–Sat 8pm–3am.

Birthdays 33–35 Stoke Newington Rd, N16 8BJ ☎020 7923 1680, 🕸birthdaysdalston.com; ⊖Dalston Kingsland; map p.187. Two floors, a big soundsystem, and cheap, often free gigs and nights, the tie-ups with Vice brand Noisey are a good indicator of the cool crowd in residence.

★**Dalston Superstore** 177 Kingsland High St, E8 2PB ☎020 7254 2273, 🕸dalstonsuperstore.com; ⊖Dalston Kingsland; map p.187. The Superstore has maintained its role as Dalston's capital with picky door staff, fashionable straight/gay clientele and a hedonistic mix of disco, house and party tunes. Bar daily, club usually Wed–Sun 9pm–3am.

★**Dance Tunnel** 95 Kingsland High St, E8 2PB ☎020 7249 7865, 🕸dancetunnel.com; ⊖Dalston Kingsland; map p.187. Superstore's sister venue – it would be just a dingy basement if the music wasn't so impeccably designed to get people moving. Home to dubstep night FWD>>. Usually Thurs–Sat 10pm–3am.

The Nest 36 Stoke Newington Rd, N16 7XJ ☎020 7354 9993, 🕸ilovethenest.com; ⊖Dalston Kingsland; map p.187. Electro-house and disco for the arty crowd. Long sets from decent names and cheap drinks and entry on Thursday. Usually Thurs–Sat 10pm–4am.

Oval Space 29–32 The Oval, E2 9DT ☎020 7183 4422, 🕸ovalspace.co.uk; ⊖Bethnal Green; map p.187. Huge multipurpose venue with a great soundsystem, fun crowds and a chilled-out back balcony. Nights are frequent but irregular and often earlier in the evening than most venues.

25

NOTTING HILL

Notting Hill Arts Club 21 Notting Hill Gate, W11 3JQ ☎ 020 7460 4459, ⓦ nottinghillartsclub.com; ⊖ Notting Hill Gate; map pp.276–277. Groovy dressed-down basement club-bar playing everything from funk through to soul and guitar music. Usually Wed–Sun 7pm–2am.

CAMDEN, KING'S CROSS AND ISLINGTON

EGG 200 York Way, N7 9AX ☎ 020 7871 7111, ⓦ egglondon.net; ⊖ King's Cross; map pp.284–285. Three floors and a decent outdoor space host a mixed crowd for house and rave, including lots of new tunes but often kicking it old school. Fri 11pm–8am, Sat 11pm–10am.

Electric Ballroom 184 Camden High St, NW1 8QP ☎ 020 7485 9006, ⓦ electricballroom.co.uk; ⊖ Camden Town; map pp.284–285. Historic club and rock venue, hosting rock or disco (Fri) and cheese nights (Sat), plus mid-tier gigs earlier in the evening. Fri & Sat 10.30pm–3am.

Proud Camden Stables Market, NW1 8AH ☎ 020 7482 3867, ⓦ proudcamden.com; ⊖ Camden Town; map pp.284–285. Crossing the dance/rock spectrum with live celebrity acts, ideal for when you want the feel of a student night in an old horse hospital. Club usually till 2.30am.

Scala 275 Pentonville Rd, N1 9NL ☎ 020 7833 2022, ⓦ scala.co.uk; ⊖ King's Cross; map p.127. This cavernous former cinema, full of hidden corridors and atmospheric balconies, stages fine gigs and weekend club nights covering everything from rock and soca to dub and cheese. Club usually Fri–Sun 10pm–6am.

Slimelight at Electrowerkz 7 Torrens St, EC1V 1NQ ☎ 020 7837 6419, ⓦ slimelight.com; ⊖ Angel; map pp.284–285. If you're into goth, aggrotech and other dark scene genres best displayed by the colour black, here should be your first port of call. Sat 11pm–7.30am.

SOUTH LONDON

★**Bussey Building** 133 Rye Lane, SE15 4UJ ☎ 020 7732 5275, ⓦ clfartcafe.org; ⊖≋Peckham Rye; map pp.308–309. The heart of Peckham's cool, Bussey delivers three floors of mixed bills with loads of space to dance, a friendly crowd and lots of afrobeat and disco vibes. The fortnightly Soul Train is big fun at a small price. Usually Thurs 8pm–2am, Fri & Sat 10pm–4am.

Coronet 28 New Kent Rd, SE1 6TJ ☎ 020 7701 1500, ⓦ coronettheatre.co.uk; ⊖ Elephant and Castle; map pp.226–227. Theatre-turned-cinema-turned-music venue, with a gorgeous Art Deco interior, regular club nights and gigs, catering for a vaguely more knowing crowd than nearby Ministry. Until 6am on club nights.

★**Corsica Studios** 5 Elephant Rd, SE17 1LB ☎ 020 7703 4760, ⓦ corsicastudios.com; ⊖ Elephant & Castle; map pp.226–227. Faintly scuzzy and very cool mid-sized venue that worships the bass, with breaks, dubstep, electro and techno. Try signature night Troublevision. Usually Fri–Sun 10pm–6am.

Ministry of Sound 103 Gaunt St, SE1 6DP ☎ 0870 060 0010, ⓦ ministryofsound.com/club; ⊖ Elephant & Castle; map pp.226–227. The vast headquarters of this clubbing brand may sometimes seem peopled by corporate clubbers and gawping visitors, but the soundsystem is exceptional and it gets the pick of visiting house and trance DJs. Usually Fri 10.30pm–6am, Sat 11pm–7am.

Prince of Wales 467 Brixton Rd, SW9 8HH ☎ 020 7383 7788, ⓦ pow-london.com; ⊖ Brixton; map pp.308–309. Sister club to its namesake pub downstairs. Join rooftop partying high above the hubbub of Brixton. Lots of urban and house nights. Usually open until 4am.

LONDON'S MUSIC FESTIVALS

Several new festivals have come and gone in the last few years with some notable disasters, so the following represent the tried, tested and trustworthy names.

Camden Rocks May ⓦ camdenrocksfestival.com. Replacing longstanding multi-venue festival the Camden Crawl, over 20 venues host 150 bands across one weekend.

Field Day June ⓦ fielddayfestivals.com. Victoria Park's hipster day out, where people are there as much to be seen as to see artists like Savages or Kindness.

British Summer Time June ⓦ bst-hydepark.com. Provides a series of megagigs in Hyde Park from the likes of Taylor Swift and Chic.

Calling Festival June ⓦ callingfestival.co.uk. Classic rock festival in Clapham, with recent headliners including Bruce Springsteen and Noel Gallagher.

Wireless June ⓦ wirelessfestival.co.uk. For the biggest names in international R&B, try Hyde Park's Wireless, recently featuring Drake in the headline slot.

Lovebox July ⓦ loveboxfestival.com. Groove Armada are the big name behind the long-running Lovebox, bringing dance and urban music to east London's Victoria Park.

South West Four Aug ⓦ southwestfour.com. Head down south for DJs like Faithless and Skrillex making the most of the sunshine on Clapham Common.

LGBT London

London's lesbian and gay scene today is so huge, diverse and well established that it's easy to forget just how fast it has grown and been accepted into the mainstream over the last couple of decades. Political progress has been accompanied by a depoliticized scene, as pink power has given way to the pink pound and gay liberation to gay lifestyle. As a result, straight Londoners tend to be a fairly homo-savvy bunch and are happy to embrace and even dip into the city's queer offerings. While Soho remains gay London's spiritual heart and Vauxhall is home to the big clubs, Shoreditch and Dalston draw a mixed younger crowd.

26

In central London, Soho's **Old Compton Street** (see p.99) is, so to speak, its main drag; traditional gay pubs rub alongside cafés and clubs, while hairdressers, letting agencies, sex boutiques and spiritual health centres offer a vast range of gay-run services, with lesbian bars completing the diverse mix in Soho.

The biggest and best **clubs** are now found just south of the river in **Vauxhall**, catering for every musical, sartorial and sexual taste, but there are well-established venues all over the city. Both Soho and Vauxhall have lost a considerable number of venues in the last couple of years, often at short notice, so check websites before a night out. **Clapham** also hosts a smaller gay contingent for the south.

In **east and northeast London**, the clubs and bars of Shoreditch and particularly Dalston cater for a younger, cooler and substantially more mixed crowd, to the point you can struggle to tell the gay and straight nights – and clienteles – apart from each other. Head further north again for London's main lesbian contingent in Stoke Newington and Hackney.

Despite some recent homophobic attacks, you may see some gay couples holding hands around town. Still, it's probably wise not to follow suit until you have a feel for any given area.

ESSENTIALS

LESBIAN AND GAY MEDIA

PRINT

While glossy print titles have to appeal to a broader UK audience, the free magazines have excellent London listings. Pick them up in gay bars around town. Paid-for titles include **Attitude** (ⓦ attitude.co.uk) and rival **Gay Times** (ⓦ gaytimes.co.uk) with **Diva** (ⓦ divamag.co.uk) aimed squarely at the lesbian market. As for the freebies, check out **Boyz** (ⓦ boyz.co.uk) and **qx** (ⓦ qxmagazine .com), which are also available in full on their websites.

ONLINE

Where print media has wilted, online sources have filled the void.

ⓦ **pinknews.co.uk** All the LGBT news that's fit to publish.
ⓦ **g3mag.co.uk** Former lesbian print title's online home.
ⓦ **gaytoz.com** Directory of LGBT-friendly organizations and businesses.
ⓦ **gingerbeer.co.uk** Reviews of bars, clubs and events

for lesbians, with excellent listings of occasional nights.

HELPLINES

London Lesbian & Gay Switchboard ☎ 0300 330 0630, ⓦ llgs.org.uk. Whether you need to talk through coming out or other personal problems, find legal advice and counselling, or just get some information from their massive database, call LLGS. Lines are open 365 days a year, 10am to 11pm: keep trying if you can't get through, or try email or instant messaging via the website.

THT Direct ☎ 0808 802 1221, ⓦ tht.org.uk. Helpline for anyone worried about HIV, STIs and sexual health.

TOURS

A good introduction to Soho's lesbian and gay history is offered by the walking tour (2–4pm) organized by Centred most Sundays (☎ 020 7437 6063, ⓦ centred.org.uk to check it is running; £5) – meet outside the *Admiral Duncan* pub (see opposite).

HOTELS

You shouldn't expect homophobia in mainstream hotels, but these hotels are specifically gay run. London's best-known gay accommodation options cater mostly for men, though all are lesbian friendly. Self-catering apartments are available through the gay-run Outlet Gay Accommodation, 32 Old Compton St, W1 (☎ 020 7287 4244; ⓦ outlet4holidays.com).

Fitzbb 15 Colville Place, W1T 2BN ☎ 07834 372866, ⓦ fitzbb.me.uk; ⊖ Goodge St; map p.97. This townhouse is stumbling distance from Soho but only has two rooms, so book ahead. Minimum booking of three nights **£75**.

Griffin House Holiday Apartments 22 Stockwell Green, SW9 9HZ ☎ 020 7096 3332, ⓦ griffinhouse.info; ⊖ Stockwell; map pp.308–309. Highly rated self-catering accommodation, 10min walk from the Vauxhall scene. Apartments **£120**.

ARTS

If you want something more Bellini than appletini, then London's gay art scene has plenty to offer. First among equals is the monthly Polari (ⓦ polariliterarysalon.co.uk), a lively but warm literary art salon that has even spawned its own book prize. **On stage**, Vauxhall's Above The Stag (ⓦ abovethestag.com) is London's only LGBT theatre, and it premieres new writing at £18 a show. Wider bills make up Tuesdays' Bar Wotever at the *Royal Vauxhall Tavern*, providing live music, cabaret and more from guest and resident performers. **On screen**, March sees the British Film Institute host Flare, the new name for the Lesbian and Gay Film Festival (ⓦbfi.org.uk/flare), which celebrates new cinema from around the world. Vogue Fabrics (ⓦvoguefabricsdalston.com) also has a hefty dose of arts programming aimed at the Dalston cool crowd. For more arts check out the local gay press (see opposite), or check radical gay arts group LeftFrontArt (ⓦleftfrontart.com) for more pointers.

CAFÉS, BARS AND PUBS

There are loads of lesbian and gay eating and watering holes in London, many of them operating as cafés by day and transforming into drinking dens by night. Lots have cabaret or disco nights and are open until the early hours, making them an affordable alternative to clubs. Most have free admission, though a few levy a charge after 10.30pm (expect to pay about £5) if there's music, cabaret or a disco. The places below represent a selective list of the best and most accessible, from self-consciously minimalist bars to shabby old pubs. We use "mixed" to mean places for both gays and lesbians, though most are primarily frequented by men.

26

MIXED CAFÉS, BARS AND PUBS

SOHO

The Admiral Duncan 54 Old Compton St, W1D 4UB ☎020 7437 5300; ⊖ Leicester Square; map p.101. Unpretentious, traditional-style gay bar in the heart of Soho, popular and busy with the post-work crowd. Expect cocktails and camp classics on the jukebox. Mon–Thurs 2–11.30pm, Fri & Sat noon–midnight, Sun noon–10.30pm.

Balans 34 Old Compton St, W1D 4TS ☎020 7439 3309; 60 Old Compton St, W1D 4UG ☎020 7439 2183; ⓦbalans.co.uk; ⊖ Leicester Square; map p.101. Balans has spawned several branches across the city but these two remain a Soho institution, serving a menu that includes a lengthy hangover-busting breakfast and brunch section. No. 34 24hr; no. 60 Mon–Thurs 7.30am–5am, Fri & Sat 7.30am–6am, Sun 7.30am–2am.

Circa 62 Frith St, W1D 3JN ☎020 7734 6826, ⓦcircasoho.com; ⊖ Tottenham Court Road; map p.101. Unpretentious boy bar that's quickly become a standard stop-off point on the Soho circuit. Daily 1pm–1am.

City of Quebec 12 Old Quebec St, W1H 7AF ☎020 7629 6159, ⓦcityofquebec-marylebone.co.uk; ⊖ Marble Arch; map p.89. An older crowd enjoys the gay answer to London's old man pubs, complete with Thursday pub quiz. Mon–Thurs noon–2am, Fri & Sat noon–3am, Sun noon–1am.

★Duke of Wellington 77 Wardour St, W1D 6QA ☎020 7439 1274; ⊖ Piccadilly Circus; map p.101. Traditional pub on two floors in the heart of Soho, with cheap lager and real ale on pump and a down-to-earth, male-dominated crowd, keen on chatting and socializing. Mon–Fri noon–midnight, Sat 11am–midnight, Sun noon–11.30pm.

The Edge 11 Soho Square, W1D 3QE ☎020 7439 1313, ⓦedgesoho.co.uk; ⊖ Tottenham Court Road; map p.101. Sister to *The Yard*, it may be a regular Soho bar by night, but by day it's a useful stop for food. Mon–Wed 4pm–1am, Thurs 3pm–1am, Fri & Sat noon–3am, Sun 4–11.30pm.

Freedom 66 Wardour St, W1F 0TA ☎020 7734 0071, ⓦfreedombarsoho.com; ⊖ Piccadilly Circus; map p.101. Hip, metrosexual place, popular for cheap weekday after work drinks or a fun dance spot at the weekend. Mon–Thurs 4pm–3am, Fri & Sat 2pm–3am, Sun 2–10.30pm.

G-A-Y Bar 30 Old Compton St, W1D 4UR ☎020 7494 2756, ⓦg-a-y.co.uk; ⊖ Leicester Square; map p.101. Vast video bar that attracts a young, fashionable, pre-G-A-Y crowd. There is a basement bar for women and guests only in the evening. Daily noon–midnight.

Ku Bar 30 Lisle St, WC2H 7BA ☎020 7437 4303; 25 Frith St, W1D 5LB ☎020 7437 4303, ⓦku-bar.co.uk; ⊖ Leicester Square; map p.101. The Lisle Street original is one of Soho's largest and best-loved gay bars, serving a scene-conscious yet low-attitude clientele. Ruby Tuesdays are for lesbians only. The Frith Street sister bar is a calmer cocktail spot. Lisle St: Mon–Sat noon–3am, Sun noon–midnight; Frith St: Mon–Thurs noon–11pm, Fri & Sat noon–midnight, Sun noon–10.30pm.

★Rupert Street 50 Rupert St, W1D 6DR ⓦrupert-street.com; ⊖ Piccadilly Circus; map p.101. Come to see and be seen at this smart, mainstream bar attracting a mixed after-work crowd, but with a more pre-club vibe at weekends. Ideal central location to start a Soho night out; happy hour lasts until 8pm. Mon–Fri noon–11pm, Sat noon–midnight, Sun noon–10.30pm.

Village Soho 81 Wardour St, W1D 6QD ☎020 7478 0530, ⓦvillage-soho.co.uk; ⊖ Piccadilly Circus; map p.101. Three floors of cafe-bar fun, with a decent happy hour to boot: it's clean and modern on the ground floor, with a stylish basement and a plush, comfortable upstairs boudoir. Mon–Sat 4pm–1am, Sun 4–11.30pm.

The Yard 57 Rupert St, W1D 7PL ☎020 7437 2652, ⓦyardbar.co.uk; ⊖ Piccadilly Circus; map p.101. The only central alfresco gay bar, it has a sociable atmosphere for an often older crowd. Expect a packed-out varied post-work crowd when the sun is out. Mon–Wed 4–11.30pm, Thurs 3–11.30pm, Fri & Sat 2pm–midnight, Sun 2–10.30pm.

26

COVENT GARDEN

Retro Bar 2 George Court (off Strand), WC2N 6HH ☎020 7839 8760, ⓦretrobarlondon.co.uk; ➌Charing Cross; map p.108. Friendly bar tucked down a quiet alleyway off the Strand, playing classic indie, rock and pop. Mon–Fri noon–11pm, Sat 2–11pm, Sun 2–10.30pm.

KING'S CROSS AND BLOOMSBURY

Central Station 37 Wharfdale Rd, N1 9SD ☎020 7278 3294, ⓦcentralstation.co.uk; ➌King's Cross St Pancras; map p.127. Late-opening pub that swings from low-key sports bar to weekend cabaret – something for everyone. Downstairs is deep fetish bar Underground Club. Sun–Wed noon–1am, Thurs–Fri noon–2am, Sat noon–3am, Sun noon–midnight.

New Bloomsbury Set 76 Marchmont St, WC1N 1AG ☎020 7383 3084, ⓦnewbloomsburyset.co.uk; ➌Russell Square; map p.127. Hit happy hour at the right time and get cheap and cheerful cocktails in this 21+ basement bar. Best enjoyed by securing one of their cute and cosy snugs to enjoy its speakeasy vibe. Mon–Sat 4–11.30pm, Sun 4–10.30pm.

SHOREDITCH

George & Dragon 2–4 Hackney Rd, E2 7NS ☎020 7012 1100; ➌Old Street; map pp.190–191. Dandies, fashionistas and locals meet in this lively, often rammed east London hangout. The interior set-up is small and traditional, but the attitudes are not. Daily 5pm–midnight.

DALSTON

★**Dalston Superstore** 117 Kingsland High St, E8 2PB ☎020 7254 2273, ⓦdalstonsuperstore.com; ➌Dalston Junction; map p.187. The hottest late-night destination in east London, catering for a fashionably mixed but often gay crowd, with some nights gayer than others; try out Little Gay Brother for the boys, or Clam Jam and Club Lesley for the girls. Daytimes bring music, art and food. Bar daily, club usually Wed–Sun 9pm–3am.

VAUXHALL

Counter South Lambeth Road, SW8 1RH ☎020 3693 9600, ⓦcounterrestaurants.com; ➌Vauxhall; map pp.308–309. A welcome addition to Vauxhall, the front brasserie provides a classy menu of food and cocktails, while Back Counter has a rolling schedule of cabaret and entertainment.

DOCKLANDS

Old Ship 17 Barnes St, E14 7NW ☎020 7791 1301, ⓦoldship.net; ➌Limehouse DLR; map p.187. Even Londoners are surprised the first time they encounter the *Old Ship*: an old school pub with what's probably the cheapest pint (from £2.80) in gay London, with raucous weekend cabaret. Mon–Wed 11am–1pm, Thu–Sun midday-midnight.

SOUTH LONDON

Bridge 8 Voltaire Rd, SW4 6DH ☎020 3632 6426, ⓦbridgewinebar.com; ➌Clapham North; map pp.308–309. Brash train arch bar, mixing cocktails and tunes for a buff Clapham crowd. Sun–Thurs 4pm–midnight, Fri & Sat 4pm–3am.

Kazbar 50 Clapham High St, SW4 7UL ☎020 7622 0070, ⓦkazbarclapham.com; ➌Clapham North; map pp.308–309. Modern, mostly buff boyz, split-level bar; upstairs is a lounge area, while there is popular alfresco eating out front. A touch of Soho in south London. Mon & Tues 5–11pm, Wed & Thurs 5pm–midnight, Fri 5pm–1am, Sat 4pm–1am, Sun 1pm–midnight.

★**The Royal Vauxhall Tavern** 372 Kennington Lane, SE11 ☎020 7820 1222, ⓦrvt.org.uk; ➌Vauxhall; map pp.308–309. This huge, disreputable, divey drag and cabaret pub is home to legendary alternative night Duckie

---

FESTIVALS

London's biggest gay events – Pride and the Lesbian and Gay Film Festival – have both had cash woes the last few years, but remain centrepieces of the calendar. London's **Pride** lands in late June, taking over central London and featuring a massive rally in Trafalgar Square, a colourful, whistle-blowing march through the city streets, live cabaret in Leicester Square and a women's stage in Soho. Full details on the website ⓦprideinlondon.org.

There are also festivals that are centred around bringing the best of Vauxhall-style clubs outside during summer: **As One In The Park** (ⓦfacebook.com/AsOneInThePark) has hopped around the calendar but is currently delivering big sounds at Easter, while weekender **Lovebox** (July, ⓦloveboxfestival.com) is at its gayest on Sundays with stellar populist line-ups.

Out On The Dock brings several gay clubs together in the Docklands in both winter and summer editions. The format has varied wildly in its short life, but you can expect Berlin-scale soundsystems out in Tobacco Docks.

on Saturdays. The rest of the week brings a changing calendar of performance that attracts a varied but often older crowd. Mon–Thurs 7pm–midnight, Fri 7pm–2am, Sat 9pm–2am, Sun 3pm–midnight.

Two Brewers 114 Clapham High St, SW4 7UJ ☎ 020 7819 9539, 🖥 the2brewers.com; ⊖ Clapham Common; map pp.308–309. Big, long-established and popular south London pub, with nightly cabaret in the front bar and a more cruisey dancefloor in the back that stays open late. Sun–Thurs 5pm–2am, Fri & Sat 5pm–4am.

WEST LONDON

The Imperial Arms 8 Lillie Rd, SW6 1TU ☎ 07854 451 511; ⊖ West Brompton; map pp.252–253. A new opening in the former gay ghetto of Earls Court, this old brewery pub serves food all day, plus roasts and karaoke on Sundays. Mon–Thurs 7am–midnight, Fri–Sat 7am–1am, Sun 1pm–midnight.

LESBIAN CAFÉS, BARS AND PUBS
SOHO

Muse Soho 23 Frith St, W1D 4RR ☎ 0207 734 9404, 🖥 musesoho.com; ⊖ Tottenham Court Road; map p.101. Restaurant and lounge providing classy cocktails and food, plus weekly acoustic music sessions (previously called Labels). Thurs–Sat 6pm–4am.

★ She Soho 23a Old Compton St, W1D 5JL ☎ 0207 437 4303, 🖥 she-soho.com; ⊖ Tottenham Court Road; map p.101. Remarkably, this is Old Compton Street's first and only lesbian bar. Opening not long after *Candy Bar* closed, this basement bar is a somewhat smarter proposition, with DJs at the weekend. Mon–Thurs 4–11.30pm, Fri & Sat 4pm–12.30am, Sun 4–10.30pm.

Star at Night 22 Great Chapel St, W1F 8FR ☎ 020 7494 2488, 🖥 thestaratnight.com; ⊖ Tottenham Court Road; map p.101. Mixed but female-led venue, popular with a slightly older crowd who want somewhere to sit, a decent glass of wine and good conversation. Tues–Sat 6–11.30pm.

Titania 75 Charing Cross Rd, WC2H 0NE ☎ 020 7287 2616, 🖥 titaniasoho.com; ⊖ Leicester Square; map p.101. Homely bar with a regular schedule of events from karaoke to open mic. Tues–Thurs 3–11.30pm, Fri & Sat 3pm–midnight, Sun 3–10.30pm.

EAST LONDON

Blush 8 Cazenove Rd, Stoke Newington, N16 6BD ☎ 020 7923 9202; ⇌ Stoke Newington; map p.187. Two floors of fun with quizzes, games nights and Friday karaoke make this local popular among lesbians. Tues–Sat 5.30pm–12.30am, Sun 4pm–12.30am.

GAY MEN'S CAFÉS, BARS AND PUBS
SOHO

Comptons of Soho 51–53 Old Compton St, W1D 6HN ☎ 020 3238 0163, 🖥 fauceinn.com/comptons; ⊖ Leicester Square; map p.101. This large, traditional-style pub attracts a butch, cruising yet relaxed 25-plus crowd. Upstairs is more chilled and draws younger folks. Mon–Thurs noon–11.30pm, Fri & Sat noon–midnight, Sun noon–10.30pm.

The King's Arms 23 Poland St, W1F 8QL ☎ 020 7734 5907; ⊖ Oxford Circus; map p.97. London's best-known and perennially popular bear bar, with a traditional London pub atmosphere. Head down on Sundays for the raucous karaoke night. Mon–Thurs noon–11pm, Fri & Sat noon–midnight, Sun 1pm–11pm.

COVENT GARDEN

Halfway 2 Heaven 7 Duncannon St, WC2N 4JF ☎ 020 7484 0736, 🖥 halfway2heaven.net; ⊖ Charing Cross; map p.108. Friendly, traditional pub off Trafalgar Square, featuring cabaret, karaoke and more. Attracts a largely male crowd older than that in Soho. Mon–Sat noon–midnight, Fri & Sat noon–3am, Sun noon–11pm.

CLUBS

London's club nights tend to open up and shut down with surreal frequency, so do check location, times and prices online before heading out. Places are listed by club name if this is well known and long lived, and by venue where there's a variety of changing theme nights. Entry **prices** start at around £3–5, but are more often between £10 and £16 for all-nighters, rising to around £35 or even £50 for special events like New Year's Eve extravaganzas. A shrinking number of places offer student concessions; picking up a flyer may help you save a few quid instead, especially for venues with attached bars. Most clubs **open** at around 11pm (although some don't get going until the small hours) and close between 3am and 6am, while after-hours clubs provide somewhere to dance the next morning.

MIXED CLUBS
SOHO

G-A-Y Late 5 Goslett Yard, WC2H 0EA ☎ 020 7494 2756, 🖥 g-a-y.co.uk; ⊖ Tottenham Court Road; map p.101. No-frills cheese and pop princesses at the late-night sister bar to G-A-Y – grab a flyer there first for free entry. Licensing means it's members only Sundays. Daily 11pm–3am.

COVENT GARDEN

Heaven Villiers St, WC2N 6NG ☎ 020 7930 2020, 🖥 heavennightclub-london.com; ⊖ Charing Cross; map p.108. Said to be the UK's most popular gay club, this two

26

SAUNAS AND GYMS

The following saunas are large sites, although there are more intimate venues around town. There have been some high-profile incidents in London saunas so be safety-minded. They all charge around £10–15.

Chariots 1 Fairchild St, EC2A 3NS, ⊖ Liverpool Street; 63–64 Albert Embankment, SE1 7TP, ⊖ Vauxhall; 101 Lower Marsh, SE1 7AB, ⊖ Waterloo; 292 Streatham High Rd, SW16 6HG; ⇌ Streatham. ☎ 020 7247 5333, ⓦ chariots.co.uk. London's Roman sauna chain has four locations: the Waterloo branch never closes, while the rest have long hours. Expect steam, sweat and videos. The Shoreditch branch is the largest and has a heated pool.

Pleasuredrome Sauna Arch 124, Alaska St, SE1 8XE ☎ 020 7633 9194, ⓦ pleasuredrome.com; ⊖ Waterloo. Refurbished facilities include two saunas, two steam rooms, dark areas and private rooms, plus café-bar and spa. Open 24hr.

The Stable 29 Endell St, WC2H 9BA ☎ 020 7836 2236, ⓦ thestable.london; ⊖ Covent Garden. Very central, this friendly place offers the usual facilities, along with masseurs and a bar. Mon–Fri 11.30am–11.30pm, Sat noon–11.30pm, Sun noon–10pm.

Sweatbox 1–2 Ramillies St, W1F 7LN ☎ 020 3214 6014, ⓦ sweatboxsoho.com. There's a line of argument that says lots of gyms in central London are gay gyms. Well, it's a little more explicit at gym/sauna Sweatbox. If you want to get pumped before a big night out, you can pick up a one-day pass for £17 – it's valid for 24 hours so you can make the most of it – and there are weekly foam parties too.

---

thousand-capacity venue is now home to G-A-Y from Thursdays to Saturdays, with big-name DJs and PAs – expect lots of Drag Race rejects – plus Popcorn Monday brings the weekday pop fun till 5.30am.

THE CITY

WayOut Club 64–73 Minories, EC3N 1JL; Mary Janes, 124–127 Minories, EC3N 1NT; ⊖ Tower Hill; ☎ 07778 157 290, ⓦ thewayoutclub.com; map pp.152–153. Long-established Saturday night for the transgendered crowd and friends that now runs across two nearby venues, offering a warm welcome, changing rooms, video screens and cabaret until 4am.

SHOREDITCH AND EAST LONDON

The Backstreet Wentworth Mews, Mile End, E3 4UA ☎ 020 890 8557 ⓦ thebackstreet.com; ⊖ Mile End; map p.187. Leather and rubber bar at the weekends until 3am, plus naked/underwear nights earlier in the evening.

East Bloc 217 City Rd, EC1V 1JN ☎ 020 7253 0367, ⓦ eastbloc.co.uk; ⊖ Old Street; map pp.190–191. Retaining its cool as most of the area goes mainstream, *East Bloc* brings electro to its cute basement site. Look out for the guaranteed cool beats of Dish.

★The Glory 281 Kingsland Rd, E2 8AS ⓦ theglory .co; ⊖ Haggerston; map p.187. Drag legend Jonny Woo's meld of lip-syncingly excellent performance, booze and a basement club for disco queens.

Savage Metropolis Strip Club, 234 Cambridge Heath Rd, E2 9NN ⓦ facebook.com/SheisSavage; ⊖ Bethnal Green; map p.187. A night in three floors of a strip club was never going to be respectable. Saturday night stripper chic

brought by gay disco dons Sink The Pink until 5am – and only a fiver.

★Vogue Fabrics 66 Stoke Newington Rd, N16 7XB, ⓦ voguefabricsdalston.com; map p.187. Dalston's favourite disco basement ranging across an array of arts events and disco fun for a fashion crowd. Highlights including genderqueer performance night Icy Gays and grrls Cherry Bomb.

NORTH LONDON

Choose Yr Own Adventure New Unity, 277a Upper Street, N1 2TZ ⓦ on.fb.me/1jLZzmf; ⊖ Angel; map pp.284–285. Find the London scene a little intoxicated? The first Saturday of every month sees this sober LGBTQ party spin tunes to get you moving.

Club Kali The Dome, 2 Dartmouth Park Hill, NW5 1HL ⓦ clubkali.com; ⊖ Tufnell Park; map pp.296–297. Held on the third Friday of every month, Kali offers bhangra, Bollywood, Arabic, r'n'b and dance flavours for an attitude-free crowd.

Exilio Latino Latin Groove, 1 Archway Rd, N19 3TD ☎ 07956 983230, ⓦ exilio.co.uk; ⊖ Archway; map pp.296–297. Long-running night playing Latin beats for a mixed crowd.

SOUTH LONDON

Bootylicious Electric Brixton, Town Hall Parade, Brixton Hill, SW2 1RJ ⓦ bootylicious-club.co.uk; ⊖ Brixton; map pp.308–309. Despite London's large black community, this is the capital's only dedicated gay and lesbian urban music/BME night, held every third Saturday of the month and featuring r'n'b, hip-hop, dancehall, house and classic vibes.

★Duckie Royal Vauxhall Tavern (see p.408), 372 Kennington Lane, SE11 5HY ☎020 7737 4043, ⓦduckie.co.uk; ⊖Vauxhall. Duckie's mix of regular live art performances and theme nights, plus cult DJs The Readers Wifes playing everything from Kim Wilde to the Velvet Underground, has kept the night going strong for nearly 20 years.

LESBIAN CLUBS
NORTH LONDON
Blue Monday Boogaloo, 312 Archway Rd, N6 5AT ⓦtheboogaloo.co.uk/bluemonday; ⊖Highgate; map pp.296–297. Live indie music night for lesbians and bisexuals on the second Mon of every month. Events are streamed live on the internet.

Waltzing with Hilda Jacksons Lane Arts Centre, 269a Archway Rd, N6 5AA ☎07939 072958, ⓦhildas.org.uk; ⊖Highgate; map pp.296–297. Women-only Latin and ballroom dancing club with classes for beginners and the more experienced. Held on the second Sat of every month (7.30–11.30pm) but closed in Aug.

GAY MEN'S CLUBS
THE CITY
Brüt Steel Yard, 13–15 Allhallows Lane, EC4R 3UL; ⊖Cannon Street; map pp.152–153. Brand-new all-nighter selling its wares in the heart of the City to bears, blokes, cubs and hunks.

SOHO
Room Service Miabella, 12–13 Greek St, W1D 4DJ ⓦclubroomservice.com; ⊖Tottenham Court Road; map p.101. Created by legendary party maker Jodie Harsh in late 2010, this weekly Thursday night event is the latest attempt to re-create 1970s New York in old London town. Probably only worth it if you're feeling confident in your abs… and you can get on the guest list.

Shadow Lounge 5 Brewer St, W1F 0RF ☎020 7317 9270, ⓦtheshadowlounge.co.uk; ⊖Piccadilly Circus; map p.101. Classier than the general Soho vibe, expect bubbles with your beautiful boys. Weekends have long been fun; Jodie Harsh is shaking up Wednesday nights with Ultraviolet.

SOUTH LONDON
★The Eagle 349 Kennington Lane, SE11 5QY ☎020 7793 0903, ⓦeaglelondon.com; ⊖Vauxhall; map pp.308–309. Home to the excellent disco Sunday-nighter Horse Meat Disco, the vibe here is a loose, friendly

re-creation of late 1970s New York, complete with facial hair, checked shirts and a pool table – more Italo disco and bear-y sorts than you can shake a moustache at. Friday night Men Inc also attracts a handsome crowd.

★Fire South Lambeth Rd, SW8 1RT ☎020 3242 0040, ⓦfirelondon.net; ⊖Vauxhall; map pp.308–309. Fire is London's superclub of choice for disco bunnies and hardboyz. All-nighters – and often all-dayers if you're making a proper weekend of it – every weekend.

The Hoist 47b–47c South Lambeth Rd, SW8 1RH ☎020 7735 9972, ⓦthehoist.co.uk; ⊖Vauxhall; map pp.308–309. London's biggest and best-known leather/dress code bar for men with few inhibitions. The Hoist also hosts regular nights for rubber and other fetishes, as well as NBN and SBN: Nearly/Stark Bollock Naked.

Union 66 Albert Embankment, SE1 7TW ☎07970 193236, ⓦfacebook.com/UnionVauxhall; ⊖Vauxhall; map pp.308–309. With semi-clothed, arousing nights, this venue appeals to the unabashedly cruisey late every night of the week. Also offers Saturday after-hours night Wrong!, and Suzie Krueger's celebrated raunchy fetish/dance club night Hard-On, which has a very strict dress code.

XXL Pulse, The Arches, Southwark St, SE1 9UF ⓦxxl-london.com; ⊖Southwark; map pp.228–229. Massively popular Saturday dance club for big, burly men and their fans, attracting a diverse crowd with its two dance floors, two bars and a chill-out area.

WEST LONDON
Ted's Place 305 North Rd, W14 9NS ☎0207 385 9359, ⓦtedsplace.co.uk; ⊖West Brompton; map pp.252–253. West London basement space famous for its TV/TS nights – it's party night Thursday and chill-out night Sunday. Closed Wed and Sat.

West 5 Popes Lane, W5 4NT ☎020 8579 3266, ⓦwest5ealing.co.uk; ⊖Northfields; map pp.252–253. A vintage brewery pub in South Ealing may not be the obvious place for a big night out, but if you're after ridiculous, no-judgement fun – and an endless carousel of Drag Race contestants – it delivers.

KING'S CROSS AND AROUND
The Vault 139–143 Whitfield St, W1T 5EN ☎020 7388 5500, ⓦvault139.com; ⊖Warren Street; map p. 97. The cruisiest club around, with about half its schedule handed over to fully stripped nights.

ENGLISH NATIONAL BALLET'S SWAN LAKE AT THE COLISEUM

Classical music, opera and dance

With established venues like the Southbank Centre, the Barbican and Wigmore Hall offering year-round appearances by first-rate musicians, and numerous smaller venues providing a stage for less-established or more specialized performers, the capital should satisfy most devotees of classical music. What's more, in the annual Proms, London has one of the world's greatest, most democratic music festivals. Opera has an enthusiastic following, too, with live screenings and fringe performances making it increasingly accessible to those who can't afford full-price tickets at the grand opera houses. You'll also find a broad spectrum of ambitious dance performances in a range of excellent venues to suit all pockets.

London is spoilt for choice when it comes to **orchestras**. On most days you should be able to catch a concert by one of the many world-class major orchestras, or more specialized ensembles, based in the city, and prices aren't too high. While the **Royal Opera House** (ROH) can attract top international stars, the downside is the prohibitive price (and availability) of most of the tickets. The nearby **English National Opera** (ENO) is often slightly less expensive, and can be more adventurous in its repertoire and productions. Small-scale and intimate productions have brought opera to the masses, while many of the off-West End theatres (see p.419) extend the boundaries of contemporary classical music and physical theatre in lively ways. As for dance, your first stop should be **Sadler's Wells**, where some of the world's outstanding companies regularly appear. Fans of classicism can revel in the **Royal Ballet**, a company with some of the most accomplished dancers in Europe.

CLASSICAL MUSIC

Unless a glamorous guest conductor is wielding the baton, or one of the world's high-profile orchestras is giving a performance, you should be able to attend a **classical concert** for around £15 (the usual range is about £12–50), and a good few concerts are **free**; check ⓦ cityevents.org.uk for a guide to free concerts in the City's many churches. In addition to the venues listed below, check the music schedules at Wilton's, a fabulous Victorian music hall in the East End (see p.420), which occasionally stages classical and avant-garde concerts.

27

THE PROMS AND OTHER CLASSICAL MUSIC FESTIVALS

THE PROMS

The **BBC Henry Wood Promenade Concerts** (Royal Albert Hall; ☎0845 401 5040, ⓦbbc .co.uk/proms; ⊖ South Kensington), better known simply as the **Proms**, tend to be associated with the raucous "Last Night", when the flag-waving audience sings its patriotic heart out to *Land of Hope and Glory*. In fact, this jingoistic knees-up is untypical of the season (mid-July to mid-Sept; tickets on sale from mid-May), which features around 75 concerts with an exhilarating mix of favourites and new or recondite works, along with alternative "Late Night" gigs (from the Philharmonic playing bhangra to grime shows and DJ sessions). The unique aspect of the Proms is that seats in the arena, and the upper gallery, are removed to create up to 1350 **standing places** – these "Promming" places cost £5, even on the last night, and must be bought on the door, on the day. Alternatively, you can buy a Promming pass (season tickets, which include the last night, cost £200; "half-season" options £120; weekend passes £9–27), which guarantee you entrance up to twenty minutes before a show. Seated **tickets** cost £7.50–95; those for the last night, which start at £57, are largely allocated by ballot, with priority given to customers who have bought tickets to at least five other concerts, and two hundred more in an open ballot. Some are also sold on the night. The acoustics aren't the world's best – OK for orchestral blockbusters, less so for small-scale works – but the performers are generally outstanding, the atmosphere is uplifting and the hall is so vast that even if you turn up on the day you have a good chance of getting in. A handful of chamber music matinee concerts are also held in Cadogan Hall, just off Sloane Square, while a "Proms Extra" series includes talks and family events at the Royal College of Music.

OTHER FESTIVALS

London has several more important classical music festivals. The most prestigious is probably the **City of London Festival** (ⓦcolf.org), which takes place in the City's churches, music venues, open spaces and livery halls for three weeks from late June. St Leonard's (Shoreditch) Church, Spitalfields, is at the centre of several music events. The largest of them, **Spitalfields Music Summer Festival** in June (ⓦspitalfieldsmusic.org.uk), features shows in a variety of intriguing venues, from private houses to arts centres in east London; the same organizers also put on a winter festival in December. Other annual festivals to look out for include the **Festival of Baroque Music** (ⓦlfbm.org.uk), in May, which has some concerts in Westminster Abbey, and the **Early Music Festival and Exhibition** (ⓦearlymusicfestival.com), held in November in Greenwich's beautiful Old Royal Naval College.

27

MAJOR VENUES

Barbican Centre Silk St, EC2 8DS ☎ 020 7638 8891, ⓦ barbican.org.uk; ⊖ Barbican or Moorgate. With the outstanding resident London Symphony Orchestra (ⓦ lso .co.uk) and the BBC Symphony Orchestra (ⓦ bbc.co.uk/ orchestras) as associate orchestra, and top foreign orchestras, ensembles and big-name soloists in regular attendance, the Barbican is one of London's best places to enjoy top-notch classical music.

Cadogan Hall 5 Sloane Terrace, SW1X 9DQ ☎ 020 7730 4500, ⓦ www.cadoganhall.com; ⊖ Sloane Square. This handsome neo-Byzantine building, built in 1901 as a Christian Science church, now serves as a 950-seat concert hall with outstanding acoustics. The Royal Philharmonic (ⓦ rpo.co.uk) is its resident orchestra and it hosts Proms chamber concerts (see box, p.413).

Kings Place 90 York Way, N1 9AG ☎ 020 7520 1490, ⓦ kingsplace.co.uk; ⊖ King's Cross St Pancras. This modern, purpose-built venue, by the canal behind King's Cross, has two performance spaces. It's headquarters of the London Sinfonietta (ⓦ londonsinfonietta.org.uk), one of the world's finest contemporary classical music groups, along with resident companies the innovative Aurora Orchestra (ⓦ auroraorchestra.com) and the Orchestra of the Age of Enlightenment (ⓦ oae.co.uk), who play on period instruments. The London Chamber Music Society (ⓦ londonchambermusic.org.uk) also hosts concerts (usually Sunday evening).

LSO St Luke's 161 Old St, EC1V 8NG ☎ 020 7638 8891, ⓦ lso.co.uk/lso-st-lukes; ⊖ Old Street. Within this Hawksmoor church is the Jerwood Hall, a fabulously converted 450-seat performance/rehearsal space that hosts the London Symphony Orchestra (ⓦ lso.co.uk) and its splendid young associate Aurora Orchestra (ⓦ auroraorchestra.com). It's actually used for a wide variety of concerts from world music to experimental jazz. Popular chamber recitals (£10), recorded for BBC Radio 3, are held here on Thursday lunchtimes, and there's a summer series of free lunchtime world music concerts in the garden.

St John's Smith Square, SW1P 3HA ☎ 020 7222 1061, ⓦ sjss.org.uk; ⊖ Westminster. Built in 1728 and firebombed in 1941, this striking Baroque church is home to an exceptional concert hall, with fine acoustics and a great organ. Its varied season includes orchestral and choral concerts, chamber music and solo recitals, from domestic and visiting companies. Shows are mostly in the evenings but also on some Thursday lunchtimes (£10) and Sunday afternoons (£14).

Southbank Centre Belvedere Rd, South Bank, SE1 8XX ☎ 020 7960 4200, ⓦ southbankcentre.co.uk; ⊖ Waterloo or Embankment. The Southbank has three concert venues, none of which is exclusively used for classical music. The 2500-seat Royal Festival Hall (RFH) is tailor-made for large-scale choral and orchestral works and home to the Philharmonia (ⓦ philharmonia.co.uk and the London Philharmonic (ⓦ lpo.co.uk). The Queen Elizabeth Hall (QEH) is the prime location for chamber concerts, solo recitals, opera and choirs, while the intimate Purcell Room, in the QEH building, sees chamber music and recitals by up-and-coming instrumentalists and singers. Other resident orchestras at the Southbank include the experimental Orchestra of the Age of Enlightenment (ⓦ oae.co.uk) and the superb London Sinfonietta (ⓦ londonsinfonietta.org.uk).

Wigmore Hall 36 Wigmore St, W1U 2BP ☎ 020 7935 2141, ⓦ wigmore-hall.org.uk; ⊖ Bond Street or Oxford Circus. With its near-perfect acoustics, the intimate Wigmore Hall – built in 1901 as a hall for the adjacent Bechstein piano showroom – is a favourite with artists and audiences alike, so book well in advance. It's brilliant for piano recitals and chamber music, but best known for its song recitals by some of the world's greatest vocalists. Some lunchtime (generally Mon and Thurs) and Sunday daytime performances.

CHURCHES AND FREE CONCERTS

BBC SO Studio Concerts Delaware Rd, W9 2LG ⓦ bbc .co.uk/orchestras; ⊖ Warwick Avenue or Maida Vale. Though they are more often to be found doing the rounds of the other major venues, the BBC Symphony Orchestra and Singers do stage a few free concerts at the Maida Vale studios.

Royal Academy of Music Marylebone Rd, NW1 5HT ☎ 020 7873 7300, ⓦ ram.ac.uk; ⊖ Baker Street. The academy's excellent "Free on Fridays" lunchtime concerts, featuring a variety of performers and music styles, are a firm fixture on its concert schedule (book in advance), along with free chamber concerts on Tuesday and Thursday lunchtimes (no booking required).

Royal College of Music Prince Consort Rd, SW7 2BS ☎ 020 7591 4300, ⓦ rcm.ac.uk; ⊖ South Kensington. The RCM hosts regular concerts of an amazingly high standard, many of them free, on site and in venues around the capital from concert halls to churches and parks. Booking generally required.

St James Piccadilly 197 Piccadilly, W1J 9LL ☎ 020 7734 4511, ⓦ sjp.org.uk; ⊖ Piccadilly Circus. Wren church with high-quality free lunchtime piano and chamber recitals (Mon, Wed and Fri), plus evening concerts (admission charged).

St Lawrence Jewry Guildhall Yard, EC2V 5AA ☎ 020 7600 9478, ⓦ stlawrencejewry.org.uk; ⊖ Bank or St Paul's. Free concerts in this Wren church include piano (Mon lunchtime) and organ (Tues) recitals, and a special summer season.

St Martin-in-the-Fields Trafalgar Square, WC2N 4JJ ☎ 020 7766 1100, ⓦ stmartin-in-the-fields.org;

Charing Cross or Leicester Square. St Martin's has a fine musical pedigree (guest musicians have included Handel and Mozart). Free lunchtime recitals (Mon, Tues and Fri) are excellent, featuring anything from choral works to saxophone to the *Goldberg Variations*, while fee-charging candlelit evening concerts feature acclaimed musicians, including – occasionally – the orchestra of the Academy of St Martin-in-the-Fields (ⓦ asmf.org).

St Mary-at-Hill Lovat Lane, EC2R 8EE ☎ 020 7626 4184, ⓦ musicathill.org.uk; ⊖ Monument. As well as free lunchtime recitals (Monday) and Bach vespers (Sunday evening), this venerable City church, with a long tradition of musical virtuosity, hosts a Bach festival each July.

St Olave's 8 Hart St, EC3 7NB ☎ 020 7488 4318, ⓦ sanctuaryinthecity.net; ⊖ Tower Hill. Medieval St Olave's, where Samuel Pepys is buried, is an atmospheric setting for chamber pieces or solo recitals (Wed & Thurs lunchtimes).

St Sepulchre-without-Newgate Holborn Viaduct, EC1A 2DQ ☎ 020 7236 1145, ⓦ stsepulchres.org; ⊖ St Paul's. The "Musicians' Church" holds free piano recitals, chamber and organ concerts (Wed lunchtimes) and fee-charging evening performances.

St Stephen Walbrook 39 Walbrook, EC4N 8BN ☎ 020 7626 9000, ⓦ ststephenwalbrook.net; ⊖ Bank. Free lunchtime concerts (recitals Tues; sung Eucharist from the professional choir Thurs; organ concerts Fri) in one of the finest of all Wren's churches.

OPERA

27

Of London's two main companies, the **Royal Opera House** is the place to go to see the top international stars, while **English National Opera** showcases largely home-grown talent and lively, sometimes radical productions. Other, smaller venues, including a number of theatres listed in our "Theatre, comedy and cinema" chapter (see p.419) provide more intimate and less expensive alternatives – Hackney's Arcola Theatre (see p.419) even hosts an alternative "Grimeborn" festival – while **fringe companies**, including Size Zero (ⓦ sizezeroopera.com), Ensemble Serse (ensembleserse.com), Erratica (ⓦ erratica.org), Diva Opera (ⓦ divaopera.com) and Opera Up Close (ⓦ operaupclose.com), produce consistently interesting work.

MAJOR COMPANIES AND VENUES

Barbican Centre Silk St, EC2 8DS ☎ 020 7638 8891, ⓦ barbican.org.uk; ⊖ Barbican or Moorgate. The Barbican's regular operatic events include innovative works from the ENO and baroque operas from the Academy of Ancient Music (ⓦ aam.co.uk).

English National Opera London Coliseum, St Martin's Lane, WC2N 4ES ☎ 0207 845 9300, ⓦ eno.org; ⊖ Leicester Square or Charing Cross. The ENO is committed to keeping opera accessible, with operas sung in English, an adventurous repertoire, dazzling modern productions and non-prohibitive pricing (£25–105). Discount options include buying a secret seat – worth at least £25, and often considerably more – for £20, or the "Access all Arias" scheme, offering discounts to under-30s and students; occasional standbys for students, senior citizens, under-16s and the unemployed go on sale 3hr before the performance. The Coliseum itself, a classic Edwardian variety theatre, is a glorious confection of gilt and red velvet.

Opera Holland Park Holland Park, Kensington High St

☎ 0300 999 1000, ⓦ www.operahollandpark.com; ⊖ High Street Kensington or Holland Park. Opera takes to the great outdoors (albeit covered by a canopy) in leafy Holland Park (June–Aug). Standard repertoire is the order of the day, and productions range unpredictably from the inspired to the ordinary. Tickets £45–67.50.

Royal Opera House Bow St, WC2E 9DD ☎ 020 7304 4000, ⓦ roh.org.uk; ⊖ Covent Garden. The ROH, one of the world's leading opera houses, puts on wonderfully lavish productions, with slightly more experimental shows staged in the Linbury Studio Theatre. All are performed in the original language with surtitles. Most tickets are more than £40 (reaching as high as £250), though there is some restricted-view seating (or standing room), which isn't as all bad, from around £5, and various special offers. Student standby tickets (subject to availability) can be bought for £10 online, and 67 day seats (at various prices) go on sale from 10am on the day of a performance (not from visiting companies); these are restricted to one per person, and you need to buy them at the ticket office (get there before 9am for popular shows).

DANCE

The ongoing craze for urban **street dance** and high-camp ballroom dancing has seen high-energy, populist dance shows take to the stage at a number of **West End theatres** (see p.418). For classical ballet, the esteemed **Royal Ballet**, with a number of outstanding principal dancers, is based at the Royal Opera House, while the **English National Ballet** (ⓦ ballet.org.uk) regularly performs at **Sadler's Wells** and the Coliseum. Sadler's Wells also features contemporary, sometimes challenging, work, as do a number of smaller, more intimate venues. The biggest of London's annual dance festivals, **Dance Umbrella** (ⓦ danceumbrella.co.uk), stages a season (Oct/Nov) of fresh new work at various venues around town. For an exhaustive **round-up** of the city's dance events, check ⓦ londondance.com.

COMING SOON TO A SCREEN NEAR YOU...

If you are hungry for high culture, have very low funds, and don't mind being one step removed from the live experience, simply head to the pictures. Many **cinemas** in the capital screen live performances of the finest ballets, operas and theatrical productions – beamed from gilded London venues including the Royal Opera House and the Coliseum, or from esteemed stages around the world – for little more than the price of a movie ticket. It's an odd feeling, giving a rousing round of applause to performers who can't see or hear you, but the acoustics and HD visuals tend to be superb, and the cost can't be argued with. Check the venues' websites to see which of the season's shows are being captured on screen.

VENUES

Barbican Centre Silk St, EC2 8DS ☎ 020 7638 8891, ⓦ barbican.org.uk; ⊖ Barbican or Moorgate. As part of its mixed programming the Barbican regularly stages contemporary dance by top international companies.

Battersea Arts Centre 176 Lavender Hill, SW11 5TN ☎ 020 7223 2223, ⓦ bac.org.uk; ⇌ Clapham Junction. It's worth checking the schedules at this terrific arts centre/theatre (see p.419) to find some top-notch modern dance and physical theatre.

Laban Creekside, SE8 3DZ ☎ 020 8463 0100, ⓦ trinitylaban.ac.uk; ⊖ Cutty Sark DLR or ⇌ Deptford or Greenwich. The Trinity Laban Conservatoire of Music and Dance, in deepest Deptford, has a name for staging progressive dance works – mainly, but not exclusively, student shows – in its cutting-edge, 350-seat Herzog & de Meuron-designed theatre.

London Coliseum St Martin's Lane, WC2N 4ES ☎ 0207 845 9300, ⓦ eno.org; ⊖ Leicester Square or Charing Cross. Superb and often spectacular shows from the English National Ballet and prestigious visiting companies, along with big-name soloists.

The Place 17 Duke's Rd, WC1H 9PY ☎ 020 7121 1100, ⓦ theplace.org.uk; ⊖ Euston. The Place, home to a conservatoire and a touring company, has long been one of London's most important centres for dance, showing the work of contemporary choreographers and student performers.

Rich Mix 35–47 Bethnal Green Rd, E1 6LA ☎ 020 7613 7498, ⓦ richmix.org.uk; ⊖ Shoreditch High Street. Powerful physical theatre and dance, with some emphasis on black companies and choreographers, from this cutting-edge arts venue in the East End.

Royal Opera House Bow St, WC2E 9DD ☎ 020 7304 4000, ⓦ roh.org.uk; ⊖ Covent Garden. Based at the Opera House, the world-renowned Royal Ballet puts on the very best in classical dance. Tickets for the main house may be cheaper than for opera (£5–120); more experimental work can be seen in the smaller Linbury Studio Theatre. It's best to book early.

Sadler's Wells Theatre Rosebery Ave, EC1R 4TN ☎ 0844 412 4300, ⓦ sadlerswells.com; ⊖ Angel. With a number of resident contemporary dance companies – including Matthew Bourne's New Adventures and the ZooNation hip-hop outfit – Sadler's Wells also hosts many of the finest international troupes and celebrates everything from flamenco to Bollywood. The Lilian Baylis Theatre, tucked around the back, stages smaller productions, while the Peacock Theatre in Holborn adds some populist shows to the mix.

Southbank Centre Belvedere Rd, South Bank, SE1 8XX ☎ 020 7960 4200, ⓦ southbankcentre.co.uk; ⊖ Waterloo or Embankment. The Southbank Centre's three venues (see p.217) see an impressive roster of dance shows – you might just as easily see a night of kathakali as a performance from the Ballet Rambert.

Theatre, comedy and cinema

London has enjoyed a reputation for quality theatre since the time of Shakespeare and still provides platforms for innovation and new writing. The West End is the heart of London's "Theatreland", with Shaftesbury Avenue its main drag; the less mainstream, "Off-West End" theatres, and the smaller, edgier places on the fringe are often more interesting. The capital's comedy scene remains lively, too, whether you want to keep things low-key in an intimate pub or pay top dollar for high-profile shows with huge audiences. As for film, the city abounds in offbeat little clubs screening obscure, classic and cult movies, along of course, with scores of multiplexes and trendy chains where you can sip wine and snuggle up on velvet sofas in front of the silver screen.

THEATRE

London's answer to Broadway has had a stellar run in recent years with headline hits like *Wicked* and *The Lion King* playing alongside a constantly changing cast of new musicals. *Les Misérables* is the longest-running musical, on the go since 1985, closely followed by *The Phantom of the Opera*, which opened in 1986; both are mere babies, though, compared with *The Mousetrap* by Agatha Christie, which began its West End run in 1952, and is the longest-running play in the world. The **Royal Shakespeare Company** (Ⓦ rsc.org.uk), which tours in London each year, and the **National Theatre** (Ⓦ nationaltheatre.org.uk) stage challenging performances of mainstream masterpieces, and there is original, exciting work found in what have become known as the **Off-West End** theatres. At the **fringe** theatres, more often than not pub venues, quality is variable (and ticket prices are lower).

Information For details and news about the West End shows, along with tickets and promotions, see Ⓦ officiallondontheatre.co.uk. Also check *Time Out* (Ⓦ timeout.com/london/theatre) for listings.

Prices For West End shows the box-office average is around £25–40, with £50–110 the usual top price, but bargains can be found. If you want to buy from the theatre direct it's best to go to the box office in person; you'll probably be charged a booking fee if you book over the phone or online. Cheap Monday nights or standbys are often very good value, and some major theatres do keep some to sell on the door on the day; check the website of the venue, and be prepared to put up with a restricted view. Students, senior citizens and the unemployed can get concessionary rates on tickets, including standbys, for most shows. Ticket agencies such as Ticketmaster (Ⓦ ticketmaster.co.uk) get seats for West End shows well in advance, but can add hefty booking fees.

Discount tickets Whatever you do, avoid the touts and the ticket agencies that abound in the West End – there's no guarantee that they are genuine. The Society of London Theatre (Ⓦ officiallondontheatre.co.uk) offers online discounts and special offers on West End shows and runs a very useful booth in Leicester Square called "tkts" (Mon–Sat 10am–7pm, Sun 11am–4.30pm; Ⓦ tkts.co.uk), which sells on-the-day tickets for the West End shows at discounts of up to fifty percent. These tend to be in the top end of the price range and are limited to four per person, and prices include a service charge of £3 per ticket. Tkts also sells some tickets up to a week in advance, some of them discounted. Another option is the Encore London theatre passport, which costs £27 and can be redeemed for seats at weekday or matinee performances of some of the West End's most popular shows. Buy the pass from the Visit Britain website (Ⓦ visitbritain .com) and redeem it on the day of the show you want to see at the Encore booth opposite the Garrick Theatre (11a Charing Cross Rd; Mon–Sat 10am–6.30pm, weekends 10am–6pm; avoid school holidays and busy periods).

Live screenings Check out the capital's cinema screenings (see p.416), when you can watch performances from the NT (Ⓦ ntlive.nationaltheatre.org.uk) and other prestigious companies as they happen, or see recorded past productions from the likes of Shakespeare's Globe (Ⓦ onscreen .shakespearesglobe.com) for a fraction of the cost of the real thing – expect to pay cinema ticket prices, around £7–10.

Festivals The excellent Vault festival brings theatre, comedy and performance together in the tunnels beneath Waterloo for six weeks at the start of the year, at cheap prices (Ⓦ vaultfestival.com); it's also the venue for November's Mimetic fest for mime, puppetry and cabaret (Ⓦ mimeticfest.com). Mimefest (Ⓦ mimelondon.com) is covers similar territory in January. LIFT (Ⓦ liftfestival.com) is a summer jamboree of innovative international productions, while the Greenwich and Docklands International Festival brings free theatre in June/July (Ⓦ festival.org).

WEST END THEATRES

Barbican Silk St, EC2Y 8DS ☎ 020 7638 8891, Ⓦ barbican .org.uk; ⊖ Barbican. Tucked away in the Barbican is the excellently designed Barbican Theatre and the much smaller Pit, which put on a wide variety of shows from puppetry and musicals to new drama and twists on old classics. Box office Mon–Sat 10am–9pm, Sun midday–9pm; phone bookings Mon–Sat 10am–8pm, Sun 11am–8pm.

★ **National Theatre** Southbank Centre, South Bank, SE1 9PX ☎ 020 7452 3000, Ⓦ nationaltheatre.org.uk; ⊖ Waterloo. The vast NT complex consists of three separate theatres: the raked, 1150-seat Olivier, the proscenium Lyttelton and the experimental Dorfman. The country's top actors and directors come together in an ambitious programme ranging from Greek tragedies to Broadway musicals. Tickets needn't break the bank – and on special "Travelex" performances seats go for as cheap as £12. Some productions sell out months in advance, but £15 day tickets go on sale on the morning of each performance – get to the box office at least an hour early for the popular shows (two tickets per person). Cheap preview tickets are also available. Box office Mon–Sat 9.30am–8pm, Sun noon–6pm.

Old Vic The Cut, SE1 8NB ☎ 0844 871 7628, Ⓦ oldvictheatre.com; ⊖ Waterloo. Since 1818 the venerable Old Vic has brought a programme of classics and new works, with a reliance on big stars. There are 100 £12 tickets for under-25s every performance. Box office Mon & Sun 10am–6pm, Tue–Sat 10am–7pm; phone bookings Mon–Fri 9am–7.30pm, Sat 9am–4pm, Sun 9.30am–4pm.

Royal Court Sloane Square, SW1W 8AS ☎ 020 7565 5000, Ⓦ royalcourttheatre.com; ⊖ Sloane Square. The Royal Court's programme includes the most ambitious and radical new writing in town. All tickets £10 on Monday. Box office and phone bookings Mon–Sat 10am–6pm.

★**Shakespeare's Globe** 21 New Globe Walk, SE1 9DT ☎020 7401 9919, ⓦshakespearesglobe.com; ⊖London Bridge, Blackfriars or Southwark. This open-roofed replica Elizabethan theatre uses only natural light and the minimum of scenery to stage superb Shakespearean shows as they were originally conceived, as well as works from the Bard's contemporaries and occasional new historical works. Seats around £17–40, with standing tickets around a fiver. The Globe is closed over winter, but the site's Jacobean-style Sam Wanamaker Theatre offers candlelit performances all year. Box office daily 10am–6pm.

OFF-WEST END

Almeida Almeida St, N1 1TA ☎020 7359 4404, ⓦalmeida.co.uk; ⊖Highbury & Islington. Popular little Islington venue that premieres excellent new plays and excitingly reworked classics from around the world, and has attracted some big Hollywood names including Benedict Cumberbatch and Ben Whishaw.

Battersea Arts Centre 176 Lavender Hill, SW11 5TN ☎020 7223 2223, ⓦbac.org.uk; ⇌Clapham Junction from Victoria or Waterloo. It's not the easiest theatre to get to, but it's worth making the effort for its wide-ranging programme of contemporary productions, from radical drama and physical theatre to cabaret.

Bush 7 Uxbridge Rd, W12 7LJ ☎020 8743 5050, ⓦbushtheatre.co.uk; ⊖Shepherd's Bush Market. This lively local theatre, housed in an old library, is London's most reliable venue for new writing after the Royal Court (see opposite).

Donmar Warehouse 41 Earlham St, WC2H 9LX ☎0844 871 7624, ⓦdonmarwarehouse.com; ⊖Covent Garden. Long home to excellent writing, the Donmar has in recent years garnered attention with big-name performers. Best bet for a decent play in Covent Garden.

The Gate The Prince Albert, 11 Pembridge Rd, W11 3HQ ☎020 7229 0706, ⓦgatetheatre.co.uk; ⊖Notting Hill Gate. Seating around seventy, this small producing pub-theatre has a huge reputation for its excellent new writing and innovative revivals of international classics.

Hampstead Theatre Eton Ave, NW3 3EU ☎020 7722 9301, ⓦhampsteadtheatre.com; ⊖Swiss Cottage. A prestigious, modern two-stage theatre with a reputation for successfully cultivating new playwrights. The programme has become more ambitious in recent years, with some transfers to the West End.

Menier Chocolate Factory 53 Southwark St, SE1 1RU ☎020 7378 1713, ⓦmenierchocolatefactory.com; ⊖London Bridge. Great name, great venue, with a decent bar and restaurant attached – pick up a meal and a show as part of a decent meal deal. Plays tend towards showy casting but interesting works do appear here.

Open Air Theatre Regent's Park, Inner Circle, NW1 4NU ☎0844 826 4242, ⓦopenairtheatre.com; ⊖Baker Street. If the weather's good, there's nothing like a dose of alfresco theatre at this beautiful space in Regent's Park. The tourist-friendly summer programme features Shakespeare and family favourites.

★**Soho Theatre** 21 Dean St, W1D 3NE ☎020 7478 0100, ⓦsohotheatre.com; ⊖Tottenham Court Road. Great, central theatre with three spaces featuring new writing from around the globe at affordable prices. Alternative comedy and cabaret, plus the popular, starry bar, make this a veritable melting pot of artistic endeavour.

Theatre Royal Stratford East, Gerry Raffles Square, E15 1BN ☎020 8534 0310, ⓦstratfordeast.com; ⊖Stratford. Beautiful Victorian theatre in the East End, where the community-pleasing shows include excellent Christmas panto, comedy and new writing.

Tricycle Theatre 269 Kilburn High Rd, NW6 7JR ☎020 7328 1000, ⓦtricycle.co.uk; ⊖Kilburn. Dynamic venues with a great space to stage new plays, often focusing on political issues or analyzing multicultural Britain. Also houses a good programme of arthouse cinema.

Unicorn Theatre 147 Tooley St, SE1 2HZ ☎020 7645 0560, ⓦunicorntheatre.com; ⊖London Bridge. London's theatre for kids and youth audiences, delivering tales for nursery kids up to new works for teens.

Young Vic 66 The Cut, SE1 8LZ ☎020 7922 2922, ⓦyoungvic.org; ⊖Waterloo. Vibrant contemporary programme, concentrating on the work of young directors. There's fierce competition for the venue's many cheap tickets so book ahead.

FRINGE AND OCCASIONAL VENUES

★**Arcola Theatre** 24 Ashwin St, E8 3DL ☎020 7503 1646, ⓦarcolatheatre.com; ⊖Dalston Junction. Exciting fringe theatre housed in an old Dalston factory and a pop-up tent space. The theatre includes politically charged, challenging plays – classics and modern works – with shows from young, international companies, and a wider performance remit including cabaret in the tent. Some "pay what you can" tickets on Tuesday nights.

King's Head Theatre 115 Upper St, N1 1QN ☎020 7226 8561, ⓦkingsheadtheatre.com; ⊖Angel or Highbury & Islington. Between here, the *Hen and Chickens* and the *Old Red Lion*, Islington has London's best pub theatres. This intimate space stages exciting contemporary productions and brand-new works from emerging writers.

Rich Mix 35–47 Bethnal Green Rd, E1 6LA ☎020 7613 7498, ⓦrichmix.org.uk; ⊖Shoreditch High Street. Offers a stimulating mix of new theatre, spoken word, comedy and dance, with emphasis on black and minority works.

Roundhouse Chalk Farm Rd, NW1 8EH ☎0300 678 9222, ⓦroundhouse.org.uk; ⊖Chalk Farm. Camden's Victorian engine repairs shed provides a stunning backdrop

28

for ambitious stagings: cutting-edge theatre, performance art, contemporary circus and spoken word. Its annual spoken word festival in May is well worth a look.

Southwark Playhouse 77–85 Newington Causeway, SE1 8BD ☎020 7407 0234, ⓦsouthwarkplayhouse. co.uk; ⊖Elephant and Castle. A new home for the Playhouse has put rocket boosters on the theatre's ambition. Two spaces concentrate on new and young

writers, reinterpreting old classics and contemporary plays.

★**Wilton's Music Hall** Grace's Alley, off Cable St, E1 8JB ☎020 7702 2789, ⓦwiltons.org.uk; ⊖Aldgate East. The world's oldest surviving music hall, built in 1858, is a crumbling, hugely atmospheric space, with a stunning old bar. A wonderful venue for innovative theatre, comedy, poetry and variety as well as magic shows, cinema and raucous nights out for a cool east London crowd.

COMEDY

From the big-name, big-theatre, big-ticket shows, to old favourites like the **Comedy Store** – at the heart of the alternative comedy movement of the 1980s – you're never too far away from a chuckle in London. There are big-name TV stars at venues like the **O2** and the **Hammersmith Apollo**, but we've focused on the cheaper gigs around town – expect to pay £5–15 for most shows. Note that many venues only have gigs on Friday and Saturday nights, and that August can be a lean month, as much of London's talent heads north for Edinburgh. (On the upside, that means July in London is full of cheap or often free comedy previews.) See also **Rich Mix** (p.419), **Union Chapel** (p.400), and **Wilton's Music Hall** (p.420), all of which host excellent comedy nights. First among equals, though, is the **Soho Theatre** (see p.419), with an unstoppable programme of the finest comedy shows. Check *Time Out* for listings.

Aces & Eights 156–158 Fortress Rd, NW5 2HP ☎020 7485 4033, ⓦacesandeightssaloonbar.com; ⊖Tufnell Park. There are many pub comedy nights that draw big names at a fraction of the club prices. The starrier members of leftfield comedy often wash up at Aces & Eights – check the well-named Shambles to see the seedy underbelly of comedy at its best/worst.

Amused Moose locations vary, check website for details ⓦamusedmoose.com. Top-notch stand-up programmed at venues around town, including Piccadilly, with robust bills of well-chosen acts.

★**Angel Comedy** The Camden Head, 2 Camden Passage, N1 8DY ⓦangelcomedy.co.uk; ⊖Angel. This would be a recommended venue for its great crowd, shepherded by organizer/comedian Barry Ferns, and excellent daily schedule of full shows and new material, even if it weren't free. Unmissable – just don't be fooled by the address, this is in Islington, not Camden.

Banana Cabaret The Bedford, 77 Bedford Hill, SW12 9HD ☎07467 027592, ⓦbananacabaret.co.uk; ⊖Balham. Friday and Saturday showcases of big names with an old-school comedy club vibe. Friendly crowd in an authentic south London boozer.

Boat Show Comedy Club Tattershall Castle, Victoria Embankment, SW1A 2HR ☎07932 658895, ⓦboatshow comedy.co.uk; ⊖Embankment. The paddlesteamer venue opposite the London Eye isn't just a novelty – big names try out new material here, although it isn't the cheapest.

Camden Comedy Club The Camden Head, 100 Camden High St, NW1 0LU ☎020 7485 4019, ⓦcamdencomedyclub.com; ⊖Camden Town. Consistently good nightly comedy, with up-and-coming acts on weekdays and bigger bills Saturday.

Canal Café Theatre The Bridge House, Delamere Terrace, W2 6ND ☎020 7289 6054, ⓦcanalcafetheatre .com; ⊖Warwick Avenue. Home of the fast-paced NewsRevue (Thurs–Sun), delivering a reasonable hit rate of topical gags and sketches.

Comedy Store 1a Oxendon St, SW1Y 4EE ☎0844 871 7699, ⓦthecomedystore.co.uk; ⊖Piccadilly Circus. The jokes may not always be fresh, but the birthplace of alternative comedy still pulls in the crowds. Monday's King Gong is recommended as a bargain raucous bear pit of newbie heckling; Fridays and Saturdays are very busy with two shows, at 7.30pm and 11pm – book ahead.

Downstairs at the King's Head 2 Crouch End Hill, N8 8AA ☎020 8340 1028, ⓦdownstairsatthekingshead .com; bus #W7 from ⊖Finsbury Park. Friendly, long-running comedy night where stand-up, cabaret and new material from decent bills are played out in a cosy basement on Thurs, Sat & Sun.

★**Invisible Dot** 2 Northdown St, N1 9BG ☎020 7424 8918, ⓦtheinvisibledot.com; ⊖King's Cross. See a new wave of young, exciting acts that are helping to thoughtfully reshape comedy in a cosy, cool studio space. It's a good spot to find respected acts who have made it big – such as Simon Amstell and Stewart Lee – testing out new material for bargain prices.

★**Laugh Out London** Various venues, ⓦlaughoutlondoncomedyclub.co.uk. Acts love the LOL guys for their keen eye for exciting line-ups and for creating excellent, low-cost nights across town.

Leicester Square Theatre 6 Leicester Place, WC2H 7BX ☎020 7734 2222, ⓦleicestersquaretheatre.com; ⊖Leicester Square. Avoid the Leicester Square comedy touts and try this comedy theatre for big names – like Stewart Lee, Doug Stanhope, Bill Bailey – performing new material.

Old Rope The Phoenix, 37 Cavendish Sq, W1G 0PP ⓦfacebook.com/oldropecomedy, ⊖Oxford Circus.

Want to see new jokes first? Old hands try out new material at this bargain Monday night – check the Facebook page for the excellent, extensive line-ups.

Pleasance Theatre North Rd, N7 9EF ☎ 020 7609 1800, ⓦ pleasance.co.uk; ⊖ Caledonian Road. Comedy and theatre hub that comes into its own during spring as acts trial shows and low-cost new material before August's Edinburgh Fringe.

CINEMA

There are an awful lot of cinemas in London, especially the **West End**. The biggest are on and around Leicester Square, including the **Empire Leicester Square** (ⓦ empirecinemas.co.uk), a former Victorian variety theatre whose 1330-seat main auditorium has a state-of-the-art soundsystem, and the 1700-seat **Odeon Leicester Square** (ⓦ odeon.co.uk), a favourite for celeb-packed premieres. These concentrate on Hollywood crowd-pleasers and new releases, but be warned that they will cost around £15; head to the outer zones for cheaper cinemas. There are three chains that show more offbeat screenings – check out the **Picturehouse** (ⓦ picturehouses.co.uk), **Curzon** (ⓦ curzoncinemas.com) and **Everyman** (ⓦ everymancinema.com) websites for a wide variety of locations right across the city. Many of London's more cultish **arthouse** cinemas may have gone, but the gap has been filled somewhat in recent years by a rash of **indie film clubs**, which colonize pub basements, back rooms and pop-up spaces all over the city.

Tickets West End screens and multiplexes will charge at least £12 for a standard adult ticket; independent cinemas may be a little cheaper and arthouse shows can be a lot less. Concessionary rates are offered for some shows at virtually all cinemas, usually at off-peak times on weekdays.

INDEPENDENT AND ARTHOUSE CINEMAS

Barbican Silk St, EC2Y 8DS ☎ 020 7638 8891, ⓦ barbican.org.uk; ⊖ Barbican. Comfy seats, three screens and a terrific rota of obscure classics and world cinema plus silent movies with live music accompaniment and excellent festivals, talks and seasons.

★ **BFI Southbank** Belvedere Rd, South Bank, SE1 8XT ☎ 020 7928 3232, ⓦ bfi.org.uk; ⊖ Waterloo. Exhaustive, eclectic programmes based around themed seasons, showing between seven and fourteen films daily on four screens. The BFI, in association with Odeon, also runs the IMAX (☎ 0330 333 7878, ⓦ bfi.org.uk/imax), a huge glazed drum in the middle of Waterloo roundabout where the colossal screen (20m high by 26m wide) is not recommended for anyone with vertigo.

Cinema Museum 2 Dugard Way, SE11 4TH ☎ 020 7840 2200, ⓦ cinemamuseum.org.uk; ⊖ Elephant & Castle. A lovingly assembled movie memorabilia collection is the backdrop for screenings – typically critical favourites and talking points – supported by discussions. Note that the collection is generally open only by appointment.

Curzon Soho 99 Shaftesbury Ave, W1D 5DY ☎ 0330 500 1331, ⓦ curzoncinemas.co.uk, ⊖ Leicester Square. Flagship of the arthouse chain, offering first looks at the best in specialist cinema. It has seven sister venues, including the world cinema specialist Bloomsbury site.

Electric 191 Portobello Rd, W11 2ED ☎ 020 7908 9696, ⓦ electriccinema.co.uk; ⊖ Notting Hill Gate. One of the

28

MOVIES ALFRESCO

A new wave of alfresco movie-watching has swept the capital in recent years. The following is a list of the more established events.

Film4 Summer Screen Somerset House, Strand, WC2R 1LA ⓦ somersethouse.org.uk/film; ⊖ Temple. This is the big one: for ten days or so in late July and early August, this magnificent setting (see p.115), is a venue for classic, indie and new movies, with DJs and "behind the screen" talks and events; bring your own cushion. Tickets sell out fast.

More London Free Film Festival Near Tower Bridge, SE1 ⓦ morelondon.com; ⊖ London Bridge. Set next to City Hall on the side of the Thames, More London's vibrant annual festival in mid-September screens free, family-friendly films in The Scoop, an eight hundred-seat, riverside amphitheatre.

Nomad Cinema ⓦ whereisthenomad.com.

Showing classics, arthouse movies and fond old favourites, this peripatetic screen might turn up anywhere – often in the city's parks – complete with superb food and drink from London's best street food sellers. Profits go to The Sustainability Institute, a sustainable living charity based in South Africa.

Rooftop Film Club ⓦ rooftopfilmclub.com; Queen of Hoxton, 1 Curtain Rd, EC2A 3JX; ⊖ Liverpool Street; Bussey Building, 133 Rye Lane, SE15; ⊖ ⇌ Peckham Rye. Settle down in a comfy seat, grab a cocktail and hook up to your own wireless headphones for cultish blockbusters in atmospheric rooftop spaces. Around five nights a week May–Sept, plus extra screenings in Kensington and Stratford.

oldest cinemas in the country (opened 1911), the Electric has added eclectic seating to the old school atmosphere that even includes a few double beds. There's fresh donuts or a retro diner next door for the hungry. The programme concentrates on mainstream hits, with more offbeat offerings on Sundays.

ICA Cinema Nash House, The Mall, SW1Y 5AH ☎020 7930 3647, ⊚ica.org.uk; ⊖Charing Cross. Tastefully chosen avant-garde, world, underground movies and docs on two screens in the seriously hip HQ of the Institute of Contemporary Arts, some with talks. Closed Mon.

Lexi 194b Chamberlayne Rd, NW10 3JU ☎0871 704 2069, ⊚thelexicinema.co.uk; ⊖Kensal Green. Calling itself the "UK's first social enterprise independent boutique digital cinema", this friendly little volunteer-run place has a film-club feel, screening the best contemporary and indie films and donating all profits to charity.

Peckhamplex 95 Rye Lane, SE15 4ST ☎0844 567 2742, ⊚peckhamplex.com; ⊖≷Peckham Rye. The screens and soundsystems desperately need a tune-up but you can't beat the £5 ticket price, all day, every day, to see mainstream hits and special events. Arrive early.

Phoenix 52 East Finchley High Rd, N2 9PJ ☎020 8444 6789, ⊚phoenixcinema.co.uk; ⊖East Finchley. Run by a charitable trust, this beautiful Art Deco cinema, open since 1910, is a neighbourhood favourite that pulls audiences from all over London for its intelligent mix of indies and classics, themed seasons and events.

★ Prince Charles 7 Leicester Place, WC2H 7BY ☎020 7494 3654, ⊚princecharlescinema.com; ⊖Leicester Square. Two screens in the heart of the West End, with great prices (tickets start at £8 with special pricing for double bills) and a daily-changing, lively programme of newish movies, classics and cult favourites, plus marathons, all-nighters and participatory "quotealong" romps.

Rio 107 Kingsland High St, E8 2PB ☎020 7241 9410, ⊚riocinema.ndirect.co.uk; ⊖Dalston Kingsland. This Art Deco beauty, with a cosy screening room, offers a good mix of the most interesting current US releases, world cinema, arthouse classics and documentaries. Frequent Q&As and special themed events and festivals, with excellent Sunday matinees.

FILM CLUBS

Duke Mitchell Film Club Phoenix, 1 Phoenix St, WC2 ⊚thedukemitchell.uk; ⊖Tottenham Court Road. Free monthly screenings of quirky movies, often based on obscure themes, from April Fools to Sensory Excess.

The Flicker Club Locations vary ⊚theflickerclub .com. Special guests from Richard Curtis to Sir Ian McKellen have given readings at this flim club before screenings of classic movies. All profits go to charity. Runs irregularly at spots around the city.

Sands Films Cinema Club 82 St Marychurch St, SE16 4HZ ☎020 7231 2209, ⊚sandsfilms.co.uk; ⊖Rotherhithe. There couldn't be a more atmospheric venue than this old movie studio – settle down to enjoy anything from wartime musicals to world cinema classics. Tickets are free, allocated first-come, first-served; sign up for weekly emails and reserve by email. Tues 8.30pm and daytime screenings on first Thurs of the month.

28

FILM FESTIVALS

East End Film Festival ⊚eastendfilmfestival.com. High-profile event in late June/early July, bursting with international premieres, workshops and live happenings. Its day-long "fringe event", Cine East, uses a host of quirky East End venues for exciting, immersive free screenings.

Free Film Festivals ⊚freefilmfestivals.org. Seven festivals operating primarily across south London through spring and autumn. The free screenings, often in atmospheric outdoor spaces that range from velodromes to cemeteries, are often popular and sometimes ticketed.

Human Rights Watch Film Festival ⊚ff.hrw.org/london. Documentary gets less of a look-in on the London film scene than in other cities, but festivals go some way to compensate for that – this March festival brings a variety of hard-hitting international docs together, including many UK premieres.

London Film Festival ⊚bfi.org.uk/lff. One of the major players on the world movie festival circuit, the LFF is held over a fortnight in late Oct, with movies shown across ten or so West End cinemas. Many sell out soon after publication of the programme in early Sept.

London International Animation Festival ⊚liaf .org.uk. Hundreds of animated shorts, features, documentaries and retrospectives shown during this ten-day festival, held at various venues in Oct/Nov.

London Short Film Festival ⊚shortfilms.org.uk. January sees the finest shorts get an airing over ten days and 25 venues. It's earned itself a world-class reputation for its selections.

Raindance Festival ⊚raindance.org. Major independent film festival, held over two weeks in late Sept/early Oct, showing new work by indie directors from across the globe.

Sundance London ⊚sundance-london.com. London's branch of the international festival, featuring darlings of leftfield cinema and shorts, held at the Picturehouse Central as of 2015.

BLITZ, SHOREDITCH

Shops and markets

From the *folie de grandeur* that is Harrods to the scruffy street markets of the East End, London is a shopper's playground – whether you want to spend enormous amounts of money, loading yourself up with posh bags of designer gear, or to rifle around rickety stalls seeking out quirky treasures for a few quid. As befits a city of villages, London's shopping neighbourhoods all have their own flavour, and many of them are known for their specialities – Oxford Street's the place to head for chains and department stores; Jermyn Street for upmarket gentlemen's outfitters; Charing Cross Road for used books; Brick Lane for vintage, for example. In the sections that follow, we've listed shops according to what they sell, rather than by area, and have erred away from chain stores unless they display some distinctive style.

29

ESSENTIALS

Sales The cheapest time to shop in London is during one of the two big annual sale seasons, centred on January and July, when prices are routinely slashed by anything between twenty and seventy percent. An increasing number of mid-season sales mean that you may be lucky whenever you visit. The best place to find details of other discount events is in *Time Out* (⊕ timeout.com).

Cash, cards and exchange Market stalls tend to take cash only. Always keep receipts: whatever the shop may tell you, the law allows a full refund or replacement on purchases which turn out to be faulty. There's no such legal protection if you just decide you don't like something, but some retailers are happy to exchange and most will at least offer a credit note.

VAT Overseas (non-EU) visitors can sometimes claim back the value-added tax (VAT) that applies to most goods sold in British shops, although you will need to spend well over £100 for this to be worthwhile. Check ⊕ hmrc.gov.uk/vat/sectors/consumers/overseas-visitors.htm for the latest details.

CLOTHES AND SHOES

Our reviews concentrate on the home-grown and local rather than the ubiquitous international names, listing individual designer flagships along with **concept stores** where a curated selection of fashion pieces rubs shoulders with homeware and accessories. If it's global **designer wear** you're after, bear in mind that nearly all the department stores stock lines from major and up-and-coming names. For designer-style fashion at lower prices, try the more upmarket high-street **chains** such as Jigsaw and Whistles, or the less expensive Topshop, Mango, Zara, Monsoon, H&M (and their cooler younger sister & Other Stories) and Warehouse. London's **markets** (see p.433), meanwhile, the hippest of which have become breeding grounds for indie shops and one-offs, are good places to hunt down street and clubwear, along with **vintage** clothes, an area in which London excels.

WHERE TO GO

In the centre of town, **Oxford Street** is the city's hectic chain-store heartland and, together with **Regent Street**, offers pretty much every mainstream clothing label you could wish for. Just off Oxford Street expensive designer outlets clutter **St Christopher's Place** and **South Molton Street**, with even pricier designers and jewellers lining chic **Bond Street**. To the north, **Marylebone High Street** offers a pretty (and upmarket) village oasis in the middle of town – a slightly more laidback place to get all your labels, treats and gifts away from the bustle.

Tottenham Court Road is the place for electrical goods, sportswear and, in its northern section, furniture and design shops, while **Charing Cross Road** remains at the centre of London's book trade, both new and secondhand. On the west side of Charing Cross Road, stretching down to Piccadilly, **Soho** may be heading mainstream but still offers funky gift shops, specialist record stores, delis and the odd old-fashioned fabric retailer, while the streets surrounding **Covent Garden**, east of Charing Cross Road, yield a good crop of art/design, fashion and shoes, plus camping gear; the streets around **Seven Dials** are best for indie designers and offbeat stores.

Just off Piccadilly, **St James's** is the domain of the quintessential English gentleman, with the shops of **Jermyn Street** in particular dedicated to his tailoring. Swanky **Knightsbridge**, further west, is home to Harrods and the big-name fashion stores of **Sloane Street** and **Brompton Road,** while the **King's Road**, having all but lost any raffish edge it once had, is now lined with upmarket fashion stores, expensive home furnishing shops and high-street chains. You can still find some offbeat shops in Notting Hill and Kensington Church Street; this rather smart part of town is enlivened by **Portobello Road**, which has been a hotspot for antique and vintage for decades, and its offshoot, Golborne Road.

Hampstead, in a luxurious and leafy world of its own north of the centre, is a great place to browse upmarket fashion stores, posh delis and patisseries, antiquarian booksellers and tasteful arts and crafts shops. Across the river and a world away, **Brixton** maintains a firmly community, multicultural feel in its local, old-fashioned shops and its thriving market. **Greenwich**, also south of the river, is swankier, with an eclectic range of shops and markets, while **Richmond**, out to the west, is posher still, offering mainstream chains and one-off boutiques in a moneyed riverside setting. For an edgier experience, head east, where independent stores and markets in and around **Brick Lane**, **Shoreditch** and **Dalston** specialize in quirky one-offs and vintage gear for hip young things; this is by far the coolest neighbourhood to shop in London. **Spitalfields** and the surrounding area has gone upmarket but still offers some offbeat finds; other popular market areas (see p.433) are also good hunting grounds for small independent stores and vintage outlets.

CLOCKWISE FROM TOP HARRODS FOOD HALL (P.427); PORTOBELLO ROAD (P.434); BROADWAY MARKET (P.433) >

29

DESIGNER FASHION

Alexander McQueen 4–5 Old Bond St, W1S 4PD ☎ 020 7355 0088, ⍟ alexandermcqueen.co.uk; ⊖ Bond Street; map p.78. The flagship store for the haute concept McQueen brand, which, since the maverick designer's suicide in 2011, has been headed by Sarah Burton. Mon–Wed, Fri & Sat 10am–6pm, Thurs 10am–7pm, Sun noon–6pm.

★ **Antoni & Alison** 43 Rosebery Ave, EC1R 4SH ☎ 020 7833 2141, ⍟ antoniandalison.co.uk; ⊖ Chancery Lane; map p.147. This cult design duo sell their whimsical, fashion-forward and wearable creations, many of them emblazoned with trompe l'oeil digital prints and doodles, from an arty little store a little way off the fashionista track. There's a café – *Ye Olde Worlde Super Modern Tearoom* – on site too. Thurs 10.30am–6pm, Fri 11.30am–7.30pm, Sat 12.30–5.30pm.

Browns 24–27 South Molton St, W1K 5RD ☎ 020 7514 0016, ⍟ brownsfashion.com; ⊖ Bond Street; map p.78. A reliable choice for a huge range of designer wear and accessories, handpicked with impeccable taste from all the major labels, from international names to hip young things. This is the flagship store, including the edgy "Focus" collection; Browns Menswear is at no. 23 (☎ 020 7514 0038). Both branches Mon–Wed, Fri & Sat 10am–6.30pm, Thurs 10am–7pm.

★ **Dover Street Market** 17–18 Dover St, W1S 4LT ☎ 020 7518 0680, ⍟ london.doverstreetmarket.com; ⊖ Green Park; map p.78. Your go-to store for fashion-forward style: a six-floor designer market-cum-megastore showcasing directional names such as Comme des Garçons and Sacai, young Turks including Molly Goddard and ChristopHer Kane, and classic perennials from Givenchy to Paco Rabanne. Mon–Sat 11am–7pm, Sun noon–5pm.

Kokon to Zai 57 Greek St, W1 3DX ☎ 020 3601 1414, map p.101; 86 Golborne Rd, W10 5PS ☎ 020 8960 3736; ⊖ Tottenham Court Rd or Ladbroke Grove; map pp.276–277. ⍟ kokontozai.co.uk. Ready-to-wear pieces from the edgy KTZ line, beloved by fashionistas and clued-up musos. Greek St: Mon–Sat 11am–7.30pm, Sun noon–6pm; Golborne Rd: Mon–Sat 10am–6pm.

The Laden Showroom 103 Brick Lane, E1 6SE ☎ 020 7247 2431, ⍟ laden.co.uk; ⊖ Aldgate East or Shoreditch High Street; map pp.190–191. A favourite with the hipper London celebs, this East End showroom showcases loads of independent designers, and is great for exuberant dressers on a budget. Mon–Fri 11am–6.30pm,

Sat 11am–7pm, Sun 10.30am–6pm.

Paul Smith Westbourne House, 122 Kensington Park Rd, W11 2EP ☎ 020 7727 3553; ⊖ Notting Hill Gate or Ladbroke Grove, map pp.276–277; 40–44 Floral St, WC2E 9TB ☎ 020 7379 7133; ⊖ Covent Garden, map p.108; ⍟ paulsmith.co.uk. Though there are branches throughout London – including in Borough Market, on Marylebone High St and on Albemarle St near Green Park – Nottingham-born designer Paul Smith's Notting Hill shop-in-a-house, and his cosily contemporary Covent Garden store, are both particularly worth a visit. Ever so English in Smith's quirky way, they sell a broad range of his well-tailored and whimsical clothes and accessories for men, women and children. Notting Hill: Mon–Fri 10am–6pm, Sat 10am–6.30pm, Sun noon–5pm; Floral St: Mon–Wed 10.30am–6.30pm, Thurs & Fri 10.30am–7pm, Sat 10am–7pm, Sun 12.30–5.30pm.

The Shop at Bluebird 350 King's Rd, SW3 5UU ☎ 0207 351 3873, ⍟ www.theshopatbluebird.com; ⊖ Sloane Square; map p.267. Huge concept store in a stunning Art Deco warehouse that extends its high-design aesthetic from luxury (Victoria Beckham, Carven, Helmut Lang) to edgy (Avelon, Fornasetti, Dagmar) and up-and-coming brands, in clothes, shoes, homeware and cosmetics. Mon–Sat 10am–7pm, Sun noon–6pm.

Vivienne Westwood 44 Conduit St, W1S 2YL ☎ 020 7439 1109, ⍟ viviennewestwood.co.uk; ⊖ Oxford Circus, map p.78; 430 King's Rd, SW10 0LJ ☎ 020 7352 6551, ⍟ worldsendshop.co.uk; ⊖ Sloane Square, map p.267. Rightly revered by the international fashion pack, this quintessentially English rebel is as outrageous as ever. Conduit St is home to the flagship ready-to-wear store, but punks-at-heart with money to burn should make for the historic World's End shop on the King's Rd, imbued with her personal stamp since she took it over with Malcolm McLaren in the 1970s, and now selling classic and new pieces and samples, some of them recycled or created from leftover fabrics. Conduit St: Mon–Wed, Fri & Sat 10am–6pm, Thurs 10am–7pm, Sun noon–5pm; World's End: Mon–Sat 10am–6pm.

Wolf and Badger 46 Ledbury Rd, W11 2AB ☎ 020 7229 5698; ⊖ Notting Hill Gate, map pp.276–277; 32 Dover St, W1S 4NE ☎ 020 7229 4848; ⊖ Green Park, map p.78; ⍟ wolfandbadger.com. Notting Hill shop selling cutting-edge pieces – clothes, jewellery, accessories, homeware – from young independent designers; a good place to come to sniff out the next big thing. There's another branch in Dover St, Mayfair. Ledbury Rd: Mon–Fri 10am–6pm, Sat 10am–6.30pm, Sun 11am–5pm; Dover St: Mon–Wed 11am–6.30pm, Thurs–Sat 11am–7pm, Sun noon–5pm.

BUDGET AND MID-RANGE FASHION

Present 140 Shoreditch High St, E1 6JE 020 ☎ 7033 0500, ⍟ present-london.com; ⊖ Shoreditch

---

TOP 5 ENGLISH CLASSICS

A Gold See p.431
Hatchards See p.429
House of Hackney See p.433
Liberty See box opposite
Vivienne Westwood See above

29

Street; map pp.190–191. This men's casual designer wear store covers all the lifestyle bases – from tea bags to man bags, desert boots to dungarees – from their own range and on-trend brands both major and niche. Mon–Fri 10.30am–7pm, Sat 11am–6.30pm, Sun 11am–5pm.

Stumper and Fielding 107 Portobello Rd, W11 ☎020 7295 5577; ⊖Notting Hill Gate; map pp.276–277. The dry English wit of the name says it all: high-style hipster-gentleman come here to get suited and booted in hand-sewn leather brogues, well-cut tweeds, retro top hats and natty

bow ties. Everything is presented beautifully, with vintage typewriters and rusty old bikes adding to the whimsical nostalgia. Mon–Fri & Sun 10am–6pm, Sat 9am–7pm.

Tatty Devine 236 Brick Lane, E2 7EB ☎020 7739 9191; ⊖Shoreditch High Street, map pp.190–191; 44 Monmouth St, WC2H 9EP ☎020 7836 2685, ⊖Covent Garden, map p.108; ⓦtattydevine.com. Keeping its East End indie aesthetic even while expanding into a prime West End location, Tatty Devine remains as fresh and playful as it did when it set up in 2001. Its colourful

DEPARTMENT STORES

Although all London's **department stores** offer a huge range of high-quality goods under one roof, most specialize in fashion and food. The fanciest places are worth visiting just to admire the scale, architecture, window displays and interior design, and the majority have good cafés and restaurants.

Fortnum & Mason 181 Piccadilly, W1A 1ER ☎020 7734 8040, ⓦfortnumandmason.com; ⊖Green Park or Piccadilly Circus; map p.78. Beautiful 300-year-old store with heavenly murals, cherubs, chandeliers and fountains as a backdrop to its quintessentially English offerings. Starting out as a humble grocer, it is famous today for its fabulous, pricey food, luxury hampers and fancy afternoon teas (see p.378), but it also sells upmarket designer clothes, furniture, luggage and stationery, with fabulous jewellery at prices that *will* break the bank. Mon–Sat 10am–9pm, Sun noon–6pm.

Harrods 87–135 Brompton Rd, Knightsbridge, SW1X 7XL ☎020 7730 1234, ⓦharrods.com; ⊖Knightsbridge; map pp.252–253. Vast, expensive and a little stuffy, with a number of of lah-dee-dah quirks – you may fall foul of the dress code if you wear a backpack or clothes that "may reveal intimate parts of the body", for example – Harrods is most notable for its Art Nouveau tiled food hall, the huge toy department and its swanky designer labels. And, of course, its memorial statue of Princess Diana and Dodi, erected by Dodi's father, previous owner Mohamed Al-Fayed. Mon–Sat 10am–9pm, Sun noon–6pm.

Harvey Nichols 109–125 Knightsbridge, SW1X 7RJ ☎020 7235 5000, ⓦharveynichols.com; ⊖Knightsbridge; map pp.252–253. Absolutely fabulous, sweetie, "Harvey Nicks" has eight floors of designer collections and casual wear. The renowned cosmetics department is frequented by A- and Z-listers alike, while the fifth-floor food hall offers luxury goodies at high prices. Mon–Sat 10am–8pm, Sun noon–6pm.

John Lewis 300 Oxford St, W1C 1DX ☎020 7629 7711, ⓦjohnlewis.co.uk; ⊖Oxford Circus; map p.78. Famous for being "never knowingly undersold", this reliable, much-loved and trusted institution can't

be beaten for basics. Every kind of button, pen, mug and rug can be found here, along with reasonably priced and well-made clothes, furniture and electronics, and an enormous beauty department. Mon–Wed, Fri & Sat 9.30am–8pm, Thurs 9.30am–9pm, Sun noon–6pm.

★**Liberty** 210–220 Regent St, W1B 5AH ☎020 7734 1234, ⓦliberty.co.uk; ⊖Oxford Circus; map p.78. A glorious emporium of luxury with a dash of Art Nouveau bohemia, this exquisite store, with its mock-Tudor exterior, is most famous for its fabrics, design and accessories, but also has an excellent reputation for both mainstream and high fashion. The perfume, cosmetics, gift and household departments are recommended, too, and there's a good kids' section. Mon–Sat 10am–8pm, Sun noon–6pm.

Marks & Spencer 458 Oxford St, W1C 1AP ☎020 7935 7954, ⓦmarksandspencer.com; ⊖Marble Arch; map p.78. London's largest branch of this cosy British institution (with more than one thousand outlets worldwide) offers a good range of own-brand clothes, food, homeware and furnishings. The underwear is essential, the food a little luxurious, and the clothes well made and reliable, if sometimes unexciting. Mon–Sat 8am–9pm, Sun noon–6pm.

★**Selfridges** 400 Oxford St, W1A 1AB ☎ 0800 123 400, ⓦselfridges.com; ⊖Bond Street; map p.78. This huge, airy palace of clothes, food and furnishings was London's first great department store and remains its best. The vast mens- and womenswear departments offer designer gear and casual lines – check out the never-ending denim collection – alongside hipper, younger names and labels, with prices to suit most budgets. There's a good children's department, and the food hall is the best in town. Mon–Sat 9.30am–9pm, Sun noon–6pm.

29

statement jewellery, much of it created from Perspex or wood, and all handmade in Britain, has given rise to a host of imitators, but the original is still the best. Brick Lane: Mon–Fri 10am–6.30pm, Sat 11am–6pm, Sun 10am–5pm; Monmouth St: Mon–Sat 10.30am–7pm, Sun 11.30am–5pm.

VINTAGE, RETRO AND SECONDHAND

Absolute Vintage 15 Hanbury St, E1 6QR ☏ 020 7247 3883; ⊖ Liverpool Street or Aldgate East, map pp.190–191; 79 Berwick St, W1F 8TL ☏ 020 7434 1544; ⊖ Tottenham Court Road, map p.101; ⓦ absolutevintage .co.uk. Spitalfields treasure trove full of affordable 1920s to 1990s clobber – some of it in the style of the era rather than genuine – with a good collection of shoes and bags. There's a slightly more glamorous sister store, Blondie just around the corner on Commercial St, selling preloved women's designer pieces (same hours), and another, smaller, Absolute Vintage in Soho, which has lots of shoes and men's gear. Spitalfields: daily 11am–7pm; Soho: Mon–Sat 10am–7pm, Sun noon–6pm.

Beyond Retro 110–112 Cheshire St, E2 6EJ ☏ 020 7613 3636; ⊖ Liverpool St or Shoreditch High Street, map pp.190–191; 58 Great Marlborough St, W1F 7JY ☏ 020 7434 1406, map p.97; 92–100 Stoke Newington Rd, N16 7XB ☏ 020 7923 2277, map p.187; ⓦ beyondretro.com. Cavernous warehouse of twentieth-century classics, with thousands of well-priced goodies including faded jeans, 1950s frocks, battered cowboy boots, punk gear and 1920s evening gowns. Their sister store in Great Marlborough St, Soho, glams it up a bit, while the huge Dalston branch provides the same excellent service – and a cool café. Cheshire St: Mon–Wed, Fri & Sat 10am–7pm, Thurs 10am–8pm, Sun 11.30am–6pm; Soho: Mon–Wed & Sat 10.30am–7.30pm, Thurs & Fri 10.30am–8.30pm, Sun 11am–6pm; Dalston: Mon, Tues & Sat 10am–7pm, Wed–Fri 10am–8pm, Sun 11.30am–6pm.

★**Blitz** 55–59 Hanbury St, E1 5JP ☏ 020 7377 8828, ⓦ blitzlondon.co.uk; ⊖ Shoreditch High Street; map pp.190–191. This self-styled vintage department store spreads across two floors of a Victorian brick warehouse, filled with not only clothes, shoes and accessories but also vinyl and furniture – there's a coffee bar, too. It's difficult to leave empty-handed. Mon–Wed 11am–7pm, Thurs–Sat 11am–8pm, Sun noon–6pm.

Reign Wear 12 Berwick St, W1F 0PN ☏ 020 3417 0276; ⊖ Oxford Circus; map p.101. Something slightly different, this little shop sources its second-hand gear from Europe, with a great selection of Italian pieces, pleasingly organized and displayed by colour and at good prices. Mon–Sat 11am–8pm, Sun 11am–5pm.

Rellik 8 Golborne Rd, W10 5NW ☏ 020 8962 0089, ⓦ relliklondon.co.uk; ⊖ Westbourne Park; map pp.276–277. Just off Portobello Rd, at the foot of the iconic Trellick Tower, Rellik sells cut-above vintage clobber to a moneyed west London set, with a good stash of cut-price couture and designer names. Tues–Sat 10am–6pm.

Rokit 101 & 107 Brick Lane, E1 6SE ☏ 020 7375 3864, ☏ 020 7247 3777; ⊖ Aldgate East or Shoreditch High Street, map pp.190–191; 225 Camden High St, NW1 7BU ☏ 020 7267 3046, map pp.284–285; 42 Shelton St, WC2H 9HZ ☏ 020 7836 6547, map p.108; ⓦ rokit.co.uk. Spreading its influence around London, Rokit offers a superb selection, nicely presented – from sparkly knits and cocktail dresses to petticoats and roller skates, plus men's gear dating back to the 1940s–80s. It's not the cheapest in town, but quality is high. Brick Lane branches: Mon–Fri 11am–7pm, Sat & Sun 10am–7pm; Camden: daily 10am–7pm; Covent Garden: Mon–Wed, Fri & Sat 10am–7pm, Thurs 10am–8pm, Sun 11am–6pm.

What the Butler Wore 108 Lower Marsh, SE1 7AB ☏ 020 7261 1968, ⓦ whatthebutlerwore.co.uk; ⊖ Waterloo or Lambeth North; map p.218. Colourful 1960s/70s boutique, evoking the groovy spirit of Carnaby St with its Mod dresses, shiny patent accessories and super-slim men's suits, and the occasional designer piece from the likes of Ossie Clark or Nina Ricci. Mon–Sat 11am–6pm.

SHOES

★**Irregular Choice** 35 Carnaby St, W1F 7DP ☏ 020 7494 4811; ⊖ Oxford Circus, map p.97; 209 Chalk Farm Rd, NW1 8AB ☏ 020 7483 3090; ⊖ Chalk Farm, map pp.284–285; ⓦ irregularchoice.com. Women's footwear doesn't get much more flamboyant, or frivolous, than this: a Mad Hatter's tea party of flowers, fruit, ribbons and knick-knacks adorning patterned pumps, flats, wedges and stilettos, all with wonderful names like Can't Touch This and Abigail's Party. Carnaby St: Mon–Sat 10am–8pm, Sun 11am–7pm; Camden Town daily 10am–7pm.

The Natural Shoe Store 70 Neal St, WC2H 9PA ☏ 020 7240 2783, ⓦ thenaturalshoestore.com; ⊖ Covent Garden; map p.108. A stalwart on shoe-shop-lined Neal St, selling socially responsible and ecologically sound shoes – mostly stylish, always comfortable and sometimes strange, with a great selection of Birkenstocks. Good value, but not necessarily cheap. Mon–Wed, Fri & Sat 10am–7pm, Thurs 10am–8pm, Sun noon–6pm.

★**Tracey Neuls** 29 Marylebone Lane, W1U 2NQ ☏ 020 7935 0039; ⊖ Bond Street, map p.89; 73 Redchurch St, E2 7DJ ☏ 020 7018 0872, map pp.190–191; ⓦ traceyneuls.com. Tracey Neuls' lovingly crafted, sculptural shoes are playful, comfortable and inspired, with genius innovations (heels that look higher than they are) and witty details. There's a second branch on Redchurch St in the East End. Marylebone: Mon–Fri 11am–6.30pm, Sat noon–6pm, Sun noon–5pm; Redchurch St: Tues–Sun 11am–6pm.

Vivobarefoot 64 Neal St, WC2H 9PQ ☎ 020 7379 5959, Ⓦ vivobarefoot.com; ⊖ Covent Garden; map p.108. A temple to the "barefoot shoe", with its ultra-thin, puncture resistant and allegedly health-giving soles. Lots of funky running shoes, of course, but also pumps, sandals and boots, many made with vegan materials. Mon–Sat 10.30am–7pm, Sun noon–6pm.

BOOKS

Along with the few surviving chains, London remains blessed, for now, with a number of local, independent and specialist bookshops. **Bloomsbury** and **Charing Cross Road** are excellent hunting grounds; the latter, in particular, along with **Cecil Court** (Ⓦ cecilcourt.co.uk) – the little lane that runs between Charing Cross Road and St Martin's Lane – is particularly good if you're looking for secondhand oddities and rare titles.

GENERAL INTEREST AND CHAINS

Blackwell's 50 High Holborn, WC1V 6EP ☎ 020 7292 5100, Ⓦ bookshop.blackwell.co.uk; ⊖ Holborn; map p.140. The new London flagship of Oxford's academic bookshop has a wider range than you might expect. Its academic stock is, unsurprisingly, excellent, but so too is the range of travel, fiction, history and biography titles. There's a café on site. Mon–Fri 8am–6.30pm, Sat 10am–4pm.

Foyles 107 Charing Cross Rd, WC2H 0DT ☎ 020 437 5660, Ⓦ foyles.co.uk; ⊖ Tottenham Court Road; map p.101. It may have moved down the road, but this long-established, huge and famous London bookshop continues to offer a splendid selection of titles on all subjects across its four miles of shelves, including antiquarian books. The store also houses a café and Ray's Jazz Shop for music; frequent readings and events include a monthly book club and music performances. There are smaller branches under the RFH on the South Bank and in Waterloo Station. Mon–Sat 9.30am–9pm, Sun noon–6pm.

Hatchards 187 Piccadilly, W1J 9LE ☎ 020 7439 9921, Ⓦ hatchards.co.uk; ⊖ Piccadilly Circus; map p.78. A little overshadowed by the colossal Waterstones down the road, and actually part of the Waterstones group, the venerable Hatchards, founded in 1797, holds its own when it comes to quality fiction, biography, history and travel. The regal interiors are only fitting for a bookseller by appointment to HM the Queen. There's a mini branch in St Pancras International train station. Mon–Sat 9.30am–7pm, Sun noon–6pm.

★ Waterstones 203–206 Piccadilly, W1J 9HD ☎ 020 7851 2400, Ⓦ waterstones.com; ⊖ Piccadilly Circus; map p.78. This flagship bookshop, Europe's largest, occupies the former Simpson's department store building – a Modernist classic – and boasts a café, bar and gallery as well as six floors of books. Various events include readings and signings. Many other branches around town. Mon–Sat 9am–10pm, Sun noon–6.30pm.

INDEPENDENT AND SPECIALIST

Arthur Probsthain 41 Great Russell St, WC1B 3PE ☎ 020 7636 1096, Ⓦ apandtea.co.uk; ⊖ Tottenham Court Road; map p.127. With another branch in the nearby School of Oriental and African Studies, this impressive old store, opposite the British Museum, specializes in books on the arts and cultures of Africa, Asia and the Middle East, with a small art gallery and tearoom downstairs. Mon–Fri 9.30am–5.30pm, Sat noon–4pm.

Bookmarks 1 Bloomsbury St, WC1B 3QE ☎ 020 7637 1848, Ⓦ bookmarks.uk.com; ⊖ Tottenham Court Road; map p.127. Leftist and radical books, with a wide range of political biography, history, theory and assorted socialist campaigning ephemera. Mon noon–7pm, Tues–Sat 10am–7pm.

★ Books for Cooks 4 Blenheim Crescent, W11 1NN ☎ 020 7221 1992, Ⓦ booksforcooks.com; ⊖ Ladbroke Grove; map pp.276–277. You'll dig up anything and everything to do with food at this splendid new and used bookshop, which also has a tiny, highly recommended café (see p.382). Tues–Sat 10am–6pm.

★ Daunt Books 83 Marylebone High St, W1U 4QW ☎ 020 7224 2295, Ⓦ dauntbooks.co.uk; ⊖ Bond Street or Baker Street; map p.89. A wide and inspirational range of travel literature, guidebooks, maps and more, in the beautiful, galleried interior of this famous Edwardian shop. Other branches around town. Mon–Sat 9am–7.30pm, Sun 11am–6pm.

Gay's the Word 66 Marchmont St, WC1N 1AB ☎ 020 7278 7654, Ⓦ gaystheword.co.uk; ⊖ Russell Square; map p.127. Venerable community bookshop, famed for weekly lesbian discussion groups, and offering an extensive collection of lesbian and gay classics, pulps, contemporary fiction and nonfiction, plus cards and calendars. Mon–Sat 10am–6.30pm, Sun 2 noon–6pm.

Gosh! 1 Berwick St, W1F 0DR ☎ 020 7636 1011, Ⓦ goshlondon.com; ⊖ Tottenham Court Road; map p.101. All manner of graphic novels, comics and art/design books for the casually curious and the serious collector alike, including vintage items, small-press gems, European titles and superhero classics. Daily 10.30am–7pm.

Idler Academy 81 Westbourne Park Rd, W2 5QH ☎ 020 7221 1960, Ⓦ idler.co.uk; ⊖ Royal Oak or Westbourne Park; map pp.276–277. With its aim to promote "cultivated leisure", this is a delightfully quirky little bookshop/café whose "academy" hosts events and courses ranging from handwriting improvement and supper clubs to instruction in taxidermy and mosaic making. Wed–Sat 10am–6pm.

29

John Sandoe 10 Blacklands Terrace, SW3 2SR ☎020 7589 9473, ⓦjohnsandoe.com; ⊖Sloane Square; map p.267. One of London's finest literary bookshops, with a personally selected range of titles crammed into three floors of an eighteenth-century building; whether you're after classic genre fiction or obscure tomes on psychology, this is the place to come. Mon–Sat 9.30am–6.30pm, Sun 11am–5pm.

London Review Bookshop 14 Bury Place, WC1A 2JL ☎020 7269 9030, ⓦlrbshop.co.uk; ⊖Tottenham Court Road; map p.127. All the books reviewed in the august literary journal and many more in this excellent Bloomsbury bookshop. Particularly strong on literary fiction, poetry, history, politics and current affairs, it hosts regular readings and events and has a nice little coffee and cake shop. Mon–Sat 10am–6.30pm, Sun noon–6pm.

Lutyens & Rubinstein 21 Kensington Park Rd, W11 2EU ☎020 7229 1010, ⓦlutyensrubinstein.co.uk; ⊖Ladbroke Grove; map pp.276–277. Classy bookstore, established by the literary agents of the same name, selling a hand-selected range of classics, works in translation, fiction, poetry, children's titles and art books, with unusual literary gifts to boot. Mon & Sat 10am–6pm, Tues–Fri 10am–6.30pm, Sun 11am–5pm.

★**Persephone Books** 59 Lamb's Conduit St, WC1N 3NB ☎020 7242 9292, ⓦpersephonebooks.co.uk; ⊖Russell Square or Holborn; map p.127. Lovely bookshop offspring of a publishing house that specializes in neglected early and mid-twentieth-century writing, mainly by women. The books are beautifully produced, all with endpapers in a textile design from the relevant period. Mon–Fri 10am–6pm, Sat noon–5pm.

★**Society Club** 12 Ingestre Place, W1F 0JF ☎020 7437 1433, ⓦthesocietyclub.com; ⊖Piccadilly Circus; map p.101. Very cool little Soho spot – bookshop, gallery, bar, members' club – with friendly resident dogs and the feel of a bohemian salon. Stock includes Soho-specific titles, vintage erotica and Charles Bukowski, along with new small-press fiction and first editions from authors as varied

as Daphne du Maurier, Vladimir Nabokov and Groucho Marx. Shop: Mon–Fri noon–6pm, Sat 2.30–6pm.

Stanfords 12–14 Long Acre, WC2E 9LP ☎020 7836 1321, ⓦstanfords.co.uk; ⊖Covent Garden; map p.108. The world's largest specialist travel and map bookshop, selling pretty much any map of anywhere, plus a huge range of books, guides, literature, travel accessories and gifts. There's a small café. Mon–Fri 9am–8pm, Tues 9.30am–8pm, Sat 10am–8pm, Sun noon–6pm.

SECONDHAND AND ANTIQUARIAN

Any Amount of Books 56 Charing Cross Rd, WC2H 0QA ☎020 7836 3697, ⓦanyamountofbooks.com; ⊖Leicester Square; map p.101. Sprawling secondhand bookshop stocking everything from obscure £1 bargains to rare and expensive first editions. Especially strong on fiction, crime, the arts and literary biography. Daily 10.30am–9.30pm.

★**Pleasures of Past Times** 11 Cecil Court, WC2N 4EZ ☎020 7836 1142; ⊖Leicester Square; map p.97. An absolute treasure, open for some fifty years and focusing on showbiz titles and ephemera from the 1960s–80s. You'll also find nineteenth-century fairy-tale collections, curious conjuring manuals and prewar children's fiction along with music hall paraphernalia, playbills and theatrical postcards, and a little vinyl record store at the back, selling groovy discs from the 1950s to the 1970s. Tues–Fri 10.30am–6.30pm, Sat noon–6.30pm.

Quinto 72 Charing Cross Rd, WC2H 0BB ☎020 7379 7669, ⓦquintobookshop.co.uk; ⊖Leicester Square; map p.101. Another Charing Cross Rd treasure, this secondhand bookshop has a huge choice, from battered paperbacks to precious first editions, and regularly refreshes its stock. Mon–Sat 9am–9pm, Sun noon–8pm.

South Bank Book Market Under Waterloo Bridge on the South Bank, SE1; ⊖Waterloo; map p.218. Alfresco book market by the Thames, opposite the BFI Southbank, offering everything from last season's and pulp fiction to obscure textbooks and modern European poetry. Daily 10am till late.

FOOD AND DRINK

As you'd expect of a city that has some of the best restaurants in the world, London offers great shopping for the most discerning of food buffs. In the centre of town, **Soho** and **Marylebone**, in particular, are a gourmand's delight: the former is particularly good for Chinese supermarkets and Italian delicatessens. The major department-store food halls (see box, p.427) are good hunting grounds for luxury snacks and picnic foods, while **specialist stores** and the many local **food markets** (see p.433) – Borough Market, Broadway Market and Maltby Street have the highest profile – offer an atmospheric shopping experience. The specialist **beer, wine and spirits** outlets listed are the pick of central London's numerous retailers, but you'll also find ever-improving ranges in the main supermarkets.

PATISSERIE AND CHOCOLATE

Lily Vanilli 6 The Courtyard, Ezra St, E2 7RH ⓦlilyvanilli.com; ⊖Bethnal Green; map pp.190–191. Many of the more elaborate cakes at this popular little bakery have an Alice in Wonderland whimsy, decorated

(appropriately enough, given the location in the heart of the Columbia Road flower market) with flowers and gilded fruits. At heart, though, Lily Jones wears her home-baking credentials with pride, celebrating old-fashioned traditions with sponges, Bakewell tarts, bite-sized fairy cakes and flaky bacon and sausage rolls. Sun 8.30am–4pm.

★ **Paul A Young** 143 Wardour St, W1F 8WA ☎ 020 7437 0011, ⓦ paulayoung.co.uk; ⊖ Oxford Circus; map p.101. Artisan chocolate beyond your wildest dreams, handmade daily and with seasonal flavours including fennel seed and stem ginger, goat's cheese with lemon and thyme, bakewell tart truffle, and honey and rose caramels. Pick and mix a box of four for £7, or of nine for £15.50. Branches in Islington, Fitzrovia and the City. Mon–Wed, Fri & Sat 10am–8pm, Thurs 10am–9pm, Sun noon–7pm.

Southerden Patisserie 72 Bermondsey St, SE1 3UD ☎ 020 7378 1585, ⓦ southerden.com; map pp.226–227. Stylish patisserie/bakery opposite the Fashion and Textile Museum in Bermondsey's foodie heartland, serving exquisite cakes, artisan breads and contemporary treats – savoury eclairs, vodka pastry pies, the signature "choumert" bun, topped with crumble and filled with crème patisserie – plus baking ingredients, Monmouth coffees, sandwiches and salads. Mon–Fri 8am–5pm, Sat 9am–7pm, 9.30am–5pm.

CHEESE

★ **Neal's Yard Dairy** 17 Shorts Gardens, WC2H 9AT ☎ 020 7240 5700; ⊖ Covent Garden, map p.108; 6 Park St, Borough Market, SE1 9AB ☎ 020 7367 0799; ⊖ Borough, map pp.228–229; ⓦ nealsyarddairy .co.uk. Pungent store packed to the rafters with quality artisan cheeses from around the British Isles, with a couple of good choices from France, Italy and Greece. You can taste before you buy. Covent Garden: Mon–Sat 10am–7pm; Borough: Mon–Sat 9am–6pm.

Paxton & Whitfield 93 Jermyn St, SW1Y 6JE ☎ 020 7930 0259, ⓦ paxtonandwhitfield.co.uk; ⊖ Piccadilly Circus; map p.67. Quintessentially English, 200-year-old gourmet cheese shop offering a traditional range of English and European varieties, plus fine wines and ports, and fabulous cheesy gifts. Regular cheese tasting and matching events. Mon–Sat 9.30am–6pm, Sun 11am–5pm.

COFFEE AND TEA

Algerian Coffee Stores 52 Old Compton St, W1D 4PB ☎ 020 7437 2480, ⓦ algcoffee.co.uk; ⊖ Leicester Square; map p.101. With its original dark wood fittings and glass display cases, and its rich, dark fragrance, this unassuming old Soho store, here since 1887, looks and feels much as it must have done when it opened. Choose from around eighty coffees – from house blends to rare beans – and (a big local secret, this) grab a quick espresso for just £1. More than one hundred teas, too, plus confectionery from around the world. Mon–Wed 9am–7pm, Thurs & Fri 9am–9pm, Sat 9am–8pm.

The Tea House 15 Neal St, WC2H 9PU ☎ 020 7240 7539, ⓦ teahouseltd.com; ⊖ Covent Garden; map p.108. The distinctive red-tiled and black facade conceals two aromatic floors of teas – black, green, white, herbal,

flowering and caffeine-free – with a wealth of accessories including infusers, teapots and cosies. Mon–Wed 10am–7pm, Thurs–Sat 10am–8pm, Sun 11am–7pm.

WORLD FOOD

A. Gold 42 Brushfield St, E1 6AG ☎ 020 7247 2487, ⓦ agoldshop.com; ⊖ Liverpool Street; map pp.190–191. Next door to Jeanette Winterson's Verde's (see p.378), A. Gold is a similarly classy old establishment, a "village shop" selling peculiarly British foodstuffs: mint balls, Camp coffee, London honey, home-made scotch eggs, Henderson's relish and the like. On weekday lunchtimes they offer delicious overstuffed artisan sandwiches, salads and daily hot specials to take away, too. Mon–Fri 10am–4pm, Sat & Sun 11am–5pm.

★ **Brindisa** Floral Hall, Stoney St, Borough Market, SE1 9AF ☎ 020 7407 1036, ⓦ brindisa.com; ⊖ Borough; map pp.228–229. If you're craving Ibérico ham, boquerones, Marcona almonds, manchego and salt cod, this upmarket contemporary Spanish deli is the place for you. They offer ham-carving classes, too. Mon 10am–4pm, Tues–Thurs 10am–5.30pm, Fri 10am–6pm, Sat 8.30am–5pm.

I. Camisa & Son 61 Old Compton St, W1 ☎ 020 7437 7610, ⓦ icamisa.co.uk; ⊖ Leicester Square; map p.101. The whole classic Italian deli range packed into one small, wonderfully old-fashioned Soho space. Excellent cheeses, salamis, pastas and dried foods, plus Italian wines and spirits. Mon–Sat 8.30am–6pm.

Loon Fung Supermarket 42–44 Gerrard St, W1D 5QG ☎ 020 7437 7332, ⓦ loonfung.com; ⊖ Leicester Square; map p.101. This warren of a supermarket in the heart of Chinatown offers every kind of Chinese food item you can imagine, and probably some you can't. There's also a range of Chinese foods and groceries in neighbouring Newport St, Newport Place and Lisle St. Daily 10am–8pm.

Taj Stores 112 Brick Lane, E1 6RL ☎ 020 7377 0061, ⓦ tajstores.co.uk; ⊖ Aldgate East; map pp.190–191. Big Bangladeshi supermarket established in 1936, offering everything from halal meats, herbs and spices to fish, fresh fruit and veg, plus ingredients from other countries including India, Thailand, Malaysia, Lebanon and Jamaica. Daily 9am–9pm.

BEER, WINE AND SPIRITS

Berry Bros & Rudd 3 St James's St, SW1A 1EG ☎ 020 7022 8973, ⓦ bbr.com; ⊖ Green Park; map p.67. A venerable wine merchant, on this site since 1698, housing a huge range of fine wines – from £10 to £25,000 – in a ravishing seventeenth-century building. Mon–Fri 10am–6pm, Sat 10am–5pm.

BottleDog 69 Gray's Inn Rd, WC1X 8TP ☎ 020 7242 7808, ⓦ brewdog.com/bars/uk/bottledog; ⊖ King's Cross; map p.127. It's craft beer heaven at this artisan off-licence from the BrewDog brewery – more than 250 bottles

29

and cans, takeaway draught beer from BrewDog and guests, plus homebrew gear, manuals and ingredients, regular tastings and food pairings. Mon–Fri noon–9pm, Sat noon–8pm, Sun noon–6pm.

★ **Gerry's** 74 Old Compton St, W1D 4UW ☎ 020 7734 4215, ⓦ gerrys.uk.com; ⊖ Leicester Square; map p.101. Characterful old Soho store, crammed with the best, most eclectic and sometimes downright weirdest range of spirits you'll find anywhere in London, including sake, schnapps and absinthe. Mon–Thurs 9am–6.30pm, Fri & Sat 9am–7.30pm, Sun noon–6pm.

The Real Ale Shop 371 Richmond Rd, TW1 2EF ☎ 020 8892 3710, ⓦ realale.com; ⊖ Richmond; map p.340. Microbrews and craft beers from around the world, including ciders, perries and smoked beers, and regularly changing cask ales from local breweries. Mon noon–8pm, Tues–Sat 10am–9pm, Sun 11am–7pm.

Vintage House 42 Old Compton St, W1D 4LR ☎ 020 7437 2592, ⓦ vintagehouse.co.uk; ⊖ Leicester Square; map p.101. The creaking shelves of this old, family-run drinker's paradise in the heart of Soho are crammed with rums, brandies and more than 1350 malt whiskies. Mon–Fri 9am–11pm, Sat 10am–11pm, Sun noon–11pm.

MUSIC

Following the demise of the big record stores, music lovers are currently on a roll in London, with many of the markets (see opposite) and a number of neighbourhood shops catering for nostalgics hunting down **vinyl** and **CDs**. Soho – especially Berwick St and around – has traditionally been a good bet for independent and specialist music shops; the neighbourhood is under increasing threat from developers, however, so get there while you can.

Gramex 104 Lower Marsh, SE1 7AB ☎ 020 7401 3830; ⊖ Waterloo; map p.218. A splendid find for classical music and jazz fans, this eccentric record store – "it might not be good, but it's rare!" – is a treasure trove of new and secondhand CDs, with friendly owners and low prices. Mon–Sat 11am–7pm.

Harold Moores Records 2 Great Marlborough St, W1F 7HQ ☎ 020 7437 1576, ⓦ hmrecords.co.uk; ⊖ Oxford Circus or Tottenham Court Road; map p.97. Two welcoming floors of CDs and vinyl, mostly classical and jazz, with rare releases and lots of contemporary, avant-garde selections. Mon–Sat 10am–6.30pm.

★ **Honest Jon's** 278 Portobello Rd, W10 5TE ☎ 020 8969 9822, ⓦ honestjons.com; ⊖ Ladbroke Grove or Westbourne Park; map pp.276–277. This west London stalwart offers a fine selection of blues, soul, jazz, funk, R&B, rare groove, reggae, world music and more, with current releases, secondhand finds and reissues. Mon–Sat 10am–6pm, Sun 11am–5pm.

Phonica 51 Poland St, W1F 7LZ ☎ 020 7025 6070, ⓦ phonicarecords.com; ⊖ Oxford Circus; map p.97. One-stop shop for specialist sounds, specializing in electronic music but ranging from krautrock via nu disco to synthwave and radical poetry, with well-informed, friendly staff. Mon–Wed & Sat 11.30am–7.30pm, Thurs & Fri 11.30am–8pm, Sun noon–6pm.

Rough Trade 130 Talbot Rd, W11 1JA ☎ 020 7229 8541; ⊖ Ladbroke Grove, map pp.276–277; Rough Trade East: 91 Brick Lane, E1 6QL ☎ 020 7392 7788; ⊖ Aldgate East or Shoreditch High Street, map pp.190–191; ⓦ roughtrade.com. This historic west London specialist has a dizzying array of indie – not all of it obscure – music from electronica to hardcore and beyond. There's a second, huge, branch, Rough Trade East, in the Old Truman Brewery. Regular in-store events at both. Rough Trade: Mon–Sat 10am–6.30pm, Sun 11am–5pm; Rough Trade East: Mon–Thurs 8am–9pm, Fri 8am–8pm, Sat 10am–8pm, Sun 11am–7pm.

★ **Sister Ray** 75 Berwick St, W1F 8TG ☎ 020 7734 3297, ⓦ sisterray.co.uk; ⊖ Tottenham Court Road; map p.101. A sizeable, long-established and well-informed vinyl specialist, specializing in cool music from the 1960s up to the present, with a stream of customers rummaging through anything from spacerock to psychobilly. There's a second, vinyl-only branch attached to the *Ace Hotel* in Shoreditch (see p.359). Mon–Sat 10am–8pm, Sun noon–6pm.

Sounds that Swing 88 Parkway, NW1 7AN ☎ 020 7267 4682, ⓦ nohitrecords.co.uk; ⊖ Camden Town; map pp.284–285. The bricks and mortar outlet of the No Hit Records label, with a very Camden Town rockabilly vibe, this colourful vinyl and CD store offers an eclectic range from blues/folk via rockabilly to garage punk. Mon–Sat 11am–6pm, Sun noon–6pm.

GIFTS

Ignore the Beefeater teddy bears and tacky comedy T-shirts – London can be a splendid place for **souvenirs**. In addition to the city's many fabulous **museum shops** (those at the V&A, London Transport Museum, the Wellcome Collection and the Southbank Centre, by the Royal Festival Hall, yield particularly rich pickings), and its **department stores** (see box, p.427) – Liberty and Selfridges are the best for gifts – London has plenty of offbeat places that are perfect for out-of-the-ordinary presents.

House of Hackney 131 Shoreditch High St, E1 6JE ☎020 7739 3901, ⊛houseofhackney.com; ⊖Shoreditch High Street; map pp.190–191. These playful, colourful and high-fashion homeware, wallpapers, textiles and clothing, all designed and made – with impeccable attention to detail and craft – in England, combine pretty with edgy, floral with funky, to eye-popping effect. Mon–Sat 10am–7pm, Sun 11am–5pm.

★ **International Magic** 89 Clerkenwell Rd, EC1R 5BX ☎020 7405 7324, ⊛internationalmagic.com; ⊖Chancery Lane or Farringdon; map p.147. Eccentric, family-owned magic store selling more tricks and accessories, along with instruction manuals and DVDs, than it is possible to imagine (unless you're a mind-reader). Mon–Fri 11.30am–6pm, Sat 11.30am–4pm.

★ **Labour and Wait** 85 Redchurch St, E2 7DJ ☎020 7729 6253, ⊛labourandwait.co.uk; ⊖Shoreditch High Street; map pp.190–191. Galvanized buckets, tins of twine, wooden brushes and Marseille soap flakes become objects of supreme desire in this cult hardware-cum-concept store. Kitchen chores never seemed so cool, but even the slobbier shopper will lust after the polka dot hankies, beauty products, books, toys and more – all with the same simple, functional and soothingly old-fashioned good looks. Tues–Sun 11am–6pm.

Limelight Movie Art 313 King's Rd, SW3 5EP ☎020 7751 5584, ⊛limelightmovieart.com; ⊖South Kensington; map p.267. Though the generally high prices mean it's geared mainly towards serious collectors, you can still pick up original movie posters and lobby cards – from Bowie to Buster Keaton – from £75 at this Chelsea shop. Mon–Sat 11.30am–6pm.

Lomography Gallery Store 3 Newburgh St, W1F 7RE ☎020 7434 1466, ⊛lomography.com; ⊖Oxford Circus, map p.97. For anyone who thinks photography lost its soul when it went digital, this swish Soho store/hangout sells all the cult analogue cameras, with lots of affordable models too. Mon–Sat 11am–7pm, Sun noon–5pm.

Magma 29 Shorts Gardens, WC2H 9AP ☎020 7240 7970; ⊖Covent Garden, map p.108; 16 Earlham St, WC2H 9LN ☎020 7240 7571; ⊖Covent Garden, map p.147; 117–119 Clerkenwell Rd, EC1R 5BY ☎020 7242 9503; ⊖Chancery Lane; ⊛magmabooks.com. It's almost impossible to leave these stores empty-handed, filled as they are with beautifully designed, innovative and affordable gifts, toys and homeware, stationery, art and design books and journals, posters and all manner of gizmos – from four-leaf clover kits to Japanese paper earrings or space age egg cups. Short's Gardens: Mon–Sat 10am–7pm, Sun noon–8pm; Earlham St: Mon–Sat 11am–7pm, Sun noon–6pm; Clerkenwell: Mon–Sat 10am–7pm.

MARKETS

London's markets are more than just a cheap alternative to high-street shopping: you haven't really got to grips with the city unless you've rummaged through the junk at Brick Lane on a Sunday morning, haggled over a leather jacket at Camden or stuffed your face with artisan goodies from the rash of street food stalls that have mushroomed through all of them. For more on London's **foodie markets**, see our Cafés and restaurants chapter (see box, p.370).

★ **Alfie's Antique Market** 13–25 Church St, NW8 8DT ☎020 7723 6066, ⊛alfiesantiques.com; ⊖Marylebone; map p.89. Vast indoor flea market offering fantastic vintage and antiques from Art Deco earrings to priceless modernist ceramics. There's a good rooftop café, too. Tues–Sat 10am–6pm.

Bermondsey (New Caledonian) Bermondsey Square, SE1 3UN; ⊖London Bridge; map pp.226–227. Antiques from obscure nautical instruments to pricey furniture. The serious collectors arrive at dawn. Fri 6am–2pm.

Berwick Street Berwick and Rupert streets, W1; ⊖Piccadilly Circus; map p.101. This famous fruit and veg market – here since the 1770s – is a fast-disappearing slice of Soho history. The notoriously noisy vendors who once worked the crowds like showmen are quieter nowadays, as gentrification runs rampant and the artisan coffee outlets and restaurants, rather than cheap bags of apples and pears, bring in the crowds, but this is still a welcome central oasis to pick up fresh produce – for now. Mon–Sat 9am–6pm.

Borough 8 Southwark St, SE1 1TL ☎020 7407 1002, ⊛boroughmarket.org.uk; ⊖London Bridge; map pp.228–229. Fine-food heaven – gourmet suppliers from all over the UK converge to sell organic and artisan goodies from around the world. The Victorian structure, with its slender wrought-iron columns, is lovely. Prices are high, and Saturdays can be a crush; go early. Wed & Thurs 10am–5pm, Fri 10am–6pm, Sat 8am–5pm.

Brick Lane Brick Lane, Dray Walk, Cygnet and Sclater streets, E1; ⊖Aldgate East or Liverpool Street or Shoreditch High Street; map pp.190–191. Huge, sprawling and frenzied, the famous East End market has become a fixture on the hipster circuit. Knock-off bikes, household tat, antique furniture, rockabilly on vinyl, home-made cakes, edgy fashion, jazzy rugs, broken spectacles – it's hard to say what you can't find here – and the street food is fabulous, too. The coolest gear is sold in and around the Old Truman Brewery, at the Backyard Market (⊛backyardmarket.co.uk), the Tea Rooms (⊛bricklane-tearooms.co.uk) and the Sunday Upmarket (⊛sundayupmarket.co.uk). Brick Lane: Sun 9am–5pm; Backyard/Tea Rooms: Sat 11am–6pm, Sun 10am–5pm; Upmarket: Sun 10am–5pm.

29

★**Brixton** Electric Ave, Pope's, Brixton Station and Atlantic rds, SW9 ⓦ brixtonmarket.net; ⊖ Brixton; map pp.308–309. Centred on Electric Ave, and spilling out along the neighbouring streets, this huge, energetic market (see p.307) still offers inexpensive fruit and veg, African and Caribbean foods, beauty products, records, clothes and fabrics to a local clientele. Brixton Station Rd also sees a farmers' market on Sunday (10am–2pm) and themed markets each Sat (10am–5pm), while cool vintage shops, food vendors and restaurants cluster in the ever-gentrifying "Brixton Village" and Market Row, the arcades off Atlantic Rd and Coldharbour Lane. Arcades: Mon 8am–6pm, Tues–Sun 8am–11.30pm; street stalls: Mon, Tues & Thurs–Sat 8am–6pm, Wed 8am–3pm; shops: daily 8am–7pm.

Broadway Broadway Market, E8 ⓦ broadwaymarket .co.uk; ⊖ Bethnal Green; map p.187. Running from the Regent's Canal down to London Fields, this trendy foodie favourite offers terrific organic and artisan produce, and you can pick up fabrics, books, vintage and one-off accessories – along with good coffee and food – in the shops and cafés alongside. For a slightly quieter mini-version of the same scene, head to Netil Market, around the corner on Westgate Street at the London Fields end (Sat 11am–6pm, Sun noon–5pm). Stalls: Sat 8am–7pm.

Camden Camden High St to Chalk Farm Rd, NW1 ⓦ camdenlock.net; ⊖ Camden Town; map pp.284–285. This legendary market, once beloved of hippies, punks and goths, and still a firm favourite with young European tourists, is actually a gaggle of markets, a mass of hundreds of stalls – arts, crafts and clubwear, records, furniture, trinkets and jewellery, and, in the Stables Market area especially, excellent vintage/antique stuff – segueing into each other to create one enormous shopping district. Lively shops add hip designers, antique dealers, restaurants, bars and booksellers to the mix. Daily, roughly 9.30am–6pm, with more stalls at the weekend.

★**Columbia Road** Columbia Rd, E2 ⓦ columbiaroad .info; ⊖ Shoreditch High Street or Hoxton; map pp.190–191. Fabulous, fragrant flower market in the heart of the East End, with bargains galore, especially late in the day. Get here early, grab breakfast in one of the local cafés or delis, and check out the area's hip indie shops, spread in the streets all around. Sun 8am–3pm.

Greenwich Greenwich High Rd, SE10 ⓦ greenwichmarketlondon.com; ⊖ ⇄ Greenwich from Charing Cross or ⊖ Cutty Sark DLR; map p.313. Sprawling set of covered flea markets with some 150 stalls selling everything from bric-a-brac to bangles to board games, with antiques and crafts, food and vintage clothes. The surrounding streets, and the shops inside the covered market, offer more treasures. Stalls: Tues–Sun 10am–5.30pm.

Portobello Portobello and Golborne rds, W10 and W11 ⓦ shopportobello.co.uk; ⊖ Ladbroke Grove or Notting Hill Gate; map pp.276–277. Probably the best way to approach this enormous market, or rather markets – beloved of tourist crowds – is from the Notting Hill end, winding your way through the junky antiques and bric-a-brac down to the fruit and veg, and then via the fashion stalls under the Westway to the thriving vintage (Fri & Sun) and fashion scene at Portobello Green (ⓦ portobellofashionmarket. com). The Golborne Road market is cheaper and less crowded, with antique and retro furniture on Fri and Sat (food and produce Mon–Thurs). Roughly 8am–6pm, till 1pm on Thurs; antiques Fri & Sat; Portobello Green Fri–Sun; Golborne Road Mon–Sat.

Ridley Road Ridley Rd, E8 2NP; ⊖ Dalston Kingsland; map p.187. A bustling, astonishingly cheap food and clothes market in the heart of Hackney. African and Caribbean fruit, veg and fish predominate, but there are also Turkish and Asian staples and shops offering fabrics, hair and beauty products, old gospel albums, cheap shoes and much else. Mon–Thurs 6am–6pm, Fri & Sat 6am–7pm.

Spitalfields Commercial St, between Brushfield and Lamb streets, E1 ⓦ spitalfields.co.uk; ⊖ Liverpool St; map pp.190–191. The East End's historic Victorian fruit and veg hall feels rather more like an upmarket mall nowadays, but there are interesting things to be found among its designer/makers, crafts, gifts and clothes stalls. Plenty of bars and restaurants all around, too, along with independent shops, and street food stalls on Wed lunchtime. Stalls: Mon–Fri 10am–5pm, Sat 11am–5pm, Sun 9am–5pm.

WIMBLEDON

Activities and sports

Many of the crucial international fixtures of football, rugby and cricket take place in the capital, and London also hosts one of the world's top tennis tournaments, Wimbledon. London is the only city to have hosted the Olympics three times, and the 2012 Olympics supplied a number of new world-class arenas in the Queen Elizabeth Olympic Park (see p.205). Domestically, football (soccer) remains the most popular sport, with London clubs Chelsea and Arsenal among Europe's top teams. The rest of the sporting calendar is chock-full of quality events, from the sedate pleasures of county cricket to a night at the "dogs" (greyhound racing). For those who'd rather compete than spectate, there's a wide range of facilities, including inexpensive access to swimming pools and lidos, gyms, tennis courts, while even golf enthusiasts can find a course within the city limits.

SPECTATOR SPORTS

For top international events, it's tough to track down a ticket without paying over the odds through a ticket agency. You can often fall back on **TV or radio coverage**: BBC Radio 5 live (digital; also 909 & 693 Mhz) has live commentaries on almost all major sporting events, while one of the free-to-view TV channels nearly always carries live transmission of international rugby and soccer. To watch some sports (including live Premier League football), you'll need to find a TV that has the paid-for stations – many pubs show these games.

30

FOOTBALL

The English **football** (soccer) season runs from mid-Aug to early May, finishing off with the **FA Cup Final** at Wembley. There are four professional leagues: at the top is the twenty-club Premier League, followed by the Championship and Leagues One and Two, each of which has 24 clubs. There are London clubs in every division, with around five or six in the Premier League at any one time. Over the decades, London's most successful club has been **Arsenal**. However, since the arrival of Russian oil tycoon Roman Abramovich, **Chelsea** has had a resurgence, winning the league for the first time in fifty years in 2005, and another three times since then.

Tickets Tickets for most Premier League games start at £40–50 and are virtually impossible to get hold of on a casual basis, though you may be able to see one of the Cup fixtures. It's a lot easier and cheaper to see a game in the Championship or one of the lower leagues, or to go on a stadium tour (see club websites for details).

Fixtures Most Premier League fixtures kick off at 3pm on Saturday, though there's also an early and late kick-off on Saturday, plus a couple on Sunday and the occasional midweek match. Matches are broadcast live on paid-for TV; in theory, the Saturday 3pm kick-offs are not shown live, though plenty of pubs find ways around this.

NATIONAL STADIUM

Wembley Stadium Wembley Way (90,000 capacity) HA9 0WS ☎0800 169 2007, ⓦwembleystadium.com; ⊖ Wembley Park or Wembley Central. The new stadium, designed by Norman Foster and featuring a massive steel arch, is the world's most expensive football ground, but it'll never reach the iconic status of the old stadium, constructed for the 1924 British Empire Exhibition, and the main focus of the 1948 Olympic Games. The stadium's most famous features were its "twin towers", forever associated with England's victory here in the 1966 World Cup Final. Guided tours are available (daily 10am–4pm; £19, under-16s £11).

FOOTBALL CLUBS

Arsenal (Premier League) Emirates Stadium, Hornsey Rd, N7 7AJ (60,400 capacity) ☎020 7619 5000, ⓦarsenal.com; ⊖ Arsenal.

Barnet (League Two) The Hive Stadium, Camrose Ave, HA8 6AG (5200 capacity) ☎020 8381 3800, ⓦbarnetfc.com; ⊖ Canons Park.

Brentford (Championship) Griffin Park, Braemar Rd, TW8 0NT (12,800 capacity) ☎0845 345 6442, ⓦbrentfordfc.co.uk; ⇌Brentford from Waterloo. Note that a ground move is in the pipeline.

Charlton Athletic (Championship) The Valley, Floyd Rd, SE7 8BL (27,000 capacity) ☎03330 14 44 44, ⓦcafc.co.uk; ⇌Charlton from Charing Cross or London Bridge.

Chelsea (Premier League) Stamford Bridge, Fulham Rd, SW6 1HS (41,800 capacity) ☎020 7958 2190 (general), ☎0871 984 1905 (tickets), ⓦchelseafc.com; ⊖ Fulham Broadway.

Crystal Palace (Premier League) Selhurst Park, Whitehorse Lane, SE25 6PU (26,300 capacity) ☎020 8768 6000 (general), ☎08712 000071 (tickets), ⓦcpfc.co.uk; ⇌Selhurst from Victoria or ⊖ Clapham Junction.

Dagenham & Redbridge (League Two) Victoria Road, Dagenham, RM10 7XL (6100 capacity) ☎020 8592 1549, ⓦdaggers.co.uk; ⊖ Dagenham East.

Fulham (Championship) Craven Cottage, Stevenage Rd, SW6 6HH (25,700 capacity) ☎0843 208 1222, ⓦfulhamfc.com; ⊖ Putney Bridge.

Leyton Orient (League One) Matchroom Stadium, Brisbane Rd, E10 5NF (9200 capacity) ☎0871 310 1881, ⓦleytonorient.com; ⊖ Leyton.

Millwall (League One) The Den, Zampa Rd, SE16 3LN (20,100 capacity) ☎020 7232 1222, ⓦmillwallfc.co.uk; ⇌South Bermondsey from London Bridge.

Queens Park Rangers (Championship) Loftus Road Stadium, South Africa Rd, W12 7PJ (18,400 capacity) ☎020 8743 0262, ⓦqpr.co.uk; ⊖ White City.

Tottenham Hotspur (Premier League) White Hart Lane Stadium, Tottenham High Rd, N17 0AP (36,300 capacity) ☎0344 499 5000, ⓦtottenhamhotspur.com; ⇌White Hart Lane from Liverpool Street.

West Ham United (Premier League) Upton Park, Green St, E13 9AZ (35,000 capacity) ☎020 8548 2748, ⓦwhufc.com; ⊖ Upton Park. Moving to the former Olympic Stadium in time for the start of the 2016/2017 season.

AFC Wimbledon (League Two) Cherry Red Records Stadium, Kingston-upon-Thames, KT1 3PB (4850 capacity) ☎020 8547 3528, ⓦafcwimbledon.co.uk; ⇌Norbiton from Waterloo.

CRICKET

The cricket (ⓦecb.co.uk) season runs from April to September. The best introduction to the sport is to go to an inter-county **Twenty20** knock-out match, which take place in the evening, lasts three hours and represents the game at its most frenetic. The other option is to attend a match, either in one of the **one-day competitions** or in the old-fashioned **county championship**. Games in the latter take place over the course of four days and are never sold out. Two county teams are based in London: **Middlesex** (⊚ middlesexccc.com), who play at Lord's, and **Surrey** (⊚ kiaoval.com), who play at The Oval. Two international sides visit each summer and play a series of **Test matches** against England, which last up to five days. There's also a series of **one-day internationals**, two of which are usually held in London.

Tickets Test match and one-day international tickets can be difficult unless you book months in advance, and cost £50 and upwards. However, not all test matches last the full five days, so tickets for the fifth day are usually sold on the day and can cost as little as £20. Tickets for Twenty20 matches and county championship matches cost in the region of £17–25.

CRICKET GROUNDS

Lord's St John's Wood, NW8 8QN (28,000 capacity) ☎ 020 7616 8500, ⊚ lords.org; ⊖ St John's Wood.
The Oval Kennington Oval, SE11 5SS (23,500 capacity) ☎ 0844 375 1845, ⊚ kiaoval.com; ⊖ Oval.

RUGBY

There are two types of rugby played in England. Thirteen-a-side **Rugby League** is played almost exclusively in the north of England. The main London team in this form of the game, **London Broncos** (⊚ londonbroncosrl.com), were relegated from the Super League to the Championship in 2014. The season runs from February to September, and games typically take place on Sundays at 3pm, but there are now matches on other days too. The final of the knock-out Challenge Cup is traditionally held at Wembley Stadium (see opposite).

In London, however, virtually all rugby clubs play fifteen-a-side **Rugby Union**. Two teams in the Premier League play in London: **Harlequins** (⊚ quins.co.uk), who play at Twickenham Stoop, and **Saracens** (⊚ saracens.com), who play at the Allianz Park in Hendon. Despite their names, **London Wasps** and **London Irish** play outside the city. Matches are traditionally on Saturdays at 3pm and the season runs from September until May, finishing off with the two knock-out finals organized by the European Rugby Cup – the European Rugby Champions Cup and the European Rugby Challenge Cup

Tickets International matches are played at Twickenham Stadium, but unless you're affiliated to a rugby club, it's tough (and expensive) to get a ticket. A better bet is to go and see a Premier League game, where there's bound to be an international player or two on display – Saracens and Harlequins tickets go for £25–55.

MAJOR RUGBY STADIUMS AND CLUBS

Harlequins Twickenham Stoop Stadium, Twickenham, TW2 7SX (14,800 capacity) ☎ 020 8410 6010, ⊚ quins .co.uk; ⇌ Twickenham from Waterloo.
Twickenham Stadium Whitton Rd, Twickenham, TW2 7BA (82,000 capacity) ☎ 0871 222 2120, ⊚ englandrugby .com/twickenham; ⇌ Twickenham from Waterloo.

TENNIS

Tennis in England is synonymous with **Wimbledon** (⊚ wimbledon.com), the only Grand Slam tournament still played on grass. The Wimbledon championships last a fortnight, in the last week of June and the first week of July. An easier opportunity to see big-name players is the Men's Championship at **Queen's Club** in Hammersmith, which finishes a week before Wimbledon.

Tickets Getting hold of a ticket for Wimbledon is a bit of a palaver. Ticketmaster (⊚ ticketmaster.co.uk) makes several hundred Centre Court and Court 3 tickets available at 9am the day before play. Otherwise, you really need to camp overnight if you want to get one of the five hundred day tickets for the show courts (prices from around £40–160). If you don't want to camp, you should get admission to the outside courts if you get there by 9am (where you'll catch some top players in the first week of the tournament), which costs £5–25. Avoid the middle Saturday, when thousands of people camp overnight, and don't bother queuing for Centre Court tickets on the last four days as all seats are pre-sold. For advance tickets, you have to enter a public ballot: see ⊚ wimbledon.com for how to go about this. Queen's tickets are sold on a first-come, first-served basis (☎ 0844 209 7356, ⊚ lta.org.uk/aegon-championships). There are also ground tickets (£10–20), which do not give access to Centre Court or Court One.

TENNIS CLUBS

All England Lawn Tennis and Croquet Club Church Rd, Wimbledon, SW19 5AE ☎ 020 8944 1066, ⊚ wimbledon.com; ⊖ Southfields or Wimbledon Park.
Queen's Club Palliser Rd, Hammersmith, W14 9EQ ☎ 020 7386 3400, ⊚ queensclub.co.uk; ⊖ Barons Court.

GREYHOUND RACING AND MOTORSPORT

Wimbledon Plough Lane, SW17 0BL ☎ 0870 840 8905, ⊚ lovethedogs.co.uk/wimbledon; ⊖ Wimbledon Park or ⇌ Earlsfield from Waterloo. For greyhound racing (Fri from 6.30pm & Sat from 5.30pm), trackside admission costs £7. The first race is at 7.30pm on a Fri and at 6.30pm on a Sat, with meetings generally including around a dozen races and ending at 10.30pm. The stadium also hosts stock-car and banger races, every Sunday from October to April (⊚ spedeworth.co.uk), with tickets from £14.

PARTICIPATING SPORTS

The following section lists most of the **sporting activities** possible in the capital. Three of the most popular facilities at the

30

Queen Elizabeth Olympic Park are the **VeloPark** (Ⓦ www.visitleevalley.org.uk/velopark), where you can experience everything from track and BMX to road and mountain biking (and sometimes watch elite cyclists in training); the Zaha Hadid-designed **London Aquatics Centre** (Ⓦ londonaquaticscentre.org), where records were broken in 2012; and the **Lee Valley White Water Centre** (Ⓦ gowhitewater.co.uk), where you can shoot the rapids in a raft, canoe or kayak.

GOLF

At most places you don't need to be a member – a pay-and-play round costs in the region of £15–20 – but it's advisable to book ahead at the weekend. There are also a few cheaper though often quite transitory places closer to the centre. For more information visit Ⓦ londongolf.info.

Central London Golf Centre Burntwood Lane, SW17 0AT ☎ 020 8871 2468, Ⓦ clgc.co.uk; ⇌ Earlsfield from Vauxhall. "Central" might be stretching it, but still a decent nine-hole pay-and-play course and a floodlit driving range. Daily 7am to 1hr before sunset; driving range Mon–Thurs 8am–9.30pm, Fri & Sat 8am–8.30pm, Sun 8am–7.30pm.

Lee Valley Golf Course Meridian Way, N9 0AR ☎ 020 8803 3611, Ⓦ visitleevalley.org.uk; ⇌ Ponders End from Liverpool Street. Public eighteen-hole course set in the watery landscape along the River Lea. Mon–Fri 8am to dusk, Sat & Sun 7am to dusk.

Richmond Park Golf Club Roehampton Gate, Priory Lane, SW15 3SA ☎ 020 8876 3205, Ⓦ richmondparkgolfclub.org.uk; ⇌ Barnes from Waterloo or bus #371 or #65 from ⊖ Richmond. Two long-established eighteen-hole courses and a driving range; call ahead to book. Daily 7am to 30min before sunset.

HORSERIDING

It costs to **saddle up** in the capital – £25/hr is the average – and you'll need your own shoes or boots with a heel.

Hyde Park Stables 63 Bathurst Mews, W2 2SB ☎ 020 7723 2813, Ⓦ hydeparkstables.com; ⊖ Lancaster Gate. The only stables in central London, situated on the north side of Hyde Park. An hour's ride or lesson in a group costs from £85, or £95–125 for a private lesson. Adult/children prices the same. Mon–Fri 7.30am–4pm, Sat & Sun 9am–4pm.

Lee Valley Riding Centre 71 Lee Bridge Rd, E10 7QL ☎ 020 8556 2629, Ⓦ visitleevalley.org.uk; ⇌ Clapton from Liverpool St. Northeast London stables, by the River Lea. A 1hr class will cost around £29.50 (£15.50/21.50 for juniors/children), whereas private lessons cost upwards of £39/30min. Mon–Thurs 7.15am-9pm, Fri–Sun 8am–7pm.

Wimbledon Village Stables 24 High St, SW19 5DX ☎ 020 8946 8579, Ⓦ wvstables.com; ⊖ Wimbledon. Hack over the wilds of Wimbledon Common and Richmond Park from £60/hr (Tues–Fri only). Hour-long group/private lessons available from British Horse Society-approved instructors from £40/85. Tues–Sun 9.30am–4.30pm.

TENNIS

There are loads of outdoor **courts** in council-run parks, costing around £8–10/hr; the downside is that they're rarely perfectly maintained. If you want to book in advance, you might have to join the local borough's scheme (£20–30/year); we've given phone numbers for courts in the main central London parks or visit Ⓦ londontennis.co.uk. During the day it's generally possible to turn up and play within half an hour or so, except in July and August.

Battersea Park Millennium Area Albert Bridge Rd, SW11 4NJ (19 floodlit courts) ☎ 020 8871 7542, Ⓦ batterseapark.org; ⇌ Battersea Park from Victoria.

Highbury Fields Baalbec Rd, N1 (11 courts, 7 of them floodlit) ☎ 020 7226 2334; ⊖ Highbury & Islington.

Holland Park W8 (6 courts) ☎ 020 7602 2226; ⊖ High Street Kensington.

Hyde Park Tennis and Sports Club South Carriage Drive, W2 2UH (6 courts) ☎ 020 7262 3474, Ⓦ royalparks .gov.uk; ⊖ South Kensington or Knightsbridge.

CLIMBING WALLS

Indoor climbing centres are run by serious climbers, and you must be a registered climber to climb unsupervised. Registration is fairly straightforward, however, and you can rent helmet, harness and footwear when you get there; total novices should book themselves on a course.

The Castle Green Lanes, N4 2HA ☎ 020 8211 7000, Ⓦ castle-climbing.co.uk; ⊖ Manor House. Housed in a Victorian water pumping station that looks like a Hammer Horror Gothic castle. Mon–Fri noon–10pm, Sat & Sun 9am–7pm.

Mile End Climbing Wall Haverfield Rd, E3 5BE ☎ 020 8980 0289, Ⓦ mileendwall.org.uk; ⊖ Mile End. Smaller climbing centre housed in an old pipe-bending factory. Mon–Thurs 10am–9.30pm, Fri 10am–9pm, Sat & Sun 10am–6pm.

Westway Climbing Centre Crowthorne Rd, W10 6RP ☎ 020 8969 0992, Ⓦ sports.westway.org; ⊖ Latimer Road. Large-scale climbing centre in a leisure centre, tucked under the Westway flyover. Mon–Fri 9.30am–10pm, Thurs 8am–10pm, Sat & Sun 8am–8pm.

OPEN-AIR SWIMS

If you fancy an alfresco dip, a swim will cost you £5 or less at the places listed below:

Brockwell Lido Brockwell Park, SE24 0PA ☏ 020 7274 3088, ⓦ fusion-lifestyle.com/centres/brockwell_lido; ⇌ Herne Hill from Victoria or St Pancras. Laidback lido at the heart of Brixton's Brockwell Park. May & Sept Mon–Fri 6.30–1pm & 4–8pm, Sat & Sun 8am–6pm; June–Aug Mon–Fri 6.30am–8pm, Sat 8am–5pm, Sun 8am–6pm; check website for reduced winter hours.

Hampstead Ponds Hampstead Heath, NW3 ☏ 020 7332 3773, ⓦ cityoflondon.gov.uk; ⊖ Hampstead. The Heath has three natural ponds: the Women's and Men's ponds are on the Highgate side (bus #214 from ⊖ Kentish Town), while the Mixed Bathing pond is nearer Hampstead. Daily: 7/7.30am to dusk (check online for precise times).

Hampton Pool Hampton High St, Hampton TW12 2ST ☏ 020 8255 1116, ⓦ www.hamptonpool.co.uk; ⇌ Hampton from Waterloo. Heated outdoor pool on the western edge of Bushy Park, about a mile's walk from Hampton Court Palace. Open all year; phone or check website for hours, though public swimming in summer is generally Mon–Fri 6–9/10am & noon–5/9pm, Sat & Sun 9am–5pm.

London Fields Lido London Fields, E8 3EU ☏ 020 7254 9038, ⓦ better.org.uk/leisure/london-fields-lido; ⇌ London Fields from Liverpool Street. Refurbished interwar lido with a 164ft heated outdoor pool. Open daily all year round, but hours vary (Tues eve women only); check online calendar or phone.

Oasis 32 Endell St, WC2H 9AG ☏ 020 7831 1804, ⓦ better.org.uk/leisure/oasis-sports-centre; ⊖ Covent Garden. The outdoor pool is small, but the water is a bath-like temperature and it's open all year. Other facilities include a gym, a health suite with sauna and sunbed, massage and squash courts. Mon–Fri 6.30am–10pm, Sat & Sun 9.30am–6pm.

Parliament Hill Lido Gordon House Rd, NW5 1NA ☏ 020 7332 3773, ⓦ cityoflondon.gov.uk; ⊖ Gospel Oak. Beautiful 200ft by 90ft open-air pool with Art Deco touches and notoriously chilly water. Daily: May to mid-Sept 7am–6.30pm (also 6.45–8pm Mon, Thurs & Fri); mid-Sept to April 7am–noon.

Pools on the Park Old Deer Park, Richmond, TW9 2SF ☏ 020 8940 0561, ⓦ springhealth.net/richmond; ⊖ Richmond. Not in Richmond Park, but in the Old Deer Park near the Thames, adjacent to a modern leisure centre. Easter to Sept: Mon 6.30am–7.45pm, Tues–Fri 6.30am–8pm, Sat & Sun 7am–5.45pm.

Serpentine Lido Hyde Park, W2 2UH ☏ 020 7706 3422, ⓦ royalparks.org.uk; ⊖ Knightsbridge. Offers 110yd of swimming in Hyde Park's lake, plus a paddling pool; deck chairs and sun loungers for rent. May Sat, Sun & Bank Holidays 10am–6pm; June to Aug daily 10am–6pm.

Tooting Bec Lido Tooting Bec Rd, SW16 1RU ☏ 020 8871 7198; bus #249 from ⊖ Tooting Bec. At 300ft by 100ft, this is England's (and one of Europe's) largest freshwater, open-air pools. May–Aug daily 6am–7.45pm; Sept daily 6am–4.45pm.

30

Islington Tennis Centre Market Rd, N7 9PL (2 floodlit outdoor and 6 indoor courts) ☏ 020 3793 6880, ⓦ better.org.uk/leisure/islingtontc; ⊖ Caledonian Road.

Lee Valley Hockey and Tennis Centre Queen Elizabeth Olympic Park, E20 3AD (6 outdoor courts, 4 indoor courts) ☏ 08456 770 604, ⓦ visitleevalley.org.uk; ⊖ Stratford.

Lincoln's Inn Fields WC2A 3TL (3 courts) ☏ 07525 278647; ⊖ Holborn.

Paddington Recreation Ground Randolph Ave, W9 1PD (12 floodlit courts) ☏ 020 7641 3642, ⓦ better.org.uk/leisure/paddington-recreation-ground; ⊖ Maida Vale.

Will to Win Regent's Park York Bridge, Inner Circle, NW1 4NU (12 courts, 4 floodlit) ☏ 020 7486 4216, ⓦ www.willtowin.co.uk; ⊖ Baker Street.

SPAS AND LEISURE CENTRES

Below are two of the best-equipped and most central multipurpose **leisure centres**: both have gyms, fitness classes and pools.

Ironmonger Row Baths 1 Norman St, EC1 3QF ☏ 020 3642 5521, ⓦ better.org.uk; ⊖ Old Street. Recently refurbished, this place consists of a spa area (with steam rooms, saunas, therapy rooms and a hammam; ⓦ spa-london.org) and a gym and a large pool facility (ⓦ better.org.uk). See websites for opening hours.

Porchester Spa Porchester Rd, W2 5HS ☏ 020 7792 3980, ⓦ better.org.uk; ⊖ Bayswater or Queensway. Built in the 1920s, these baths are well worth a visit for the Art Deco tiling alone. Admission is £28 for a three-hour session, and entitles you to use the saunas, steam rooms, plunge pool, jacuzzi and swimming pool. Men: Mon, Wed & Sat 10am–10pm; Women: Tues, Thurs & Fri 10am–10pm, Sun 10am–2pm; Mixed Sun 4–10pm.

DIANA MEMORIAL PLAYGROUND

Kids' London

London is a great place for children and it needn't overly strain the parental pocket. Magicians, jugglers and human statues provide free entertainment at Covent Garden (see p.107) and the South Bank (see p.216), where a traffic-free riverside walk stretches from the London Eye to Tower Bridge. And if you don't fancy the walk, plenty of boats stop off at piers along the way (see p.24). The spread of children's shows is at its best during school holidays, and at Christmas there's a glut of traditional British pantomimes, stage shows based on folk stories or fairy tales, invariably featuring a showbiz star, and often with an undercurrent of innuendo for the adults. If that's too passive, there are plenty of parks and indoor play centres where kids can burn off excess energy. And of course, London Zoo (p.287) and the Aquarium (see p.221) are sure-fire winners.

THEATRE, PUPPETRY AND CIRCUSES

Shows that appeal to children play in the West End all the time. What follows is a selective rundown of theatre, puppetry and circuses that are aimed at kids.

Half Moon Young People's Theatre 43 White Horse Rd, E1 0ND ☎ 020 7709 8900, ⓦ halfmoon.org.uk; ⊖ Limehouse DLR or Stepney Green. Well-established theatre that hosts touring youth shows, produces and tours its own work and runs a programme of workshops and theatre sessions. Generally Mon–Fri 10am–6pm (later on performance days; check website) & Sat 10am–4pm (performance days); all tickets £6.

Little Angel Puppet Theatre 14 Dagmar Passage, off Cross St, N1 2DN ☎ 020 7226 1787, ⓦ littleangeltheatre .com; ⊖ Angel. Puppet theatre specializing in table-top, rod and glove puppetry, with shows usually taking place Tues–Sun at 11am and 2pm. Adults £14, children £12.

Polka Theatre 240 The Broadway, SW19 1SB ☎ 020 8543 4888, ⓦ polkatheatre.com; ⊖ Wimbledon or South Wimbledon. Specially designed junior arts centre aimed at kids aged up to 12, with two theatres, a playground, a café and a toyshop. Storytellers, puppeteers and mime artists make regular appearances. Tickets from £11.50.

Puppet Theatre Barge Little Venice, W9 2PF ☎ 020 7249 6876, ⓦ puppetbarge.com; ⊖ Warwick Avenue. Wonderfully imaginative string marionette shows on a unique fifty-seat barge moored in Little Venice from October to July, and at Richmond from the end of July to the end of September. Shows start around 3pm at weekends and in the holidays. Adults £12, children £8.50.

Unicorn Theatre 147 Tooley St, SE1 2HZ ☎ 020 7645 0560, ⓦ unicorntheatre.com; ⊖ London Bridge. The oldest professional children's theatre in London lives in modern, purpose-built premises near City Hall in Southwark. Shows run the gamut from storytelling sessions and traditional plays to creative-writing workshops, dance, mime and puppetry. adults from £12 under-18s from £8.

Zippo's Circus ☎ 0871 210 2100, ⓦ zippos.co.uk. Zippo's Circus performs in and around London for much of the year. A traditional, big-top circus offering a variety of acts from clowning and tightrope walking to frolicking horses and daredevil motorbike tricks. Tickets £7–25 (according to quality of view), family ticket £60.

PARKS, GARDENS AND PLAYGROUNDS

Right in the centre of the city, there are plentiful green spaces, such as **St James's Park** (see p.66) and **Regent's Park** (see p.286), providing playgrounds and ample room for general mayhem. If you want something more unusual than ducks and squirrels, head for one of London's several **city farms** (see p.442). Below is a list of the best parks and playgrounds.

Battersea Park Albert Bridge Rd, SW11 4NJ ⓦ batterseapark.org; ⇌ Battersea Park or Queenstown Road from Victoria. The park has an excellent free adventure playground and adjacent children's playground, a boating lake and a children's zoo (see p.326). Park and playgrounds daily 8am to dusk; free. Zoo: summer daily 10am–5.30pm; winter closes 4.30pm; adults £8.95, under-16s £6.95.

Camley Street Natural Park 12 Camley St, N1C 4PW ☎ 020 7833 2311, ⓦ wildlondon.org.uk; ⊖ King's Cross St Pancras. Canalside wildlife haven, run by the London Wildlife Trust. See p.137. Summer daily 10am–5pm; winter closes 4pm. Free.

Coram's Fields 93 Guilford St, WC1 ☎ 020 7837 6138, ⓦ coramsfields.org; ⊖ Russell Square. Big, centrally located park with lots of water and sand play, an adventure playground, and a mini-farm with chickens, rabbits, goats and birds. There's also a youth centre and a children's centre (activities at both free; see website for details). See p.130. Daily 9am to dusk. Free.

MUSEUMS FOR MINORS

Many of the big museums **museums** are free of charge. The **Science Museum** (see p.259), the **Natural History Museum** (see p.262), the **London Transport Museum** (see p.107) and the **National Maritime Museum** (see p.316) have hands-on sections that will keep young kids busy for hours. At the other end of the scale, the **London Dungeon** (see p.222) and **Madame Tussauds**, with its infamous Chamber of Horrors (see p.93), remain popular, but are very expensive.

Smaller museums specifically designed with children in mind include the **Horniman Museum** (see p.311), which houses an aquarium, and the **London Museum of Water and Steam**, which runs a miniature steam train at weekends (see p.333). There are also museums devoted to childhood and toys, from the atmospheric **Pollock's Toy Museum** (see p.104) to the much larger V&A outpost, the **Museum of Childhood** (see p.200).

31

31

MUSIC FOR YOUNG EARS

Most of the established orchestras run special **children's concerts**: look out for the London Philharmonic Orchestra (🌐 lpo.co.uk), London Symphony Orchestra (🌐 lso.co.uk) and National Children's Orchestra (🌐 nco.org.uk). The Barbican (see p.402) lays on excellent family-focused concerts (often involving the LSO and BBC Symphony Orchestra), as does the Royal Festival Hall at the South Bank (see p.402).

Dalston Eastern Curve 13 Dalston Lane, E8 3DF 🌐 dalstongarden.org; ⊖ Dalston Junction. A tucked-away community garden that kids love to explore (when they're not rummaging in the sand pit). Runs child-focused workshops and nature days. Free wi-fi. See p.201. Mon–Thurs & Sun 11am–7pm, Fri & Sat 11am–11pm.

Hampstead Heath Parliament Hill Playground, NW3 ☎ 020 7433 1917, adventure playground ☎ 020 7482 2116 🌐 cityoflondon.gov.uk; ⊖ Hampstead, Gospel Oak or ≷ Hampstead Heath. Nine hundred acres of grassland and woodland, with superb views of the city. Plenty of playgrounds, sports facilities and music events. See p.299. Open daily 24hr.

Hyde Park/Kensington Gardens W2 2UH ☎ 0300 061 2000, 🌐 royalparks.org.uk; ⊖ Hyde Park Corner, Knightsbridge, Lancaster Gate or Queensway. Hyde Park (daily 5am–midnight) is central London's main open space and home to the Diana Fountain where kids can dip their feet (daily 10am to dusk); in Kensington Gardens (daily 6am to dusk), adjoining its western side, you can find the famous Peter Pan statue and a playground dedicated to Princess Diana. See p.246.

Kew Gardens Richmond, Surrey TW9 3AB ☎ 020 8332 5655, 🌐 kew.org; ⊖ Kew Gardens. Open spaces, glasshouses and a small aquarium in the basement of the Palm House. Adults £15, children aged 4–16 £3.50. See p.336. Daily 10am to between 4.15 and 7.30pm depending on season; see website.

Richmond Park Richmond, Surrey TW10 5HS ☎ 0300 061 2200, 🌐 royalparks.org.uk; ⊖ Richmond or ≷ Richmond from Waterloo. A fabulous stretch of countryside, with opportunities for duck-feeding, deer-spotting and cycling. Playground situated near Petersham Gate or toddlers' play area near Kingston Gate. Bike hire available. See p.342. Daily 24hr except during Feb & Nov deer cull, when 7.30am–8pm.

Tumbling Bay Playground Queen Elizabeth Olympic Park, Stratford E20 2ST ☎ 0800 0722 110, 🌐 queenelizabetholympicpark.co.uk; ⊖ Stratford. An inventive playground with treehouses and bridges, sand pits and rock pools, plus the usual equipment. See p.205. Daily 24hr.

CITY FARMS

The website 🌐 farmgarden.org.uk is also worth a visit for details of other gardens and wildlife havens in London.

Brooks Farm Skelton's Lane Park, Leyton, E10 5BS ☎ 020 8509 4636, 🌐 forestymca.org.uk/brooksfarm; ⊖ Leyton Midland Road. This farm has cows, goats, Shetland ponies, llamas and a pygmy hedgehog, as well as its own allotments and an adventure playground. Tues–Sun (also Bank Holiday Mon) 10am–5pm. Free.

Freightliners Farm Sheringham Rd, N7 8PF ☎ 020 7609 0467, 🌐 freightlinersfarm.org.uk; ⊖ Highbury & Islington or Holloway Road. Small with goats, hens, guinea fowl, sheep, bees and giant rabbits. Farm shop and veggie *Strawbale* café (Thurs–Sun only). Tues–Sun (also Bank Holiday Mon) 10am–4pm (4.45pm in summer). Free.

Hackney City Farm 1a Goldsmith's Row, E2 8QA ☎ 020 7729 6381, 🌐 hackneycityfarm.co.uk; ⊖ Hoxton. This converted brewery houses calves, sheep, pigs, hens, guinea pigs, bees and donkeys, plus the *Frizzante* café. Tues–Sun 10am–4.30pm. Free.

Kentish Town City Farm 1 Cressfield Close, off Grafton Rd, NW5 4BN ☎ 020 7916 5421, 🌐 ktcityfarm.org.uk; ⊖ Chalk Farm or Kentish Town. Five acres of farmland with cows, pigs, goats and chickens. Daily activities,

including pony rides at weekends (1.30pm; £2; call to book at noon on the day). Daily 9am–5pm. Free.

Mudchute City Farm Pier St, E14 3HP ☎ 020 7515 5901, 🌐 mudchute.org; ⊖ Mudchute, Crossharbour or Island Gardens DLR. One of the largest city farms in Europe, with over two hundred fowl and animals, llamas, alpacas, an aviary, an equestrian centre and a "pets' corner". *Mudchute Kitchen* café, too. Farm daily 9am–5pm, park daily dawn to dusk, café Tues–Fri 9.30am–3pm, Sat & Sun 9.30am–5pm. Free.

Spitalfields City Farm Buxton St, E1 5AR ☎ 020 7247 8762, 🌐 spitalfieldscityfarm.org; ⊖ Shoreditch High Street. A tiny farm (with a shop and café) housing sheep, donkeys, geese, rabbits and guinea pigs. Also runs a number of gardens and a café and holds a Sunday market (summer only). Farm Tues–Sun 10am–4pm, café Wed–Sun 10am–4pm. Free.

Stepney City Farm Stepney Way, E1 3DG ☎ 020 7790 8204, 🌐 stepneycityfarm.org; ⊖ Stepney Green. A working farm with plenty of animals, plus a "rural arts centre" featuring a blacksmith, potter and woodworker; a café and farm shop;

KIDS GO FREE

Don't underestimate the value of London's **public transport** as a source of fun – and remember kids travel free (see p.22). **The Underground** is a buzz for a lot of kids, and you can get your bearings while entertaining your offspring by installing them in the front seats on the top deck of a red **double-decker bus**. The driverless **Docklands Light Railway** (see p.212) is another source of amusement, too – grab a seat at the front of the train and pretend to be the driver.

and a Saturday farmers' market (10am–3pm). Tues–Sun 10am–4pm. Free (charge for some rural arts activities).
Surrey Docks Farm Rotherhithe St, SE16 5ET ☎020 7231 1010, ⓦsurreydocksfarm.org.uk; ⊖Surrey Quays. All manner of animals, plus bees in hives, a smithy, veg and herb gardens and the *Piccalilli* café (Tues–Sun).

Daily 10am–5pm; closes 4pm in winter; £3.
Vauxhall City Farm 165 Tyers St, SE11 5HS ☎020 7582 4204, ⓦvauxhallcityfarm.org; ⊖Vauxhall. Little city farm with lots of furry residents (including Shetland ponies). Riding lessons, and other activities at weekends and on holidays. Wed–Sun 10.30am–4pm. Free.

INDOOR ADVENTURE PLAY CENTRES AND SWIMMING POOLS

Bramley's Big Adventure 136 Bramley Rd, W10 6SR ☎020 8960 1515, ⓦbramleysbigadventure.co.uk; ⊖Latimer Road or Ladbroke Grove. Indoor play centre with equipment suitable for children up to 11. Play sessions £2–7.75. Mon–Fri 10am–6pm, Sat & Sun 10am–6.30pm.
Discover 385–387 Stratford High St, E15 4QZ ☎020 8536 5555, ⓦdiscover.org.uk; ⊖Stratford. A hands-on creative learning centre with a great outdoor play garden,

aimed at story-building for under-11s. £5 per adult/child. Tues–Fri 10am–5pm, Sat & Sun 11am–5pm.
Waterfront Leisure Centre High St, Woolwich, SE18 6DL ☎020 8317 5010, ⓦbetter.org.uk; ⊖Woolwich Arsenal DLR. Massive adventure swimming pool with 100ft-plus slide, wave machine and waterfall. Under-3s free; tickets from around £4.50. Mon–Fri 6.30am–10.30pm, Sat & Sun 8am–8pm.

SHOPS

In addition to the city's many fabulous museum shops and department stores (see box, p.427) – Harrods' "Toy Kingdom", with lots of interactive possibilities, is hard to beat – London has plenty of kid-focused shops.

Forbidden Planet 179 Shaftesbury Ave, WC2H 8JR ☎020 7420 3666, ⓦforbiddenplanet.com; ⊖Tottenham Court Road; map p.97. A superstore of sci-fi, cult and fantasy interests that will appeal to teenagers. Mon & Tues 10am–7pm, Wed, Fri & Sat 10am–7.30pm, Thurs 10am–8pm, Sun noon–6pm.
Hackney Pirates Ship of Adventures 38 Kingsland High Street, E8 2NS ☎020 3327 1777, ⓦhackneypirates .org; ⊖Dalston Kingsland; map p.187. A literacy-focused young people's charity which looks like the interior of a (pirate's) ship. There's a café and books for sale too, plus a fancy dress box. Tues–Fri 8.30am–6.30pm, Sat 11am–6pm, Sun noon–6pm.
Hamleys 188–196 Regent St, W1B 5BT ☎0871 704 1977, ⓦhamleys.com; ⊖Oxford Circus; map p.97. This 250-year-old London landmark has no less than seven floors of fun, from rocking horses to Wii U games. Mon–Fri 10am–9pm, Sat 9.30am–9pm, Sun noon–6pm.
★ **International Magic** 89 Clerkenwell Rd, EC1R 5BX ☎020 7405 7324, ⓦinternationalmagic.com; ⊖Chancery Lane or Farringdon; map p.147. Eccentric, family-owned little magic store selling tricks and accessories. Mon–Fri 11.30am–6pm, Sat 11.30am–4pm.
The Moomin Shop 43 Covent Garden Market, WC2E 8RF ☎020 7240 7057, ⓦthemoominshop.com; ⊖Covent

Garden; map p.108. A cupboard-sized shrine to Tove Jansson's creations upstairs at Covent Garden Market. Mon–Sat 10am–8pm, Sun 10am–7pm; an hour later in Dec.
Paddington Bear Shop Paddington Station, W2 1RH ☎020 7402 5209, ⓦthisispaddington.com/article/paddington-bear-shop; ⊖Paddington; map pp.276–277. Sited on the mezzanine level of Paddington Station, our hero's spiritual home (not counting Peru), you'll find this trove of Paddington Bear-themed items. Mon–Fri 7.30am–7.30pm, Sat & Sun 9am–7pm.
Pollock's Toyshop Central Ave, South Piazza, Covent Garden, WC2E 8RF ☎020 7379 7866, ⓦpollocks-coventgarden.co.uk; ⊖Covent Garden; map p.108. If Hamleys feels a bit commercial, head for this tiny cupboard of a place on Covent Garden piazza, where the toys – Victorian curiosities, toy theatres, wooden games, vintage puzzles – appeal to adults as much as to kids. Mon–Wed 10.30am–6pm, Thurs–Sat 10.30am–6.30pm, Sun 11am–6pm.
The Toy Box 223 Victoria Park Rd, E9 7HD ☎020 8533 2879, ⓦthetoyboxshop.co.uk; ⇌London Fields or Cambridge Heath station; map p.187. A lovely independent toy shop with plenty of traditional toys and games but also a fine line in slightly more off-the-wall stuff. Mon–Sat 9am–6pm, Sun 10am–5pm.

31

Contexts

History

The citizens of London are universally held up for admiration and renown for the elegance of their manners and dress, and the delights of their tables… The only plagues of London are the immoderate drinking of fools and the frequency of fires.
                                                                                    William Fitzstephen, companion of Thomas Becket

Conflagrations and drunkenness certainly feature strongly in London's complex two-thousand-year history. What follows is a highly compressed account featuring riots and revolutions, plagues, fires, slum clearances, lashings of gin, Boris Johnson and the London people. For more detailed histories, see our book recommendations (see p.462).

Roman Londinium

Although there is evidence of scattered Celtic settlements along the Thames, no firm proof exists to show that central London was permanently settled before the arrival of the Romans. **Julius Caesar** led two small cross-Channel incursions in 55 and 54 BC, but it wasn't until nearly a century later, in **43 AD**, that a full-scale invasion force of some forty thousand Roman troops landed in Kent. Britain's rumoured mineral wealth was certainly one motive behind the Roman invasion, but the immediate spur was the need of Emperor Claudius, who owed his power to the army, for an easy military triumph. The Romans, under Aulus Plautius, defeated the main Celtic tribe of southern Britain, the Catuvellauni, on the Medway, southeast of London, crossed the Thames and then set up camp to await the triumphant arrival of Claudius, his elephants and the Praetorian Guard.

It's now thought that the site of this first Roman camp was, in fact, in Westminster – the lowest fordable point on the Thames – and not in what is now the City. However, around 50 AD, when the Romans decided to establish the permanent military camp of **Londinium** here, they chose a point further downstream, building a bridge some 50yd east of today's London Bridge. London became the hub of the Roman road system, but it was not the Romans' principal colonial settlement, which remained at **Camulodunum** (modern Colchester) to the northeast.

In 60 AD, the East Anglian people, known as the Iceni, rose up against the invaders under their queen **Boudicca** (or Boadicea) and sacked Camulodunum, slaughtering most of the legion sent from Lindum (Lincoln) and making their way to the ill-defended town of Londinium. According to archeological evidence, Londinium was burnt to the ground and, according to the Roman historian Tacitus, whose father-in-law was in Britain at the time (and later served as its governor), the inhabitants were "massacred, hanged, burned and crucified". The Iceni were eventually defeated, and Boudicca committed suicide (62 AD).

In the aftermath, Londinium emerged as the new commercial and administrative (though not military) **capital of Britannia**, and was endowed with a military fort for around a thousand troops, an imposing basilica and forum, a governor's palace,

122	200	296	312
Emperor Hadrian visits Londinium	The Romans build a defensive wall around the city	Emperor Constantius ends the civil war in Britain and northern Gaul	Christianity becomes the state religion throughout the Roman Empire

LEGENDS

Until Elizabethan times, most Londoners believed that London had been founded around 1000 BC as New Troy or *Troia Nova* (later corrupted to Trinovantum), capital of Albion (aka Britain), by the Trojan prince **Brutus**. At the time, according to medieval chronicler Geoffrey of Monmouth, Britain was "uninhabited except for a few giants", several of whom the Trojans subsequently killed. They even captured one called Goemagog (more commonly referred to as Gogmagog), who was believed to be the son of Poseidon, Greek god of the sea, and whom one of the Trojans, called Corineus, challenged to unarmed combat and defeated.

For some reason, by late medieval times, Gogmagog had become better known as two giants, **Gog and Magog**, whose statues can still be seen in the Guildhall (see p.166) and on the clock outside St Dunstan-in-the-West (see p.154). According to Geoffrey of Monmouth's elaborate genealogical tree, Brutus is related to Leir (of Shakespeare's *King Lear*), Arthur (of the Round Table) and eventually to **King Lud**. Around 70 BC, Lud is credited with fortifying New Troy and renaming it *Caer Ludd* (Lud's Town), which was later corrupted to Caerlundein and finally London.

temples, bathhouses and an amphitheatre (see p.167). Archeological evidence suggests that Londinium was at its most prosperous and populous from around 80 AD to 120 AD, during which time it is thought to have evolved into the empire's fifth largest city north of the Alps.

Between 150 AD and 400 AD, however, London appears to have sheltered less than half the former population, probably due to economic decline. Nevertheless, it remained strategically and politically important and, as an imperial outpost, actually appears to have benefited from the chaos that engulfed the rest of the empire during much of the third century. In those uncertain times, **fortifications** were built, three miles long, 20ft high and 9ft thick, whose Kentish ragstone walls can still be seen near today's Museum of London (see p.165), home to many of the city's most significant Roman finds.

In 406 AD, the Roman army in Britain mutinied for the last time and invaded Gaul under the self-proclaimed Emperor Constantine III. The empire was on its last legs, and the Romans were never in a position to return, officially abandoning the city in **410 AD** (when Rome was sacked by the Visigoths), and leaving the country and its chief city at the mercy of the marauding Saxon pirates, who had been making increasingly persistent raids on the coast since the middle of the previous century.

Saxon Lundenwic and the Danes

Roman London appears to have been more or less abandoned from the first couple of decades of the fifth century until the ninth century. Instead, the **Anglo-Saxon** invaders, who controlled most of southern England by the sixth century, appear to have settled, initially at least, to the west of the Roman city. When Augustine was sent to reconvert Britain to Christianity, the Saxon city of **Lundenwic** was considered important enough to be granted a bishopric in 604, though it was Canterbury, not London, that was chosen as the seat of the Primate of England. Nevertheless, trade flourished once more during this period, as attested by the Venerable Bede, who wrote of London in 730 as "the mart of many nations resorting to it by land and sea".

410	604	878	1066
The Romans withdraw from Britain	Mellitus, the first Bishop of London, begins the first St Paul's Cathedral	King Alfred defeats the Vikings and England is divided into Danelaw and Wessex	William the Conqueror defeats King Harold at the Battle of Hastings

In 841 and 851 London suffered Danish Viking attacks, and it may have been in response to these raids that the Saxons decided to reoccupy the walled Roman city. By 871 the **Danes** were confident enough to attack and established London as their winter base, but in 886 Alfred the Great, King of Wessex, recaptured the city, rebuilt the walls and formally re-established London as a fortified town and a trading port. After a lull, the Vikings returned once more during the reign of Ethelred the Unready (978–1016), attacking in 994, 1009 and 1013. Finally the Danes, under Swein Forkbeard, captured London, and Swein was declared King of England. He reigned for just five weeks before he died, allowing Ethelred to reclaim the city in 1014, with help from King Olaf of Norway.

In 1016, following the death of Ethelred, and his son, Edmund Ironside, the Danish leader Cnut (or Canute), son of Swein, became King of All England, and made London the **national capital** (in preference to the Wessex base of Winchester), a position it has held ever since. Danish rule lasted only 26 years, however, and with the death of Cnut's two sons, the English throne returned to the House of Wessex, and to Ethelred's exiled son, **Edward the Confessor** (1042–66). Edward moved the court and church upstream to Thorney Island (or the Isle of Brambles), where he built a splendid new palace so that he could oversee construction of his "West Minster" (later to become Westminster Abbey). Edward was too weak to attend the official consecration and died just ten days later: he is buried in the great church he founded, where his shrine became a place of pilgrimage for centuries. Of greater political and social significance, however, was his geographical separation of power, with royal government based in the **City of Westminster**, while the **City of London** remained the commercial centre.

1066 and all that

On his deathbed, in the new year of 1066, the celibate Edward made **Harold**, Earl of Wessex, his appointed successor. Having crowned himself in the new abbey – establishing a tradition that continues to this day – Harold went on to defeat his brother Tostig (who was in cahoots with the Norwegians), but was himself defeated by **William of Normandy** (aka William the Conqueror) and his invading Norman army at the Battle of Hastings. On Christmas Day of 1066, William crowned himself king in Westminster Abbey. Elsewhere in England, the Normans ruthlessly suppressed all opposition, but in London, William granted the City a charter guaranteeing to preserve the privileges it had enjoyed under Edward. However, as an insurance policy, he also built three forts in the city, of which the sole remnant is the White Tower, now the nucleus of the **Tower of London**.

Over the next few centuries, the City waged a continuous struggle with the monarchy for a degree of self-government and independence. After all, when there was a fight over the throne, the support of London's wealth and manpower could be decisive, as **King Stephen** (1135–54) discovered, when Londoners attacked his cousin and rival for the throne, Mathilda, daughter of Henry I, preventing her from being crowned at Westminster. Again, in 1191, when the future **King John** (1199–1216) was tussling with William Longchamp over the kingdom during the absence of Richard the Lionheart (1189–99), it was the Londoners who made sure Longchamp remained cooped up in the Tower. For this particular favour, London was granted the right to

1089	1189	1209	1215	1290
Cluniac monastery established in Bermondsey	Henry Fitz-Ailwin becomes the first Mayor of London	Old London Bridge completed	Magna Carta signed – Mayor of London is one of the signatories	Jews expelled from London

elect its own sheriff, or lord mayor, an office that was officially acknowledged in the Magna Carta of 1215.

Occasionally, of course, Londoners backed the wrong side, as they did when they turned up at Old St Paul's to accept **Prince Louis of France** (the future Louis VIII) as ruler of England during the barons' rebellion against King John in 1216, and again with Simon de Montfort, when he was engaged in civil war with **Henry III** (1216–72) during the 1260s. As a result, the City found itself temporarily stripped of its privileges. In any case, London was chiefly of importance to the medieval kings as a source of wealth, and traditionally it was to the Jewish community, which arrived in 1066 with William the Conqueror (see box, p.456), that the sovereign turned for a loan. By the second half of the thirteenth century, however, the Jews had been squeezed dry, and in 1290, after a series of increasingly bloody attacks, **London's Jews** were expelled by Edward I (1272–1307), who turned instead to the City's Italian merchants for financial assistance.

From the Black Death to the Wars of the Roses

London backed the right side in the struggle between Edward II (1307–27) and his queen, Isabella, who, along with her lover Mortimer, succeeded in deposing the king. Edward and Isabella's son Edward III (1327–77) was duly crowned, and London enjoyed a period of relative peace and prosperity, thanks to the wealth generated by the wool trade. All this was cut short, however, by the arrival of the Europe-wide bubonic plague outbreak, known as the **Black Death**, in 1348. This disease, carried by black rats and transmitted to humans by flea bites, wiped out something like two-thirds of the capital's 75,000 population in the space of two years. Other epidemics followed in 1361, 1369 and 1375, creating a volatile economic situation that was worsened by the financial strains imposed on the capital by having to bankroll the country's involvement in the Hundred Years War with France.

Matters came to a head with the introduction of the poll tax, a head tax imposed in the 1370s on all men regardless of means. During the ensuing **Peasants' Revolt** of 1381, London's citizens opened the City gates to Wat Tyler's Kentish rebels and joined in the lynching of the archbishop, plus countless rich merchants and clerics. Tyler was then lured to meet the boy-king Richard II at Smithfield, just outside the City, where he was murdered by Lord Mayor Walworth, who was subsequently knighted for his treachery. Tyler's supporters were fobbed off with promises of political changes that never came, as Richard unleashed a wave of repression and retribution.

After the Peasants' Revolt, the next serious disturbance was **Jack Cade's Revolt**, which took place in 1450. An army of 25,000 Kentish rebels – including gentry, clergy and craftsmen – defeated King Henry VI's forces at Sevenoaks, marched to Blackheath, withdrew temporarily and then eventually reached Southwark in early July. Having threatened to burn down London Bridge, the insurgents entered the City and spent three days wreaking vengeance on their enemies before being ejected. A subsequent attempt to enter the City via London Bridge was repulsed, and the army was dispersed with yet more false promises. The reprisals, which became known as the "harvest of heads", were as harsh as before – Cade himself was captured, killed and brought to the capital for dismemberment.

1337–1453	1380	1381	1415
Hundred Years War	Chaucer's *Canterbury Tales* published	The peasants' revolt reaches London	Henry V wins the Battle of Agincourt against the French

---

JOHN WYCLIFFE AND THE LOLLARDS

Parallel with the social unrest of the 1370s were the demands for clerical reforms made by the scholar and heretic **John Wycliffe**, whose ideas were keenly taken up by Londoners. A fierce critic of the papacy and the monastic orders, Wycliffe produced the first translation of the Bible into English in 1380. He was tried for heresy at Lambeth Palace, and his followers, known as **Lollards**, were harshly persecuted. In 1415, the Council of Constance, which burned the Czech heretic Jan Hus at the stake, also ordered Wycliffe's body to be exhumed and burnt.

A decade later, the country was plunged into more widespread conflict during the so-called **Wars of the Roses**, the name now given to the strife between the cousins within the rival noble houses of Lancaster and York. Londoners wisely tended to sit on the fence throughout the conflict, only committing themselves in 1461, when they opened the gates to the Yorkist king Edward IV (1461–70 and 1471–83), thus helping him to depose the mad Henry VI (1422–61 and 1470–71). In 1470, Henry, who had spent five years in the Tower, was proclaimed king once more, only to be deposed again a year later, following Lancastrian defeats at the battles of Barnet and Tewkesbury.

Tudor London

The **Tudor** family, which with the coronation of **Henry VII** (1485–1509) emerged triumphant from the mayhem of the Wars of the Roses, reinforced London's pre-eminence during the sixteenth century, when the Tower of London and the royal palaces of Whitehall, St James's, Richmond, Greenwich, Hampton Court and Windsor provided the backdrop for the most momentous events of the period. At the same time, the city's population, which had remained constant at around fifty thousand since the Black Death, increased dramatically, trebling in size during the course of the century.

One of the crucial developments of the century was the English **Reformation**, the separation of the English Church from Rome, a split initially prompted not by doctrinal issues, but by the failure of Catherine of Aragon, first wife of **Henry VIII** (1509–47), to produce a male heir. In fact, prior to his desire to divorce Catherine, Henry, along with his lord chancellor, Cardinal Wolsey, had been zealously persecuting Protestants. However, when the Pope refused to annul Henry's marriage, Henry knew he could rely on a large amount of popular support, as anti-clerical feelings were running high. By contrast, Henry's new chancellor, Thomas More, wouldn't countenance divorce, and resigned in 1532. Henry then broke with Rome, appointed himself head of the English Church and demanded both citizens and clergy swear allegiance to him. Very few refused, though More was among them, becoming the country's first Catholic martyr with his execution in 1535. One consequence was the **Dissolution of the Monasteries**, a programme to close down the country's monasteries and appropriate their assets, commenced in 1536. Medieval London boasted over a hundred places of worship and some twenty religious houses, with two-thirds of the land in the City belonging to the Church. The Dissolution changed the entire fabric of the city and the country: London's property market was flooded with confiscated estates, which were quickly snapped up by the Tudor nobility.

1422	1455–85	1476	1483
Riot ensues after victory of City of London over the City of Westminster in a wrestling match	Wars of the Roses	William Caxton sets up the first printing press in the precincts of Westminster Abbey	Death of the Princes in the Tower, Edward V and his brother the Duke of York

Henry may have been the one who kickstarted the English Reformation, but he was a religious conservative, and in the last ten years of his reign he succeeded in executing as many Protestants as he did Catholics. Religious turmoil only intensified in the decade following Henry's death. First, Henry's sickly son, **Edward VI** (1547–53), pursued a staunchly anti-Catholic policy. By the end of his short reign, London's churches had lost their altars, their paintings, their relics and virtually all their statuary. After an abortive attempt to secure the succession of Edward's Protestant cousin, Lady Jane Grey, the religious pendulum swung the other way for the next five years with the accession of "**Bloody Mary**" (1553–58). This time, it was Protestants who were martyred with abandon at Tyburn and Smithfield.

Despite all the religious strife, the Tudor economy remained in good health for the most part, reaching its height in the reign of **Elizabeth I** (1558–1603), when the piratical exploits of seafarers Walter Raleigh, Francis Drake, Martin Frobisher and John Hawkins helped to map out the world for English commerce. London's commercial success was epitomized by the millionaire merchant Thomas Gresham, who erected the **Royal Exchange** in 1571, establishing London as the premier world trade market.

The 45 years of Elizabeth's reign also witnessed the efflorescence of a specifically **English Renaissance**, especially in the field of literature, which reached its apogee in the brilliant careers of **Christopher Marlowe**, **Ben Jonson** and **William Shakespeare**. The presses of **Fleet Street**, established a century earlier by William Caxton's apprentice Wynkyn de Worde, ensured London's position as a centre for the printed word. Beyond the jurisdiction of the City censors, in the entertainment district of Southwark, whorehouses, animal-baiting pits and theatres flourished. The carpenter-cum-actor James Burbage designed the first purpose-built playhouse in 1576, eventually rebuilding it south of the river as the **Globe Theatre**, where Shakespeare premiered many of his works. The theatre has since been reconstructed (see p.230).

From Gunpowder Plot to Civil War

On Elizabeth's death in 1603, James VI of Scotland became **James I** (1603–25) of England, thereby uniting the two crowns and marking the beginning of the **Stuart dynasty**. His intention of exercising religious tolerance after the anti-Catholicism of Elizabeth's reign was thwarted by the public outrage that followed the **Gunpowder Plot** of 1605, when Guy Fawkes and a group of Catholic conspirators were discovered attempting to blow up the king at the state opening of Parliament. James, who clung to the medieval notion of the divine right of kings, inevitably clashed with the landed gentry who dominated Parliament, and tensions between Crown and Parliament were worsened by his persecution of the Puritans, an extreme but increasingly powerful Protestant group.

Under James's successor, **Charles I** (1625–49), the animosity between Crown and Parliament came to a head. From 1629 to 1640 Charles ruled without the services of Parliament, but was forced to recall it when he ran into problems in Scotland, where he was attempting to subdue the Presbyterians. Faced with extremely antagonistic MPs, Charles attempted unsuccessfully to arrest several of their number at Westminster. Acting on a tip-off, the MPs fled by river to the City, which sided with Parliament. Charles withdrew to Nottingham, where he raised his standard, the opening military

1512	1534	1553–58	1561	1571
Royal Dockyards established in Woolwich	Henry VIII breaks with the Roman Catholic Church	Queen Mary reinstates Catholicism	Lightning strikes Old St Paul's and the spire falls to the ground	The opening of the Royal Exchange in the City

act of the **Civil War**. London was the key to victory, and as a **Parliamentarian stronghold** it came under attack almost immediately from Royalist forces. After Charles defeated the Parliamentary troops to the west of London at **Brentford in** November 1642, the way was open for him to take the capital. Londoners turned out in numbers to defend their city, some 24,000 assembling at **Turnham Green**. A stand-off ensued, Charles hesitated and in the end withdrew to Reading, thus missing his greatest chance of victory. A complex system of fortifications was thrown up around London, but was never put to the test. In the end, the capital remained intact throughout the war, which culminated in the execution of the king outside Whitehall's Banqueting House in January 1649.

For the next eleven years England was a **Commonwealth** – at first a true republic, then, after 1653, a Protectorate under **Oliver Cromwell**, who was ultimately as impatient of Parliament and as arbitrary as Charles had been. London found itself in the grip of the Puritans' zealous laws, which closed down all theatres, enforced observance of the Sabbath and banned the celebration of Christmas, which was considered a papist superstition.

Plague and fire

Just as London proved Charles I's undoing, so the ecstatic reception given to **Charles II** (1660–85) helped ease the **Restoration** of the monarchy in 1660. The "Merry Monarch" immediately caught the mood of the public by opening up the theatres, and he encouraged the sciences by helping the establishment of the **Royal Society** for Improving Natural Knowledge, whose founder members included **Christopher Wren**, **John Evelyn** and **Isaac Newton**.

The good times that rolled in the early period of Charles's reign came to an abrupt end with the onset of the **Great Plague** of 1665. Epidemics of bubonic plague were nothing new to London – there had been major outbreaks in 1593, 1603, 1625, 1636 and 1647 – but the combination of a warm summer and the chronic overcrowding of the city proved calamitous in this instance. Those with money left the city (the court moved to Oxford), while the poorer districts outside the City were the hardest hit. The extermination of the city's dog and cat population – believed to be the source of the epidemic – only exacerbated the situation by allowing the flea-carrying rat population to explode. In September, the death toll peaked at twelve thousand a week, and in total an estimated hundred thousand lost their lives.

A cold snap in November extinguished the plague, but the following year London had to contend with yet another disaster, the **Great Fire** of 1666. As with the plague, outbreaks of fire were fairly commonplace in London, whose buildings were predominantly timber-framed, and whose streets were narrow, allowing fires to spread rapidly. However, this particular fire raged for five days and destroyed some four-fifths of the City of London (see box, p.452).

Within five years, nine thousand houses had been rebuilt with bricks and mortar (timber was banned), and fifty years later **Christopher Wren** had almost single-handedly rebuilt all the City churches and completed the world's first purpose-built Protestant cathedral, **St Paul's**. Medieval London was no more, though the grandiose masterplans of Wren and other architects had to be rejected due to the legal intricacies of property

1588	1599	1605	1642–51	1643
Defeat of the Spanish Armada	Globe Theatre opens on Bankside	Gunpowder Plot foiled	Civil War	Cheapside Cross torn down by iconoclasts

---

THE GREAT FIRE

In the early hours of September 2, 1666, the **Great Fire** broke out at Farriner's, the king's bakery in Pudding Lane. The Lord Mayor refused to lose any sleep over it, dismissing it with the line "Pish! A woman might piss it out." Pepys was also roused from his bed, but saw no cause for alarm. Four days and four nights later, the Lord Mayor was found crying "like a fainting woman", and Pepys had fled, having famously buried his Parmesan cheese in the garden: the Fire had destroyed some four-fifths of the City of London, including 87 churches, 44 livery halls and 13,200 houses. The medieval city was no more.

Miraculously, there were only eight recorded fatalities, but one hundred thousand people were made homeless. "The hand of God upon us, a great wind and the season so very dry", was the verdict of the parliamentary report on the Fire, but Londoners preferred to blame Catholics and foreigners. The poor baker eventually "confessed" to being an agent of the pope and was executed, after which the following words, "but Popish frenzy, which wrought such horrors, is not yet quenched", were added to the Latin inscription on the Monument (see p.174), and only erased in 1830.

---

rights within the City. The **Great Rebuilding**, as it was known, was one of London's most remarkable achievements – and all achieved in spite of a chronic lack of funds, a series of very severe winters and continuing wars against the Dutch.

Religious differences once again came to the fore with the accession of Charles's Catholic brother, **James II** (1685–88), who successfully put down the Monmouth Rebellion of 1685, but failed to halt the "Glorious Revolution" of 1688, which brought the Dutch king William of Orange to the throne, much to most people's relief. **William** (1689–1702) and his wife **Mary** (1689–95), daughter of James II, were made joint sovereigns, having agreed to a Bill of Rights defining the limitations of the monarch's power and the rights of his or her subjects. This, together with the Act of Settlement of 1701 – which among other things barred Catholics, or anyone married to one, from succession to the throne – made Britain the first country in the world to be governed by a **constitutional monarchy**, in which the roles of legislature and executive were separate and interdependent. A further development during the reign of **Anne** (1702–14), second daughter of James II, was the Act of Union of 1707, which united the English and Scottish parliaments, a union most recently tested with the 2014 Scottish referendum on independence but that – for the time being – holds.

Georgian London

When Queen Anne died childless in 1714 (despite having given birth seventeen times), the Stuart line ended, though pro-Stuart or Jacobite rebellions continued on and off until 1745. In accordance with the Act of Settlement, the succession passed to a non-English-speaking German, the Duke of Hanover, who became **George I** (1714–27) of England. As power leaked from the monarchy, the king ceased to attend cabinet meetings (which he couldn't understand anyway), his place being taken by his chief minister. Most prominent among these chief ministers or "prime ministers", as they became known, was **Robert Walpole**, the first politician to live at **10 Downing Street**, and effective ruler of the country from 1721 to 1742.

1645	1649	1649–60	1652
Archbishop of Canterbury, William Laud, executed on Tower Hill	King Charles I executed in Whitehall	The Commonwealth of England	Pasqua Rosée opens the first coffee house in London

THE GIN CRAZE

It's difficult to exaggerate the effects of the gin-drinking orgy which took place among the poorer sections of London's population between 1720 and 1751. At its height, **gin consumption** was averaging two pints a week for every man, woman and child, and the burial rate exceeded the baptism rate by more than 2:1. The origins of this lay in the country's enormous surplus of corn, which had to be sold in some form or another to keep the landowners happy. Deregulation of the distilling trade was Parliament's answer, thereby flooding the urban market with cheap, intoxicating liquor, which resulted in an enormous increase in crime, prostitution, **child mortality** and general misery among the poor. Papers in the Old Bailey archives relate a typical story of the period: a mother who "fetched her child from the workhouse, where it had just been 'new-clothed', for the afternoon. She strangled it and left it in a ditch in Bethnal Green in order to sell its clothes. The money was spent on gin." Eventually, in the face of huge vested interests, the government was forced to pass an Act in 1751 that restricted gin retailing and brought the craze to a halt.

Meanwhile, London's expansion continued unabated. The shops of the newly developed **West End** stocked the most fashionable goods in the country, the volume of trade more than tripled and London's growing population – it was by now the largest city in the world, with a population rapidly approaching one million – created a huge market for food and other produce, as well as fuelling a building boom. In the City, the **Bank of England** – founded in 1694 to raise funds to conduct war against France – was providing a sound foundation for the economy. It could not, however, prevent the mania for financial speculation that resulted in the fiasco of the **South Sea Company**, which in 1720 sold shares in its monopoly of trade in the Pacific and along the east coast of South America. The "bubble" burst when the shareholders took fright at the extent of their own investments, and the value of the shares dropped to nothing, reducing many to penury and almost wrecking the government, which was saved only by the astute intervention of Walpole.

Wealthy though London was, it was also experiencing the worst mortality rates since records began in the reign of Henry VIII. Disease was rife in the overcrowded immigrant quarter of the East End and other slum districts, but the real killer during this period was **gin** (see box above).

Policing the metropolis was an increasing preoccupation for the government. It was proving a task far beyond the city's three thousand beadles, constables and nightwatchmen, who were, in any case, "old men chosen from the dregs of the people who have no other arms but a lantern and a pole", according to one French visitor. As a result, **crime** continued unabated throughout the eighteenth century, so that, in the words of Horace Walpole, one was "forced to travel even at noon as if one was going into battle". The government imposed draconian measures, introducing **capital punishment** for the most minor misdemeanours. The prison population swelled, transportations began and 1200 Londoners were hanged at Tyburn's gallows.

Despite such measures, and the passing of the Riot Act in 1715, rioting remained a popular pastime among the poorer classes in London. Anti-Irish riots had taken place in 1736; in 1743 there were further riots in defence of cheap liquor; and in the 1760s there were more organized mobilizations by supporters of the great agitator

1665	1666	1694	1702
The Great Plague kills 100,000 people	The Great Fire of London	Bank of England established	*The Daily Courant*, the world's first daily newspaper, published on Fleet Street

John Wilkes, calling for political reform. The most serious insurrection of the lot, however, were the **Gordon Riots** of 1780, when up to fifty thousand Londoners went on a five-day rampage through the city. Although anti-Catholicism was the spark that lit the fire, the majority of the rioters' targets were chosen not for their religion but for their wealth. The most dramatic incidents took place at Newgate Prison, where thousands of inmates were freed, and at the Bank of England, which was saved only by the intervention of the military – and John Wilkes, of all people. The death toll was in excess of three hundred, 25 rioters were subsequently hanged, and further calls were made in Parliament for the establishment of a proper police force.

Nineteenth-century London

The **nineteenth century** witnessed the emergence of London as the capital of an empire that stretched across the globe. The world's largest enclosed **dock system** was built in the marshes to the east of the City; Tory reformer **Robert Peel** established the world's first civilian **police force**; and the world's first public-transport network was created, with horse-buses, trains, trams and an underground railway.

The city's population grew dramatically from just over one million in 1801 (the first official census) to nearly seven million by 1901. **Industrialization** brought pollution and overcrowding, especially in the slums of the East End. Smallpox, measles, whooping cough and scarlet fever killed thousands of working-class families, as did the cholera outbreaks of 1832 and 1848–49. The **Poor Law** of 1834 formalized **workhouses** for the destitute, but these failed to alleviate the problem, in the end becoming little more than prison hospitals for the penniless. It is this era of slum life and huge social divides that Dickens evoked in his novels.

Architecturally, London was changing rapidly. **George IV** (1820–30), who became Prince Regent in 1811 during the declining years of his father, George III, instigated several grandiose projects that survive to this day. With the architect **John Nash**, he laid out London's first planned processional route, Regent Street, and a prototype garden city around **Regent's Park**. The Regent's Canal was driven through the northern fringe of the city, and Trafalgar Square began to take shape. The city already boasted the first secular public museum in the world, the **British Museum**, and in 1814 London's first public art gallery opened in the suburb of Dulwich, followed shortly afterwards by the National Gallery, founded in 1824. London finally got its own university, too, in 1826.

The accession of **Queen Victoria** (1837–1901) coincided with a period in which the country's international standing reached unprecedented heights, and as a result Victoria became as much a national icon as Elizabeth I had been. Though the intellectual achievements of Victoria's reign were immense – typified by the publication of Darwin's *The Origin of Species* in 1859 – the country saw itself above all as an imperial power founded on industrial and commercial prowess. Its spirit was perhaps best embodied by the great engineering feats of **Isambard Kingdom Brunel** and by the **Great Exhibition** of 1851, a display of manufacturing achievements from all over the world, which took place in the Crystal Palace, erected in Hyde Park.

Despite being more than twice the size of Paris, London did not experience the political upheavals of the French capital – the terrorists who planned to wipe out the cabinet in the **1820 Cato Street Conspiracy** were the exception (see p.86). Mass

1710	1720	1750	1751
Completion of St Paul's Cathedral, designed by Christopher Wren	The South Sea Bubble causes financial ruin for many	Westminster Bridge opens	The Gin Act brings the decades of London's Gin Craze to an end

---

THE CHARTIST MOVEMENT IN LONDON

The **Chartist movement**, which campaigned for universal male suffrage (among other things), was much stronger in the industrialized north than in the capital, at least until the 1840s. Support for the movement reached its height in the revolutionary year of 1848. In March, some ten thousand Chartists occupied Trafalgar Square and held out against the police for two days. Then, on April 10, the Chartists organized a mass demonstration on Kennington Common. The government panicked and drafted in eighty thousand "special constables" to boost the capital's four thousand police officers, and troops were garrisoned around all public buildings. In the end, London was a long way off experiencing a revolution: the demo took place, but the planned march on Parliament was called off.

---

demonstrations and the occasional minor fracas preceded the passing of the **1832 Reform Act**, which acknowledged the principle of popular representation (though few men and no women had the vote), but there was no real threat of revolution. London doubled its number of MPs in the new parliament, but its own administration remained dominated by the City oligarchy.

The birth of local government

The first tentative steps towards a cohesive form of metropolitan government were taken in 1855 with the establishment of the **Metropolitan Board of Works** (**MBW**). Its initial remit only covered sewerage, lighting and street maintenance, but it was soon extended to include gas, fire services, public parks and slum clearance. The achievements of the MBW – and in particular those of its chief engineer, **Joseph Bazalgette** – were immense, creating an underground sewer system (much of it still in use), improving transport routes and wiping out some of the city's more notorious slums.

In 1888 the **London County Council** (**LCC**) was established. It was the first directly elected London-wide government, though as ever the City held on jealously to its independence (and in 1899, the municipal boroughs were set up deliberately to undermine the power of the LCC). The arrival of the LCC coincided with an increase in working-class militancy within the capital. In 1884, 120,000 gathered in Hyde Park to support the ultimately unsuccessful London Government Bill, while a demonstration held in 1886 in Trafalgar Square in protest against unemployment ended in a riot through St James's. The following year the government banned any further demos, and the resultant protest brought even larger numbers to Trafalgar Square. The brutality of the police in breaking up this last demonstration led to its becoming known as "Bloody Sunday".

In 1888 the Bryant & May matchgirls won their landmark **strike action** over working conditions, a victory followed up the next year by further successful strikes by the gasworkers and dockers. Charles Booth published his seventeen-volume *Life and Labour of the People of London* in 1890, providing the first clear picture of the social fabric of the city and shaming the council into action. In the face of powerful vested interests – landlords, factory owners and private utility companies – the LCC's Liberal leadership attempted to tackle the enormous problems, partly by taking gas, water,

1759	1760	1780	1811	1812
British Museum opens	City of London gates demolished	Gordon Riots	London's population exceeds one million	Prime Minister Spencer Perceval becomes the first (and so far) last PM to be assassinated

electricity and transport into municipal ownership, a process that took several more decades to achieve. The LCC's ambitious housing programme was beset with problems, too. Slum clearances only exacerbated overcrowding, and the new dwellings were too expensive for those in greatest need. Rehousing the poor in the suburbs also proved unpopular, since there was a policy of excluding pubs, traditionally the social centre of working-class communities, from these developments.

While half of London struggled to make ends meet, the other half enjoyed the fruits of the richest nation in the world. Luxury establishments such as *The Ritz* and Harrods belong to this period, which was personified by the dissolute and complacent Prince of

LONDON'S JEWS

William the Conqueror invited the first **Jews** to England in 1066. After a period of relatively peaceful coexistence and prosperity, the small community increasingly found itself under attack, financially milked by successive monarchs and forced eventually to wear a distinguishing mark or *tabula* on their clothing. The Crusades whipped up further religious intolerance, with London's worst recorded incident taking place in 1189, when thirty Jews were killed by a mob during the coronation of Richard I. In 1278 Edward I imprisoned the capital's entire community of around six hundred on a charge of "clipping coins" (debasing currency by shaving off bits of silver), executing 267 at the Tower, and finally, in 1290, expelling the rest.

For nearly four centuries thereafter, Judaism was outlawed in England. Sephardic (ie Spanish or Portuguese) Jews fleeing the Inquisition began arriving in small numbers from 1540 onwards (often via Amsterdam), though they had to become, or pretend to be, Christians until 1656, when Oliver Cromwell tolerated Jews meeting privately and worshipping in their own homes. The Jews who arrived immediately following this **Readmission** were in the main wealthy merchants, bankers and other businessmen. As a beacon of (relative) tolerance and economic prosperity, London quickly attracted further Jewish immigration by poorer Sephardi families and, increasingly, Ashkenazi settlers from eastern and central Europe.

By far the largest influx of **Ashkenazi Jews** arrived after fleeing pogroms that followed the assassination of the Russian Tsar Alexander II in 1881. The more fortunate were met by relatives at the Irongate Stairs by Tower Bridge; the rest were left to the mercy of the boarding-house keepers or, after 1885, found shelter in the Jewish Temporary Shelter. They found work in the sweatshops of the East End: cabinetmaking, shoemaking and tailoring. By 1901, over 45 percent of London's Jews worked in the garment industry.

Perhaps the greatest moment in Jewish East End history was the **Battle of Cable Street**, which took place on October 4, 1936, when Oswald Mosley and three thousand of his black-shirted fascists attempted to march through the East End. More than twice that number of police tried to clear the way for Mosley with baton charges and mounted patrols, but they were met with a barrage of bricks and stones from some one hundred thousand East Enders chanting the slogan of the Spanish Republicans: "*No pasaran*" (They shall not pass). Eventually the police chief halted the march – and another East End legend was born. A mural on the side of the old Shadwell town hall on Cable Street commemorates the event.

After World War II, more and more Jews moved out to the suburbs of north London, and the largest Orthodox Jewish communities are now to be found in Golders Green and Stamford Hill, with one hundred and seventy thousand Jews across the city as a whole. In 2014 antisemitic violence rose alarmingly in the UK, with more than double the recorded incidents of the previous year.

1814	1826	1836	1851
The last Frost Fair takes place on the frozen River Thames	London University opens	The first railway is built in London between London Bridge and Greenwich	Great Exhibition held in Hyde Park

Wales, later **Edward VII** (1901–10). For the masses, too, there were new entertainments to be enjoyed: music halls boomed, public houses prospered and the circulation of populist newspapers such as the *Daily Mirror* topped one million. The first "Test" cricket match between England and Australia took place in 1880 at the Kennington Oval in front of twenty thousand spectators, and during the following 25 years nearly all of London's professional football clubs were founded.

From World War I to World War II

Public patriotism peaked at the outbreak of **World War I** (1914–18), with crowds cheering the troops off from Victoria and Waterloo stations, convinced the fighting would all be over by Christmas. In the course of the next four years London experienced its first aerial attacks, with Zeppelin raids leaving some 650 dead, but these were minor casualties in the context of a war that destroyed millions of lives and eradicated whatever remained of the majority's respect for the ruling classes.

At the war's end in 1918, the country's social fabric was changed drastically as the voting franchise was extended to all men aged 21 and over and to women of 30 or over. Equal voting rights for women – hard fought for by the radical **Suffragette** movement led by Emmeline Pankhurst and her daughters before the war – were only achieved in 1928, the year of Emmeline's death.

Between the wars, London's population increased dramatically, reaching close to nine million by 1939, and representing one-fifth of the country's population. In contrast to the nineteenth century, however, there was a marked shift in population out into the **suburbs**. Some took advantage of the new "model dwellings" of LCC estates in places such as Dagenham in the east, though far more settled in "Metroland", the sprawling new suburban districts that followed the extension of the Underground out into northwest London.

In 1924 the **British Empire Exhibition** was held, with the intention of emulating the success of the Great Exhibition. Some 27 million people visited the show, but its success couldn't hide the tensions that had been simmering since the end of the war. In 1926, a wage dispute between the miners' unions and their bosses developed into the **General Strike**. For nine days, more than half a million workers stayed away from work, until the government called in the army and thousands of volunteers to break the strike.

The economic situation deteriorated even further after the crash of the New York Stock Exchange in 1929, with unemployment in Britain reaching over three million in 1931. The Jarrow Marchers, the most famous protesters of the **Depression** years, shocked London on their arrival in 1936. In the same year thousands of British fascists tried to march through the predominantly Jewish East End, only to be stopped in the so-called **Battle of Cable Street** (see box opposite). The end of the year brought a crisis within the Royal Family, too, when Edward VIII abdicated following his decision to marry Wallis Simpson, a twice-divorced American. His brother, **George VI** (1936–52), took over.

There were few public displays of patriotism with the outbreak of **World War II** (1939–45), and even fewer preparations were made against the likelihood of aerial bombardment. The most significant step was the evacuation of six hundred thousand of London's most vulnerable citizens (mostly children), but around half that number had drifted back to the capital by the Christmas of 1939, the midpoint of the "phoney

1858	1863	1908	1911
The Great Stink when the smell of untreated waste in the Thames reached an unprecedented level	The first section of the Underground opens between Paddington and Farringdon	London hosts the Olympic Games and Britain wins the most medals	London population exceeds seven million

THE BLITZ

The Luftwaffe bombing of London in World War II – commonly known as the **Blitz** – began on September 7, 1940, when in one night alone some 430 Londoners lost their lives, and over 1600 were seriously injured. It continued for 57 consecutive nights, then intermittently until the final and most devastating attack on the night of May 10, 1941, when 550 planes dropped over one hundred thousand incendiaries and hundreds of explosive bombs in a matter of hours. The death toll that night was over 1400, bringing the total killed during the Blitz to between twenty thousand and thirty thousand, with some 230,000 homes wrecked. Along with the East End, the City was particularly badly hit: in a single raid on December 29 (dubbed the "Second Fire of London"), 1400 fires broke out across the Square Mile. Some say the Luftwaffe left St Paul's standing as a navigation aid, but it came close to destruction when a bomb landed near the southwest tower; luckily the bomb didn't go off, and it was successfully removed to the Hackney marshes where the 100ft-wide crater left by its detonation is still visible.

The authorities were ready to build mass graves for potential victims, but were unable to provide adequate air-raid shelters to prevent widespread carnage. The corrugated steel **Anderson shelters** issued by the government were of use to only one in four London households – those with gardens in which to bury them. Around 180,000 made use of the tube, despite initial government reluctance, by simply buying a ticket and staying below ground. The cheery photos of singing and dancing in the Underground which the censors allowed to be published tell nothing of the stale air, rats and lice that folk had to contend with. And even the tube stations couldn't withstand a direct hit, as occurred at Bank in January 1941, when over a hundred died. The vast majority of Londoners – some sixty percent – simply hid under the sheets and prayed.

war". The Luftwaffe's bombing campaign, known as the **Blitz** (see box above), lasted from September 1940 to May 1941. Further carnage was caused towards the end of the war by the pilotless V-1 "doodlebugs" and V-2 rockets, which caused another twenty thousand casualties.

Postwar London

The end of the war in 1945 was followed by a general election, which brought a landslide victory for the Labour Party under **Clement Attlee**. The Attlee government created the **welfare state**, and initiated a radical programme of **nationalization**, which brought the gas, electricity, coal, steel and iron industries under state control, along with the inland transport services. London itself was left with a severe accommodation crisis, with some eighty percent of the housing stock damaged to some degree. In response, prefabricated houses were erected all over the city, some of which were to remain occupied for well over forty years. The LCC also began building huge housing estates on many of the city's numerous bombsites, an often misconceived strategy which ran in tandem with the equally disastrous New Towns policy of central government.

To lift the country out of its gloom, the **Festival of Britain** was staged in 1951 on derelict land on the south bank of the Thames, a site that was eventually transformed into the Southbank Arts Centre. Londoners turned up at this technological funfair in their thousands, but at the same time many were abandoning the city for good, starting

1926	1936	1948	1951	1952
The General Strike lasts for nine days	Police, fascists and anti-fascist protesters clash in the Battle of Cable Street in the East End	London hosts the Olympic Games	Festival of Britain held on the South Bank	London's tram system is abandoned

slow process of population decline that has continued ever since. The consequent labour shortage was made good by mass **immigration** from the former colonies, in particular the Indian subcontinent and the West Indies. The first large group to arrive was the 492 West Indians aboard the SS *Empire Windrush*, which docked at Tilbury in June 1948. The newcomers, a large percentage of whom settled in London, were given small welcome, and within ten years were subjected to **race riots**, which broke out in Notting Hill in 1958.

The riots are thought to have been carried out, for the most part, by "Teddy Boys", working-class lads from London's slum areas and new housing estates, who formed the city's first postwar youth cult. Subsequent cults, and their accompanying music, helped turn London into the epicentre of the so-called **Swinging Sixties**, the Teddy Boys being usurped in the early 1960s by the "Mods", whose sharp suits came from London's Carnaby Street. Fashion hit the capital in a big way, and, thanks to the likes of The Beatles, The Rolling Stones and Twiggy, London was proclaimed hippest city on the planet on the front pages of *Time* magazine.

Life for most Londoners, however, was rather less groovy. In the middle of the decade London's local government was reorganized, the LCC being supplanted by the **Greater London Council** (**GLC**), whose jurisdiction covered a much wider area, including many Tory-dominated suburbs. As a result, the Conservatives gained power in the capital for the first time since 1934, and one of their first acts was to support a huge urban motorway scheme that would have displaced as many people as did the railway boom of the Victorian period. Luckily for London, Labour won control of the GLC in 1973 and halted the plans. The Labour victory also ensured that the Covent Garden Market building was saved for posterity, but this ran against the grain. Elsewhere, whole areas of the city were pulled down and redeveloped, and many of London's worst tower blocks were built.

Thatcherite London

In 1979 **Margaret Thatcher** won the general election for the Conservatives, and the country and the capital would never be quite the same again. Thatcher went on to win three general elections, steering Britain into a period of ever greater social polarization. While taxation policies and easy credit fuelled a consumer boom for the professional classes (the yuppies of the 1980s), the erosion of the manufacturing industry and weakening of the welfare state created a calamitous number of people trapped in long-term unemployment, which topped three million in the early 1980s. The Brixton riots of 1981 and 1985 and the Tottenham riot of 1985 were reminders of the price of such divisive policies, and of the long-standing resentment and feeling of social exclusion rife among the city's black youth.

Nationally, the Labour Party went into sharp decline, but in London the party won a narrow victory in the GLC elections on a radical manifesto that was implemented by its youthful new leader **Ken Livingstone**, or "Red Ken" as the tabloids dubbed him. Under Livingstone, the GLC poured money into projects among London's ethnic minorities, into the arts and, most famously, into a subsidized fares policy. His popular brand of socialism was too much for the Thatcher government, who, in 1986, abolished the GLC, leaving London as the only European capital without a directly elected body to represent it.

1953	1956	1966	1971	1973
Coronation of Queen Elizabeth II	Clean Air Act	England wins the World Cup at Wembley	Decimal currency introduced	Britain joins the EEC

During the 1980s **homelessness** returned to London in a big way for the first time since Victorian times, and the underside of Waterloo Bridge was transformed into a "Cardboard City", sheltering up to two thousand vagrants on any one night. Great efforts were made by nongovernmental organizations to alleviate homelessness, not least the establishment of a weekly magazine, the *Big Issue*, which continues to be sold by the homeless right across London, earning them a small wage. At the same time, the **Big Bang** of 1986 abolished a whole range of restrictive practices on the Stock Exchange, while whole swathes of the East End were redeveloped into a new business quarter around Canary Wharf (see p.213).

Thatcher's greatest folly, however, was the introduction of the **Poll Tax**, a head tax levied regardless of means, which hit the poorest sections of the community hardest. The tax also highlighted the disparity between the city's boroughs. In wealthy, Tory-controlled Wandsworth, Poll Tax bills were zero, while those in poorer, neighbouring, Labour-run Lambeth were the highest in the country. In 1990, the Poll Tax provoked the first full-blooded riot in central London for a long time, and played a significant role in Thatcher's downfall later that year.

Twenty-first-century London

On the surface at least, the **twenty-first-century** has been one of London's most successful periods. Funded by money from the National Lottery and the Millennium Commission, the face of the city changed for the better around the start of the new millennium: the city's national museums were transformed into state-of-the-art visitor attractions, and all of them are free; pedestrian bridges were built over the Thames, and more are planned; and Tate Modern's opening in 2000 was a landmark, a beacon of optimism over the South Bank.

The creation of the **Greater London Assembly** (**GLA**), along with a directly elected **Mayor of London**, ended fourteen years without a city-wide authority. The Labour government, which came to power on a wave of enthusiasm in 1997, did everything it could to prevent the election of the former GLC leader **Ken Livingstone** as the first mayor, but, despite being forced to leave the Labour Party and run as an independent, he won a resounding victory in the 2000 mayoral elections.

One of his lasting legacies was **transport**. As well as introducing more buses, he successfully introduced a **congestion charge** for every vehicle entering central London (see p.25). As a result, traffic levels in central London reduced, at least for a time.

Livingstone was also instrumental in winning the **2012 Olympics** for London, by emphasizing the Games' regenerative potential for a deprived area of London's East End. For a moment, London celebrated wildly – the euphoria was all too brief. A day after hearing the news about the Olympics, on **July 7, 2005**, London was hit by four Islamist extremist **suicide bombers** who killed themselves and over fifty innocent commuters in four separate explosions: on tube trains at Aldgate, Edgware Road and King's Cross and one on a bus in Tavistock Square. Two weeks later a similar attack was unsuccessful after the bombers' detonators failed.

Londoners have repeatedly voted for mavericks and independents for mayor and Livingstone was succeeded by the charismatic Conservative politician **Boris Johnson** in 2008, who became the – slightly puffy – face of the city. Though both mayors

1986	1991	2000	2005
GLC abolished leaving London without a central government	The first buildings at Canary Wharf completed	Establishment of the Greater London Authority (GLA)	July 7 a series of terrorist bombs across the London transport network leaves 56 dead

championed cycling when in office, it was Boris who became synonymous with the bike-hire scheme implemented under his watch; Ken may have brought the Olympics to London, but Boris, haplessly dangling from a zip-wire waving a flag, became its mascot.

The **2010 general election** produced no overall winner and resulted in a hung parliament for only the second time since World War II. The Conservatives formed a coalition with the Liberal Democrats and began the harshest series of spending cuts since 1945. In August 2011, against a background of deepening economic hardship, London suffered the worst **riots** since the 1980s, not just in areas such as Tottenham, following the fatal police shooting of a 29-year-old black man Mark Duggan. (The police had intelligence that he had bought a gun, but beyond this the exact sequence of events leading up to the shooting remain disputed.) From Tottenham, they rapidly spread across the capital, from Bromley to Waltham Forest.

2012 proved a great year for London, with the celebrations of the Queen's **Diamond Jubilee** (sixty years on the throne), and a very successful and distinctive **Olympic Games**, further boosting London's international status and the mood of the city. The **2015 general election** saw inner London vote Labour, Scotland vote SNP (the Scottish National Party) and the outer suburbs and much of the rest of the country – outside Labour heartlands of the North – vote Conservative, the first Tory outright win since 1992. The May 2016 mayoral election – when Boris Johnson will stand down – will be a test of whether the city really does vote Labour and Boris, or whether other Tories have a chance.

Just over a decade ago, Ken Livingstone, speaking after the July 7 attacks and aiming his comments directly to the terrorists, said: "In the days that follow look at our airports, look at our sea ports and look at our railway stations and, even after your cowardly attack, you will see that people from the rest of Britain, people from around the world will arrive in London to become Londoners and to fulfil their dreams and achieve their potential." He could not have been more prescient.

In recent times London's population has grown rapidly, reaching 8.6 million in 2015 and speeding towards its all-time high reached in 1939 of nine million; estimates put it at eleven million by 2050. London is also the world's most visited city for tourists. While the city booms, many Londoners debate the cost to the city's fabric and the consequences for less wealthy residents, as infrastructure and resources creak under the weight of the city's own success. The biggest problems are transport – even with immense projects like Crossrail (see p.105) underway – other public services, such as schools, and, above all, **housing**. From luxury flats in Battersea to Bank's new skyscrapers, twenty-first-century London is one great big building site, but affordable housing is thin on the ground, and some imaginative thinking is needed if a full-blown accommodation crisis is to be avoided.

2008	2011	2012	2015
Boris Johnson becomes Mayor of London	August riots in London	London hosts the Olympic Games	General election returns majority Conservative government for first time in 23 years

Books

Given the enormous number of books on London, the list below is necessarily a selective one, with books marked ★ being particularly recommended. London still has many excellent independent bookshops (see p.429). Most of the books listed here are in paperback, but the more expensive books can often be bought secondhand online.

TRAVEL, JOURNALS AND MEMOIRS

★**James Boswell** *London Journal*. Boswell's diary, written in 1792–93 when he was lodging in Downing Street, is remarkably candid about his frequent dealings with the city's prostitutes, and is a fascinating insight into eighteenth-century life.

John Evelyn *The Diary of John Evelyn*. In contrast to his contemporary, Pepys, Evelyn gives away very little of his personal life, but his diaries are full of inside stories of court life from James II to Queen Annie.

Ford Madox Ford *The Soul of London*. Experimental, impressionist portrait of London published in 1905 by the author of *Parade's End*.

Doris Lessing *Walking in the Shade 1949–62*. The second volume of Lessing's autobiography, set in London in the 1950s, deals with the literary and theatre scenes and party politics, including her association with the Communist Party, with which she eventually became disenchanted.

George Orwell *Down and Out in Paris and London*. Orwell's tramp's-eye view of the 1930s, written from first-hand experience. The London section is particularly harrowing.

★**Samuel Pepys** *The Diary of Samuel Pepys*. Pepys kept a voluminous diary while he was living in London from 1660 until 1669, recording the fall of the Commonwealth, the Restoration, the Great Plague and the Great Fire, as well as describing the daily life of the nation's capital. Penguin's *The Diary of Samuel Pepys*, although abridged from eleven volumes, is still massive; but contains a selection of all the best bits.

Christopher Ross *Tunnel Visions*. Witty and perceptive musings of popular philosopher Ross as he spends a year working as a station assistant on the tube at Oxford Circus.

Iain Sinclair *Hackney, That Rose-Red Empire: a Confidential Report; Liquid City; London Orbital; London Overground*. Sinclair is one of the most original (and virtually unreadable) London writers of his generation. *Hackney* is an absorbing biography of the author's favourite borough. *Liquid City* contains beautiful photos and entertaining text about London's hidden rivers and canals; *London Orbital* is an account of his walk round the M25, delving into obscure parts of the city's periphery, while *London Overground* does the same for the route of the "ginger line".

HISTORY, SOCIETY AND POLITICS

Peter Ackroyd *Dickens; Blake; Sir Thomas More; Thames: Sacred River; London: The Biography* and *London Under*. Few writers know quite as much about London as Ackroyd does, and London is central to all three of his biographical subjects – the result is scholarly, enthusiastic and eminently readable. *London: The Biography* is the massive culmination of a lifetime's love affair with a living city and its intimate history.

Paul Begg *Jack the Ripper: The Definitive History*. This book, whose author has given talks to the FBI on the subject, sets the murders in their Victorian context and aims to debunk the myths.

Piers Dudgeon *Our East End: Memoirs of Life in Disappearing Britain*. Packed with extracts from written accounts and diaries as well as literary sources, this is a patchwork of the East End with its legendary community spirit and a dash of realism.

Juliet Gardiner *The Blitz: the British Under Attack*. A far-reaching account of the Blitz which dispels some of the myths, combining first-hand accounts with some surprising statistics.

Jonathan Glancey *London Bread and Circuses*. In this small, illustrated book, the *Guardian*'s architecture critic extols the virtues of the old LCC and visionaries like Frank Pick, who transformed London's transport in the 1930s, discusses the millennium projects (the "circuses" of the title) and bemoans the city's creaking infrastructure.

★**Ed Glinert** *The London Compendium*. Glinert dissects every street, every park, every house and every tube station and produces juicy anecdotes every time. The same author's *East End Chronicles: Three Hundred Years of Mystery and Mayhem* is a readable revelation of all the nefarious doings of the East End, sorting myth from fact, and hoping the spirit will somehow survive in spite of Docklands.

Rahila Gupta *From Homebreakers to Jailbreakers: Southall Black Sisters*. The story of a radical Asian women's group which, against all the odds, was founded in London in 1979 and became internationally famous for campaigning for all disempowered black women.

Sarah Hartley *Mrs P's Journey: The Remarkable Story of the*

Woman Who Created the A–Z Map. The tale of Phyllis Pearsall, the indomitable woman who survived a horrific childhood and went on to found London's most famous mapmaking company – you won't feel the same about the A–Z again.

Rachel Lichtenstein and Iain Sinclair Rodinsky's Room. A fascinating search into the Jewish past of the East End, centred on the nebulous figure of David Rodinsky.

Jack London The People of the Abyss. The author went undercover in 1902 to uncover the grim reality of East End poverty.

Henry Mayhew London Labour and the London Poor. Mayhew's pioneering study of Victorian London, based on research carried out in the 1840s and 1850s.

Roy Porter London: A Social History. This immensely readable history is one of the best books on London published since the war, particularly strong on the saga of the capital's local government.

Stephen Porter The Great Plague of London. Drawing on various contemporary sources, Porter paints a vivid picture of what it was like to live with a horror which killed seventy thousand Londoners.

Maude Pember Reeves & Polly Toynbee Round About a Pound a Week. From 1909 to 1913, the Fabian Women's Group, part of the British Labour Party, recorded the daily budget of thirty families in Lambeth living in extreme poverty. This is the accompanying comment, which is both enlightening and enlightened.

John Stow A Survey of London. Stow, a retired tailor, set himself the unenviable task of writing the first-ever account of the city in 1598, for which he is now rightly revered, though at the time the task forced him into penury.

Judith R. Walkowitz City of Dreadful Delight: Narratives of Sexual Danger in Late-Victorian London. Weighty feminist tract on issues such as child prostitution and the Ripper murders, giving a powerful overview of the image of women in the fiction and media of the day.

★**Ben Weinreb & Christopher Hibbert** The London Encyclopaedia. More than a thousand pages of concisely presented information on London past and present, accompanied by the odd illustration. The most fascinating book on the capital.

Jerry White London in the Eighteenth Century; London in the Nineteenth Century; London in the Twentieth Century and Zeppelin Nights: London in the First World War. Comprehensive histories of the most momentous periods in the city's history.

ART, ARCHITECTURE AND ARCHEOLOGY

T.M.M. Baker London: Rebuilding the City after the Great Fire. In 1666 the heart of the City of London was destroyed; this book covers not only Wren churches but other less well-known public and private buildings and is beautifully illustrated.

Reuel Golden London: Portrait of a City. A treasure trove of photographs sourced from archives worldwide as well as from such famous names as Bailey, Beaton and Cartier Bresson, this book captures London from Victorian times through the Swinging Sixties, from the Festival of Britain to the 2012 Olympics.

Elaine Harwood & Andrew Saint London. Part of the excellent Exploring England's Heritage series, sponsored by English Heritage. It's highly selective, though each building is discussed at some length and is well illustrated.

Leo Hollis The Stones of London. An illuminating social history of London illustrated by studying twelve of the city's buildings ranging from the iconic (Westminster Abbey) to the obscure (a tower block in the East End).

Derek Kendall The City of London Churches. A beautifully illustrated book, comprised mostly of colour photos, covering the remarkable City churches, many of them designed by Wren after the Great Fire.

Andrew Kershman London's Monuments. A stroll around some of the well-known and the more obscure monuments of the city.

Mark Ovenden London Underground by Design. Celebrating 150 years of the tube, this book illustrates its impact on design – the maps, the font, the roundel, the station design and marketing posters.

Nikolaus Pevsner and others The Buildings of England. Magisterial series, started by Pevsner, to which others have added, inserting newer buildings but generally respecting the founder's personal tone. London comes in six volumes, plus a special volume on the City churches.

Arnold Schwartzman London Art Deco: A Celebration of the Architectural Style of the Metropolis During the Twenties and Thirties. Generously illustrated, this book bears witness to the British version of Art Deco in the likes of the Savoy and the Hoover building.

Anthony Sutcliffe Architectural History of London. A weighty tome, extensively illustrated, which traces the history of building in London from the Romans to the twenty-first century.

Richard Trench & Ellis Hillman London under London. Fascinating book revealing the secrets of every aspect of the capital's subterranean history, from the lost rivers of the underground to the gas and water systems.

LONDON IN FICTION

Peter Ackroyd English Music; Hawksmoor; The House of Doctor Dee; The Great Fire of London; and Dan Leno and the Limehouse Golem. Ackroyd's novels are all based on arcane aspects of London, wrapped into thriller-like narratives, and conjuring up kaleidoscopic visions of various ages of English culture. Hawksmoor, about the great church architect, is the most popular and enjoyable.

★**Monica Ali** *Brick Lane*. Acute, involving and slyly humorous novel about a young Bengali woman who comes over with her husband to live in London's East End.

Martin Amis *London Fields*; *Yellow Dog*. Short sentences and cartoon characters, Amis's novels tend to provoke extreme reactions in readers. Love 'em or hate 'em, these two are set in London.

J.G. Ballard *The Drowned World*; *Concrete Island*; *The Millennium People*; *High Rise*. Wild stuff. *The Drowned World*, Ballard's first novel, is set in a futuristic, flooded and tropical London. In *Concrete Island*, a car crashes on the Westway, leaving its driver stranded on the central reservation, unable to flag down passing cars. In *The Millennium People* the middle classes turn urban terrorist. In *High Rise*, the residents of a high-rise block of flats in east London go slowly mad.

Samuel Beckett *Murphy*. Nihilistic, dark-humoured vision of the city, written in 1938, and told through the eyes of anti-hero Murphy.

Elizabeth Bowen *The Heat of the Day*. Bowen worked for the Ministry of Information during World War II, and witnessed the Blitz first-hand from her Marylebone flat; this novel perfectly captures the dislocation and rootlessness of wartime London.

Anthony Burgess *A Dead Man in Deptford*. Playwright Christopher Marlowe's unexplained murder in a tavern in Deptford provides the background for this historical novel, which brims over with Elizabethan life and language.

Angela Carter *The Magic Toyshop*; *Wise Children*. The *Magic Toyshop* was Carter's celebrated 1967 novel, about a provincial woman moving to London, while *Wise Children*, published a year before her untimely death, is set in a carnivalesque London.

G.K. Chesterton *The Napoleon of Notting Hill*. Written in 1904, but set eighty years in the future, in a London divided into squabbling independent boroughs – something prophetic there – and ruled by royalty selected on a rotational basis.

★**Arthur Conan Doyle** *The Complete Sherlock Holmes*. Deerstalkered sleuth Sherlock Holmes and dependable sidekick Dr Watson penetrate all levels of Victorian London, from Limehouse opium dens to millionaires' pads. *A Study in Scarlet* and *The Sign of Four* are based entirely in London.

Joseph Conrad *The Secret Agent*. Conrad's wonderful spy story is based on the botched anarchist bombing of Greenwich Observatory in 1894, and exposes the hypocrisies of both the police and the anarchists.

Daniel Defoe *Journal of the Plague Year*. An account of the Great Plague seen through the eyes of an East End saddler, written some sixty years after the event.

Charles Dickens *Bleak House*; *A Christmas Tale*; *Little Dorrit*; *Oliver Twist*. The descriptions in Dickens' London-based novels have become the clichés of the Victorian city: the fog, the slums and the stinking river. *Little Dorrit* is set mostly in Borough and contains some of his most trenchant pieces of social analysis. Much of *Bleak House* is set around the Inns of Court that Dickens knew so well.

Maureen Duffy *Capital*. First published in 1975, the novel is like a many-layered sandwich full of startling flavours, as the focus shifts from the central character, an unbalanced squatter with an obsession with London's past and future, to vivid slices of history.

Nell Dunn *Up the Junction*; *Poor Cow*. Perceptive and unsentimental account of the downside of London life in the 1950s and 1960s.

Helen Fielding *Bridget Jones's Diary*. Originally a column in the *Independent* newspaper, then a phenomenally successful book and film, Fielding's creation is a satirical but affectionate take on 1990s London life, booze, fags and all.

George Gissing *New Grub Street*; *The Nether World*. *New Grub Street* is a classic 1891 story of intrigue and jealousy among London's Fleet Street hacks. *The Nether World* is set among the poor workers of Clerkenwell.

Graham Greene *The Human Factor*; *It's a Battlefield*; *The Ministry of Fear*; *The End of the Affair*. Greene's London novels are all fairly bleak, ranging from *The Human Factor*, which probes the underworld of the city's spies, to *The Ministry of Fear*, which is set during the Blitz.

Patrick Hamilton *Hangover Square*; *Twenty Thousand Streets Under the Sky*. The first is a story of unrequited love and violence in Earl's Court in the 1940s, while the latter is a trilogy of stories set in seedy 1930s London.

Neil Hanson *The Dreadful Judgement*. A docu-fiction account in which modern scientific methods and historical knowledge are applied to the Fire of London so vividly you can almost feel the heat.

Aldous Huxley *Point Counter Point*. Sharp satire on London's high-society wastrels and dilettantes of the Roaring Twenties.

Hanif Kureishi *The Buddha of Suburbia*. The *Buddha of Suburbia* is a raunchy account of life as an Anglo-Asian in late-1960s suburbia, and the art scene of the 1970s.

Andrea Levy *Small Island*. A warm-hearted novel in which postwar London struggles to adapt to the influx of Jamaicans who in turn find that the land of their dreams is full of prejudice.

★**Hilary Mantel** *Wolf Hall*; *Bring up the Bodies*. Tudor London is majestically conjured up in Mantel's re-telling of the story of Thomas Cromwell, Henry VIII's chief minister and fixer, who traverses all London society, from his Putney origins and the merchants of the City of London to Henry's court. As well as visiting Hampton Court, *Wolf Hall* completists may want to make the trip to Hackney's Sutton House (see p.203), the home of the real Rafe Sadler (or

Ralph Sadleir), Cromwell's clerk.

Somerset Maugham *Liza of Lambeth*. Maugham considered himself a "second-rater", but this early novel, written in 1897, about Cockney lowlife, is packed with vivid local colour.

Ian McEwan *Saturday*. Set on the day of a protest march against the war in Iraq, this book captures the mood of London post-9/11, as the main character is forced to consider his attitude to this and many other issues.

Timothy Mo *Sour Sweet*. Very funny and very sad story of a newly arrived Chinese family struggling to understand the English way of life in the 1970s, written with great insight by Mo, who is himself of mixed parentage.

Michael Moorcock *Mother London*. A magnificent, rambling, kaleidoscopic portrait of London from the Blitz to Thatcher by a once-fashionable, but now very much underrated, writer.

Iris Murdoch *Under the Net; The Black Prince; An Accidental Man; Bruno's Dream*. *Under the Net* was Murdoch's first, funniest and arguably her best novel, published in 1954, starring a hack writer living in London. Many of her subsequent works are set in various parts of middle-class London and span several decades of the second half of the twentieth century.

George Orwell *Keep the Aspidistra Flying*. Orwell's 1930s critique of Mammon is equally critical of its chief protagonist, whose attempt to rebel against the system only condemns him to poverty, working in a London bookshop and freezing his evenings away in a miserable rented room.

Jonathan Raban *Soft City*. An early work from 1974 that's both a portrait of, and paean to, metropolitan life.

Derek Raymond *Not till the Red Fog Rises*. A book which "reeks with the pervasive stench of excrement" as Iain Sinclair put it, this is a lowlife spectacular set in the seediest sections of the capital.

Barnaby Rogerson (ed) *London: Poetry of Place*. A delightful pocket-sized book complete with potted biographies of the poets.

Edward Rutherfurd *London*. A big, big novel (perhaps too big) that stretches from Roman times to the twentieth century and deals with the most dramatic moments of London's history. Masses of historical detail woven in with the story of several families.

Will Self *The Book of Dave*. What would happen if a dystopian society 500 years in the future were devoted to following the ramblings of a disgruntled twentieth-century London cabbie? That's precisely the premise of Self's ambitious novel.

Samuel Selvon *The Lonely Londoners*. "Gives us the smell and feel of this rather horrifying life. Not for the squeamish",

ran the quote from the *Evening Standard* on the original cover. This is, in fact, a wry and witty account of the African-Caribbean experience in London in the 1950s.

Iain Sinclair *White Chappell, Scarlet Tracings; Downriver; Radon Daughters*. Sinclair's idiosyncratic and richly textured novels are a strange mix of Hogarthian caricature, New Age mysticism and conspiracy-theory rant.

Zadie Smith *White Teeth; NW*. *White Teeth* is her highly acclaimed and funny first novel about race, gender and class in the ethnic melting pot of north London. *NW* follows the fortunes of four Londoners from a council estate through the labyrinth of urban life in northwest London.

John Sommerfield *May Day*. Set in the revolutionary fervour of the 1930s, this novel is "as if Mrs Dalloway was written by a Communist Party bus driver", in the words of one reviewer.

Muriel Spark *The Bachelors; The Ballad of Peckham Rye*. Two London-based novels written by the Scots-born author, best known for *The Prime of Miss Jean Brodie*.

Edith Templeton *Gordon*. A tale of sex and humiliation in postwar London, banned in the 1960s when it was published under a pseudonym (Louisa Walbrook).

Rose Tremain *The Road Home*. The moving story of Lev, an Eastern European economic migrant, who heads for London and finds the streets are not paved with gold in the late twentieth century.

★ **Sarah Waters** *Tipping the Velvet; Affinity; Fingersmith; The Night Watch; The Paying Guests*. Waters' novels – compelling, intricately plotted period pieces, usually with lesbian protagonists – range across different periods and social settings. Her earliest ones are set in Victorian London: *Affinity* in the spiritualist milieu, *Fingersmith* focuses on an orphan girl, while *Tipping the Velvet* is about lesbian love in the music hall. *The Night Watch* is the tale of a London ambulance driver during World War II, while *The Paying Guests* explores love and social upheaval in 1920s Camberwell.

Evelyn Waugh *Vile Bodies*. Waugh's target, the "vile bodies" of the title, are the flippant rich kids of the Roaring Twenties, as in Huxley's *Point Counter Point* (see opposite).

P.G. Wodehouse *Jeeves Omnibus*. Bertie Wooster and his stalwart butler, Jeeves, were based in Mayfair, and many of their exploits take place with London showgirls and in the Drones gentlemen's club.

★ **Virginia Woolf** *Mrs Dalloway*. Woolf's novel relates the thoughts of a London society hostess and a shell-shocked war veteran, with her "stream-of-consciousness" style in full flow. *The London Scene* consists of six musings on Woolf's favourite London walks, originally written for *Good Housekeeping* in 1932.

SPECIALIST GUIDES

Jill Billington *London's Parks and Gardens*. An expensive coffee-table item, but the photos are beautiful.

Judi Culbertson & Tom Randall *Permanent Londoners*. An illustrated guide to the finest of London's cemeteries,

LONDON IN FILM THROUGH THE DECADES

As early as 1889 Wordsworth Donisthorpe made a primitive motion picture of Trafalgar Square, and since then London has been featured in countless films. Below is a snapshot selection of films culled from each decade since the 1920s.

Blackmail (Alfred Hitchcock, 1929). The first British talkie feature film, this thriller stars the Czech actress Anny Ondra and has its dramatic finale on the dome of the British Museum.

The Adventures of Sherlock Holmes (Alfred Werker, 1939). The Baker Street detective has made countless screen appearances, but Basil Rathbone remains the most convincing incarnation. Here Holmes and Watson (Nigel Bruce) are pitted against Moriarty (George Zucco), out to steal the Crown Jewels.

Passport to Pimlico (Henry Cornelius, 1948). The quintessential Ealing Comedy, in which the inhabitants of Pimlico, discovering that they are actually part of Burgundy, abolish rationing and closing time. Full of all the usual eccentrics, among them Margaret Rutherford in particularly fine form as an excitable history don.

The Ladykillers (Alexander Mackendrick, 1955). Delightfully black comedy set somewhere at the back of King's Cross (a favourite location for filmmakers). Katie Johnson plays the nice old lady getting the better of Alec Guinness, Peter Sellers and assorted other crooks.

Blow-Up (Michelangelo Antonioni, 1966). Swinging London and some less obvious backgrounds (notably Maryon Wilson Park, Charlton) feature in this metaphysical mystery about a photographer (David Hemmings) who may unwittingly have recorded evidence of a murder.

Jubilee (Derek Jarman, 1978). Jarman's angry punk collage, in which Elizabeth I finds herself transported to the urban decay of late twentieth-century Deptford.

My Beautiful Laundrette (Stephen Frears, 1985). A surreal comedy of Thatcher's London, offering the unlikely combination of an entrepreneurial Asian (Gordon Warnecke), his ex-National Front boyfriend (Daniel Day-Lewis) and a laundrette called Powders.

Naked (Mike Leigh, 1993). David Thewlis is brilliant as the disaffected and garrulous misogynist who goes on a tour through the underside of what he calls "the big shitty" – life is anything but sweet in Leigh's darkest but most substantial film.

Dirty Pretty Things (Stephen Frears, 2002). Entertaining romantic thriller set in London's asylum-seeking, multicultural underbelly, shot through with plenty of humour and lots of pace.

The King's Speech (Tom Hooper, 2011). Moving, funny account of King George VI's battle to overcome his stammer, after finding himself catapulted onto the throne following the abdication of Edward VIII.

from Westminster Abbey and St Paul's to the Victorian splendours of Highgate and Kensal Green. Very good on biographies of the deceased, too.

Andrew Duncan *Secret London*. With boundless enthusiasm, Duncan takes you along the lost rivers, unmasks the property tycoons, exposes dead tube stations and uncovers just about every undiscovered nook and cranny in the city.

David Fathers *The London Thames Path*. A charming, illustrated guide to walking the Thames Path on both sides of the river.

Paul Goldsack *River Thames: In the Footsteps of the Famous*. Written in conjunction with English Heritage this is a racy romp up the river, spotting connections with the famous and the infamous.

David Long *Hidden City: The Secret Alleys, Courts and Yards of London's Square Mile*. This book will send you scurrying through narrow alleyways in search of historical relics.

★**Helena Smith** *The Rough Guide to Walks in London & the Southeast*. The perfect companion guide to this one, detailing delightful walks in London and the wider region; all can be reached on public transport and include recommendations for good pub lunches.

Roger Tagholm *Walking Literary London*. Twenty-five walks in central and outer London, visiting birthplaces, homes and tombstones. Good maps, photos and transport details.

Christian Wolmar *The Subterranean Railway*. A fascinating history of the tube, the world's first underground railway and product of the vision of Victorian pioneers.

Glossaries

ARCHITECTURAL TERMS

Aisle Clear space parallel to the nave of a church, usually with lower ceiling than the nave.

Altar Table at which the Eucharist is celebrated, at the east end of a church. (When the church is not aligned to the geographical east, the altar end is still referred to as the "east" end.)

Ambulatory Passage behind and around the chancel.

Apse The curved or polygonal east end of a church.

Arcade Row of arches on top of columns or piers, supporting a wall.

Baldachin Canopy over an altar.

Barbican Defensive structure built in front of the main entry to a fortress.

Barrel vault Continuous rounded vault, like a semi-cylinder.

Blue plaque English Heritage plaques placed on a building associated with a prominent figure (who must have been dead for at least 25 years).

Boss A decorative carving at the meeting point of the lines of a vault.

Buttress Stone or brick structure strengthening a wall; some buttresses are wholly attached to the wall, others, known as "flying buttresses", take the form of a tower with a connecting arch.

Capital Uppermost section of a column or pillar, usually decorative.

Chancel Section of a church where the altar is located.

Choir Area in which the church service is conducted; next to or same as chancel.

Clerestory Upper storey of nave, containing a line of windows.

Coffering Regular recessed spaces set into a ceiling.

Corbel Jutting stone support, often carved.

Crenellations Battlements with square indentations.

Fan vault Late Gothic form of vaulting, in which the area between walls and ceiling is covered with stone ribs in the shape of an open fan.

Finial Any decorated tip of an architectural feature.

Gallery A raised passageway or extended balcony often open on one side.

Hammer-beam Type of internal roofing in which horizontal beams support vertical timbers that connect to and support the roof.

Lady Chapel Chapel dedicated to the Virgin, often found at the east end of major churches.

Lantern Structure on top of a dome or tower, often glazed to let in light.

Listed building A building which has been put on English Heritage's protected list; buildings are classed (in descending order of importance) Grade I, Grade II* and Grade II.

Misericord Carved ledge below a tip-up seat, usually in choir stalls.

Nave The main part of a church on the other (usually western) side of the crossing from the chancel.

Oriel Projecting window.

Palladian Eighteenth-century classical style adhering to the principles of Andrea Palladio.

Pediment Triangular space above a colonnade, window or doorway.

Perpendicular Late Gothic style, about 1380–1550.

Piano nobile Principal floor of a large house usually located above the ground floor.

Pilaster Flat column set against a wall.

Reredos Painted or carved panel at the back of an altar.

Rood screen Wooden screen supporting a crucifix (or rood), separating the choir from the nave; few survived the Reformation.

Rose window Large, circular window, divided into vaguely petal-shaped sections.

Stalls Seating for clergy in the choir area of a church.

Tracery Pattern formed by narrow bands of stone in a window or on a wall surface.

Transept Sections of the main body of a church at right angles to the choir and nave.

Tympanum Panel over a doorway, often with low-relief sculpture in medieval churches.

Vault Arched ceiling.

BRITISH TERMS

Bill	Restaurant check	**Chemist**	Pharmacist
Biscuit	Cookie or cracker	**Chips**	French fries
Bonnet	Car hood	**Coach**	Bus
Boot	Car trunk	**Crisps**	Potato chips
Caravan	Trailer	**Dodgy**	Suspect or unreliable
Car park	Parking lot	**Dustbin**	Trash can
Cheap	Inexpensive	**First floor**	Second floor

COCKNEY RHYMING SLANG

The term **Cockney** originally meant cock's egg or misshapen egg such as a young hen might lay, in other words, a lily-livered townie as opposed to a strong countryman. From the seventeenth century, it was used as a pejorative term for any Londoner, but was later appropriated by Londoners to describe themselves (and their accent). Traditionally, to be a true Cockney, you had to be born within earshot of the **Bow Bells** (see p.160), an area estimated to be roughly a five-mile radius around the City. However, with increased traffic noise, and no maternity ward in the near vicinity, this traditional definition is of little use nowadays.

As for **Cockney rhyming slang**, it's basically a coded language, where a word is replaced by two or more words, the last one of which rhymes with the original. For example, instead of the word "stairs" you have "apples and pears"; a piano (pronounced "pianner") is a "Joanna"; and pinch becomes "half-inch". The general theory is that it evolved in the criminal underworld of the **East End** as a secret means of communication, and many folk nowadays think of Cockney rhyming slang as a bit of a joke. In actual fact, it's alive and well, you just need to know a few basic rules. For a start, Londoners often don't use the part of the phrase which rhymes with the original at all. In other words, rather than say "butcher's hook" (for "look"), they say "Have a butcher's at that"; instead of "loaf of bread" (for "head"), you hear "Use your loaf!", and when it's cold, it's "'tat'ers" not "potatoes in the mould". Rhyming slang is constantly evolving, too, with public figures providing rich pickings: Brad Pitt (shit), Posh & Becks (specs) and Gordon Brown (clown). For the latest rhyming slang, and all the old favourites, visit Ⓦ cockneyrhymingslang.co.uk.

Fiver	Five-pound note	**Queue**	Line
Flat	Apartment	**Quid**	Pound (money)
Fortnight	Two weeks	**Return ticket**	Round-trip ticket
Ground floor	First floor	**Roundabout**	Rotary interchange
High Street	Main Street	**Single ticket**	One-way ticket
Hire	Rent	**Stalls**	Orchestra seats
Jam	Jelly	**Stone**	Fourteen pounds (weight)
Jelly	Jell-O	**Subway**	Pedestrian passageway
Jumper	Sweater	**Sweets**	Candy
Leaflet	Pamphlet	**Tap**	Faucet
Lift	Elevator	**Tenner**	Ten-pound note
Lorry	Truck	**Tights**	Pantyhose
Motorway	Highway	**Tory**	Conservative (politics)
NHS	National Health Service	**Trainers**	Sneakers
Off-licence	Liquor store	**Trousers**	Pants
Pants	Underwear	**Tube/Underground**	Subway (train)
Petrol	Gasoline	**Whig**	Liberal (politics, historic term)
Pudding	Dessert		

Small print and index

A ROUGH GUIDE TO ROUGH GUIDES

Published in 1982, the first Rough Guide – to Greece – was a student scheme that became a publishing phenomenon. Mark Ellingham, a recent graduate in English from Bristol University, had been travelling in Greece the previous summer and couldn't find the right guidebook. With a small group of friends he wrote his own guide, combining a highly contemporary, journalistic style with a thoroughly practical approach to travellers' needs.

The immediate success of the book spawned a series that rapidly covered dozens of destinations. And, in addition to impecunious backpackers, Rough Guides soon acquired a much broader readership that relished the guides' wit and inquisitiveness as much as their enthusiastic, critical approach and value-for-money ethos.

These days, Rough Guides include recommendations from budget to luxury and cover more than 120 destinations around the globe, as well as producing an ever-growing range of ebooks.

Visit **roughguides.com** to find all our latest books, read articles, get inspired and share travel tips with the Rough Guides community.

ABOUT THE AUTHORS

Samantha Cook (samanthacookeditorwriter.weebly.com) was born in London and has lived in the capital all her life. A freelance writer and editor, she has written many Rough Guides, including travel guides to the USA; New Orleans; Paris; Kent, Sussex and Surrey; the Best Places to Stay in Britain on a Budget, and Vintage London. She also wrote the *Rough Guide to Chick Flicks* and contributed to a number of Rough Guides' film titles.

Neil McQuillian has updated and edited various Rough Guides, authored the Wallpaper City Guides to Liverpool and Manchester, and written travel features for publications including *The Independent*, *The Telegraph* and *The Sunday Times Travel Magazine*. His work on this guide is for his sister Louisa, whose trips to east London with Ella always made things a lot more fun.

Andrew Mickel is a London-based freelance journalist specializing in travel, nightlife and comedy.

Matt Norman was born in Kent, London's back garden, and has lived in London for around 25 years. He has lived in the south, north and west of the city but his heart is in the south east. He works at The National Archives in Kew.

Alice Park is a freelance writer and editor. She has edited numerous guidebooks, and written about Germany and Austria, as well as her native South London. When not editing travel guides she dabbles in studying politics.

Rough Guide credits

Editor: Greg Dickinson
Layout: Ankur Guha
Cartography: Ed Wright
Picture editors: Marta Bescos and Michelle Bhatia
Proofreader: Jennifer Speake
Managing editor: Mani Ramaswamy
Assistant editor: Sharon Sonam

Production: Jimmy Lao
Cover design: Nicole Newman, Dan May, Ankur Guha
Editorial assistant: Freya Godfrey
Senior pre-press designer: Dan May
Programme manager: Gareth Lowe
Publisher: Keith Drew
Publishing director: Georgina Dee

Publishing information

This eleventh edition published February 2016 by
Rough Guides Ltd,
80 Strand, London WC2R 0RL
11, Community Centre, Panchsheel Park,
New Delhi 110017, India
Distributed by Penguin Random House
Penguin Books Ltd, 80 Strand, London WC2R 0RL
Penguin Group (USA), 345 Hudson Street, NY 10014, USA
Penguin Group (Australia), 250 Camberwell Road,
Camberwell, Victoria 3124, Australia
Penguin Group (NZ), 67 Apollo Drive, Mairangi Bay,
Auckland 1310, New Zealand
Penguin Group (South Africa), Block D, Rosebank Office
Park, 181 Jan Smuts Avenue, Parktown North, Gauteng,
South Africa 2193
Rough Guides is represented in Canada by DK Canada, 320
Front Street West, Suite 1400, Toronto, Ontario M5V 3B6
Printed in Singapore
© Rough Guides 2016
Maps © Rough Guides
Contains Ordnance Survey data © Crown copyright and
database rights 2016

MIX
Paper from
responsible sources
FSC www.fsc.org FSC™ C018179

Acknowledgements

Samantha Cook Thanks to Greg Dickinson for excellent,
smooth and creative editing, to Rob Humphreys, without
whom this guide wouldn't exist and who was sorely
missed during the updating of this edition, to all my co-
authors, and above all to Greg Ward, fellow Londoner and
fellow traveller, for everything and more.

Neil McQuillian Tim Whittaker; Richard Meunier; Erica
Davies; Hannah Talbot, Liz Selby and Jo Rosenthal; Chaya
Spitz; Gareth Bell-Jones; Claire and Natalie Suckall; Carien
Kremer; Nancy Loader; Laura Parker; Richard Bray; Kate
Berman; James Gray; Elle Potter; Sam Parry; Richard
Meunier; David Milne and Lindsay Friend; Dave Stuart; Alex
O'Neill; Grant McCahon; Tamsin O'Hanlon; Michelle Bhatia;
Alistair Maddox; Andy Rider and Fay Cattini; Carolyn Fuest;
Paul Bloomfield-Bray; Chris Cleeve; Marcus Nodder; Eleanor
Aldridge; Ed Aves; Rachel Mills; Olivia Rawes; the Bowyers
and Phillipses; Jacqueline Passmore; Patricia Mediavilla;
Lindsay McQuillian; Corinne Bannister; co-authors Sam
Cook and Alice Park for tips; Greg Dickinson, our excellent
editor. And insights gleaned from Ed Glinert's *East End
Chronicles* and *London 5: East* (Cherry O'Brien and Pevsner).

Andrew Mickel Thanks to Nicky Phillips for her unparalleled
knowledge of London's lesbian scene, both old and new.

Matt Norman Thanks to Ian Lacey; Will Stanley; Simon
Josiffe; Heather Farwell and Sally Dobinson; Laura
Hutchinson and Pauline Stobbs; Amaya Wang; Ed Holmes;
Sophie Lawrenson; Sylvia Ross and Neil Evans; Emily
Butcher; Murray MacKay; Laura Quinton; Debbie Challis;
also to Greg Dickinson for being a real pleasure to work
with. Special thanks to Juliette Desplat for bringing her
expertise and enthusiasm to bear on the British Museum
review and for making trips to Bloomsbury so enjoyable;
and to my mum, Lesley Norman, for the insights and
knowledge that a lifetime's worth of visits to the National
Gallery and Tate Britain brought to this guide.

Alice Park Thank you to Carol Bombata and Su Whiting
at Visit Greenwich for all their help. Thanks to everyone at
Rough Guide headquarters in London and Delhi, especially
Greg and Rachel for editorial mastery, and to my super co-
authors: Samantha, Neil, Matt and Andrew. A cap doffed
to the original London author, Rob Humphreys, for ten
editions to live up to. Finally many thanks to all my fellow
South Londoners who joined me on my exotic travels,
especially Mum, Dad and Sophie, and to mini-adventurer
Inigo, who braved scary sharks, fearsome dinosaurs and a
very large walrus, all in the name of research.

Help us update

We've gone to a lot of effort to ensure that the eleventh edition of **The Rough Guide to London** is accurate and up-to-date. However, things change – places get "discovered", opening hours are notoriously fickle, restaurants and rooms raise prices or lower standards. If you feel we've got it wrong or left something out, we'd like to know, and if you can remember the address, the price, the hours, the phone number, so much the better.

Please send your comments with the subject line "Rough Guide London Update" to mail@uk.roughguides.com. We'll credit all contributions and send a copy of the next edition (or any other Rough Guide if you prefer) for the very best emails.

Find more travel information, connect with fellow travellers and plan your trip on ⓦroughguides.com.

Readers' updates

Thanks to all the readers who have taken the time to write in with comments and suggestions (and apologies if we've inadvertently omitted or misspelt anyone's name):

Ali Bell; Johanne Decary; Ingmar Hemsen; Ed Hutchings; Trina King

Photo credits

All photos © Rough Guides except the following:
(Key: t-top; c-centre; b-bottom; l-left; r-right)

p.1 Alamy/Simon Turner
p.2 AWL Images/Jon Arnold
p.4 Alamy/ilpo musto (t)
p.6 Getty Images/Justin Guariglia
p.7 Alamy/Nigel Dickinson
p.9 Getty Images/AWL Images RM (t); Getty Images/Frank Whitney (c); AWL Images/Travel Pix Collection (b)
p.10 Alamy/John Kellerman
p.11 Alamy/Monica Wells (c); Alamy/Alex Segre (b)
p.12 Alamy/Roger Hutchings (t); Axiom Photographic Agency/Marc Jackson (b)
p.13 Getty Images/Fraser Hall (t); Getty Images/Doug McKinlay (c)
p.14 Alamy/Ian Shaw (t); Alamy/Carolyn Jenkins (cl); SuperStock/Alan Copson (cr); Getty Images/Latitudestock (b)
p.15 Alamy/John Kellerman (t); Alamy/VIEW Pictures Ltd (c)
p.16 Alamy/Drew Buckley (t)
p.17 Alamy/Scott Hortop Travel
p.18 Getty Images/Jeremy Walker
p.34 Getty Images/Peter Adams
p.43 Corbis/Demotix/Mark Thomas (c); Corbis/Steven Vidler (b)
p.57 Getty Images/Future Light (tr); Axiom Photographic Agency/James Morris (bl); Corbis/Steven Vidler (br)
p.65 AWL Images/Jon Arnold
p.69 Corbis/Atlantide Phototravel
p.76 SuperStock/Sara Janini
p.87 Corbis/Loop Images/Ricky Leaver
p.95 Alamy/PjrTravel
p.106 Getty Images/Photononstop RM
p.113 SuperStock (bl)
p.118 Robert Harding Picture Library/Eurasia
p.123 Getty Images/Travel Ink (t); Interfoto (bl); Alamy/Imagepast (br)
p.138 Getty Images/Ed Pritchard
p.144 SuperStock/Phil Robinson
p.150 Getty Images/Dominic Burke

p.157 Alamy/Paul Carstairs (tl)
p.173 Getty Images/Rudi Sebastian (t)
p.176 SuperStock
p.185 Alamy/Piero Cruciatti
p.195 Alamy/Rudolf Abraham (t); Getty Images/Maremagnum (br)
p.207 Alamy/Brian Anthony
p.216 SuperStock/Joe Fox
p.225 Robert Harding Picture Library/Peter Barritt
p.231 Alamy/Monica Wells (t)
p.240 Alamy/A.P.S. (UK)
p.250 Getty Images/Eric Nathan
p.261 Alamy/Peter D Noyce (tr); Alamy/Tracey Whitefoot (br)
p.281 Alamy/ilpo musto
p.291 Alamy/Nando Machado (t)
p.306 Alamy/Chris Lawrence
p.351 Alamy/Nature Picture Library
p.354 The Zetter Townhouse/Andreas von Einsiedel
p.361 Ace Hotel London Shoreditch/Andrew Meredith (tl)
p.371 Alamy/Helen Cathcart (tl); Alamy/Matthew Chattle (tr); Dishoom (b)
p.386 Alamy/Cath Harries
p.393 Alamy/Steve Vidler (bl)
p.395 The Jerusalem Tavern (t)
p.405 Alamy/Steven Vidler
p.412 Getty Images/Ian Gavan
p.417 Alamy/Patrick Ward
p.423 Blitz
p.425 Alamy/Bjanka Kadic (br)
p.435 Getty Images/Clive Brunskill
p.440 Dorling Kindersley/Max Alexander
p.444 Getty Images/Imagno

Front cover & spine Dr. Martens © AWL Images/Hemis
Back cover Hyde Park © AWL Images/Jon Arnold (t); Tower Bridge © AWL Images/Travel Pix Collection (bl); Sky Garden © Alamy/Steve Tulley (br)

Index

Maps are marked in grey

D

E

F

Map index

Listings key

■ Accommodation
● Restaurant/café
■ Bar/pub/club
● Shop

City plan

The **city plan** on the pages that follow is divided as shown:

0   500
yards

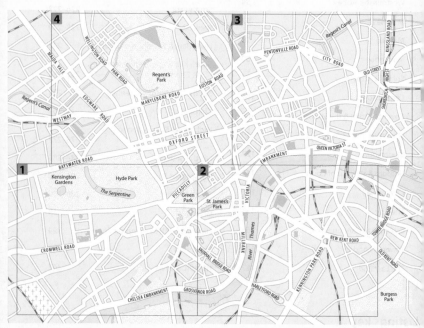

Map symbols

T	Toilets	♦	Place of interest	▲	Peak		Building
✉	Post office	@	Internet café	⛴	Boat		Church
ⓘ	Tourist information	ⵙ	Gardens/fountain	⩲O	Train station	◯	Stadium
✛	Hospital	⊙	Statue	⊖	Underground station	⬚	Park
☪	Mosque	⌣	Bridge	⊖	Overground station	⊞	Christian cemetery
✡	Synagogue	⊠	Gate	⊖	DLR station	●–•●	Cable car

Key bus routes in central London

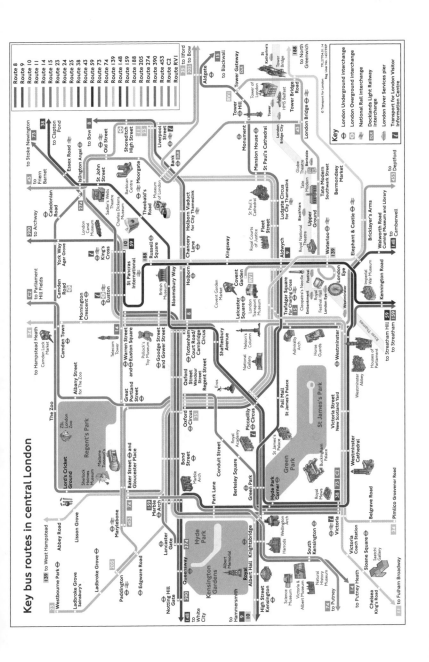

| Route 8 |
| Route 9 |
| Route 10 |
| Route 11 |
| Route 14 |
| Route 15 |
| Route 23 |
| Route 24 |
| Route 25 |
| Route 38 |
| Route 43 |
| Route 59 |
| Route 73 |
| Route 74 |
| Route 139 |
| Route 148 |
| Route 159 |
| Route 188 |
| Route 205 |
| Route 274 |
| Route 390 |
| Route 453 |
| Route C2 |
| Route RV1 |

Key

⊖ London Underground interchange
⊖ London Overground interchange
≠ National Rail interchange
DLR Docklands Light Railway interchange
↯ London River Services pier
ℹ Transport for London Visitor Information Centre

© Transport for London.
TfL 27784.01 / 14
Reg. User No.: 14/2730/P

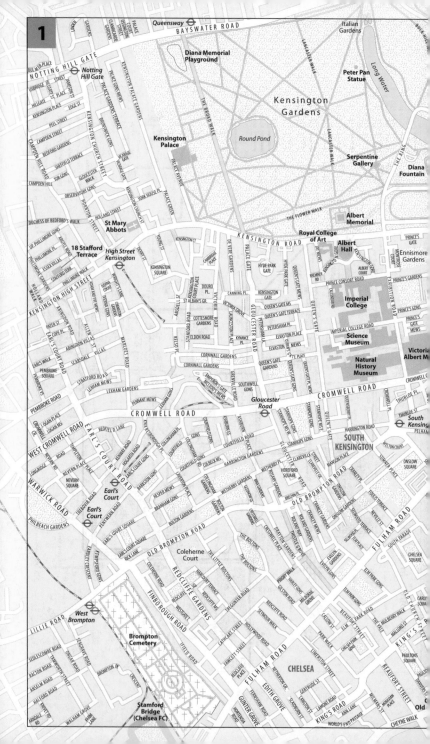

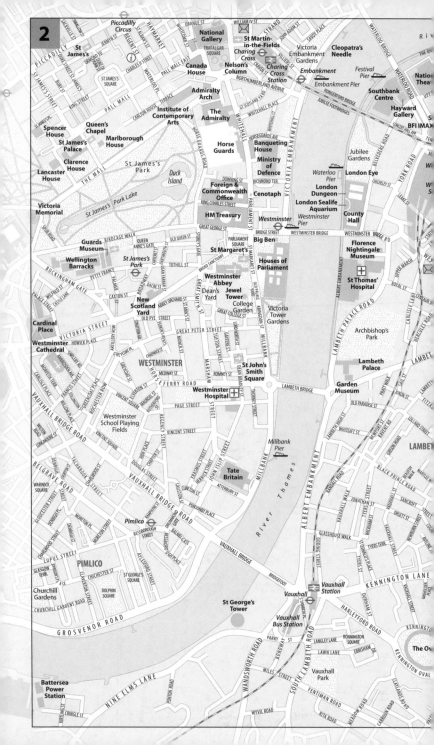

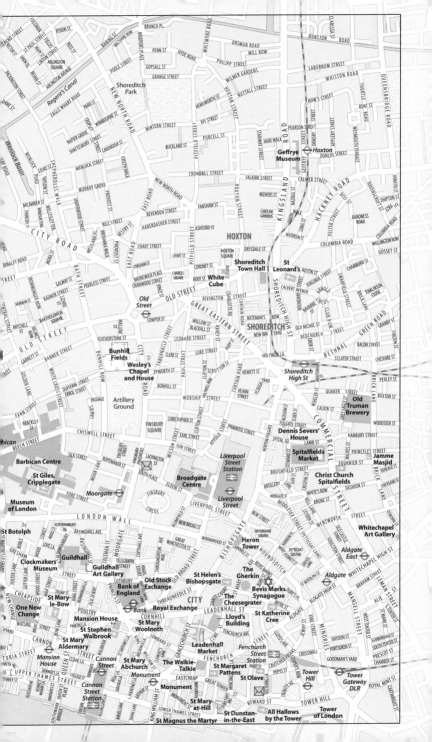

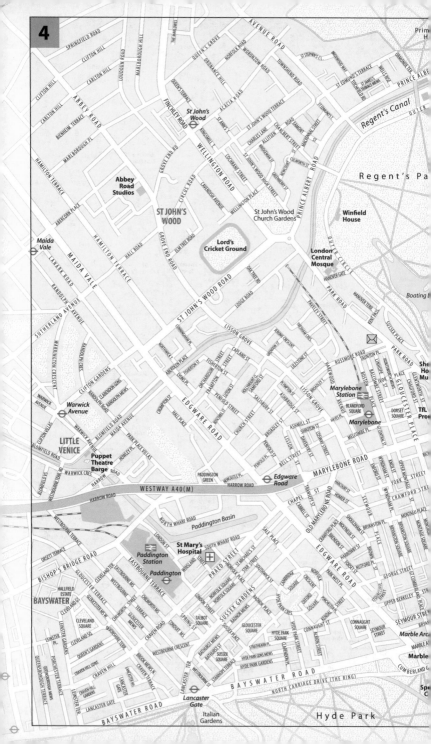

SPRINGFIELD ROAD
CLIFTON HILL
CARLTON HILL
CLIFTON HILL
ABBEY ROAD
CARLTON HILL
BLENHEIM TERRACE
MARLBOROUGH PL
HAMILTON TERRACE
ABERCORN PLACE
MARLBOROUGH HILL
LOUDOUN ROAD
QUEEN'S GROVE
AVENUE ROAD
NORFOLK ROAD
WORONZOW ROAD
TOWNSHEND ROAD
THE MARLOWES
ORDNANCE HILL
QUEEN'S TERRACE
FINCHLEY ROAD
KINGSMILL
St John's Wood
ACACIA ROAD
ST ANN'S
ST JOHN'S WOOD TERRACE
CHARLES LANE
ST STEPHEN'S CL.
NUGENT TERR.
ST JAMES' TERRACE MEWS
ST EDMUND'S TERRACE
WELLINGTON ROAD
GROVE END RD
CAVENDISH AVENUE
CIRCUS ROAD
COCHRANE STREET
CUNWORTH ST
ST JOHN'S WOOD HIGH STREET
CHARLBERT STREET
ALLITSEN ROAD
PRINCE ALBERT ROAD
Regent's Canal
PRINCE ALBE

Abbey Road Studios
ST JOHN'S WOOD
HAMILTON TERRACE
MAIDA VALE
HALL ROAD
GROVE END ROAD
ELM TREE ROAD
St John's Wood Church Gardens
Regent's Pa
Winfield House

Maida Vale
LANARK ROAD
RANDOLPH AVENUE
SUTHERLAND AVENUE
WARRINGTON CRESCENT
Lord's Cricket Ground
ST JOHN'S WOOD ROAD
LODGE ROAD
OAK TREE RD
PARK ROAD
HANOVER GATE
London Central Mosque
OUTER CIRCLE
HANOVER TERR.
Boating

CLIFTON GARDENS
RANDOLPH CRES.
CLIFTON GARDENS
WARWICK AVENUE
Warwick Avenue
BLOMFIELD ROAD
MAIDA AVENUE
RANDOLPH ROAD
CLARENDON GDNS
RANDOLPH MEWS
LISSON GROVE
CUNNINGHAM PL
NORTHWICK
WARWICK
AVENUE
ABERDEEN PLACE
FISHERTON ST
FRAMPTON ST
CAPLAND ST
ORCHARDSON STREET
ASHBRIDGE ST
TRESHAM CRES.
JEROME CRESCENT
LILESTONE ST
GREGORY PL.
PENFOLD ST
PENFOLD ST
SALISBURY ST
ROSSMORE ROAD
TAUNTON PL.
SHROTON ST
BOSTON PLACE
LINDFORD ST
NUTFORD PLACE
BLANDFORD
SQUARE
Marylebone Station
GLOUCESTER PLACE
She
Ho
Mu

LITTLE VENICE
BLOMFIELD ROAD
WARWICK AVENUE
PARK PLACE VILLAS
HONKLEY ST
CROMPTON ST
HALL PLACE
CHURCH STREET
EDGWARE ROAD
BROADLEY ST
BELL STREET
CONNAUGHT STREET
DARLINGTON PL.
MELCOMBE PL.
Marylebone
DORSET SQUARE
TfL Pro

Puppet Theatre Barge
BLOMFIELD
CLIFTON VILLAS
WARWICK CRES.
HARROW ROAD
PADDINGTON GREEN
NEWCASTLE PL.
HARROW ROAD
Edgware Road
MARYLEBONE ROAD
HARCOURT ST
UPPER MONTAGU ST
YORK STREET
BUCK

WESTWAY A40(M)
HARROW ROAD
NORTH WHARF ROAD
Paddington Basin
CHAPEL ST
CABBELL ST
OLD MARYLEBONE ROAD
MONTAGU PLACE
CRAWFORD STREET
SEYMOUR
BRYANSTON SQUARE
MONTAGU SQUARE

BISHOP'S BRIDGE ROAD
ORSETT TERRACE
WESTBOURNE TERRACE
Paddington Station
Paddington
LONDON ST
SOUTH WHARF ROAD
St Mary's Hospital
PRAED STREET
SALE PLACE
EDGWARE ROAD
GEORGE STREET

BAYSWATER
HALLFIELD ESTATE
CLEVELAND TERRACE
GLOUCESTER TERRACE
EASTBOURNE TERRACE
EASTBOURNE MS
WESTBOURNE
CHILWORTH STREET
SPRING ST
NORFOLK SQUARE
LONDON STREET
ST MICHAEL'S ST
STAR STREET
SOUTHWICK ST
CAMBRIDGE SQUARE
HYDE PARK CRES.
NORFOLK CRESCENT
PARK WEST P
OXFORD
SQUARE
CONNAUGHT SQUARE
UPPER BERKELEY ST
SEYMOUR STRE

CLEVELAND SQUARE
CLEVELAND SQ
DEVONSHIRE TER
GLOUCESTER MEWS
CONDUIT MEWS
CONDUIT ST
TALBOT SQUARE
SUSSEX GARDENS
BATHURST MEWS
GLOUCESTER SQUARE
SUSSEX SQUARE
RADNOR MEWS
HYDE PARK SQUARE
GLOUCESTER SQUARE
STRATHEARN PL
KENDAL ST
ALBION STREET
CONNAUGHT STREET
SEYMOUR STREET
Marble Arc

LEINSTER GARDENS
QUEEN'S GARDENS
LEINSTER PL.
CRAVEN HILL GARDENS
CRAVEN ROAD
BROOK MEWS NORTH
CRAVEN TERRACE
WESTBOURNE CRESCENT
SUSSEX PLACE
HYDE PARK GARDENS MEWS
HYDE PARK GARDENS
ST
BRYAN
CUMBERLAND G
Marble

PORCHESTER TERRACE
QUEENSBOROUGH TERRACE
PORCHESTER MEWS
CRAVEN HILL
CRAVEN HILL GARDENS
LANCASTER GATE
LANCASTER TERRACE
LANCASTER TER.
Lancaster Gate
BAYSWATER ROAD
NORTH CARRIAGE DRIVE (THE RING)
Spe
C

BAYSWATER ROAD
Italian Gardens
Hyde Park

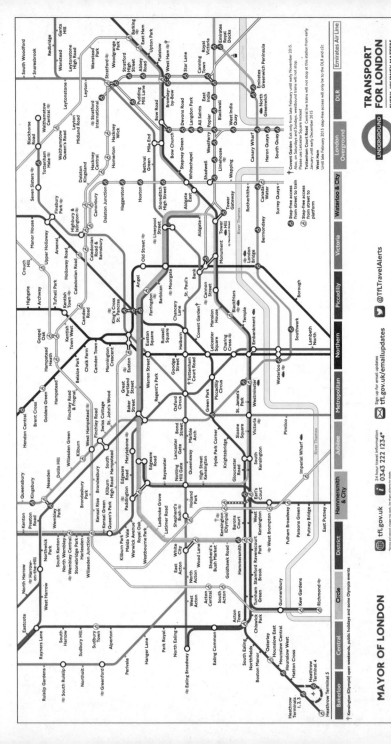